D1524978

SAGE was founded in 1965 by Sara Miller McCune to support the dissemination of usable knowledge by publishing innovative and high-quality research and teaching content. Today, we publish over 900 journals, including those of more than 400 learned societies, more than 800 new books per year, and a growing range of library products including archives, data, case studies, reports, and video. SAGE remains majority-owned by our founder, and after Sara's lifetime will become owned by a charitable trust that secures our continued independence.

Los Angeles | London | New Delhi | Singapore | Washington DC | Melbourne

Community Psychology

Community Psychology
Theories and Applications

Sibnath Deb

Director, Rajiv Gandhi National Institute of Youth Development, Ministry of Youth Affairs and Sports, Government of India; Formerly Professor at the Department of Applied Psychology, Pondicherry University

Aleena Maria Sunny

PhD Scholar, Department of Applied Psychology, Pondicherry University, Kalapet, Puducherry

Nilanjana Sanyal

Retired Professor, Department of Psychology, University of Calcutta, Kolkata, West Bengal

Los Angeles I London I New Delhi
Singapore I Washington DC I Melbourne

First published in 2020 by

SAGE Publications India Pvt Ltd
B1/I-1 Mohan Cooperative Industrial Area
Mathura Road, New Delhi 110 044, India
www.sagepub.in

SAGE Publications Inc
2455 Teller Road
Thousand Oaks, California 91320, USA

SAGE Publications Ltd
1 Oliver's Yard, 55 City Road
London EC1Y 1SP, United Kingdom

SAGE Publications Asia-Pacific Pte Ltd
18 Cross Street #10-10/11/12
China Square Central
Singapore 048423

Published by Vivek Mehra for SAGE Publications India Pvt Ltd. Typeset in 10.5/12.5 pt Berkeley by AG Infographics, Delhi.

Library of Congress Control Number: 2020942525

ISBN: 978-93-5388-404-8 (PB)

SAGE Team: Indrani Dutta, Amit Kumar, Aishna Bhatt, Ankit Verma and Rajinder Kaur

Thank you for choosing a SAGE product!
If you have any comment, observation or feedback,
I would like to personally hear from you.

Please write to me at **contactceo@sagepub.in**

Vivek Mehra, Managing Director and CEO, SAGE India.

Bulk Sales

SAGE India offers special discounts
for bulk institutional purchases.

For queries/orders/inspection copy requests,
write to **textbooksales@sagepub.in**

Publishing

Would you like to publish a textbook with SAGE?
Please send your proposal to **publishtextbook@sagepub.in**

Subscribe to our mailing list

Write to marketing@sagepub.in

This book is also available as an e-book.

Contents

Detailed Contents

List of Figures

List of Tables

List of Abbreviations

ADB	Asian Development Bank
ADHD	Attention-deficit/hyperactivity disorder
AIDS	Acquired immunodeficiency syndrome
ART	Antiretroviral therapy
ASD	Autism spectrum disorder
ASHA	Accredited social health activist
AUD	Alcohol use disorder
BMI	Body Mass Index
BMTPC	Building Materials and Technology Promotion Council
BPL	Below poverty line
CAM	Complementary and alternate medicine
CAP	Contingency action plan
CARA	Central Adoption Resource Authority
CBR	Community-based rehabilitation
CBSE	Central Board of Secondary Education
CCS	Cabinet Committee on Security
CD	Conduct disorder
CDP	Community development programme
CIP	Central Institute of Psychiatry
CMG	Crisis management group
CMH	Community mental health
CMIG	Calcutta Metropolitan Institute of Gerontology
CP	Corporal punishment
CPAI	Community Psychology Association of India
CRC	Central Relief Commissioner
CRF	Calamity Relief Fund
CRPD	Convention on the Rights of Persons with Disabilities
CSW	Commercial sex worker
DALY	Disability-adjusted life years
DDMA	District Disaster Management Authority
DDP	Desert Development Program
DMHP	District Mental Health Program
DOHaD	Developmental origins of health and diseases
DPAP	Drought Prone Area Program

DRDA	District Rural Development Agency
DSM	Diagnostic and Statistical Manual of Mental Disorders
EBP	Evidence-based practice
ECT	Electroconvulsive therapy
ESIS	Employment State Insurance Scheme
FGD	Focus group discussion
FTT	Fairy Tale Test
GFATM	Global Fund to Fight AIDS, Tuberculosis and Malaria
GHQ	General Health Questionnaire
HIV	Human immunodeficiency virus
HRG	High-risk group
ICD	International classification of diseases
ICPS	Integrated Child Protection Scheme
ICT	Information and communications technology
ICTC	Integrated counselling and testing centre
ICZMP	Integrated Coastal Zone Management Project
ILO	International Labour Organization
IPC	Indian Penal Code
IPOP	Integrated Programme for Older Persons
IQ	Intelligence quotient
ISPCAN	International Society for Prevention of Child Abuse and Neglect
ISR	Institution social responsibility
KV	Kendriya Vidyalaya
LA	Land acquisition
LD	Learning disability
MSM	Men who have sex with men
MWPSC	Maintenance and Welfare of Parents and Senior Citizens
NACO	National AIDS Control Organization
NACP	National AIDS Control Programme
NBC	National Building Code
NCCF	National Calamity Contingency Fund
NCMC	National Crisis Management Committee
NCRB	National Crime Records Bureau
NCRMP	National Cyclone Risk Mitigation Project
NDMA	National Disaster Management Authority
NDMF	National Disaster Mitigation Fund
NDRF	National Disaster Response Force
NEC	National Executive Committee
NERMP	National Earthquake Risk Mitigation Project
NFRMP	National Flood Risk Mitigation Project
NGO	Non-governmental organization
NIDM	National Institute of Disaster Management
NIMHANS	National Institute of Mental Health and Neurosciences
NMHP	National Mental Health Policy·

NMHS	National Mental Health Survey
NPAG	Nutrition Program for Adolescent Girls
NPHCE	National Programme for Healthcare of the Elderly
NRHM	National Rural Health Mission
NUHM	National Urban Health Mission
NVBDCP	National Vector Borne Disease Control Program
ODD	Oppositional defiant disorder
OI	Opportunistic infection
PEP	Post-exposure prophylaxis
PG	Postgraduate
PHCs	Primary health centres
PHCs	Private healthcare systems
PLWHA	People living with HIV/AIDS
PMMVY	Pradhan Mantri Matru Vandana Yojana
PMSMA	Pradhan Mantri Surakshit Matritva Abhiyan
PMSSY	Pradhan Mantri Swasthya Suraksha Yojana
PPTCT	Prevention of parent to child transmission
PRA	Participatory rural appraisal
PTSD	Post-traumatic stress disorder
PWD	Persons with Disabilities
QUT	Queensland University of Technology
RBSK	Rashtriya Bal Swasthya Karyakram
RCI	Rehabilitation Council of India
RGNIYD	Rajiv Gandhi National Institute of Youth Development
RMNCH+A	Reproductive, maternal, newborn, child and adolescent health
RR	Rehabilitation and resettlement
RSBY	Rashtriya Swasthya Bima Yojana
SCHIS	Senior Citizen Health Insurance Scheme
SCRA	Society for Community Research and Action
SDGs	Sustainable Development Goals
SDMA	State Disaster Management Authority
SDRF	State Disaster Response Force
SEOC	State Emergency Operation Centre
SIMS	Strategic information management systems
SLDs	Specific learning disabilities
STI	Sexually transmitted infection
SUBI	Subjective Well-being Inventory
TB	Tuberculosis
UG	Undergraduate
UNCRC	United Nations Convention on the Rights of the Child
UNCRPD	United Nations Convention on the Rights of Persons with Disabilities
UNISDR	United Nations Office for Disaster Risk Reduction
WESW	Women engaged in sex work
WHO	World Health Organization

Foreword

The text *Community Psychology: Theories and Applications* by Sibnath Deb, Aleena Maria Sunny and Nilanjana Sanyal has six distinctive features. First, it provides readers with a comprehensive overview of the field of community psychology beginning with its origins at the Swampscott Conference in 1963. The book describes the application of community psychology to a wide range of social problems: physical health, mental health and vulnerable populations such as children, elderly, differently abled, persons with HIV/AIDS, disaster victims and persons displaced by government and business development projects. Second, the authors provide extensive evidence-based support for the need for a community psychology approach. Each chapter is followed by a valuable reference list of current research relevant to the practice of community psychology. Third, this book provides extensive examples of the application of community psychology principles to India, as well as other countries around the world. The authors show a strong grasp of community psychology globally. Fourth, each chapter contains concrete suggestions for how a particular community problem—whether dealing with a disaster causing massive loss of life or physical illness affecting a particular strand of the community—can be remedied using a community psychology approach. Especially noteworthy are the recommendations for how to use school-based interventions to build community resilience. The authors emphasize the importance of strength-based interventions that are participatory and build community resilience. Fifth, each chapter contains figures and diagrams, mostly developed by the authors, that are useful teaching aids that focus on critical community psychology variables. In addition, each chapter provides, at the end, useful questions arranged in increasing degree of challenge for higher-education classroom discussion. Sixth, the book contains a practical introduction to conducting community psychology research. The authors favour a research approach that integrates qualitative research with quantitative research, and they provide a comprehensive overview of how to initiate a community psychology research project that is participatory and multiculturally sensitive.

In summary, the book is a valuable introductory text on community psychology. It is comprehensive, practical and evidence based. Just as the discipline of family therapy had a revolutionary effect on the practice of mental health by showing us that individuals must be viewed in a family context, so too does the discipline of community psychology have a revolutionary effect by directing our attention to the community as a focus of intervention. The book is an outstanding introduction to this important discipline.

Brian A. Gerrard,
PhD, Chief Academic Officer,
Western Institute for Social Research,
Berkeley, CA.
Chair, Institute for School-Based Family Counseling.
Emeritus Faculty, Counseling Psychology Department,
University of San Francisco,
San Francisco, CA.

Preface

Rapid changes in social and community life, due to technological advancements, have made life much easier in terms of academic advancement, comforts in daily life and industrial growth and development. Technological advancement has connected people easily and made information regarding various issues available to common people, through different search engines, social networking sites, WhatsApp and other means. However, despite scientific advancements, common people are continuously facing various challenges, which need attention of the policymakers for review of existing policies and programmes. In addition, academic institutes should teach about such contemporary issues so that students and scholars are exposed to the right information and, in turn, they develop interest on the subject/issue and play a significant role as a professional after the completion of their studies. Here lies the role of community psychology, like public health, to disseminate among students knowledge and information, based on evidence, about various emerging community-related issues. Keeping this background in mind, the authors have attempted to come out with this volume since no such work exists covering the issues that have been addressed here.

Let us look at the broad objective of community psychology. It primarily focuses on problems and challenges of the common people, at the community level, through a participatory and collaborative approach for giving them relief from the sufferings and improving their overall quality of life in the given situation. In other words, community psychologists attempt to understand the quality of life of individuals within groups, organizations and institutions, communities in particular, and the society at large.

In addressing these issues and challenges in community life—such as social stigma attached to mental health, physical health challenges, issues and challenges of elderly people, challenges faced by the students and children in disadvantaged conditions and with disabilities, people with HIV/AIDS, and people affected by natural calamities and development projects—the role of community psychology goes beyond an individual focus and integrates social, cultural, economic, political and environmental aspects in understanding the problems from an insider's perspective and holistically with a view to bringing a positive change in behaviour, attitude and perception of common people about various issues through sensitization and empowerment of people at different levels.

Cultural beliefs and practices play a major role in certain aspects of community behaviour such as child upbringing, disciplining children, mental and physical health, disabilities and HIV/AIDS. Wrong cultural beliefs and practices act as a barrier for quality of life and misguide people in wrong directions. It is very difficult to change cultural beliefs and practices. However, it is not impossible. It requires continuous efforts, and in this regard, the younger educated generations of the same community should be mobilized to take proactive measures in bringing positive changes in the community.

Nevertheless, this subject is yet to get proper attention from the policymakers and academics in developing countries like India. However, of late, the academic community and policy members have started realizing the importance of the role of community psychology in resolving issues and challenges, at the community level, with community participation and collaboration.

There is also a need to carry out more collaborative and interdisciplinary empirical research on various contemporary and emerging issues to understand the situation better from different angles and from the insiders' perspectives, and, in turn, the insiders' perspectives of issues and challenges will guide the programme planner and policymakers to consider need-based policies and programmes, which will really benefit the community. Therefore, it may be stated that community psychologists play an integral role in promoting the health and well-being of the common people of the society.

The document on community psychology is scanty in developing countries like India. The subject is in its infancy, as compared to in developed countries. Perhaps, this is the first initiative by Indian authors to write a book on community psychology, explaining theoretical perspectives and their application and practices, thus covering some emerging areas based on empirical evidence with case studies, for a better understanding of the subject. We are sure that academics, researchers, students and non-governmental organization (NGO) personnel working at the community level as well as policymakers will find the book informative and useful.

The first author of the book has extensive field and research experience on all the areas covered in the book, both nationally and internationally, which prompted him to think of coming out with a volume on community psychology. The second author does not require any introduction for her significant contribution in mental health, especially on counselling and psychoanalysis. She is an academic, known well both nationally and internationally for her significant contribution in academics. The second author of the book is the direct scholars of the first author and worked with him in different projects on social and community issues and gained substantial experience. The book is the outcome of the hard work and collaborative efforts of all the authors.

It attempts to focus on both theoretical concepts of community psychology and its applications in day-to-day life, by providing an in-depth analysis of different concepts based on evidence. It is written in a lucid language with a lot of examples and has been provided with case studies for better understanding of the subject by the students. Additionally, a number of conceptual models are provided in different chapters for better illustration.

There are 11 chapters in this book, which are covered under three broad themes, namely Part A: Concepts and Frameworks, Part B: Community Interventions and Part C: Research and Practice. Chapter 1 gives an overview of community psychology in addition to various theoretical concepts with special reference to mental health, organizational health and social justice. Benefits of participatory and collaborative approaches and empowerment are discussed at length in the chapter with practical examples. It also focuses on various preventive measures and challenges of community psychology. Chapter 2 is about community-based intervention for mental health, in which an overview of mental health and mental illness is provided extensively with special emphasis on myths and misconceptions attached to mental health and what needs to be done. Evidence concerning global epidemic of mental disorders, with special reference to India, is provided in addition to discussion about treatment gaps and other related issues and role of mental health professionals. Chapter 3 focuses on the concept of community health with special reference to health habits, common diseases, risk and health-seeking behaviour and preventive measures. Chapter 4 comprises definitions of disability, broad types and symptoms of disabilities, disability assessment and preventive and intervention methods for different types of disabilities. Likewise, Chapter 5 focuses on issues and challenges of elderly people in the society, and at the end, it talks about family-based intervention programmes and social support for elderly people. The need for old-age homes and palliative care is also discussed in the chapter from a practical point of view. A large number of children in developing countries, like India, are in disadvantaged and vulnerable conditions. Chapter 6 emphasizes on a community-based approach for taking care of disadvantaged and at-risk children, highlighting their various challenges with examples. Chapter 7 discusses the problems caused by development projects and rehabilitation of project-affected people through a participatory approach. First, this chapter starts discussing the definition of project-affected people and reasons for taking up development projects and its consequences, and then it emphasizes on developing people-friendly rehabilitation packages based on evidence and with the participation of the local people.

Natural calamities are evident, and these affect the lives of people in different manners. Despite disaster management systems in different states, the sufferings of disaster victim people are countless. Chapter 8 highlights the plight of disaster-affected people and puts special emphasis on mental health intervention for addressing post-traumatic stress disorder. HIV/AIDS, a global public health challenge, affected about 37 billion people worldwide. It is not only the loss of human resources, but this pandemic has also caused a lot of health expenditure. Therefore, preventive measures need special attention in national and international programmes for combating HIV/ AIDS. Extending quality care towards people with HIV/AIDS must be the priority for every nation. This issue is discussed at length in Chapter 9.

Chapter 10 explains the need for school-based intervention programmes for addressing the challenges faced by school students, their motivation, safety measures in schools and disciplining methods. It also discusses the role of parents and teachers in creating student-friendly school environment with quality education. Finally, Chapter 11 elaborates upon community-based research and its importance in taking actions for resolving various issues and challenges through a collaborative approach.

At the end of each chapter, some exercises are provided for the students. We hope that postgraduate (PG) and undergraduate (UG) students would be able to answer these logically. This book would not only be useful for the PG and UG students, but PhD scholars and academics on community psychology, social psychology, health psychology, public health, sociology, social work, anthropology, social exclusion, women studies, psychiatry, NGO personnel, legal professionals and policymakers would also benefit from it. Very few universities teach the same subject in India. After reading this volume, it can be hoped that academics would like to introduce community psychology in their discipline and join hands with government and other allied organizations for moving ahead and making a 'new, prosperous and progressive India' as part of institution social responsibility (ISR).

There are many more issues which need the attention of academics to cover in future volumes on community psychology such as the role and impact of Swachh Bharat Abhiyan, since cleanliness and hygiene have high correlation with good physical and mental health as well as overall well-being of a community. Another area could be empowerment of rural women through self-help groups and/or skill-based training for improving their economic condition. Social stigma related to physical and health issues and its impact need attention in future volumes. Rampant usage of plastic bags and burning of waste materials openly are causing environmental pollution. This issue may also be accommodated in future volumes on community psychology, explaining its role for changing the behaviour of common people and their practices through community mobilization. For all those issues, community psychologists could visit different educational institutions and deliver a professionally developed and brief presentation on each subject, with latest evidence to create awareness, motivate students and engage them in action-oriented activities.

Although every effort has been made to come out with a volume on community psychology, covering various emerging areas with proper illustrations and case studies, we welcome every suggestion for further improvement of the volume.

Acknowledgements

Writing a volume on a subject like community psychology was very challenging, as evidence and information about the subject is very limited. The first author of the book, Professor Sibnath Deb, undertook extensive research on various issues covered in the book, in addition to organizing training programmes on mental and physical health, as well as on HIV/AIDS. He was also a part of different academic and policymaking bodies, which prompted him to conceptualize the idea of writing the present book, and, in turn, he invited one of his bright scholars Aleena Maria Sunny and one senior academic Professor Nilanjana Sanyal from the University of Calcutta for his support. The joint effort and hard work, put in from all corners, made it possible to write the volume. However, for writing this volume, different academics, NGO personnel and researchers were consulted to learn from their experiences, and all of them were very generous to share their experiences with us. We thank all of them from the core of our heart for helping us in writing the book. We are also grateful to all the previous researchers whose work we referred to in the volume with proper citations.

The library staff of Pondicherry University and the University of Calcutta extended full support in various manners while writing the volume. We are indebted to all the staff of the library of Pondicherry University, namely Dr R. Samyuktha, Librarian; Mr Z. Olirvel, Computer Information Scientist; and Dr Vijayakumar, Assistant Librarian, as well as of the University of Calcutta, namely Dr Soumitra Sarkar, Librarian, for their support and cooperation.

Technical support and professional input from our friend Kaustuv Chakraborti, a bright research scholar from the Department of English, Pondicherry University, was really helpful in producing this volume. Encouragement from the staff of SAGE also deserves special appreciation, especially that of Amit Kumar and Anveshi Gupta, for bringing out this volume. Feedback from the reviewers helped us to improve the volume further, and, in turn, it improved its overall presentation. We extend our gratitude to all the reviewers of this volume for their valuable suggestions. Finally, it would be a lapse on our part if we do not acknowledge the support of our family members while writing this volume.

About the Authors

Professor Sibnath Deb, PhD and DSc, is the Director of the Rajiv Gandhi National Institute of Youth Development (RGNIYD), Ministry of Youth Affairs and Sports, Government of India, Sriperumbudur, Tamil Nadu. Prior to joining RGNIYD, he was teaching in Pondicherry University and the University of Calcutta. In 1994, he completed an intensive course on 'HIV/AIDS and Qualitative Research' from the University of Western Australia. From April to August 2009, he visited the School of Public Health and Social Work, Queensland University of Technology (QUT), Brisbane, Australia, as a visiting faculty. Currently, he is also an Adjunct Professor at the School of Justice, Faculty of Law at QUT. From 2004 to 2008, he was a council member of the International Society for Prevention of Child Abuse and Neglect (ISPCAN). He has 29 years of teaching, research and administrative experience and has published a large number of research articles in leading national and international journals as well as in edited books. He has written eight books and edited six. Some of his latest books include (a) *Disadvantaged Children in India: Empirical Evidence, Policies and Actions* (2020); (b) *Social Psychology in Everyday Life* (2019); (c) *Childhood to Adolescence: Issues and Concerns* (2019); (d) *Positive Schooling and Child Development: International Perspectives* (2018); (e) *Child Safety, Welfare and Well-being* (2016); and (f) *Distance Education: Prospects, Challenges and Way Forward* (2018). His research interests include child safety, students' mental health, adolescent reproductive health, family relationships, childcare, happiness and applied social psychology. He has received three international and five national awards for his contribution in academics and research including an award from the Asiatic Society, Kolkata (an institute of national importance under the Ministry of Culture, Government of India) in 2018 and 'Visitor's Award 2019' from the Honourable President of India for his contribution in the field of child protection, students' mental health and HIV/AIDS. He can be reached at sibnath23@gmail.com.

Aleena Maria Sunny is a full-time PhD scholar under the supervision of Professor Sibnath Deb at the Department of Applied Psychology, Pondicherry University. She holds an Master's degree in Applied Clinical Psychology in applied clinical psychology from Tata Institute of Social Sciences and a Bachelor's (Honours) Degree (Honours) in psychology from Christ University, Bengaluru. Recently, she co-authored two books titled (a) *Disadvantaged Children in India: Empirical Evidence, Policies and Actions* (2020) and (b) *Childhood to Adolescence: Issues and Concerns* (2019) with Professor Sibnath Deb. Her research interests include clinical psychology, neuro-cognitive psychology and child development.

Professor Nilanjana Sanyal, PhD, is currently a retired professor of the Department of Psychology, University of Calcutta. She is also a practising psychoanalyst for the last 36 years. She has imparted training in counselling in various governmental institutions and NGOs, both nationally and internationally, and is consistently involved in mass media programmes for awareness generation regarding mental health issues. She is also a columnist in different national dailies and magazines. She has authored a book, *Positivism, Positive Psychology and Spirituality*, edited two books and is a co-author of a test manual. She has over 180 international and national publications including 28 book chapters to her credit till date. Her research interests include psychoanalysis and psychodynamic psychotherapy, personality, clinical and spiritual psychology and interpersonal relationships. She is a co-researcher for the creation of a registered assessment methodology, namely the Fairy Tale Test (FTT) with Dr Carina Coulacouglou, University of Athens, Greece. She is a member of International Psychoanalytical Association and an honorary member of the FTT Society, Greece, apart from her membership in other national and international professional bodies. She is a gold medallist of the University of Calcutta, at both UG and PG levels. She received the Jubilee Merit Prize and Jawaharlal Nehru Award from the Government of India along with the Suhashini Basu Memorial Prize from the Indian Psychoanalytical Society for excellence of a research paper. Apart from other awards, she is also the recipient of the Professor Maya Deb Memorial Award (2012) from the Asiatic Society, Kolkata.

PART A
Concepts and Frameworks

Theoretical Concepts of Community Psychology

ABSTRACT

Homo sapiens are social beings and cannot thrive in isolation. It becomes mandatory for individuals to relate to the wider environment and the community at large to ensure quality living. The need is felt to understand the principles of behaviour in the relational matrix with the community being the context. This is adopted by the relatively nascent branch of community psychology which has certain ingrained values. The wellness model is observed to replace the illness/medical paradigm, thus making it possible for preventive measures and competence development to come to the foreground as major objectives of the discipline. Community psychology appears to be a *linking science* as well as a *linking practice*. Empowerment and citizen participation are highlighted to bring forth the optimization of resources in the community. Its historical development has been explained by taking into consideration the different theoretical perspectives, for example, the biopsychosocial model. A sense of community is expected to develop among the citizens, thus making them perceive the community as one. The implications and challenges of the discipline are also discussed.

Keywords: Community psychology; prevention; competence development; empowerment

1.1. INTRODUCTION

The presence of an individual in any social platform presents him/her as a figure in the backdrop of a community whose existence and identity are derived from the connections in the community. Except in the case of emotional withdrawal, no one is alone in this world. Society and community hold us through our life. Indeed, human beings are social animals. One cannot simply thrive in the world in isolation. This is because the individual's and community's lives are intertwined in nature. There is a necessity to understand human behaviour in the context of the larger community as a whole with which the individual relates. This is because behaviour possesses its dynamic community backdrop factor. The focus needs to be on the neighbourhood—the community and the society—to promote a sense of well-being rather than intervening only when a problem arises. In fact, the present era is adorned by strong linkages that reveal disease aetiology to arise out of behaviour in personal as well as in community space (Detels & Breslow, 1997). Hence, in order to achieve the target of illness prevention, the establishment of health-promotive environments at the community level becomes palpable and should be the focus of the current times. Progress in this fashion requires time, which nevertheless would eventually solve several social problems step by step (Weick, 1984). Anyhow, sound theoretical analyses of key concepts such as 'health', 'wellness', 'wellness promotion' and 'healthy environments' are essential prerequisites for developing effective environmental designs and public policy programmes so as to create healthy surroundings (Webster, 1989). Collective well-being and optimal state of wellness are the terms often used in modern parlance. Such concepts of health or wellness promotion differ essentially from disease-prevention orientation by laying greater emphasis on the role of individuals, groups and organizations as active agents in shaping health practices and policies. A dire necessity is felt to change the individualistic perspective rather than their environments, organizations or institutions. Health habits and lifestyles are also getting modified. The community as a whole needs to address its mental health. The present chapter will attempt to explore the nuances of wellness and optimization of health by using the psychological lens to focus on the community as a whole.

1.2. FUNDAMENTALS OF COMMUNITY PSYCHOLOGY

1.2.1. COMMUNITY: A CONCEPTUAL OVERVIEW

A community is understood to be a social group of people belonging to a specified area who share common geography, culture, government or personal characteristics. This may be pictorially presented as in Figure 1.1.

Warren (1977) opines that different facets of a community need to be considered in perceiving a better comprehension of any community. They provide a framework for comparing different

FIGURE 1.1
Diagrammatic Illustration of Community

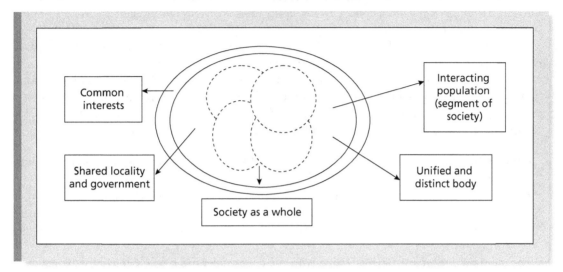

communities as well as helping to draw the similarities (Kazdin, 2000). The various ways of understanding a specific community are as follows:

- **The community as a space:** It is defined by not only a physical space but also a psychological space.
- **The community as people who thrive in the space:** The population of a distinct community is defined by different demographic data available with census boards (e.g., number and percentage of people hailing from different ethnic and/or racial groups, age, sex distributions and so on).
- **The community as shared institutions and values:** A community may be regarded as an institution that is shared by a unique pattern of living and value systems among the individuals against a specific cultural/subcultural backdrop.
- **The community as an interaction:** The association of individuals with each other is of great importance along with the behaviour associated with different community institutions such as temples, churches, mosques, schools, family and neighbourhood.
- **The community as a distribution of power:** It relates to the play of power dynamics in a community set-up.
- **The community as a social system:** It involves taking into consideration the communication patterns, boundary maintenance, systemic linkage or interdependence of units in a particular community, socialization processes, mechanisms of social control, institutionalization or predictability of organization and social actions in the community.

This may be explained by the ecological perspective, wherein the 'person-in-context' (where context is seen as being multi-level) is the unit of analysis and change, and has become a guiding principle of community psychology. Problems are seen as faulty adaptations to the natural environment, rather than solely the deficiencies of the individuals. This aids to develop new progressive insights (Burton & Kagan, 2000; Levine & Perkins, 1997). Community-health professionals attempt to understand citizens amid their societal environment so as to promote quality of life for individuals as a whole.

The scientific concern and practice of ecology is a relatively new enterprise, whose ideas have been stimulated from concepts of public health. The social ecological perspective is an approach in health research, which draws upon concepts from multiple disciplines of medical and behavioural sciences. Social ecological approach stresses on curative strategies that are present throughout the community—for holistic wellness—and not just to work in the purview of an individual. This perspective incorporates behavioural and social science emphasis in such a manner that

- Individuals and groups play an active role in modifying their own health, behaviour and well-being.
- Theoretical models describing people–environment transactions are developed and tested.
- Evaluative studies are conducted to assess overall wellness and not just the cure of an illness (Henderson & Scutchfield, 1989; Winett et al., 1989).

The interrelationships of the individual with the environment as a whole may be schematically represented by Figure 1.2.

FIGURE 1.2
Individual Self in Relation to the Environment

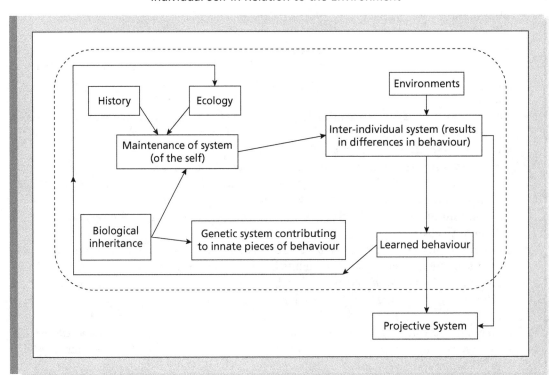

It is to be noted that culture is the sum of the maintenance system, environments and inter-individual context. It virtually influences every aspect of our existence (Fiske et al., 1998; Kim & Markus, 1999). In other words, cultures elaborate upon a variety of social organizations to deal with basic life problems. Cultures can be conceptualized as providing a 'tool kit' of habits, skills, styles, perspectives, norms, roles and values, out of which, each individual can construct a potentially unique strategy for action. Trickett (1996) locates the development of human activities within a socio-historical and cultural context of meanings and relationships. This has been supported by Dalton et al. (2001). Behaviour can be understood better if the context in which it takes place is comprehended.

In sum

A community is understood to be a social group of people belonging to a specified area, who share a common geography, culture, government or personal characteristics. Community can be understood as (a) a space, (b) people, (c) shared institutions, (d) an interaction, (e) the distribution of power and (f) a social system.

1.2.2. COMMUNITY ECOLOGY: A FOUNDATION OF COMMUNITY PSYCHOLOGY

A community holds the interplay of varied forces, which account for community dynamics that gives it its distinct character. Many factors come into play, some being community history, social action, advocacy, social change movements, the ethnic composition of a specific area, its crime rate, extent of poverty, human rights, social policy and a sense of cohesion or belongingness to the community (Prilleltensky & Nelson, 1997). As represented in Figure 1.3, community is a cultural representative of a group of human beings. A society is run by community values and prescribed norms and its rituals, which constitute the basic framework of community psychology. It is community dynamics that shapes the different experiences of individuals and underlies the basis of different interventions addressed to the community at large. Community psychology is a branch in growing demand, as it seeks to understand people and their behaviour in their contexts. It attempts to connect the individuals and their context to draw valid inferences. It is thus the understanding of the individual, being embedded in their social context. The ultimate aim is to attain betterment at the macro level and to have advancement in the society at large.

Uneven stratification of our social world in terms of wealth, class, race, gender, ethnicity and sexuality reflects the key assumptions of the need of a specialized subdiscipline within a psychology that addresses the structure of unequivalence (Prilleltensky, 2001). The need to acknowledge the community framework for intervening in social issues like inclusion–exclusion or mental health is rightly addressed through the theories of community psychology by professionals.

1.2.2.1. Principles of Social Ecological Model

Kelly (1971) suggested the presence of four principles from biological ecology to guiding community psychologists' assessment of natural social environments. Please refer to Figure 1.4.

FIGURE 1.3

Psychological Intervention Continuum

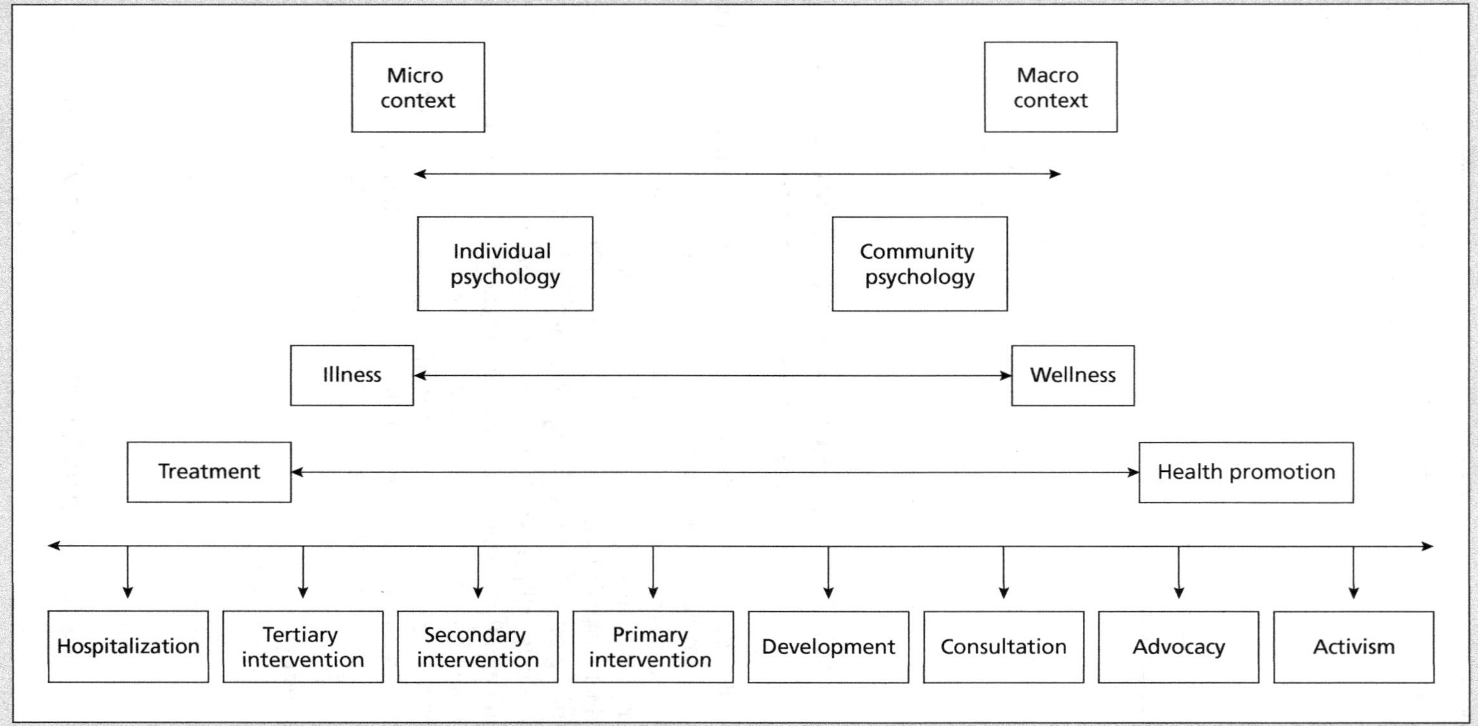

Source: Naidoo et al. (2004).

- **Principle of interdependence:** The social ecological model holds that multiple components of any social context are interrelated and influence each other. Alterations in a particular subsection of the system are likely to bring about changes in other areas as well. Collaborating at the community level requires a challenging endeavour since it takes time not only to assess the local community but also to build relationships between the professionals and various interdependent segments of the community. This is—in turn—mandatory for creating a realistic and workable system of different layers of social structures that exist within a geographical area.
- **Principle of distribution of resources:** Communities are different in terms of the resources they possess, as proposed by the social ecological model, some of which may comprise money, time and human resources. Each and every place has people who are resources for others. Besides, different forms of interventions and their distribution may be influenced by the creation of varied resources in a community. Cycling of resources within a community is fostered, which also helps to solve many of its problems. Thus, it becomes important to realize that all participants of the social system and their shared culture can become resources for the community at large. Another important ecological premise is that the trained professionals need to be open to be educated by the community as the problems often remain outside or beyond the methods sanctioned by the formal training. One often requires collaboration with individuals from other disciplines and models about how to relate to and create a variety of appropriate resources for any problem.
- **Principle of adaptation:** The process by which people constantly cope with available or changing resources in their environments is referred to as adaptation. Different skills or competencies are necessary to successfully adapt to the demands of each community. Problem behaviour is seen as a failure or mental illness, rather than simply a deficiency of an individual or a mental illness. What appears to be problematic behaviour may be quite appropriate in different situations.
- **Principle of succession:** Succession refers to the orderly process, wherein the community changes with the new situations successively as they keep arising. In the natural course of things, all communities change. They must adapt to the changes in the external environment. The role of a community psychologist is not simply to help the community mobilize its resources but also to solve current problems and help it prepare for future changes.

These principles can be helpful in understanding a community through its functioning and this, in turn, helps in conceptualizing community-based research and practice.

FIGURE 1.4
Principles of Social Ecological Model

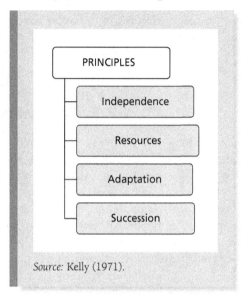

Source: Kelly (1971).

> **In sum**
>
> The four principles of the social ecology model suggested by Kelly (1971) to guide community psychologists' assessment of natural social environments are: (a) principle of interdependence, (b) principle of distribution of resources, (c) principle of adaptation and (d) principle of succession.

1.2.3. COMMUNITY PSYCHOLOGY: AN OVERVIEW

Community psychology is a derivative in the discipline of psychology that studies individuals from the context of community interactions; the transactions between individuals and their environment is the prime lesson in this discipline. The ultimate aim is to bring about a sense of improved well-being and functionality of the community of individuals. It is thus an emerging branch of applied psychology (Naidoo et al., 2007). It is also to be noted that lack or deficit of different resource points such as poverty, estrangement and loneliness would affect the overall well-being of the community. This specialized discipline of psychology—which views people in context—is essentially a research-oriented and action-oriented field. It essentiates a number of principles:

1. Social–environmental factors are crucial influencers of the behavioural patterns observed in the community.
2. Community interventions can promote overall health and prevent illness in any social institution.
3. Community intervention should give equal consideration for illness prevention among population at high risk as well as for rehabilitation for population prone to any hazard.
4. Attainment of social competence should be the goal of community intervention, and through it the reduction of distress could be attained.
5. Community clinicians should adapt to the need of the community at work and be available to the community by all means.
6. Availability of the clinicians in terms of socio-demographic factors such as distance, place and time should be flexible to meet the need of the community members.
7. Human resources within the community—such as professional or non-professionals who are community members—should be amply utilized for the benefit of the community.
8. Application of novel ideas and models in a community set-up is highly encouraged.
9. The need and issues of the community members should be the first in the priority list.
10. The range of community intervention programmes should be vast and maximally effective.
11. Knowledge dissemination and provision of psychoeducation on matters of social concerns are highly valued.
12. Social reformation and community well-being are the chief objectives of community psychologists.
13. Community interventions should be developed from the findings of research outcomes that are naturalistic and ecologically favourable.

The field of community psychology is often regarded as a *linking science* and a *linking practice* (Stark, 2009). It is a *linking science* because it studies micro–macro levels of analysis to have a better understanding of how the individual's well-being can be maintained. At the same time, it is a *linking practice* because it helps to bring together multiple stakeholders to take account of community issues (Kloos et al., 2007). It helps in theory building and research from a social context. Community is a value that needs to be inculcated by every individual to become better citizens of the global community. It works on a meta-value system with comradeship, love, acceptance and tolerance as the sub-values within the value of community. It would be a ground where diversity is celebrated, mistakes are tolerated and potentials are nurtured. It is the place where its members are unconditionally accepted. It is thus a specific field of psychology, which is suggestive of important underlying values, social analyses and community psychological practices to enable the liberation of the individuals.

1.2.4. Prominent Models in Community Psychology

1.2.4.1. Biopsychosocial Model

Popular for its broad framework, the biopsychosocial model developed by George L. Engle explains the interaction between the biological, psychological and social factors, which explains all the health and illness outcomes of an individual. The model believes in the influence of multiple causal factors and considers the dynamics between an individual's genetic build-up, the psychological dynamics (cognitive, emotional, attitudinal and behavioural factors) and the environment/context in explaining health outcomes (Lehman et al., 2017). Research has found several benefits of this model in the healthcare system; improvement in patient satisfaction and speedy recovery have been found in patients, which was understood to result from holistic and inclusive interpretation of illness aetiology. This model is rightly called holistic, as any information pertaining to the patient is sought and perceived as a cue to healthcare. The model advocates for the involvement of experts from multiple disciplines. Lack of informed and committed professionals as well as financial crunch are the chief barriers to the practice of the biopsychosocial model.

1.2.4.2. Bronfenbrenner's Ecological Model

Adopting the ecological systems perspective, the best-known theory is that of Bronfenbrenner (1979), who described the environment to be a system where development is a nested system placed one over the other. The ecology of human development theory propounded by Bronfenbrenner (1979) has been defined as the 'mutual accommodation between an active, growing human being and the changing properties of the immediate context where the individual person develops'. It is influenced by the interrelationships among the different settings in which the context is situated as depicted in Figure 1.5. The model categorized the context into four different systems. These systems include micro, meso, exo and macro systems. Later, a fifth system was added, known as the chrono system. An individual learns to survive through an ever-evolving context.

The micro system relates to the immediate environment of the child, which includes relationships/institutions of regular interactions such as home and school. It is understood that the quality of the relationship and that of these systems of interactions are mutually inclusive of each

FIGURE 1.5

Interrelationships of Micro, Meso, Exo and Chrono Systems

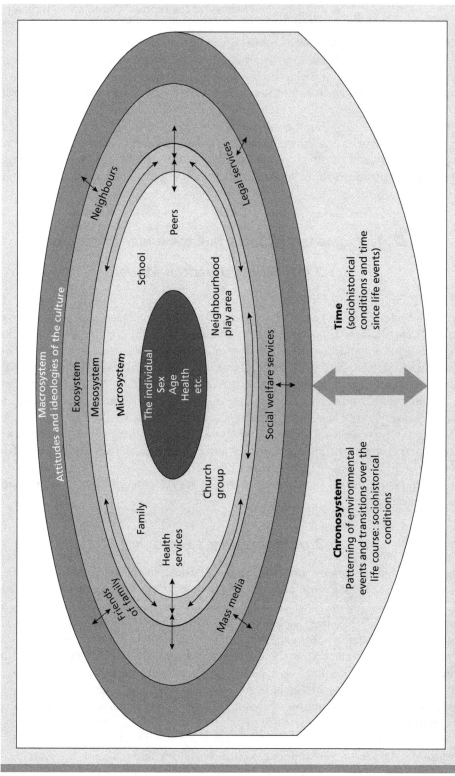

other. The meso system—the next tier—is comprised of the nature of linkages between the micro systems in which the individual is located. The exo system could be the extended systems/ institutions of interaction such as neighbourhood and extended family members, with whom the child's interaction may not be so regular. At the macro-system level, relationships/institutions which are at the most remote status, such as government or economy, could still exert their influence on the developmental outcomes of that child.

Bronfenbrenner (1979) therefore recognized the influence of sociocultural and economic factors such as poverty and oppression, as well as large-scale social change or behavioural patterns. The chrono system 'reflects the cumulative experiences a person has over the course of his/her lifetime' and includes environmental events/major transitions (Santrock, 2011), that is, marriage, divorce, birth of a baby and so on. This system may thus imbibe a change in the family structure, address and parent's employment status, in addition to immense societal changes such as economic cycles and wars. It thus becomes comprehensible that any conflict or change in any one system will automatically affect all other systems. Therefore, it is important to consider the child, their immediate environment as well as their interaction with each other to have a glimpse of the whole scenario (Rhodes, 2013).

By studying the different systems that simultaneously influence a child, the ecological systems theory is able to demonstrate the diversity of interrelated influences on the child's development. It is envisioned that the environment relates to a series of nested structures that includes, but extends beyond, home, school and neighbourhood settings in which children spend their everyday lives. It is suggested that an individual's perception of the environment is often more important than the 'objective reality', and such perceptions influence the individual's expectations and activities. As such, this theory recognized the influence of the wider environment and higher-order systems on human behaviour. One of the resourceful contributions of an ecological endeavour lies in the fact that such enquiries may illuminate the factors that come into play for some individuals and not others (Kelly, 2006).

There are at least four drawings that can be drawn from the above-mentioned ecological model to be applied in the community. These are as follows:

- For a tailor-made intervention to be successful, the current and past requirements of the specific community need to be taken into consideration.
- The intervention programme should aim at a social change, and longitudinal assessment should be done to assess its impact.
- The anticipated effects of the interventions could be in two directions: It could be to enhance the positive effects and also to reduce the negative effects of the interventions on the community.
- Alternative intervention strategies should be developed to tackle the negative effects, which should be a novel idea away from stereotypical methods.

The ecological model of mental health has three different dimensions, which may be represented as in Figure 1.6.

As can be understood from the model, mental health of an individual as well as the overall mental health of a community could be strongly determined by their physical and social environment. It is important to understand that each of these dimensions has its own ecological system within

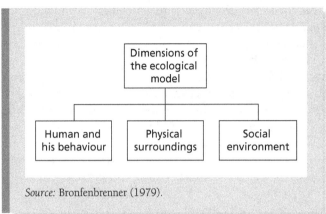

FIGURE 1.6
Dimensions of the Ecological Model of Mental Health

Source: Bronfenbrenner (1979).

it—which are within the individual and between individuals—and at various stages of organizations, community and the bigger society. Thus, ecological practice is a hard-wired endeavour which helps create a local community leadership structure that gives the work both authenticity and a grounded quality. It also necessitates creating supportive groups for community participation to reduce strains and frustrations of individuals as far as practicable. However, the ecological model has its drawbacks as well.

- The model chiefly lays its foundation only on the values of the local conditions of the community.
- The model has widened the definition of 'human environment' as a result of which drawing precise conclusions becomes taxing.
- The levels beyond the meso system are hardly given any prominence in the development of interventions.
- Circular causality and interdependence fail to address the influence of power differences in the ecosystem.
- This model also requires a new definition of the criterion for the psychologist's work in the community as well as the educational set-up involving research in the field of community psychology.
- The naturalistic and evolutionary perspectives of the model leave no space for the creation of forces for any change in the community.

In sum

Community psychology is a derivative in the field of psychology that studies individuals from the context of community interactions. The ultimate aim is to bring about a sense of improved well-being and functionality of the community. The prominent models in community psychology are (a) biopsychosocial model and (b) Bronfenbrenner's ecological model. The systems of Bronfenbrenner's ecological model are micro system, meso system, exo system, macro system and chrono system.

1.2.5. CORE VALUES IN COMMUNITY PSYCHOLOGY

The essence of community psychology lies in its core values. However, it is to be noted that the *original spirit* of community psychology—which was dominant at the very inception of the field—has been lost because of many reasons. It entails not only a feeling of passion but also personal vision,

FIGURE 1.7
Core Values of Community Psychology

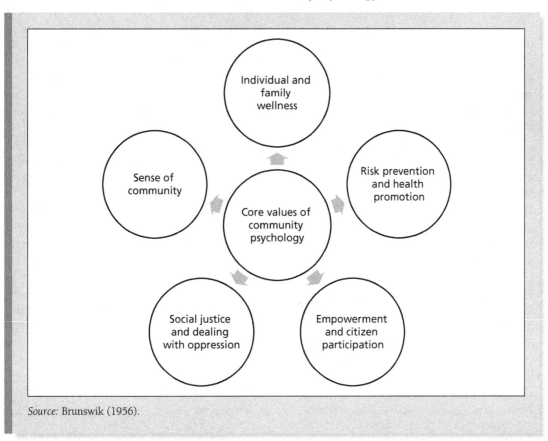

Source: Brunswik (1956).

ideology, a sense of empowerment, resilience, persistence, humour, spirituality and transcendence (Coon, 2000; Hill, 2000; Sarason, 1994). These components may be regarded as resources for social activism (Abdul-Adil, 1999; Balcazar, 1999; Molock & Douglas, 1999, Potts, 1999; Ramos, 1999; Rodriguez & Quellette, 1999). Thus, spirit is a multifaceted, multidimensional concept which varies from person to person and ecology to ecology (Brunswik, 1956; Hammond, 1966).

The core values of a sense of community, respect for human diversity, social justice, individual and family wellness, collaboration and community strengths, along with empirical grounding, empowerment and citizen participation, as presented in Figure 1.7, help members to be related to the global context and enjoy quality through interdisciplinary contributions. Empirical grounding relates to the integration of research with community action as far as practicable. This is expected to make community action more effective and the research more valid in the long run. It is also to be noted that the psychologist engaged in studying community processes often serves as a *participant-conceptualizer*, who is actively involved in the community and also attempts to understand and explain the intricate nuances of its working. Thus, he/she remains an *active agent* as well as an *objective onlooker* of the process—being both an *insider* and an *outsider* (Bennett et al., 1966).

1.2.6. HUMAN DIVERSITY

In today's society, human diversity is a reality because of increasing trend of population; scarcity of basic facilities such as education, health and job opportunities in all locations; and changing social structure and migration for survival. In the past, people were mostly dependent on agriculture and preferred to settle down in their birthplace. Now, the advancement of science and technology and enhanced awareness among common people about various facilities has created an urge among the younger generation to go out of their native place for higher education. Subsequently, after higher studies, people prefer to settle down in a new place with a job for better comfort.

Human diversity in occupation, industry and community has both advantages and disadvantages. Advantages include getting exposed to another culture, knowing about the practices of another culture, generating creative ideas in workplace and enhanced outcomes. Nowadays, in every business organization, top management wants people from diverse backgrounds so that they can satisfactorily address the issues of the customers from different perspectives in terms of proper communication and pushing a product. Whenever a customer comes across a salesperson from their community in another geographical location, they are more likely to become dependent on them in decision-making and in selecting any item, with a notion that they will guide them in purchase. In that way, for business promotions, recruitment of a salesperson from another cultural background is beneficial. In the industry, there is a common notion that during brainstorming sessions, employees from diverse backgrounds would be able to bring in their own ideas and experiences in the new workplace, which might be beneficial for policy decision. The disadvantages of human diversity are many. For example, people from another culture struggle to adjust in new culture, and their social acceptability is also low. Second, some people do not feel mentally happy when they settle down in another place. They feel alienated and become vulnerable to social discrimination and boycott. Third, children also struggle to adjust in new cultural set-ups, since they do not find children from their own community. Fourth, during any crisis, people feel very helpless.

1.2.7. SOCIAL JUSTICE

The term 'social justice' has a significant meaning in ensuring the well-being of common people in the society. It is based on the concept of human rights and equality, as outlined in the Indian Constitution; that is, every individual in a society should enjoy equal national wealth, opportunities and privileges. The principles of social justice should be applicable in every aspect of community life. There are four broad principles of social justice and they are equity, access, participation and rights. Every individual born in a country/community should enjoy equal opportunity in all respects, irrespective of their social, cultural and religious backgrounds. It is the obligation of the federal and local government to bring appropriate legislation towards this end and implement them. Social justice in terms of legislation, policy and practice would ensure equality among all, and thereby every individual will lead a quality life. Nevertheless, it is quite likely that an individual with better talent and quality will enjoy better life, since their demand will be higher as compared to those of a person with low talent, poor knowledge and skills. In some societies, in the name of rendering social justice to disadvantaged population, some section of poor people from the so-called upper social caste or community remain deprived from government programmes and facilities, since, officially, they are from the upper social groups. This issue needs debate and discussion to ensure social justice to economically backward groups of people, irrespective of social, cultural and religious identities. It we look at the philosophy of the Indian Constitution, it talks about equality and equity. In reality, do people of all the sections of the society enjoy equity and equality, including the people of the upper social strata, with poor economic conditions?

1.2.8. SENSE OF COMMUNITY

It focuses on the *experience of community* rather than its structural features. It refers to a perception of belongingness, interdependence and mutual commitment that links individuals in a collective manner (Kloos et al., 2007). It forms the pedestal of collective unity (McMillan & Chavis, 1986). It assists as a standard for the judgement of social capital; the creation of social policies; the evolvement of social and geographical societies; and the assessment of community capacity building. Community psychologists regard the sense of community as predominant to their value-based practices for the promotion of social justice and social change (Sarason, 1974). Community organizations, from time to time, at grassroots levels, help the citizens to identify local issues and decide how to address them. Different forms of community coalitions bring citizens and institutions of the community together to address different community problems. Some examples include religious congregations, schools, police, business and government.

The sense of community often has 'creases' of different kinds, if intrapersonal or interpersonal relationships are not maintained smoothly. The need is then felt to mend them delicately with skilled hands. One pertinent proactive avenue in this regard is provided by counselling. The technique is explained in detail in the following section with suitable illustrations as seen in Figure 1.8.

1.2.9. EMPOWERMENT

Empowerment means providing self-confidence to people and imparting knowledge and skills among them so that they can take their own decision in a given situation. However, the term 'empowerment' has different connotations in different situations. For example, in the case of school-based reproductive health education for adolescents, empowerment means dissemination of correct and complete knowledge among adolescents about various aspects of reproductive health such as nutrition, health and hygiene, functions of reproductive organs, family planning methods, modes of transmission and prevention of HIV/AIDS, and consequences of risk behaviours. If scientific information based on evidence is shared with the adolescents about all these issues and it is reinforced twice or thrice, it is expected that most of the adolescents will not indulge in any risk behaviour and will follow healthy lifestyles for good health and better career growth. The reason for healthy lifestyle is empowerment of adolescents with correct and complete knowledge about the issues.

FIGURE 1.8
Factors for Sense of Community

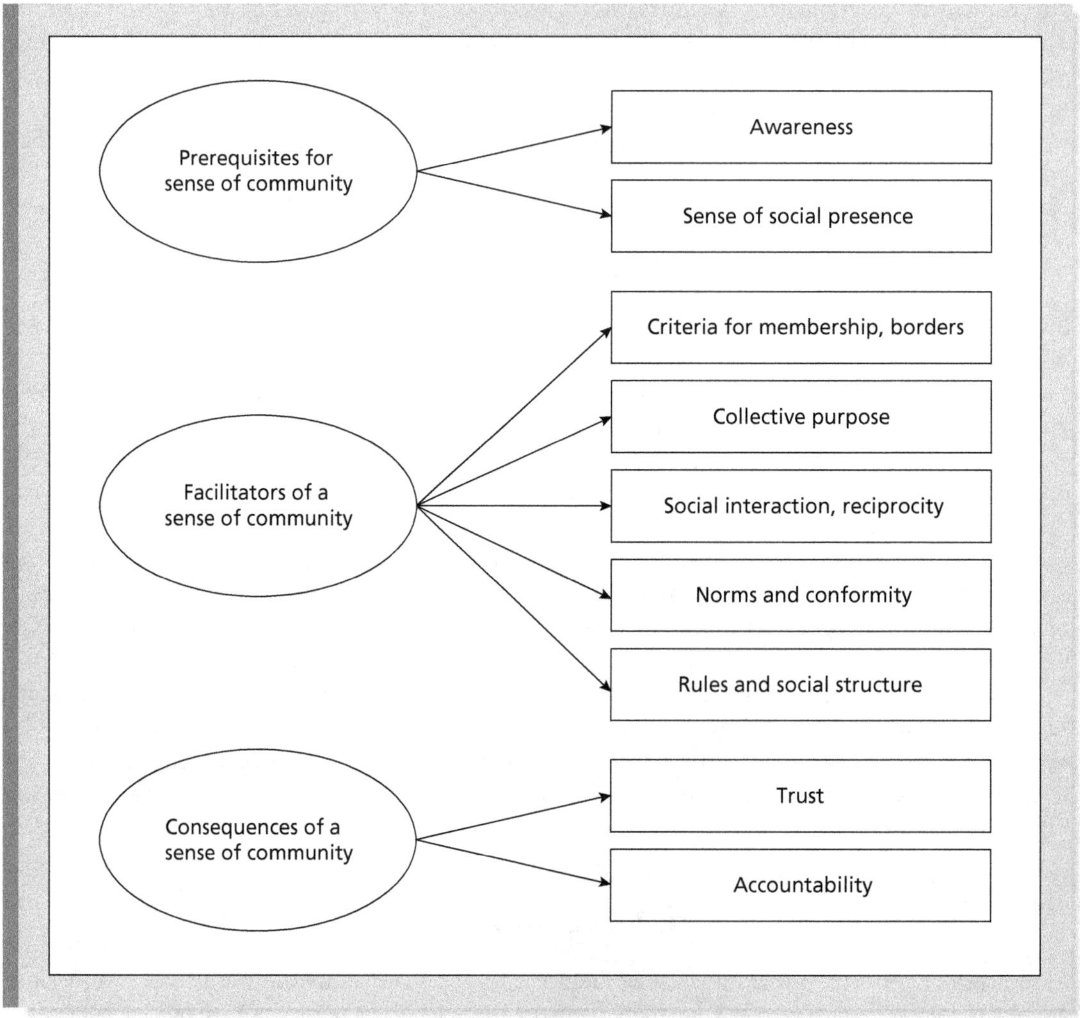

Let us have a look at another example in case of community-based intervention programmes. One NGO is going to help people living below the poverty line—especially women—for forming a self-help group. The NGO is acting as a facilitator for getting funds from the rural bank for running the self-help group. NGO personnel discussed modalities to form a self-help group with the poor rural women and asked them to come out with an idea for running a small business which has a market for selling the products and how to share the responsibilities jointly. They helped in preparing the documents and went to the bank for sanction of funds under a government scheme and finally got the fund. They also monitored the implementation of the scheme and ensured that the women of the self-help group were able to make some profit out of their business and save some part of it after sharing the profit. In that way, they moved ahead and were able to flourish and sustain their business. The initial support provided by a local NGO—with information about government scheme for supporting poor women for the formation of self-help groups—helped the poor women to improve their economic conditions and find a meaningful life.

1.2.10. COMMUNITY PARTICIPATION IN COMMUNITY-BASED INTERVENTION PROGRAMMES

For success of any community-based intervention programme, community participation is a prerequisite. Therefore, it is the duty of the programme manager of any welfare or government organization to involve all the community members from the beginning of conceptualization of any community-based intervention programme. Community members need to be informed about the ground reality pertaining to any issue which is bothering the common people and their views, and suggestions should be sought to design the need-based intervention programme. Once they are convinced and involved in the programme at the development stage, they will have better understanding about the efficacy of the programme and will perceive it as their own. In turn, community members will give full support for effective implementation of the programme. For monitoring the progress of implementing the programme, a committee should be formed by a group of people in which there should be representatives from the community as selected by the community members. The involvement of the community representatives in the committee will help to develop a trust-building relationship with the local community. There are several examples of positive outcome of community involvement in intervention programmes. For example, in an intervention programme aimed at rehabilitating the children of commercial sex workers (CSWs) by keeping them with their mothers in the same locality, other people of the same locality and the neighbouring community, as well as public representatives, that is, local counsellors and Member of Legislative Assembly, were involved in various capacities in the implementation. Local community leaders were briefed about the objectives of the intervention programme and their support was sought for a good cause; they were empowered to implement the project while the project staff had given them guidance regarding implementing the project. The support which was received from the local community included a space (local club premise) for children's study during the evening when their mothers remain busy in their business, teaching and guiding children by community volunteers, generating funds for excursions, and organizing games and sports for them in which children from neighbouring communities were invited to participate. Supervision of children mobility for safety, taking children to health camps for immunization, admitting children of CSWs in local schools and monitoring their performance and so on were also taken care of. The most important aspect is acceptance of the children of CSWs by the larger society which would give them self-confidence and a sense of belongingness.

In sum

The broad core values in community psychology are (a) human diversity, (b) social justice, (c) sense of community and (d) empowerment. Community participation is a crucial agent for the success of community-based intervention programmes.

1.2.11. EVOLUTION OF PERSPECTIVES OF COMMUNITY PSYCHOLOGY

There are multicultural and multifaceted approaches to enable the creation of preventive social interventions pertaining to the varied cultural, social and ethnic needs of each community. It is to be noted that the origin of studies related to community psychology had its genesis after the Second World War. It was then that the concepts of prevention began to be stated as salient for the field of mental health. The provision of services before a problem arose in a specific individual was a novel approach in this field. This is referred to as the *seeking mode of treatment* unlike the traditional *waiting modality of treatment*. It is the mental health professionals who seek contact with the community at large to offer treatment options in the former version. In contrast, the waiting mode of treatment ensures that the clients wait for their turn in seeking treatment from mental health professionals. Before the Second World War, the services were available *after* the individual, family members, friends or public officials recognized the appearance of personal difficulties. That was the initial point of the seeking mode of treatment. The founding of the field hails back to the Boston Conference on the Education of Psychologists for Community Mental Health at Swampscott, Massachusetts (4–8 May 1963). This is more commonly referred to as the Swampscott Conference (Bennett et al., 1966), during which the term 'community psychology' was coined. Psychiatrists Erich Lindemann and Gerald Caplan were two of the foremost thinkers regarding translating concepts from the individual to the community. Consultant–consultee relationship was highlighted to a great extent. The publication of two journals, namely the *American Journal of Community Psychology* (Charles Spielberger, founding editor, 1973) and the *Journal of Community Psychology* (Frederick C. Thorne, founding editor, 1973), enabled research publications in this area (Iscoe et al., 1977; Levine & Perkins, 1997).

Five different forces appear to play a pivotal role in increasing community-oriented thinking, namely (a) interests in preventive perspectives, (b) reforms in mental health systems, (c) developments in group dynamics, (d) research and action; movements for social change and liberation and (e) an undercurrent of optimism about social change efforts (Levine et al., 2005). Public health was much influenced due to the preventive perspectives on problems in living. Preventive measures can be of different forms such as sanitation, vaccination, education and early detection of illness and treatment. The second force involving varied reforms in mental health systems began with the Second World War and continued into the 1960s. The Veteran's Administration and the National Institute of Mental Health relied heavily on psychological principles to be applied in the community set-up. Further, Kurt Lewin initiated studies on group dynamics and action research traditions, which served as yet another influential factor in being the third force for community psychology. Movements for social change and liberation reached a crescendo during the 1960s and early 1970s, serving as the next impetus for the same. People became inspired to think globally and act locally. Finally, optimism about the ability to find different solutions for problems at the societal level influenced job training and employment programmes, as well as local community action organizations. It is also to be noted that the field had its identity solidified with the establishment of the Society for Community Research and Action (SCRA) in 1987 and included several groups of varying research interests. The SCRA continues to promote theory and practice of community psychology over various topics of research interests.

The field of community psychology—while developing its identity—started defining problems differently and had different kinds of interventions. Some of the pivotal ones are as follows:

1. Cowen (1973) identified a number of interventions—principally dealing with child or youth development—and often focused on disadvantaged populations and collaborations with local citizens.
2. Trickett et al. (1972) proposed that ecological concepts could enhance the understanding of how individual coping or adaptation techniques varied in social environments with differing psychosocial qualities.
3. Sarason (1974) opined the concept of 'psychological sense of community' by abandoning the individualistic focus on mental health services.
4. Rappaport (1977) persuaded that community psychology needs to focus on its values to guide research and social action.

The specific field of community psychology has a number of implications as follows (Rappaport & Seidman, 2000; Snowden, 1987):

- It helps in providing knowledge regarding how to design and evaluate community-based interventions.
- It talks about generating effective social support systems that enhance a sense of positive well-being.
- It deals with bringing about the implementation of a large number of preventive mental health programmes.
- It mentions bringing about the evaluation of self-help groups and how to carry out participatory research.

1.2.11.1. The Community as a Teacher

Community psychology has now advanced into a broader context and may be regarded as an experienced teacher preaching the members precisely about what competencies are required to solve a problem and how to reap the harvests from the inductive process. A pupil of community psychology is provided with rich experiential folds that mend the gaps in training. For this, it becomes mandatory that the community worker identifies with the total community. It can then help the members to preach how it is organized and how it works, who the real members are and where they are heading. Different emerging issues of the environment, such as global warming, climate change and increasing pollution need to be probed into by adopting a mature outlook, which is, in fact, done by the community at large. As such, it is the community which reflects much of its life lessons upon its inmates. It does so by facilitating the pupil to become sufficiently involved in a community to find out the first-hand skills required to manage a particular problem. This makes them enriched with experiential wisdom to address the problem from a mature perspective (Kelly, 2006). The community, as such, becomes a useful vehicle for setting priority, evaluating past efforts and, most importantly, planning on the part of the community worker for the future. The need is felt to create health-promotive environments by the wellness worker, the details of which are narrated in the upcoming section.

1.2.12. COMMUNITY PSYCHOLOGY IN PRACTICE

1.2.12.1. Prevention of Problems to Restore Well-being

Community psychology is essentially targeted towards *prevention of problems* rather than their treatment. Prevention of problems within a community is premised to be tackled through the alteration of the social systems within the community. One chief target of such intervention is inclusion of all community members, and it has a holistic perspective to embrace the society as a whole and sees individuals against their strengths and competencies instead of focusing only on their lacunae. Thus, community psychology is more a way of thinking and looking at the canvas of life rather than mere show of theories. The spectrum of issues addressed by this discipline works in close association with the social relevance as well as curative practices. For this reason, a community psychologist studies the sociocultural, political and environmental factors of that community and stresses on the theory-based research as well as applied service delivery. Their tasks include connecting individuals to their community (particularly the disadvantaged community members), understanding the need of the community and prevalent social issues concerning the community, implementing and assessing action-oriented interventions. They work with families, educational institutions, hospitals or even with governmental bodies to ensure effective functioning and actively conduct research studies in all human service sectors.

Community psychology counts prevention of illness as one of its prime motives and is designed to modify/alter a running process that creates high risk of problems in living (Rappaport & Seidman, 2000). It may be of different types.

1. **Primary prevention:** Primary prevention targets to prevent the actual occurrence of any illness among the people at risk. For instance, immunization against polio is carried on towards preventing the incidences of polio among newborn children of a community. Primary prevention does not single out certain individuals for special treatment. Instead, intervention is done on a mass scale, targeting an entire population, that is, a school system, factory and community, even a nation. The goal is to reduce the occurrence of problems and promote adjustment within the whole target population. It could involve legislative and social policies (at social action levels) or interpersonal levels through the interaction of community members, through which incidences of new cases are kept under control. The reduction in social and emotional problems associated with the occurrence of such illness are also to be added to the positive outcomes of primary prevention.
2. **Secondary prevention:** Secondary prevention focuses on early identification and intervention. Quick and accurate assessment by the community—physicians, teachers, clergymen, police officers, court officials, social workers—allows remedial procedures to begin early.
3. **Tertiary prevention:** Tertiary prevention involves providing services to individuals who have already developed problems. It also seeks to reduce the long-term consequences of having a disorder; for example, mental health workers help those who have recovered from mental illness to participate fully in the occupational and social life of the community. This may be depicted by a schematic representation as seen in Figure 1.9.

As such, health promotion is much focused in community psychology. 'Health is essentially viewed as a state of complete physical, mental and social well-being and not simply the absence of disease' (World Health Organization, 1986). This definition entirely covers the construct of health

FIGURE 1.9
Leavell and Clark's Level of Prevention

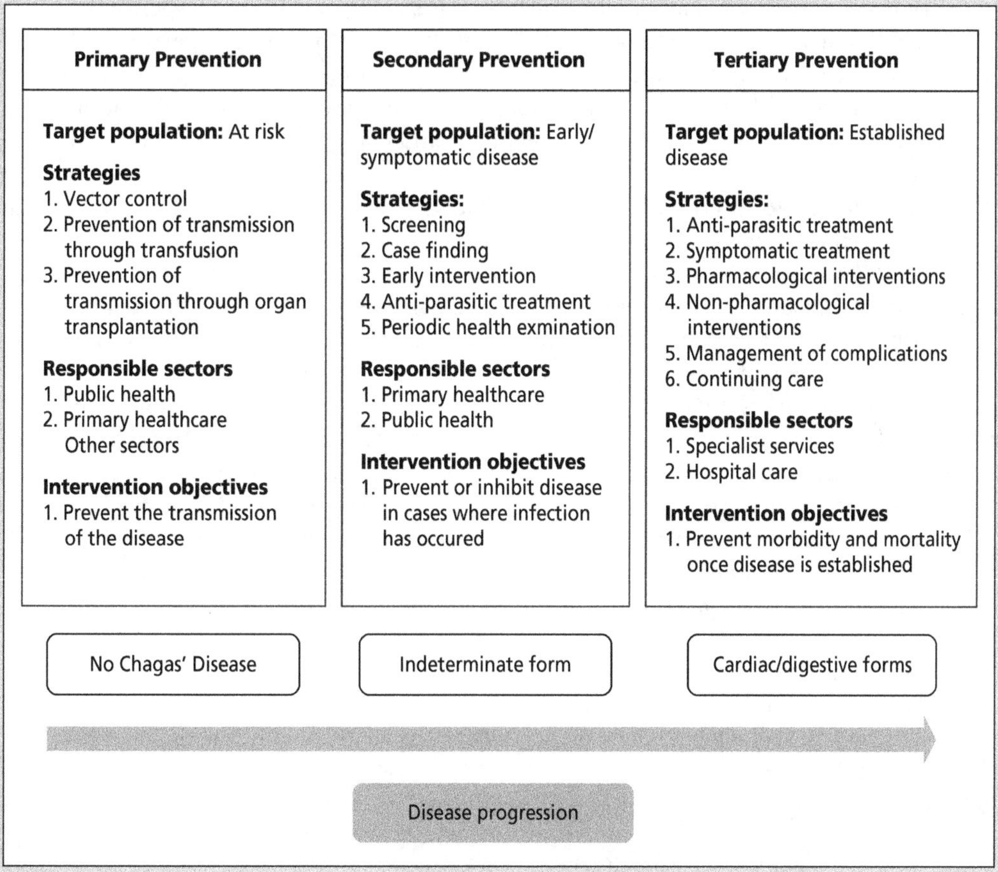

Primary Prevention	Secondary Prevention	Tertiary Prevention
Target population: At risk **Strategies** 1. Vector control 2. Prevention of transmission through transfusion 3. Prevention of transmission through organ transplantation **Responsible sectors** 1. Public health 2. Primary healthcare Other sectors **Intervention objectives** 1. Prevent the transmission of the disease	**Target population:** Early/symptomatic disease **Strategies:** 1. Screening 2. Case finding 3. Early intervention 4. Anti-parasitic treatment 5. Periodic health exmination **Responsible sectors** 1. Primary healthcare 2. Public health **Intervention objectives** 1. Prevent or inhibit disease in cases where infection has occured	**Target population:** Established disease **Strategies:** 1. Anti-parasitic treatment 2. Symptomatic treatment 3. Pharmacological interventions 4. Non-pharmacological interventions 5. Management of complications 6. Continuing care **Responsible sectors** 1. Specialist services 2. Hospital care **Intervention objectives** 1. Prevent morbidity and mortality once disease is established
No Chagas' Disease	Indeterminate form	Cardiac/digestive forms

Disease progression

Source: Leavell and Clark (1979).

and also attempts to combine both the educational and environmental support that are conductive to health (Donald et al., 2006). The World Health Organization (1986) identifies five major actions that constitute the core of health promotion, which are '(a) building healthy public policy, (b) creating supportive environments, (c) strengthening community action and participation, (d) developing personal skills and (e) re-orienting health services'.

1.2.12.2. Competence Development among Community Members and Professionals

Competence development is yet another pertinent aim of community psychology. It involves promoting positive human development and includes one's sense of control over life and feeling of satisfaction and well-being. It is essentially associated with one's sense of personal control in life and thereby, one's extent of controllability awareness (Heth & Somer, 2002). Competence can be understood as a construct with four dimensions, which are:

1. **Personal control:** The individual's belief on one's ability to manage responsibility.
2. **Shared control:** The individual's belief on one's ability to manage interpersonal situations which have shared responsibility.
3. **Others in control:** The individual's ability to accept the outcome from another person's responsibility. In such situations, individual participation and responsibility are found to decrease.
4. **Uncontrollable/unpredictable:** The individual's ability to accept outcomes that are unpredictable or uncontrollable.

According to Erikson (1968)—from the lifespan perspective—personal competence in children develops during school age, specifically during the stage of industry vs. inferiority. It occurs between 6 and 11 years of age and corresponds to the latency stage in Freudian theory. Children begin to participate in an organized programme of learning. Industry—the ability to work and acquire skills—is the keynote of the stage, which children develop when they begin to comprehend their own potentials through attending school and gradual workmanship. This period is associated with the child's powers of deductive reasoning and self-discipline as well as the ability to relate to peers according to prescribed rules. Children learn that they are able to make things to be able to master and complete a task. A sense of inadequacy and inferiority—the potential negative outcome of this stage—may result from different sources.

1. Children may be discriminated at school.
2. They may be told that they are inferior.
3. They may be overprotected at home, or excessively dependent on the emotional support of their families.
4. They may compare themselves unfavourably with the same sex parent.

Thus, industry includes a feeling of being interpersonally competent—the confidence that one can exert positive influences on the social world in the quest of becoming a meaningful individual and achieving social goals. The psychosocial strength of competence (that finally develops into workmanship) thus underlies the basis for participation in the socio-economic-political order. It is characterized by formal ritualization; its counterpart being referred to as formalism.

Another approach to competence development is that of *empowerment* (Burton & Kagan, 1996; Rappaport, 1981, 1987). It is gaining a sense of control over one's life which relates to both psychological as well as social process as it includes collective action to have access to societal resources which are equitably distributed (Zimmerman, 2000). Empowerment is the central value and strategy used in community psychology (Rappaport & Seidman, 2000). Citizen participation is central to empowerment. It relates to effective:

- Role relationships
- Participation
- Access to resources

Empowerment is targeted in community development to enhance local power and well-being of its inmates (Christens, 2012). Psychosocial benefits are reaped by the participants in terms of well-being and resilience, which in turn have compounding effects on the psyche. Global mental health gets promoted consequently. This also has its behavioural manifestations among the most marginalized and least powerful of societies, women, minorities, the poor and the young, to name a few, who tend to suffer from much instabilities, being vulnerable subgroups in the community (Anand & Lee, 2011; Santiago et al., 2011). Marginalization in different aspects and its relationship with mental health extend beyond race, gender and socio-economic status. Hence, the cry of the present day is to make these subgroups empowered physically and psychologically so that wellness of the community is maintained (Rojas, 2011). It also relates to the mechanism by means of which people, organizations and communities gain mastery over their daily lives and environment, acquire valued resources and basic rights, achieve important life goals and reduced societal marginalization (Maton, 2008; Rappaport, 1977, 1987). This automatically calls forth empowerment of individuals at the psychological level in the long run. Consequently, citizens of a community adopt more proactive approaches in the communities and develop critical understandings of their socio-political environments (Zimmerman, 1995). It includes skill-building, increasing one's motivation to make social and political changes and so on. This can be promoted by means of collective efforts to resist unwanted change and to bring about alterations, and challenge the status quo where needed.

1.2.12.3. Needed Skills of Community Psychologists

Stark (2009) outlined different skills which need to be present among community psychologists or scholars engaged in the wellness paradigm. They may be classified as *action skills* (e.g., consulting, community organizing, community development, coalition building, conducting evaluation and research), and *social skills* (e.g., active listening, rapport building, conscientiousness, group facilitation and conflict resolution). These are expected to improve the expertise and focus of such professionals.

1.2.13. CREATION OF HEALTH-PROMOTIVE ENVIRONMENTS

Adaptive personal behaviours are highlighted to enhance physical health and reduce the risk of illness (Cataldo & Coates, 1986; Green, 1984). Such behaviours need to be considered, not only at the individual level but in terms of dynamic transaction between individuals, groups and their socio-physical milieu. It essentiates explicit analysis of the interplay between the environmental resources available in any particular area and the specific health habits and lifestyles of the inhabitants (Lindheim & Syme, 1983).

It is also to be comprehended that the health promotion adheres to both personal and collective achievement on the part of the individual (Stokols, 2001). The biopsychosocial model of health needs to be taken into consideration at this juncture. Health promotion requires developing a repertoire of good health habits on the part of the individual—early in life—so as to carry them forward throughout adulthood and old age (Sanyal, 2019). *Health behaviours* are of much importance at this juncture. They refer to the behaviours undertaken by people to enhance or maintain their health. Poor health behaviours appear to accumulate unwanted materials in the

TABLE 1.1
A Few Dimensions of Health-promotive Environments

Dimensions of Health and Well-Being	External Life Resources and Opportunities	Behavioural, Psychological and Physiological Impact
Physical health	Being resistant to any form of injury, physically comfortable, non-pathogenic, non-toxic and ergonomically sound	Physiological health and well-being, absence of illness symptoms
Mental and emotional well-being	Environmental controllability, social support, economic and personal stability	Sense of fulfilment and happiness, little feeling of stress, feeling of belongingness in the community, greater productivity and involvement, injury prevention and environmentally protective behaviour.

body and contribute to illness. A *health habit* is a health-related behaviour which is often internalized on the part of the individual without their own awareness. These habits usually develop in childhood and begin to stabilize around 11 or 12 years of age (Cohen et al., 1993) like brushing teeth, eating a healthy diet, running playfully or having lot of physical movements. The habits are generally introduced by the caregivers. Hence, health awareness is an epitome of the mature 'elder-mind.' A few dimensions of health-promotive environment is given in Table 1.1.

Mental well-being is essentially brought forth by means of building positive psychological and personal resources that enable individuals to be satisfied with their lives by balancing one's emotionality, having unconditional acceptance of oneself, finding purpose and meaning in life; seeking personal growth, autonomy and competence; having a sense of personal control and generally experiencing optimism on the whole (ODPHP, 2016). As such, individuals with sound well-being are likely to transform life's myriad problems into moderate and beneficial challenges by means of their coping skills (Szabo et al., 2012). Different factors such as family, education, spiritual activities, recreation, supportive interpersonal relationships, employment and commuting are found to contribute much to whether the environment is health-promoting or not (Cohen & Syme, 1985; Sarason & Sarason, 1985). This holds true in the workforce, industrial set-up or any other organizational setting.

At this juncture, it is worth noting that 'salutogenesis' refers to aetiologic processes that tend to enhance emotional and physical well-being of individuals by highlighting on the health domain in terms of positivity (Antonovsky, 1979). Many personal and environmental factors have been found to serve as mediators in human health. Personal factors may be further classified into biogenetic, psychological and behavioural processes. Environmental factors include different types of socio-physical environment, such as geographic, architectural/technological and socio-cultural processes that influence health. Thus, the environment enjoys certain characteristics which account for health promotion or otherwise of its inhabitants.

- Both the physical and social environment may operate in a different manner for transmitting different diseases.
- The environment can also serve as a stressor, source of safety or danger.
- It may also be viewed as an enabler of health behaviour.
- The environment serves as a provider of health resources to its members.

Thus, wellness may be regarded as an ecological enterprise which involves the intricate relationship between personal and community spheres (Kelly, 2006). This accounts for the emergence of resilient coping among the inmates of any given community (Seligman, 1998). A different epistemology is invoked and the new enterprise may be considered as the province of the wellness domain which is mainly concentrated on situations and their impact on individuals. A scholar of this domain uses many methods to examine the diversity of the individuals acting in a variety of situations. He is engrossed with the following five ideologies.

1.2.13.1 An Agenda for Situated Enquiry in the Form of Contextual Thinking

It necessitates the wellness scholar to be involved in the deep understanding of individuals so that they become familiar with their unfamiliar aspects. Traditions, social norms and expectations for behaviour—established within and across specific social settings are analysed in detail—to probe into the nuances of individual-environment fitness (Kingry-Westergaard & Kelly, 1990; McLoyd, 1998). Situated enquiry of a context takes into consideration the linguistic and cognitive constructions that are used by people in everyday encounters to have a better understanding of social constraints and resources. Thus, the unique micro-social processes applicable to each participant are of much concern through this mode of enquiry (Seaburn et al., 1994).

It also has its implications in organizational psychology and specifically, workplace behaviour. In fact, the individuals' sense of optimism, humanitarian acts, civility, generative thinking and so on are impacted by the unique qualities of everyday work environments (Taylor et al., 1997). The ecological work opines that people can not only influence the social conditions which tend to limit their freedom, dignity and opportunities for growth, but can also preserve the traditions and rituals that endanger health in nature. One also needs to possess interdependent contextual thinking with intradisciplinary and interdisciplinary thinking.

1.2.13.2. New Disciplinary Connections and Pluralistic Methods

The utility of pluralistic methodologies has been advocated by many wellness scholars to address issues of situational effects (Cronbach, 1986). Situated enquiry is open-ended in nature and the pluralistic process of the ingrained methodology helps in facilitating the understanding of the phenomenon. Personal, social and historical factors of behaviour need to be taken into consideration by the scholar in his enquiry. This requires the scholar to be open-ended and flexible so that he attends everyday events and daily interactions of people. It is also desirable to have concordance with other allied disciplines to have a better comprehension of the microsocial underpinnings.

1.2.13.3. Adopting a Novel Perspective of Learning with Others Instead of Assessing Them

The wellness scholar needs to adopt new ways of doing their work so as to gain insight into the sources of everyday behaviour of inmates of a community (Anderson, 1990; Leiblinch & Josselson, 1994). Research venues, portfolios of techniques and criteria for truth are changed from time to time by the scholar who adopts new directions and listens to the stories of the participants taking their own perspectives. Autobiographies, oral histories and narratives are often used to assess their stories and personal tales (Conway, 1998; Denzin & Lincoln, 1994). The scholar is also encouraged towards collaborative enquiry by inculcating major qualities like openness to new experiences, investment in learning about new concepts, and the ability to expend energy in the working relationship, creating a listening ambience and social support groups too. A good listener tends to get salient and deep data which reflects the participant's stories. The wellness scholar is also desirable to be a distant, detached and objective observer who has genuine interest and care for the participant and his environment. A conjoint process of conversing and listening needs to be understood by the wellness scholar to comprehend the behaviour in situ. He becomes a learner in the process. The situated enquiry is also a relationship of trust between the two parties.

1.2.13.4. Learning about Resilient and Competent Communities

Expression of health-endangering experiences and listening to such collective stories of resilient groups and communities help to develop insights on the part of the wellness scholar to affirm core values of participation, justice and dignity. The underlying social fabric can then be deciphered by wellness scholars in this regard. Wandersman and Florin (1990) and McKnight (1995) are some scholars who have worked in the arena of resilient and competent community development. *Social norms and boundary spanning* are concepts from social psychology and organizational psychology to clarify how shared values and informal standards of behaviour affect wellness behaviour (Kelly et al., 2000; Opp, 1982). If information and the exchange of resources are health-promoting and efficacious to the group, then the wellness of the community is restored. The group thereby has greater ability to adapt.

1.2.13.5. The Analysis of Variety and Quality

It takes into consideration each and every participant in the community and analyses their inherent variety. In fact, examining patterns of diversity in wellness behaviour can serve as a constructive force to extend the boundaries of the concept of wellness in the community. The patterns of variability can provide an alternative frame of reference as well. Thus, knowledge about wellness is a process of enquiry which is cross-disciplinary in nature and has a personal flavour. Understanding wellness needs to take into consideration the different ways in which individuals construct meaning, create social ties and establish a workable cohesive culture. Then only can a sense of global community be well developed. Its concept is elaborated in the forthcoming section.

1.2.13.6. Counselling

Conceptually in Feltham's and Horton's (2006) verbose,

> Counselling is mainly though not exclusively, listening-and-talking based method of addressing psychological and psychosomatic problems and change, including situational dilemmas, deep and prolonged human suffering, crises and developmental needs and aspirations towards the realization of human potential.

In contrast to biomedical approaches, counselling operates largely without medication or other physical interventions and is concerned with not only mental health but with spiritual, philosophical, social and other aspects of living.

In its functional bearing, counselling is not a fixed entity, but a 'fluid' process in which the counsellor continuously tries to adjust the course of development to accommodate the unique and emerging needs of the client. The venture should provide a point of reference to chart an effective dealing strategy in each personal context. In its functional fold, counselling is:

- A 'relationship' that emphasizes the quality of the relationship offered to the counselee. The relationship has non-passive warmth, genuineness and a sensitive understanding of the counselee's thoughts and feelings.
- It involves a 'repertoire' of skills. The interventions need to focus on feeling, thinking and acting.
- It emphasizes 'choice'. Helping aims to help the counselee become better choosers in life.
- It focuses on 'problems of living'.
- It is a 'process', that denotes movement, flow and interaction of at least two people in which each is being influenced by the behaviour of the other. The process ideally involves two people but gradually emerges to be a 'self-help process'.

Major dichotomous issues in counselling are:

- **Autonomy vs heteronomy:** The distinction between self-control and control by others. Aim of counselling is to promote self-dependence.
- **Domination vs submission:** Counselling pinpoints this polarity to be situation-specific where submission is comfortable but at times assertion, not domination. This should be the aim.
- **Meaning vs futility:** When meaning is lost in life or a specific situation, the individual grapples in the darkness of depression. Counselling tries to erase the futile approach of withdrawal and shows the meaning of life in other dimensions.
- **Individuation vs group identity:** Counselling proposes that a person should develop their talents and pursue their interests and not stay as 'merely' a member of a group.
- **Socialization vs alienation:** Counselling pinpoints that socialization relates to adaptability—the pillar of strength in personality—whereas alienation is closure of the mind.

Counselling is a 'communicative therapy' to improve relationship perspectives in our lives. In a counselling set-up, communicative pattern-wise, the professional

- Listens to all concerned (empathetic listening)
- Avoids premature judgements, comments
- Avoids harsh, humiliating, ridiculing, abusive language.
- Avoids assumptions of client's lying, stealing, pretending and so on
- Avoids derogatory references, particularly regarding the significant social members
- Has unconditional acceptance of the client even if their behaviour seems socially unacceptable
- Avoids a sense of superiority or expressing contempt regarding the client's background, motive and so on

Communication in counselling calls for 'good listening' which makes the client feels affirmed, accepted, safe, understood and is motivated to give more information about oneself. The counsellor's communicative mode 'helps' clients to develop self-help skills; to experience and express feelings; to own responsibility, to solve problems, and reduces the client's defensiveness, and increases 'owning'. Hence, in a 'relationship breakage', the counsellor acts as a mediator between 'me' and 'myself in the other', to develop 'insight' into the self, to develop a 'positive self-perspective', to help rely on 'self-resources', to 'cut down expectations' regarding others and to help locate 'self-importance' amidst others in 'my-own-reality'. Encouraging healthy habits like detoxifying the environment helps a long way too in improving qualitative community life. Elaboration of the same follows in the upcoming section.

1.2.14. COMMUNITY-BASED REHABILITATION (CBR) MATRIX

CBR is a means of empowerment for differently abled individuals through the provision of equal opportunities in the community, thereby invoking among them a feeling of inclusion and acceptance. It was initially installed by WHO in the mid-1970s for people from underdeveloped countries which face a huge dearth in professional resources, where opportunities in educational, social and occupational arenas as well as health services were rendered. The professionals working in CBR develop CBR services for disabled people through the support of their families, communities and stakeholders. These rehabilitations are proven to enhance the quality of life of people with disabilities and their families by meeting their basic needs. The workers of CBR could involve psychologists, social workers, volunteers or even family members who are in direct contact with the community. These CBR personnel could act as a bridge between the people in need and the service by providing them the needed health services and guidelines. Most of the times, these personnel need to be trained to equip them with the needed knowledge and skills. The workers may be segregated into non-professionals and paraprofessionals. Those trained professionals, who can deal with the issues of the community to a great extent, can be helpful in being updated about the status of the community.

A South Kolkata NGO called Iswar Sankalpa can be taken as an example of community programme server. Their aim is to help the mentally disturbed people on the streets. Being equipped with skilled professionals, they undertake training programmes to develop paraprofessional groups. With the help of these participants, they take up the programme of locating such clients on the streets. With the help of the psychiatrists, they administer medicines along with food that is given to them by the participants/trainees. When the client improves with regular help, they are brought into Iswar Sankalpa's clinic for the continuation of their treatment. They also have provisions to keep a certain number of clients as an inpatient system. With sufficient improvement in their mental health, the NGO tries to relocate them to their families.

They have another programme of holding a monthly campaign in certain areas of Kolkata where a number of such clients have been identified. They organize a half-day-long programme including the locals of the area to orient them to such mental problems and help them understand the implications of regular community treatments. They have been quite successful in having the help from the local boys and girls, the paan sellers or grocers to imbibe into their programmes who have taken the responsibility of administering medicines and food to such clients, initially under the supervision of paraprofessionals and later on their own. Hence, a number of non-professionals have also been included in their community programme.

However, the use of non-professionals and paraprofessionals is not free of drawbacks.

- They lack elaborate knowledge, training and skills needed for providing rehabilitation services.
- The personnel may behave impulsively based on little knowledge and could result in severe repercussions.
- Sometimes, the training may not empower the individual to compete against people who have gone through intensive training in the same field. They may not have a secure career.

Therefore, mentoring of these paraprofessional forces is very crucial in communicating the correct concepts and true spirit of the CBR. They should be under regular supervision and monitoring of the skilled professionals is mandatory. Such community guides may often correct the wrong orientations and make the non-professionals and paraprofessionals quite fruitful in the adopted programme.

1.3. INCULCATING THE HABIT OF DE-CLUTTERING THE COMMUNITY

De-cluttering one's immediate surroundings in terms of homes, work space and so on engages one to be relieved of innumerous stimuli impinging in the sensory field which otherwise would have competed for neural-image representation in the brain, producing chaos and restricting one's ability to focus and process further information. Clutter steals one's focus, making the individual feel overwhelmed, distracted and agitated (Sanyal, 2019). The momentary pleasures that could have been experienced by the self are robbed off by means of clutter.

A person can engage himself in this de-cluttering exercise by first beginning from where they spend most of the time. One can also set-up a schedule which may be regularly maintained to clean the 'clutter'. They also need to deal with indecision on a moment-to-moment basis so as to successfully de-clutter the external space. They require inculcating practices to be able to enjoy the process by simplifying their digital/virtual life as far as practicable. One needs to be cautious about the duration spent in such activities, the relevance of such activities, to prioritize one's activity frame, to de-clutter devices from time to time as well and to become aware of one's own digital mindset (Scott and Davenport, 2016).

Simplifying one's activities can be done by focusing on three important daily goals, building in 'sacred time' (where the individual simply does absolutely nothing, and just remains as he 'is'), leaving work on time, taking a 'digital sabbatical' (in terms of usage of smart phones, laptops, iPads and so on), harnessing the power of flow and focus, monitoring one's emotional state and so on. Procrastination may be overcome through understanding one's own priorities, removing distractions as much as practicable, simplifying one's distractions by planning ahead, engaging in mindfulness practice and so on. Further actions may be simplified by eating meals mindfully, cleaning the house mindfully, walking mindfully, experiencing nature mindfully, paying attention to different parts of the body mindfully, exercising mindfully and so on. Thus, disciplining oneself is like decluttering one's house, which needs to be done regularly. Managing one's thoughts requires commitment and practice on a moment-to-moment basis. Hence, attaining self-control over one's impulses appears to help an individual to remain healthy in the community.

The field of community psychology is still nascent and has a long way to go. Nevertheless, it is confronted with certain major challenges which are brought to the foreground in the following section.

***

In sum

Some applications of community psychology are prevention of illness, community competence development, provision of counselling services, creation of health promotive environment, learning about the resilient community, and analysis of variety and quality. Leavell and Clark (1940) categorized prevention into primary, secondary and tertiary. The components of competence are (a) personal control, (b) shared control, (c) others in control and (d) uncontrollable/unpredictable.

1.4. CHALLENGES IN COMMUNITY PSYCHOLOGY

Individuals are still faced with the traditions of the larger field of psychology where they are taught to be self-directed and to achieve individual status and recognition for their work and talents. This automatically reduces the opportunities for shared, reciprocal learning in the stifling competitive world. Often, it results in different psychosocial problems. Hence, there is a need for community psychology by involving new ways of understanding the processes of community change. It is to be noted that the original spirit of community psychology may then once again be re-evaluated to make it more viable by means of:

- Encouraging and continuing education in the field of community psychology.
- Improving family communication, encouraging discussion groups and so on.
- Creating time to share stories about community work.
- Creating safe settings to enlarge one's spirit.

It is then that the quality of social life is expected to be much enhanced by creating social settings that are safe for intellectual exchanges. In fact, the ideal spirit of this specialized sub-field of psychology is to listen, appraise and generate ideas based on the ideas of all participants where each and every participant is considered as a potential resource.

1.5. CONCLUSION AND IMPLICATIONS

Human beings thrive in terms of personal resources, no doubt. But the vibrancy of these resources does not take place in vacuum. The interactions and communications of the social members, so to say specific community members, are the supportive platform to create vibrant ripples in one's life. The community serves as the mirror to look at oneself, realize the meaninglessness of isolated living and understand the implications of integrated group life. Community is the most important resource for everybody. In today's world, this new dimension of psychology has its focal point of interest in deducing resource generation and resource utilization from balanced, positive group life. Community psychology offers a protective shield for everybody in terms of offering assurances of help from group life. Psychology gives us theories to understand the self- and identity-creation processes. Community psychology prompts us to understand community security in terms of group identification and group empathy. Hence, in today's world of competition and chronic diseases, community workers seem to be the assets in the society to create the ambience of assurance and help. Century-wise, life is progressing. It cannot live on a single dot of 'self'. It has to have its wings spread to embrace 'we' in the group-rim.

The subject of community psychology has many implications. It ensures addressing emerging issues in the community as a facilitator, trainer and therapist. The chapters in the book are tailored to address the prominent inferences of community psychology. The need, scope and practice of community-based intervention for mental illness, physical illness, differently abled people, aged people, school-going children, vulnerable kids, at-risk children, project-affected people, victims of calamities and HIV-AIDS patients are extensively discussed in this book. Although the subject is relatively new in India, it is slowly getting attention as it takes interest on common issues of the community with a view towards improving the overall quality of life through a participatory approach.

EXERCISES

One-mark Questions

1. What is a community?
2. Define community psychology.
3. Mention any two core values of community psychology.
4. What do you understand by empowerment?
5. What are the different types of prevention?
6. Define 'sense of community'.
7. What does counselling mean?
8. What do you understand by the biopsychosocial model of health?
9. Define wellness.
10. What is meant by active listening?

Five-mark Questions

1. Why is community psychology regarded as a *linking science* and a *linking practice*?
2. Mention the skills that are prerequisite in a community psychologist.
3. Discuss the role of cultural context in community psychology.
4. Discuss the role of community members in community development activities.

Ten-mark Questions

1. How can competence development be made possible in a community?
2. Discuss the significance of preventive interventions in community psychology.

Reflexive Questions

1. Critically stipulate the future of community psychology.
2. Discuss the implications of community psychology.
3. Is community psychology pertinent to current society? Discuss.

REFERENCES

Abdul-Adil, J. K. (1999). Inner-city Muslim action network: Islam as a resource in revitalizing urban communities. *Community Psychologist, 32*, 29–31.

Anand, P., & Lea, S. (2011). The psychology and behavioural economics of poverty. *Journal of Economic Psychology, 32*(2), 284–293.

Antonovsky, A. (1979). *Health, stress, and coping.* Jossey-Bass.

Balcazar, F. E. (1999). Lessons from liberation theology. *Community Psychologist, 32*, 19–24.

Bennett, C. C., Anderson, L. S., Cooper, S., Hassol, L., Klein, D. C., & Rosenblum, G. (Eds.). (1966). *Community psychology: A report of the Boston conference on the education of psychologists for community mental health.* Boston University Press.

Bronfenbrenner, U. (1979). *The ecology of human development.* Harvard.

Brunswik, E. (1956). *Perception and the representative design of psychological experiments* (2nd ed.). University of California Press.

Burton, M., & Kagan, C. (1996). Rethinking empowerment: Shared action against powerlessness. In I. Parker & R. Spears (Eds.). *Psychology and society: Radical theory and practice.* Plenum.

Burton, M., & Kagan, C. (2000). *'Edge' effects and resource utilization in community psychology.* Paper presented at the European Community Psychology Conference, Bergen, Norway.

Cataldo, M. F., & Coates, T. J. (Eds.) (1986). *Health and industry: A behavioral medicine perspective.* John Wiley and Sons.

Christens, B. D. (2012). Targeting empowerment in community development: A community psychology approach to enhancing local power and well-being. *Community Development Journal, 47*(4), 538–554.

Cohen, S., & Syme, S. L. (Eds.). (1985). *Social support and health.* Academic Press.

Cohen, S., Tyrrell, D. A. J., & Smith, A. P. (1993). Negative life events, perceived stress, negative effect, and susceptibility to the common cold. *Journal of Personality and Social Psychology, 64*, 131–140.

Conway, J. K. (1998). *When memory speaks: Reflections on autobiography.* Knopf.

Coon, D. (2000). Salvaging the self in a world without soul: William James's The Principles of Psychology. *History of Psychology, 3*, 83–103.

Cowen, E. L. (1973). Social and community interventions. *Annual Review of Psychology, 24*, 423–472.

Cronbach, L. J. (1986). Social inquiry by and for earthlings. In D. W. Fiske & R. A. Shweder (Eds.), *Meta-theory in social science* (pp. 83–107). University of Chicago Press.

Dalton, J., Elias, M., & Wandersman, A. (2001). *Community psychology: Linking individuals and communities.* Wadsworth/Thomson Learning.

Denzin, N. K., & Lincoln, Y. S. (Eds.). (1994). *Handbook of qualitative research.* SAGE Publications.

Detels, R., & Breslow, L. (1997). Current scope and concerns in public health. In R. Detels, W. W. Holland, J. McEwen, & G. Omenn (Eds.), *Oxford textbook of public health, Volume 1: The scope of public health* (3rd ed., pp. 3–17). Oxford University Press.

Donald, D., Lazarus, S., & Lolwana, P. (2006). *Educational psychology in social context* (3rd ed.). Oxford University Press.

Erikson, E. H. (1968). *Identity: Youth and crisis.* Norton.

Feltham, C., & Horton, I. (2006). *The SAGE handbook of counselling and psychotherapy.* SAGE Publications.

Fiske, A. P., Kitayama, S., Markus, H. R., & Nisbett, R. E. (1998). The cultural matrix of social psychology. In D. T. Gilbert, S. Fiske, & G. Lindzey (Eds.), *Handbook of social psychology* (4th ed., Vol. 2, pp. 915–981). McGraw-Hill.

Green, L. W. (1984). Modifying and developing health behavior. *Annual Review of Public Health, 5*, 215–236.

Hammond, K. (Ed.). (1966). *The psychology of Egon Brunswik.* Holt.

Henderson, D. A., & Scutchfield, F. D. (1989). Point-counterpoint: The public health versus medical model of prevention. *American Journal of Preventive Medicine, 5*, 113–119.

Heth, T. J., & Somer, E. (2002). Characterizing stress tolerance: Preliminary results from a new approach to controllability and its relationship to perceived stress and reported health. *Personality and Individual Differences, 33*(6), 883–895.

Hill, J. L. (2000). A rationale for the integration of spirituality into community psychology. *Journal of Community Psychology, 28*, 139–149.

Iscoe, I., Bloom, B., & Spielberger, C. (Eds.). (1977). Community psychology in transition. *Proceedings of the national conference on training in community psychology.* Hemisphere.

Kazdin, A. E. (Ed.) (2000). *Encyclopedia of psychology.* (Vol. 2). Oxford University Press.

Kelly, J. G. (1971). Qualities for the community psychologist. *American Psychologist, 26*, 897–903.

Kelly, J. G. (Ed.). (2006). *Becoming ecological: An expedition into community psychology.* Oxford University Press.

Kelly, J. G., Altman, B. E., Ryan, A. M., & Stelzner, S. (2000). Understanding and changing social systems. In J. Rapapport & E. Seidman (Eds.), *The handbook of community psychology* (pp. 133–159). Plenum.

Kim, H., & Markus, H. R. (1999). Deviance or uniqueness, harmony or conformity? A cultural analysis. *Journal of Personality and Social Psychology, 77*, 785–800.

Kingry-Westergaard, C., & Kelly, J. G. (1990). A contextualist epistemology for ecological research. In P. Tolan, C. Keys, F. Chertok, & L. Jason (Eds.), *Researching community psychology: Issues of theory and methods* (pp. 23–31). APA.

Kloos, B., Hill, J., Thomas, E. Wandersman, A., Elias, M. J., & Dalton, J. H. (2007). *Community psychology: Linking individuals and communities* (3rd ed.). Wadsworth Cengage Learning.

Leavell, H. R., & Clark, E. G. (1979). *Preventive medicine for the doctor in his community* (3rd ed.). Robert E. Krieger Publishing Company.

Lehman, B. J., David, D. M., & Gruber, J. A. (2017). Rethinking the biopsychosocial model of health: Understanding health as a dynamic system. *Social and Personality Psychology Compass, 11*(8), 1–17. https://doi.org/10.1111/spc3.12328

Levine, M., Perkins, D. D., & Perkins, D. V. (2005). *Principles of community psychology: Perspectives and applications* (3rd ed.). Oxford University Press.

Levine, M., & Perkins, D. V. (1997). *Principles of community psychology: Perspectives and applications* (2nd ed.). Oxford University Press.

Lieblich, A., & Josselson, R. (Eds.). (1994). *Exploring identity and gender: The narrative study of lives* (Vol. 2). SAGE Publications.

Lindheim, R., & Syme, S. L. (1983). Environments, people, and health. *Annual Review of Public Health, 4*, 335–354.

Maton, K. I. (2008). Empowering community settings: agents of individual development, community betterment, and positive social change. *American Journal of Community Psychology, 41*, 4–21.

McKnight, J. (1995). *The careless society.* Basic Books.

McLoyd, V. (1998). Socio-economic disadvantage and child development. *American Psychologist, 53*(2), 185–204.

McMillan, D. W., & Chavis, D. M. (1986). Sense of community: Definition and theory. *Journal of Community Psychology, 14*, 6–23.

Molock, S. D., & Douglas, K. B. (1999). Suicidality in the Black community: A collaborative response from a womanist theologian and a community psychologist. *Community Psychologist, 32*, 32–35.

Naidoo, A., Pillay, J., & Bowman, B. (2007). *Community psychology: Analysis, context and action.* UCT Press.

Naidoo, A. V., van Wyk, S. B., & Carolissen, C. (2004). Community mental health. In L. Swartz, C. de la Rey, & N. Duncan (Eds.), *Psychology: An introduction.* Oxford University Press.

ODPHP (Office of Disease Prevention and Health Promotion). (2016). *Health-related quality of life and well-being.* ODPHP. http://www.healthy people.gov/2020/topics-objectives/topic/health-related-quality-of-life-well-being

Opp, K. D. (1982). The evolutionary emergence of norms. *British Journal of Social Psychology, 21*, 139–149.

Potts, R. (1999). The spirit of community psychology: Spirituality, religion and community action. *Community Psychologist, 32*, 17–18.

Prilleltensky, I. (2001). Value-based praxis in community psychology: Moving toward social justice and social action. *American Journal of Community Psychology, 29*, 747–778.

Prilleltensky, I., & Nelson, (1997). Community psychology: Reclaiming social justice. In D. Fox & I. Prilleltensky (Eds.), *Critical psychology: An introduction.* SAGE Publications.

Ramos, C. M. (1999). Faith at work: Reflections on Catholic social teaching and community psychology. *Community Psychologist, 32*, 36–37.

Rappaport, J. (1977). *Community psychology: Values, research, and action.* Holt, Rinehart and Winston.

Rappaport, J. (1981). In praise of paradox: A social policy of empowerment over prevention. *American Journal of Community Psychology, 9*, 1–25. Reprinted In Revenson, T., D'Augelli, A., French, S. E., Hughes, D., Livert, D., Seidman, E., Shinn, M., & Yoshikawa, H. (Eds.). (2002). *A quarter century of community psychology* (pp. 121–145). Kluwer Academic/Plenum.

Rappaport, J. (1987). Terms of empowerment/exemplars of prevention: Toward a theory for community psychology. *American Journal of Community Psychology, 15*, 121–144.

Rappaport, J., & Seidman, E. (2000). *Handbook of community psychology.* Kluwer.

Rhodes, S. (2013). *Bronfenbrenner's ecological theory.* http://uoit.blackboard.com

Rodriguez, E. M., & Quellette, S. C. (1999). The metropolitan community church of New York: A community of gay and lesbian Christians. *Community Psychologist, 32*, 24–29.

Rojas, M. (2011). Poverty and psychological distress in Latin America. *Journal of Economic Psychology, 32*(2), 206–217.

Santiago, C. D. C., Wadsworth, M. E., & Stump, J. (2011). Socioeconomic status, neighborhood disadvantage, and poverty-related stress: Prospective effects on psychological syndromes among diverse low-income families. *Journal of Economic Psychology, 32*(2), 218–230.

Santrock, J. W. (2011). *Life-span development* (13th ed). McGraw-Hill. http://voices.yahoo.com/bronfenbrenners-ecological-theory-human-development–7630190.html?cat=72

Sanyal, N. (2019). De-cluttering of lifestyle through self-control: The most needed track to health attainment. *Journal of Health Studies, 1*(1), 21–39.

Sarason, I. G., & Sarason, B. R. (Eds.). (1985). *Social support: Theory, research, and applications.* Martinus Nijhoff Publishers.

Sarason, S. B. (1994). *Psychoanalysis, general custer, and the verdicts of history: And other essays on psychology in the social scene.* Jossey-Bass.

Scott, S. J., & Davenport, B. (2016). *De-clutter your mind: How to stop worrying relieve anxiety, and eliminate negative thinking.* Oldtown Publishing LLC.

Seaburn, D. B., Lorenz, A. D., Gunn, W. B., Jr., Gawinski, B. A., & Mauksch, L. B. (1994). *Models of collaboration* (pp. 3–350). New Harbinger Publishing.

Seligman, M. E. P. (1998). President's column. *APA Monitor, 29*, 2–5.

Snowden, L. R. (1987). The peculiar successes of community psychology: Service delivery to ethnic minorities and the poor. *American Journal of Community Psychology, 15*, 575–586.

Stark, W. (2009).*Community psychology in Europe: Potentials and challenges.* Plenary presentation at the 7th European Congress of Community Psychology, Paris.

Stokols, D. (2001). Creating health-promotive environments. In M. S Jamner & D. Stokols (Eds.), *Promoting human wellness: New frontiers for research, practice and policy.* University of California Press.

Szabo, S., Tache, Y., & Somogyi, A. (2012). The legacy of Hans Selye and the origins of stress research: A retrospective 75 years after his landmark brief 'letter' to the editor of Nature. *Stress, 15*(5), 472–478. doi:10.3109/10253890. 2012.710919

Taylor, S. E., Repetti, R. L., & Seeman, T. (1997). Health psychology: What is an unhealthy environment and how does it get under the skin? *Annual Review of Psychology, 48*, 411–447.

Trickett, E. J. (1996). A future for community psychology: The contexts of diversity and the diversity of contexts. *American Journal of Community Psychology, 24*, 209–234. Reprinted in Revenson, T., D'Augelli, A., French, S. E., Hughes, D., Livert, D., Seidman, E., Shinn, M., & Yoshikawa, H. (Eds.). (2002). *A quarter century of community psychology* (pp. 513–534). Kluwer Academic/Plenum.

Trickett, E. J., Kelly, J. G., & Todd, D. M. (1972). The social environment of the school: Guidelines for individual change and organizational redevelopment. In S. Golann & C. Eisdorfer (Eds.), *Handbook of community mental health* (pp. 331–406). Appleton-Century-Crofts.

Wandersman, A., & Florin, P. (1990). Citizen participation, voluntary organizations and community development: Insights for empowerment and research. *American Journal of Community Psychology, 18*(1), 41–54.

Warren, R.L. (1977). *The community in America.* Rand-McNally.

Webster, I. (1989). *Webster's encyclopedic unabridged dictionary of the English language.* Portland House.

Weick, K. E. (1984). Small wins: Re-defining the scale of social problems. *American Psychologist, 39*, 40–49.

Winett, R. A., King, A. C., & Altman, D. G. (1989). *Health psychology and public health: An integrative approach.* Pergamon Press.

World Health Organization (1986, 21 November). *Ottawa charter for health promotion.* Paper presented at First International Conference on Health Promotion, Europe.

Zimmerman, M. A. (1995). Psychological empowerment: Issues and illustrations. *American Journal of Community Psychology, 23*(5), 581–599.

Zimmerman, M. A. (2000). Empowerment theory: Psychological, organizational and community levels of analysis. In J. Rappaport & E. Seidman (Eds.), *Handbook of community psychology* (pp. 43–63). Kluwer/Plenum.

RECOMMENDED READINGS

Kloos, B., Hill, J., Thomas, E. Wandersman, A., Elias, M. J., & Dalton, J. H. (2007). *Community psychology: Linking individuals and communities* (3rd ed.). Wadsworth Cengage Learning.

Rappaport, J., & Seidman, E. (Eds.) (2000). *Handbook of community psychology.* Kluwer/Plenum.

Reich, S. M., Riemer, M., Prilleltensky, I., & Montero. (2007). *International community psychology: History and theories.* Springer.

Shinn, M., & Toohey, S. M. (2003). Community contexts of human welfare. *Annual Review of Psychology, 54,* 427–460.

Trickett, E. (2009). Community psychology: Individuals and interventions in community context. *Annual Review of Psychology, 60,* 395–419.

PART B
Community Interventions

Community-based Intervention for Mental Health

ABSTRACT

Standards in understanding mental health and illness in India are catching up with the contemporary changes in the world. Appreciating the investment of societal backgrounds in human thought and behaviour has resulted in utilizing community involvement for defining, altering and intervening in the various dimensions of mental health. Community mental health is a complex process of decentralizing the mental health service delivery, wherein it will be accessible to every community member. This chapter aims at introducing the concept of community mental health to its readers by deliberating upon the updated definitions of mental health and illness. The chapter also discusses the myths, misconceptions and social stigma attached to mental health, challenges concerning prevention and identification as well as treatment gaps especially in the developing countries. A detailed account of age-specific mental health conditions, as seen among people, is also stated along with reference to its prevalence. The chapter further explains the concept of community-based rehabilitation and its range of outcomes. To better equip the reader, a brief timeline of events that have been taking place in the Indian legislation, in the forms of policies and Acts, is provided. The chapter ends with an elaborate model, which has community participation at its core and the paraprofessional force in psychology at its lead, to address the common mental health issue of the nation along with prompting mental health and well-being.

Keywords: Mental health; mental illness; community; rehabilitation; community mental health

2.1. INTRODUCTION TO COMMUNITY MENTAL HEALTH

Like physical health, mental health is also very important for every individual to realize their quality of life. A person with good mental health is able to adjust with others and can lead a productive life and finally can contribute to the family and society. If a person suffers from any major mental health problem, they would not be able to lead a well-adjusted life and will fail to contribute to the family and society. Over and above, they create problems for others, and their productivity is also affected when they come in interaction with people who have mental health challenges. Therefore, there is a need to address the mental health problems, promptly, just as physical health problems.

Indices of mental health are now given due importance, and cautious investments are done in terms of defining and recognizing them. Intervention in mental-health-related matters is seen around the globe. A healthy development in the efforts to comprehend mental health is the addition of the 'wellness' component, which is understanding mental health as a growing process where an individual strives to attain mental hygiene. To detail this, continuous progression cannot be achieved in isolation. Rather, persistent socialization and community life that an individual indulges in can help in achieving the desired outcome. In line with the World Health Organization (WHO) definition of mental health, striving for mental wellness has components such as good interpersonal skills, positive interpretation and outlook on daily life events, responsible and productive thinking and behaviour, and maintenance of peace and harmony with oneself and the society. Hence, understanding mental illness as one among the several components and not the only component of mental health has been taking shape. A better advertence to developing intervention strategies has evolved, which encourages community involvement into mental healthcare delivery without which successful and long-lasting results cannot be found. This is revolutionary in itself for several reasons: Myths and age-old misconceptions, which have their form and circulation at the community level, get scrutinized and countered within the same community itself; the fading-away of the dark and deep-rooted stigma about mental illness; reduction in the reluctance in seeking psychological help would occur steadily; issues related to non-availability of mental-health professionals in meeting the heightened demand can be tackled effectively through well-coordinated community support; comprehending mental health in relation to productivity, quality of life and happiness would cautiously be cultivated into individuals; psychological disturbance resulting from social issues such as abuse and victimization, parent–child relationships and old-age-related uneasiness could be approached sensitively which then reduce the global burden significantly; and legislative and legal support for meeting the mental-health needs of the community can be effectively pursued to ensure enduring solutions. Active community participation in mental healthcare would provide an updated understanding based on global standards and latest research findings and so parameters of good mental health can accordingly be modified. This is a crucial step in taking precautionary measures for avoiding socially induced deviant behaviour in the community and implementing interventions based on contemporary findings.

Community mental health (CMH) is a joint effort developed out of the confirmation that mental health of people, belonging to all sections of society, matters and should be addressed in ways that suit the dynamics of each community, and their characteristics such as age, gender and other demographic distributions, educational and vocational backgrounds, prevalent mental illness conditions and the possible causal factors and culture and other community-specific factors could be taken into account. However, community rehabilitation services in any form are yet to be established in many developing countries (Tinney et al., 2007) and so is the case of India as well. It requires investments in capability building, creating bridges across community assets and establishing trust with community and clients. In other words, they depend more on social capital than financial capital (Lee et al., 2018). Thus, each community can make their strategies with backgrounds of common knowledge and understanding of mental health and illnesses, which would produce the best possible outcomes. This chapter is an attempt to place mental health in the context of community and attempts to explore ways in which untapped community assets can be utilized to co-produce immediate, persistent and scientific elucidations to the unmet mental-health needs of our society.

CMH is a comprehensive paradigm where the mental-health needs of a community are addressed, met and facilitated within the community through the right usage of community resources. It can be understood as a pattern of distribution of mental healthcare services, which has its spread across the community and involves the constructive engagement of every community member. Through CMH, the mental healthcare services are intended to be decentralized from limited manpower and be distributed at the community level in order to increase the service availability. CMH aims at bridging the wide treatment gap that exists in the country by encouraging community participation and volunteering. The goals of CMH services are amiable and are as follows:

1. Promote mental health and well-being in the community
2. Prevent mental illness from the community
3. Treat mental illness in the community
4. Rehabilitate mental illness within the community

In sum

- CMH is a comprehensive paradigm where the mental health needs of a community are addressed, met and facilitated within the community through the right usage of community resources.
- The goals of CMH services are amiable and are as follows:
  1. Promote mental health and well-being in the community
  2. Prevent mental illness from the community
  3. Treat mental illness in the community
  4. Rehabilitate mental illness within the community

2.2. UNDERSTANDING MENTAL HEALTH AND MENTAL ILLNESS

Mental health and mental illness are two related but distinct concepts that are often mistakenly used as antonyms. Mental health is popularly understood as the absence of mental illness and vice versa. This understanding cannot be completely nullified since absence of mental illness is an important characteristic of mental health. As defined by WHO, mental health is a 'state of wellbeing in which the individual realizes his/her own abilities, can cope with the normal stresses of life, can work productively and fruitfully, and is able to make a contribution to his or her community' (WHO, 2005, p. 12). Clearly, mental health is lot more than just the absence of illness. Rather, it is the right combination of well-being as well as the quality of one's functioning as an individual as well as a member of their community. The progressive and substantial changes in the conceptualization of mental health beyond mental illness give enormous importance to the subjective well-being of an individual and are understood as a measure of one's functioning at both individual and community levels. Since mental health does not just involve positive emotions and behaviour, it is important to rightly understand what subjective well-being stands for. The three components of mental health identified by Keyes (2002, 2006, 2014) describe the aforementioned by compartmentalizing subjective well-being into three:

1. **Emotional well-being,** which includes the following:
   - Positive affect (happiness and interest in life)
   - Judgement of one's quality of life
2. **Psychological well-being,** which includes the following:
   - Self-acceptance (liking most of one's own personality)
   - Positive growth (attempts to become better in life)
   - Purpose in life (sense of direction and meaning)
   - Environmental mastery (being good at managing the responsibilities of daily life)
   - Autonomy (confidence to think and express own ideas and opinions)
   - Positive relations with others (having good relationships with others)
3. **Social well-being,** which includes the following:
   - Social contribution
   - Social integration (feeling part of the community)
   - Social actualization (believing that society is becoming a better place for all people)
   - Social coherence (societal functioning making sense to an individual)

This popularly sited 'tripartite structure of mental health' trivializes the misconception that a mentally healthy person should always remain happy and positively functional since mental health is multifaceted. Several studies conducted among adults (Gallagher et al., 2009) and college students (Robitschek & Keyes, 2009) have supported these components of well-being and validated its crucial contribution towards mental health. Hence, newer dimensions of mental health, emphasizing on subjectivity, have evolved.

Mental illness is also a concept that has been undergoing changes in terms of its conceptualization. Over time, the definition of mental illness has been found to be varying and is often drastically coloured by the societal stigma and ignorance. In fact, the definition given by the public is often punitive and slender than reality. The uninformed nature of the subject matter has made the society insensitive. On the one hand, emotional ups and downs associated with day-to-day life stresses are labelled as mental illness and such people may get easily targeted, but on the other hand, the tendency to trivialize anything other than psychosis as normal and not provide attention and treatment to such individuals also exist. All these points lead to the heightened need of a precise definition of mental illness and make it available to the public so as to build a sensitive and informed community. However, not as broad as mental health, defining mental illness has been approached through a more expanded outlook and the rejecting attitude is undergoing alterations. However, unlike mental health, the concept of mental illness has no established definition covering the various dimensions which are internationally approved. The American Psychiatric Association has defined mental illness as 'a health condition involving changes in emotion, thinking or behavior (or a combination of these) and is associated with distress and/or problems functioning in the social, work or family activities' (American Psychiatric Association, 2019). The WHO understands mental disorders to be characterized by 'some combination of abnormal thoughts, emotions, behaviors and relationships with others' (WHO, 2019a).

The *two continua model of mental illness and health* would rightly explain the relationship between the two: where, one continuum deals with the presence/absence of mental health, whereas the other is about the presence/absence of mental illness (Westerhof & Keyes, 2010). Similarly, the *dual-factor model of mental health* identifies mental health as a 'complete state' and finds subjective well-being as an important indicator for mental health prevention and intervention (Wang et al., 2011). Of course, culture plays a significant role in one's understanding of mental illness, and this is particularly true in a collectivist society like India. Since cultural milieus and practices are crucial in defining anchors of normality and abnormality, mental health and illness in the Indian context have to be understood in terms of its rich cultural background, systems of family, religion, politics, values, beliefs and morals that have been passed down over the years. Hence, CMH is of highest relevance in the country in order to intervene and enhance mental health and well-being of the community members.

In sum

The three components of mental health are as follows:

- *Emotional well-being:* Positive effect and judgement of one's quality of life
- *Psychological well-being:* Self-acceptance, positive growth, purpose in life, environmental mastery, autonomy and positive relations with others.
- *Social well-being:* Social contribution, social integration, social actualization and social coherence.

2.3. QUALITY OF LIFE

As long as an individual survives, it is very important that they lead a quality life; and life becomes meaningful. The meaning and definitions of quality of life varies from individual to individual. There are various dimensions of quality of life. It could be psychological, physical, environmental, social and sexual. However, it is a subjective and a multidimensional concept which speaks about some standard levels for emotional, physical, environmental and social well-being.

Nevertheless, common people perceive quality of life from different angles. For example, to some people, quality of life means earning more money while some feel happy when they are able to do something for others. Again, at different points of time, the meaning and definition of quality of life vary. During childhood, a child gets maximum happiness from games and sports or playing with another child. During adolescence, one wishes to get recognition from the peer group for any activity, and that recognition gives an adolescent more happiness.

In addition to wealth and employment, the built environment, physical and mental health, education, recreation and leisure time and social belonging are some of the standard indicators of the quality of life (Derek et al., 2009). According to the WHO, quality of life is defined as 'the individual's perception of their position in life in the context of the culture and value systems in which they live and in relation to their goals.'

2.4. MYTHS, MISCONCEPTIONS AND SOCIAL STIGMA ABOUT MENTAL HEALTH

People across the society, especially in the developing countries, possess a lot of myths and misconceptions about mental health problems. Myths, misconceptions and social stigma attached to mental health discourage common people to come forward for proper diagnosis and treatment. In general, most people prefer to remain unattended when they experience minor mental health problems instead of seeking mental health support services.

When parents notice unusual behaviour among their children, they do not draw the attention of mental health professionals. Rather, they prefer to overlook the same with an expectation that it would be automatically corrected once they grow. Some of the parents think that getting a person, suffering mental health problems, married or dependence on substances is the solution. After marriage the problem might disappear. The reality is that marriage does not help to solve the problem. Rather, it invites many more problems and the opposite partner becomes the worst victim of the situation and suffers their entire life. Thereafter, when they get one or two children, they also experience neglect, violence and abuse. Therefore, there is a need to seek mental health support services and encourage the person to undergo the same, which in turn will help to improve the situation and help to lead a quality life. After treatment, if the situation is found to have improved, parents may think of arranging the marriage of their children after consultation with the mental health professional. If mental health professional concurs with the decision, then only parents should proceed with marriage. Otherwise, it would be an unethical act on the part of the parents.

Nevertheless, in case of minor mental health challenges, some of the parents visit psychiatrists first because of misconceptions about the issue, instead of visiting a psychologist. Perhaps the problem did not require the attention of a psychiatrist; it could have been well addressed by a psychologist.

More interestingly, misconceptions also exist among some of the psychiatrists about the mode of treatment for people with mental health challenges in the developing countries. Sometimes, professional competition among various mental health professionals, especially in the developing countries, creates confusion in the minds of the common people. Some psychiatrists always prefer to start the medication without consulting a psychologist and make the patients dependent on medicine. However, as suggested by a psychiatrist, patient parties start the medication, which is pharmacological treatment. If the prognosis is not satisfactory, they discontinue the medication and do not further consult the psychiatrist or other mental health professionals.

Social stigma is so strong that if affects the marriage of an individual even if they recover from the problem and mental health professionals advise for a marriage. Marriage of other siblings is also affected. Normally, people avoid going for marriage in a family in which there is a person with mental health problem.

Feldman and Crandall (2007) remarked that 'the stigma of mental illness can be as harmful as the symptoms, leading to family discord, job discrimination, and social rejection.' In a study, authors made an attempt to understand the characteristics across various mental disorders, which lead to stigmatization and social rejection. Regarding social rejection, findings disclosed that three dimensions are essential in accounting for rejection: *personal responsibility* for the illness, *dangerousness* and *rarity* of the illness.

Corrigan and Watson (2002) stated that

Many people with serious mental illness are challenged doubly. On one hand, they struggle with the symptoms and disabilities that result from the disease. On the other, they are challenged by the stereotypes and prejudice that result from misconceptions about mental illness. As a result of both, people with mental illness are robbed of the opportunities that define a quality life: good jobs, safe housing, satisfactory health care, and affiliation with a diverse group of people.

2.5. STRATEGIES FOR CHANGING PUBLIC STIGMA

There are three possible strategies for changing public stigma and they include protest, education and contact (Corrigan & Penn, 1999). Groups protest inaccurate and hostile representations of mental illness as ways to challenge the stigmas they represent. These efforts send two messages. To the media: To 'stop' reporting inaccurate representations of mental illness. To the public: To 'stop' believing negative views about mental illness. Wahl (1995) is of the opinion that citizens are encountering far fewer sanctioned examples of stigma and stereotypes because of protest efforts. Evidence suggests that protest campaigns have been effective in getting stigmatizing images of mental illness to be withdrawn. Similarly, people should be educated with correct information about mental illness and then it will be expected that people will have better ideas about the issue and then they will change their views.

2.6. GLOBAL EPIDEMIC OF MENTAL DISORDERS WITH SPECIAL REFERENCE TO COMMON MENTAL HEALTH PROBLEMS

Mental health problems are global challenges. People across the countries are victims and are vulnerable to various mental health problems. However, the prevalence varies across countries and in different geographical locations. People living in countries with more resources and less population are less vulnerable to mental health problems as compared to people living in resource-constrained countries. Substantial evidence proves this. Higher prevalence rates of depression was reported in low- and middle-income countries such as Nigeria (5.5%; Adewuya et al., 2018), Ethiopia (17.5%; Molla et al., 2016), Malaysia (10.3%; Maideen et al., 2014), Pakistan (45.9%; Gadit & Mugford, 2007), India (15.1%; Poongothai et al., 2009) and Uganda (17.4%; Ovuga & Boardman, 2005). The scenario in the case of alcohol use disorder (AUD) is not any different as a Nepal-based cross-sectional study showed that 19.8 per cent of the men and 1.1 per cent of the women had AUD (Luitel et al., 2018). 'Alcohol use, lifetime drunkenness and alcohol-related problems' were very frequently found among the young adolescent population of countries with low- and middle-income capacity (Ma et al., 2018). A Portugal-based study found mental and behavioural disorders to be the second-most prevalent clinical condition (32%) among adolescents, followed by obesity (Abreu et al., 2018).

Mental illness is lot more than a unidimensional illness. It may take forms by the confluence of several factors and the ill are not the only victims of the condition. Hence, the burden of mental illness is huge, and it curbs an individual and their surroundings in all important arenas of their life. As per WHO reports, over 450 million people are mentally ill worldwide and contribute significantly to the global burden of diseases. Clubbing with neurological illness, mental disorder and particularly those induced by substance abuse have been reported to contribute to 14 per cent of the global burden (Saxena & Skeen, 2012). 'Increasing population sizes and growing awareness' can also be reasons for the increase in the perceived prevalence of mental health conditions (Baxter et al., 2014).

In the USA also, depression is found to be among the most prevalent mental disorders, particularly among adults, that is, 'an estimated 16.2 million adults in the United States had at least one major depressive episodes' (US Department of Health and Human Service, 2017). The *2004 Survey of Mental Health and Well-being in England* reported that 1 out of every 6 people had reported symptoms of depression or anxiety in the past week of the survey; and 'one in twenty have reported to experience suicidal thoughts in the past year' (Baker, 2018). The adults in the Latin ethno-lingual group of European countries were found to be more vulnerable to depression (Castro-Costa et al., 2007). The gender gap in depression has been a consistent finding in the mental health surveys based in European countries. 'Depression has been found to be twice as prevalent among women as it is among men' (Van de Velde et al., 2010). Alarming reports of inferior mental health from Australia should be quoted here. According to the National Survey of Mental Health and Well-being, nearly 45.5 per cent is the lifetime prevalence of mental illness in the country's population; further, 'nearly 1 million Australians had affective disorders, over 2.3 million had anxiety disorders and over, 800,000 had substance use disorders' in the year 2006 (Australian Bureau of Statistics, 2008). The prevalence of depression among children is fairly high among rural children in China as compared to their urban counterparts. However, 'children from ethnic minority, from poorer families, and whose parents are depressed are more likely to display depressive symptoms than other children' (Zhou et al., 2018). Generalized anxiety disorders were found to be prevalent (5.3%) in urban China. 'Age, gender, marital status, income level, insurance status, smoking, drinking and exercise behaviors, and comorbidity burden' were other factors which had strong associations with the illness condition (Yu et al., 2018). An assessment conducted among Chinese children and adolescents found over 50 per cent of them to be having increased risks of anxiety (Liu et al., 2018). Country-specific data indicates that people across the country have been suffering from different mental health problems. For example, a cross-sectional study in one tertiary hospital in Hanoi, Vietnam, reported that 18.5 per cent, 39.8 per cent and 13.2 per cent of the nurses were suffering from stress, anxiety and depression respectively (Tran et al., 2019).

2.7. EPIDEMIC OF MENTAL HEALTH PROBLEMS IN INDIA

Like other countries, people in India are also vulnerable to various mental health problems. Worldwide, about 56 million people suffer from depression (*The Hindu*, 2019, p. 2). Out of the 56 million, 5 per cent of them live in India where there are only about 4,000 psychiatrists to address mental health challenges like depression. Now, one can easily understand the crisis of mental health support services in a country like India. Vulnerability to mental health problems is more for the Indian population because of a number of factors such as stress in daily life, illiteracy, poverty, family violence, lack of social support and support services and diverse cultural beliefs and practices. Not much research is carried out in India on this issue. Therefore, lack of epidemiological study makes it hard to draw estimations on the right statistics of mental illness in India. However, the findings of limited regional studies are helpful to assess India's mental health status.

2.7.1. CHILD MENTAL HEALTH

Ensuring psychological well-being of children is crucial to their overall growth and development. A well-recognized concept in itself, nevertheless, child mental health problems are significantly contributing to the global burden of the time. In India, there is hardly any provision for child mental health. They are mostly confined to the urban areas, which are inaccessible, fragile and poor in service delivery (Ronad et al., 2017). Poverty is still India's reality and so malnutrition and anaemia among mothers and the resultant intrauterine growth retardation of children would reveal the pressing status of the nation. It is unfortunate but a child born into poverty (particularly a girl child) in India would grow up facing exploitation from multiple dimensions, which include family and school and could be subjected to physical, psychological and sexual torture. This would result into the child feeling worthless and developing a poor self-concept. It is important to be available to the extreme vulnerability of this population; such that, child mental health cannot be disturbed by any unhealthy environmental stressors such as 'death of a family member, marital discord or separation, environmental disasters and economic disadvantages' (Ronad et al., 2017).

Child mental health in India is an underresearched area. Given the lack of epidemiological studies, the existing investigations show a wide variation on the prevalence rate ranging from 0.48 per cent to 29.40 per cent (Malhotra & Patra, 2014). Studies estimated the prevalence rate of child mental illness to be 12.5 per cent in Bangalore (Srinath et al., 2005), 9.4 per cent in Kerala (Hackett et al., 1999) and 6.3 per cent in Chandigarh (Malhotra et al., 2002). Mental disorder prevalence was found to be 13.8 per cent among children between 0 and 3 years. Mental retardation, pica and expressive language disorder were found to be most prominent (Venkatashivareddy et al., 2013). Mental illness among children (4–16 years) were enuresis, phobia, stuttering and oppositional defiant disorders (Srinath et al., 2005). In a North India-based study conducted on children between the age of 4 and 11, the annual incidence rate of mental illness was calculated as 18/1,000, out of which 60 per cent of the cases were illness conditions which were considered to be adult psychiatric disorders such as depression, anxiety and personality disorders (Malhotra et al., 2013). Absence of empirical data in child mental health issues curbs the scientific nature of the subject matter to be presented for policymaking. Lack a national statistics of mental health, in general, and child mental health, in particular, makes the task stressful to derive at a firm estimation. Understanding mental health conditions within the brackets of culture is the need of the time in India; and so more and more systematic researches have to be encouraged. It has to be noted that several prospective and retrospective studies have, time and again, proved that most of the severe adult mental illness would have its roots from childhood (Kessler et al., 2007), highlighting the need to pay immediate and cautious attention in understanding child psychiatric epidemiology. India should target to work on its child development strategies by 'early childhood intervention like preschool psychosocial activities, nutritional and psychosocial help' (Venkatashivareddy et al., 2013) by holding its string roots in the community.

2.7.2. ADOLESCENT MENTAL HEALTH

The increasing sensitivity towards adolescent mental health in India, which constitutes a quarter of the country's population, is indeed a progress but, it is nowhere close to the actual need of the hour. As data is limited in this field, so a generalization couldn't be done to the whole nation. This limited data shows disturbing statistics on the prominence of mental illness among this population. The onset of more than 50 per cent of psychiatric illness is understood to be before the age of 14 (Kessler et al., 2005; Patel et al., 2007). So this is a pressing rationale to retaliate on adolescent mental health. A recent nation-wide study revealed that nearly 9.8 million Indian adolescents are in dire need of active interventions and 7.3 per cent was the prevalence of mental illness among this population (NIMHANS, 2016). Further, crucial findings of this study are: prevalence of mental illness was nearly double in urban metros (13.5%) as compared to rural India (6.9%). The common illness conditions that were found are mood disorder, particularly 'Depression (2.6%), Agoraphobia (2.3%), Intellectual Disability (1.7%), Autism Spectrum Disorder (1.6%), Phobic Anxiety Disorder (1.3%) and Psychotic Disorders (1.3%)' (NIMHANS, 2016). Some vigorous Indian-based study has found 3–4 per cent prevalence of mood disorder among Indian adolescents and attention-deficit hyperactivity disorder (ADHD), oppositional defiant disorder (ODD) and conduct disorder (CD) have been found to be the comorbid disorders (Gautam et al., 2019). In a study, based on Indian-university students, 37.7 per cent, 13.1 per cent and 2.4 per cent of the students were found to be depressed moderately, severely and extremely severe respectively (Deb et al., 2016). Neuropsychiatric conditions are another leading cause of disability among young adults across the world (WHO, 2019b) and obsessive compulsive and spectrum disorders are prevalent neuropsychiatric disorders affecting this population (Geller, 2006). A study conducted to analyse emotional and behavioural problems among adolescents held in Bangalore went on to mention, '9% risk for emotional symptoms, 13% for conduct problems, 12.6% for hyperactivity/inattention and 9.4% for peer problems' (Bhola et al., 2016). Substance abuse among adolescents can be considered as the most dangerous of all. For its complex prognosis, addiction and substance abuse would either occur in isolation or as a comorbid condition. A cross-sectional study conducted in North India found that substance use is 52.7 per cent prevalent among students who belong to the 19–21 age group: alcohol (53.5%), smoking (27.3%), tobacco (8.2%), cannabis (6.8%) were the common addictions found (Gupta et al., 2013). At least 50 per cent of the boys, around the age of 15, would have tried at least one substance of abusive nature (Ramachandran, 1991; Singh et al., 2017). Such addictions are usually found to cause behavioural changes and many a times, mental ill-health such as 'depression, anxiety, thought disorders like schizophrenia, as well as antisocial personality disorders' (Sharma & Tyagi, 2016). Despite repeated warnings and clear understanding, adolescents tend to succumb to addictive behaviour (Pal et al., 2010). This is where the comprehensive role of family and community comes into the picture.

Let us get into a few figurative understandings:

The WHO reports, 'Mental Health Stats of Adolescents in South-East Asia: Evidence for Action' suggested that, 'at least 25% of India's adolescents report being depressed for 2 weeks or more in a row' (Singh, 2017). Twenty per cent of the world's adolescents and children are said to be sufferers of disabling metal illness (WHO, 2000) and suicide was identified as a leading cause of adolescent deaths worldwide (WHO, 2001). A Gujarat-based cross-sectional study detected high risk of mental illness in at least one out of every eight adolescents involved in the study (Nair et al., 2017). Undisputedly, mental illness can potentially curb the growth, education, social life and development of these youngsters at such young ages, worsening the burden on their lives. Initiatives such as 'tackling bullying, provision of education to increase awareness of mental health issues and to improve the recognition of children's emerging needs, and provision of support for those children with particular needs' (Ronad et al., 2017), which can ease the process of early identification, timely intervention and support, are the only means to tackle the issue.

2.7.3. ADULT MENTAL HEALTH

'150 million Indians aged 18 and above are suffering from various mental health dispute and are in need of mental care services' (Chatterjee, 2016; NIMHANS, 2016). National Mental Health Survey (NMHS) 2016 further found mental problems to be mostly prominent within the age range of 30–49 and/or above 60. A meta-analysis of 13 psychiatric epidemiological studies found the prognosis of the following illness conditions: organic psychosis (0.4%), schizophrenia (2.7%), affective disorders (12.3%), mental retardation (6.9%), neurotic disorders (20.7%), epilepsy (4.4%) and addiction (6.9%) (Reddy & Chandrashekar, 1998). Of late, increased attention is being paid to issues concerning women and girls in the country, who are at higher risks of suicide. However, social- and gender-specific factors alter the prognosis, course and prevalence of mental illness (Malhotra & Shah, 2015). Substance abuse and addiction are other challenges that the nation is facing with '62.5 million alcohol users, 8.7 million cannabis users and 2 million opiate users' (Sidana, 2018). The burden of such illness conditions is enormous, which can have other comorbidity and/or disability that follow. Quality of life, productivity, economic stability and well-being of an individual gets downgraded. NMHS 2016 report validates this understanding by stating that mentally ill health is followed by disability in all aspects of that individual's life: work, social and family, in case of three out of four people.

2.7.4. GERIATRIC MENTAL HEALTH

The Census 2001 estimated the elderly population of the country to be 7.1 per cent of the total population. Further, a 10 per cent increase in their proportion by 2021 was also predicted in the same report. Therefore, growing India needs significant attention (Prakash & Kukreti, 2013). Epidemiological studies estimates that 20.5 per cent, that is, 17.31 million population of India are facing difficulties in their old age due to mental illness (Tiwari & Pandey, 2012). Cerebral pathology, physical health deterioration, changes in the family system, lack of independence (physical and economical), social isolation and so on burden the mental health of elderly people. Depression, dementia and anxiety were found to be the most prevalent illness conditions among the elderly (Marwaha et al., 2014; Mathur, 2017; Prakash & Kukreti, 2013), along with other affective disorders, delirium, neurocognitive disorder, sleep disorder, adjustment disorders as the commonly found geriatric mental illnesses (Marwaha et al., 2014). They are also found to be prone to abuse: physical, verbal, psychological and sexual abuse. Spouses, sons-in-law, daughters-in-law were found to be the perpetrators (Ingle & Nath, 2008).

Factors that established significant roles in the causation and/or enhancement of illness included 'female sex, low education, absence of life partner (widow/widower/divorcee), medical co-morbidities, poor socioeconomic status and disability' (Mathur, 2017). Various psychosocial and biological factors can influence the mental health status of the Indian elderly, such as retirement, housing issues, financial dependence, lack of transport, physical distance between the parents and children (parents in India and children abroad; Lodha & Sousa, 2018). This population is at heightened risk of further agony and pain, and indisputably requires attention and intervention. Further, discussion of the role of community psychology among the elderly would be discussed in a following chapter.

2.8. PREVENTION OF MENTAL HEALTH PROBLEM AT THE COMMUNITY LEVEL

Given the increasing rate of various types of mental health problems, there is an urgent need to think of preventive measures at the community level by creating awareness about mental health issues and improving the quality of family functioning. Healthy family environment, good interpersonal relationships among the family members and availability of support facilities would definitely create a healthy psychological ambience to remain happy and reduce stress among people. Good family environment discourages an individual to become dependent on substance and getting involved in socially undesirable activities and becoming dependent on peer group members for sharing of personal issues and concerns. Rather, they would prefer to share their issues and concerns with the family members; and thus, they would be guided properly.

The general trend seen in most of the middle- and low-income countries is an extremely slow process in mental health service delivery (Srivastava et al., 2016) and India isn't any different. The treatment gap in such countries were found to be high and lay between 76 and 85 per cent (Lepine et al., 2004). Poorly decided priorities in the existing health services in the country, unavailability of funds, non-involvement of the country's primary care setup in mental health service delivery, extremely low number of trained professionals and lack of leaders, who are sensitive to mental health needs of the people, are a few of the major barriers that has led to the present condition in India (Saraceno et al., 2007). One such community-based prevention programme in Tohoku, Japan, aimed at a four-action programme which included the following objectives, 'An outline of the four action programs was as follows: to raise awareness about suicide prevention, to increase opportunities for mental health consultation, to promote both primary and secondary prevention of depression, and to create a supportive environment for mental health promotion' (Motohashi et al., 2004). India faces challenges both in terms of human resources and other logistical facilities like infrastructure (Thirnavukarasu, 2011). Hence, 'task-shifting to non-specialist community health workers has been recommended as an effective strategy for delivery of efficacious treatments in low resource settings' (Patel et al., 2009). This could be through periodic home visits by the health worker (accredited social health activist [ASHA] worker) of each locality, taking the help of the *Anganwadi* workers. Brief preventive interventions are found to be effective in managing conditions such as excessive drinking habits, trauma and depression. Through this 'cost-effective and integrative framework for care of children and adults,' (Patel et al., 2007) preventive efforts at community level, for instance, providing antiretroviral drugs for human immunodeficiency virus/acquired immunodeficiency syndrome (HIV/AIDS) can work wonders. This could be helpful in grasping both the physical and mental framework of each member of the community. Preventive measures at primary, secondary and tertiary levels can be implemented through such home visits and community gathering.

2.9. IDENTIFICATION AND TREATMENT OF MENTAL HEALTH PROBLEM AT THE COMMUNITY LEVEL

'Building or sustaining healthy communities is now considered an important weapon in a state's strategy to prevent mental illness' (Silva et al., 2005). In other words, the most effective way of reaching out to every individual is through community involvement. For identification of various mental health problems at the community level, there is a need to create awareness among Local-Level health workers, social workers, primary and secondary school teachers about the signs and symptoms, especially about the problems which are highly prevalent, so that, whenever they will come across similar cases, they can refer those to the specialists for proper diagnosis. Proper diagnosis, by following scientific methods, would ensure appropriate treatment and faster prognosis.

2.10. COMMUNITY-BASED REHABILITATION

Management of mental illness is majorly done through rehabilitation where the term literally stands for the individuals who are made to undergo a restoration process, at the end of which they return to their original state of being. 'Total quality of life in terms of wellness, happiness and satisfaction in fulfilling the demands, freedom of movements, independence, expression of self (with respect to age, sex, and culture), relationships and ability to ensure independent economic existence' (Tinney et al., 2007) are also taken care of in rehabilitation. The complex and intricate process generally involves the application of suited and scientific treatment and management techniques on an individual in a very amiable environment that is sensitive to the condition of the individual. In CMH, this environment is targeted to be created in one's own community itself. This would be made possible only through the coming together of multiple groups, starting from families, communities and governments as well as sectors of education, health and social services. Undoubtedly, the shift of paradigm from institution to the community (deinstitutionalization) is our current topic of discussion, which has been widely propagated and practised across the world. Psychosocial rehabilitation, which is the 'therapeutic approach that encourages a mentally ill person to develop his/her fullest capacities through learning and environmental support' (Chandrashekar et al., 2010; Bachrach, 1992), has been found successful and is widely incorporated as a significant component of mental healthcare service along with pharmacology. Community based rehabilitation (CBR) uses the application of psychosocial rehabilitation models and adapts according to the nature and characteristics of the community. CBR is a brainchild of WHO and was conceptualized in the mid-1970s. This was the result from the attempts made to address issues related to shortage of healthcare facilities in general; and hence, the idea of benefiting from local resources, for the betterment of the locality, took shape (Hartley et al., 2009). In a short span of time, this initiative caught the international attention and had been accepted as a global style of rehabilitation in the developed countries. CBR model was found to effectively cause an attitudinal shift through its integration between the traditional and the contemporary (Kendall et al., 2000). For many reasons, this is unlike the case in developing and underdeveloped countries despite the passage of time.

Numerous researches have been conducted on the outcomes of CBR, for illnesses ranging from physical to psychological, and their results have been mostly positive. Advantages of CBR are many: In cases of severe mental illness, CBR has caused significant reduction in the time spent in institutional rehabilitation as well as the frequency of seeking medical help; the recovery is sooner and their quality of life is enhanced (Coldwell & Bender, 2007; Lockwood & Marshall, 2000). Most optimistic outputs of CBR are the reduction and prevention of relapse as well as significant improvement in housing stability found among the rehabilitants (Brekke et al., 2007; Keith et al., 2001; Mueser et al., 1995). Further, improving access to such projects based on CBR was found to hasten and enhance individual recovery goals and provide support and hope for the caregivers, along with being cost-effective as well (Mueser et al., 2003). An evaluation study of CBR in rural India found that the model is feasible to fit in the Indian scenario to rehabilitate people suffering from chronic schizophrenia, where resources are poor (Chatterjee et al., 2003). In a study conducted on people with schizophrenia and their caregivers in India, collaborative community-based care and facility-based care intervention was found to be effective in reducing disability in psychosis (Chatterjee et al., 2014). Another exhaustive study in rural India would provide insights into the practicality of CBR. This CBR package is described to involve medicine, psychoeducation, psychosocial rehabilitation and support for livelihood. The study found a significant change in the disability scores of its participants who were 256 people with schizophrenia and bipolar affective disorder (Chatterjee et al., 2009).

In sum

- CBR is an intervention method aimed at rehabilitating the mentally ill within one's own community under the supervision of their own community members who are informed and sensible in mental healthcare.
- Objectives of community-initiated mental health service delivery are prevention of mental illness, early identification of mental illness in individuals and guiding them towards further treatment options, rehabilitating the individual, mostly in an institution, after which, rehabilitation can be provided within the community and follow-up and aftercare is provided with caution and support.

2.11. CMH CARE SERVICES BY THE PARAPROFESSIONAL FORCE IN PSYCHOLOGY

The foremost barrier that our country faces in mental healthcare delivery is the limited trained manpower for service provision. The shortage of trained mental health professionals is so severe that there are only 4,000 psychiatrists in the country of 1.2 billion (Ashraf, 2018). The number of institutions which provide specialization for advanced courses in mental healthcare are also very few in the country and so are the number of seats they offer. Taking cognizance of the situation, mental health services can be made available to the common people only through a community movement, where responsibility is equally divided amongst every individual member of the community. The generic objective of the community-initiated mental health service delivery is to promote mental well-being in the community. As discussed earlier, the course of action of this system of service would be the prevention of mental illness, early identification of mental illness in individuals and guiding them in further treatment, rehabilitating the individual in an institution; after which, rehabilitation can be provided within the community and follow-up and aftercare is provided with caution and support (see Figure 2.1).

The paraprofessional force in psychology is a unique feature of the CMH programme. This force, at its most effective form, can function in communities by instigating its potential for group work towards a common cause. Here, institutions of education, workplace and specific communities of living (rural and urban) can be the spheres where mental-health-related initiatives can be efficiently carried out for a large number of people. The nature, number and strategies of the paraprofessional force in psychology should be specific to that community and should inculcate the characteristics of the community in which they function. Upon the service of the force on the members of the community, several outcomes, both direct and indirect, would take place. In fact, all the objectives of the CMH programmes (as detailed in the beginning of this chapter) would be met through the effective intervention of the paraprofessional force in

FIGURE 2.1
Impact of the Paraprofessional Force in Psychology on the Community

FIGURE 2.1
Impact of the Paraprofessional Force in Psychology on the Community

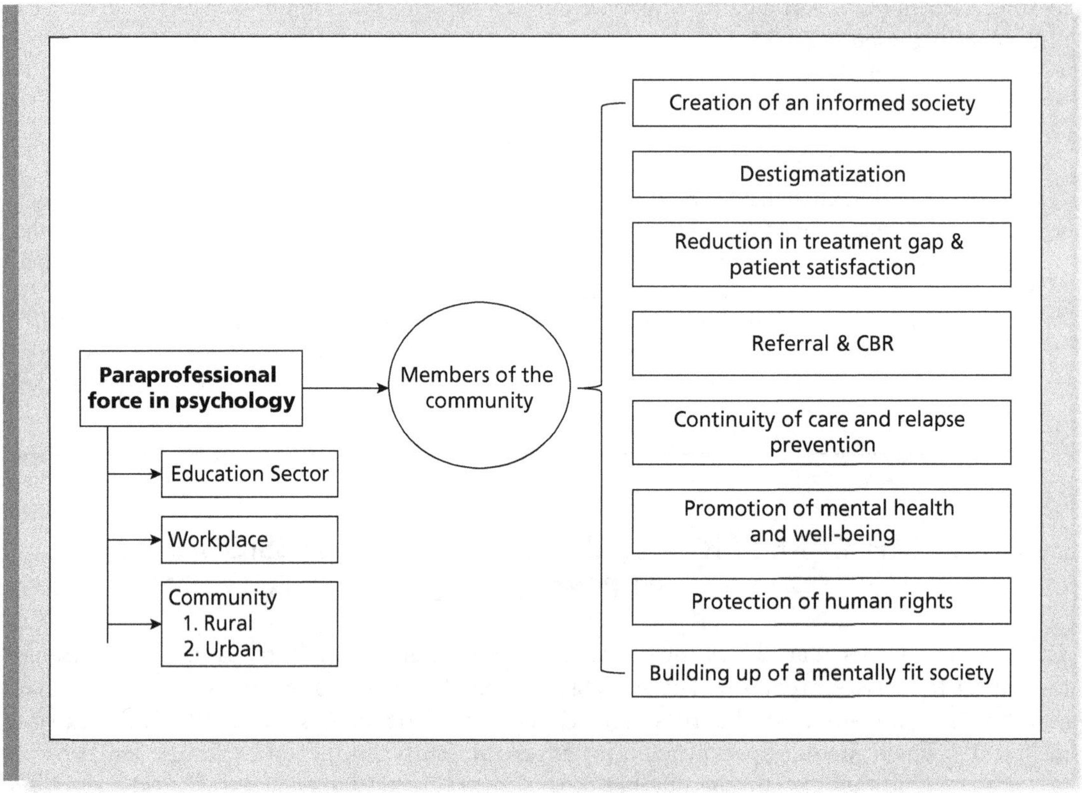

psychology along with the cooperation of the entire community. A detailed explanation of the role of CMH in each of these three spheres is given below.

2.11.1. MENTAL HEALTH IN THE EDUCATION SECTOR

Dissemination of information about mental health and illness would rightly start from school through systematic delivery of the right content. Inclusion of mental health curriculum in school education is lately a hot topic of discussion in India (Parikh, 2019). In India, depression and suicide rates are increasing among adolescents, more than ever, and their vulnerability to other mental illnesses are growing higher due to several psychosocial stressors such as academic pressure, media exposure and so on, which are often ignored. Body shaming issues, poor self-esteem, identity crisis and adolescent-age-related challenges are other factors that would contribute to the burden they carry. Broadly, the curriculum should aim at creating awareness about positive mental health, destigmatizing the society and sensitizing the students who require mental healthcare and support (*India Today*, 2019). Bhutan has already attracted attention and appreciation for their 'happiness curriculum', which would be implemented from the next academic session, for their

FIGURE 2.2
School Mental Health Programme Model by WHO

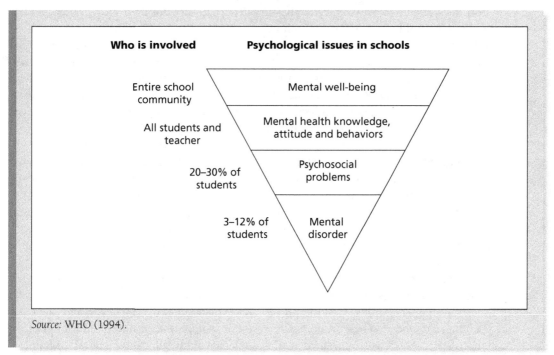

Source: WHO (1994).

effort to ensure happiness and satisfaction among their students (Matharu, 2019). In cognizance of the importance of the issues, the WHO in 1994 has proposed a model framework for school mental health programmes, which includes the students, teachers and the entire school community, as depicted in Figure 2.2.

1. *At schools:* Ironically, it took over 25 years for our nation to understand the need to expose the society to the concepts of mental illness through school education. As can be seen, through this process, the entire school community is involved and through this process, they would be exposed to mental-health-related facts. The young students would understand the need to regulate, maintain and optimize mental health and also become aware of the prevalent mental illnesses and the available treatment options for the same. In the process, they would gather ideas about the times/feelings/thoughts/behaviours that require help. They would also be informed about the reliable sources from where they can seek help. A parallel and gradual process that would occur is the destigmatization and installation of the right kind of knowledge, attitude and behaviour in the community. Being aware of the importance of positive mental health, the children can be saved from acting on impulse and falling prey to abuse and violence; they can be taught the skills required to deal with their day-to-day stress. Information regarding specific mental illnesses that are prevalent or could have its onset during adolescence can be delivered in a simple manner. This would help them to remain sensible and alert enough to act in the right direction. Issues and challenges

faced by adolescents are many, most of them being age specific. There is no better option than school to address such issues from the right perspective and hence encourage and support the students to overcome such barriers. This can ease out their growth process from the right spirit and be supportive to each other.

2. *At universities:* More number of news on student suicides in Indian colleges and universities are being heard every day, which speaks volumes about mental health challenges faced by young Indians. Symptoms of severe depression are found among one in every three college students (Taehtinen & Kristjansdottir, 2018). Anxiety, substance abuse and impulsive behaviour, issues in academics and relationships, trouble in sleep and appetite and lack of productivity (Hunter, 2019), campus violence, ragging menace, alcohol and drug addiction (Janetius, 2016) are other main issues observed among this population. As understood, this is a period of transition where students are struggling to strike a balance between education and social interaction, a time when they get to enjoy more freedom and exposure, a time that requires the backup of more social support and care (Dogan, 2012). Despite this issue, barely any institution of higher learning in our country provides options for counselling and mental healthcare. Mental wellness is hardly a topic of discussion in any classroom. In fact, such students struggle with poor coping skills, indecisiveness, unhealthy lifestyle, addictive behaviour, poor academic performance and dropout. Therefore, inclusion of a mental health curriculum, installation of counselling centres for mental health and promotion of activities towards mental wellness should be made mandatory in every institution of higher learning. Conducting researches on student mental health and execution of scientific and evidence-based intervention would upgrade the quality of education of the nation. Teachers who will be trained in this subject would gain better understanding and knowledge on such matters and hence would be sensitive to issues related to students, in particular, and the society, in general. This would act as a powerful tool for them to identify matters that require attention to provide timely involvement and needed intervention, and in required cases, to suggest appropriate referrals for further mental health support in a professional manner. They could also create a conducive school environment which would instigate the right spirit, a curiosity to learn and promote healthy competition among students according to their calibre and interests. They can turn into a powerful support system for students who require help and support by providing them counselling services, special classes, life-skill training and similar activities. Teachers equipped with such skills and attitude towards mental health can deliberate mental-wellness-related matters to the parents of the students as well through the exchange of ideas on the importance of promotion and maintenance of positive mental health among students and also provide support and guidance in seeking professional help when needed. In one way or the other, teachers would also benefit from this and learn to deal with issues/stress related to their profession. The paraprofessional force in psychology in the school could be the school/university counsellor, teachers and a few student representatives from each class, who can act as sensitive filters in identifying and reaching out to the students and institutional staff in need. Equipping the school community with right information, skills and attitude would reveal its impact in due course of time and will be seen in the societal approaches towards mental health and illness. Such a congenial school community would unknowingly set examples for their students about being sensible, accommodating and healthy on issues related to mental health.

2.11.2. MENTAL HEALTH AT WORKPLACE

Mental health challenges are an under-discussed topic at Indian workplaces, despite its severity. As high as 46 per cent of employees in India were found to be suffering from stress of any form and its associated difficulties in a large-scale study held in 2016. They also found 30 per cent increase in the proportion as compared to a similar study conducted in 2014 (Bhattacharyya & Vijayaraghavan, 2016). *The Wall Street Journal* publication titled 'Indian Millennials Clock Way More Work Hours Than Their Global Competition' found that the Indian employees work for 52 hours a week which is more than the time spent at work in any other country (Bhattacharya, 2016). Apart from psychological disturbances associated with work pressure, workplace harassment and bullying are prominently reported in the organized sectors, like the case of the #metoo campaign that the nation has witnessed. Fall in productivity, disturbed sleep-wake cycle (which are also due to unscientifically followed work schedules and shifts), disturbances faced by women at work such as the class-ceiling effect and work-life balance, racism, gender discrimination and high absenteeism are unfortunately not considered important amidst deadlines, appraisals, feedback, targets and competitions. It would not be inappropriate to say that a great proportion of Indians go to work with mental illness. However, baseline studies conducted in India are very few and some of them could be mentioned. These include hazardous drinking habits among industrial workers (Silva et al., 2003), psychological disturbances faced by medical professionals from treating chronic illness and death (Lambert & Lambert, 2008), poor subjective well-being and job satisfaction among bank employees (Alam & Rizvi, 2012), occupational stress and professional burnout among university professors (Reddy & Poornima, 2012) and occupational stress in armed forces (Sharma, 2015) are a few of the studies.

Workplace of any nature would develop a community out of it, be it big or small/active or passive. Therefore, psychological contracts would develop in this space and can rightly be channelized as potential mental health support. Hence, employee assistance programmes targeting the mental health of the employees as well as workplace counselling services should be made mandatory in every workplace. Developing relevance and voice for mental health concerns at workplace is important in establishing the need to speedily address human relation problems. This could have both direct and indirect outcomes as depicted in Figure 2.3.

Creation of a pro-mental health environment could be the by-product of a joint venture of the entire workplace community. It is about disseminating skills and awareness about the prevalent mental illnesses that occur at a workplace, including its course, prognosis and treatment methods. Through this process, an environment which is receptive to the mental health needs of the workplace community is created and the idea that it is important to talk about mental health would get introduced, thereby curbing and dissolving the stigma associated with seeking mental healthcare support. Basic training and skills provided on various work-related activities such as communication skills, time management, stress management and assertive skill training could empower the workplace community in being a support for oneself and their own community. In order to raise the mental health services, the timely visit and consultation of a trained mental health professional would be appropriate. This could extend to services beyond the workplace in cases that require further care and intervention. Therefore, the paraprofessional force in psychology at the workplace, constituting the mental health consultant, the HR wing of the organization/company and a few sensible and interested employees can be watchful in providing mental-health

FIGURE 2.3
Impact of Mental-Health Services at Workplace

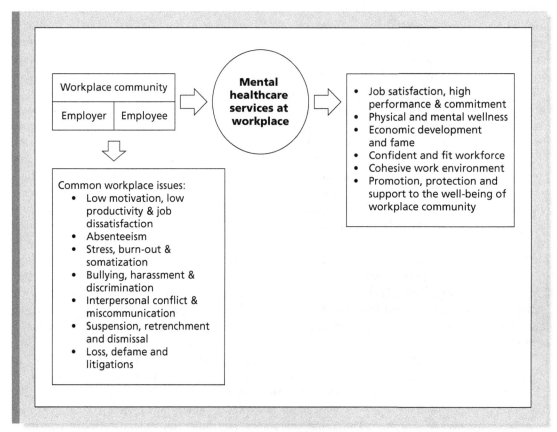

services to its employees and can work towards building a congenial work environment. Otherwise, the cases of mental health challenges can be sorted out within the workplace and well-being can be promoted within the community.

2.11.3. MENTAL HEALTH AT THE COMMUNITY LEVEL

To optimize mental health and the well-being of every individual in society, a wider and large-scale care service should be provided. This isn't as easy as it may sound, unless the full engagement of all citizens is involved. Mental health at the community level can be viewed as a movement where every member of the community in whatever role(s) they serve, takes responsibility for the mental health of their own community. This can only be achieved through a systematic planning and execution of a pool of activities which would enhance community well-being. For the ease of understanding and for the difference in their formulas, communities in India are of two types: rural and urban. As mentioned earlier, the constitution of mental health issues of these two communities are varied, so are the modes of intervention to be used.

1. ***CMH in urban India:*** In urbanization, with the demographic movement of people, changes in social, economic and psychological build-up of an individual would also take place (Srivastava, 2009). The profound changes in family patterns, social interaction, schedules of the day and environmental factors, such as overcrowding, polluted environment and apartment culture as well as social factors like increased crime rates and violence, would have strong impacts on the mental health of an individual. For such reasons and also due to better reporting standards, urban areas would show higher prevalence rates in terms of mental illness as compared to rural India. However, the NMHS 2015–16 found that the availability of psychiatrists in the country would vary from 0.05 to 1.2 for every 100,000 people who need mental healthcare. The deviance found among the urban population are huge with depression, substance abuse, alcoholism, family disintegration and alienation, dementia and anxiety found to figure prominently (Srivastava, 2009). Hence, here too, community involvement would be the only immediate, long-term and effective mode of service rendering. Urban population has a different dynamic as compared to the rural population, for which, a strategical approach is necessary to reach the entire population. A good majority of the urban population could be effectively sensitized through mental healthcare activities done in educational institutions and workplaces. Accessing the otherwise occupied community in the urban setup, for instance, homemakers and retired people, various pre-planned programmes such as talk shows, workshops and symposiums under the banner of the community's educational, institutional, residential associations and clubs or places of worship can be arranged. Social media is another effective mode of communication through the smart usage of which, even mass movements have flourished in a matter of minutes. The status of education and the knowledge-seeking attitude of the urban population are a boon and are majorly easing out the spread of information across the community. Considering the diversity among people, areas of expertise and position in the society, CMH care provisions could be multisectoral. Universities or any institution of higher learning in association with the Ministry of Public Health and Social Welfare could take up the responsibility to plan and coordinate activities to promote mental health. The various departments of universities, particularly those of psychology and social work, can volunteer to coordinate with the mental health professionals of their community in communicating basic information regarding mental health. The active participation and input from the departments of mass communication and public relations of the university in utilizing the professional and social-media platforms can make huge impacts in accessing the community members. Celebrity involvement and endorsements could be the effective campaigning techniques and have always been successful in India. They could be used for knowledge dissemination and promotion of mental health. Hence, every member of the community can, in one way or the other, be the paraprofessional force in psychology and responsibly ensure mental hygiene in places.

2. ***CMH in rural India:*** As is the case about accessibility to mental health professionals, awareness about mental illnesses is also feeble among the rural population of the country. Lack of education and poverty has not left the interiors of India. When it comes to mental illness, age-old beliefs, myths and misperceptions about the nature and course of the treatment remain unscientific. Such is the case that people fail to identify mental illnesses within their community by its symptomatology; and hence, timely intervention is hardly provided. Hence, a child with severe learning difficulties or an adolescent with alcohol addiction or a woman experiencing severe depression after childbirth would remain untreated as mental health conditions, such

as learning disability (LD), substance abuse or postpartum depression, remain unidentified. The situation is such that people would still choose some of the bizarre (indigenous) healing practices for the cure of mental illnesses even today. Newspapers keep reporting deaths caused due to such unsolicited practices. 'Increase in population, changing lifestyle, unemployment, lack of social support and increasing insecurity' have also contributed to the massive mental health concerns in rural India (Kumar, 2011). The scarcity of mental health professionals further deepens their ignorance and stigma around mental illnesses in rural India, such that 'persons with mental illness in rural India are unable to receive quality care due to limited awareness, availability, accessibility, and affordability' (The MINDS Foundation, 2017). A positive change can only be brought about through the effective involvement of the community as a whole. CMH in rural India can be envisaged as a process where knowledge dissemination is effectively done in order to reach every corner of the country. This could be made possible by the participation of everybody in the community under the guidance/leadership of the village panchayat. A paraprofessional force in psychology could be created at the community level, which would be a team of responsible and committed community members, possibly including a few selected members who are respected and valued in the community, such as a retired teachers or doctors, *Anganwadi*/ASHA workers and volunteers who might be students/adults who can effectively communicate the matter to even the uneducated in the community. This paraprofessional force in psychology thus identified and having undergone training under the supervision of the *Panchayati Raj* system of the village could be used to spread basic awareness about mental health among the community members. The force needs to be rightly equipped with information needed for identification of mental illness, immediate course of action, referral systems, community rehabilitation and reintegration, aftercare and follow-up. Through special lectures, talks and discussions, field visits, case management and individual care, baseline studies, research and publication, the paraprofessional force in psychology could reach, teach, sensitize and be involved with the community members on mental-health-related matters. The potential receivers of this initiative should not be restricted to students or working-class people. Rather, non-working women, school dropouts, retried community members, farmers and similar people of the community who work in similar unorganized sectors, people who are uneducated/under-educated, migrants and so on should be targeted. Spiritual leaders of the locality can also utilize their space and time in effectively sensitizing their followers about the importance of understanding mental illness through the right perspective. In this manner, the community becomes self-sufficient in terms of mental healthcare.

As depicted in Figure 2.4, this is a cycle of processes where clear-cut boundaries cannot be drawn between each of these four stages. Here, one step flows into the next; and thus, in this cyclic-model, the mental health and well-being of the community are preserved intact. The four-phase community intervention programme is depicted in the Figure 2.4. The objective is to take care of four broad areas that need immediate attention:

1. *Prevention of mental illness:* This objective could be met by the propagation of information regarding basic mental-health issues and challenges, their possible causal and contributory factors and the precautionary measures to be taken. Information being spread should be

FIGURE 2.4
Phases of Community Mental-Health Service Delivery

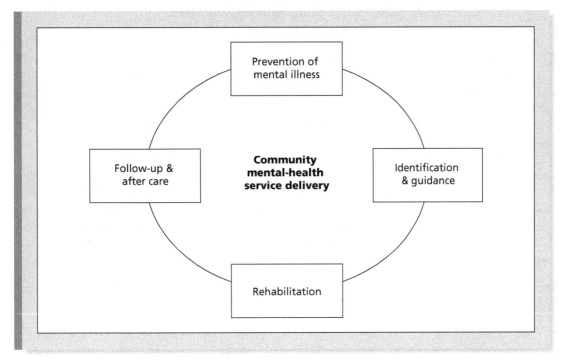

based on latest research findings, and the measure adopted should be based on evidence. This is also about creating an environment, which is free and distant from newer incidents of mental illness. This would provide a space for thorough and careful watch on people, who have recovered from mental illness, to prevent relapse. At this level, the community can encourage more research studies to be conducted in their community, so that difference based on culture and system, specific to the community, would be taken care of.

2. ***Identification, treatment and guidance:*** Early detection of illness based on symptomatology is always in the best interests of the patient. Skilled and confident paraprofessional force in psychology could easily identify the illness and provide guidance for immediate course of action. This would avoid further worsening of the condition. Also, they could lead the individuals and their caregivers to further mental health intervention through the referral system.

3. ***Rehabilitation:*** As discussed earlier, rehabilitation can be of two types: institutional-based and community-based. The activities conducted towards awareness creation would build a community which is stigma free and capable of taking care of the sick. Hence, in such cases, the community itself will be the rehabilitation centre for the individual; and hence, the patient's satisfaction level and speed of recovery would be faster. In cases, where institutional care is required, the individual can be discharged early in order to be rehabilitated in one's own community.

4. *Follow-up and aftercare:* Any intervention would be successful when relapse is prevented. Challenges related to relapse are effectively taken care of in the CMH setup. Presence of informed caregivers, who remain as shields around the mentally ill, would make aftercare effective and long lasting.

The outcomes of such initiatives at the community level (both urban and rural) are many. CMH can maximize the health outcomes of the community to greater levels by providing high-quality care and support in cases of emergency within the community. Hence, unwanted complications and worsening of illness through faulty immediate care can be avoided till right medical supervision is provided. In other words, this can be understood as a reduction in the emergency admissions to the hospitals itself, since such close monitoring by the community would secure the individual from such situations. The wholehearted engagement of the citizens would provide sustainability in the care model followed by the community, which has the potential to improve the quality of life, an all-round development, personal growth and mental well-being of the individual. If meticulously followed, CMH services can secure additional years of life for the individual members of the community by treating the ill, promoting the vulnerable and by maintaining/enhancing the others. Through the spread of specialist services, care and support is made available and accessible to a large number of people.

In sum

The paraprofessional force in psychology is the unique feature of the CMH programme and functions in communities by instigating its potential for group work towards a common cause. The nature, number and strategies of paraprofessional force in psychology should be specific to that community and should inculcate the characteristics of the community in which they function. It can function in the education sectors, workplace and also at both rural and urban communities. CMH service delivery focuses on:

- Prevention
- Identification, treatment and guidance
- Rehabilitation
- Follow-up and aftercare

2.12. TREATMENT GAP

Treatment gap in mental illnesses is universally large and significantly higher across all countries of both strong and weak economic backgrounds. A review based on several community-based epidemiological studies clearly substantiates this understanding, and the treatment gap median of various mental illness conditions are the following: 'non-affective psychosis: 32.2%, depression: 56.3%, dysthymia: 56.0%, bipolar disorder: 50.2%, panic disorder: 55.9%, Generalized Anxiety Disorder: 57.5%, Obsessive Compulsive Disorder: 57.3% and Alcohol abuse and Dependence (AUD): 78.1%' (Kohn et al., 2019). As can be understood from the above data, AUD is the most neglected mental illness condition in both high- and low-income countries (National Council on Alcoholism and Drug Dependence, 2010; Olesji et al., 2010; Rathod et al., 2016). The condition in low- and middle-income countries are extremely severe and the estimated treatment gap in such countries is around 95 per cent (Np et al., 2017; Rathod et al., 2016; Zewdu et al., 2019).

The reasons for such wide gaps can be many, including reasons like 'poor accessibility and availability of services, lack of knowledge about the features and treatability of the disorder, ignorance about accessing assessment and treatment, prejudice against people who have the disorder and, expectations of discrimination against people who have a diagnosis' (Zewdu et al., 2019). Lack of support services for mental health problems as compared to need and non-availability of services, especially in rural areas, are lack of follow-up or referral services. These are barriers that need immediate address. Non-availability of a directory of mental health specialists, in the developing countries is another helpless situation for parents having children with mental health problems. Recognition of mentally ill health is extremely low at the community level and hence educating the community is important in order to enhance the 'public's ability to recognize mental illness in the community and suggest sources to help set a baseline for assessments' (Huang et al., 2019). Mental health education is essentially important, as research confirms a positive correlation between higher levels of education and social support status, in association with CMH knowledge (Gebrekidan et al., 2018). 'Addressing gaps in current practice will require assuring collaboration with service users, utilizing implementation science methods, creating tools to facilitate community services and evaluate competencies of providers, and developing standardized reporting for community-based programs'. Given the lack of trained manpower to identify and treat such mental-health conditions, interventions targeting the public to reduce stigma and screening at the community level can provide help to a great extent.

2.13. ROLE OF PSYCHIATRIST, PSYCHOLOGISTS, PARENTS, HEALTH/GUARDIANS AND SOCIAL WORKERS AS WELL AS NGOs IN ADDRESSING THE PROBLEM

Ideally, for assessing the mental health status of an individual, a team of professionals should work together, and they include general physicians, psychiatrists, psychologists and social workers. However, their role varies at the community level. The most important cause for the huge treatment gap is the unavailability of mental health professionals, who are trained for service delivery. Long-term plans to tackle this issue of non-availability include establishment of more national- and state-level institutions for higher learning in mental health, which can also serve the purpose of prevention and treatment as well as increase the number of seats available at the educational and training institutions for creating efficient psychiatrists and psychologists. However, efficient and collaborative short-term plans are the need of the hour which would be possible in collaboration with the existing mental health professionals. Moreover, it is important to be aware that research findings talk about the societal prejudices that mental health personnel show towards mental illness, which in itself is doubly negative in nature. Hence, it is also important to correctively modulate these attitudinal differences within the professional community to assure quality in care (Del Olmo-romero et al., 2018).

'Given the dire shortage in numbers of psychiatrists, psychologists, psychiatric nurses, and social workers; piggy-banking on primary care systems and employing innovative force-multipliers are future courses of action' (Srivastava et al., 2016). Therefore, at the community level, psychiatrists and psychologists can create a pool of available professionals such as the medical force at the primary health centre, social workers available in the community and train them in active and vigilant service delivery along with the mental health domains of the community. An auxiliary team that can include responsible and sensible community members who would be serving multiple roles such as parents/guardians, teachers, local NGOs, social activists, retired/elderly population and other reputed professionals of the community are also needed. In this manner, a community as an entity can work towards prevention, identification and intervention of mental illness. Moreover, destigmatization would, at its best shape, be made possible through such collaborative efforts.

2.14. MENTAL HEALTH EDUCATION AND AWARENESS AND ROLE OF MEDIA

Inclusion of media in our day-to-day life has been the latest trend in human civilization, which had its initiation from newspapers and books. The involvement of media has evolved ever since; and today, it has grown into such a form that every individual can develop their own content in their respective social media platforms and communicate their ideas. The consequences of power of this sort are widely discussed; but the most outrageous implication of these platforms is the space that it creates in the virtual world to spread a word about mental illness.

Of late, many social media users have been fighters of several mental illnesses and they are using their platforms to spread awareness about such illnesses using their own life experiences. They use these platforms to openly discuss the illness, which in other ways, pave way for many to gain more confidence to deal with it themselves. This is the latest and most effective way to reconstruct stigma and spread awareness. A lot of people, including celebrities, have been lately using this mode to create awareness. These messages get shared instantly across the world and give an enormous reach and audience. Positive impact can be understood as this has led to the creation of a generation which is cautious about their health and fitness and determined towards a happy and healthy life. The concept of mental health has also gained popularity among the youth and the messages kept spreading. Hence, through the smart and appropriate utilization of media, mental health education and awareness can be easily established, given the fact that the cost involved would be effective and the audience would be maximum.

2.15. MENTAL HEALTH IN INDIA: AN OVERVIEW

Indian texts can probably be the oldest documentation of mental illness. Indian epics and ancient literature such as *Charaka Samhita, Sushruta Samhita, Atharva Veda*, Bhagavad Gita, Ramayana and Mahabharata have extracts, which documents various mental illness and their treatment regime (Nizamie & Goyal, 2010). Medical systems such as Siddha, Unani and Ayurveda had developed and followed various treatment modules for psychiatric illness. From witchcraft and practices like trephining, our country had a long way to travel to finally adapt to modern medicine and psychotherapy that we practise today. Lunatic asylums, Lunacy Act, establishment of institutions such as the Central Institute of Psychiatry (CIP), Ranchi and the All India Institute of Mental Health (currently known as National Institute of Mental Health and Neurosciences [NIMHANS]) are few of the milestones that our country has achieved in the field of mental health (Nizamie & Goyal, 2010). The Mental Health Act of India, 1987 and the National Mental Health Policy that followed subsequently are the major advancements in the field of mental health post-Independence.

2.15.1. MENTAL HEALTH POLICIES IN INDIA

The Indian Mental Health Act came into effect in April 1993. It was established with the objective of equalizing mental health treatment and practice to any physical illness. The act aimed at minimizing mental illness in the society as well as regulating the admission to psychiatric hospitals and nursing homes. Followed by this was the 1983 National Health Policy, later revised in 2002. This policy intended to uplift the treatment standards by installing newer systems in place of the older ones. Decentralization of the health system is another highlight of the policy upon which upgradation of mental hospital infrastructure was attempted.

The NMHP is a significant initiative in India, which aimed at working along the blueprint that was set with prevention and rehabilitation as its centre, along with emphasizing on the promotion of mental health in the community. The policy was launched by the Government of India in 1982 with three main components, namely:

1. Treatment of the mentally ill
2. Rehabilitation
3. Prevention and promotion of mental health.
   The District Mental Health Program (DMHP) was also introduced in 1996, using which early detection of illness and stigma reduction was aimed at in the community. NMHP-2003 is the re-strategized version of the same programme which added two other schemes to NMHP, namely
4. Modernization of state mental hospitals
5. Upgradation of psychiatric wings of medical colleges/general hospitals.
   In 2009, a sixth component was added on as a part of the programme:
6. Manpower development schemes

NMHP worked towards ensuring the accessibility of minimum mental healthcare facilities to everyone, which is understood to be possible through community participation and integration. This is where the importance of spreading mental health knowledge is promoted along with aiming at enhancing the human resources of other mental health specialties (Ministry of Health & Family Welfare, 2014). The latest version of the policy is the NMHP-2017 which is to 'inform, clarify, strengthen and prioritize the role of the Government in shaping the health systems in all its dimensions' (Ministry of Health and Family Welfare, 2017). In the mental health dimensions, the policy takes action towards increasing the creation of mental health professionals in the public system, creating a network of community members in order to provide needed psychosocial support for the people and to leverage the benefits of digital technology in rendering services.

2.15.2. THE MENTAL HEALTHCARE ACT, 2017

The Mental Healthcare Act (MHCA) is the latest development in mental healthcare services provided by the country and has come into force in 2018. 'An Act is to provide for mental healthcare and services for persons with mental illness and to protect, promote and fulfil the rights of such persons during delivery of mental healthcare and services and for matters connected therewith or incidental thereto' (Ministry of Law and Justice, 2017). MHCA, 1987, was, of course, superseded and MHCA, 2017, is the only upgradation done to the same. The distinct feature of MHCA, 2017, is the clarity it had given to defining mental illness as, the law that understands mental illness as 'in accordance with nationally and internationally accepted medical standards (including the latest edition of the International Classification of Diseases [ICD] of WHO) as may be notified by the Central Government' (Ministry of Law and Justice, 2017). Decriminalization of 'attempt to commit suicide', attempts to fulfil the international mandate for the Convention on Rights of Persons with Disabilities and Its Optional Protocol, restrictions brought into the usage of electroconvulsive therapy (ECT) to only rare cases of emergency are a few of the salient features of the MHCA, 2017, (Neredumilli et al., 2018). Further destigmatization, provision for the registration of mental healthcare institutions and empowering people to take a decision about their health are also to be noted.

There are a number of lacunas in the MHCA, 2017. First, it does not discuss anything about punishment for the people who deny the treatment to people with mental health challenges on account of social stigma and arrange their marriage secretly when one is grown up which cause lifelong sufferings to an innocent partner who got married without knowing the mental health condition of the person. Second, children of the same person/couple experience neglect, abuse and maltreatment. Third, the innocent life partner who is a victim of the situation experiences further victimization in the hand of in-laws. Even in some cases when an innocent person expresses their sufferings and expressed desire to go for separation, in-laws blackmail demanding huge money for signing in the divorce paper. The first-hand experience of the first author in dealing with such cases in the Service Program Unit of the Department of Applied Psychology, University of Calcutta, opened his eyes on the issue and witnessed the suffering of innocent persons. Therefore, this issue needs special attention of the policymakers for keeping some provision to safeguard the interest of an innocent person.

2.16. SUICIDES IN INDIA

Suicide is understood as 'a leading cause of mortality, accounting to nearly 1 million deaths globally every year' (Sinyor et al., 2017). Suicide rates in India are also very alarming. Among this, 'agricultural pesticide poisoning has been a leading contributor to the global burden of suicide'. 'Suicides among farmers is a public health problem that require immediate and serious intervention' (Behere & Behere, 2008). As per the reports of the National Crime Records Bureau (NCRB), 'the annual suicide numbers among farmers 'lie between 13,600 and 18,300 during the 1997–2007 (Gruère & Sengupta, 2011). In this light, a study based in the Sundarbans, India, rightly recommended for an 'inter-sectoral approach linking the interests of public health, mental health and agriculture in order to reduce morbidity and mortality from unintentional and intentional self-injury in low income agricultural communities' (Chowdhury et al., 2007).

Adolescence and young adulthood is found to be the period of heightened risk of suicides (Vijayakumar et al., 2005). Suicide among Indian adolescents has become a leading cause of death

(Aaron et al., 2004) and can be due to several factors of mental health conditions such as mood distress or substance abuse. In rural India, suicide is found to be the reason for 50–75 per cent of the deaths among females between the age of 10 and 19 years (Radhakrishnan & Andrade, 2012). The collective nature of family units in Indian culture is found to have both positive and negative impacts (Samuel & Sher, 2013). A study found the association between 'female gender, not attending school or college, independent decision making, premarital sex, physical abuse at home, lifetime experience of sexual abuse, and probable common mental disorders' to be the primary causes for suicidal tendencies among young people of the country (Pillai et al., 2009).

Studies investigating its epidemiological and prevalence rates are happening worldwide and it calls for the attention of policymakers to develop suicide prevention programmes based on this evidence. A systematic review, based on the results of the national ban implemented by 5 low- and middle-income countries and 11 high-income countries on commonly ingested pesticides, was performed. The analysis showed that such a preventive step has brought positive results as there has been a significant reduction in the overall suicide rates in these 15 countries except Greece. Therefore, implementation of effective preventive measures is an immediate need in India.

Decriminalization of suicide attempts has come into effect in India from July 2018 as per the MHCA, 2017. As a first step in understanding the psychological build of people attempting suicide, the Supreme Court of India amended Section 309 of IPC to decriminalize suicide and would target at the care and treatment of those who attempted suicide in order to avoid recurrence (*NDTV*, 2018). The act has further held the government the responsibility of providing care and rehabilitation (if required) to the person who is under stress after a failed suicide attempt, thus attempting to reduce the risk of any more attempt. The act provides free treatment and care for such people who are homeless or are under below poverty line (BPL) category. This is a much-appreciated step taken by the country through the act and is also an attempt to redefine mental health and illness in the country. In this regard, the newly introduced MHCA 2017 stands as an eye-opener to the society on their perception and behaviour towards people suffering from various forms of mentally ill health in the country.

In sum

Important mental health policies of India are as follows:

1. National Mental Health Policy
2. Mental Health Act
3. Mental Healthcare Act

2.17. RECOMMENDATIONS

CMH care and service delivery are multidimensional and would be the following:

1. *Creation of an informed society:* Most of the society-driven mishaps that we hear about are due to limited knowledge; and so the rate of mental health imbalance in the country is increasing at alarming rates. Uninformed and poorly equipped society, in the grassroots level,

needs to be addressed. The attitude of our current society to mental illness is driven by misinterpretations and ignorance, and since these wrong belief systems have been long-standing, correcting them is tedious. Historically, mentally ill people have been ostracized and subjected to multiple victimization and torture. Of course, progressive changes and acceptance are slowly taking its shape even though in minimal terms. Whatever little progress that is taking place is the result of the spread of information and knowledge related to mental illness in society. Taking cognizance of this, creation of an informed society would be the only key to clarify and thereby rightly address the issues related to mental illness. The CMH programmes and service, through its intentions, would create awareness among the communities, thereby paving ways to build a sensible, informed and knowledgeable community. Most importantly, this would also create a sense of care and responsibility in the community to take care of the overall mental health of its members.

2. *Destigmatization:* The outcomes of such an initiative can be huge. Destigmatization of the society attempts that, which have mostly been let-downs or can be effectively tackled through this, with accuracy and spread. Information which is scientific and systematic would reveal the right picture, which would make anyone sensitive to the matter. Slowly, misconceptions and mistaken beliefs would be clear and so would be stigma. In fact, there is no better treatment for stigma that would be as powerful and effective as this. Destigmatization in itself can anchor into great changes, in terms of the well-being of the patient and their family, increased responsiveness from the mental health professionals and receptiveness shown by the community and governments. It wouldn't be inappropriate to perceive a stigma-less community to be the best possible niche for rehabilitation. The society which has been enlightened in such a manner would uphold its strong sense of ownership on mental health and well-being of its own community. Undoubtedly, CMH would stand out particularly because it would also induce feelings of belongingness, responsibility and care on each and every community member.

3. *Reduction in the treatment gap:* Reduction in the treatment gap would be the immediate and direct target of CMH care services. The huge demand for mental healthcare is unmet in India due to limited trained manpower and inadequate mental health training centres in the country. Here again, CMH can be systematically used to successfully tackle the issue immediately by making use of the community as a watchguard for the mental health of its people. This is where the involvement of every member of the community can be made use of, which would ensure the identification of individuals who require care and right treatment. Hence, systematic and timely intervention under guidance, and monitoring and care by one's own community would yield highly positive results in preventing and controlling mental illness, by identifying illness symptoms and guiding them towards right diagnosis and treatment, providing aftercare services and monitoring and finally by providing rehabilitation within the community a congenial environment for recovery and progress gets created.

4. *Patient satisfaction:* Patient satisfaction cannot be attained in isolation. A mixture of surrounding aspects, such as immediate access to healthcare, responsiveness from mental healthcare professionals, quick and accurate diagnosis, provisions for effective treatment and interpersonal aspects of care and support should fall in place. Studies have found a significant positive correlation between patient satisfaction and recovery, thereby highlighting the importance of its enhancement. CMH programmes, by its nature, organization and structure, takes complete care of this by adapting an individual-centric, community-based approach.

Through this process, an individual, in need of care and medical assistance, would be the prime focus around whom a network of caregivers, at various levels, starting from the immediate family, school/workplace, community and the medical system would render their time, effort, money and care for the fast recovery of an individual. The involvement of all these levels of caregivers would optimally ensure the satisfaction of the patient, both physically and psychologically, which would hasten the recovery process. The high probability of rehabilitation, to be taken care of within the community, would be another factor that adds up to patient satisfaction. If otherwise the case, then too, the period of institutional-based rehabilitation can be cut short to soon bring the individual back to their community. A detailed discussion on rehabilitation in CMH would be found elsewhere in this chapter.

5. *Community-based rehabilitation:* As have been the findings of several researches, rehabilitation and the best recovery happens at the patient's own environment (Wade, 2003). Hence, in CMH, which highlights on community inclusion through CBR, the most ideal environment for a speedy recovery can be provided to the individuals. This mode of rehabilitation has several features:
   a. Well-informed team of caregivers at various levels of care provision
   b. Round-the-clock check and monitoring of the individual
   c. Stigma-free congenial environment for recovery and growth
   d. Assured continuity of care
   e. Control over other psychosocial stressors that would lead to relapse
   f. Swiftness in the reintegration with the family/community after recovery

   This is a long-term approach where psychiatric care and health services are taken from the hospital to the community and are successfully carried out through teamwork and community participation. Hence, manageable individuals, who require attention, can be rehabilitated within their own community under the supervision of an informed network of people within one's comfort zone. Even in cases where institutionalized care is required, the individual can rejoin their own family soon enough as the symptoms and illness become manageable. Hence, it can be understood that reintegration with the community, which is otherwise a crucial matter of concern for the long-term functioning of an individual, is effectively taken care of in CBR.

6. *Continuity of care and relapse prevention:* CBR is the best mode to render aftercare services. In fact, this is the long-term advantage of CMH; since the functional level of the individual would be monitored by the circle of caregivers around them. Through correct knowledge dissemination and capacity building, a caregiver can rightly identify the nature, prognosis and symptomology of mental illness. Hence, timely intervention and rehabilitation can be effectively carried out, in addition to systematically handling follow-ups.

7. *Promotion of mental health and well-being:* CMH works towards the overall idea of promoting the mental health and well-being of all of its members. It is more than one topic and includes:
   a. *Enhancement of the overall mental health of the community on a general ground:* This includes building up of a healthy and well-functional community that would optimize the overall quality of the community. This is also about being sensitive towards issues of the time and being updated about possible mental health issues, people of any age might develop. A watchful society can manage to enhance the situation in such a way that the psychosocial stressors, which would lead to malfunctioning, can be controlled.

b. **Knowledge dissemination and incidence control:** This can be achieved by investing time, effort, skills and money in training the human capital about the basics of prominent mental health and illness conditions, their prognosis, identification and immediate actions to be taken. Along with the community, one can educate the community towards sectors of education, workplace, media and politics, thereby creating an informed community, which remain sensitive and alert to issues of mental health. Another important outcome of this would be the reduction in the incidence of mental illness rooted in situational causes due to increased awareness. Reduction in stigma is another attribute that would further ameliorate the community's mental health. The impact of this would be seen in the prevalence rates of the prominent mental illnesses which are caused/stimulated by any common reason such as board examination results or death of a loved one, natural calamities and so on.

c. **Early detection and intervention:** The next step to CMH is equipping the community to be able to identify and intervene in cases that require help. This is the most crucial stage that would explicitly decide the success of this initiative. Mental health professionals and trained volunteers would be assigned their duties and responsibilities based on their knowledge and expertise to sequentially carry out care delivery. The combination of informal manpower and specialists would be effectively integrated with the current system of psychiatric care in the country (Padmavati, 2005). In India, the role of NGOs is pivotal in filling the huge treatment gap in a cost-effective manner. However, the country has a lot to work towards the right usage of this system of serving the mental health needs of its population with the limited existing manpower. An effective model to carry out CMH service delivery is proposed in the following session.

d. **Rehabilitation, follow-up and aftercare:** Decentralization of mental health services to the community level would allow the delivery of resources locally (Olaogun et al., 2009). Hence, the quality of these services would be heightened and would speed up the recovery process and functioning levels. The community would then become the space for growth in terms of education, vocation, family and community. An expanded discussion on the CBR is provided later in this chapter.

8. **Protection of human rights:** Across the globe, the range of discrimination and violation of human rights that is faced by the mentally ill are many and the most important of all is the inaccessibility to healthcare services. In countries where community-based mental healthcare services are absent, the violation of human rights is even severe. Lack of right understanding among the community members on mental health would further exclude the mentally ill from the community context, which further leads to denial of basic human rights such as food, shelter, housing, education or employment (WHO, 2019c). Taking into account these situations, it can be understood that CMH initiatives would significantly contribute towards the protection of basic human rights by providing services at local levels and destigmatization.

9. **Building up a mentally healthy society:** This is the ultimate aim of CMH, which could be accomplished through systematic and effective execution of CMH initiative by sensitizing, training and equipping every member of a community into a responsible, sensible and informed human being. Ultimately, the target is the building up of a healthy society where the mental health of every individual receives equal respect, care and attention.

2.18. CONCLUSION AND IMPLICATIONS

The world is shifting its paradigm in mental healthcare from the institutions to the community. Inviting community involvement and encouraging community participation can result in enduring solutions to the mental-health-related problems the country is facing. Through knowledge dissemination and diffusion, responsibility among the community members should be focused. This team effort would not only benefit in reducing the prevalence and incidence of mental illness but also help in promoting mental hygiene and establishing a mentally fit society.

There are numerous implications of CMH preventive measures and interventions as well as findings of secondary studies. First, prevention of mental health problems at the community level by adopting different strategies, such as strengthening family functioning, creating awareness about signs and symptoms of common mental health challenges through health workers and the paraprofessional force in psychology as well as community psychologists, would help to reduce the burden of mental health diseases, thereby optimizing the productivity of common people. Second, the identification of cases with mental health challenges and extension of need-based intervention would help to improve the condition by enabling an individual to lead a productive and quality life. Third, the CBR approach would ensure quality care and faster prognosis of the problem. Fourth, the findings of secondary data would help in designing effective community-based intervention programmes considering the need of the people. Fifth, policymakers would be able to allocate resources in terms of funds and professional manpower for addressing the issue at the community level. Finally, findings of the secondary study also highlight the need for carrying out more systematic studies on various aspects of CMH with special reference to suicide prevention in developing countries like India.

EXERCISES

One-mark Questions

1. Define CMH.
2. Give two key features of CMH.
3. What is the definition of mental health according to WHO?
4. Write any one feature of the MHCA, 2017.
5. What are the types of rehabilitations available in mental health services?
6. Explain relapse prevention.
7. Elaborate NMHP.
8. What are the components of CMH service delivery?
9. What do you understand by the term 'destigmatization'?
10. What is paraprofessional force in psychology?

Five-mark Questions

1. Elaborate the history of mental health services in India.
2. How should education sectors participate in CMH service delivery?
3. Explain the four components of CMH service delivery.

4. Elaborate CBR.
5. How can mental health in workplace be promoted?
6. What is the role of media in disseminating knowledge of mental health?

Ten-mark Questions

1. What are the features of CMH?
2. How is community intervention different in rural and urban India?
3. What is the role of paraprofessional force in psychology in CMH?
4. Patient satisfaction would be higher in CBR. Explain.
5. How do you understand mental health and mental illness?
6. Write an account on the prevalent mental illnesses in India.

Reflexive Questions

1. How do you sensitize the larger society about mental health issues so that when people experience the same problem, they may come forward for mental health support services?
2. Is it necessary to establish a Mental Health Accreditation Council in India for certification?
3. Are mental health support services beneficial?
4. There is a necessity of mandatory recruitment of psychologists in every educational institution for addressing the mental needs of the students. Discuss.

REFERENCES

Aaron, R., Joseph, A., Muliyil, J., Abraham, S., George, K., Prasad, J., Minz, S., Abraham, V. J., & Bose, A. (2004). Suicides in young people in rural southern India. *The Lancet*, 363(9415), 1117–1118. https://doi.org/10.1016/S0140-6736(04)15896-0

Abreu, N., Dias, I., Cascais, M., Luz, A., & Moleiro, P. (2018). What are the most frequent diagnoses in adolescence? The reality of an adolescent medicine clinic. *Einstein Sao Paulo*, 16(2), 1–11. https://doi.org/10.1590/s1679-45082018ao4225

Adewuya, A. O., Atilola, O., Ola, B. A., Coker, O. A., Zachariah, M. P., Olugbile, O., Fasawe, A. A., & Idris, O. (2018). Current prevalence, comorbidity and associated factors for symptoms of depression and generalised anxiety in the Lagos State Mental Health Survey (LSMHS), Nigeria. *Comprehensive Psychiatry*, 81, 60–65.

Alam, S., & Rizvi, K. (2012). Psychological well-being among bank employees. *Journal of the Indian Academy of Applied Psychology*, 38(2), 242–247.

American Psychiatric Association. (2019). What is mental illness? https://www.psychiatry.org/patients-families/what-is-mental-illness

Ashraf, N. A. (2018, 3 April). There are less than 4000 psychiatrists in India: Is medical education to blame? *The News Minute*. https://www.thenewsminute.com/article/there-are-less-4000-psychiatrists-india-medical-education-blame-78952

Australian Bureau of Statistics. (2008). *National survey of mental health and wellbeing: Summary of results, 2007*. https://www.abs.gov.au/AUSSTATS/abs@.nsf/Lookup/4326.0Main+Features32007?OpenDocument

Bachrach, L. L. (1992). Psychosocial rehabilitation and psychiatry in the care of long-term patients. *American Journal of Psychiatry*, 149(11), 1455–1455.

Baker, C. (2018). *Mental health statistics for England: Prevalence, services and funding*. UK Parliament.

Baxter, A. J., Scott, K. M., Ferrari, A. J., Norman, R. E., Vos T., & Whiteford, H. A. (2014). Challenging the myth of an 'epidemic' of common mental disorders: Trends in the global prevalence of anxiety and depression between 1990 and 2010. *Depression and Anxiety*, 31(6), 506–516. https://doi.org/10.1002/da.22230

Behere, P. B., & Behere, A. P. (2008). Farmers 'suicide in Vidarbha region of Maharashtra state: A myth or reality? *Indian Journal of Psychiatry, 50*(2), 124–127. https://doi.org/10.4103/0019-5545.42401

Bhattacharya, S.. (2016, 31 May). Indian millennials clock way more work hours than their global competition. *The Wall Street Journal.* https://blogs.wsj.com/indiarealtime/2016/05/31/indian-millennials-clock-way-more-work-hours-than-their-global-competition/

Bhattacharyya, R., & Vijayaraghavan, K. (2016, 11 June). 46% of workforce in firms in India suffer from some or the other form of stress: Data. *The Economic Times,* 1–24. https://economictimes.indiatimes.com/jobs/46-of-workforce-in-firms-in-india-suffer-from-some-or-the-other-form-of-stress-data/articleshow/52696795.cms?from=mdr

Bhola, P., Sathyanarayanan, V., Rekha, D. P., Daniel, S., & Thomas, T. (2016). Assessment of self-reported emotional and behavioral difficulties among pre-university college students in Bangalore, India. *Indian Journal of Community Medicine, 41*(2), 146–150. https://doi.org/10.4103/0970-0218.177536

Brekke, J. S., Hoe, M., Long, J., & Green, M. F. (2007). How neurocognition and social cognition influence functional change during community-based psychosocial rehabilitation for individuals with schizophrenia. *Schizophrenia Bulletin, 33*(5), 1247–1256. https://doi.org/10.1093/schbul/sbl072

Castro-Costa, E., Dewey, M., Stewart, R., Banerjee, S., Huppert, F., Mendonca-Lime, C., Bula, C., Reisches, F., Wancata, J., Ritchie, K., Tsolaki, M., Mateos, R., & Prince, M. (2007). Prevalence of depressive symptoms and syndromes in later life in ten European countries: The SHARE study. *British Journal of Psychiatry, 191*(5), 393–401. https://doi.org/10.1192/bjp.bp.107.036772

Chandrashekar, H., Prashanth, N. R., Kasthuri, P., & Madhusudhan, S. (2010). Psychiatric rehabilitation. *Indian Journal of Psychiatry, 52*(1), 1–5. https://doi.org/10.4103/0019-5545.69250

Chatterjee, S. (2016, October 22). 150 million adult Indians suffer from mental disorder: NMHS. *Times of India,* pp. 1–22. https://timesofindia.indiatimes.com/india/150-million-adult-Indians-suffer-from-mental-disorder-NMHS/articleshow/55036009.cms

Chatterjee, S., Naik, S., John, S., Dabholkar, H., Balaji, M., Koschorke, M., Varghese, M., Thara, R., Weiss, H. A., Williams, P., McCrone, P., Patel, V., & Thornicroft, G. (2014). Effectiveness of a community-based intervention for people with schizophrenia and their caregivers in India (COPSI): A randomised controlled trial. *The Lancet, 383*(9926), 1385–1392. https://doi.org/10.1016/S0140-6736(13)62629-X

Chatterjee, S., Patel, V., Chatterjee, A., & Weiss, H. A. (2003). Evaluation of a community-based rehabilitation model for chronic schizophrenia in rural India. *The British Journal of Psychiatry, 182*(1), 57–62.

Chatterjee, S., Pillai, A., Jain, S., Cohen, A., & Patel, V. (2009). Outcomes of people with psychotic disorders in a community-based rehabilitation programme in rural India. *The British Journal of Psychiatry, 195*(5), 433–439.

Chowdhury, A. N., Banerjee, S., Brahma, A., & Weiss, M. G. (2007). Pesticide practices and suicide among farmers of the Sundarban region in India. *Food and Nutrition Bulletin, 28*(2), 381–391.

Corrigan, P. W., & Watson, A. C. (2002). Understanding the impact of stigma on people with mental illness. *World Psychiatry, 1*(1), 16–20.

Corrigan, P. W., & Penn, D. L. (1999). Lessons from social psychology on discrediting psychiatric stigma. *American Psychologist, 54*(9), 765.

Coldwell C. M., & Bender W. S. (2007). The Effectiveness of assertive community treatment for homeless populations with severe mental Illness: A meta-analysis. *The American Journal of Psychiatry, 164*(3), 1–16.

Deb, S., Banu, P. R., Thomas, S., Vardhan, R. V., Rao, P. T., & Khawaja, N. (2016). Depression among Indian university students and its association with perceived university academic environment, living arrangements and personal issues. *Asian Journal of Psychiatry, 23,* 108–117. https://doi.org/10.1016/j.ajp.2016.07.010

Del Olmo-romero, F., Gonzalez-Blanco, M., Sarro, S., J, G., Martin-Carrasco, M., Martinez-Cabezón, A. C., Perna, G., Pomarol-Clotet, E., Varandas, P., Ballesteros-Rodríguez, J., Rebolleda-Gil, C., Vanni, G., González-Fraile, E., & INTER NOS group. (2018). Mental health professionals' attitudes towards mental illness: Professional and cultural factors in the INTER NOS study. *European Archive of Psychiatry and Clinical Neuroscience, 269*(3), 325–339. https://doi.org/10.1007/s00406-018-0867-5

Derek, G., Johnston, R., Pratt, G., Watts, M. J., & Whatmore, S. (Eds.). (2009). Quality of Life. *The dictionary of human geography 5th edition.* Wiley-Blackwell.

Dogan, T. (2012). A long-term study of the Counselling needs of Turksih univeristy students. *Journal of Counselling and Development*, 90(1), 91–96.

Feldman, D. B., & Crandall, C. S. (2007). Dimensions of mental illness stigma: What about mental illness causes social rejection? *Journal of Social and Clinical Psychology*, 26(2), 137–154. https://doi.org/10.1521/jscp.2007.26.2.137

Gadit, A. A. M., & Mugford, G. (2007). Prevalence of depression among households in three capital cities of Pakistan: Need to revise the mental health policy. *PloS One*, 2(2), e209.

Gallagher, M. W., Lopez, S. J., & Preacher, K. J. (2009). The hierarchical structure of well-being. *Journal of Personality*, 77(4), 1025–1050.

Gautam, S., Jain, A., Gautma, M., Gautam, A., & Jagawat, T. (2019). Clinical practice guidelines for bipolar affective disorder (BPAD) in children and adolescents. *Indian Journal of Psychiatry*, 61(8), 294–305.

Gebrekidan Abbay, A., Tibebe Mulatu, A., & Azadi, H. (2018). Community knowledge, perceived beliefs and associated factors of mental distress: A case study from Northern Ethiopia. *International Journal of Evnironmental Research and Public Health*, 15(11). https://doi.org/10.3390/ijerph15112423

Geller, D. A. (2006). Obsessive-compulsive and spectrum disorders in children and adolescents. *Psychiatric Clinics of North America*, 29(2), 352–370.

Gruère, G., & Sengupta, D. (2011). Bt cotton and farmer suicides in India: An evidence-based assessment. *The Journal of Development Studies*, 46(2), 316–337. https://doi.org/10.1080/00220388.2010.492863

Gupta, A., Sarpal, S., Kumar, D., Kaur, T., & Arora, S. (2013). Prevalence, pattern and familial effects of substance use among the male college students: A North Indian study. *Journal of Clinical and Diagnostic Research*, 7(8), 1632–1636. https://doi.org/10.7860/JCDR/2013/6441.3215

Hackett, R., Hackett, L., Bhakta, P., & Gowers, S. (1999). The prevalence and associations of psychiatric disorder in children. *Journal of Child Psychology and Psychiarty and Applied Disciplines*, 40(5), 801–807.

Hartley, S., Finkenflugel, H., Kuipers, P., & Thomas, M. (2009). Community-based rehabilitation: Opportunity and challenge. *The Lancet*, 374(9704), 1803–1804.

Huang, D., Yang, L. H., & Pescosolido, B. A. (2019). Understanding the public ' s profile of mental health literacy in China: A nationwide study. *BMC Psychiatry*, 19(20), 1–12.

Hunter, C. (2019). The Importance of promoting mental health in universities. Women's Health Research Institute. https://www.womenshealth.northwestern.edu/blog/importance-promoting-mental-health-universities

India Today. (2019, 12 February). Here's why schools should include mental health education in curriculum. *India Today*, pp. 1–10. https://www.indiatoday.in/education-today/featurephilia/story/here-s-why-schools-should-include-mental-health-education-in-curriculum-1454266-2019-02-12

Ingle, G. K., & Nath, A. (2008). Geriatric health in India: Concerns and solutions. *Indian Journal of Community Medicine*, 33(4), 214–218.

Janetius, S. (2016). Evidence-based counselling model for college students. *The International Journal of Indian Psychology*, 3(4), 1–14.

Lepine, J. P., Demyttenaere, K., Bruffaerts, R., Posada-Villa, J., Gasquet, I., Kovess, V., Angermeyer, M. C., Bernert, S., de Girolamo, G., Morosini, P., Polidori, G., Kikkawa, T., Kawakami, N., Ono, Y., Takeshima, T., Uda, H., Karam, E. G., Fayyad, J. A., Karam, A. N., … Mneimneh, Z. N. (2004). Prevalence, severity, and unmet need for treatment of mental disorders in the World Health Organization World Mental Health. *JAMA*, 291(21), 2581–2590. https://doi.org/10.1001/jama.291.21.2581

Keith, S. J., Bustillo, Juan, R., Lauriello, John, & Horan, William, P. (2001). Reviews and overviews psychosocial treatment of schizophrenia: An update. *American Journal of Psychiatry*, 158(2), 1–21.

Kendall, E., Buys, N., & Larner, J. (2000). Community-based service delivery in rehabilitation: The promise and the paradox. *Diasbility and Rehabiliation*, 22(10), 435–445. https://doi.org/10.1080/09638280050045901

Kessler, R., Amminger, G., Aguilar-Gaxiola, S., Alonso, J., Lee, S., & Ustun, T. (2007). Age of onset of mental disorders: A review of recent literature. *Current Opinion in Psychiatry*, 20(4), 359–364. https://doi.org/10.1097/YCO.0b013e32816ebc8c

Kessler, R. C., Berglund, P., Demler, O., Jin, R., Merikangas, K. R., & Walters, E. E. (2005). Lifetime prevalence and age-of-onset distributions of. *Archives of General Psychiatry*, 62(6), 593–768.

Keyes, C. L. M. (2002). The mental health continuum: From languishing to flourishing in life. *Journal of Health and Social Behaviour, 43*(2), 207–222.

Keyes, C. L. M. (2006). Mental health in adolescence: Is America's youth flourishing? *American Journal of Orthopsychiatry, 76*(3), 395–402.

Keyes, C. L. M. (2014). Mental health as a complete state: How the salutogenic perspective completes the picture. In G. F. Bauer & O. Hämmig (Eds.), *Bridging occupational, organizational and public health: A transdisciplinary approach* (pp. 179–192). Springer. Kohn, R., Saxena, S., Levav, I., & Saraceno, B. (2019). The *treatment gap in mental health care. Bulletin of World Health Organization, 82*(11), 858–866.

Lambert, V. A., & Lambert, C. E. (2008). Nurses' workplace stressors and coping strategies. *Indian Journal of Palliative Care, 14*(1), 38–44. https://doi.org/10.4103/0973-1075.41934

Lee, J., Yu, F., Augong, H., & Chok, S. (2018). *Community-based approaches to the prevention, rehabilitation and reintegration of drug offenders.* The Singapore Anti-Narcotics Association. https://lkyspp.nus.edu.sg/docs/default-source/ips/abstract_and_executive_summary_ips-csu-case-study_070318-(1).pdf

Liu, H., Shi, Y., Auden, E., & Rozelle, S. (2018). Anxiety in rural Chinese children and adolescents: Comparisons across provinces and among subgroups. *International Journal of Environmental Reserach and Public Health, 15*(10), 1–19. https://doi.org/10.3390/ijerph15102087

Lockwood, A., & Marshall, M. (2000). Assertive community treatment for people with severe mental disorders. *Cochrane Database of Systematic Reviews, 2,* 1–2. https://doi.org/10.1002/14651858.CD001089

Lodha, P., & de Sousa, A. (2018). Geriatric mental health: The challenges for India. *Journal of Geriatric Mental Health, 5*(1), 16–29. http://www.jgmh.org/text.asp?2018/5/1/16/235372

Luitel, N. P., Baron, E. C., Kohrt, B. A., Komproe, I. H., & Jordans, M. J. D. (2018). Prevalence and correlates of depression and alcohol use disorder among adults attending primary health care services in Nepal: A cross sectional study. *BMC Health Services Research, 18*(215), 1–10.

Ma, C., Bovet, P., Yang, L., Zhao, M., Liang, Y., & Xi, B. (2018). Alcohol use among young adolescents in low-income and middle-income countries: A population-based study. *The Child and Adolsecent Health, 2*(6), 415–429. https://doi.org/10.1016/S2352-4642(18)30112-3

Marwaha, S., Kaur, R., & Kaur, I. (2014). Mental health of elderly in india: A study. *International Journal of International Law, 2*(1), 188–205.

Malhotra, S., Kohli, A., & Arun, P. (2002). Prevalence of psychiatric disorders in school children in Chandigarh, India. *Indian Journal of Medical Research, 116,* 21–28.

Malhotra, S., & Patra, B. N. (2014). Prevalence of child and adolescent psychiatric disorders in India: A systematic review and meta-analysis. *Child and Adolescent Psychiatry and Mental Health, 8*(1), 22. https://doi.org/10.1186/1753-2000-8-22

Malhotra, S., & Pradhan, B. K. Kohli, A., & Kapoor, M. (2013). Childhood psychiatric disorders in North-India: Prevalence, incidence and implication. *Indian Journal of Psychiatry, 51*(2), 87–89. https://doi.org/10.4103/0019-5545.49449

Malhotra, S., & Shah, R. (2015). Women and mental health in India: An overview. *Indian Journal of Psychiatry, 57*(2), 205–211. https://doi.org/10.4103/0019-5545.161479

Maideen, S. F. K., Sidik, S. M., Rampal, L., & Mukhtar, F. (2014). Prevalence, associated factors and predictors of depression among adults in the community of Selangor, Malaysia. *PloS One, 9*(4), e95395.

Matharu, A. (2019). The pursuit of happiness: Delhi govt schools to combat mental health issues. *The Wire,* pp. 1–8. https://thewire.in/education/pursuit-happiness-delhi-govt-schools-combat-mental-health-issues

Mathur, A. (2017). Mental health in old age. *Journal of the Indian Academy of Geriatrics, 13*(1), 1–2. https://www.jiag.org/jiagpdf/editorial_3_4

Ministry of Health & Family Welfare. (2014). *National Mental Health Policy of India 2014.* https://nhm.gov.in/images/pdf/National_Health_Mental_Policy.pdf

Ministry of Health and Family Welfare. (2017). *National Health Policy, 2017.* https://www.nhp.gov.in/nhpfiles/national_health_policy_2017.pdf

Ministry of Law and Justice. (2017). *Mental Healthcare Act 2017.* http://egazette.nic.in/WriteReadData/2017/175248.pdf

Molla, G., Sebhat, H., ZN, H., Mekoneh, A., Mersha, W., & Yimmer, T. (2016). Depression among Ethiopian adults: Corss-sectional study. *Psychiatry Journal.* https://doi.org/10.1155/2016/1468120

Motohashi, Y., Kaneko, Y., & Sasaki, H. (2004). Community-based suicide prevention program in Japan using a health promotion approach. *Environmental Health and Preventive Medicine, 9*(1), 3–8. https://doi.org/10.1265/ehpm.9.3

Mueser, K. T., Bond, G. R., Drake, R. E., & Resnick, S. G. (1995). Models of community care for severe mental illness: A review of research on case management. *Schizophrenia Bulletin, 24*(1), 37–74.

Mueser, K. T., Torrey, W. C., & Lynde, D., Singer, P., & Drake, R. E. (2003). Implementing evidence-based practices for people with severe mental illness. *Behaviour Modification, 27*(3), 387–411. https://doi.org/10.1177/0145445503027003007

Nair, S., Ganjiwale, J., Kharod, N., Varma, J., & Nimbalkar, S. M. (2017). Epidemiological survey of mental health in adolescent school children of Gujarat, India. *BMJ Paediatr Open, 1*(1), 2–15.

National Council on Alcoholism and Drug Dependence. (2010). *Alcohol and drug addiction is one of the most serious health problems facing our society today.*

NDTV. (2018, 30 June). Government decriminalises suicide, notifies new law, 2–3. https://www.ndtv.com/india-news/government-decriminalises-suicide-notifies-new-law-1861575

Neredumilli, P. K., Padma, V., & Radharani, S. (2018). Mental Health Care Act 2017: Review and upcoming issues. *Archives of Mental Health, 19*(1), 9–14. https://doi.org/10.4103/AMH.AMH_8_18

NIMHANS. (2016). *National mental health survey of India, 2015–16: Prevalence, pattern and outcomes.* Bengaluru. http://indianmhs.nimhans.ac.in/Docs/Report2.pdf

Nizamie, S. H., & Goyal, N. (2010). History of psychiatry in India. *Indian Journal of Psychiatry, 52*(1), 7–12. https://doi.org/10.4103/0019-5545.69195

Np, L., Mjd, J., Ba, K., Sd, R., & Ih, K. (2017). Treatment gap and barriers for mental health care : A cross-sectional community survey in Nepal. *PLoS ONE, 12*(8). https://doi.org/10.1371/journal.pone.0183223

Olaogun, M. O., Nyante, & Ajediran, A. (2009). Overcoming the barriers for participation by the disabled: An appraisal and global view of community-based rehabilitation in community development. *AJPARS, 1*(1), 24–29.

Olesji, J., Mota, N., Cox, B., & Sareen, J. (2010). Perceived need for care, help seeking, and perceived barriers to care for alcohol use disorders in a national sample. *Psychiatric Services, 61*(12), 1223–1231. https://doi.org/10.1176/ps.2010.61.12.1223

Ovuga, E., & Boardman, J. (2005). The prevalence of depression in two districts of Uganda. *Social Psychiatry and Psychiatric Epidemiology, 40*, 439–445. https://doi.org/10.1007/s00127-005-0915-0

Padmavati, R. (2005). Community mental health care in India. *International Review of Psychiatry, 17*(2), 103–107.

Pal, R., Dasgupta, A., & Tsering, D. (2010). Substance use among adolescent high school students in India: A survey of knowledge, attitude, and opinion. *Journal of Pharmacy And Bioallied Sciences, 2*(2), 137. https://doi.org/10.4103/0975-7406.67005

Parikh, S. (2019, 3 February). Getting mental health into the curriculum. *The Hindu*, 2–5. https://www.thehindu.com/sci-tech/health/getting-mental-health-into-the-curriculum/article26163579.ece

Patel, V., Araya, R., Chatterjee, S., Chisholm, D., Cohen, A., De Silva, M., Hosman, C., McGuire, H., Rojas, G., & van Ommeren, M. (2007). Treatment and prevention of mental disorders in low-income and middle-income countries. *Global Mental Health, 370*(9591), 991–1005.

Patel, V., Flisher, A., S, H., & McGorry, P., & Hetrick, S. (2007). Mental health of young people: A global public-health challenge. *The Lancet, 369*(9569), 10–11. https://doi.org/10.1016/S0140-6736(07)60368-7

Patel, V., Goel, D., & Desai, R. (2009). Scaling up services for mental and neurological disorders in low-resource settings. *International Health, 1*(1), 37–44. https://doi.org/10.1016/j.inhe.2009.02.002

Pillai, A., Andrews, T., & Patel, V. (2009). Violence, psychological distress and the risk of suicidal behaviour in young people in India. *International Journal of Epidemiology, 38*(2), 459–469. https://doi.org/10.1093/ije/dyn166

Poongothai, S., Pradeepa, R., Ganesan, A., & Mohan, V. (2009). Prevalence of depression in a large urban South Indian population: The Chennai urban rural epidemiology study (Cures-70). *PLoS ONE, 4*(9), 1–9.

Prakash, O., & Kukreti, P. (2013). State of geriatric mental health in India. *Current Translational Geriatrics and Gerontology Reports, 2*(1), 1–6. https://doi.org/10.1007/s13670-012-0034-1

Radhakrishnan, R., & Andrade, C. (2012). Suicide: An Indian perspective. *Indian Journal of Psychiatry, 54*(4), 304–319. https://doi.org/10.4103/0019-5545.104793

Ramachandran, V. (1991). The prevention of alcohol-related problems. *Indian Journal of Psychiatry, 33*(1), 3–10.

Rathod, S. D., de Silva, M. J., Ssebunnya, J., Breuer, E., Murhar, V., Luitel, N. P., Medhin, G., Kigozi, F., Shidhaye, R., Fekadu, A., Jordans, M., Patel, V., Tomlinson, M., & Lund, C. (2016). Treatment contact coverage for probable depressive and probable alcohol use disorders in four low-and middle-income country districts: The PRIME cross-sectional community surveys. *PLoS ONE.* https://doi.org/10.1371/journal.pone.0162038

Reddy, G. L., & Poornima, R. (2012). Occupational stress and professional burnout of university teachers in South India. *International Journal of Educational Planning & Administration, 2*(2), 109–124.

Reddy, M. V., & Chandrashekar, C. R. (1998). Prevalence of mental and behavioural disorders in India: A meta-analysis. *Indian Journal of Psychiatry, 40*(2), 149–157.

Robitschek, C., & Keyes, C. L. M. (2009). Keyes's model of mental health with personal growth initiative as a parsimonious predictor. *Journal of Counseling Psychology, 56*(2), 321–329.

Ronad, S. V, Babu, R. B., Patali, C. S., Shrinivas, K., Ugargol, S. S., & Shridhar, H. (2017). Child and adolescent mental health in Indian context. *Research in Medical & Engineering Sciences,* 1–6. https://doi.org/10.31031/RMES.2017.02.000548

Samuel, D., & Sher, L. (2013). Suicidal behavior in Indian adolescents. *International Journal of Adolescence Mental Health, 25*(3), 207–212. https://doi.org/10.1515/ijamh-2013-0054

Saraceno, B., van Ommeren, M., Batniji, R., Gureje, O., Mahoney, J., Sridhar, D., & Underhill, C. (2007). Barriers to improvement of mental health services in low-income and middle-income countries. *The Lancet, 370*(9593), 1164–1174. https://doi.org/10.1016/S0140-6736(07)61263-X

Saxena, S., & Skeen, S. (2012). No health without mental health: Challenges and opportunities in global mental health. *African Journal of Psychiatry, 15*(6), 397–400.

Sharma, P., & Tyagi, A. (2016). A study on adolescent drug abuse in India. *American International Journal of Research in Humanites, Arts and Social Sciences, 16*(244), 119–121.

Sharma, S. (2015). Occupational stress in the armed forces: An Indian army perspective. *IIMB Management Review, 27*(3), 185–195. https://doi.org/10.1016/j.iimb.2015.06.002

Sidana, A. (2018). Community psychiatry in India: Where we stand? *Journal of Mental Health and Human Behaviour, 23*(1), 4–11. http://www.jmhhb.org/text.asp?2018/23/1/4/244922

Silva, M. C., Gaunekar, G., Patel, V., Kukalekar, D. S., & Fernandes, J. (2003). The prevalence and correlates of hazardous drinking in industrial workers: A study from Goa, India. *Alcohol and Alcoholism, 38*(1), 79–83.

Silva, M. J. De, Mckenzie, K., Harpham, T., & Huttly, S. R. A. (2005). Social capital and mental illness: A systematic review. *Journal of Epidemiology and Community Health, 59*(8), 619–627. https://doi.org/10.1136/jech.2004.029678

Singh, A. (2017, 10 October 10). World Mental Health Day 2017: Mental health status among adolescents in India; possible solutions. *NDTV.* https://www.ndtv.com/education/mental-health-status-among-adolescents-in-india-possible-solutions-1761025

Singh, M., Bala, N., Garg, P. D., Bansal, S., Bumrah, S., & Attri, A. (2017). Substance abuse in Children and adolescent: A retrospective study. *International Journal of Medical Research and Review, 5*(3), 1–8.

Sinyor, M., Tse, R., & Pirkis, J. (2017). Global trends in suicide epidemiology. *Current Opinion in Psychiatry, 30*(1), 1–6. https://doi.org/10.1097/YCO.0000000000000296

Srinath, S., Girmaji, S., Gururaj, G., Seshadri, S., Subhakrishna, D., Kumar, N., & Bhola, P. (2005). Epidemiological study of child & adolescent psychiatric disorders in urban & rural areas of Bangalore, India. *Indian Journal of Medical Research, 122*(1), 67–69.

Srivastava, K. (2009). Urbanization and mental health. *Industrial Psychiatry Journal, 18*(2), 75–76. https://doi.org/10.4103/0972-6748.64028

Srivastava, K., Chatterjee, K., & Bhat, P. S. (2016). Mental health awareness: The Indian scenario. *Industrial Management and Data Systems, 25*(2), 131–134. http://www.industrialpsychiatry.org/text.asp?2016/25/2/131/207856

Tahtinen, R., & Kristjansdottir, H. (2018). The influence of anxiety and depression symptoms on help-seeking intentions in indivisual sport athletes and non-athletes: The role of gender and athlete status. *Journal of Clinical Sport Psychology, 13*(1), 1–31.

The Hindu. (2019, 18 February). Efficacy of deep brain stimulation highlighted. https://www.thehindu.com/news/cities/chennai/efficacy-of-deep-brain-stimulation-highlighted/article26298851.ece

The MINDS Foundation. (2017, 21 April). What rural and urban India can teach each other about mental healthcare. The Better India. https://www.thebetterindia.com/96308/mental-healthcare-rural-india-urban-india-contrast/

Thirnavukarasu, M. (2011). Closing the treatment gap. *Indian Journal of Psychiatry, 53*(3), 199–201. https://doi.org/10.4103/0019-5545.86803

Tinney, M., Chiodo, A., Haig, A., & Wiredu, E. (2007). Medical rehabilitation in Ghana. *Disability and Rehabilitation, 29*(11), 921–927.

Tiwari, S. C., & Pandey, N. M. (2012). Status and requirements of geriatric mental health services in India: An evidence-based commentary. *Indian Journal of Psychiatry, 54*(1), 8–14. https://doi.org/10.4103/0019-5545.94639

Tran, T. T. T., Nguyen, N. B., Luong, M. A., Bui, T. H. A, Phan, T. D., Tran, V. O., Ngo, T. H., Minas, H., & Nguyen, T. Q. (2019). Stress, anxiety and depression in clinical nurses in Vietnam: A cross-sectional survey and cluster analysis. *International Journal of Mental Health Systems, 13*(3). https://doi.org/10.1186/s13033-018-0257-4

US Department of Health and Human Service. (2017). *The national survey on drug use and health: 2017 national survey on drug use and health (NSDUH).* https://www.samhsa.gov/data/sites/default/files/cbhsq-reports/NSDUHDetailedTabs2017/NSDUHDetailedTabs2017.pdf

Van de Velde, S., Bracke, P., & Levecque, K. (2010). Gender differences in depression in 23 European countries: Cross- national variation in the gender gap in depression. *Social Science & Medicine, 71*(2), 305–313. https://doi.org/10.1016/j.socscimed.2010.03.035

Venkatashivareddy, B., Gupta, A., Lohiya, A., & Kharya, P. (2013). Mental health issues and challenges in India: A review. *International Journal of Scientific and Research Publications, 3*(2), 1–4.

Vijayakumar, L., John, S., Pirkis, J., & Whiteford, H. (2005). Suicide in developing countries (2): Risk factors. *Crisis, 26*(2), 112–119. https://doi.org/10.1027/0227-5910.26.3.112

Wade, D. (2003). Community rehabilitation, or rehabilitation in the community? *Disability and Rehabiliation, 25*(15), 875–881. https://doi.org/10.1080/0963828031000122267

Wahl, O. F. (1995). *Media madness: Public images of mental illness.* Rutgers University Press.

Wang, X., Zhang, D., & Wang, J. (2011). Dual-factor model of mental health: Surpass the traditional mental health model. *Psychology, 02*(08).

Westerhof, G. J., & Keyes, C. L. M. (2010). Mental illness and mental health: The two continua model across the lifespan. *Journal of Adult Development, 17*(2), 110–119.

WHO. (2000). *The world health report 2000 health systems : Improving Performance.* https://www.who.int/whr/2000/en/

WHO. (2001). *The world health report mental health: New understanding, new hope.* https://www.who.int/whr/2001/en/

WHO. (2005). *Promoting mental health: Concepts, emerging evidence, practice* (Vol. 51). https://www.who.int/mental_health/evidence/MH_Promotion_Book.pdf

WHO. (2019a). *Mental disorders.* https://www.who.int/mental_health/management/en/

WHO. (2019b). *Child and adolescent mental health.* https://www.who.int/mental_health/maternal-child/child_adolescent/en/

WHO. (2019c). *Mental health, human rights & legislation.* https://www.who.int/mental_health/policy/legislation/en/

Yu, W., Singh, S. S., Calhoun, S., Zhang, H., Zhao, X., & Yang, F. (2018). Generalized anxiety disorder in urban China: Prevalence, awareness, and disease burden. *Journal of Affective Disorders, 234*, 89–96. https://doi.org/10.1016/j.jad.2018.02.012

Zewdu, S., Hanlon, C., Fekadu, A., Medhin, G., & Teferra, S. (2019). Treatment gap, help-seeking, stigma and magnitude of alcohol use disorder in rural Ethiopia. *Substance Abuse Treatment, Prevention and Policy, 14*(4), 1–10.

Zhou, M., Zhang, G., Rozelle, S., Kenny, K., & Xue, H. (2018). Depressive symptoms of Chinese children: Prevalence and correlated factors among subgroups. *International Journal of Evnironmental Research and Public Health, 15*(2), 1–10. https://doi.org/10.3390/ijerph15020283

RECOMMENDED READINGS

Cutting, A. R. (1970). An approach to community mental health education. *Social Casework, 51*(8), 475–480. http://ovidsp.ovid.com/ovidweb.cgi?T=JS&PAGE=reference&D=psyc2&NEWS=N&AN=1971-08856-001

Mair, H. (1972). Community mental health services. *Public Health, 86*(2), 73–78. https://doi.org/10.1016/S0033-3506(72)80005-2

Mueser, K. T., Bond, G. R., Drake, R. E., & Resnick, S. G. (1995). Models of community care for severe mental illness: A review of research on case management. *Schizophrenia Bulletin, 24*(1), 37–74.

Padmavati, R. (2005). Community mental health care in India. *International Review of Psychiatry, 17*(2), 103–107.

Community-based Intervention for Physical Health

LEARNING OBJECTIVES

- Understanding community physical health
- Identifying health risk across lifespan
- Defining health-seeking behaviour and its determinants
- Identifying the role and functions of community psychologists in India
- Proposing a community need-based intervention model

ABSTRACT

Changes in everyday life have their direct impact on the nature, course and manifestation of illnesses. It demands for more research and practice in the field of health to smartly tackle the numerous issues in curative science. While the developed nations are burdened by non-communicable diseases, underdeveloped countries fight malnutrition and communicable diseases spreading through unsafe living environment. Health and health-seeking behaviour are influenced by an array of determinants ranging from categorical variables such as age and gender to community-specific factors such as stigma and cultural practices. Illness, now, has to be understood from a holistic perspective, and treatment has to be tailored accordingly to see positive outcomes. Community health and the role of community psychologists have become a topic of hope especially due to these reasons. This chapter is devoted to understanding physical health in India from the realm of our socio-economic, political and cultural context and is exhaustively based on empirical evidence. Causal and risk factors of prominent illnesses reported in the country, our health-seeking behaviours and their determinants, the need and scope of community psychologists and existing health policies in the country are detailed in this chapter. The chapter also proposes a framework for community need-based intervention programmes and a few relevant recommendations, which would address the key issues pertaining to accessibility, availability and affordability of healthcare services in the country.

Keywords: Community health; illness; health-seeking behaviour; community psychologist

3.1. INTRODUCTION

The Sustainable Development Goals (SDGs; 2015) have undertaken the promotion of health and wellness as one of their key preferences and have committed to 'ensure healthy lives and promote well-being for all at all ages' by 2030. The current conceptualization of health as 'a state of complete physical, mental and social wellbeing and not merely the absence of diseases or infirmity' is a holistic outlook; now, health is no more an isolated concept; rather, it is perceived as an idea propagating towards a productive life by all means. Nevertheless, this interpretation of health could also be counterproductive, as this inadvertently increases the proportion of people who can be labelled as 'ill' (Huber et al., 2011). The need for a pragmatic understanding about health and illness is desired because now, both the bearers and receivers of healthcare show high preference for value-based care over mere symptom management. The dynamicity of health as a concept demands it to be placed in the context of its prevalence to define, estimate, manage and intervene from the right perspective. Health, being the function of the community, calls for the applicability of community health to force. It is difficult to emphatically define this notion of service; however, Mckenzie et al. (2011) explained community health as 'the health status of a defined group of people and the actions and conditions, both private and public (governmental), to promote, protect, and preserve their health'. This frame of community health encompasses certain key areas of focus, such as the locus (common geographical area), the contextual concept of health and the application of multi-professional expertise involved in the process (Goodman et al., 2014). The space thus created would function in a continuum of health promotion and wellness at one end and prevention, intervention and rehabilitation of illness at the other. In fact, this is the sustainable healthcare management procedure that has the potential to build on a strong health capital for any economy. The reflection of socio-economic and legal benefits of upholding individuals' health and well-being is such that one-fourth of the economy's growth of low-middle-income countries during 2000–2011 was the result of evidence-based health intervention (Every Women Every Child, 2016).

Manifestation of health and illness are concomitantly varying with the overall changes in the lifestyle across the world. Apart from the rising incidence of new medical conditions, the variations in the age, onset, aetiology and management of familiar illness conditions are placing the healthcare system in an alarming state. As long as equity-equality issues in health service delivery pertain, the high demand for tailor-made treatment regimen is far beyond the scope in a country like India. Implementation of community healthcare services is one true solution to the many health services issues faced by the country, as it tackles problems related to availability, accessibility and affordability of health services to the public. Community health in India gains its prominence from the 1978 Alma-Ata Declaration when the key role of primary healthcare in healthcare delivery was recognized (WHO, 1978). The team of community healthcare facilitators can function in different roles and responsibilities suiting to their community need which includes assisting the medical professionals in healthcare activities such as immunization, medical camps or medical needs during disaster/crisis management (Scott & Shanker, 2010), rendering services to the underprivileged/marginalized population, addressing the financial and human resource problems in resource-poor areas (UNAIDS, 2008), intermediating between the community's culture and existing healthcare system (Lehmann et al., 2004) and facilitating community participation in social issues pertaining to health.

This chapter is exclusively dedicated to understand the various health-related requirements of the community in the Indian context. In order to fully capture the scenario, the chapter has dwelt into the possible causes of prominent illness in the country and identified biological, behavioural, psychosocial, environmental and occupational risk factors of illness. The session on 'health conditions across lifespan' discusses the recent age-related illness conditions prevalent in the country with the help of relevant empirical data. Health-seeking behaviours in India and its determinants are extensively examined by cooperating verbatim responses and case studies. The doctor–patient relationship, role of community psychologist and health policies in India are other topics that are broadly discussed. This chapter also proposes a framework for need-based community intervention plan as well as provides a set of pragmatic recommendations relevant to community physical health. This book is an effort to place health in the context of community and understand health and illness from a lifespan perspective instead of merely rating illness in terms of its severity and framing health as an isolated mechanism to target.

In sum

The team of community healthcare facilitators can function in different roles and responsibilities suiting to their community needs which include the following:

1. Assisting the medical professionals in healthcare activities such as immunization, medical camps or medical needs during disaster/crisis management
2. Rendering services to the underprivileged/marginalized population, addressing the financial and human resource problems in resource-poor areas
3. Intermediating between the community's culture and the existing healthcare system
4. Facilitating community participation in social issues pertaining to health

---

3.2. RISK FACTORS OF ILLNESS

Knowledge on the aetiology of illness expands with the development of investigative techniques and procedures in medical science. This has been proven to be helpful in the prevention, intervention and rehabilitation stages of illness management. As per WHO estimation, 4.1 million child deaths in 2004 were due to preventable illness caused due to 'micronutrient deficiencies, underweight, suboptimal breastfeeding and preventable environmental risks' (WHO, 2009). A USA-based risk assessment study found smoking and high blood pressure to cause the largest number of deaths in the USA; 'poor diet, physical inactivity, excessive alcohol consumption, uncontrolled high blood pressure, and hyperlipidaemia' (Bauer et al., 2014) also largely contribute to the chronic disease burden of the country. Another recent estimation conducted in the country indicated that approximately 'one in three premature heart disease deaths, one in five premature cancer deaths, two out of five chronic lower respiratory diseases death and one out of three stroke deaths' (Yoon et al., 2014) were due to modifiable risk factors and could be prevented. Empirical data from across the world reinstates these understandings with region-specific alterations. These several casual factors can be categorized in terms of their nature into the following subtypes:

3.2.1. Biological Risk Factors

Genes can either be directly involved in the incidence of a health condition or indirectly influence a determinant of a health condition (Mackenbach, 2005). Conditions such as Down syndrome, cystic fibrosis and haemophilia are known to be genetic in nature, which are understood to be inherited health conditions and are caused due to DNA abnormalities. However, it is equally important to understand the indirect involvement of genetic factors in the occurrence of illness conditions such as obesity, coronary heart diseases, diabetics and several other prominent illnesses. Explanation regarding bioengineering behind such illness is beyond the scope of this chapter.

3.2.2. Behavioural Factors

The findings of the analysis and estimation of disease from 2002 to 2030 by the WHO identified the four key behavioural outcomes to disease burden worldwide, namely (a) smoking, (b) alcohol consumption, (c) excess body weight and (d) dietary factors (Mathers & Loncar, 2006). Alcohol consumption is identified as the leading contributor to the global health burden and is the cause of 30 major health conditions which include chronic liver and pancreas diseases, infectious diseases, cancer, diabetes, neuropsychiatric diseases, cardiovascular disease and unintentional and intentional injury as well as social issues such as domestic violence and abuse (Rehm, 2011). 'Lung cancer, heart disease, stroke, chronic respiratory diseases and other breathing difficulties resulting from both active and passive smoking are also increasing; smoking during pregnancy still continues to be an issue on concerns particularly in developed countries' (Jacob et al., 2017). The two latter factors potentially lead to high blood pressure as well as high cholesterol and sugar deposits in the blood, thus resulting in major illnesses such as coronary heart disease and diabetes. The population at high vulnerability to these behavioural factors is, unfortunately, the adolescent and elderly population (WHO, 2018).

3.2.3. Psychosocial Factors

Attempts to study the psychosocial contributors to health and illness have found several factors which may exert an influence of various degrees on an individual's health outcomes. A study undertaking along the lifespan developmental perspective found health inequalities in terms of age, gender, race/ethnicity, childhood experiences, educational status and socio-economic status to control health outcomes (Alwin & Wray, 2005). In fact, the very first principle of this perspective is a lifelong impact of social status on the health of an individual (Jacob et al., 2017). Along with environmental factors, educational attainment, income level and employment status were found to have a distinctive and measurable effect on the vulnerability to cardiovascular health (Schultz et al., 2018), Body Mass Index (BMI; Akil & Ahmad, 2011) and diabetes mellitus (Suwannaphant et al., 2017) among individuals. Further, empirical evidence relates to positive affect and protective psychosocial factors such as 'greater social connectedness, perceived social support, optimism and preference for adaptive coping responses' which was found to be linked to behaviours like regular exercise. The association between adverse childhood experience and poor health status in later life is a proven fact: a recent cross-sectional study conducted in China has identified lifetime drinking and smoking habit, depression and post-traumatic stress disorder (PTSD) to be the health outcomes of adverse childhood experience in/of later life (Chang et al., 2019).

3.2.4. ENVIRONMENTAL RISKS

Illness associated with poor environmental conditions is increasing in its severity, outcome and manifestation. They can be 'all physical, chemical and biological factors external to a person and all the related factors impacting behaviours' (Bircher & Kuruvilla, 2014). WHO, in a recent worldwide report, linked air pollution to one out of eight deaths across the world; this includes pneumonia which is a leading cause (50%) of death among children as well as ill health including intellectual disabilities (600,000 new cases every year) due to lead exposure (Every Women Every Child, 2016). Unsafe drinking water, contaminated air, poor sanitation facilities, industrial waste, climate change, greenhouse gas emission and other environmental hazards are undoubtedly contributing significantly to poor health outcomes. Environmental risks are, in fact, the biggest agents of communicable diseases such as malaria, dengue and tuberculosis (TB). Environmental risks such as, for instance, the Endosuflan tragedy in Kerala which caused several deaths and severe health consequences such as neurobehavioural disorders and malformations in newborn children (Mathew, 2009), has the potential to persist across generations.

3.2.5. OCCUPATIONAL AND OTHER RISKS

Evaluation of health hazards due to occupational risk factors is difficult because of the lack of any global data in this matter. However, occupational risk factors, single-handedly account for over 1.7 per cent of disability-adjusted life years (DALY) lost across the globe (WHO, 2009). Especially in developed countries, work-related stresses are linked with mental health conditions such as depression (Tennant, 2001) and coronary heart diseases (CSDH, 2008). Occupational exposure to (a) carcinogens and biochemical agents causes cancers (Takala, 2015), (b) airborne particulates cause pulmonary diseases, neurodegeneration, diabetes and other similar conditions (Dimakakou et al., 2018) (c) ergonomic stressors cause musculoskeletal disorders such as aches in the lower back and shoulder (Niu, 2010), loss/disturbances of vision and hearing due to work-related exposure (Iregren et al., 2002) are prominent health outcomes of work-related hazards.

Equally important is to know about people's perception of the causes of illness: a recent study based in Ethiopia is helpful in explaining the need and impact of such investigations. Participants of the study perceived the causes to be related to supernatural, natural (environmental, biological and psychological) and societal factors (trust, family environment, violation of taboo and so on;

Kahissay et al., 2017). Knowing people's perception of the causes of illness would be helpful for policymakers in developing appropriate programmes that can target modification of unscientific beliefs and investment of congruent interventions. It is important also because health information behaviour is also strongly correlated with peoples beliefs and perception about the illness, which in turn affect their health outcome (Katavić et al., 2016). In cases of people suffering from stigma-attached illness, correction of such wrong perception by the public could be ensured only by rightly analysing people's perception of illness aetiology (Gedzi, 2013).

In sum

The risk factors of illness can be divided as follows:

1. Biological risk factors
2. Behavioural risk factors
3. Psychosocial risk factors
4. Environmental risk factors
5. Occupational risk factors

3.3. HEALTH CONDITIONS ACROSS LIFESPAN

Biological programming, which is the role of exposures as early as in utero and early infancy, is now an established influencer of later life health and well-being condition; this is the very basis of the contemporary branch of science known as Developmental origins of health and diseases (DOHaD). Experimental findings from this field see the initiation of any long-term risk of diseases to be rooted in the early adaptive responses given by the foetus or the infant (Gluckman et al., 2008). Hence, early life responses linked to maternal nutrition and hyperglycaemia and gestational diabetes mellitus (Darnton-Hill et al., 2004) are found to be linked with obesity, Type 2 diabetes and cardiovascular diseases (Ben-shlomo & Kuh, 2002). A study conducted in India has proved the association between low birth weight and insulin resistance in the baby (Bavdekar et al., 1999), another study called the Pune Maternal Nutrition Study also proved that deficiencies of micronutrients can lead to low birth weight and leaves the baby in high risk of diabetes (Yajnik et al., 2008). Various methods of scientific enquiries have proven the powerful influence of early life experiences in predicting an individual's susceptibility to certain illnesses conditions. A growing body of research understands an individual's early life factors, such as maternal diet or childhood experiences, to play 'as antecedents of later-life health conditions' (Jacob et al., 2017), and scientists have begun to employ those factors in predicting quotients related to disease morbidity and mortality. Hence, familiarizing with the various health condition from a developmental perspective would be helpful in both learning and research.

3.3.1. CHILDHOOD

As childhood is the most sensitive period in lifespan, issues pertaining to each year of childhood are complex and hence must be studied separately. Here, we consider childhood to start from the time of conception up to adolescence, and so common health conditions seen during these phases is subdivided under the following three age groups:

Prenatal: The maternal mortality rate is unexpectedly high, and a good majority of these deaths are preventable. The close inextricable relationship between maternal and newborn health is established by several strong empirical evidence; it is the most crucial time period for both the mother and the child in terms of their health (Lassi et al., 2013). Nearly 75 per cent of these complications are due to severe bleeding, infection and pre-eclampsia (high blood pressure during pregnancy). Common health problems seen in mothers during the prenatal period that can severely affect the health of the baby are iron deficiency/anaemia (Tandon et al., 2018; Vindhya et al., 2019), gestational diabetes (Li et al., 2018; Mishra et al., 2018), antepartum mental health conditions such as depression and anxiety (Johnson et al., 2018; Priya et al., 2018), foetal problems related to movement or size, gestational hypertension (Magee et al., 2019), infections like HIV/AIDS (Nayak et al., 2017; Shah et al., 2017), maternal placental conditions such as hyperemesis gravidarum, placenta previa, placental abruption (Bolin et al., 2013) and preterm labour that has both short-term and long-term impact including cerebral palsy, visual and auditory impairment and poor growth pattern in later life (Drljan et al., 2016). Providing quality treatment during childbirth fetches 'triple return on investment' (Every Women Every Child, 2016), as in the process both the mother and child are taken care of, which in effect reduces stillbirths or prevents other related disabilities. As per predictions, this would prevent '113,000 maternal deaths, 531,000 stillbirths and 1.3 million neonatal deaths annually by 2020' (Human Reproduction Programme, 2015).

Breastfeeding the child up to 2 years of age is found to have many benefits: apart from reducing undernutrition, it lessens deaths in children under five to 12 per cent (WHO, 2014). Despite the fact, the percentage of children breastfed is declining due to several reasons: ill health and anaemia in mothers as seen in low-income countries to an increasing number of work-related demands of working mothers in high-income countries could be the range of reasons. Whatever be the causes, WHO understands 'suboptimal breastfeeding to be held responsible for 45% neonatal infectious deaths, 30% of diarrheal deaths and 18% of acute respiratory deaths in children under 5 years' (WHO, 2009). The importance of prenatal maternal care is an age-old understanding; the clear association between infant mortality rates and absence of antenatal care is also established along with other contributing factors such as the literacy level of the mother, her age, occupation, characteristics of her socio-demography and so on (Chandrasekar et al., 1998). Maternal folate insufficiency and maternal Vitamin B deficiencies were found to be significantly associated with adverse pregnancy outcomes such as developmental disabilities including mental retardation and cretinism in their offspring (WHO, 2009).

Children under five: WHO identified preterm birth, intrapartum complications such as asphyxia and birth trauma (breathing difficulty during birth; Bassani & Jha, 2010; Sankar et al., 2016), infections and birth defects as the leading causes of death in 2017; childhood pneumonia (Gothankar et al., 2018; Rodrigues & Groves, 2018), diarrhoea (Lakshminarayanan & Jayalakshmy, 2015), tropical fevers (Ogoina, 2011), birth defects and congenital anomalies (Kar, 2014; Mathur & Mukherjee, 2017; Sharma, 2013), measles (Shrivastava et al., 2015), malaria (Kaushik et al., 2012; Kumar et al., 2007) and associated malnutrition (Sahu et al., 2015) are the leading illness conditions during the first five years of life (WHO, 2019). Undernutrition (nutritional deficiencies particularly that of iodine, iron, zinc and Vitamin A are often reported) continue to be the case in several low-income countries and hence it would not be surprising to know that 'underweight and suboptimal breastfeeding' are the leading causes of death among children (WHO, 2009).

Late childhood: Some common ailments found during this time period are cold and cough, fever, headache, vomiting, constipation, worm infection, skin infections such as boils and scabies, eye/ear infection and pain in abdomen; common childhood diseases include whooping cough, diphtheria, measles, chickenpox, mumps, diarrhoea, dysentery, respiratory illness, paediatric HIV (Nath, 2017), polio and TB.

3.3.2. ADOLESCENCE

The WHO has identified the following as the main health issues causing death and disability in the order of their incidence among the population, which is backed up by several other empirical findings: (a) unintentional injuries (Han et al., 2019), (b) mental health conditions such as depression, suicidal tendencies (Radhakrishnan et al., 2012; Trivedi et al., 2016), (c) interpersonal violence (Sarkar, 2010; UNICEF, 2017), (d) HIV/AIDS (Joshi et al., 2017; Mehra et al., 2016), (e) other infectious diseases such as diarrhoea, lower respiratory tract infections and meningitis (Troeger et al., 2018), (f) early pregnancy and childbirth (Kulkarni et al., 2017; Ghose & John, 2017) (g) alcohol, tobacco and drug abuse (Dhawan et al., 2017; Jaisoorya et al., 2016; Pal et al., 2010), (h) malnutrition and micronutrient deficiencies (Deka et al., 2015; Gonmei & Toteja, 2018), (i) obesity (Goyal et al., 2010; Patnaik et al., 2015) and (j) lack of physical activity (Gulati et al., 2014; Satija et al., 2018).

The majority of adolescents who survive from this haphazard will be left affected even during their adult life and be unable to attain their full potential. In India 'lack of accurate information, absence of proper guidance, parent's ignorance, lack of skills and insufficient services from healthcare delivery system' are the primary barriers faced by this population (Sivagurunathan et al., 2015). Hence, adolescents are a special population who require due attention and care and can be monitored through (a) education: health education including sexual and reproductive health information, prevention of harmful practices such as substance abuse, prevention of injuries caused due to impulsivity and reckless behaviour, (b) management: management of communicable and non-communicable diseases specific to the adolescent population, immunization, vaccination, provision of nutrition and (c) psychological support: supportive parenting and other psychosocial support required for their academic, personal and social life. These remedial measures, if taken seriously, could be helpful in altering the modifiable risk factors and avert health risks from this population.

3.3.3. EARLY AND MIDDLE ADULTHOOD

The Global Burden of Diseases 2017 as reported by the Institute of Health Metrics and Evaluation (2018) identified the following to be the leading causes of health condition in India: ischemic heart disease and stroke (Gupta et al., 2016; Krishnan, 2012; Prabhakaran et al., 2016;

Prabhakaran et al., 2018), chronic obstructive pulmonary disease (Rajkumar et al., 2017; Saleem et al., 2017; Salvi et al., 2018), diarrhoeal disease (Joseph et al., 2016; Nilima et al., 2018), lower respiratory infections (Chavan et al., 2015; Krishnan et al., 2019), TB (Aggarwal et al., 2015; Moonan et al., 2018; Sarin et al., 2018), asthma (Aggarwal et al., 2006; Bhalla et al., 2018), diabetes (Kaveeshwar & Cornwall, 2014; Tripathy et al., 2017) and chronic kidney disease (Kokila & Chellavel Ganapathi, 2019; Shyam et al., 2007; Varma, 2015). Cancer (Dhillon et al., 2018; Rajpal et al., 2018), unintentional injuries, digestive diseases, malaria, typhoid, asthma (Kumar & Ram, 2017; Lalu et al., 2017), epilepsy, nervous system injuries, Alzheimer's disease (Das et al., 2012; Mathuranath et al., 2012), and depression (Buvneshkumar et al., 2018) were quoted to be other leading illnesses faced by adults in the country.

3.3.4. OLDER ADULTHOOD/ELDERLY

Advancement in the medical field has made the concept of 'extended old-age' into a reality, and so medical science has accordingly advanced into newer dimensions of health and illness. Normal ageing itself is associated with changes in every aspect of bodily functions, such as (a) sensory changes such as hearing loss, changes in visual acuity and muscle strength (Amieva et al., 2015; Davis et al., 2016), (b) cognitive changes such as mild memory loss, delay in information processing (Blazer et al., 2015) and (c) changes in physical functions such as mobility disability or disability in carrying out activities of daily living. Somatic diseases and multiple chronic conditions such as cardiovascular disease (Odden et al., 2014), hypertension, cancer (Siu, 2016; Walter & Covinsky, 2001), osteoporosis, arthritis, diabetes mellitus (Oiwa & Komatsu, 2015), psychological, cognitive and neurodegenerative conditions like depression (Steptoe et al., 2009), dementia, sleeping disorders, Alzheimer's disease, Parkinson's disease (Jaul & Barron, 2017), sarcopenia, obstructive pulmonary disease (Franceschi et al., 2018) are commonly found in older adults. A detailed discussion about health problems faced by the aged population of our country is discussed in detail in Chapter 5.

An interesting observation is that, globally, the rate of disease mortality due to non-communicable diseases, such as respiratory diseases or hypertension, has outnumbered the communicable diseases to a notable degree over the past century (Lopez et al., 2006). According to WHO, the leading causes of mortality across all income groups of countries are 'high blood pressure (13%), tobacco use (9%), high blood glucose (6%), physical inactivity (6%) and overweight and obesity (5%; WHO, 2009); around two-third of deaths worldwide is due to non-communicable conditions (Bauer et al., 2014). The rise in proneness to diseases due to lifestyle imbalances are found to be primarily associated with general factors such as the country's socio-economic status (Mathers & Loncar, 2006) and individual factors such as diet and physical activity or substance abuse (WHO, 2009). It may be out of this critical understanding, that the 2030 SDGs have aimed to 'reduce by one-third premature mortality from non-communicable diseases through prevention and treatment' (United Nations, 2018).

It is important to be aware about the various mental illness conditions as they may occur at different points in time and could be triggered by different causal factors. Also, occurrence of disorders with physical or mental ill health is also increasingly being noticed from childhood to adulthood (Rockville, 2012). Hence, balancing of an individual's mental health across their lifespan is also equally fundamental in the overall health well-being dyad, and is elaborately discussed in

Chapter 2. One has to be sensitive above health issues that are exclusively faced by women and people from minority communities and understand their aetiology and management in the context of their daily lives.

3.4. HEALTH-SEEKING BEHAVIOUR

Health-seeking behaviour is 'any activity undertaken by individuals who perceive themselves to have a health problem or to be ill for the purpose of finding an appropriate remedy' (Patle & Khakse, 2015; Ward et al., 1997). It is the 'decision or an action taken by an individual to maintain, attain, or regain good health and to prevent illness' (Chauhan et al., 2015). Conceptualization of their own illness by an individual, the analysis made regarding its cause and effect and all the probable outcomes would determine the steps to be taken by them towards health (Ahmed et al., 2005). There is an array of responses one shows as reaction to an illness which could vary from being depressed and locking oneself in a room to actively seeking medical help. These responses to health-seeking behaviour vary from individual to individual because these are the product of various decisive factors such as age and gender to one's belief system. With the help of Figure 3.1 and the explanation following it, we are attempting to explain the possible determinants of health-seeking behaviour and its outcome relevant to Indian context.

FIGURE 3.1
Determinants and Outcomes of Health-seeking Behaviours

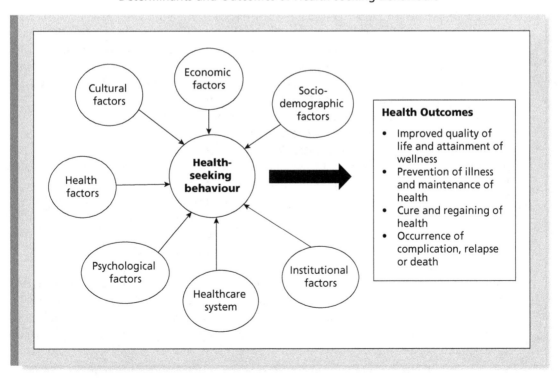

3.5. DETERMINANTS OF HEALTH-SEEKING BEHAVIOUR

1. *Socio-demographic factors:* The influence of certain socio-demographic factors is crucial in deciding the direction of health-seeking behaviour. Age and gender of a person, if considered as such a factor, have a strong involvement in the efforts taken by an individual to attain, maintain or regain health (Deeks et al., 2009). In terms of age, children and their mothers and people in old age are the phases when maximum engagement in health-seeking activities are observed. Children up to their adolescent period are taken for medical support under the initiative of their parents; care is taken to provide children with nutritional food, clean drinking water, vaccinations, preventive medicines and regular health checkup are all ways to health-seeking behaviours. This is exactly why malnourishment and deficiencies are considered to be illness conditions. Old age can be an interesting determinant as it can lead to either more active seeking of health service due to old-age-related difficulties (explaining the increasing life expectancy index in India) or prevent people from such behaviour due to poor financial status and lack of support (Barua et al., 2017; Patle & Khakse, 2015). Adolescent girls and women of reproductive age also require medical assistance to tackle their reproductive health (Deeks et al., 2009); thus, gender and marital status playing determining role in health-seeking behaviour. On the basis of our discussion on the rural-urban disparity, it is evident that the area of residence is undoubtedly a strong determinant. As discussed earlier, this disparity is visible in the availability of services, quality of available services and huge direct-indirect cost of treatment (Gupta & Dasgupta, 2013). The influence of the type of family to which one belongs can be observed from the day-to-day activities one follows, for instance, individuals who had grown up with their grandparents tend to imbibe some traditional practices or home remedies in their day-to-day life. Of late, several studies have claimed the crucial role played by the 'family type' (nuclear/joint family) in geriatric literature, with the changing social setup of the nuclear family makes the older population vulnerable to several insecurities, which indirectly influence their attitude towards health (Central Statistics Office, 2011). Another determinant could be religion, whose influence might be one way of explaining the success of yoga and indigenous healing practices in the country.

   Of course, the influence of education level in an individual's health-seeking behaviour is understood in itself and is found to override the influence of any other socio-demographic factor. Several studies are reinstated that educated people who have better knowledge about illnesses and the various treatment options available tend to indulge in pro-health behaviours as compared to their counterpart. Moreover, they are found to be responsive to health maintaining behaviours as well. As per the findings of the study based in Bangladesh, the education level of the patients would determine the preferred treatment modality they take up; educated people were found to avoid self-treatment and drugstore salesperson and chose allopathic practices (Ahmed et al., 2005). The overall influence of education of an individual's immediate social support on their health-seeking behaviour would be an interesting research which can bring out impactful findings. The importance of accessibility to healthcare services in terms of physical distance as discussed earlier is crucial because in almost all cases what people would seek is immediate care and quick relief. In several rural-India-based studies, inconvenient location and the long distance to government hospitals have seldom come up as the topic of concern which makes the people in the peri-urban area to prefer private hospitals and clinic despite the treatment charges they quote (Chauhan et al., 2015; Patle & Khakse, 2015). People from rural India, as discussed, would be left with poor quality services.

2. ***Economic factors:*** Interference of financial stability in one's health-seeking behaviour has interesting dynamics. The wealth index of a person has high predictability in the patterns of behaviours and options of services chosen by an individual. An interesting observation observed in more than study-based on rural India has to be described. One main reason for people in rural India to relay on self-treatment and unscientific faith healers was the cost of treatment. Apart from bearing indirect costs such as travel fare, doctors and other healthcare professionals in government hospitals were reported to ask for money even for free services (Vargese et al., 2013). Seeking the assistance of private hospitals is beyond the scope of people from lower economic strata, hence people from poor economic conditions refrain from seeking such services. There are studies which have found socio-economic indicators such as wealth index and income to be the 'single most pervasive determinant of health-seeking behaviour' particularly among the elderly population (Ahmed et al., 2005); similarly, the income level of the family was found to be one of the two primary predictors for health-seeking behaviour in sick children of Kerala (Pillai et al., 2003). Health insurance coverage, another source of economic stability in terms of healthcare is also poorly distributed in India; a 2013 study conducted among lowest economy category household found less than 3 per cent to have health insurance coverage (Shijith & Sekher, 2013). Pregnant women from sound socio-economic backgrounds were found to make more frequent visits and were more likely to get antenatal care as compared to pregnant women from poor and uneducated backgrounds in north India (Pallikadavath et al., 2004). As can be understood, occupation status and family income, social capital and associated benefits such as power and influence and so on are a few other economic factors that determine health-seeking behaviour. In fact, this strong association between socio-economic factors and health-seeking behaviour is found to be capable of explaining treatment delay and the severity of the illness when medical help is sort (Ashwani & Deepika, 2011).

3. ***Cultural factors:*** Cultural beliefs and practices can be both helpful and hurtful depending on the context and time period of practice. For instance, in Indian culture, there exists an elaborate 90-day procedure in taking care of a new mother to help her body and mind adapt to the changes that she has gone through. Even though there are differences in the customs that each locality/community follows, these rituals continue to be followed with great importance in majority of Indian households. While it is the same cultural norms that put restrictions on some women to decide whether it is acceptable to deliver her baby in the hospital as some are adamant about childbirths to take place in their own homes with the help of midwives. This is one example of how culture influences an individual's decisions to opt for health-seeking behaviours (Griffiths & Stephenson, 2001).

Prevailing stigma can restrict someone from seeking medical help for illness conditions which are labelled to be incurable. A systematic study conducted on the health-seeking behaviours among TB patients in India reported the following findings which have resulted out of the fear of social stigma: (a) concealment of symptoms from even close family, (b) resistance to start or continue treatment (Kulkarni et al., 2013) and (c) interrupting medication during treatment and defaulting from the treatment itself (Uplekar & Rangan, 1996); depicting the whole range of social factors that can hinder an individual from seeking help when affected by TB (Samal, 2016). In a study covering south of India among people suffering from HIV/AIDS, the curtailing influence of social stigma affecting all aspects of their lives was often stressed. The respondent emphasized on stigma to (a) prevent from disclosing to family and friends, (b) resulting in avoidance and cornering at workplace which led to losing/quitting their jobs, (c) develop depression and anxiety, (d) delay seeking medical help and (e) continue seeking treatment (Balasundaram et al., 2014). Similarly, numerous studies have discussed the role of stigma in seeking help when affected by even minor mental disturbances (Shidhaye & Kermode, 2013). Undoubtedly, social stigma could be a paramount reason for delay in illness representation by individuals affected by life-threatening/communicable/labelled illnesses.

Medical science is growingly acknowledging the importance of spiritual concerns in understanding the health-related behaviour of an individual (Chatters, 2000). The influence of religion and spirituality, can be viewed as a cultural factor, as it lays the foundation of many cultural beliefs, influences the style of pro-health behaviours in India. Several empirical studies have suggested the positive association between spirituality and positive treatment outcome in India, stressing in the need for Indian medical practitioners to acknowledge the spiritual sentiments of the patients in attaining a better treatment outcome (Chattopadhyay, 2007). Thus, if the practitioner and the patient could establish each other's vantage point on religion, it would be highly beneficial especially for patients fighting with terminal illness towards positive health-seeking behaviours (Rumun, 2014). It is the great significance of spirituality in India that give greater scope to Ayurveda and other complementary and alternate medicine (CAM) as probable treatment options (Gupta, 2010).

4. ***Status of health:*** Health-seeking behaviour is understood to have three general targets, which are: to attain, maintain and regain. Hence, the status of health would decide the target and the modus of operation chosen by the individual. Any healthy individual is recommended to involve in activities towards maintaining their health through routine check-up, exercise and diet. They are also expected to be aware of health-related updates and current affairs so as to keep themselves prepared through vaccination and preventive medicines; this would also help them to be watchful about conditions/environment to be avoided to prevent the spread of illness. The target of attaining the optimal level could also be clubbed with this behaviour, which has to do with BMI, deficiency of essential vitamins and minerals. Adolescent girls and women in reproductive age are often found to be involved in routine medical check-up to tackle issues related to iron deficiency (Kumari et al., 2017), Vitamin D deficiency (Khadilkar, 2010), low-dietary calcium (Harinarayan et al., 2004) and reproductive health issues. Appreciably, the relevance of a healthy lifestyle is gaining the attention of the student community and young adults, showing great enthusiasm in body building and eating healthy. This is a growing trend among students and young adults from sound economic backgrounds who are also a group where prominent lifestyle illnesses are also often reported. But most of the times, seeking healthcare help happens only when one falls sick. Health-seeking behaviours to regain health would vary according to the nature and severity of the illness condition as well as the various treatment modalities available. This is the phase where people show active participation in search of immediate relief. What is ironic here is that a good proportion of illness conditions arise when people skip the health-seeking behaviours to maintain and attain health. Comorbidity or presence of other illness

conditions may aggravate the condition and can influence the decisions taken regarding measure to be taken to regain health.

5. *Psychological factor:* An individual as well as the decision-maker (it could be parents of son/ daughter in the case of children or elderly) can take decisions regarding various health-seeking behaviours. Hence, the interference of their cognition, personality traits and other psychological correlated factors will influence the choice of their health-seeking behaviour. Let us discuss a few such factors. Perception about the nature and severity of the illness by these individuals is one such factor based on which they would approach a treatment plan. Trust developed on the doctor and the chosen treatment plan, compliance and cooperation are some of the essentials with which the doctor works. Their knowledge such as understanding about the particular illness, the procedures involved in the treatment plan, the scope and success rates of the treatment plan can be crucial in the treatment choice made. Individuals' own ideology about health and wellness, its importance would influence their treatment option; for instance, people who believe in the curative power of nature would avoid allopathic medicine and opt for Ayurveda or other such CAM. Psychological factors such as hope, optimism and determination, certain characteristic features such as the will to strive, perseverance, resilience and the coping mechanism would show greater relevance in cases of severe illness.

6. *Healthcare system:* The type of medical system chosen would further determine other associated behaviours to be followed for better outcome. It could be allopathic medicine, CAM, home remedies, self-treatment methods, indigenous healing or any others. Depending on the choice made, the individual would be asked to indulge in pro-health activities such as exercise and dietary changes, charting of routine activities and lifestyle changes, periodic check-up, intake of medicines for a period of time and later regularizing it or sometimes adopting certain way-of-life practices such as Yoga. The evidence of success rates of these treatment plans as well as the acceptance of it among the public would further determine the initiation and later continuation of these behaviours. Other chief determining features such as the attitude of the healthcare provider and the doctor–patient relationship is discussed in detail elsewhere in this chapter.

7. *Institutional factors:* Type and nature of the institution, such as government or private hospital, primary health centres, clinics, dispensaries, community health centres, doctors private practice centres and so on can determine the choice of the individual in opting for any of these options. This choice is significantly associated with the quality of the service provided such as professionalism, quality of care and facilities provided at the institution, its reputation and specialization and cost of treatment. Several studies have quoted that the cost associated with treatment at these institutions to be a very important determinant of health-seeking behaviour. Cost of treatment is associated with reduced use by people from the lower economic group (Pate et al., 2010), whereas the quality of care is linked with the lower utilization of public healthcare facilities (Ahmad, 2019).

As mentioned in the figure, the resulting outcomes of health-seeking behaviour could be (a) improved quality of life and attainment of wellness, (b) prevention of illness and maintenance of health, (c) cure and regain of health and (d) occurrence of complication, relapse or death. Explaining the causal factors responsible for each of these outcomes is beyond the scope of this chapter.

3.6. HEALTH-SEEKING BEHAVIOUR IN INDIA

India is known for its diverse healthcare systems which have super-specialty hospitals and modern medicine at one end while shrines and deities of health and well-being at the other. This is where exploring the various health-seeking behaviour of the country becomes complex and cannot be done without placing it in the cultural context. Appreciably, the concept of *arogya* was understood as the holistic wellness of an individual even from the time of Indus Valley civilization (Roy, 1985); this proves that Indian curative care culture worked with clarity and precision. Despite the systems of medicine which are of Indian origin, a few foreign branches could also well assimilate into the country, resulting into distinctive categories of curative culture. Apart from modern medicine, there exist Ayurveda, Unani, naturopathy, homoeopathy and siddha as prominent health-seeking options along with several faith healers and indigenous practices (Ravishankar & Shukla, 2007). But what is surprising here is, despite the prevalence of these treatment options, the WHO's universal health coverage remains a challenging target to achieve (Bader, 2018). The factors that influence the health-seeking behaviour among the individuals are many and crucial in developing a cooperative attitude among the public. To increase the overall efficiency of the country's healthcare system, knowing a few corollaries, such as the degrees of awareness about health and wellness among the public, commonly observed health-seeking attitudes and the reasons for those behaviours, common beliefs about various healthcare systems and the preferred choices made, problems in the healthcare systems that keep people away from seeking help and so on, is very crucial. A general trend observed among a normal Indian household on health-seeking behaviours is interesting to discuss. Health continues to be understood only in terms of illness and not as well-being among the majority of the population in the country, and hence, health-seeking behaviours work unidirectional, that is in line of controlling/curing the illness or its symptoms.

At an initial stage of any common illness such as fever, cough or a common cold, a good majority of individuals are seen to resort to home remedies by using indigenous plant derivatives with medicinal values or such traditional means. For instance, a commonly seen home remedy for cold or cough is black coffee with turmeric, *tulsi* leaves and pepper. This trend is prevalent in rural areas and would be a passed-down knowledge of healthcare. Neha, a 19-year-old engineering student, says that she prefers home remedies and traditional medicines for most of the mild medical requirements, as she goes:

> Personally, I have developed a trust in traditional medicines, as they are homely and been widely used by many. They are cheap, lacks side effects and are easily accessible. Moreover, many of these medicinal properties are scientifically proven.

In urban areas too, for mild illness conditions people prefer taking popularly used and readily available medicines, such as Dolo 650 or Cetirizine, over consulting a doctor. An IT professional, named Ashok, finds modern medicines to give quicker results. He says,

> I always carry Allegra (a commonly used tablet to treat allergic reactions) in my wallet as I am prone to allergies. I tried all the traditional methods but for me nothing gave such immediate relief as allopathy medicine. These tablets come in handy and are available everywhere.

Some people approach private medical store pharmacists to prescribe medication for their illness condition. A recently reported case from Chennai should be discussed in this regard; a man died after getting an injection for pain from a local pharmacy owner (Selvaraj, 2019). One should not be surprised to know that this is a commonly observed trend in the country. Despite being a risky affair, people tend to practice the same to avoid hospitals. Here are the words of Cyriac, a banker:

> My whole day will get wasted at the hospital as I have to stand in long queues, be around so many sick people and get poorly treated by the hospital staff to finally see a doctor who would prescribe me more or less the same set of medicines that I can buy without prescription from a pharmacy. If it is a mild illness, I would any day prefer getting them from a medical store.

A common theme in all of the above-mentioned cases is the reluctance in meeting a doctor. A fact that has to be considered is that some of these symptoms which are perceived to be mild could be the indication of some other severe illness condition which is losing its chance to be detected by a doctor at an early stage. This is when the case of Hari Kumar, an LIC agent from Kerala, holds its relevance.

Case I: Mr Hari Kumar was only 55 when he died of cancer. According to Anjana, his daughter, Hari was found to be tired and falling sick more often than before, but he never took it seriously. Anjana said, 'Appa was reluctant to go to a doctor to get himself checked and used to treat himself by relying on home remedies and other traditional medicines.' When his health conditions showed a significant deterioration he was taken to a doctor who after initial investigation and tests diagnosed him with Stage 3 lung cancer. Within a month, he passed away, as it was already too late to do anything.

Developing the habit of regularly meeting a doctor to do routine check-up in whichever medical system one believes is important. There are complex sets of reasons why people avoid hospitals in India; in order to make hospitals a favourable place for people to approach, employment of a large workforce from different sectors is needed. Due to the need to link these factors to many associated issues, this topic is discussed in detail elsewhere in this chapter.

Most of the times, it is only when the disease hinters with one's daily functioning or when all the preliminary 'self-treatment' seems to have failed that medical help is sought by the individual. By then, the illness would have grown in the individual that he is now a patient who needs professional healthcare services. As mentioned, an individual in India has to choose between the available medical systems to carry forward the treatment; an interesting interplay of a number of factors are involved here as well that determines an individual's perception towards each system of medicine. Like in any other country, modern medicine enjoys its upper hand in India with the upsurge of a greater number of public and private hospitals, medical colleges and research centres. A study based in Malaysia (another Southeast Asian country) found that more people prefer modern medicine as it gives immediate results, employs scientific and sophisticated technology to form precise diagnosis and have clear evidence that has led to the diagnosis (Maung et al., 2019). In line with this is a verbatim by Shikha whose mother underwent a knee transplantation surgery a few months ago:

> We tried all the possible options that were available for my mother to get rid of the pain. Not just that nothing worked in favour of her, but that we were left with an only option, which was the surgery. It was a tough decision to make as my mother had other medical conditions too, and even tougher to convince mom that she will be alright. What helped me was the confidence I gained on the team of doctors specialized in different fields of medicine who jointly did the surgery as well as the number of knee transplantation success stories.

The opinion of Shikha holds relevance too because it represents a good proportion of people who seeks modern medical care when all the alternatives are closed, and no other curative care techniques give any result. Why is it so, even when modern medicine is widely accepted across the world? Let us discuss some of the possible reasons relevant to the Indian context. Accessibility to healthcare services, which is the complex dynamics of 'availability, supply and utilization of healthcare services' (Kasthuri, 2018) is the first and foremost barricade. In the case of health-seeking behaviours, inaccessibility would not just have to do with geographical access (Munjanja et al, 2012), but also be influenced by the 'financial, organizational, social and cultural domains' (Gulliford et al., 2002). This is easier to understand, when placed in the context of women and habitants of rural India (Hooda, 2017; Ladusingh, Mohanty, & Thangjam, 2018). Following is the description of a pertinent case study which has resulted from the interplay of most of the above-mentioned domains which make healthcare services inequitable.

Case II: The plight of Majhi from a rural village in Odisha had caught the attention of humanitarians across the world. It was reported that he had carried the dead body of his wife, Late Mrs Dana Majhi, for 12 km because the hospital failed to provide ambulance service to take her dead body back home. She died of TB in a district hospital on the day of her admission, (Sahu, 2008). 'I kept pleading with the hospital staff to provide a vehicle to carry my wife's body, but to no avail. Since I am a poor man and could not hire a private vehicle, I had no choice but to carry her body on my shoulder,'(Sahu, 2008) he reported to journalists who approached him.

It would not be right to blame poverty as the only villain in his story; the case of Majhi is a clear example of the disabling power of the deeply interwoven socio-economic and political condition of India.

Unavailability of human power in healthcare is so severe, that a 2011 study estimated that there are only 20 health worker for 10,000 people who require service (Balarajan et al., 2011); undoubtedly, this situation is significantly hindering the healthcare services in the country. The availability and distribution of these limited resources are also causing problems; and again, rural India is at a disadvantage. Healthcare professionals are generally found to prefer working in fairly developed areas for better and easier living conditions; further, healthcare professionals, mainly doctors are attracted by the high salary of private hospitals and other offers, that the public sector of healthcare in the country work suboptimally. Thus, when people from rural India or people who cannot afford the medical expenditure of private hospitals seek health services from government hospitals or health centres, qualified and experienced hand may not be available at their delivery points. The *2015 Rural Health Statistics* substantiates this understanding as they have reported that 27 per cent of doctors, which is more than one-third of the available posts for primary health centre remains vacant (Ministry of Health and Family Welfare, 2015). Apart from unavailability of resources, the quality of the available care at the delivery point is also under question. Unfortunately, poor and inadequate medical facilities due to unskilled and unprofessional doctors are becoming an everyday story. Reports from across the country and outside validates these miserable status, such as the one from Uttar Pradesh where children admitted for encephalitis were either dead or left with severe health condition due to poor diagnosis and misplaced prescription (Shukia, 2018); from Chhattisgarh where 11 women died and 34 women in critical condition after undergoing surgery at a free sterilization camp (Dahat, 2014); from Banda, where an 11-year-old boy died because the family could not pay the bribe amount of ₹5,000 to the doctor at the government medical college (Press Trust of India, 2018); international reports on Indian doctors being bribed by pharmaceutical companies to improve the sales of their products (Davies et al., 2019) and Indian healthcare system via medical tourism to gain 'the reputation of one of the most dishonest in the world' by Transparency International (*TOI Editorial*, 2014). Affordability and needlessly high cost of medical care with cases of doctors prescribing for unnecessary diagnostic tests to add up to huge out-of-pocket expenditure, remain another matter of concern that results in inequity of services. Concerns regarding poor safety measures in hospitals are a formidable challenge that affects the credibility of doctors in India; '1.6 million Indians died due to poor quality care in 2016, nearly twice as many as due to non-utilization of healthcare services' (Yadavar, 2018). One of the news headlines that left the country in shock in this regard was the death of 41 newborns over a span of six days in a hospital in Kolkata for which the rural healthcare system was blamed (Hayden, 2014). The death rate in India (122/100,000) due to poor quality of care is significantly worse than that of neighbouring countries such as Pakistan (46), Bangladesh (93) and Sri Lanka (51; Kruk et al., 2018). The Gorakhpur tragedy where 30 children died in a week due to disruption in oxygen supply is another example of the poor safety measures of our hospitals (Jadid, 2017).

For reasons such as these and many more, a good set of people opt for CAM, let us explore some of those. Considering India's cultural background, people incorporate CAM, particularly Ayurveda in their health-seeking behaviour because of its strong association with religious philosophies (Menniti-Ippolito et al., 2002). People who want to avoid the tedious fear-inducing and expensive treatment procedures involved in allopathic treatment also tend to seek healthcare services from CAM. However, CAM due to lack of general awareness about the various treatment options, various clinical trials and its scientific basis and outcome evidence could hinder its popularity among the public. Nevertheless, CAM is knowingly or unknowingly practised by most of the Indian households; there are several treatment and wellness tips that everyone knows, for instance, garlic is known for its effect to control diabetics and so is found to be included in one's diet, similarly, the antibacterial properties of turmeric are put to use when injured or one develops mouth ulcer. Similarly, yoga as a way of life as well as a treatment modality for illness condition is also gaining popularity in India.

In sum

- Health-seeking behaviour is 'any activity undertaken by individuals who perceive themselves to have a health problem or to be ill for the purpose of finding an appropriate remedy'. It is the 'decision or an action taken by an individual to maintain, attain, or regain good health and to prevent illness'.
- The determinants of health-seeking behaviours are socio-demographic factors, economic factors, cultural factors, the status of health, psychological factor, healthcare system and institutional factors.

3.7. DOCTOR–PATIENT RELATIONSHIP

An integral part of health-seeking behaviour is the nature of doctor–patient relationships: even though unquantifiable, it is one of the most responsive dynamics that determines continuity and betterment of health outcomes. Like any other relationships, the characteristics of both the doctor and the patient determine the dynamics. Communication between doctor and patient contributes to the participation and cooperation from the patient; this would also determine the treatment outcome as well. The doctor who is pleasant in his approach and personality opens a comfortable platform for the patient to express their concern. It is on this premises that the doctor would be able to take up the role of an in-depth interviewer/researcher who attempts to understand the health status of the patient. In order to improve the quality of care to be provided, it is imperative for the doctor to respect the views, preferences and ideologies of the patient on health and illness to behave congruently to the needs of the patient. A doctor who takes effort to ensure physical comfort of the patient and provide psychological support by addressing their fear and anxieties tend to succeed in choosing the right treatment strategy. Many a times, it is the patient who initiates the consultation and not the doctor; often patient's dissatisfactions arise out of this cold and abrasive attitude of the doctor. The doctor is expected to be empathetic to the patients and provide them with information, confidence and hope. A correlation study conducted in the USA substantiates this understanding, as it was found that 'receiving an explanation of the likely cause as well as expected duration of the presenting symptom' would increase patient satisfaction (Jackson et al., 2001). Patients should be managed with respect and dignity; they should be explained about their health in simple language by avoiding medical jargon. Several studies have been recommending the need for patient-centred approach, that is, an approach where shared decision-making is welcomed and patient's experiences and opinions are acknowledged, especially in health conditions that have stigma attached to them (Fochsen et al., 2006). When medicines are prescribed the doctor should explain the uses, side effects and consequences of the medicine/treatment plan so that the patient and his family remain informed. This would enhance patient cooperation and treatment outcome. Hence, it is very important to initiate orientation programmes on interpersonal and communication skills for medical professionals in medical colleges (Singh, 2016); an experimental study found 1.62 times higher adherence among patients whose physicians were trained in communication skills (Zolnierek & Dimatteo, 2010). Further, doctors should be guided by ethics. Corruption, kickbacks, abuse of medical investigative equipment for money and other such malpractices ruin the trust and reliability on the medical profession in the country (Berger, 2014). Widespread corruptions which work in alliance with pharmaceutical companies for unnecessary prescription of medicine and highly charged medical tourism also add to the situation. In these circumstances, news of doctors being arrested for bribery allegations would not be surprising. Discrimination on the grounds of class, religion and race are also widespread across the country.

Equally important to treatment outcome is the attitude and behaviour of the patients. The success rate of treatment is high among patients who are compliant to the doctor. General awareness about health and illness, status and severity of illness condition, level of pain and inconvenience and several such factors could contribute to patient compliance. Factors relating to one's personality, for instance, conscientiousness (a popular personality trait; Smith, 1995) have been found to be linked to patient compliance. Active participation of the patient is equally important as is the case with the doctor; the patient should communicate with the doctor with the intention of clarifying one's understanding about one's health conditions, they should provide feedback on the effectiveness of the treatment plan which is being adopted, involve in the decision-making process and show accountability for it. Moreover, the patient should approach the doctor with respect and should have trust in their skills and decision. But unfortunately, the attitude of the public towards healthcare professionals is badly affected due to several reasons and has become threatful. Violence against doctors are now very frequently reported, the recent incident that caught national attention was about an intern doctor who was in critical condition due to skull fracture after being attacked by a patient family in a medical college in Kolkata hospital (Loiwal, 2019). An unhealthy circumstance like this negates the decorum of the medical care system. Incidences as mentioned above should probe the society to condemn as well as act out in order to bring humane in medical practice.

An interesting framework depicting the overlapping and conflicting doctor-patient interest has been proposed by Goold and Lipkin (1999) in an article on doctor–patient relationship was found to be very relevant to our topic of discussion. The model contains three bodies or components: the doctor, the patient and health plans. The circles seen in the following figure represents the 'interests' of each of these components. As depicted in Figure 3.2 the interest of these three bodies may interact at varying degrees, depending on which congruence/conflict in the doctor–patient relationship could result. A doctor, who is aided by professional ethics, would attempt to attain maximum congruence with the interests of the patient. However, when health plan interests put forward by hospitals for their profits and benefits, it would exert force on the doctors to adopt actions against the interest of the patients and it would range with the extent of overlap.

The most ideal situation would be when all the three circles completely overlap each other, that is, when the interest of the doctor, the patient and the plan would be the exact same (Goold & Lipkin, 1999). Even though this is a very ideal situation, this could be done if plans keep the

FIGURE 3.2
Overlapping and Conflicting Interests

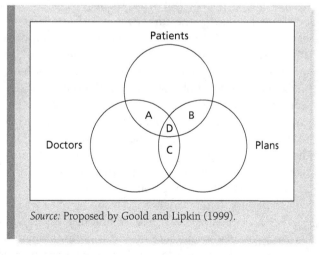

Source: Proposed by Goold and Lipkin (1999).

patient's well-being and satisfaction as the core agenda and pay little attention to profit as the prime target.

3.8. COMMUNITY PSYCHOLOGY AND PHYSICAL HEALTH

In simple terms, community health psychology works towards the promotion of the health of community through the employment of various theories and methods. Assessment of an individual with their high-impact contexts and working in/with the communities are the methodologies of community psychology since several decades (Trickett, 2009). The current society probes the need of this subject matter to go beyond the periphery and indulge into the deeper dynamics of the community. The impact of the collective movement is becoming a method on popular demand for health-based interventions in communities; in this regard, identification of effective mediators for social change becomes crucial, as it is this partnership that instruments community-level action plans (Campbell & Murray, 2004).

The impact of 'collectives' is gaining its popularity primarily because it has proven to be a very powerful aid for social change. Time and again, it is reinstated that both the people and the determinants of health-seeking behaviour are contoured by the bigger social context. Thus, if addressing the existing inequalities and inequities in health is the aim, there should be mediators to correlate between the community and health. This is exactly where the principles of community health psychology and the practice of the community psychologist become relevant. Since the predominant role of psychological process in health and illness is an empirically proven fact, community health psychology can utilize outcomes of its research and practice in designing social policies and intervention. Here community health psychology is significant for two reasons: (a) it depicts the damaging effects of these social determinants on health and also (b) maps out ways to challenge these influences. One mechanism that could counter-react against these negative influences on health is popularizing the concept of 'healthy community' through collective movement. The topic that needs sensitization and interference are many, and the list would be unending. It is not that our country is facing human resources crunch or that our scientific understanding is poor but what we require is psychosocial mediators who can bridge the gap between the known the unknown. Community psychologist can play the role of an effective psychosocial mediator for social change suitable for the society at work, whose need and relevance are pressing in an overly populated society like India. Let us utilize this space to envisage the scope of community psychology in tackling existing health inequalities.

Community psychologists are trained professionals who can create responsible platforms for learning, sensitization, research and discussion for the public. By invoking the spirit of 'healthy community', they can create an environment for knowledge dissemination. The proposed outline to be discussed works within the framework of the 'paraprofessional force in psychology' that we discussed in Chapter 2 of this textbook. The community psychologist in the field, in an environment like that of India, would be required to adopt a community level analysis of the situation. The findings of baseline studies conducted on various topics that is found to be the need of the area will be the first-hand evidence for planning effective intervention strategies. As proposed (refer to Section 2.11 of Chapter 2), the community psychologist utilizes the association with education sectors, workplaces and community at both rural and urban levels to effectively reach the people. The proposed framework for need-based community intervention plan is given in Figure 3.3.

Common physical health issues of a community could be identified through area-wise analysis of the primary and secondary data; hospitals, panchayaths and some NGOs could be approached for authentic information regarding the health status of the community. Key informants' interview, survey and case histories could be helpful in quantifying the evidence. The planned intervention strategy should be based on the community development approach and be culturally sensitive and should employ interprofessional expertise and skills. To enhance its reachability, intervention can be delivered through channels, namely institutions and community. Institutions of significance

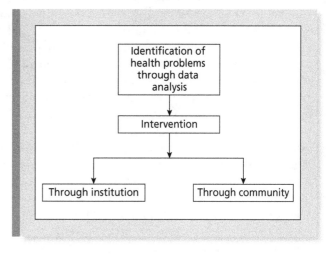

FIGURE 3.3
Proposed Framework for Need-based Community Intervention Plan

in a locality, such as educational institutions, hospitals, institutions such as children's home, old age home and home for poor and religious places such as churches and temples could be the access points to the public where knowledge dissemination could be successful. The systems in place in these institutions could be used to create a platform for spreading information about health and illness. Apart from this, areas of intervention could be decided based on the target population to be intervened, which in most of the cases be children, pregnant women and older adults. But this alone would not serve the purpose. Access points to everybody in a community should be ensured, and this can be done through camps/classes conducted in open spaces by professionals from relevant specializations of health on holidays. Free medical camps could be organized under the initiatives of private healthcare systems (PHCs), panchayat, local police station, religious institutions and so on in spaces which are open to the public such as open grounds and marketplace on prior information. This could be a very effective community activity as it would ensure convenience and participation from maximum community members. Community activities could be the free medical check-ups, deliberations by goodwill ambassadors, group activities such as cleanliness drive, information leaflet distribution or home visits. The community psychologist takes up the role of an effective facilitator in collaborating with various bodies to ensure the availability of these services to the community members. These strategies, if adapted to suit the context to be intervened, could be very successful in terms of effectiveness and reachability.

3.9. PREVENTION AND INTERVENTION

The range of health-related problems that need professional interference is extensive. Theories of community psychology have acquired the potential to adapt to the context to which the issue is tied to. Severity and status of the illness, socio-economic and political capital of the community, the strength and dynamics of community in which they are involved are other characteristics that can determine the effectiveness of the intervention. Hence, the role of community psychologist is dynamic and demands the psychologist to be attentive to the needs of the community, sensitive to the context of the issue, and develop newer models of intervention suiting the need of the community. These frameworks of intervention should be grounded in the very spirit of 'collective' and should be governed by the community. They should be culturally sensitive and should appreciate the integration of interprofessional skills and etiquettes. Community psychologist can intervene at any stage of healthcare, be in prevention and intervention.

Community psychology targets on prevention of illness and promotion of well-being as a strategy and works along the belief that 'prevention is better than cure'. Optimization of competencies and strengths of individuals in a community as well as alteration of existing maladaptive social systems are the approaches adopted in addressing real-life challenges during this phase. As widely understood, primary prevention could be targeting to avoid the onset of or future incidence of any specific condition. This could also be called as universal prevention, as the target could be a whole population, for instance, community psychologist can educate every woman in a community, who have crossed 30 years, about issues related to calcium deficiency. They can involve in programmes targeting people at high risk through issue-specific intervention (selective intervention), for instance, initiating school-based support for children who face academic difficulties. Indicated prevention could be helping an adolescent with body image issues to address his concerns with bodyweight management and self-esteem, that is, targeting individuals who are detected from early signs of disturbance in order to control its impact. The assessment reports by WHO (2009) recommended that a reduction in the following six identified factors, which are, 'childhood underweight, unsafe sex, alcohol use, unsafe water and sanitation and high blood pressure' can result in an increase of 5 years in global life expectancy rates across the world (WHO, 2009); and these findings speak for itself. Associated with prevention is the employment of health promotion activities which a community psychologist can employ and includes (a) primary promotion could be universal strategies to promote overall health such as emphasizing on the need for physical exercise for overall quality of physical health, (b) secondary promotion would be to targeting empowerment and upliftment of a community, for instance, advocacy for the transgender community and (c) tertiary promotion which has a higher meaning to achieve such as meeting high levels of well-being lie in self-actualization for a group of people (Edwards, 2017). However, the case, the primary prevention methods are hardly put into practice and there is need to facilitate the incorporation of primary prevention as agenda of national and state policies. One has to understand that, preventive services and health promotion activities include issues related to physical and mental health, and also all social concerns such as climate change, war or pollution, that can have a direct or indirect effect on the well-being of a community.

For effective intervention, a country to should identify its place in the risk transition of diseases that would affect its population. One has to understand that as the country progresses economically, there would be an associated transition in the illness conditions it had to face from epidemics of communicable nature to diseases which are non-communicable and caused due to poor lifestyle practices. This so happens due to improvement in the country's medical care systems and public health interventions such as vaccinations, clean drinking water and waste disposal mechanisms and so on; issues associated with poverty and undernutrition would be gradually addressed and tackled. As discussed earlier, problems that would increasingly pester modern society would be those arising from a poor lifestyle such as obesity, alcohol and substance dependency and physical inactivity. Hence, understanding the status of the nation in this risk trajectory is crucial in planning effective intervention. Countries like India suffers from double burden, as it has to tackle problems associated with malnutrition and poor sanitation as well as those associated with economic development such as air pollution, poor eating habits and physical inactivity. Hence, intervention strategies planned in our nation should address the population at all the levels of economic standards. Addressing the causal and contributory factors are also important and so intervention strategies should target those. In relation to intervening the causal line, multiple distal risk factors such as education or social security can be modified or altered to amplify its impact on proximal factors of illnesses. Hence, fundamental enhancement of health and lifestyle can be brought in through smart modification of such environmental and behavioural risk factors (CSDH, 2008). When it comes to targeting people, those who are at high risk as well as the entire population, would be necessary, as the nature and manifestation of illness, in the case of non-communicable disease, are such. For strategies like improving nutrition is essential for improving global health or intervening at early childhood to adolescence stage would be double beneficial as it would take care of the health of the future adults as well as the next generations—their offsprings.

Here is an attempt to understand the administration of community need-based intervention programme conducted for the school children in a community (Figure 3.4).

FIGURE 3.4
Model for a Community Need-based Intervention among School Children

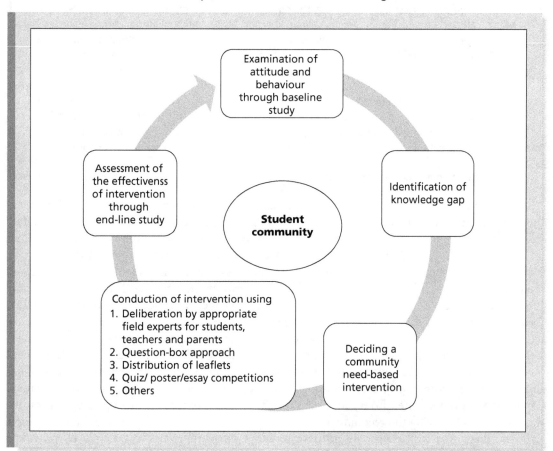

A hypothetical case study would be useful to understand the role of a community psychologist in equipping adolescent girls in a rural community with needed information on reproductive health.

Case III: Ms Sahirah is a community psychologist who is working in a rural locality of Andhra Pradesh. As a trained psychologist, she decided to identify various health needs of her locality, and so she tactfully employed some of the inspective techniques such as case studies, focus group discussions and interviews in her preliminary investigative study. This helped her to develop a list of common health-related concerns of the locality on a priority basis. She has taken into account some other characteristics such as the existing political scenario, current affairs, presence of epidemic/communicable diseases reported, social mishaps, new governmental schemes on health and wellness and the list continues, based on which she identified 'reproductive health among adolescent girls' as the topic of study. By employing her research skills, practical knowledge and literature reviews, she developed tools for the baseline survey. She has targeted two groups for her study which were the adolescent girls between the age of 9–16 years. Hence, the tool developed was a basic aptitude test which contained questions that would assess the level of knowledge the test taken has on reproductive health. By utilizing the association with the schools in the locality, the paraprofessional force in psychology administered the baseline study and analysed the data. Based on the inferences drawn, Sahirah developed a module on 'reproductive health and associated concerns' which was a four-week session with topics such as puberty, menstruation, reproductive health, safe sex, early/unwanted pregnancy and abortion, STDs, family planning, rape and violence and existing government policies and laws as its contents. Sahirah identified influential community members and trained them on these modules. Deliberations of professionals from associated fields, provisions for a question-box approach to address queries, conduction of competitions such as quizzes, essay writing and poster making were also employed to educate the students. To make parents and teachers play effective mediator roles, special sessions for discussions and information dissemination were also conducted. In associations with the schools, teachers, students and their parents were given a platform for learning and discussion. An end-line study was also administered, and the data was used for effectiveness study, documentation, research and publication.

Community intervention for terminal illness could be provided all throughout the illness not just for the individual, but also for the family. Community psychologists can facilitate need-based intervention strategies suiting the nature of the illness. Let us examine the roles and responsibilities of community psychologist in dealing with cancer. To work towards prevention of cancer, the community psychologist can provide group and one-to-one education about healthy habits and behaviours, controllable risk factors contributing to cancer, the signs and symptoms for early detection, enhanced community engagement for the avoidance of tobacco, recommended routine health check-up and share scientifically proven cancer prevention recommendations among the communities. A community study conducted in Korea was successful in reducing breast-cancer-related myths and motivating women to undertake mammography in their health check-up (Park et al., 2011). Through knowledge dissemination and encouragement for screening, community-based interventions can help early identification of illness and thus reducing the health burden. People who have recovered from cancer should be reminded of their follow-up as well as on the importance of following the recommended cancer prevention techniques. Intervention for people who are diagnosed with cancer would have to adopt other intervention strategies by providing physical and emotional assistance in dealing with the condition. Denial, acceptance, coping mechanism and hope are concepts associated with dealing with cancer. Help can also be provided in dealing with the pain, side effects of chemotherapy, financial management, transportation, reducing out-of-pocket expenditure, caregiver burnout and dealing with stigma and labelling. For individuals who are at the terminal stage of cancer, the community can offer support for the individual and the family to accept the reality, manage the pain and the suffering and offer palliative care.

Likewise, the range of problems that can be sorted through their involvement could be many, such as:

- Encouraging the community to build self-sufficient homes which have their own vegetable garden and poultry farming, proper rainwater harvesting and waste management system, solar power panel and biogas plant.
- Emphasizing the importance of clean drinking water, hygienic and organic food consumption, balanced diet, eating habits and exercise.
- Educating young mothers on antenatal and post-natal care, good child-rearing practices, breastfeeding, vaccinations and other health-related factors.
- Sensitizing the adolescent and young-adult population about academic stress and anxiety, addiction and substance abuse, eating disorders and obesity, reproductive health, early pregnancy by keeping into account the existing socio-political environment in the country such as adolescent mental health issues such as depression and suicide, rape, paedophilia and so on.
- Discussing topics such as work-life balance and financial management, family planning, contraceptives and associated governmental policies, dependency on substance and country-made liquor, social issues such as domestic violence and dowry, to adults of marriageable age.
- Deliberating on issues such as empty nest, loneliness, work-related stress and burnout, problems at workplace, income-generating opportunities for homemakers and so on with middle-aged adults.
- Reflecting on the importance of physical activity and routine health check-ups, potential health risks and its management, caregiver burnout, dealing with the death of the spouse and bereavement, mental health challenges and coping skills and so on with older adults.
- Promoting periodic health check-up for everyone in a family, particularly children, pregnant women and older adults.
- Providing warning on the probable health conditions/epidemic due to seasonal changes or other factors and prevent/control the spread by organizing camps for vaccination and preventive medicines.
- Normalizing mental illness and other similar 'labelled' health conditions through dissemination of correct information to the public.

The efficacy of such population-centred intervention strategies can be improved when the responsibility is fully or partially shifted to the legislation and governmental bodies. Like in many developed countries, the governments can adopt strategies that would accommodate the strong contribution of socio-economic factors towards health and well-being and intervene through taxing systems, subsides and similar health-promotion incentives, free and mandatory health check-ups or even through engineering solutions (WHO, 2009). Such initiatives could yield the maximum outcome only when government and mediators of psychosocial change join hands to move towards achieving community well-being.

3.10. HEALTH POLICIES IN INDIA

Health status of a country exerts a direct effect on the economy of any nation; despite the case, in most of the countries health sector is untapped and ignored. The *Human Development Index Report 2018* ranked India at the 130th position out of 189 countries which is a sign of great grievance and shame. Owing to poor infrastructure (in public hospitals), peculiar demography of the country, deficient financial resources, dearth in human resource, high population and diversity in terms of socio-economic and cultural milieu, the healthcare system in the country faces several critical challenges (Garg, 2018). The National Rural Health Mission (NRHM) was launched in 2005 to address the issues related to lack of healthcare professionals and services in rural India, and the National Urban Health Mission (NUHM) targets the primary healthcare facilitates for urban population through its three tiers which are (a) community level, (b) urban health centre level and (c) secondary/tertiary level through public-private sector partnerships. Moreover, the Government of India has launched several schemes under the National Health Mission by targeting the population of varying needs. Reproductive, maternal, newborn, child and adolescent health (RMNCH+A), Pradhan Mantri Matru Vandana Yojana (PMMVY), Pradhan Mantri Surakshit Matritva Abhiyan (PMSMA), Janani Shishu Suraksha Karyakaram for pregnant women, Rashtriya Bal Swasthya Karyakram (RBSK) for early identification of birth defects, deficiencies, disease and developmental delays in children, Pulse Polio, the Rashtriya Kishor Swasthya Karyakram for adolescent population, Mission Indradhanush for ensuring overall coverage of immunization, Pradhan Mantri Swasthya Suraksha Yojana (PMSSY) for ensuring the availability of tertiary medical care services for all, Rashtriya Arogya Nidhi for seeking financial assistance for BPL patients, Rashtriya Swasthya Bima Yojana to provide health insurance, National AIDS Control Organization, Revised National TB Control Program, National Leprosy Eradication Programs, National Mental Health Programs, National Tobacco Control Program, Integrated Child Development Services (ICDS) are the prominent schemes provided by the Indian government. Success of these programmes in terms of feasibility, reach and implementation is challenging due to the country's population density, unique demographic and social constitution.

3.11. HEALTH INSURANCE AND ITS OBJECTIVE

As the climate, living conditions and environment deteriorates, India is becoming home to a number of illnesses which are capable of imposing huge physical, mental and financial burden on any family. It is therefore suggested that one essential factor to keep individuals/families prepared to address the illness is medical insurance. Health insurance is an effective method to avail appropriate treatment options for an illness without spending a huge proportion of one's income and savings. The choice of health insurance determines its coverage and thus reduces the financial distress. Governments across the world address 'universal health coverage' through either through their legislation or by the utilization of taxes. In some countries like Australia, free public hospital systems have been instituted form the 1940s onwards. The Indian government also provides national health insurance schemes such as the Rashtriya Swasthya Bima Yojana (RSBY) for hospitalization up to ₹30,000, the Employment State Insurance Scheme (ESIS) for government employees and their dependents, the Central Government Health Scheme for central government employees, the Aam Aadmi Bima Yojana for poor and rural households in the country, the Universal Health Insurance Scheme, the Janashree Bima Yojana for a set of specified professional group, the Senior Citizen Health Insurance Scheme (SCHIS) and the Ayushman Bharat (National Health Protection Mission).

3.12. RECOMMENDATIONS

Based on evidence and first-hand field experience, a number of issues are recommended for improving the health status of common people keeping their economic condition in mind. Issues include:

- Government hospitals and medical colleges should be instituted in rural areas and enforce the medical students to serve the medical college and its sub-centres (district hospitals, community health centres, primary health centres and other sub-centres) for a mandatory time period. This would ensure the availability of doctors at all time.
- Government should determine a range of price for medical investigative methods administered in hospital and should make this information available for both the hospitals and the public. This would ensure the affordability of health service to all.
- Conduction and review of nutrition-sensitive programmes for mothers and babies during conception period (such as PMMVY and PMSMA) and for children and adolescents (mid-day meals and Nutrition Program for Adolescent Girls (NPAG) in schools should be made mandatory.
- Community health centres should be mandated to circulate guidelines on guidelines on pre-pregnancy, pregnancy and post-pregnancy care for women and encourage paternal involvement in childcare through education and sensitization; 'paternal education increases routine antenatal care utilization and that child health improves as a result' (Halim et al., 2011). This remedial measure would reduce maternal-child mortality rate as well as domestic violence faced by women.
- Educational institution should be involved in inculcating positive health behaviour and habits in children and adolescents. Similarly, public space (including social media) and resources should be utilized to disseminate information regarding positive health behaviour, health habits and importance of healthy lifestyle, especially healthy childhood, healthy pregnancy and healthy ageing.

3.13. CONCLUSION AND IMPLICATIONS

Elucidating illness in terms of its social, economic, political and psychological corollaries is an appreciable shift in illness aetiology as this has been helpful in placing the individual in the context of their families and culture. This new attitude has opened newer dimensions to the prevention, intervention and rehabilitation aspect of health and illness. 'Developing countries increasingly face a double burden from the risks for communicable diseases and maternal and child outcomes that traditionally affect the poor combined with the risks for non-communicable conditions' (WHO, 2009). This is where the need for tailor-made medicine/treatment becomes important as well as community psychology. Public health policies should be thoughtfully updated targeting the comprehensive integration of healthcare and its promotion within the existing healthcare delivery system (Kapadia, 2012). Ensuring community participation and development of community-need-based intervention can address issues related to treatment as well as equality-equity. Wellness of all ages should be the top priority of any government and need-based policies should be adopted and implemented.

There are several implications about the role of community psychologists. Community psychologists not only creates awareness about various common public physical health issues which affect common people especially people from rural belt who are not aware of the same issues, but they also mobilize the community leaders such as panchayat members, school teachers and spiritual leaders in sensitizing the larger society since they have a direct connection with grassroots-level people. Community psychologists also play the role of facilitators for diagnosis of the common health problem and necessary treatment through referral services and help poor people with fund through community mobilization.

EXERCISES

One-mark Questions

1. Define community health.
2. Give two key roles of community psychologist.
3. What is the definition of health according to WHO?
4. Write any two health policies in India.
5. What is coronary heart disease?
6. Explain health-seeking behaviour.
7. Differentiate between communicable and non-communicable diseases with examples.
8. What are the components of doctor–patient communication?
9. What do you understand by the term 'primary promotion'?
10. Elaborate two common geriatric illnesses?

Five-mark Questions

1. Elaborate on the features of community health psychology.
2. How should the education sector participate in community service delivery?
3. Explain how intervention of terminal illness be done in community setting.
4. Elaborate CBR.
5. What are environmental and occupation risk factors?
6. Analyse health-seeking behaviour in India.

Ten-mark Questions

1. What are the determinants of health-seeking behaviours?
2. How is community intervention different in rural and urban India?
3. What is the role of psychosocial mediator in community health?
4. How to tackle the issues related to availability, affordability and accessibility of healthcare system in the country?

5. How do you understand illness across lifespan?
6. Write an account on the health policies in India.

Reflexive Questions

1. Do healthcare providers at rural hospitals extend proper care and support services?
2. How to ensure equal opportunity of health services to all, irrespective of location of residence?
3. Is it possible to come out with a policy to standardize price for all diagnostic tests across all private health service centre?
4. Do common people of India realize the value of periodic health check-ups?

REFERENCES

Aggarwal, A. N., Chaudhry, K., Chhabra, S. K., Souza, G. A. D., Gupta, D., Jindal, S. K., Katiyar, S. K., Kumar, R., Shah, B., Vijayan, V. K., & Asthma Epidemiology Study Group. (2006). Prevalence and risk factors for bronchial asthma in Indian adults: A multicentre study. *The Indian Journal of Chest Disease & Allied Sciences*, 48, 13–22.

Aggarwal, Ashutosh N., Gupta, D., Agarwal, R., Sethi, S., Thakur, J. S., Anjinappa, S. M., Chadha, V. K., Kumar, R., Sharma, M., Behera, D., & Jindal, S. K. (2015). Prevalence of pulmonary tuberculosis among adults in a North Indian district. *PLoS ONE*, 10(2), 25695761. https://doi.org/10.1371/journal.pone.0117363

Ahmad, A. (2019). Health-seeking behavior and its determinants among mine workers in the Karauli district of Rajasthan in India. *Dubai Medical Journal*, 226013, 1–10. https://doi.org/10.1159/000500495

Ahmed, S. M., Tomson, G., Petzold, M., & Kabir, Z. N. (2005). Socioeconomic status overrides age and gender in determining health-seeking behaviour in rural Bangladesh. *Bulletin of the World Health Organization*, 83(2), 109–117.

Akil, L., & Ahmad, H. A. (2011). Effects of socioeconomic factors on obesity rates in four southern states and Colorado. *Ethinicity & Diseases*, 21(1), 9–10.

Alwin, D. F., & Wray, L. A. (2005). A life-span developmental perspective on social status and health. *The Journals of Gerontology Series B: Psychological Sciences and Social Sciences*, 60(Special Issue 2), S7–S14.

Amieva, H., Ouvard, C., Giulioli, C., Meillon, C., Rullier, L., & Dartigues, J. F. (2015). Self-reported hearing loss, hearing aids, and cognitive decline in elderly adults: A 25-year study. *Journal of American Geriatrics Society*, 63(10), 1–2.

Ashwani, A. K. A., & Deepika, S. (2011). Treatment delay in oral and oropharyngeal cancer in our population: The role of socio-economic factors and health-seeking behaviour. *Indian Journal of Otolaryngol and Head & Neck Surgery*, 63(2), 145–150. https://doi.org/10.1007/s12070-011-0134-9

Bader, S. (2018, 4 September). In India, can universal health care become a reality ? *Devex*, 1–6. https://www.devex.com/news/in-india-can-universal-health-care-become-a-reality-92650

Balarajan, Y., Selvaraj, S., & Subramanian, S. (2011). Health care and equity in India. *The Lancet*, 377(9764), 505–515. https://doi.org/10.1016/S0140-6736(10)61894-6

Balasundaram, A., Sarkar, S., Hamide, A., & Lakshminarayanan, S. (2014). Socioepidemiologic profile and treatment-seeking behaviour of HIV/AIDS patients in a tertiary-care hospital in South India. *Journal of Health, Population and Nutrition*, 32(4), 587–594.

Barua, K., Borah, M., Deka, C., & Kakati, R. (2017). Morbidity pattern and health-seeking behavior of elderly in urban slums: A cross-sectional study in Assam, India. *Journal of Family Medicine and Primary Care*, 6(2), 345. https://doi.org/10.4103/2249-4863.220030

Bassani, D. G., & Jha, P. (2010). Causes of neonatal and child mortality in India: A nationally representative mortality survey. *The Lancet*, 376(9755), 1853–1860. https://doi.org/10.1016/S0140-6736(10)61461-4

Bauer, U. E., Briss, P. A., Goodman, R. A., & Bowman, B. A. (2014). Prevention of chronic disease in the 21st century: Elimination of the leading preventable causes of premature death and disability in the USA. *The Lancet, 384*(9937), 45–52.

Bavdekar, A., Yajnik, C. S., Pandit, A., & Joglekar, C. (1999, December). Insulin resistance syndrome in 8-year-old Indian children. *Diabetes, 48*(12), 2422–2429. https://doi.org/10.2337/diabetes.48.12.2422

Ben-shlomo, Y., & Kuh, D. (2002). A life course approach to chronic disease epidemiology: Conceptual models, empirical challenges and interdisciplinary perspectives. *International Journal of Epidemiology, 31*(2), 285–293.

Berger, D. (2014). Corruption ruins the doctor–patient relationship in India. *BMJ Journal, 348* (3169). https://doi.org/10.1136/bmj.g3169

Bhalla, K., Nehra, D., Nanda, S., Verma, R., Gupta, A., & Mehra, S. (2018). Prevalence of bronchial asthma and its associated risk factors in school-going adolescents in tier-III north. *Journal of Family Medicine and Primary Care, 7*, 1452–1457. https://doi.org/10.4103/jfmpc.jfmpc_117_18.

Bircher, J., & Kuruvilla, S. (2014). Defining health by addressing individual, social, and environmental determinants: New opportunities for health care and public health. *Journal of Public Health Policy, 35*(3), 363–386.

Blazer, D. G., Yaffe, K., & Karlawish, J. (2015). Cognitive aging: A report from the Institute of Medicine. *Journal of the American Medical Association, 313*(21). https://doi.org/10.1001/jama.2015.4380

Bolin, M., Åkerud, H., Cnattingius, S., Stephansson, O., & Wikström, A. K. (2013). Hyperemesis gravidarum and risks of placental dysfunction disorders: A population-based cohort study. *BJOG: An International Journal of Obstetrics and Gynaecology, 120*(5), 541–547. https://doi.org/10.1111/1471-0528.12132

Buvneshkumar, M., Jogn, K. R., & Logaraj, M. (2018). A study on prevalence of depression and associated risk factors among elderly in a rural block of Tamil Nadu. *Indian Journal of Public Health, 62*(2), 89–94. https://doi.org/10.4103/ijph.IJPH_33_17

Campbell, C., & Murray, M. (2004). Commubity health psychology: Promoting analysis and action for social change. *Journal of Health Psychology, 9*(2), 187–195.

Central Statistics Office. (2011). Situation Analysis Of The Elderly in India. Ministry of Statistics and Programme Implementation. http://mospi.nic.in/sites/default/files/publication_reports/elderly_in_india.pdf

Chandrasekar, S., Roa, R. S. P., Nair, N. S., & Kutty, P. R. (1998). Socio-demographic determinants of antenatal care. *Tropical Doctor, 8*, 1–2. https://journals.sagepub.com/doi/pdf/10.1177/004947559802800406

Chang, X., Jiang, X., Mkandarwire, T., & Shen, M. (2019). Associations between adverse childhood experiences and health outcomes in adults aged 18–59 years. *PLoS ONE, 14*(2), e0211850. https://doi.org/10.1371/journal.pone.0211850

Chatters, L. M. (2000). Religion and health: Public health research and practice in Africa. *Annual Review of Public Health, 21*(1), 335–367. https://doi.org/10.4081/jphia.2010.e1

Chattopadhyay, S. (2007). Religion, spirituality, health and medicine: Why should Indian physicians care? *Journal of Postgraduate Medicine, 53*(4), 262–266. https://doi.org/10.4103/0022-3859.33967

Chauhan, R. C., Kandan, M., Purty, A. J., Samuel, A., & Singh, Z. (2015). Determinants of health care seeking behavior among rural population of a coastal area in South India. *International Journal of Scientific Reports, 1*(2), 118. http://dx.doi.org/10.18203/issn.2454-2156.IntJSciRep20150218

Chavan, R. D., Kothari, S. T., Zunjarrao, K., & Chowdhary, A. S. (2015). Surveillance of acute respiratory infections in Mumbai during 2011–12. *Indian Journal of Medical Microbiology, 33*(1), 43–50. https://doi.org/10.4103/0255-0857.148376

CSDH. (2008). *Closing the gap in a generation: Health equity through action on the social determinants of health.* World Health Organization. https://www.who.int/social_determinants/final_report/csdh_finalreport_2008.pdf

Dahat, P. (2014). 11 women die after sterilisation surgeries in Chhattisgarh. *The Hindu,* 1. http://www.thehindu.com/news/national/other-states/8-women-dead-in-botched-surgeries-at-chhattisgarh-govt-camp/article6586425.ece

Darnton-Hill, I., Nishida, C., & James, W. P. T. (2004). A life course approach to diet, nutrition and the prevention of chronic diseases. *Public Health Nutrition, 7*(1A), 101–121. https://doi.org/10.1079/PHN2003584

Das, S. K., Pal, S., & Ghosal, M. K. (2012). Dementia: Indian scenario. *Neurology India, 60*(6), 618–624. https://doi.org/10.4103/0028-3886.105197

Davies, M., Meesaraganda, R., & Stockton, B. (2019, 21 August). Indian medical representatives are giving quacks cash and gifts to sell antibiotics. *THe Bureau of Investigative Jounralism*. https://scroll.in/article/934538/in-india-medical-representatives-are-giving-quacks-cash-and-gifts-to-sell-antibiotics

Davis, A., McMahon, C. M., Pichora-Fuller, K. M., Russ, S., Lin, F., Olusanya, B. O., Chaddha, S., & Tremblay, K. L. (2016). Aging and hearing health: The life-course approach. *Gerontologist*, 56(S2), S256–S267. https://doi.org/10.1093/geront/gnw033

Deeks, A., Lombard, C., Michelmore, J., & Teede, H. (2009). The effects of gender and age on health related behaviors. *BMC Public Health*, 9, 1–8. https://doi.org/10.1186/1471-2458-9-213

Deka, M., Malhotra, A., Yadav, R., & Gupta, S. (2015). Dietary pattern and nutritional deficiencies among urban adolescents. *Journal of Family Medicine and Primary Care*, 4(3), 364. https://doi.org/10.4103/2249-4863.161319

Dhawan, A., Pattanayak, R. D., Chopra, A., Tikoo, V. K., & Kumar, R. (2017). Pattern and profile of children using substances in India: Insights and recommendations. *National Medical Journal of India*, 30(4), 224–229. https://doi.org/10.4103/0970-258X.218679

Dhillon, P. K., Mathur, P., Nandakumar, A., Fitzmaurice, C., Kumar, G. A., Mehrotra, R., Shukla, D. K., Rath, G. K., Gupta, P. C., Swaminathan, R., Thakur, J. S., Dey, S., Allen, C., Badwe, R. A., Dikshit, R., Dhaliwal, R. S., Kaur, T., Kataki, A. C., Visweswara, R. N., Gangadharan, P., Dutta, E., Furtado, M., Varghese, C. M., Bhardwaj, D., Muraleedharan, P., Odell, C. M., … Dandona, L. (2018). The burden of cancers and their variations across the states of India: The global burden of disease study 1990–2016. *The Lancet Oncology*, 19(10), 1289–1306. https://doi.org/10.1016/S1470-2045(18)30447-9

Dimakakou, E., Johnston, H. J., Streftaris, G., & Cherrie, J. W. (2018). Exposure to environmental and occupational particulate air pollution as a potential contributor to neurodegeneration and diabetes: A systematic review of epidemiological reserach. *International Journal of Environmental Reserach and Public Health*, 15(8), 1704. https://doi.org/10.3390/ijerph15081704

Drljan, Č. D., Mikov, A., Filipović, K., Todorović, S. T., Knežević, A., & Krasnik, R. (2016). Cerebral Palsy in Preterm Infants. *Vojnosanitetski Pregled*, 73(4), 343–348. https://doi.org/10.2298/VSP140321019D

Edwards, S. D. (2017). *Health promotion: Community psychology and indigenous*. University of Zululand.

Every Women Every Child. (2016). *The global strategy for women's, children's and adolescents' health (2016–2030)*. https://www.who.int/life-course/partners/global-strategy/globalstrategyreport2016-2030-lowres.pdf

Fochsen, G., Deshpande, K., & Thorson, A. (2006). Power imbalance and consumerism in the doctor-patient relationship: Health care providers' experiences of patient encounters in a rural district in India. *Qualitative Health Research*, 16(9), 1236–1251. https://doi.org/https://doi.org/10.1177/1049732306293776

Franceschi, C., Garagnani, P., Morsiani, C., Conte, M., Santoro, A., Grignolio, A., Monti, D., Capri, M., & Salvioli, S. (2018). The continuum of aging and age-related diseases: Common mechanisms but different rates. *Frontiers in Medicine*, 5(61). https://doi.org/10.3389/fmed.2018.00061

Garg, S. (2018). *Healthcare policy in India: Challenges and remedies*. Sajeev Sirpal Academic and Creativity Excellence Award. https://www.iima.ac.in/c/document_library/get_file?uuid=f4758624-d359-4608-82e7-abb73ad2f51f&groupId=52123

Gedzi, V. S. (2013). Societal perception of illness and relationship with ill persons. *European Scientific Journal*, 9(14), 1–2.

Ghose, S., & John, L. B. (2017). Adolescent pregnancy: An overview. *International Journal of Reproduction, Contraception, Obstetrics and Gynecology*, 6(10), 4197–4203.

Gluckman, P. D., Harison, M. A., Cooper, C., & Thornburg, K. L. (2008). Effect of in utero and early-life conditions on adult health and disease. *The New England Journal of Medicine*, 359(1), 61–73.

Gonmei, Z., & Toteja, G. S. (2018). Micronutrient status of Indian population. *Indian Journal of Medical Research*, 148(5), 511–521. https://doi.org/10.4103/ijmr.IJMR_1768_18

Goodman, R. A., Bunnell, R., & Posner, S. F. (2014). What is 'community health'? Examining the meaning of an evolving field in public health. *Preventive Medicine*, 67(S1), S58–S61. https://doi.org/10.1016/j.ypmed.2014.07.028

Goold, S. D., & Lipkin, M. (1999). The doctor-patient relationship. *Journal of General Internal Medicine*, 14(S1), 26–33. https://doi.org/10.1046/j.1525-1497.1999.00267.x

Gothankar, J., Doke, P., Dhumale, G., Pore, P., Lalwani, S., Quraishi, S., Murarkar, S., Patil, R., Waghachavare, V., Dhobale, R., Rasote, K., Palkar, S., & Malshe, N. (2018). Reported incidence and risk factors of childhood pneumonia in India: A community-based cross-sectional study. *BMC Public Health*, *18*(1), 1111. https://doi.org/10.1186/s12889-018-5996-2

Goyal, R. K., Shah, V. N., Saboo, B. D., Phatak, S. R., Shah, N. N., Gohel, M. C., Raval, P. B., & Patel, S. S. (2010). Prevalence of overweight and obesity in Indian adolescent school going children: Its relationship with socioeconomic status and associated lifestyle factors. *Journal of Association of Physicians of India*, *58*(3), 151–158.

Griffiths, P., & Stephenson, R. (2001). Understanding users' perspectives of barriers to maternal health care use in Maharashtra, India. *Journal of Biosocial Science*, *33*(3), 339–359. https://doi.org/10.1017/S002193200100339X

Gulati, A., Hochdorn, A., Paramesh, H., Paramesh, E. C., Chiffi, D., Kumar, M., Gregori, D., & Baldi, I. (2014). Physical activity patterns among school children in India. *Indian Journal of Pediatrics*, *81*(1), 47–54. https://doi.org/10.1007/s12098-014-1472-x

Gulliford, M., Figueroa-munoz, J., Morgan, M., Hughes, D., Gibson, B., & Beech, R. (2002). What does 'access to health care' mean? *Journal of Health Services Research and Policy*, *7*(3), 186–188. https://doi.org/10.1016/s0031-9406(05)66922-2

Gupta, I., & Dasgupta, P. (2013). Health-seeking behavior in urban Delhi: An exploratory study. *World Health & Population*, *3*(2). https://doi.org/10.12927/whp..17580

Gupta, R., Mohan, I., & Narula, J. (2016). Trends in coronary heart disease epidemiology in India. *Annals of Global Health*, *82*(2), 307–315. https://doi.org/10.1016/j.aogh.2016.04.002

Gupta, V. B. (2010). Impact of culture on healthcare seeking behavior of Asian Indians. *Journal of Cultural Diversity*, *17*(1), 13–19.

Halim, N., Bohara, A. K., & Ruan, X. (2011). Healthy mothers, healthy children: Does maternal demand for antenatal care matter for child health in Nepal? *Heath Policy and Planning*, *26*, 242–256. https://doi.org/10.1093/heapol/czq040

Harinarayan, C. V., Ramalakshmi, T., & Venkataprasad, U. (2004). High prevalence of low dietary calcium and low vitamin D status in healthy south Indians. *Asia Pacific Journal of Clinical Nutrition*, *13*(4), 359–364.

Hayden, M. E. (2014, 1 April). Rural health care blamed for infant deaths in Kolkata. *The New York Times*. https://india.blogs.nytimes.com/2014/04/01/rural-health-care-blamed-for-infant-deaths-in-kolkata/

Hooda, S. K. (2017). Out-of-pocket payments for healthcare in India: Who have affected the most and why? *Journal of Health Management*, *19*(1), 1–15. https://doi.org/10.1177/0972063416682535

Huber, M., Knottnerus, J. A., Green, L., Van Der Horst, H., Jadad, A. R., Kromhout, D., Leonard B, Lorig, K., Loureiro, M. I., van der Meer, J. W., Schnabel, P., Smith, R., van Weel, C., & Smid, H. (2011). How should we define health? *BMJ*, *343*(7817), 1–3. https://doi.org/10.1136/bmj.d4163

Human Reproduction Programme. (2015). *Strategies toward ending preventable maternal mortality (EPMM)*. https://apps.who.int/iris/bitstream/handle/10665/153540/WHO_RHR_15.03_eng.pdf?sequence=1

Institute of Health Metrics and Evaluation. (2018). *Findings from the global burden of disease study 2017*. http://www.healthdata.org/sites/default/files/files/policy_report/2019/GBD_2017_Booklet.pdf

Iregren, A., Andersson, M., & Nylen, P. (2002). Color vision and occupational chemical exposures: I. An overview of tests and effects. *Neurotoxicology*, *23*(6), 719–733.

Jackson, J. L., Chamberlin, J., & Kroenke, K. (2001). Predictors of patient satisfaction. *Social Science & Medicine*, *52*(4), 609–620.

Jacob, C. M., Baird, J., Barker, M., Hanson, M., & Cooper, C. (2017). The Importance of a life course approach to health: Chronic disease risk from preconception through adolescence and adulthood. https://www.who.int/life-course/publications/life-course-approach-to-health.pdf

Jadid, A. (2017, 13 August). Gorakhpur tragedy: 60 children die in Baba Raghav Das Medical College in a week amid oxygen supply disruption. *Hindustan Times*. https://www.hindustantimes.com/india-news/up-30-dead-in-48-hours-due-to-disruption-of-oxygen-supply-in-gorakhpur-hospital/story-TwMrMJxhAZzIkn3pXcZEMN.html

Jaisoorya, T. S., Beena, K. V., Beena, M., Jose, D. C., Ellangovan, K., Thennarasu, K., & Benegal, V. (2016). Prevelence & correlated of tobacco use among adolescents in Kerala, India. *Indian Journal of Medical Research*, *144*(5), 704–711. https://doi.org/10.4103/ijmr.IJMR_1873_14

Jaul, E., & Barron, J. (2017). Age-related diseases and clinical and public health implications for the 85 years old and over population. *Frontiers in Public Health, 5*(335). https://doi.org/10.3389/fpubh.2017.00335

Johnson, A. R., George, M., Goud, B. R., & Sulekha, T. (2018). Screening for mental health disorders among pregnant women availing antenatal care at a government maternity hospital in Bengaluru city. *Indian Journal of Psychological Medicine, 40*(4), 343–348. https://doi.org/10.4103/IJPSYM.IJPSYM_41_18.

Joseph, N., Suvarna, P., Hariharan Bharadwaj, S., Dhanush, K. S., Raeesa, F., Mohamed Jasir, K. K., Joseph, N., Kotian, S. M., & Rai, S. (2016). Prevalence, risk factors and treatment practices in diarrhoeal diseases in south India. *Environmental Health and Preventive Medicine, 21*(4), 248–257. https://doi.org/10.1007/s12199-016-0521-7

Joshi, K. S., Bhaware, B. D., & Pazare, A. R. (2017). Indian adolescent living with HIV-AIDS: Current clinical scenario. *Journal of Association of Physicians of India, 65*(7), 41–46.

Kahissay, M. H., Fenta, T. G., & Boon, H. (2017). Beliefs and perception of ill-health causation: A socio-cultural qualitative study in rural North-Eastern Ethiopia. *BMC Public Health, 17*(1), 124. https://doi.org/10.1186/s12889-017-4052-y

Kapadia, F. (2012). Health and wellness across the life span. *American Journal of Public Health, 102*(11), 1–2. https://doi.org/10.2105/AJPH.2012.301026

Kar, A. (2014). Birth defects in India: Magnitude, public health impact and prevention. *Journal of Krishna Institute of Medical Sciences University, 3*(2), 7–16.

Kasthuri, A. (2018). Challenges to health care in India: The five A's. *Indian Journal of Community Medicine, 43*(3), 141–143. https://www.ncbi.nlm.nih.gov/pmc/articles/PMC6166510/

Katavić, S. S., Tanacković, S. F., & Badurina, B. (2016). Illness perception and information behaviour of patients with rare chronic diseases. *Information Research, 21*(1). https://files.eric.ed.gov/fulltext/EJ1094564.pdf

Kaushik, J. S., Gomber, S., & Dewan, P. (2012). Clinical and epidemiological profiles of severe malaria in children from Delhi, India. *Journal of Health, Population and Nutrition, 30*(1), 113–116. https://doi.org/10.3329/jhpn.v30i1.11291

Kaveeshwar, S., & Cornwall, J. (2014). The current state of diabetes mellitus in India. *Australasian Medical Journal, 7*(1), 45–48. https://doi.org/10.4066/AMJ.2013.1979

Khadilkar, A. V. (2010). Vitamin D deficiency in Indian adolescents. *Indian Pediatrics, 47*(9), 755–756. https://doi.org/10.1007/s13312-010-0110-6

Kokila, K., & Chellavel Ganapathi, K. (2019). A study on prevalence of chronic kidney disease and its risk factors among adults in selected slums of Chennai. *International Journal of Community Medicine and Public Health, 6*(2), 504. https://doi.org/10.18203/2394-6040.ijcmph20190059

Krishnan, A., Kumar, R., Broor, S., Gopal, G., Saha, S., Amarchand, R., Choudekar, A., Purkayastha, D. R., Whitaker, B., Pandey, B., Narayan, V. V., Kabra, S. K., Sreenivas, V., Widdowson, Marc-Alain, Lindstrom, S., Lafond, K. E., & Jain, S. (2019). Epidemiology of viral acute lower respiratory infections in a community-based cohort of rural north Indian children. *Journal of Global Health, 9*(1). https://doi.org/10.7189/jogh.09.010433

Krishnan, M. N. (2012). Coronary heart disease and risk factors in India: On the brink of an epidemic? *Indian Heart Journal, 64*(4), 364–367. https://doi.org/10.1016/j.ihj.2012.07.001

Kruk, M. E., Gage, A. D., Joseph, N. T., Danaei, G., García-Saisó, S., & Salomon, J. A. (2018). Mortality due to low-quality health systems in the universal health coverage era: A systematic analysis of amenable deaths in 137 countries. *The Lancet, 392*(10160), 2203–2212. https://doi.org/10.1016/S0140-6736(18)31668-4

Kulkarni, P., Kulkarni, A., Akarte, S., Bhawalkar, J., & Khedkar, D. (2013). Treatment seeking behavior and related delays by pulmonary tuberculosis patients in E-ward of Mumbai Municipal Corporation, India. *International Journal of Medicine and Public Health, 3*(4), 286. https://doi.org/10.4103/2230-8598.123474

Kumar, A., Valecha, N., Jain, T., & Dash, A. P. (2007). Burden of malaria in India: Retrospective and prospective view. *Defining and Defeating the Intolerable Burden of Malaria III: Progress and Perspectives,* supplement to *American Journal of Tropical Medicine and Hygiene, 77*(6), 69–78.

Kumar, P., & Ram, U. (2017). Patterns, factors associated and morbidity burden of asthma in India. *PLoS ONE, 12*(10), 1–18. https://doi.org/10.1371/journal.pone.0185938

Kumari, R., Bharti, R. K., Singh, K., Sinha, A., Kumar, S., Saran, A., & Kumar, U. (2017). Prevalence of iron deficiency and iron deficiency anaemia in adolescent girls in a tertiary care hospital. *Journal of Clinical and Diagnostic Research*, *11*(8), BC04–BC06. https://doi.org/10.7860/JCDR/2017/26163.10325

Ladusingh, L., Mohanty, S. K., & Thangjam, M. (2018). Triple burden of disease and out of pocket healthcare expenditure of women in India. *PLoS ONE*, *13*(5), 1–17. https://doi.org/10.1371/journal.pone.0196835

Lakshminarayanan, S., & Jayalakshmy, R. (2015). Diarrheal diseases among children in India: Current scenario and future perspectives. *Journal of Natural Science, Biology and Medicine*, *6*(1), 24–28. https://doi.org/10.4103/0976-9668.149073

Lalu, J., Rakesh, P., & Leelamoni, K. (2017). Prevalence of bronchial asthma and factors associated with it among higher secondary school children in Ernakulam district, Kerala, Southern India. *Journal of Family Medicine and Primary Care*, *6*(2), 311. https://doi.org/10.4103/2249-4863.220026

Lassi, Z. S., Majeed, A., Rashid, S., Yakoob, M. Y., & Bhutta, Z. A. (2013). The interconnections between maternal and newborn health: Evidence and implications for policy. *The Journal of Maternal-Fetal & Neonatal Medicine*, *26*(1), 3–53. https://doi.org/10.3109/14767058.2013.784737

Lehmann, U., Friedman, I., & Sanders, D. (2004). *Review of the utilisation and effectiveness of community-based health workers in Africa* (Working Paper of the Joint Learning Initiative), 1–44. https://pdfs.semanticscholar.org/7a0c/fd44975b00b045c7957c9327a87c9fcc6b63.pdf

Li, K. T., Naik, S., Alexander, M., & Mathad, J. S. (2018). Screening and diagnosis of gestational diabetes in India: A systematic review and meta-analysis. *Acta Diabetologica*, *55*(6), 613–625. https://doi.org/10.1007/s00592-018-1131-1

Loiwal, M. (2019, 11 June). Doctors protest at Kolkata hospital after intern attacked, beaten by patient's kin. *India Today*. https://www.indiatoday.in/india/story/doctors-protest-hospital-intern-attacked-beaten-patient-kin-1546726-2019-06-11

Lopez, A. D., Mathers, C. D., Ezzati, M., Jamison, D. T., & Murray, C. J. (2006). Global and regional burden of disease and risk factors, 2001: Systematic analysis of population health data. *The Lancet*, *367*(9524), 1747–1757.

Mackenbach, J. P. (2005). Genetics and health inequalities: Hypotheses and controversies. *Journal of Epidemiology and Community Health*, *59*(4), 268–273. https://doi.org/10.1136/jech.2004.026807

Magee, L. A., Sharma, S., Nathan, H. L., Adetoro, O. O., Bellad, M. B., Goudar, S., Macuacua, S. E., Mallapur, A., Qureshi, R. Sevene, E., Sotunsa, J., Valá, A., Lee, T., Payne, B. A., Vidler, M., Shennan, A. H., Bhutta, Z. A., & von Dadelszen, P. (2019). The incidence of pregnancy hypertension in India, Pakistan, Mozambique, and Nigeria: A prospective population-level analysis. *PLoS Medicine*, *16*(4). https://doi.org/10.1371/journal.pmed.1002783

Mathers, C. D., & Loncar, D. (2006). Projections of global mortality and burden of disease from 2002 to 2030. *PLoS Medicine*, *3*(11). https://doi.org/10.1371/journal.pmed.0030442

Mathew, R. (2009, 25 October). No end to Endosulfan tragedy. *The Hindu*. https://www.thehindu.com/news/cities/Thiruvananthapuram/No-end-to-Endosulfan-tragedy/article16888527.ece

Mathur, S. B., & Mukherjee, S. B. (2017). Congenital malformations to birth defects: The Indian scenario. *Indian Pediatrics*, *54*(7), 587–588.

Mathuranath, P. S., George, A., Ranjith, N., Justus, S., Kumar, M. S., Menon, R., Sarma, P. S., & Verghese, J. (2012). Incidence of Alzheimer's disease in India: A 10 years follow-up study. *Neurology India*, *60*(6), 625–630. https://doi.org/10.4103/0028-3886.105198

Maung, T. M., Deborah, S., & Tun, A. A. (2019). Traditional medicine vs modern medicine in rural area of Kedah state, Malaysia. *IOSR Journal of Pharmacy and Biological Sciences*, *14*(1), 5–8. https://www.semanticscholar.org/paper/Traditional-Medicine-Vs-Modern-Medicine-in-Rural-of-Maung-Deborah/6b21e04394cf39dfdb1e7caf0cb4c3912d654f4b#paper-header

Mckenzie, J. F., Pinger, R. R., & Kotecki, J. E. (2011). *An introduction to community health* (7th ed.). Jones & Bartlett Learning. https://doi.org/10.1108/ijhcqa.2002.06215bae.004

Mehra, B., Bhalla, P., & Rawat, D. (2016). Indian adolescents and human immunodeficiency virus: A pilot study from Delhi. *Journal of Family Medicine and Primary Care*, *5*(1), 187. https://doi.org/10.4103/2249-4863.184665

Menniti-Ippolito, F., Gargiulo, L., Bologna, E., Forcella, E., & Raschetti, R. (2002). Use of unconventional medicine in Italy: A nation-wide survey. *European Journal of Clinical Pharmacology*, *58*(1), 61–64. https://doi. org/10.1007/s00228-002-0435-8

Ministry of Health and Family Welfare. (2015). Health management information system. Government of India. https:// www.nrhm-mis.nic.in/Pages/RHS2015.aspx?RootFolder=%2FRURAL HEALTH STATISTICS%2F%28A% 29RHS-2015&FolderCTID=&View=%7BC50BC181-07BB-4F78-BE6FFCE916B64253%7D

Mishra, S., Bhadoria, A. S., Kishore, S., & Kumar, R. (2018). Gestational diabetes mellitus 2018 huidelines: An update. *Journal of Family Medicine and Primary Care*, *7*(6), 1169–1172. https://doi.org/10.4103/jfmpc.jfmpc_178_18

Moonan, P. K., Nair, S. A., Agarwal, R., Chadha, V. K., Dewan, P. K., Gupta, U. D., Ho, C. S., Holtz, T. H., Kumar, A. M., Kumar, N., Kumar, P., Maloney, S., Mase, S. R., Oeltmann, J. E., Paramasivan, C. N., Parmar, M. M., Rade, K. K., Ramachandran, R., Rao, R., … Khaparde, S. D. (2018). Tuberculosis preventive treatment: The next chapter of tuberculosis elimination in India. *BMJ Global Health*, *3*(5), e001135. https://doi.org/10.1136/ bmjgh-2018-001135

Munjanja S. P., Magure, T., & Kandawasvika, G. (2012). Geographical access, transport and referral systems. In J. Hussein, A. McCaw-Bins, & R. Webber (Eds.), *Maternal and perinatal health in developing countries* (pp. 139–154). http://www.transaid.org/wp-content/uploads/2015/06/Geographical-Access-Transport-and-Referral-Systems.pdf

Nath, A. (2017). Pediatric HIV in India: Current scenario and the way forward. *Indian Journal of Public Health*, *61*(2), 124–130. https://doi.org/10.4103/ijph.IJPH_314_15

Nayak, A. K., Jain, M. K., Dhivya, S., & Hota, S. (2017). A study on prevalence of HIV infection among pregnant women attending antenatal clinic in a tertiary care hospital, Cuttack, India. *International Journal Of Community Medicine and Public Health*, *4*(5), 1504. https://doi.org/10.18203/2394-6040.ijcmph20171547

Nilima, Kamath, A., Shetty, K., Unnikrishnan, B., Kaushik, S., & Rai, S. N. (2018). Prevalence, patterns, and predictors of diarrhea: A spatialoral comprehensive evaluation in India 11 Medical and Health Sciences 1117 Public Health and Health Services. *BMC Public Health*, *18*(1). https://doi.org/10.1186/s12889-018-6213-z

Niu, S. (2010). Ergonomics and occupational safety and health: An ILO perspective. *Applied Ergonomics*, *41*(6), 744–753. https://doi.org/10.1016/j.apergo.2010.03.004

Odden, M. C., Shlipak, M. G., Whitson, H. E., Katz, R., Kearney, P. M., Defilippi, C., Shastri, S., Sarnak, M. J., Siscovick, D. S., Cushman, M., Psaty, B. M., & Newman, A. B. (2014). Risk factors for cardiovascular disease across the spectrum of older age: The Cardiovascular Health Study. *Atherosclerosis*, *237*(1), 336–342. https:// doi.org/10.1016/j.atherosclerosis.2014.09.012

Ogoina, D. (2011). Fever, fever patterns and diseases called 'fever' : A review. *Journal of Infection and Public Health*, *4*(3), 108–124. https://doi.org/10.1016/j.jiph.2011.05.002

Oiwa, A., & Komatsu, M. (2015). Diabetes in older adults. *Nihon Rinsho. Japanese Journal of Clinical Medicine*, *73*(12), 2027–2031. https://europepmc.org/article/med/26666148

Pal, R., Dasgupta, A., & Tsering, D. (2010). Substance use among adolescent high school students in India: A survey of knowledge, attitude, and opinion. *Journal of Pharmacy and Bioallied Sciences*, *2*(2), 137. https://doi. org/10.4103/0975-7406.67005

Pallikadavath, S., Foss, M., & Stones, R. W. (2004). Antenatal care: provision and inequality in rural North India. *Social Science & Medicine*, *59*(6), 1147–1158.

Park, K., Hong, W. H., Kye, S. Y., Jung, E., Kim, M. H., & Park, H. G. (2011). Community-based intervention to promote breast cancer awareness and screening: The Korean experience. *BMC Public Health*, *11*. https://doi. org/10.1186/1471-2458-11-468

Pate, P. B., Trivedi, K., Nayak, S. N., & Patel, P. (2010). Health seeking behaviour of peri-urban community of Chandkheda. *National Journal of Community Medicine*, *1*(1), 35–36.

Patle, R. A., & Khakse, G. M. (2015). Health-seeking behaviour of elderly individuals: A community-based cross-sectional study. *The National Medical Journal of India*, *28*(4), 181–184.

Patnaik, L., Pattanaik, S., Sahu, T., & Venkata Rao, E. (2015). Overweight and obesity among adolescents: A comparative study between government and private schools. *Indian Pediatrics*, *52*(9), 779–781. https://doi. org/10.1007/s13312-015-0716-9

Pillai, R. K., Williams, S. V., Glick, H. A., Polsky, D., Berlin, J. A., & Lowe, R. A. (2003). Factors affecting decisions to seek treatment for sick children in Kerala, India. *Social Science and Medicine*, 57(5), 783–790. https://doi.org/10.1016/S0277-9536(02)00448-3

Prabhakaran, D., Jeemon, P., & Roy, A. (2016). Cardiovascular diseases in India: Current epidemiology and future directions. *Circulation*, 133(16), 1605–1620. https://doi.org/10.1161/CIRCULATIONAHA.114.008729

Prabhakaran, D., Jeemon, P., Sharma, M., Roth, G. A., Johnson, C., Harikrishnan, S., Gupta, R., Pandian, J. D., Naik, N., Roy, A., Dhaliwal, R. S., Xavier, D., Kumar, R. K., Tandon, N., Mathur, P., Shukla, D. K., Mehrotra, R., Venugopal, K., Kumar G. A., … Dandona, L. (2018). The changing patterns of cardiovascular diseases and their risk factors in the states of India: The global burden of disease study 1990–2016. *The Lancet Global Health*, 6(12), e1339–e1351. https://doi.org/10.1016/S2214-109X(18)30407-8

Press Trust of India. (2018). Boy dies after government doctor denied treatment demanding bribe. *India Today*. https://www.indiatoday.in/crime/story/boy-dies-after-govt-doctor-denies-treatment-demanding-bribe-1216717-2018-04-20

Priya, A., Chaturvedi, S., Bhasin, S. K., Bhatia, M. S., & Radhakrishnan, G. (2018). Depression, anxiety and stress among pregnant women: A community-based study. *Indian Journal of Psychiatry*, 60(1), 151–152. http://www.indianjpsychiatry.org/text.asp?2018/60/1/151/228394

Radhakrishnan, R., Andrade, C., Haven, N., Associate, P., & Haven, N. (2012). Suicide: An Indian perspective. *Indian Journal of Psychiatry*, 54(4), 304–319. https://doi.org/10.4103/0019-5545.104793

Rajkumar, P., Pattabi, K., Vadivoo, S., Bhome, A., Brashier, B., Bhattacharya, P., & Mehendale, S. M. (2017). A cross-sectional study on prevalence of chronic obstructive pulmonary disease (COPD) in India: Rationale and methods. *BMJ Open*, 7(5), 1–6. https://doi.org/10.1136/bmjopen-2016-015211

Rajpal, S., Kumar, A., & Joe, W. (2018). Economic burden of cancer in India: Evidence from cross-sectional nationally representative household survey, 2014. *PLoS ONE*, 13(2), 29481563. https://doi.org/10.1371/journal.pone.0193320

Ravishankar, B., & Shukla, V. J. (2007). Indian systems of medicine: A brief profile. *African Journal of Traditional, Complementary and Alternative Medicines*, 4(3), 319–337.

Rehm, J. (2011). The risks associated with alcohol use and alcoholism. *Alcohol Research Current Reviews*, 34(2), 135–143.

Rockville. (2012). Behavioral health disroder across the lifespan. *Behavioral Health*, 1–4. https://www.ncbi.nlm.nih.gov/books/NBK174668/

Rodrigues, C. M. C., & Groves, H. (2018). Community-acquired pneumonia in children: The challenges of microbiological diagnosis. *Journal of Clinical Microbiology*, 56(3), 1–9. https://doi.org/10.1128/JCM.01318-17

Roy, S. (1985). Primary health care in India. *Health and Population: Perspectives and Issues*, 8, 135–167. https://doi.org/10.2307/3342068

Rumun, A. J. (2014). Influence of religious beliefs on healthcare practice. *International Journal of Education and Reserach*, 2(4), 37–48.

Sahu, S. (2008, August 25). Indian man carries dead wife's body for 12 km. *BBC News*. https://www.bbc.com/news/world-asia-india-37183011

Sahu, S. K., Kumar, S. G., Bhat, B. V., Premarajan, K. C., Sarkar, S., Roy, G., & Joseph, N. (2015). Malnutrition among under-five children in India and strategies for control. *Journal of Natural Science, Biology and Medicine*, 6(1), 18–23. https://doi.org/10.4103/0976-9668.149072

Saleem, M., Priya, S., Pradeep, M., & Sabeetha, K. (2017). A study on the prevalence of chronic obstructive pulmonary disease among adults in Madurai, Tamil Nadu. *International Journal Of Community Medicine And Public Health*, 4(11), 4113. https://doi.org/10.18203/2394-6040.ijcmph20174629

Salvi, S., Kumar, G. A., Dhaliwal, R. S., Paulson, K., Agrawal, A., Koul, P. A., Mahesh, P. A., Nair, S., Singh, V., Aggarwal, A. N., Christopher, D. J., Guleria, R., Mohan, B. V. M., Tripathi, S. K., Ghoshal, A. G., Kumar, R. V., Mehrotra, R., Shukla, D. K., Dutta, E., Furtado, M., Bhardwaj, D., Smith, M., Abdulkader, R. S., Arora, M., Balakrishnan, K., Chakma, J. K., Chaturvedi P., … Dandona, L. (2018). The burden of chronic respiratory diseases and their heterogeneity across the states of India: The Global Burden of Disease Study 1990–2016. *The Lancet Global Health*, 6(12), e1363–e1374. https://doi.org/10.1016/S2214-109X(18)30409-1

Samal, J. (2016). Health seeking behaviour among tuberculosis patients in India: A systematic review. *Journal of Clinical and Diagnostic Research, 10*(10). https://doi.org/10.7860/JCDR/2016/19678.8598

Sankar, M. J., Neogi, S. B., Sharma, J., Chauhan, M., Srivastava, R., Prabhakar, P. K., Khera, A., Kumar, R., Zodpey, S., & Paul, V. K. (2016). State of newborn health in India. *Journal of Perinatology, 36*(s3), S3–S8. https://doi.org/10.1038/jp.2016.183

Sarin, R., Vohra, V., Khalid, U. K., Sharma, P. P., Chadha, V., & Sharada, M. A. (2018). Prevalence of pulmonary tuberculosis among adults in selected slums of Delhi city. *Indian Journal of Tuberculosis, 65*(2), 130–134. https://doi.org/10.1016/j.ijtb.2017.08.007

Sarkar, M. (2010). A study on domestic violence against adult and adolescent females in a rural area of West Bengal. *Indian Journal of Community Medicine, 35*(2), 311–315. https://doi.org/10.4103/0970-0218.66881

Satija, A., Khandpur, N., Satija, S., Mathur Gaiha, S., Prabhakaran, D., Reddy, K. S., Arora, M., & Venkat Narayan, K. M. (2018). Physical activity among adolescents in India: A qualitative study of barriers and enablers. *Health Education and Behavior, 45*(6), 926–934. https://doi.org/10.1177/1090198118778332

Schultz, W. M., Keli, H. M., Lisko, J. C., Varghese, T., Shen, J., Sandesara, P., Quyyumi, A. A., Taylor, H. A., Gulati, M., Harold, J. G., Mieres, J. H., Ferdinand, K. C., Mensah, G. A., & Sperling, L. S. (2018). Socioeconomic status and cardiovascular: Challenges and interventions. *Circulation, 137*(20), 2166–2178. https://doi.org/10.1161/CIRCULATIONAHA.117.029652

Scott, K., & Shanker, S. (2010). Tying their hands? Institutional obstacles to the success of the ASHA community health worker programme in rural North India. *AIDS Care, 22*(S2), 1606–1612. https://doi.org/10.1080/09540121.2010.507751

Selvaraj, A. (2019, July 24). Chennai man dies after taking injection for pain at pharmacy, owner held. *Times of India*, 1–15. https://timesofindia.indiatimes.com/city/chennai/city-man-dies-after-taking-injection-for-pain-at-pharmacy-owner-held/articleshow/70354129.cms

Shah, I., Lala, M., & Damania, K. (2017). Prevalence of HIV infection in pregnant women in Mumbai, India: Experience from 1993–2004 and 2008. *Journal of Family Medicine and Primary Care, 6*(2), 240. https://doi.org/10.4103/2249-4863.219990

Sharma, R. (2013). Birth defects in India: Hidden truth, need for urgent attention. *Indian Journal of Human Genetics, 19*(2), 125. https://doi.org/10.4103/0971-6866.116101

Shidhaye, R., & Kermode, M. (2013). Stigma and discrimination as a barrier to mental health service utilization in India. *International Health, 5*(1), 6–8. https://doi.org/10.1093/inthealth/ihs011

Shijith, M., & Sekher, T. V. (2013). *Who get health insurance coverage in India? New findings from nation-wide surveys.* Paper presented at XXVII IUSSP International Population Conference, 1–26. https://iussp.org/sites/default/files/event_call_for_papers/shijith_health insurance.pdf

Shrivastava, S. R. B. L., Shrivastava, P. S., & Ramasamy, J. (2015). Measles in India: Challenges and recent developments. *Infection Ecology & Epidemiology, 5*(1), 25–27. https://doi.org/10.3402/iee.v5.27784

Shukia, N. (2018, 18 July). Unskilled doctors add to health crisis in encephalitis hit areas of Uttar Pradesh. *India Today*, 1–9. https://www.indiatoday.in/india/story/up-gorakhpur-brd-medical-college-quacks-health-encephalitis-1289672-2018-07-18

Shyam, C., Sreenivas, V., & Dakshinamurty, K. V. (2007). Chronic kidney disease in India. *Indian Journal of Medical Research, 126*(5), 485. https://doi.org/10.2215/cjn.09180817

Singh, M. (2016). Communication as a bridge to build a sound doctor–patient/parent relationship. *Indian Journal of Pediatrics, 83*(1), 33–37. https://doi.org/10.1007/s12098-015-1853-9

Siu, A. L. (2016). Screening for breast cancer: U S Preventive Aervices Task Force. *Annals of Internal Medicine, 164*(4), 279–296. https://doi.org/10.7326/M15-2886

Sivagurunathan, C., Umadevi, R., Rama, R., & Gopalakrishnan, S. (2015). Adolescent health: Present status and its related programmes in India. Are we in the right direction? *Journal of Clinical and Diagnostic Research, 9*(3), LE01–LE06. https://doi.org/10.7860/JCDR/2015/11199.5649

Smith, T. W., & Christensen, A. J. (1995). Personality and patient adherence: Correlates of the five-factor model in renal dialysis. *Journal of Behavioral Medicine, 18*(3), 305–313.

Steptoe, A., Dockray, S., & Wardle, J. (2009). Positive affect and psychobiological processes relevant to health. *Journal of Personality, 77*(6), 6494. https://doi.org/10.1111/j.1467-6494.2009.00599.x

Suwannaphant, K., Puttanapong, N., Saengsuwan, J., Phajan, T., & Laohasiriwong, W. (2017). Association between socioeconomic status and diabetes mellitus: The National Socioeconomics Survey, 2010 and 2012. *Journal of Clinical and Diagnostic Research*, *11*(7), LC18–LC22. https://doi.org/10.7860/JCDR/2017/28221.10286

Takala, J. (2015). Eliminating occupational cancer. *Industrial Health*, *53*(4), 307–309. https://doi.org/10.2486/indhealth.53-307

Tandon, R., Jain, A., & Malhotra, P. (2018). Management of iron deficiency anemia in pregnancy in India. *Indian Journal of Hematology and Blood Transfusion*, *34*(2), 204–215. https://doi.org/10.1007/s12288-018-0949-6

Tennant, C. (2001). Work-related stress and depressive disorders. *Journal of Psychosomatic Research*, *51*(5), 697–704.

TOI Editorial. (2014, 1 July). Disease of kickbacks via unnecessary tests must be cured and severe punishments prescribed. *Times of India*, 1–2. https://timesofindia.indiatimes.com/blogs/toi-editorials/disease-of-kickbacks-via-unnecessary-tests-must-be-cured-and-severe-punishments-prescribed/

Trickett, E. J. (2009). Community psychology: Individuals and interventions in community context. *Annual Review of Psychology*, *60*(1), 395–419. https://doi.org/10.1146/annurev.psych.60.110707.163517

Tripathy, J. P., Thakur, J. S., Jeet, G., Chawla, S., Jain, S., Pal, A., Prasad, R., & Saran, R. (2017). Prevalence and risk factors of diabetes in a large community-based study in North India: Results from a STEPS survey in Punjab, India. *Diabetology and Metabolic Syndrome*, *9*(1), 1–8. https://doi.org/10.1186/s13098-017-0207-3

Trivedi, D., Dhakappa, N., Ghildiyal, P., Deekonda, S., Subramaniam, S., Iyer, J. S., & Kotiyan, M. S. (2016). Depression among adolescent students in South India: How serious is the issue? *Indian Journal of Psychiatry*, *58*(3), 349–350. https://doi.org/10.4103/0019-5545.191997

Troeger, C., Blacker, B., Khalil, I. A., Rao, P. C., Cao, J., Zimsen, S. R. M., Albertson, S. B., Deshpande, A., Farag, T., Abebe, Z., Adetifa, I. M. O., Adhikari, T. B., Akibu, M., Al Lami, F. H., Al-Eyadhy, A., Alvis-Guzman, N., Amare, A. T., Amoako, Y. A., Antonio, C. A. T., … Reiner, R. C. (2018). Estimates of the global, regional, and national morbidity, mortality, and aetiologies of lower respiratory infections in 195 countries, 1990–2016: A systematic analysis for the Global Burden of Disease Study 2016. *The Lancet Infectious Diseases*, *18*(11), 1191–1210. https://doi.org/10.1016/S1473-3099(18)30310-4

UNAIDS. (2008). *Task shifting: Global recommendations & guidelines*. World Health Organization. https://www.who.int/healthsystems/TTR-TaskShifting.pdf

UNICEF. (2017). A familiar face: Violence in the lives of children and adolescents. https://www.unicef.org/publications/files/Violence_in_the_lives_of_children_and_adolescents.pdf

United Nations. (2018). *The Sustainable Development Goals report*. https://unstats.un.org/sdgs/files/report/2018/TheSustainableDevelopmentGoalsReport2018-EN.pdf

Uplekar, M., & Rangan, S. (1996). *Tackling TB: Search for solutions*. The Foundation for Research in Community Health.

Vargese, S., Mathew, P., & Mathew, E. (2013). Utilization of public health services in a rural area and an urban slum in Western Maharashtra, India. *International Journal of Medical Science and Public Health*, *2*(3), 646. https://doi.org/10.5455/ijmsph.2013.220420135

Varma, P. P. (2015). Prevalence of chronic kidney disease in India: Where are we heading? *Indian Journal of Nephrology*, *25*(3), 133–135.

Vindhya, J., Nath, A., Murthy, G. V. S., Metgud, C., Sheeba, B., Shubhashree, V., & Srinivas, P. (2019). Prevalence and risk factors of anemia among pregnant women attending a public sector hospital in Bangalore, South India. *Journal of Family Medicine and Primary Care*, *8*(1), 37–43. https://doi.org/10.4103/jfmpc.jfmpc_265_18

Walter, L. C., & Covinsky, K. E. (2001). Cancer screening in elderly patients a framework for individualized decision making. *Journal of the American Medical Association*, *285*(21), 2750–2756. https://doi.org/10.1001/jama.285.21.2750

Ward, H., Mertens, T. E., & Thomas, C. (1997). Health seeking behaviour and the control of sexually transmitted disease. *Health Policy and Planning*, *12*(1), 19–28. https://doi.org/10.1093/heapol/12.1.19

WHO. (1978). Declaration of Alma-Ata. International Conference on Primary Health Care, Alma-Ata, USSR, 6, p. 12. http://www.who.int/publications/almaata_

WHO. (2009). *Global health risks: Mortality and burden of disease attributable to selected major risks*. WHO Press. https://www.who.int/healthinfo/global_burden_disease/GlobalHealthRisks_report_full.pdf

WHO. (2014). The health of the people : What works—Health through the life course. Bulletin of the World Health Organization. https://www.who.int/bulletin/africanhealth2014/health_through_the_life_course/en/

WHO. (2018). *Global status report on alcohol and health 2018*. https://apps.who.int/iris/bitstream/handle/10665/274603/9789241565639-eng.pdf

WHO. (2019). *Children: Reducing mortality*. http://www.who.int/mediacentre/factsheets/fs178/en/

Yadavar, S. (2018, 6 September). More Indians die of poor quality care than due to lack of access to healthcare: 1.6 million. IndiaSpend. https://www.indiaspend.com/more-indians-die-of-poor-quality-care-than-due-to-lack-of-access-to-healthcare-1-6-million-64432/

Yajnik, C. S., Deshpande, S. S., Jackson, A. A., Refsum, H., Rao, S., Fisher, D. J., Bhat, D. S., Naik, S. S., Coyaji, K. J., Joglekar, C. V., Joshi, N., Lubree, H. G., Deshpande, V. U., Rege, S. S., & Faill, C. H. D. (2008). Vitamin B 12 and folate concentrations during pregnancy and insulin resistance in the offspring: The Pune Maternal Nutrition Study. *Diabetologia*, 51(1), 29–38. https://doi.org/10.1007/s00125-007-0793-y

Yoon, P. W., Bastian, B., Anderson, R. N., Collins, J. L., & Jaffe, H. W. (2014). Potentially preventable deaths from the five leading causes of death—United States, 2008–2010. *Morbidity and Mortality Weekly Report*, 63(17), 369–374.

Zolnierek, K. B. H., & Dimatteo, M. R. (2010). Physician communication and patient adherence to treatment: A meta-analysis. *Medical Care*, 47(8), 826–834. https://doi.org/10.1097/MLR.0b013e31819a5acc

RECOMMENDED READING

Mckenzie, J. F., Pinger, R. R., & Kotecki, J. E. (2011). *An introduction to community health* (7th ed.). Jones & Bartlett Learning. https://doi.org/10.1108/ijhcqa.2002.06215bae.004

Community-based Intervention for Children with Disability and Developmental Disorders

LEARNING OBJECTIVES

- Understanding disability and common developmental disorders
- Discussing the characteristic features and causal factors of disability and developmental disorders
- Introducing evidence-based practices and their importance in managing disability and developmental disorders
- Elucidating the role of community stakeholders in disability management
- Proposing a community-based intervention for disability-friendly environment
- Familiarizing with the existing legislative framework that aids disability management in the country

ABSTRACT

Disability is a social construct ingrained in the sociocultural and political ambience of a society. The layout of one's community can, to a great extent, decide the causal and influencing factors, its manifestation of symptoms, the trend of diagnosis and the effectiveness of management strategies adopted. As children with disability are dependent on their ecosystem to lead their day-to-day lives, intervening within this space can enhance their smooth functioning. This chapter attempts to introduce disability and a few childhood developmental disorders, namely LDs, intellectual disabilities, autism spectrum disorder and attention-deficit hyperactivity disorder. A brief discussion of their aetiology and characteristic symptoms is given, followed by deliberating of evidence-based practices for these conditions. In order to enhance the involvement of community stakeholders, a conceptual model which is community-driven is proposed, which is an intervention at community level that targets to create a disability-friendly environment. The chapter proceeds to discuss prominent legislative measures available in the country and ends with a few practical and relevant recommendations.

Keywords: Developmental disorders; disability; childhood; community

4.1. INTRODUCTION

Disability management as a social affair larger than any other human health condition has begun to be discussed more often than before. Identified as a state that anyone can experience, either permanently or temporarily, at any given time (not just during old age), disability management is definitely a topic that would always be relevant to be studied. According to the Convention on the Rights of Persons with Disabilities (CRPD) adopted in the year 2006, 'Persons with disabilities include those who have long-term physical, mental, intellectual or sensory impairments which in interaction with various barriers may hinder their full and effective participation in society on an equal basis with others.'

Approaches to disability have been adapting with time. Disability and developmental disorders are now understood to be multidimensional and complex due to the influence of factors other than health problems. Hence, the shift from 'medical model' to 'social model' in framing the context of disability explains the shift from a concrete 'structural' outlook to a lucid 'social' perspective of disability. More than the disabling tendencies of any particular body part, the focus has been shifted to that of the society itself in the lives of persons with disabilities. However, only a balanced approach can provide sufficient weightage to each contributing aspect, and would identify new influencers as well (Shakespeare, 2007). Time and again, experts in the field as well as scientific findings have stressed on the importance of early identification of such conditions due to several relevant reasons. Childhood provides the best possible window period for any intervention strategy to produce maximum output. This early identification is usually found to happen mostly in the cases of health conditions which have explicit symptomatology, like in the case of any physical disabilities. Hence, disabling conditions like LDs or mild intellectual retardation often go unnoticed until the environment becomes intolerable for the child. The distress and inconvenience faced by children with disability and their parents are the price to be paid for the ignorance we as a society are reluctant to work towards. The disabling tendencies of the prevailing sociocultural, economic and political spirit in the country result in lasting impressions on the health and well-being of these children. They not only lose the benefits of early intervention but also have to deal with the associated incapacitating outcomes of wrong and/no intervention. Community, in which a person with disability lives, can play an effective role through a participative attitude as well as by being aware of their significant role. Hence, understanding disability, its causes, manifestation, diagnosis and management within the community of their being could be the best framework of understanding.

The chapter attempts to introduce the concept of disability within a social framework with the help of definitions as understood by prominent international agencies. The chapter takes the help of four commonly found childhood conditions, that is, intellectual disabilities, LDs, autism spectrum disorder (ASD) and ADHD to understand the pattern of aetiology, symptomatology and evidence-based management of common developmental disorders. The chapter emphasizes the role of community stakeholders such as family, teachers, service providers and community members as important contributors for effective disability management and proposes a community-based conceptual model for creating a disability-friendly environment. An overview of current legislative measures available in the country is also given. The chapter ends with few practical recommendations which can be impactful in making their day-to-day life better.

4.2. UNDERSTANDING DISABILITY

The International Classification of Functioning, Disability and Health, a framework of WHO (2009), has defined disability as an umbrella term covering impairments, activity limitations and participation restrictions. This is an advanced definition wherein the influence of environmental factors as either a facilitator or a barrier is highly emphasized. Personal factors are also considered even though not to the extent of environmental factors.

Here in the definition, there is an emphasis on problems in three interconnected areas of functioning, which are as follows:

- *Impairment* is a problem in the body function/structure (e.g., deafness).
- *Activity limitation* is a difficulty encountered by an individual in executing a task or action (e.g., walking).
- *Participation restriction* is a problem experienced by an individual in getting involved in life situations (e.g., impairments leading to unemployment).

As seen in Figure 4.1, there should not be any demarcation between physical or mental disability, difficulty faced in any of the above-mentioned domains is understood to be a disability.

FIGURE 4.1
Representation of Disability

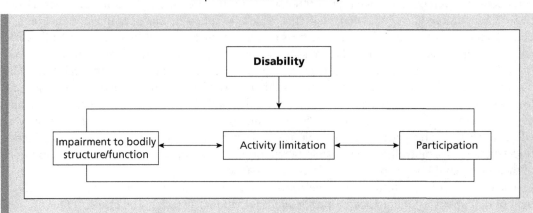

The characterization of disability has adapted with passing time, with the due involvement of psychosocial and environmental factors associated with the condition (see Figure 4.2).

Agreeably, CRPD (Gregor, 2006) identifies disability to 'result from the interaction between persons with impairments and attitudinal and environmental barriers that hinder their full and effective participation in society on an equal basis with others'. This is the reason why the same disability condition may express differently in different people. Therefore, intervention strategies are said to be developed according to an individual and not for any particular disability. This framework of understanding quotes disability along a continuum of quantity and hence disagrees with the dichotomous yes/no of ability. No special categorization of people into with and without also occurs. The premise of this chapter is also set in this explanation of disability, and so at every point of discussion, factors other than physical/mental impairment should be considered when the context is interpreted.

Children with disability are the most affected among persons with disabilities. They may be children born with disabling conditions/impairment or be children who developed disability as a result of some illness/injury at a later point. A UNICEF estimate assesses the population size to be at least 93 million (UNICEF, 2018). More than the disability, other influencing factors (see Figure 4.2) would make their experience of disability cumbersome. Let us get introduced to some very common disabilities found among children. A detailed elaboration of each of these conditions is given in the following section. Developmental disorders arise from a variety of conditions which can affect either one or all of the developmental patterns in an individual and could be of physical, cognitive or social nature. *Diagnostic and Statistical Manual of Mental Disorders* (DSM-5) has renamed this group of conditions as neurodevelopmental disorders. This is an umbrella term that includes intellectual disability, LD, ASD and ADHD. Let us get introduced to each of them.

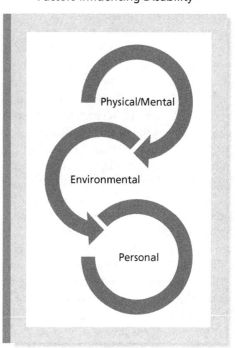

FIGURE 4.2
Factors Influencing Disability

- Intellectual disability is the condition arising out of an individual's compromised cognitive development in comparison to their age group.
- LD is a group of conditions that are characterized by 'significant limitations in both intellectual functioning and in adaptive behaviour, which covers many everyday social and practical skills' (Schalock et al., 2007).
- ASDs are a group of conditions where social communication is predominately affected. They also exhibit behavioural difficulties.
- ADHD is a condition where areas of attention and activity are compromised. The individual may express inattention and hyperactivity either in isolation or simultaneously.

Child development is linked with several factors and is not limited to a few biological or environmental domains; some are protecting/enhancing, while others are compromising in nature (Fernald et al., 2009). Linked to this condition, such children become increasingly subjected to stigma and discrimination, leading to further disabling conditions. Several studies from different geographical locations have reinstated their increased proneness to abuse and neglect, institutionalization, poor caregiver interaction and lack of access to quality care (European Agency for Development in Special Needs Education, 2005; Skelton & Rosenbaum, 2010). Poverty and disability have an explicit link; children of malnourished mothers (maternal ill health), children exposed to toxins, restricted food (malnutrition) and unhygienic environment, poor access to healthcare facilities and exposure to violence and abuse are prone to development of disabling health conditions (Walker et al., 2011). Similar contributing tendencies are put by disability on poverty as such families are required to meet the additional demands of the disabled child in the family (World Health Organization, 2012). Children with disability are the most excluded among all in their families, schools and in the larger society; this is primarily due to lack of knowledge about these disabling conditions leading to a non-inclusive and disabling space. With the severity of impairment, such children may be subjected to victimization at multiple levels which are linked to their age, gender, social status and geographical location. Hence, effective intervention strategies should address all these individual concerns and be tailored for the need of an individual child. Taking the huge population size, the feasibility of providing such individualistic care could be attainable only with the involvement of community. This chapter aims at creating such an inclusive atmosphere in communities where disability-friendly attitude and spaces will be created.

In sum

Disability is an umbrella term covering impairments, activity limitations and participation restrictions. There is emphasis on problems in three interconnected areas of functioning, which are as follows:

- *Impairment* is a problem in the body function/structure (e.g., deafness).
- *Activity limitation* is a difficulty encountered by an individual in executing a task or action (e.g., walking).
- *Participation restriction* is a problem experienced by an individual in getting involved in life situations (e.g., impairments leading to unemployment).

According to CRPD, adopted in the year 2006, persons with disabilities include those who have long-term physical, mental, intellectual or sensory impairments which in interaction with various barriers may hinder their full and effective participation in society on an equal basis with others.

4.3. MAGNITUDE AND PREVALENCE OF THE CHILDHOOD DISABILITIES

Childhood developmental disorders are a broad category of illness which includes neurodevelopmental, emotional and behavioural disorders; the impact of these conditions on children and their families is even broader in terms of the psychological and social burden it creates. Most of these disorders which initiate in childhood tend to carry forward at least some of their characteristics to their adulthood, owing to a persistent and lasting need for additional support and help from their families, educational institutions, workplaces and any space of transaction (Shaw et al., 2012). Estimation of a global prevalence of common childhood disorders, despite the difficulty in the availability of data from low- and middle-income countries, is essential for severity analysis. This chapter works around four most prevalent childhood disorders, namely LD, intellectual disability, ASD and ADHD, and so let us place our framework of understanding on the epidemiology of these conditions.

As per *The Global Burden of Disease 2004* data on children between 0 and 14 years, 93 million children suffer from 'moderate or severe disability', while nearly 13 million children suffer from 'severe disability' (World Health Organization, 2011). Ascertaining the global magnitude of intellectual disability is challenging due to many reasons: manifestation of ID is varying with age and cause of the condition and assessment of intelligence quotient (IQ) score alone will not help for accurate diagnosis (also consider the occurrence of Flynn effect). However the case, 'the prevalence of ID is often quoted at 1%' (McKenzie et al., 2016). The large population size of India makes the epidemiological estimation of ID cumbersome. Factors such as age and gender, demographical details, socio-economic condition (poverty, inaccessible health services and so on; Edwardraj et al., 2010; Lakhan & Ekúndayò, 2013), environmental factors (exposure to toxins, pollution; Emerson, 2007) varies across the country to a notable extent. Therefore, one should not be surprised to see the variation of prevalence rates found in studies conducted in India: from 1.7 cases/1,000 to 32 cases/1,000 (Lakhan et al., 2015). The magnitude of LD had shown an interesting trend in the USA; the incidence of LD in the special education sector had shown a drastic hike up to year 2000, after which there has been an annual decline of up to 2 per cent. Nevertheless, 2.4 million school students in the USA suffer from LD (Cortiella & H. Horowitz, 2014). Validating these findings, another recent study conducted in the United Kingdom found that 'up to 10 per cent of the population are affected by specific learning disabilities (SLDs), such as dyslexia, dyscalculia and autism, translating to 2 or 3 pupils in every classroom' (Butterworth & Kovas, 2013).

Epidemiological estimation of LD conducted in India has shown variation in their study findings; a recent study based in Chandigarh suggested 1.58 per cent prevalence (Arun et al., 2013), while another study conducted in the same region estimated the prevalence to be 3.03 per cent (Padhy et al., 2016). The Centers for Disease Control and Prevention has estimated the prevalence rate of ASD in India to be 0.20 per cent. A recent study conducted in the rural India setting showed the prevalence rate to be 0.11 per cent, while that in urban setting to be 0.09 per cent (Chauhan et al., 2019). 'One in 160 children has ASD' (Elsabbagh et al., 2012; World Health Organization, 2019). In a systematic analysis of several studies conducted worldwide, the median of global prevalence of autism was found to be 62/10,000 cases (Elsabbagh et al., 2012). Several studies were conducted in India to estimate the prevalence of ADHD among children: a study based in Kancheepuram district found the prevalence of ADHD to be 8.8 per cent (Catherine et al., 2019). Interestingly, a similar study conducted in an adjacent district Coimbatore revealed the ADHD prevalence rate among primary schoolchildren to be 11.33 per cent (Venkata & Panicker, 2013).

4.4. COMMON DEVELOPMENTAL DISABILITIES

The International Classification of Functioning, Disability and Health: Children & Youth has defined four broad categories of disabilities in children on the basis of areas of impairment such as (a) body functions, (b) body structures, (c) activities and participation and (d) environmental factors. From the long list of disabilities, this chapter focuses on four disabilities, namely SLDs, intellectual disabilities, ASD and ADHD. Unlike physical disabilities which are easily identifiable, these are pervasive disabilities, which even though are widely prominent, remain unidentified at an early stage due to unawareness among parents/elderly and teachers. Let us explore each of them in detail.

4.4.1. Specific Learning Disabilities

Learning abilities are the product of both genetic and environmental variables; they are different from the natural acquisition of developmental milestones as the academic skills are taught and learnt. 'Learning disabilities is a generic term used for a heterogenous group of disorders manifested by significant difficulties in the acquisition and use of listening, speaking, reading, writing, or mathematical abilities, or social skills'. SLD impairs the normal academic pursuit of a child which has nothing to do with lack of exposure or opportunities to learn. The academic performance exhibited by a child with SLD would be much below (a difference of at least 1.5 standard deviation) the average expected from the children of their age group (Medina, 2019).

The definition of LDs adopted by the Rehabilitation Council of India (RCI) is the same as given by the U.S. Department of Education (the Individuals with Disabilities Education Act of 2004), that is:

> Specific learning disability means a disorder in one or more of the basic psychological processes involved in understanding or in using language, spoken or written, which may manifest itself in an imperfect ability to listen, speak, read, spell, or to do mathematical calculations. including conditions such as perceptual handicaps, brain injury, minimal brain dysfunction, dyslexia, and developmental aphasia. Specific learning disability does not include learning problems that are primarily the result of visual, hearing, of intellectual disability, or mental retardation, emotional disturbance, or of environmental, cultural, or economic disadvantage. (US Department of Education, 2004)

The updated DSM-5 classifies developmental disorders associated with difficulties in academics as 'specific learning disorders', separately identified using specifiers. The specifiers are three different subtypes that show the predominant area of impairment such as impairment in reading (also known as dyslexia), written expression (dysgraphia) and mathematical abilities (dyscalculia). Please check DSM-5 diagnostic code 315 for the diagnostic guidelines.

4.4.2. Intellectual Disabilities

Intellectual disability is understood as a 'significantly reduced ability (a) to understand new or complex information and to learn and apply new skills and (b) to cope independently, that begins before adulthood with a lasting effect on development' (World Health Organization, 2020). Impairment in two predominant areas, namely intellectual functioning (general mental ability assessed using an IQ test) and adaptive behaviour, is the key characteristic of intellectual disability. The latter concept of adaptive behaviour 'is the collection of conceptual, social and practical skills that are learnt and performed by people in their everyday lives' (World Health Organization, 2020). Therefore, a child whose IQ falls below 70 and faces significant difficulties in carrying daily activities is identified to have an intellectual disability. WHO has classified intellectual disability into four types based on the range of IQ scores. This classification has been retained by DSM-4,

TABLE 4.1
Levels of Intellectual Disabilities

Severity Category	Case Distribution (in Percentage)	DSM-4 Criteria (IQ Range)	DSM-5 Criteria (Daily Skills)
Mild	85	50–69 (approx.)	Can live independently with minimum levels of support.
Moderate	10	36–49 (approx.)	Independent living may be achieved with moderate levels of support, like those available in group homes.
Severe	3.5	20–35 (approx.)	Requires daily assistance with self-care activities and safety supervision.
Profound	1.5	<20	Requires 24-hour care.

Source: Boat and Wu (2015).

however, in DSM-5, this criterion is based on terms of impairment in daily skills. Please refer to Table 4.1 for a clear depiction.

Apart from the genetic involvement in the development of intellectual disabilities (Coffee et al., 2009; Parker et al., 2010), 'exposure to toxic substances, nutritional deficiencies, brain radiation, childhood brain infections, traumatic brain injury and maternal infections' (Boat & Wu, 2015) and 'pre- and post-natal complications' (Gustafsson, 2003) can lead to the development of intellectual disability. Conditions such as Down syndrome, Fragile X syndrome and Prader–Willi syndrome are some of the intellectual disabilities.

4.4.3. Autism Spectrum Disorder

ASD is a pervasive neurodevelopmental disorder characterized by impairments in social communication and restricted, repetitive patterns of behaviour, interests or activities (American Psychological Association, 2013). The term 'spectrum' is needed to be used to represent the range of severity of the condition as well as the intra-individual variability in its manifestation across time and context (Weiss et al., 2016). The key characteristics found in people with ASD, according to DSM–5, are difficulty in social communication and presence of repetitive/restrictive behaviours. These symptoms if present from childhood and cause significant functional impairment, will be identified as ASD (American Psychiatric Association, 2013). A range of assessments is needed to be employed in order to diagnose ASD.

4.4.4. Attention-deficit/Hyperactivity Disorder

ADHD is one of the most commonly found condition among children. According to the American Psychiatric Association, the three characteristic symptoms of ADHD are (a) inattention (inability to focus), (b) hyperactivity (excessive movement) and (c) impulsivity (sudden hasty action without thought). In other words, 'ADHD is characterized by a persistent pattern of inattention and/or hyperactivity/impulsivity that interferes with functioning or development' (American Psychiatric Association, 2013). According to DSM-5 criteria, six or more symptoms (as listed in Table 4.2),

TABLE 4.2
Symptoms of Inattention and Hyperactivity seen in ADHD

Symptoms of Inattention	Symptoms of Hyperactivity/Impulsivity
• Often fails to give close attention to details or makes careless mistakes in schoolwork, at work or during other activities.	• Often fidgets with or taps hands or feet or squirms in seat.
• Often has difficulty sustaining attention in tasks or play activities.	• Often leaves seat in situations when remaining seated is expected.
• Often does not seem to listen when spoken to directly.	• Often runs about or climbs in situations where it is inappropriate.
• Often does not follow through instructions and fails to finish schoolwork, chores or duties in the workplace.	• Often unable to play or engage in leisure activities quietly.
• Often has difficulty organizing tasks and activities.	• Is often 'on the go', acting as if 'driven by a motor'.
• Often avoids, dislikes or is reluctant to engage in tasks that require sustained mental effort.	• Often talks excessively.
• Often loses things necessary for tasks or activities.	• Often blurts out an answer before a question has been completed.
• Is often easily distracted by extraneous stimuli.	• Often has difficulty waiting for their turn.
• Is often forgetful in daily activities.	• Often interrupts or intrudes on others.

each of inattention and hyperactivity, must be persistently seen for more than six months to be diagnosed to have ADHD in a child. For more details, please refer to DSM-5.

ADHD may be noticeable from the age of 3 but definitely starts before the age of 12. Symptoms may be brought under control as age increases, while some may never grow out of ADHD; prevalence of child ADHD is 8.4 per cent (Danielson et al., 2018), while among adults is 2.5 per cent (Simon et al., 2009). The nature and severity of the condition vary from individual to individual and is reported more in boys than girls. DSM-5 uses the labels 'mild', 'moderate' and 'severe' to mark the severity index of ADHD. A combination of genetic and environmental factors is understood to cause ADHD, however, the scientific community continues to attempt to identify clear aetiologies related to ADHD.

In sum

Common childhood developmental disorders include the following:

- Intellectual disability is a condition arising out of an individual's compromised cognitive development in comparison to their age group.
- SLD is a 'generic term used for a heterogeneous group of disorders manifested by significant difficulties in the acquisition and use of listening, speaking, ready, writing, mathematical abilities or social skills'
- ADHD is a condition where areas of attention and activity are compromised. The individual may express inattention and hyperactivity either in isolation or simultaneously.

4.5. MANAGEMENT OF DISABILITY AND DEVELOPMENTAL DISORDERS USING EVIDENCE-BASED PRACTICES

Management of children with special needs should be governed by scientifically recommended practices and interventions so as to ensure efficacy of the service provided as well as to prevent mishandling. The huge variation in the types of disabling conditions and needs of these children, as well as huge dearth in research, puts this area under stress. Nevertheless, the positive influence of early intervention on all developmental domains has been proved time and again by several studies. Practitioners and service providers are highly recommended to base their intervention plans on scientific evidence (Suhrheinrich et al., 2014). Evidence-based practice (EBP) is the outcome of interaction between scientific evidence, expert's opinion and patient's need. A metanalytical paper has identified the following as suitable EBP (alphabetically) for disability and developmental disorders among children: antecedent-based intervention; cognitive behavioural intervention; differential reinforcement of alternative, incompatible or other behaviours; discrete trial teaching; exercise; extinction; functional behavioural assessment; functional communication training; modelling; naturalistic intervention; parent-implemented intervention; peer-mediated instruction and intervention; picture exchange communication system; pivotal response training; prompting; reinforcement; response interruption/redirection; scripting; self-management; social narratives; social skills training; structured playgroups; task analysis; technology-aided instruction and intervention; time delay; video modelling and visual support (Wong et al., 2015). Elaboration of each of these practices is beyond the scope of this book.

Several studies have strongly emphasized on the powerful impact of family on the developmental domains of children with disabilities (Bruder, 2010); these findings strongly recommend adopting a family-centred management for treating these children. Evidence also stresses on the need to base the therapeutic approaches in an inclusive and natural environment so that children can easily identify with the learning process and can be encouraged to make use of all the learning opportunities available (Campbell, 2004; Woods & Lindeman, 2008). Research evidence also speaks for the need to have a collaborative team effort in service rendering so that (a) child receives help from professionals from different specialized services and (b) efficacy of the overall professional interventions would be enhanced (Bruder, 2010).

4.6. THE ROLE OF COMMUNITY STAKEHOLDERS IN THE DISABILITY MANAGEMENT

An individual cannot function in isolation. There have been countless research on the benefits of social support for the development of various psychosocial factors. Thus, involving the community, which is often perceived to play a neutral role in the management of disability, can be effectively involved. The different roles in which community members can be involved are non-administrative staff of a special school, logistical arrangements of awareness campaigns, procuring of materials that help children with disability for facilitating different therapies as well as door-to-door campaigns. Most of the special schools inducted in the present study were located in suburban areas where not everyone is involved in everyday occupation. Their familiarity with the locality and basic literacy can be streamlined and capitalized to equip them with spreading awareness. This might, in turn, make them more empathetic towards the situation and increase their support in accordance.

4.6.1. ROLE OF FAMILIES

Children with disabilities and developmental disorders are largely dependent on their families for leading their day-to-day life to a great extent in comparison to their peers. Family as a space of transaction needs to be optimally informed about illness condition so that their children can be brought up in the most suitable environment. Family can be seen as a community in itself, apart from being a point of the larger community. Parents, siblings, grandparents and extended family members influence the health of a child with disability. Dealing with a disabled child is physically and mentally challenging for the family as well, particularly the parents. The family as a whole should be willing to adapt itself to the needs of the child, free itself from the socioculturally driven stigma and work towards quality care growth of the child. 'Adults create a family unit and have ultimate responsibility for caregiving, supporting the child's development, and enhancing the quality of the child's life' (Bruder, 2000). Hence, there is a heightened need to create a supportive ground within these families where the needs (physical, psychological and professional) of both the child and their family members could be met. Each informed family can act as a unit aggregating to form an informed disability-friendly non-judgemental and accommodative community.

4.6.2. ROLE OF TEACHERS

Teachers play a crucial role in educating society. In the context of disability, teachers can play the following multiple roles:

1. Teachers in special education schools can influence a disabled child to a tremendous extent through their active engagement. Most of the times, they understand the need of the child better than their own parents; therefore, they can work hand in hand with the parents to help the child. Trained special educators can approach the child through a scientifically proven and systematic approach. They can keep themselves updated with the latest studies and research and advocate for appropriate curriculum changes and teaching methodology.
2. Teachers through their active participation and advocacy can encourage a normal school to be as disability-friendly as possible. This includes not just physical/infrastructural modification but also the modification in the attitude and behaviour of others towards children with disability. This would be particularly beneficial for a child with a mild–moderate level of disability, who can otherwise cope with the normal education system if a nurturing and accepting school environment can be created.
3. Schools can become the centre of knowledge dissemination for a community. Topics related to disability can be discussed and taught in school to its student and parent community, thereby destigmatizing disability as well as engaging a larger set of people in community-driven activities.

4.6.3. ROLE OF NGOs

Involvement of NGOs is needed the most in working closely with the government. They can be the channel between the government and the people. By basing their advocacy efforts on research conducted in communities, they can help in the execution of existing plans and policies, ample and systematic utilization of funds, working towards filling the knowledge gap in the society, advocacy for an inclusive society and appeal for the introduction and/amendment of rules of the land based on the changing need of the society.

4.6.4. ROLE OF SERVICE PROVIDERS

Medical professionals, audiologists and speech therapists, clinical psychologists, hearing aid and ear mould technicians, special educators, vocational counsellors and multipurpose rehabilitation therapists, social workers are all service providers to children with disability, whose wholehearted effort is decisive in the welfare of children and their families.

In sum

- EBP is the outcome of interaction between scientific evidence, expert's opinion and patients need.
- Community stakeholders such as families, teachers, service providers, NGOs and community as a whole are crucial in disability management.

4.7. COMMUNITY-BASED INTERVENTION FOR THE CREATION OF A DISABILITY-FRIENDLY ENVIRONMENT

Theories and practices of community psychology should be suitably used in the creation of a disability-friendly community. The attainment of an inclusive community is a long process. The model proposed in this session is generic in nature and attempts to deconstruct this process into four stages which involve participation from different dimensions of the society. Due to the fluidity of the model, stages may seem to be overlapping; also, the progress of each stage appears to be the result of the ripple effect from the previous stage. Hence, the characteristic of the illness, the locality and the community would determine the number of runs this model has to take to attain the target. For the ease of understanding, let us place our discussion in the context of our present discussion, that is, the common childhood disorders. However, this model can be adapted to the context of any intervention involving the community.

As have been discussed, awareness about common childhood disorders is lacking in our present society. The extent of this unawareness is particularly deficient in disabilities other than physical ailments which do not have explicit characteristic features. Hence, the child is unable to exercise the benefits of early identification and timely intervention. The rationale behind the need to create an informed and inclusive environment for children lies here. Community, in the context of this model, operationalizes within the systems such as family, schools, workplace and religious institutions. Since our target population includes parents, teachers and elderly, these centres can be identified as the appropriate points for knowledge dissemination.

Psycho-education is considered to be the most powerful tool in knowledge dissemination. It is a structured intervention strategy developed by field experts on specific topics of discussion whose overlay is designed suiting the nature and need of the psychoeducational group. This goal-directed approach would be the best way to disseminate basic and relevant information about the common

FIGURE 4.3
Model on Intervention for the Creation of a Disability-friendly Environment

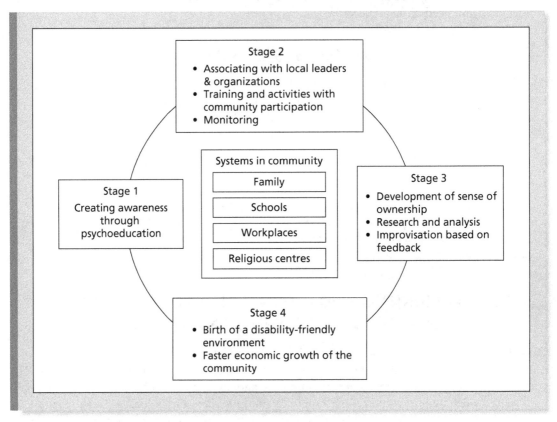

childhood disorders among the target audience. Rendering of these modules thus developed by the community psychologists is where the process begins. As depicted in Figure 4.3, this is a cyclic process where information regarding disability conditions (which includes its epidemiology, aetiology, common signs and symptoms, and management) would be provided successively. Classes, discussions, invited lectures by experts, activities, movie screening, campaigns, pamphlet distribution and so on would be the modes used for it. Online psychoeducation is also gaining popularity and is identified for its reach among a large population, particularly the youth. As the psychoeducational groups begin to gain momentum, the process further elaborates by seeking the involvement of local community leaders and representatives from local government. In a gradual fashion, the community would gain a sense of ownership about the goal to create an inclusive community. Feedback received from various ends would be beneficial for constructive decision-making. For evidence-based progress of the intervention, research is an inevitable aspect. Testimonials by parents, teachers or caregivers of children with disability could be collected and analysed to propose changes in institutions. Through this simultaneous–successive process, a disability-friendly space for children would take form where informed and sensitive agents of social change would employ their skills and efforts for an improved quality of life for our children and thus for a better economy.

The above-discussed community-based intervention has a far-reaching implication which functions at both individual and community levels.

1. *Normalizing disabilities/destigmatization:* The incapacitating attitude towards children with disabilities is situated within the social structure, in the sociocultural and religious milieu of a society. Stigma and prejudice, ignorance and segregation, overprotection or ignorance by the families, lack of opportunities in education and employment, physical and mental inaccessibility, lack of social, financial and legal aid are all by-products of this biased edifice. Conditioning of the existing ideologies by experts from medical, legal and social fronts along with advocates and social engineers is required. Breaking this age-old attitude in the society is the most challenging task which, considering the current sociopolitical set-up in the country, could be possible only through community intervention.

2. *Early identification and timely intervention:* Childhood disabilities, if identified at an early stage in life, can be managed to a great extent through evidence-based interventions suitable for each disability condition. Apart from the benefit of reduced distress management from an early phase, early intervention can prevent the development of comorbid or associated conditions. Community-based intervention for a disability-friendly environment would result in home-based learning with informed participation of the families in the child's learning process. Schools would be motivated to be inclusive for children of all abilities and greater involvement of adult community members could be expected. This would automatically invoke the need for accessibility to specialists who work hand in hand with the parents and teachers in the identification and management of childhood disabilities.

3. *Research and estimation:* The huge population size of the country affects the accuracy of prevalence estimation. This is a matter of serious concern because accurate estimation is the basis for effective policy formulation, budget allocation, logistic management and policy implementation. In India, particularly where rural–urban differences are bold, policies and programmes should be developed suiting to the needs of the area. Hence, these community spaces can be coordinated to create a platform for accurate estimation of prevalence, incidence and magnitude. If properly coordinated, all these individual focal points could be clubbed to create national data. Protective, productive and rehabilitative intervention strategies could be accordingly developed.

4. *Disability rights and policy considerations:* This platform could be effectively utilized for knowing the existing legal aids and policies available in the country. This would be helpful in seeking the benefits of these policies in treatment, education, employment and many more. Evidence collected through systematic research conducted in the space of this community intervention can, in turn, be used for the development of relevant disability-related policies and aids in the country. Logistical arrangements suiting the needs of communities can also be allotted accordingly.

4.8. IMPORTANT INTERNATIONAL AND NATIONAL POLICIES ON DISABILITY

Policies are the key players in ensuring the effective implementation of programmes crucial for an economy's growth and development. Several national and international policies to tackle the issues faced by individuals with disabilities have been developed and adopted by various governments suiting their situation. Timely updating of such policies to cater to the needs of the society is also an important aspect, leading to better utilization of a country's human resources.

4.8.1. UNITED NATIONS CONVENTION ON THE RIGHTS OF THE PERSONS WITH DISABILITIES

CRPD was adopted by the UN General Assembly in 2007. It has been signed by 158 countries and ratified by 138. It was brought into force as a result of the increasing prevalence of global disabilities. It emphasizes on the implementation of the entire existing legislative framework for persons with disabilities. It has a total of 50 articles. The general principle on which the convention is based is as follows:

- Respect for inherent dignity and individual autonomy, including the freedom to make one's own choices and independence of persons
- Non-discrimination, which includes the concept of reasonable accommodation which is the 'necessary and appropriate modification and adjustments, not imposing a disproportionate or undue burden, where needed in a particular case, to ensure to persons with disabilities the enjoyment or exercise on an equal basis with others of all human rights and fundamental freedoms'
- Full and effective participation and inclusion in society
- Respect for difference and acceptance of persons with disabilities as part of human diversity and humanity
- Equality of opportunity
- Accessibility
- Equality between men and women
- Respect for the evolving capacities of children with disabilities and respect for the right of children with disabilities to preserve their identities

In order to ensure the monitoring and implementation of the rights of persons with disabilities, national human rights institutions play important roles. They provide coordination between different parts of the government which requires multi-sectorial involvement. The purpose of such synergy is to reach the maximum number of national stakeholders that include civil society organizations, academic institutions and the private sector.

An overview of some prominent national policies related to disability and developmental disorders (without restricting to only children) are described below.

4.8.2. NATIONAL POLICY FOR PERSONS WITH DISABILITIES

National Policy for Persons with Disabilities ensures equal opportunities and effective access to rehabilitation measures. It also endeavours to provide social rehabilitation. The policy recognizes that persons with disabilities are valuable human resources for the country and seeks to create an environment that provides them with equal opportunities, protection of their rights and full participation in society. The focus of the policy shall concentrate on physical, educational and economic rehabilitation, human resource development, employment, social protection, sports recreation and creation of a barrier-free environment.

The Measures adopted to provide effective services to persons with disability should consider a holistic picture in doing so. For this purpose, the National Policy for Persons with Disabilities has proposed physical and educational resources that include counselling services provided by ASHA who addresses the grassroots-level provision of assistive devices such as prostheses and orthoses, tricycles, wheelchairs, surgical footwear and devices for activities of daily living and quality education through Sarva Shiksha Abhiyan. This programme effectively addresses the educational needs of students with disabilities. This includes education through an open learning system and open schools, alternative schooling, distance education, special schools, home-based education wherever necessary, itinerant teacher model, remedial teaching, part-time classes, CBR and vocational education. Economical needs are addressed through the Integrated Education for Disabled Children (IEDC) scheme, which provides financial assistance for development and dissemination of resources such as hostel allowance, production of instructional material, training of general teachers and equipment for resource rooms. Human resources are trained to meet the requirement of education for children with disabilities under inclusive education, special education, home-based education, pre-school education and so on. These training programmes target teachers who are willing to be a part of inclusive education, enhancing the curriculum of special education training and training of caregivers for home-based education and care services for disabled adults/senior citizens and so on.

Education of persons with disabilities has been provided with special attention under the National Policy for Persons with Disabilities. This is so because education is considered to be instrumental in effectively empowering the person with disability and it is a right-based issue for them. Our society and its tangible and intangible resources are structured in a stereotypic manner that often compromises on the right to education for this population. Hence, the National Policy for Persons with Disabilities provides for rehabilitation measures in curriculum revisions, training of educators and legal provisions in educational institutions. A gainful employment is necessary for fulfilling the basic needs of an individual. Although there are reservations for the disabled in government sectors, their problems require more concrete steps. Under this legislation, the employment opportunities have been extended to private sectors as well as home-based income generation programmes; training on skills that ensure employment has been imparted; and an accessible work environment has also been ensured. Also, for those who are self-employed, assistance is provided through appropriate agencies such as marketing boards, District Rural Development Agency (DRDA), private agencies and NGOs in the marketing of goods and services.

Public buildings (functional or recreational), transport amenities including roads, subways and pavements, railway platforms, bus stops/terminals, ports, airports, modes of transports (bus, train, plane and waterways), playgrounds, open space and so on are made accessible. Modification of the curriculum of architects and civil engineers is undertaken to include issues relating to construction of barrier-free buildings. In-service training is provided on these issues to the government architects and engineers. State transport undertakings ensure disability-friendly features in their vehicles. Railways provide barrier-free coaches in a phased manner. They have also made the platforms, buildings, toilets and other facilities barrier-free. Communication needs of the persons with disabilities are met by making information service and public documents accessible. Braille, tape service, large print and other appropriate technologies are used to provide information for the persons with visual disability.

Social security that measures the security of a person in the society aims at measuring whether he/she is living adequately. This policy covers issues such as tax-relief benefit, amount of pension and unemployment allowance and support by Life Insurance Corporation without exception for persons with disabilities. Sports and cultural activities give an opportunity to the persons with disabilities to explore and strengthen their abilities. Hence, under the policy, accessibility to the services and the travel opportunities have been emphasized upon. Identification of talent among persons with disabilities in different sports are made with the assistance of local NGOs. The representation of a person with disability is enhanced by the formation of sports organizations and cultural societies. Participation in sports and recreational activities is encouraged and reinforced with a national award for excellence in sports for persons with disabilities.

4.8.3. Persons with Disabilities (Equal Opportunities, Protection of Rights and Full Participation) Act, 1995

Passed in 1995, the Persons with Disabilities (PWD) Act covers the seven categories of disabilities. This Act was often hailed as a landmark legislation when it came to the disability movement. The person with a disability should be certified as having no less than 40 per cent of any disability. This should be certified by a medical authority to avail the benefits provided under this legislation. The disabilities covered under the PWD Act are as follows:

- *Blindness:* It is the total absence of sight or visual acuity not exceeding 6/60 or 20/200 (Snellen chart) in the better eye with corrective lenses. A limited field of vision is also included in this definition.
- *Low vision:* It includes the visual capacity to execute a task with appropriate devices.
- *Leprosy cured:* Leprosy is a contagious bacterial infection that affects eyes, skin, nose and peripheral nerves. In the PWD Act, people with three stages of the disease have been considered, these are: a person who has been cured of leprosy but has lost sensation, a person who manifests deformity but has just adequate mobility and a person with severe physical deformity that affects engagement in employment.
- *Locomotor disability:* Restriction in the limb movement of a person has also been considered under this Act. The aetiology mainly consists of disability of bones, muscles or joints. The provisions have been provided, keeping in view a substantial capability decided by the person's involvement in routine jobs and normal functioning.
- *Hearing impairment:* A person who loses the ability to hear the sounds of 60 decibels or less in the better ear has hearing impairment and can avail the measures under this Act.
- *Mental retardation:* This category specially considers those persons who have their range of intelligence below the normal. The normal range as defined by the IQ score is 90–110. Any person who has IQ less than 90 is considered to be subnormally intelligent.
- *Mental illness:* This is an umbrella term that considers any mental health issue apart from mental retardation.

Protection of rights, provision of equal opportunities and complete participation of authorities are the major areas of focus in the sectors of education, public accessibility, employment and health.

The Lok Sabha passed 'The Rights of Persons with Disabilities Rules, 2019' with a lot of improvement. Speech and language disability, SLD, acid attack victims, three blood disorders, i.e., thalassemia, haemophilia and sickle cell disease have been included. Dwarfism and muscular dystrophy have been indicated as separate classes of specified disability. In addition, the government has been authorized to notify any other category of specified disability. The new Act will bring our laws in line with the United Nations Convention on the Rights of Persons with Disabilities (UNCRPD), to which India is a signatory. This will fulfil the obligations on the part of India in terms of UNCRPD. Further, the new law will not only enhance the rights and entitlements but also provide an effective mechanism for ensuring the empowerment and true inclusion of persons with disability into the society in a satisfactory manner.

4.8.4. THE NATIONAL TRUST FOR THE WELFARE OF PERSONS WITH AUTISM, CEREBRAL PALSY, MENTAL RETARDATION AND MULTIPLE DISABILITIES ACT, 1999

The National Trust for the Welfare of Persons with Autism, Cerebral Palsy, Mental Retardation and Multiple Disabilities Act was passed by the Parliament in 1999. The major aim of this Act is to make persons with disabilities self-sufficient and prevent their isolation from society by making the community more supportive—physically, emotionally and financially. The family's support is ensured by making them empowered to care for these people as well as the appointment of guardians in case there is no family or the guardians are deceased. Ancillary support is provided by recognizing registered organizations that provide need-based services to the families of persons with disabilities. An approved programme has the following characteristics:

- Promotion of independent living in the community
- Facilitating care and support services like respite care, foster care or daycare services
- Ensuring a proper shelter of permanent or temporary nature
- Increasing social support by networking and other methods
- Constituting bodies that can ensure effective and appropriate guardianship

The board receives the financial funds allocated by the central government for the disability sector and then they further distribute the resources to implement the approved programmes. These programmes are often channelized through registered organizations. All allocations work on the basis of priority. In most of the situations, preference shall be given to women with disability, or to persons with severe disability and to senior citizens with disabilities (i.e., person above the age of 65 years).

4.8.5. REHABILITATION COUNCIL OF INDIA ACT, 1992

This Act came into being to regulate the training of rehabilitation professionals and to maintain a central rehabilitation register to certify rehabilitation professionals. By this Act, RCI has become the apex body to further professional development of those in the field of disability rehabilitation. According to this Act, the term 'rehabilitation professionals' refers to audiologists and speech therapists, clinical psychologists, hearing aid and ear mould technicians, special educators, vocational counsellors and multipurpose rehabilitation therapists. RCI mainly works for ensuring quality training to the service providers of persons with disabilities. This is mainly done through implementation of training policies, ensuring the credibility of service providers by standardizing training courses, eliciting their required qualifications as well as giving appropriate recognition to the institutes and universities which impart the necessary expertise to these potential service providers. Also, a central rehabilitation register of institutions possessing the recognized rehabilitation qualification is maintained with the council.

In sum

Some of the prominent legislative measures in the country are as follows:

- National Policy for Persons with Disabilities
- Persons with Disabilities (Equal Opportunities, Protection of Rights and Full Participation) Act, 1995
- The National Trust for Welfare of Persons with Autism, Cerebral Palsy, Mental Retardation and Multiple Disabilities Act, 1999
- Rehabilitation Council of India Act, 1992

4.9. RECOMMENDATIONS

Looking into the ground reality and available evidence, the following measures are recommended for creating an inclusive approach for children with disability and development disorders:

- Fostering community inclusion by conducting community-based activities and knowledge dissemination, resulting in destigmatization.
- Enhancing the collaboration between service providers, researchers and policymakers to develop need-based and evidence-driven strategies.
- Establishing service-delivery centres where all related services can be brought under one roof so that integrated and holistic management strategies could be planned. This would also address the issues related to conveyance and accessibility.
- Inspiring youngsters to choose courses specialized to meet the dearth in professionals; encouraging professionals to remain active in the service delivery field by providing needed funds and facilities.
- Creating inclusive and disability-friendly infrastructure and curriculum in schools; adopting newer teaching–learning practices in special schools.
- Training teachers to address the needs of children with disability by equipping them with needed skills and equipment in a monitored fashion.
- Motivating the community to tackle issues related to gaps in services, mismanagement of funds and underfunding.
- Reducing/preventing disabilities by altering lifestyle and environmental factors which are proved to cause disability.

4.10. CONCLUSION AND IMPLICATIONS

Care and support services to persons with disabilities involve resources and revisions at multiple levels. In order to utilize the human resources of people with disability, a stigma-free environment must be created, where their rights are respected and preserved, they are treated with dignity, opportunities related to education and employment are supported, their contribution for the society, however small it be, is promoted, and quality of their life is ensured. This needs help from many stakeholders, apart from the main caregivers such as communities around, local bodies of the government and other organizations that can provide infrastructural, economical and legal aids to these people. Protection of rights of children with disability, early identification of their problems and timely intervention would improve the overall quality of life of these children reducing their vulnerability to remain dependent on others, thereby experiencing neglect and leading poor quality of life.

EXERCISES

One-mark Questions

1. What is EBP?
2. Define disability.
3. Explain the term 'dyscalculia'.
4. What is meant by SLD training?
5. What are the LD classifications given by DSM-5?
6. Explain moderate intellectual disability.
7. What do you understand by 'disability-friendly environment'?
8. Expand ADHD.
9. What is community-based rehabilitation?
10. State any two legislative measures taken for disability management in India.

Five-mark Questions

1. Community involvement is the core of disability management. Justify the statement.
2. What are levels of intellectual disability?
3. Critically analyse EBPs.
4. Explain the components of disability.
5. Critically evaluate the role of community stakeholders in creating a disability-friendly environment.
6. Discuss in detail childhood developmental disorder (any two).

Ten-mark Questions

1. Analyse the community-based model on disability management.
2. With the backup of evidence, explain the importance of adopting EBPs for managing disability.
3. Explain any two policies given by the Government of India on disability.
4. Write a note on UNCRPD.

Reflexive Questions

1. How can a community play a positive as well as a negative role in disability management?
2. 'The conditions of persons with disability can be improved by enhancing our legislative frameworks'. Justify the statement with examples.
3. 'Community can play an important role in disability assessment'. Elaborate the statement with relevant examples.
4. Do you think that India, as a nation, has taken constructive steps for the disabled population? Justify.

REFERENCES

American Psychiatric Association. (2013). *Diagnostic and statistical manual of mental disorders* (5th ed.). Author.

American Psychological Association. (2013). Autism spectrum disorder. https://www.apa.org/topics/autism/

Arun, P., Chavan, B. S., Bhargava, R., Sharma, A., & Kaur, J. (2013, July). Prevalence of specific developmental disorder of scholastic skill in school students in Chandigarh, India. *Indian Journal of Medical Research*, *138*, 89–98.

Boat, T. F., & Wu, J. T. (Eds.). (2015). Clinical characteristics of intellectual disabilities. In *Mental disorder and disabilities among low-income children*. National Academics Press.

Bruder, M. B. (2000). Family-centered early intervention: Clarifying our values for the new millennium. *Topics in Early Childhood Special Education*, *20*(2), 105–116.

Bruder, M. B. (2010). Early childhood intervention: A promise to children and families for their future. *Exceptional Children*, *76*(3), 339–355. https://doi.org/10.1177/001440291007600306

Butterworth, B., & Kovas, Y. (2013). Understanding neurocognitive developmental disorders can improve education for all. *Science*, *340*(6130), 300–305. https://doi.org/10.1126/science.1231022

Campbell, P. H. (2004). Participation-based services: Promoting children's participation in natural settings. *Young Exceptional Children*, *8*(1), 20–29. https://doi.org/10.1017/CBO9781107415324.004

Catherine, T. G., Robert, N. G., Mala, K. K., Kanniammal, C., & Arullapan, J. (2019). Assessment of prevalence of attention deficit hyperactivity disorder among schoolchildren in selected schools. *Indian Journal of Psychiatry*, *61*, 232–237. https://doi.org/10.4103/psychiatry.IndianJPsychiatry

Chauhan, A., Sahu, J. K., Jaiswal, N., Kumar, K., Agarwal, A., Kaur, J., Singh, S., & Singh, M. (2019). Prevalence of autism spectrum disorder in Indian children: A systematic review and meta-Analysis. *Neurology India*, *67*(1), 100–104. https://doi.org/10.4103/0028-3886.253970

Coffee, B., Keith, K., Albizua, I., Malone, T., Mowrey, J., Sherman, S. L., & Warren, S. T. (2009). Incidence of fragile X syndrome by newborn screening for methylated FMR1 DNA. *American Journal of Human Genetics*, *85*(4), 503–514. https://doi.org/10.1016/j.ajhg.2009.09.007

Cortiella, C., & H. Horowitz, S. (2014). The state of learning disabilities: Facts, trends and emerging issues. National Center for Learning Disabilities. https://doi.org/10.1002/yd.20269

Danielson, M. L., Bitsko, R. H., Ghandour, R. M., Holbrook, J. R., Kogan, M. D., & Blumberg, S. J. (2018). Prevalence of parent-reported ADHD diagnosis and associated treatment among U.S. children and adolescents, 2016. *Journal of Clinical Child and Adolescent Psychology*, *47*(2), 199–212. https://doi.org/10.1080/15374416.2017.1417860

Edwardraj, S., Mumtaj, K., Prasad, J. H., Kuruvilla, A., & Jacob, K. S. (2010). Perceptions about intellectual disability: A qualitative study from Vellore, South India. *Journal of Intellectual Disability Research*, *54*(8), 736–748. https://doi.org/10.1111/j.1365-2788.2010.01301.x

Elsabbagh, M., Divan, G., Koh, Y. J., Kim, Y. S., Kauchali, S., Marcín, C., Montiel-Nava, C., Patel, V., Paula, C. S., Wang, C., Yasamy, M. T., & Fombonne, E. (2012). Global prevalence of autism and other pervasive developmental disorders. *Autism Research*, *5*(3), 160–179. https://doi.org/10.1002/aur.239

Emerson, E. (2007, July). Poverty and people with intellectual disabilities. *Mental Retardation and Developmental Disabilities Research Reviews, 236,* 228–236. https://doi.org/10.1002/mrdd

European Agency for Development in Special Needs Education. (2005). *Early childhood intervention: Analysis of situations in Europe: Key aspects and recommendations.* Author. https://doi.org/10.1097/00001504-199308000-00012

Fernald, L. C. H., Kariger, P. K., Engle, P., & Raikes, A. (2009). *Examining early child development in low-income countries: A toolkit for the assessment of children in the first five years of life* (pp. 1–133). The World Bank. http://documents.worldbank.org/curated/en/499021468332411850/Examining-early-child-development-in-low-income-countries-a-toolkit-for-the-assessment-of-children-in-the-first-five-years-of-life

Gregor, C. (2006). The UN Convention on the Rights of Persons with Disabilities. *Development, 49,* 158–160. https://doi.org/10.1057/palgrave.development.1100310

Gustafsson, C. (2003). *Intellectual disability and mental health problems : Evaluation of two clinical assessment instruments, occurrence of mental health problems and psychiatric care utilisation.* http://www.diva-portal.org/smash/record.jsf?pid=diva2%3A163146&dswid=9394

Lakhan, R., & Ekúndayò, O. T. (2013). Application of the ecological framework in depression: An approach whose time has come. *Andhra Pradesh Journal of Psychological Medicine, 14*(2), 103–109.

Lakhan, R., Ekúndayò, O. T., & Shahbazi, M. (2015). An estimation of the prevalence of intellectual disabilities and its association with age in rural and urban populations in India. *Journal of Neurosciences in Rural Practice, 6*(4), 523–528. https://doi.org/10.4103/0976-3147.165392

McKenzie, K., Milton, M., Smith, G., & Ouellette-Kuntz, H. (2016). Systematic review of the prevalence and incidence of intellectual disabilities: Current trends and issues. *Current Developmental Disorders Reports, 3*(2), 104–115. https://doi.org/10.1007/s40474-016-0085-7

Medina, J. (2019). Specific learning disorder. https://psychcentral.com/disorders/specific-learning-disorder/

Padhy, S. K., Goel, S., Das, S. S., Sarkar, S., Sharma, V., & Panigrahi, M. (2016). Prevalence and patterns of learning disabilities in school children. *Indian Journal of Pediatrics, 83*(4), 300–306. https://doi.org/10.1007/s12098-015-1862-8

Parker, S. E., Mai, C. T., Canfield, M. A., Rickard, R., Wang, Y., Meyer, R. E., Anderson, P., Mason, C. A., Collins, J. S., Kirby, R. S., & Correa, A. (2010). Updated national birth prevalence estimates for selected birth defects in the United States, 2004–2006. *Birth Defects Research Part A—Clinical and Molecular Teratology, 88*(12), 1008–1016. https://doi.org/10.1002/bdra.20735

Schalock, R. L., Luckasson, R. A., & Shogren, K. A. (2007). The renaming of mental retardation: Understanding the change to the term intellectual disability. *Intellectual and Developmental Disabilities, 45*(2), 116–124.

Shakespeare, T. O. M. (2007). Disability rights and wrongs. *Scandinavian Journal of Disability Research, 9*(3–4), 278–281. https://doi.org/10.1080/15017410701687543

Shaw, M., Hodgkins, P., Caci, H., Young, S., Kahle, J., Woods, A. G., & Arnold, L. E. (2012). A systematic review and analysis of long-term outcomes in attention deficit hyperactivity disorder: Effects of treatment and non-treatment. *BMC Medicine, 10*(1), 99. https://doi.org/10.1186/1741-7015-10-99

Simon, V., Czobor, P., Bálint, S., Mészáros, Á., & Bitter, I. (2009). Prevalence and correlates of adult attention-deficit hyperactivity disorder: Meta-analysis. *British Journal of Psychiatry, 194*(3), 204–211. https://doi.org/10.1192/bjp.bp.107.048827

Skelton, H., & Rosenbaum, P. (2010). *Disability and child development: Integrating the Concepts.*

Suhrheinrich, J., Hall, L. J., Reed, S. R., Stahmer, A. C., & Schreibman, L. (2014). Evidence based interventions in the classroom. In L. A. Wilkinson (Ed.), *School psychology book series* (pp. 151–172). American Psychological Association.

US Department of Education. 2004. *Individuals with Disabilities Education Act Amendments.* Author.

UNICEF. (2018). *Disabilities.* Author.

Venkata, J. A., & Panicker, A. S. (2013). Prevalence of attention deficit hyperactivity disorder in primary school children. *Indian Journal of Psychiatry, 55*(4), 338–342. https://doi.org/10.4103/0019-5545.120544

Walker, S. P., Wachs, T. D., Grantham-Mcgregor, S., Black, M. M., Nelson, C. A., Huffman, S. L., Baker-Henningham, H., Chang, S. M., Hamadani, J. D., Lozoff, B., Gardner, J. M. M., Powell, C. A., Rahman, A.,

& Richter, L. (2011). Inequality in early childhood: Risk and protective factors for early child development. *The Lancet, 378*(9799), 1325–1338. https://doi.org/10.1016/S0140-6736(11)60555-2

Weiss, J. A., Baker, J. K., & Butter, E. M. (2016). *Mental health treatment for people with autism spectrum disorder (ASD).* American Psychological Association.

Wong, C., Odom, S. L., Hume, K. A., Cox, A. W., Fettig, A., Kucharczyk, S., Brock, M. E., Plavnick, J. B., Fleury, V. P., & Schultz, T. R. (2015). Evidence-based practices for children, youth, and young adults with autism spectrum disorder: A comprehensive review. *Journal of Autism and Developmental Disorders, 45*(7), 1951–1966. https://doi.org/10.1007/s10803-014-2351-z

Woods, J. J., & Lindeman, D. P. (2008). Gathering and giving information with families. *Infants & Young Children, 21*(4), 272–284. https://depts.washington.edu/isei/iyc/21.4_woods.pdf

World Health Organization. (2009). *Disabilities.* https://www.who.int/topics/disabilities/en/

World Health Organization. (2011). *World report on disability.* Author. https://doi.org/10.1136/ip.2007.018143

World Health Organization. (2012). *Early childhood development and disability: A discussion paper.* Author. https://apps.who.int/iris/bitstream/handle/10665/75355/9789241504065_eng.pdf;jsessionid=6E38B11944FD74D615911DEA299F6FDB?sequence=1

World Health Organization. (2019). Autism spectrum disorders. https://doi.org/10.1016/j.aidsoi.2018.12.001

World Health Organization. (2020). *Intellectual disability.* https://www.who.int/topics/disabilities/en/

RECOMMENDED READINGS

Dempsey, I. J., & Nankervis, K. (Eds.). (2006). *Community disability services: An evidence-based approach to practice.* Purdue University Press.

Geisen, T., & Harder, H. G. (Eds.). (2011). *Disability management and workplace integration: International research findings.* Gower Publishing.

Mitchell, D., & Karr, V. (Eds.). (2014). *Crises, conflict and disability: Ensuring equality.* Routledge.

Rennie, J. (Ed.). (2007). *Learning disability: Physical therapy treatment and management, a collaborative approach.* John Wiley & Sons.

Rummery, K. (2017). *Disability, citizenship and community care: A case for welfare rights?* Routledge.

Community-based Intervention for the Elderly

ABSTRACT

The role of elderly people is equally important in the family and in the society, if not more like the younger ones. An elderly person's lifelong experience is a valuable asset for the next generation in every aspect. They are the sources of knowledge and guide the family members of the next generation in the right direction. Grandchildren enjoy their childhood with grandparents, who are active listeners for their grandchildren, and they enjoy each other's company. Ironically, in today's society, the concept of joint family is disappearing and grandchildren miss the opportunity to live with grandparents. This chapter intends to discuss a range of challenges experienced by the elderly people such as loneliness, neglect, humiliation, psychological and even physical violence in addition to various health-related problems. Some even require special care or palliative care. Further, the chapter emphasizes family-based intervention and social support to address the issues and challenges of the elderly people. The perception of the elderly people about available support services has also been assessed and discussed in the chapter. The issues related to positive ageing is also highlighted in the chapter, in addition to discussing the strengths and weaknesses of the National Policy for Protection of the Rights of Aged People.

Keywords: Elderly people; role; India; violence; neglect; contribution

5.1. INTRODUCTION

Ageing is a normal phenomenon in life. However, it has become a serious public health concern for policymakers and administrators worldwide since the increasing number of elderly people impacts social policy, economics and social work practice. Nevertheless, elderly people are equally resourceful, and their contribution is significant in the family and society like all other citizens. They might have retired from the services or some of them are not physically very active or dependent on others, but most valuable resources the family and society get from the elderly people are their guidance, lifelong knowledge and experience and, most importantly, their love and affection for all family members and their role as counsellors in the family. They always guide the younger members of the family for their proper upbringing, welfare and happiness. In turn, they feel happy when everybody is happy in the family. They are best friends for the grandchildren and, in turn, grandchildren also enjoy their association as they find them very good listeners and playmates and make jokes and fun with them, in addition to telling stories or sharing their childhood experiences to their grandchildren. In fact, elderly people's presence in the family is a big relief for working parents as they can leave their children under the care of the grandparents while they go for work. Indian cultural values like respecting elderly people, like other citizens, and taking care of them during their old age is highly appreciated worldwide. In general, in India, elderly people are not sent to old-age homes like in the Western countries until there is a compulsion in the family, that is, children living in urban apartments (small) or they live abroad for service. Therefore, there is a need to nurture Indian cultural values, respecting the elderly and taking care of them when they are unable to lead an independent life.

5.2. EPIDEMIOLOGY OF GLOBAL ELDERLY POPULATION

The volume of elderly people is increasing across the world because of improved health facilities and living environments. It is estimated that there were 617 million people above the age of 65 worldwide in 2015 and the number of it will jump to 1.6 billion by 2050 (United States Census Bureau, 2015). They can contribute towards social and economic development if they are active and not suffering from any major health problem. Sadly, a large number of them are suffering from some sort of old age-related problems and are not able to lead an independent life.

According to *An Aging World* report (United States Census Bureau, 2015), the global life expectancy at birth has been projected to increase by eight years, that is from 68.6 years in 2015 to 76.2 years in 2050. Further, the report projected that US's population of above 65 will become double by 2050, from 48 million to 88 million. Regarding the global oldest population, that is for people aged 80 and above, it is projected by the same report that their number would be three times or more by 2050 (from 126.5 million in 2015 to 446.6 million by 2050).

Further, the latest data from the World Population Prospects: The 2017 Revision (United Nations, 2017) highlights that the percentage of elderly people above 60 would be more than double by 2050 and more than triple by 2100, that is, increasing 962 million (13% of the global population) globally in 2017 to 2.1 billion in 2050 and 3.1 billion in 2100.

It is projected that the global elderly population will increase steadily from 962 million in 2017 to 3.1 billion by 2100 (Table 5.1).

TABLE 5.1
Projected Global Population

Year	Population in Billion
2030	1.4
2050	2.1
2100	3.1

Source: United Nations (2017).

5.3. ELDERLY PEOPLE IN INDIA

Like the global population, the number of the elderly people in India is also increasing and the same trend will continue. The percentage of elderly people above 60 is estimated to jump from 8 per cent in 2015 to 19 per cent by 2050 in India. It is also estimated that by the end of the century, about one-third of the total population of India will be the elderly people. The increasing trend of the elderly people in India varies from state to state. For example, the percentage of elderly people is highest in Kerala (12.3%), followed by Tamil Nadu (11.2%) and lowest in Assam (6.5%). Some of the states of North India, namely Himachal Pradesh (10.3%), Maharashtra (9%), Odisha (9%) and Punjab (9.7%) have a greater number of elderly people. Like Assam, Delhi (6.5%) being a union territory is also witnessing a less increasing trend of elderly people. Other states which are having less number of elderly people in India are Jharkhand (7.1%), Uttar Pradesh (7.1%), Madhya Pradesh (7.1%), Bihar (7.2%), Rajasthan (7.3%), Chhattisgarh (7.9%) and Uttarakhand (8.5%; United Nations Population Fund, 2017).

5.3.1. CHARACTERISTICS OF ELDERLY PEOPLE IN INDIA

Among the total elderly people in India, the percentage of women is more. Loss of husband during old age makes a woman more vulnerable to neglect and abuse. As per 2011 Census concerning distribution of the elderly people, it has been observed that more than two-fifth (66%) of women are currently married while 32 per cent are widowed and about 3 per cent are separated or divorced.

Interestingly, the majority (71%) of the elderly people live in rural India, except two smaller states, Goa and Mizoram. The elderly people living in rural areas confront a number of challenges since road conditions, transport facilities, poor health facilities, poor social support facilities and lack of source of earning contribute to the same.

Migration of the younger generation from the rural areas to the urban areas in search of work has badly impacted the quality of life of the elderly people, although migration met the demand of workers in the urban areas. Himachal Pradesh (92.4%) is having the maximum percentage of elderly people living in rural areas followed by Bihar (89.1%), Arunachal Pradesh (88.6%), and Orissa (86.3%) and so on. On the other hand, the states/union territories where least number of elderly people reside include Goa (40.2%), Mizoram (47.4) and Kerala (52.4%; United Nations Population Fund, 2017).

As per the report, Tamil Nadu is the state where the maximum percentage (13.7%) of elderly people live alone, followed by Nagaland (10.9%), Andhra Pradesh (8.0%) and Meghalaya (8.0%).

In sum

Ageing is a natural phenomenon in life. It is the last stage of life. Worldwide, the number of aged people is increasing. India is not an exception. The percentage of increase might vary from country to country or one geographic region to another. It is projected that 617 million elderly people worldwide in 2015 (above 65) will reach to 1.6 billion by 2050. In India, the people above 60 will jump from 8 per cent in 2015 to 19 per cent by 2050. In India, the majority of the elderly people live in rural areas and the percentage of women is more in this category. Therefore, public health policymakers should plan social and economic policies accordingly to meet the emerging challenges.

5.4. ROLE OF ELDERLY PEOPLE IN THE FAMILY

As stated in the earlier section, the role of the elderly people in the family is very important. They play multiple roles and it depends upon family structure, family size, and socio-economic background of the family. However, the overall welfare of the family members is the ultimate outlook of the elderly people. In particular, they guide their children in leading a disciplined, decent and comfortable life. They play the role of a counsellor when a crisis arises in terms of conflict in interpersonal relationship within the family, act as liaison officer with other family members and community members by keeping regular touch with them, shopping, and daily marketing, looking after grandchildren, playing with them and telling them stories. Nevertheless, the role of elderly people also varies from rural areas to urban areas. Elderly people who live in urban areas are either living in their own house or flat or do not have much work as compared to the rural people. Elderly people in rural areas work very hard. They not only look after the daily issues of the family, but they also work in the agriculture fields and look after livestock animals as long as their health permits. To them, agriculture is their mother, since it gives them bread and butter. Elderly people who are very poor work as casual workers for their survival even if their health do not permit.

5.4.1. PERCEPTION OF THE FAMILY MEMBERS ABOUT THE ROLE OF ELDERLY PEOPLE IN THE FAMILY

Perception of family members about the elderly people varies across countries and communities. In Western countries, the social structure is totally different from that of the developing countries. In Western countries like the USA and UK, the majority of the elderly people live in old-age homes after a certain age and it is a common practice. In developing countries like India, elderly people mostly live with other family members and others look after them and provide them proper care. However, over a period of time, there has been a change in the social structure. The concept of joint family has changed over time and growing trend of nuclear family has emerged due to urbanization, lack of land, poverty, and change in occupational patterns. As a result, emerging trends of nuclear family—for obvious reasons—adversely impacted the life of the elderly people and people hold different perceptions about it.

Despite the change in social structure—in some Indian communities—elderly people are highly respected. Younger generations listen to them and take their advice for their career and related issues. In these communities, elderly people are the main decision-makers. Whereas in some communities, elderly people are judged based on their physical strength and resources available with them, out of the expectation of the share of their resources. As long as elderly people are independent and are able to look after themselves, others do not consider them as a burden. The moment they become dependent for their essential tasks or fall sick, which involves money, initially the family members do the needful. Slowly, with the passage of time, family members and even their children start feeling stressed and consider them as liabilities. Like Western countries, old-age homes are coming up in most of the cities in India. Some families do not have the manpower to look after the elderly once the children go to work. In some families, elders are perceived as burdens. Therefore, due to various reasons, the people, who can afford, send their parents to old-age homes.

In sum

The role of elderly people is very important in the family and in the society. They play multiple roles if they are active. Their knowledge and lifelong experiences benefit the family and the next generation. They guide the next generation and act a counsellor during any crisis in the family and give quality time to the grandchildren in terms of telling them stories and inculcating values. In some communities, they are highly respected while in some communities, they are considered a burden if they become dependent on others.

5.5. PROBLEMS FACED BY THE ELDERLY PEOPLE IN THE FAMILY

While some elderly people enjoy their old age because of cultural values of their family, their good health and wealth and other reasons, a good number of them also experience various challenges within the family. This is very unfortunate. However, sometimes it is perceived because of a change of role in the family after retirement and sometime, it is genuine. Some elderly people after retirement feel empty and without any work, they feel idle, neglected and lose their temperament with others in the family for minor issues, which cause relationship problems. There are also instances where it has been observed that wives are unable to tolerate the presence of their husbands in the family after retirement. It happens perhaps because of certain conditioning. All these days (for a long period) wives, who were not working, became habituated to leading different lifestyles after the departure of the husband for office. They used to do different household works on their own or any outside work. All of a sudden, although the husband's retirement is expected—when he stays at home during office hours—it causes irritation for some of the wives and they are unable to accept the change in lifestyles, resulting in conflict in the relationship.

Nevertheless, a good number of elderly people experience other challenges and these include feeling of neglect, poor status in the family because of retirement or poor health conditions, lack of respect from others, ignorance by others/not consulting them for any family-related issues, not listening to their views and suggestions and even psychological and physical abuse (Acierno et al., 2010; Lachs & Pillemer, 1995). There are instances where parents were denied timely food, medical care and even confined in rooms for a long period, since they did not sign the property to the children or did not sign the cheque (Hindustan Times, 2019).

The term, elder abuse, covers a range of maltreatment of elderly people and they include mostly neglect, psychological, physical and sexual abuse, in addition to property and financial fraud. All such types of abuse are experienced by elderly people when they are financially weak, lack social support and support from extended family members, poor social network or when they become dependent on others and/or are bedridden. Most common risk factors for elderly abuse, as revealed by previous research, include age, race, low-income status, functional or cognitive impairment, a history of family violence, and stressful situation in life (Lachs et al., 1997; Paris et al., 1995).

Evidence from earlier community-based surveys demonstrate that between 3 per cent and 10 per cent of individuals over the age of 65 experience various types of elderly abuse, neglect, or both (Comijs et al., 1998; Cupitt, 1997; Hogstel & Curry, 1999). Reporting of abuse to the police or any other authority is very low because of various reasons like, not being aware where to report, fear of further abuse, having no faith in the system, not wanting to disclose the incident of abuse to outsiders as it might tarnish family image. Evidence indicates that only one in five reported the incident to appropriate authority (National Center on Elder Abuse, 1998).

A number of studies in the middle east and Arab region found elderly abuse and it was more among women (69.4%), the widowed (65.9%), or the functionally dependent (82.7%; Sharon & Zoabi, 1997; Zoabi, 1994). A study carried out among elderly Jews observed 8% fraud (Lehman, 1989).

The study of HelpAge India carried in Puducherry observed that about one-fifth (18%) of the elderly people reported experience of being abused. However, the study did not focus on the specific nature of abuse experienced by the elderly people in Puducherry. Shockingly, about half of them did experience the same for the last five years or more at the hands of their biological sons and daughters-in-law (The Hindu, 2012, p. 2). The same study further reported that lack of adjustment, psychological and economic dependence were the main reasons behind elderly abuse.

The findings of Population Ageing in India (BKPAI) survey (2011), which was carried out in seven states—Himachal Pradesh, Kerala, Maharashtra, Odisha, Punjab, Tamil Nadu and West Bengal—revealed that 'about 11% of the elderly people reported experience of different forms of abuse, mostly by the elders who lived alone and had low levels of education and poor economic status'. The perpetrators were mostly family members and neighbours, as revealed. This was a collaborative study by the Government of India and The United Nations Population Fund.

One empirical study, carried out in Kolkata, disclosed a very disturbing picture that is 87 per cent women reported feelings of insecurity at their own house as compared to 16 per cent male elderly people (p < 0.01). Further, a large number of elderly female (82%) shared that they experienced neglect at their own house. The percentage of neglect reported by male elderly people was very negligible (7%) as compared to female elderly people. It might be because of their lifestyle, that is, staying at home most of the time and not getting expected attention from the family members and younger ones in the family, while elderly male members comparatively spend some time outside the family and stay less time in the family as compared to their counterparts. Mental harassment in the hands of family members as reported by female elderly people was another issue of serious concern. About 15 per cent female and 9.0 per cent female elderly people shared that they experienced physical abuse too (Paul, 2013). This is unfortunate and it requires reporting to the police. In most of the cases, parents do not report the incidents of physical and psychological violence to the police and bear it silently. Parents do not report the incident to the police as they do not want their children's image to be tarnished. Their over affection also discourages them not to report the incident of abuse or harassment to the relatives or police. This sort of gesture of elderly people encourages their children to cross their limits and forget their duties and responsibilities towards their parents. If any such incident is reported, it would be a lesson for other children and in turn, other parents will be safer.

One recent incident in Chennai is a bright example of the status of elderly people—especially women—after death of their husbands and in the grid of their biological children. The incident did not happen in a poverty-stricken family. It happened in an educated, wealthy and well-connected family. The wife of a former Member of Parliament of Tamil Nadu was stabbed to death by her own son over a property dispute on 14 April 2019. The couple have two daughters and a son who lives in the UK. The son came to India and demanded his share from the family property. Regarding this issue, there was an argument with the mother and since his desire was not easily fulfilled, he stabbed his mother and escaped (The Hindu, 2019, p. 2). The incident is shameful and it raises a question about the security of elderly people, especially when it happens within the family and even in the hands of the biological children. The issue also raises a question about the upbringing of the children and the values imparted to the children. If one does a research on the issue, one might find some clue about the mindset of the child, which is whether he did this because of his desire for taking family share to lead a better life in the UK or he did it out of instigation from his wife to bring his share to the UK. Whatever might be the reason, this incident talks about strengthening of value-based education in the schools. If value-based education is imparted in the schools, perhaps, children will not indulge in similar shameful incidents.

Latest study by HelpAge India study disclosed that more than half (60%) of the elder persons participated in the study and confirmed that they experienced abuse. Of those who reported experience of abuse, 88 per cent of them believed its existence is high. Nearly one-fourth (25%) reported that both men and women experienced abuse in different forms like disrespect (56%), verbal abuse (49%) and neglect (33%). The main perpetrators were son (57%) and daughter-in-law (38%). About one-fifth (18%) elderly persons reported the incident (HelpAge India, 2018).

Acierno et al. (2010) undertook a study to ascertain the prevalence and correlates of emotional, physical, sexual and financial mistreatment and potential neglect experienced by people aged 60 years and above in a randomly selected 5777 national sample. Findings disclosed that 'one-year prevalence was 4.6% for emotional abuse, 1.6% for physical abuse, 0.6% for sexual abuse, 5.1% for potential neglect and 5.2% for current financial abuse by a family member. One in 10 respondents reported emotional, physical, or sexual mistreatment or potential neglect in the past year. The most consistent correlates of mistreatment across abuse types were low social support and previous traumatic event exposure'.

In general—in the Asian Countries—elder people are highly respected and adequate care is extended to them when they require it. Although respecting elder people is a cultural practice in the Asian countries. Over a period of time, social dynamics and outlook have been changing which slowly impacted the cultural values. As a result, society is witnessing degeneration of human values and people are becoming more self-centric and wish to achieve everything following a shortcut. Elderly abuse is one of the symptoms of degeneration of social values. In this regard, a number of studies have been carried out in China. One cross-sectional study by Dong et al. (2007) made an attempt to find out the prevalence of elder abuse and neglect in an urban Chinese population following self-administration method. Out of a total of 412 participants, 145 (35%) reported experiencing abuse and neglect. The mean age of the victims was 69 years and more than half (59%) were men. Elder people reported experience of neglect in the hands of the caregiver. The nature of abuse experienced by them includes financial exploitation, psychological abuse, physical abuse, sexual abuse, and abandonment. More than one-third (36%) reported multiple sufferings. So far as association of elderly abuse is concerned, data indicates that female gender, low education and low income were the risk factors for elderly abuse and neglect. After five years, Lai (2011) attempted to ascertain the incidents of abuse and neglect and the associated correlates based on the data collected from a random sample of 2,272 ageing Chinese people, who were 55 years and older in seven Chinese cities. The findings disclosed that

> 4.5% of the participants reported experiencing at least one incident of maltreatment or neglect within the past year. The most common forms of neglect and abuse experienced by the ageing Chinese include being scolded, yelled at, treated impolitely all the time, and ridiculed. Close family members such as spouses and sons are those that most commonly maltreat older Chinese. Those who were more likely to report at least one incident of maltreatment or neglect were older adults living with others; they tended to have no education, more access barriers, more chronic illnesses, less favorable mental health, and a higher level of identification with Chinese cultural values. (Lai, 2011)

Another study carried out in a major urban medical centre in Nan Jing, China by Dong et al. (2008) made an attempt to figure out depression among elder people and elderly abuse. The study found that 12 per cent of the elderly people were suffering from depression while 35 per cent of them experienced abuse and neglect. Further, multiple logistical regressions disclosed that 'the factors which were associated with elderly abuse include a feeling of dissatisfaction with life, often being bored, often feeling helpless, and feeling worthless. Multiple logistic regression modelling showed that depression is independently associated with elderly abuse and neglect. Finally, the study highlighted that depression is a significant risk factor associated with elderly abuse and neglect among Chinese elders'. In this regard, Kraaij and de Wilde (2001) found that 'negative life events experienced during childhood and adulthood had a much stronger association with depressive symptoms in later life, signifying that there is a need to gather information about adversities experienced during childhood and adulthood while dealing with mental health issues of elderly people'.

Homer and Gilleard (1990) undertook a study to ascertain the prevalence of elderly abuse by their caregivers and the characteristics of the abusers and the abused. The study disclosed that 45 per cent of carers openly admitted abusing elderly people in some form. Few patients also admitted experiencing abuse. Alcohol dependence of carers was one of the significant risk factors of elderly physical abuse. Other risk factors include poor premorbid relationship and previous abuse experienced by the caregivers over many years. Social dysfunction was also applicable to some elderly abuse. Migrant elderly people are more vulnerable to abuse as found by Iecovich (2005).

WHO conducted a *World Values Survey* covering 83,000 respondents from 57 countries to assess the level of discrimination and negative attitudes toward older adults. The study disclosed that '60% of the older people aren't respected, as reported'. Surprisingly, elder people receive the least respect in the high-income countries.

5.5.1. CRIME AGAINST ELDERLY PEOPLE IN INDIA (2015)

Crime in India data (2015) indicates that a total of 20,532 Indian Penal Code (IPC) crimes were registered by the elderly people above 60 years in India during 2015, indicating an increase of 9.7 per cent crimes against them as compared to total registered cases of crime in 2014. Cheating was the highest crime (1,867 cases) experienced by elderly people in 2015, followed by robbery (1,294 cases), murder (1,053 cases) and grievous hurt (949 cases).

If we look at the crime scenario, state and union territory-wise as registered in 2015, it has been observed that Maharashtra is on top, followed by Madhya Pradesh, Andhra Pradesh and Tamil Nadu.

So far as disposal of cases is concerned, charge sheets were submitted in case of 13,880 reported complaints out of 20,532 in 2015 while 1,649 cases ended in conviction. About 2,709 cases ended in acquittal/discharge. A total of 2,343 persons were convicted and 4,172 were acquitted or discharged (Table 5.2).

TABLE 5.2
Disposal of IPC Cases under Crime against Senior Citizens during 2015

Sl No.	Disposal Status	Cases Registered	Person Arrested
1.	Reported/Arrested	20,532	23,615
2.	Charge sheets submitted	13,880	21,401
3.	Convicted	1,649	2,343
4.	Acquitted/Discharged	2,709	4,172

Source: Crime in India (2015).
Note: Disposal during the year may include pending cases of previous year awaiting disposal.

In sum

Elderly people face a range of challenges in the family and in society. It is more in number if they become dependent. The nature of challenges faced by them includes neglect, humiliation, and even physical abuse, as disclosed by secondary evidence. Some reported that the younger generation do not respect them. Crime in India's data shows increase of crime against elderly people across the country and it is more in Maharashtra, followed by Madhya Pradesh, Andhra Pradesh and Tamil Nadu. The most common forms of crimes against elderly people are cheating, robbery, murder and grievous hurt.

5.6. MENTAL HEALTH OF ELDERLY PEOPLE

It is very important for every individual to remain psychologically healthy to enjoy life and to lead a meaningful life by contributing to the society and maintaining healthy interpersonal relationships. Good mental health of an individual depends upon a number of factors. Any individual at any age is vulnerable to any type of mental health problem. However, people during old age generally suffer from loneliness, feeling of neglect, anxiety, depression, dementia and so on. People engaged in some activities and those who are physically active are less vulnerable to mental health challenges. Also, people who are financially well off remain psychologically stronger because of financial security. Dependence on others and even biological children during old age makes a person psychologically weaker. Let us see what evidence says about mental health status of elderly people. For example, Dyer et al. (2000) undertook a case control study in Baylor College of Medicine Geriatrics Clinic at the Harris County Hospital District, Houston, Texas and found that 'there was a statistically significant higher prevalence of depression (62% vs 12%) and dementia (51% vs 30%) in victims of self-neglect, compared to patients referred for other reasons. Further, the study highlights a high prevalence of depression as well as dementia in mistreated older people'. In another study, Paluska and Schwenk (2000) observed that 'increased aerobic exercise or strength training reduces depressive symptoms significantly among elder people. However, habitual physical activity has not been shown to prevent the onset of depression. Anxiety symptoms and panic disorder also improve with regular exercise, and beneficial effects appear to equal meditation or relaxation. In general, acute anxiety responds better to exercise than chronic anxiety. It has also been found that excessive physical activity may lead to overtraining and generate psychological symptoms that mimic depression'.

There is always a debate about the benefits of faith of an individual on religion, which is, whether religiosity helps an individual to remain mentally happy. In this regard, Moreira-Almeida et al. (2006) made an attempt to find out the relationship between religiosity and mental health through meta-analysis. Findings revealed that 'the majority of well-conducted studies highlights that higher levels of religious involvement are positively associated with indicators of psychological well-being (life satisfaction, happiness, positive affect, and higher morale) and with less depression, suicidal thoughts and behaviour, drug/alcohol use/abuse. Usually, the positive impact of religious involvement on mental health is more robust among people under stressful circumstances (the elderly, and those with disability and medical illness)'. Therefore the issue may be promoted among elderly people across the society to help them remain psychologically happy and healthy.

Further, in a secondary study Koenig (2009) observed that 'religious beliefs and practices can represent powerful sources of comfort, hope, and meaning, and they are often intricately entangled with neurotic and psychotic disorders'. At the same time, Koenig remarked, based on secondary evidence, that sometimes it is difficult to determine whether religious and spiritual faith or practice are a resource or a liability.

With regard to the mental health of elderly people, Kolkata-based study disclosed that psychologically male elderly people especially were in better state of mind in terms of subjective happiness than their female counterparts (Paul, 2013). It was also observed that unmarried elderly people were more satisfied in life than their female counterparts.

Regarding the psychological adjustment of the elderly people, Guglani et al. (2000) carried out a study to compare the psychological adjustment of grandmothers from nuclear and extended families within British Hindu communities and also investigated the influence of cultural identity. The authors found that 'grandmothers were better adjusted in extended families than in nuclear families. This adjustment was, in part, mediated by the level of traditional beliefs within the family. Elders whose granddaughters had an exclusively Indian or Hindu ethnic identity were better adjusted than those whose granddaughters had a British ethnic identity'.

Social network of an individual in a every phase of life plays a very important role. Whenever somebody is upset for some reason or is in difficult situation, they can meet their friends and well-wishers and discuss the problem. In turn, they feel happy and relaxed since they could share the problem with reciprocation. In general, people with low social network and support facilities feel psychologically weak and struggle a lot when they encounter any problem. In this regard, Fiori et al. (2006) conducted a study 'to test the previous social network research and extend this work to determine if support quality is one mechanism by which network types predict mental health, covering 1,669 adults, aged 60 or above, from the Americans' Changing Lives study. Authors found two types of restricted networks, rather than just one: a non-family network and a non-friends network. Depressive symptomatology was highest for individuals in the non-friends network and lowest for individuals in the diverse network. Positive support quality partially mediated the association between network type and depressive symptomatology. Results suggest that the absence of family in the context of friends is less detrimental than the absence of friends in the context of family, and that support quality is one mechanism through which network types affect mental health'.

People of the third gender experience a range of challenges across the society because of their low social acceptance, poor social network and support facilities. Since there is not much research on the third gender, D'Augelli et al. (2001) explored the mental health status of the third gender by covering a group of 416 lesbian, gay and bisexual adults, aged 60–91 years old, who were attending social and recreational programmes. More precisely, the authors tried to understand the status of self-esteem, internalized homophobia, loneliness, alcohol and drug abuse, and suicidality. Findings revealed that 'better mental health was correlated with higher self-esteem, less loneliness, and lower internalized homophobia. Compared to women, men reported significantly more internalized homophobia, alcohol abuse, and suicidality related to their sexual orientation. Less lifetime suicidal ideation was associated with lower internalized homophobia, less loneliness, and more people knowing about participants' sexual orientation.'

5.6.1. GENERAL MENTAL HEALTH AND SUBJECTIVE WELL-BEING

Globally mental health challenges contribute to 13 per cent of the global burden of diseases which is more among the elderly people. The BKPAI survey collected data using the 12-item General Health Questionnaire (GHQ) and the 9-item Subjective Well-being Inventory (SUBI). Data collected through GHQ indicates that about 50 per cent of the older persons have been suffering from some form of psychological distress which becomes more with the advancement of age while SUBI inventory also highlights similar trends. When elderly people suffer from chronic mental health problems, it becomes a big challenge for them since it involves a lot of expenditure. Second, non-availability of trained mental health professionals is the reason for which a large number of elderly people remain unattended, both in urban and rural areas. In rural areas, they hardly receive any treatment (Alam et al., 2015).

5.6.2. Health Seeking Behaviour of Elder People for Mental Health

Generally speaking, people across society, especially in the developing countries, social stigma is attached to mental health problems, which discourages people to seek mental health support services. At the same time, the reality is that there is dearth of trained mental health professionals in the developing countries. The number of institutions for the training of mental health professionals is limited. In a country like India, where population is a major problem and about one-fourth to one-fifth people live below the poverty line, people are more vulnerable to mental health challenges. Unfortunately, elderly people are treated as burdens in the family in some communities, especially in families with poor financial conditions. Although, it is very difficult to make a generalized statement in this regard, there are families with poor financial conditions where elderly people are respected and they receive proper care from the family. However, in general, the mental health of elderly people is not the priority of the family. They remain neglected when they suffer from mental health problems. Visiting mental health professionals for mental health challenges of elderly people is a rare practice in developing countries like India, until the situation is very severe. Lack of knowledge about the problem and support facilities is another hindering factor towards seeking mental health support services.

With regard to social stigma in the context of health-seeking behaviour of elderly people related to mental health, Conner et al. (2010) examined the impact of public stigma (negative attitudes held by the public) and internalized stigma (negative attitudes held by stigmatized individuals about themselves) on racial differences in treatment-seeking attitudes and behaviours among older adults with depression. The study found that

> Stigma associated with having a mental illness has a negative influence on attitudes and intentions toward seeking mental health services among older adults with depression, particularly African American elders, than their counterparts. Interventions to target internalized stigma are needed to help engage this population in psychosocial mental health treatments. (Conner et al., 2010)

In sum

Elderly people, irrespective of gender and socio-economic backgrounds, are vulnerable to various mental health problems. Among them, a feeling of loneliness and feeling of neglect are the most common. Other mental health problems are dementia, depression and anxiety. Social stigma is the main barrier towards seeking mental health support services. Lack of availability of trained mental health professionals is another challenge for which elderly people remain unattended. Neglect of the family towards seeking mental health support services is also very common.

5.7. PHYSICAL HEALTH STATUS OF ELDERLY PEOPLE

After 65 years, an individual remains vulnerable to a range of health problems like physical disability, vision-related problems, cardiac problems, dementia and so on. People leading disciplined lives, have a balanced diet, does regular exercise, not taking much stress in early days, and are not dependent on substance, reasonably remains healthy than their counterparts. However, environment and socio-economic status of an individual plays significant roles in the physical health of an individual. People who live in a pollution-free environment and having a happy and stress-free family life enjoy good health. The quality of diet also matters. Finally, people with good financial conditions remain healthy after attaining 70 and even above as they can afford health expenditure, consult good doctors as and when required and undergo medication. A number of studies are carried out on the health status of elderly people and findings vary from country to country although there are some similarities.

Findings of a Kolkata-based study also revealed that

> 81.5% elderly people were suffering from either major or minor ailments like (i) instability, fall, arthritis, movement disorder, pain in bones and joints, osteoporosis (45.5%), (ii) urinary incontinence, constipation, nocturnal enuresis, loss of sphineteric tone (31.0%), (ii) cataract, narrowing of visual field, glaucoma, retinopathy, retinal detachment, color vision (30.0%), (iv) deafness, progressive loss of hearing, otitis media (11.5%), and so on. (Paul, 2013)

Disability is very common during old age which does not allow them to remain connected to their social network, which they develop over a period of time, resulting in dependence and becoming vulnerable to neglect. As per the Census 2011 data, 'the disability rate was 51.8 per 1,000 for the elderly and 84.1 per 1,000 for the 80-plus population as compared to 22.1 per 1,000 of the general population'. Elderly people above 80—especially women—experience more disability than their counterparts.

Wiglesworth et al. (2010) found that

> 47.3% elderly people experienced mistreatment in the hands of caregivers. The findings suggest important characteristics of older adults with dementia and their CGs that have potential for use in a clinical screening tool for elder mistreatment. Potential screening questions to be asked of CGs to the people with dementia are suggested.

In a 6-year prospective cohort study of the institutionalized elderly living in 29 of the 30 institutions for the elderly in Kitakyushu, Japan, Shimazaki et al. (2001) observed that 'poorer dentition status, especially edentulousness without dentures is the reason for deterioration in the systemic health of the aged'.

Cohen et al. (2006) intended to measure the impact of professionally conducted community-based cultural programmes on the physical health, mental health, and social activities of individuals aged 65 and above. The findings revealed positive results, that is 'intervention groups reported a higher overall rating of physical health, fewer doctor visits, less medication use, fewer instances of falls, and few other health problems than the comparison group. The intervention group also evidenced better morale and less loneliness than the comparison group. In terms of activity levels, the comparison group evidenced a significant decline in the total number of activities, whereas the intervention group reported a trend toward increased activity. The positive impact of participatory art programmes for older adults in this study on overall health, doctor visits, medication use, falls, loneliness, morale, and activities reflect important health promotion and prevention effects and a reduction of risk factors driving the need for long-term care'.

Bhutan is on top in terms of happiness index in the world. However, not much empirical evidence is available on the mental health status of elderly people in Bhutan. Given the scarcity of data on elderly people, Dorji et al. (2017) conducted a study to find out the

> associations between quality of life (QOL), spirituality, social integration, chronic diseases, and lifetime adversity among people aged 60 years and above, in Bhutan, covering 337 elder people aged between 60 to

101 years. Findings revealed that frequent back pain, memory decline, depression, mobility impairment, insomnia, and lung diseases were common among elderly people, especially among women in Bhutan. Further data analysis disclosed that "cumulative health problems, psychological distress, and social connectedness contributed significantly to the overall QOL.

In another study in Bhutan, it has been observed that 'close family integration and interpersonal harmony, respect for the older people, spirituality, chronic health conditions and adverse childhood experiences, lack of education, insufficient income and, changes in the sources of practical help in the community influenced quality of life of the elderly people' (Dorji et al., 2018).

In sum

The physical health problems that are common among the elderly people include instability, fall, arthritis, movement disorder, pain in bones and joints, osteoporosis, urinary incontinence, constipation, nocturnal enuresis, loss of sphincteric tone, cataract, narrowing of visual field, glaucoma, retinopathy, retinal detachment, colour vision, deafness, progressive loss of hearing, otitis media and so on.

5.8. ELDERLY PEOPLE: RESOURCE FOR THE SOCIETY

The knowledge and lifelong experience of elderly people are valuable assets for a family and any society. Family members are guided by the experience of elderly people, younger ones get values from them which make them well mannered, responsible, humble, generous and disciplined. At the same time, our society can also utilize their experiences and skills for the training of younger people and/or gaining knowledge from their experiences. For example, the people who retire from school, college and university, can be engaged in teaching even after retirement. Their styles of teaching and knowledge dissemination would be immensely beneficial for young students. Similarly, the people who retired from banks and other government offices may be engaged in NGOs in different capacities and NGOs will be benefitted from their first-hand work experience. The resources of the people who retired from the health sectors may also be engaged in community-based organization for addressing the health needs of the poorest of the poor or in training programmes for creating more health resource persons. These retired people will not have much expectation in terms of salary, but they should be given some honorarium as well as good status and respect. A person after retirement also wishes to be engaged in some work similar to their skills and expertise, which will keep them busy and healthy, psychologically and physically. Therefore, the larger society should utilize the services and expertise of all retired people in different positions and in turn, their contribution will help in an overall socio-economic growth of the society.

At the same time, we observe elderly people in today's society who are greedy and actively engaged in earning quick money through manipulation. They do not have any ethics and their only objective in life is to enjoy power and earn easy money using their social and political networks and probes that are more capable before others. These elderly people also teach their children directly or indirectly how to become rich overnight and manipulate the situation instead of following natural growth and development of the career. They are dangerous for society. They spread their germ and spoil the healthy life of their own children and also adversely affect social values. They become role models for a section of the youth and younger people say that if they are doing the same wrong thing at the age of 70 or above, why cannot we do the same.

In sum

Although people retire after a certain age from their job, their services could be utilized even after their retirement by engaging them in different works like teaching and NGOs or as advisors in different sectors based on their background which will benefit the society.

5.9. ROLE OF OLD-AGE HOMES AND PERCEPTION OF ELDERLY INMATES

Although the concept of old-age homes is very known in the Western countries, in India it is coming up very fast. The number of old-age homes is increasing day by day in all the metropolitan cities and in rural areas in India which shows the demand for the same. A large number of people—when they are unable to look after them or prior to that—prefer to stay in old-age homes for a number of reasons. Some come to old-age homes as they do not wish to cause problem for their children. Some come since nobody is there to look after them or children stay elsewhere for occupation while some wish to lead a life of their choice and so on. Whatever might be the reason, old-age homes are alternatives for a large number of people.

In a Kolkata-based study, it was found that an overwhelming number of the elderly were satisfied in the old-age homes—irrespective of gender—since they lived independently and also received adequate facilities and services there. However, about half of them stated that old-age homes should be neater and cleaner and the quality of food should be improved. A good number of them also suggested that there should be some recreational facilities at the old-age homes. This issue requires the attention of the Home authorities (Paul, 2013).

5.9.1. SOCIAL SUPPORT FOR ELDERLY PEOPLE

Social support is found to be beneficial during crisis in life. Elderly people require social support. In case of any problem, people generally contact their close family members. Likewise, elderly people also do the same as more than 90 per cent preferred to contact their own children and siblings in case of any problem. However, about one-fifth of the elderly people did not receive support.

The concept adopted in Switzerland—that is Time Bank—is a good initiative to make the life of the elderly people comfortable and to get necessary care and support services when they are unable to work and take care of themselves. Anybody can enlist their name for giving care and services to elderly people, who are aged and unable to look after them. Number of hours of services delivered to elderly person in a day will be deposited in their Time Bank and in turn, they can avail the same services when they require the same during old age or if anybody meets any accident. This concept has become very popular in Switzerland and a majority of the Swiss people have become a member of the same bank. The same concept may be replicated elsewhere.

In sum

Old-age homes are catering to the needs of the society. A large number of elderly people across the society find alternate homes where they find people of their age group, and there they can exchange views and discuss their life stories. In turn, they feel happy. In some homes, the quality of services is very good while in some homes, services need improvement. Elderly people who live in their own house and lack manpower need social support from relatives and neighbours. In addition, Time Bank of Switzerland could be introduced in developing countries like India.

5.10. POSITIVE AGEING

The term 'positive ageing' means remaining healthy, both physically and mentally, leading an active life through engagement in some productive activities and remaining connected to people in the community. It is also important to think positively and accept the reality and regulate oneself accordingly. In other words, it means enjoying old age actively like the other phases in life by being a part of the community and larger society to the greatest extent possible. However, there are different connotations of positive ageing in different countries. For example:

According to WHO, the meaning of positive gaining means 'the process of developing and maintaining the functional ability that enables wellbeing in older age'. In the USA, positive ageing means 'it is multidimensional, encompassing the avoidance of disease and disability, the maintenance of high physical and cognitive function, and sustained engagement in social and productive activities'(Rowe & Kahn, 1997) whereas in the UK, the meaning of positive ageing is slightly different. Positive ageing means 'a way of living rather than a state of being'.[1]

The Positive Psychology Institute of Australia defined positive ageing as 'the process of maintaining a positive attitude, feeling good about yourself, keeping fit and healthy, and engaging fully in life as you age'.

In New Zealand, the Ministry of Social Development defined positive ageing as 'reflection of the attitudes and experiences older people have about themselves and how younger generations view the process of ageing. It takes into account the health, financial security, independence, self-fulfilment, personal safety and living environment of older New Zealanders'.

In China, positive ageing denotes 'the criteria are sufficiently inclusive, encompassing physical health, mental health, social engagement, and nutritional status, which in principle are in conformity with both the WHO definition and the Rowe and Kahn model' (Zhou et al., 2018).

In Eastern Europe, 'active ageing is concerned with facilitating the rights of older people to remain healthy (reducing the costs of health and social care), remain in employment longer (reducing pension costs) while also participating in community and political life' (Foster & Walker, 2015).

5.10.1. THEORIES OF POSITIVE AGEING

There are a number of theories related to positive ageing. In the following section, some of the theories are discussed in brief:

1. **Disengagement theory:** This theory is contributed by Elaine Cumming and William E. Henry (1961). According to this theory, people withdraw themselves from social interactions when they become old with a notion that they are going to die soon. According to Elaine Cumming and William E. Henry, there are nine beliefs related to ageing. For example,
   • 'Everyone expects death. Older adults accept that they are losing abilities as they age, so they begin to leave their networks.
   • Fewer contacts create behavioural freedoms. This creates an 'I can do whatever I want' approach to their behaviour.
   • Men and women differ in their experience. Men have instrumental roles. Women do not have.
   • The ego evolves as it ages. The older adult steps aside so the younger person can take over in whatever role the elder leaves. The older person seeks out personal enjoyment.
   • Complete disengagement occurs when society is ready for it. Older adults cannot transition unless society is ready to let them.
   • Disengagement can occur if people lose their roles. Roles are gender-specific. Men do labour. Women handle domestic responsibilities. If they are unable to fulfil their role, then disengagement happens.
   • Readiness equates to societal permission. When an older adult begins pondering their death, sense a loss of status, and lose 'ego energy', then society allows disengagement.
   • Relational rewards become more diverse. Societal rewards tend to include upward mobility. Disengagement creates horizontal rewards. People look to their remaining interpersonal relationships to fill the vertical reward void.
   • This theory is independent of culture. It takes on the norms of the person's culture.'
2. **Activity theory:** This theory is offered by Robert Havighurst in 1961. According to this theory, the elderly people remain engaged in some activities, considering them as productive and enjoy ageing. This theory is similar to the self-determination theory of motivation, which emphasizes autonomy, competence, and relatedness to increase intrinsic motivation. Combining the two concepts of the two theories, one can see why a person feels happy during old age.
3. **Continuity theory:** This theory was offered by Robert Atchley in 1989. This theory is about an ability of an individual to continue the same habits, preferences, lifestyles and maintaining social networks and relationships whey they grow old, that is, they do not much differentiate their habits and lifestyles as they age. In other words, an individual carries their past knowledge, skills and experiences and uses the same, after modifications, when they are old. Continuity are of two types: internal and external. Internal is about our personality traits while external is about our environment.
4. **The life course perspective:** This theory is also known as life course theory. As a concept, a life course is defined as 'a sequence of socially defined events and roles that the individual enacts over time' (Giele & Elder, 1998, p. 22). This theory is multidisciplinary in nature which tries to understand the mental, physical and social health of individuals by incorporating both life span and life stage concepts, resulting in determining the health trajectory. Glen H. Elder Jr theorized life course based on five key principles, which are as follows:
   • '**Life-span development**: Human development and ageing are lifelong processes.
   • **Agency**: Individuals construct their own lives through the choices and actions they make within the opportunities and constraints of history and social circumstance.

- **Time and place**: The life course of individuals is embedded and shaped by the historical time and place they experience over their lifetime.
- **Timing**: The developmental antecedents and consequences of life transitions, events, and behavioural patterns vary according to their timing in a person's life.
- **Linked lives**: Lives are lived interdependently, and socio-historical influences are expressed through this network of shared relationships.'

All the theories are subjected to some forms of criticism. However, all of them have some relevance in interpreting positive ageing.

5.10.2. Living Longer with Good Health

There are different views on this issue. Let us have a look at places in different countries where the life span is more. The places where people live longer are Ikaria (Greece), Loma Linda (California), Sardinia (Italy), Okinawa (Japan), and Nicoya (Costa Rica). These places are called Blue Zones. In this regard, Buettner (2012) conducted a research to understand why people live longer in the Blue Zones and came to the conclusion that nine specific habits helped people of the Blue Zones to live longer in good health. Nine natural habits are, leading easy-going life without thinking much and doing exercises regularly, getting up early in the morning, being able to manage daily life stress easily, eating less, especially in the late afternoon or early evening, having balanced diet and eating more beans, being spiritual, living within the family and having a regular connection with their own social circles.

5.10.3. Positive Ageing Week

Positive Ageing Week is celebrated in many countries across the world which gives happiness to all elderly people. Elderly people feel happy since they get the chance to assemble in one place for celebration of the week through different activities just for them. It first started in Ireland. This year it was celebrated during 30 September to 4 October 2019.

In sum

Positive ageing has different meanings in different countries. Broadly, positive ageing means remaining healthy, both physically and mentally, leading active life through engagement in some activities and remaining connected to personal social network and also thinking positive. In addition, accepting ageing as a normal phenomenon and enjoying this stage of life without thinking too much about other issues is a prerequisite.

5.11. PALLIATIVE CARE

A good number of elderly people suffer from different forms of disability and chronic diseases. As a result, they become dependent on others and are vulnerable to neglect, humiliation and even abuse. In some families, there is manpower to look after them whereas in some families, the same facilities are not available. Some people engage nurses and/or caregivers to look after their dependent parents while some cannot afford. However, as long as a person survives, they need to be cared for by others. Palliative care means taking care of fully dependent individuals round the clock so that their quality of life remains better. According to the WHO, 'palliative care is an approach that improves the quality of life of those patients and their families which are facing life-threatening illnesses, through prevention and relief from suffering'.

This concept emerged for looking after mainly cancer patients since cancer is a terminal disease. These facilities started functioning in India during the 1980s and 1990s. After a few years, that is, in 1994, the Indian Association for Palliative Care was formed with a goal to promote affordable and quality palliative care across the country. Over a period of time, palliative care centres expanded very fast in India. As per 2012 data, about 908 palliative care service centres have been established across the country which intends to deliver home-based or out-patient-based care services. Most of the centres are established in Kerala. Given the nature of physical and mental health challenges, it was realized that there is a need for integrated care and support services by combining physical, psychological and spiritual support services for elderly people so that all their challenges can be addressed at one place.

As stated earlier, Kerala is much ahead of other states in India for providing palliative care to the elderly people who are dependent. The Neighbourhood Network of Palliative Care was established in Kerala in 2001. It was a joint venture of four NGOs and the largest network for palliative care in the world. The unique feature of the same initiative is the active involvement of home care teams. Three departments of the Government of Kerala—the State Department for Health, the Department of Social Welfare and the Local Self-Government Department—have been supporting the same programme. In addition, HelpAge India and Pallium India are also active in delivering similar services in Kerala and other parts of India. The Institute of Palliative Medicine in Kozhikode district is actively involved in training, research and outreach care purposes. This institute was also designated as the WHO Collaborating Centre for community participation in palliative and long-term care. It is important to mention here that Kerala brought the first State Palliative Care Policy in India in 2009.

There are five principles of palliative care and they include giving relief to elderly people from pain and other distressing symptoms, giving them a feel that dying is a natural and normal phenomenon and it is not possible to postpone the destiny, integrating the psychological and spiritual aspects of patient care with palliative care and helping elderly patients to lead an active life as much as possible before death.

Home-based palliative care—either full time or part-time, based on needs—is a good opportunity for comfortable care accompanied with all memories and the people you love. If needed, specialized care may also be provided.

In sum

A good number of elderly people suffer from some form of physical disability and become dependent on others. Some of them require 24-hour care. During this phase, palliative care is badly needed to take care of fully dependent persons, ensuring a reasonable quality of life. Kerala is a pioneer in delivering palliative care to elderly people in India and they first brought the policy towards this end. Every state should come out with more palliative care services and in this regard, NGOs should come forward.

5.12. ROLE OF PSYCHOLOGISTS IN ADDRESSING ISSUES OF ELDERLY PEOPLE

Psychologists have multiple roles in the case of elderly people.

First, they may extend individual counselling to elderly people who experience adjustment problem or develop a feeling of loneliness or feeling of neglect after retirement. Some of the widows also suffer from such perceived problems because of *the* death of *the* husband. Normally, women, after death of their husband, do not enjoy the same status in the family and in the society, especially non-working women, which causes some psychological problems. Individual counselling is very much required and it is found to be beneficial.

Second, the elderly people who suffer from chronic physical health problems is also affected psychologically. This issue also requires the psychological support services to give them a feel to accept the reality and undergo medication as suggested by the doctors.

Third, counselling of life partners or family members to become tolerant towards issues of elderly people and accept them. In this regard, family counselling is beneficial to improve the family functioning and/or ensuring cordial relationships within the family.

Fourth, there is a need for community awareness on issues and challenges of elderly people. In this regard, psychologists may think of better ways of creating community awareness.

Fifth, there is a need to deliver effective services in the old-age homes. Since elderly people live in old-age homes far away from the family members, it causes psychological stress and feeling of sadness. Psychologists need to help the old-age home authorities to design elderly-people-friendly intervention programmes for keeping them engaged and happy in the homes. Whole day activities should be interest-oriented and entertaining.

Sixth, during old age, spiritual practice would be helpful since they have finished most of their duties and responsibilities in *the* family. Now, they should enjoy ageing and accept this phase of life. Psychologists should arrange some discussions on spirituality for generating interest among elderly people and once they get the essence of spirituality, they will remain engaged in spiritual discussions and in turn, will enjoy ageing.

Seventh, psychologists can do research on different dimensions of elderly people and share their findings with the policymakers for bringing appropriate policies in addition to evaluation of government policies and programmes and organizing training for the service providers engaged in palliative care.

In sum

The role of psychologists in taking care of *the* needs of elderly people is very important. Psychologists can play multiple roles, right from extending counselling to elderly people, who suffer from mental health and physical challenges. Psychologists can also extend family counselling to families of elderly people to make them understand the needs of the elderly people sensitively and prepare them to cope with the stress of prolonged illness of elderly people. In addition, they can conduct awareness camps, act as a counsellor in the old-age homes and in palliative care centres and carry out research, evaluation and training.

5.13. UNITED NATIONS INITIATIVE FOR OLDER PERSONS

5.13.1. MADRID INTERNATIONAL PLAN OF ACTION ON AGEING, 2002: INTERNATIONAL MEASURES BY UN BODIES FOR ELDERLY PEOPLE

In the first International Plan of Action on Ageing in Vienna in 1991, the issue of safety and human rights of elderly people was discussed at length and resolved that independence, participation, care, self-fulfilment and dignity should be given priority in the United Nations Principles for Older Persons.

Further, the Madrid International Plan of Action on Ageing (2002) recommended a number of steps for the protection of the rights of older persons in society. One of the recommendations states that older persons must be full participants in the development process and also share in its benefits. No individual should be denied the opportunity to benefit from development. It further emphasized the need to recognize the contribution of older persons in social, cultural, economic and political spheres and proposed actions related to the same issues,

'(a) Ensure the full enjoyment of all human rights and fundamental freedoms by promoting the implementation of human rights conventions and other human rights instruments, particularly in combating all forms of discrimination; (b) Acknowledge, encourage and support the contribution of older persons to families, communities and the economy; (c) Provide opportunities, programmes and support to encourage older persons to participate or continue to participate in cultural, economic, political, social life and lifelong learning.' (Madrid International Plan of Action on Ageing, 2002)

Most of the older persons worldwide live in rural areas without much support and resources. Amongst them, the number of women is more. As a result, they experience a lot of challenges. In order to address the same issue, it is recommended by the Madrid International Plan of Action that 'policies and programmes for food security and agricultural production must take into account the implications of rural ageing'.

A number of action plans in connection with different objectives have been recommended by Madrid International Plan of Action for the welfare of older persons. Some of the objectives are

- 'Improvement of living conditions and infrastructure in rural areas.
- Alleviation of the marginalization of older persons in rural areas.
- Integration of older migrants within their new communities.
- Equality of opportunity throughout life with respect to continuing education, training and retraining, as well as vocational guidance and placement services.
- Full utilization of the potential and expertise of persons of all ages and recognizing the benefits of increased experience with age.
- Strengthening of solidarity through equity and reciprocity between generations.
- Promotion of programmes to enable all workers to acquire basic social protection/social security, including, where applicable, pensions, disability insurance and health benefits.
- Sufficient minimum income for all older persons.
- Enhanced contributions of older persons to the reestablishment and reconstruction of communities and the rebuilding of the social fabric following emergencies.

- Reduction of the cumulative effects of factors that increase the risk of disease and consequently, potential dependence in older age.
- Development of policies to prevent ill-health among elder persons.
- Access to food and adequate nutrition for all elder persons.
- Elimination of social and economic inequalities based on age, gender or any other ground.
- Creation of support services to address elder abuse.'

It is the responsibility of the concerned authorities of different countries to review and discuss the action plan as suggested by the Madrid International Plan of Action on Ageing and take appropriate policies and measures for improving the condition of elder people.

5.14. LATEST LEGISLATIVE MEASURE IN INDIA: THE MAINTENANCE AND WELFARE OF PARENTS AND SENIOR CITIZENS (MWPSC) ACT, 2007

Parents look after their children and provide them with education and all possible support for their proper upbringing so that they become a productive and responsible citizen. In turn, it is the responsibility of the children to look after their own parents when they are old and are unable to look after themselves. Unfortunately, a good number of parents do not get support from their children when they badly need it. Elderly people are also vulnerable to various challenges within the family. Therefore, reality necessitated to introduce a legislation in India in 2007 titled 'The Maintenance and Welfare of Parents and Senior Citizens Act, 2007' by the Ministry of Social Justice and Empowerment (2007), Government of India to compel children to legally look after their elder parents. In addition, this law protects the life and property of the older persons.

Section 9 of the Act talks about maintenance. According to this section, 'if children or relatives, as the case may be, neglect or refuse to maintain a senior citizen being unable to maintain himself, the Tribunal may, on being satisfied of such neglect or refusal, order such children or relatives to make a monthly allowance at such monthly rates, for the maintenance of such senior citizen, as the Tribunal may deem fit and to pay the same to such senior citizen as the Tribunal may, from time to time, direct'.

Further, there is a provision as per Section 13 to deposit maintenance amount to the account of the elder person. As per Section 13, the children or relatives shall pay the maintenance amount within thirty days from the date of the announcement by the Tribunal.

Section 19 of Chapter III of the Act talks about the establishment of old-age homes. For example, 'The State Government may establish and maintain such a number of old age homes at accessible places, as it may deem necessary, in a phased manner, beginning with at least one in each district, to accommodate in such homes a minimum of one hundred fifty senior citizens who are indignant'.

Sub-section 2 of Section 19 talks about the various types and quality of services for the elderly people in the old-age homes. In this regard, the State Government may prescribe norms for the management of old-age homes.

During old age, most of the people experience a range of physical health problems. In order to take care of health issues, Section 20 directs to provide medical services to all senior citizens. According to Section 20,

The State Government shall ensure that

1. The Government hospitals or hospitals funded fully or partially by the Government shall provide beds for all senior citizens as far as possible;
2. Separate queues be arranged for senior citizens;
3. Facility for treatment of chronic, terminal and degenerative diseases is expanded for the senior citizens;
4. Research activities for chronic elderly diseases and ageing is expanded; and
5. There are earmarked facilities for geriatric patients in every district hospital, duly headed by a medical officer with experience in geriatric care.

There are a number of legislations in the country for the welfare of the marginalized population and/or protection of the interests of the society. People hardly have any knowledge about such legislations. Until there is awareness, usages of the law would be minimal. Therefore, there is a need to create awareness about legislations among common people and law enforcement agencies. Section 21 of the MWPSC Act, 2007 emphasizes on publicity and awareness generation of the law.

As per the Section 22 of the Act, The State Government empowers the District Magistrate of a district to ensure effective implementation of the law and in turn, the District Magistrate may choose those who are subordinate to him to exercise all or any of the powers.

Further, Sub-section 2 of Section 22 has a provision for prescribing comprehensive action plan by the State Government for protection of life and property of senior citizens.

Some parents transfer their property in the name of their children with an understanding that their children will look after them. In a number of such instances, it has been observed that children did not discharge their duties properly and/or forced their parents to leave the house. To avoid similar situations, that act, kept a provision under Section 23, which is 'transfer of property to be void in certain circumstances'.

Section 24 of the Act has a provision for punishment of children or relatives, who abandon old people, with imprisonment which may extend to three months or fine. This sort of act is regarded as a cognizable offence (Section 25).

5.15. SOCIAL POLICIES FOR ELDERLY PEOPLE

5.15.1. National Policy on Older Persons

The Government of India has come out with the National Policy on Older Persons in the year 1999 for taking care of all issues related to elderly people.'The salient features of the National Policy are as follows:

*   'To support financial security, health care and nutrition, shelter, information needs, appropriate concessions and discounts etc. for the senior citizens.
*   Special attention to protect and strengthen their legal rights such as, safeguarding their life and property.
*   Recognizes persons aged above 60 as senior citizens.'

5.15.2. The Integrated Programme for Older Persons (IPOP)

The IPOP (revised) was effective from April 2016. This programme is under the Ministry of Social Justice & Empowerment, Government of India. This programme integrated the following components of Non-Plan Schemes as recommended by the Standing Finance Committee. New components include,

- 'Awareness Generation for Maintenance and Welfare of Parents and Senior Citizens (MWPSC) Act, 2007.
- Setting up of helpline for Senior Citizens at the National Level.
- Setting up of helpline for Senior Citizens at the District Level.
- Scheme for the implementation of the New National Policy on Senior Citizens.'

This programme extends financial assistance of up to 90 per cent to the NGOs for establishing and maintaining old-age homes, daycare centres, and mobile medicare units and also provides non-institutional services to older persons.

5.15.3. NATIONAL PROGRAMME FOR THE HEALTH CARE OF THE ELDERLY (NPHCE)

For addressing the various health-related issues of elderly people, the Ministry of Health and Family Welfare, Government of India launched the National Programme for the Health Care of the Elderly during the 11th plan (i.e., 2010–2011). All elderly people above 60 years, across the country, are the beneficiary of the same specialized healthcare services which Health Departments of every State is supposed to deliver. The objective of the NPHCE are:

1. 'Extending referral services through district hospitals and regional medical institutions
2. Merging with National Rural Health Mission and initiatives of the Ministry of Social Justice and Empowerment; and
3. Promoting a community-based approach, integrated with the existing primary health centres and capacity building.'

As per the programme, some beds are supposed to be reserved for elderly people in every hospital. NPHCH also emphasize on the revision of healthcare curricula in educational institutions involved in healthcare education, keeping the needs of elderly people, especially focusing on non-communicable diseases. NPHCH is a comprehensive programme in India for addressing the health need of the elderly. It also gives support to community-based services of NGOs meant for elderly people.

5.16. ROLE OF NGOs

There are a number of NGOs working across the country for taking care of issues of elderly people. A brief description of two NGOs is provided below:

5.16.1. CALCUTTA METROPOLITAN INSTITUTE OF GERONTOLOGY

The Calcutta Metropolitan Institute of Gerontology (CMIG) was established in 1988 with an objective to promote research for the better understanding of the issues and challenges of elderly people in the city. The nature of services extended by CMIG in Kolkata include daycare centres, provision of livelihood and a healthcare system based on mobile clinics in slum areas.

5.16.2 HELPAGE INDIA

HelpAge India is an NGO that was established in 1978. This NGO works for elderly people across the country. Its mission is 'to work for the cause and care of disadvantaged older persons and to improve their quality of life'. HelpAge India is extending a range of services to elderly people. The exact nature of services provided by HelpAge India is providing mobile health services, running Gram Chikitsa Centres, running accredited clinics, organizing health camps, providing geriatric physiotherapy, taking care of cancer patients, performing cataract surgeries on elderly people, running income generation programmes for the elderly, organizing elderly self-help groups, running elderly helpline and working during disasters to protect the elderly people.

In sum

The latest Legislative Measure, that is, The MWPSC Act, 2007 is a comprehensive measure to take care of the rights and safety of the elderly. It is important to create awareness about the law among all concerned and also, the respective State Governments should ensure its effective implementation. Reporting of any abuse and fraud cases is very essential. In this regard, common people of the country should play their role as responsible citizens. The Government of India has brought appropriate social policies in the line of legislative measures and they should be implemented for the welfare of elderly people. The role of some of the NGOs is highly appreciable, towards taking care of elderly people in different parts of the country. The efforts are not comparable to the needs. More and more NGOs should come forward and in this regard, the government should support them.

5.17. RECOMMENDATIONS

On the basis of the secondary data and first-hand work experience with elderly people, the following steps are suggested for creating safe and comfortable environments in the family for the elderly people.

- Ensure effective implementation of all government welfare schemes for elderly people in every state and in this regard, NGOs should play the role of advocacy.
- Awareness about the rights of elderly people and government welfare schemes meant for elderly people should be created across the society so that, elderly people who require any support may enjoy the facilities meant for them. Local media should take initiative in creating awareness about the welfare schemes.
- Legal aid services should be made available to all elderly people and mental support should be extended.
- There is a need to strengthen coordination between different NGOs working for the welfare of elderly people and between respective government departments and NGOs for delivering better services to elderly people.

- Inculcating Indian values among school students on issues like respecting and caring elderly people, being assertive, tolerant and leading an honest and decent life.
- Extending need-based support to elderly people without any discrimination and reporting of any incident of neglect, abuse and fraud to the appropriate authorities.
- Improving the quality of care and support services in the old-age homes by appointing professionals in the homes.
- Monitoring of the quality of care and support services offered in the old-age homes, periodically, by government officials.
- Periodic evaluation of styles of functioning of old-age homes by the Ministry of Social Justice and Empowerment and/or respective departments of the State Government.
- Introduction of the Time Bank concept in India. The elderly people who are in need of care and who are interested to extend services to dependent elderly people can enlist their names with an organization and, in turn, the organization will send the person and the time they have given will be deposited in their account. When they will become old, they can avail similar services from others using their Time Bank Account. This concept is very popular in Switzerland and it may be promoted in India.
- Organizing training programmes for the NGO personnel and healthcare providers for under-standing the issues of elderly people from their perspective and delivering them better services.
- More and more old-age homes should come up in all the states to meet the needs of the society with more quality of care and support services and with affordable charges since a large number of them are not financially well off.
- Along with medical care, psychological support services need to be provided to elderly people in the old-age homes, as most of them experience a variety of psychological problems like loneliness, feeling of neglect, hopelessness, depression and anxiety.
- Different Non-Government Welfare organizations should engage elderly people who are physically and mentally fit and willing to work for a social cause. They can be engaged in educational and social welfare activities. In fact, a good number of elderly people look for some engagement. They expect respectable designation and some honorarium. Since elderly people are highly experienced, their voluntary services with some honorarium would be immensely beneficial for society.
- Lifestyle choices for active ageing should start early in life. One should be careful about diet and does some physical exercise regularly.

Finally, it is worth revisiting WHO's recommendations concerning positive ageing. They include '(a) Promoting and leading a healthy lifestyle across the life-course; (b) Creating age-friendly environments and policies to engage older men and women; (c) Making primary healthcare age-friendly; (d) Ensuring access to healthcare and rehabilitation services for older people; and (e) Adapting physical environments to existing disabilities'.

5.18. CONCLUSION AND IMPLICATIONS

Ageing is a normal phenomenon and one should accept this phase in life and enjoy. Globally, the number of aged people are increasing, especially in the developed countries because of changing lifestyles and improved healthcare. Like every stage of life, there are some challenges during old age and every country and community should come out with strategies to address the challenges of elderly people in terms of bringing legislation for the protection of their property and safety and to improve their quality of life to the best extent possible.

Elderly people are highly resourceful and every community should make the best use of their lifelong knowledge and experience for social and economic gain. They should be respected and should receive proper care as and when they require. This culture should be inculcated among the younger generations from the early days of their life, through school education. Sadly, a good number of elderly people experience neglect, violence and financial fraud. Shockingly, in some communities, they undergo honour killing. The younger generation consider them as burden after a certain age and want their properties. Before death, they should hand over all resources to them. Social consciousness is required in such communities to alter practices of honour killing and the government also needs to check such practices and take appropriate measures for stopping them.

Mental harassment is the most common form of violence experienced by women, followed by neglect and physical violence. As a result, the feeling of insecurity develops among them. However, old-age homes were found to be an alternate and comfortable as well as safe place for the elderly. During old age, they experience a range of physical and mental health problems. About 69.0 per cent of them were undergoing treatment. Self-savings was the main source of money for bearing medical expenses (51.0%), followed by support from children (28.0%) and relatives (0.5%).

Male members were in better mental states during old age compared to female elderly people. Although psychological general well-being and feeling of security were higher among married elderly people, unmarried people were more satisfied and happier in life. Two forms of violence, that is, neglect and mental harassment had negative effects on two dimensions of mental disposition of elderly people, that is, subjective happiness and feeling of insecurity.

There are a number of implications related to the welfare of the elderly people. First, inculcating Indian values among younger generations to care and respect elderly people. In turn, it would help elderly people to feel happy at the dusk of their life as they did everything for their children's welfare and well-being. Otherwise, our society will witness degeneration of human values. Second, guidance from elderly people will help for the prosperity of the family. Third, right to life is a fundamental right of an individual. The cultural practice of some communities that is 'honour killing' is a violation of the fundamental right of a person. Fourth, positive ageing will bring happiness in the family and younger generations will enjoy the company of elderly people and will learn a lot from their lifelong experience.

EXERCISES

One-mark Questions

1. Whom do we call elderly people?
2. What is the projected elderly population by 2050?
3. State the characteristics of Indian elderly population.
4. How to inculcate values among younger generation to respect elderly people?
5. Will it be wise to re-employ elderly people after retirement? Justify.
6. Do women report more experience of neglect? Why?
7. In the first International Plan of Action on Ageing in Vienna in 1991, what issues were discussed?

8. State the role of psychologists in dealing with elderly people.
9. What is the benefit of counselling?
10. What is the difference between sympathy and empathy?

Five-mark Questions

1. Discuss the general perception of family members towards elderly people.
2. How to utilize the potential of elderly people?
3. Is the number of elderly people increasing? Justify your answer with logic.
4. How to ensure positive ageing?
5. What do you mean by palliative care?
6. Do health workers need training for dealing with needs of elderly people? Justify your answer.

Ten-mark Questions

1. Discuss the role of elderly people in the family.
2. Do elderly people experience any challenge in the family? Justify your answer.
3. Discuss the status of mental health during old age.
4. How to sensitize the large society to be tolerant to elderly people and taking care of them? Discuss.

Reflexive Questions

1. Are elderly people causing threat to economic development? Justify your answer.
2. State the reasons for common health problems of elderly people.
3. How to ensure effective implementation of the MWPSC Act, 2007?
4. Is monitoring of an old-age home necessary? How should it be done across the country?

NOTE

1. http://positiveageing.org.uk

REFERENCES

Acierno, R., Hernandez, M. A., Amstadter, A. B., Resnick, H. S., Steve, K., Muzzy, W., & Kilpatrick, D. G. (2010). Prevalence and correlates of emotional, physical, sexual, and financial abuse and potential neglect in the United States: The national elder mistreatment study. *American Journal of Public Health, 100*(2), 292–297.

Alam, M., Mazumdar, S., & Yadav, P. (2015). *Inequalities in elderly health and wellbeing in India: An exploration* (Working Paper No. 5). BKPAI.

Atchley, R. C. (1989). A continuity theory of normal aging. *The Gerontologist, 29*(2), 183–190.

Buettner, D. (2012). *The blue zones: 9 lessons for living longer from the people who've lived the longest.* National Geographic Books.

Crime in India. (2015). Crime against senior citizens (p. 177). https://ncrb.gov.in/sites/default/files/crime_in_india_table_additional_table_chapter_reports/Chapter%2020-15.11.16_2015.pdf

Cohen, G. D., Perlstein, S., Chapline, J., Kelly, J., Firth, K. M., & Simmens, S. (2006). The impact of professionally conducted cultural programs on the physical health, mental health, and social functioning of older adults. *The Gerontologist, 46*(6), 726–734.

Comijs, H. C., Pot, A. M., Smit, J. H., Bouter, L. M., & Jonker, C. (1998). Elder abuse in the community: Prevalence and consequences. *Journal of the American Geriatrics Society, 46*(7), 885–888.

Conner, K. O., Copeland, V. C., Grote, N. K., Koeske, G., Rosen, D., Reynolds III, C. F., & Brown, C. (2010). Mental health treatment seeking among older adults with depression: The impact of stigma and race. *The American Journal of Geriatric Psychiatry, 18*(6), 531–543.

Cumming, E., & Henry, W. E. (1961). *Growing old, the process of disengagement.* Basic Books.

Cupitt, M. (1997). Identifying and addressing the issues of elder abuse: A rural perspective. *Journal of Elder Abuse and Neglect, 8*(4), 21–30.

D'Augelli, A. R., Grossman, A. H., Hershberger, S. L., & O'connell, T. S. (2001). Aspects of mental health among older lesbian, gay, and bisexual adults. *Aging & Mental Health, 5*(2), 149–158.

Dong, X., Simon, M. A., & Gorbien, M. (2007). Elder abuse and neglect in an urban Chinese population. *Journal of Elder Abuse & Neglect, 19*(3–4), 79–96.

Dong, X., Simon, M. A., Odwazny, R., & Gorbien, M. (2008). Depression and elder abuse and neglect among a community-dwelling Chinese elderly population. *Journal of Elder Abuse & Neglect, 20*(1), 25–41.

Dorji, N., Dunne, M. P., Seib, C., & Deb, S. (2017). Quality of life among senior citizens in Bhutan: Associations with adverse life experiences, chronic diseases, spirituality, and social connectedness. *Asia Pacific Journal of Public Health, 29*(1), 35–46.

Dorji, N., Dunne, M. P., Seib, C., & Deb, S. (2018). Qualitative inquiry into quality of life among older adults in Bhutan. *Biomedical Journal of Scientific & Technical Research, 5*(4), 1–8.

Dyer, C. B., Pavlik, V. N., Murphy, K. P., & Hyman, D. J. (2000). The high prevalence of depression and dementia in elder abuse or neglect. *Journal of the American Geriatrics Society, 48*(2), 205–208.

Fiori, K. L., Antonucci, T. C., & Cortina, K. S. (2006). Social network typologies and mental health among older adults. *The Journals of Gerontology Series B: Psychological Sciences and Social Sciences, 61*(1), 25–32.

Foster, L., & Walker, A. (2014). Active and successful aging: A European policy perspective. *The Gerontologist, 55*(1), 83–90.

Giele, J. Z., & Elder, G. H. (Eds.). (1998). *Methods of life course research: Qualitative and quantitative approaches.* SAGE Publications.

Guglani, S., Coleman, P. G., & Sonuga-Barke, E. J. (2000). Mental health of elderly Asians in Britain: A comparison of Hindus from nuclear and extended families of differing cultural identities. *International Journal of Geriatric Psychiatry, 15*(11), 1046–1053.

Havighurst, R. J. (1961). The nature and values of meaningful free-time activity. In R. W. Khleemeier (Ed.), *Aging and leisure* (309–344). Oxford University Press.

HelpAge India. (2018). *Elder abuse in India: Changing cultural ethos & impact of technology.* https://www.helpageindia.org/wp-content/uploads/2018/06/ELDER-ABUSE-IN-INDIA-2018-A-HelpAge-India-report.pdf

Hindustan Times. (2019). Neglect and abuse: The reality of India's elderly people, 22 April.

Hogstel, M. O., & Curry, L. C. (1999). Elder abuse revisited. *Journal of Gerontological Nursing, 25*(7), 10–18.

Homer, A. C., & Gilleard, C. (1990). Abuse of elderly people by their carers. *British Medical Journal, 301*(6765), 1359–1362.

Iecovich, E. (2005). Elder abuse and neglect in Israel: A comparison between the general elderly population and elderly new immigrants. *Family Relations, 54*(3), 436–447.

Koenig, H. G. (2009). Research on religion, spirituality, and mental health: A review. *The Canadian Journal of Psychiatry, 54*(5), 283–291.

Kraaij, V., & de Wilde, E. J. (2001). Negative life events and depressive symptoms in the elderly: A life span perspective. *Aging & Mental Health, 5*(1), 84–91.

Lachs, M. S., & Pillemer, K. (1995). Abuse and neglect of elderly persons. *New England Journal of Medicine, 332*(7), 437–443.

Lachs, M. S., Williams, C., O'Brien, S., Hurst, L., & Horwitz, R. (1997). Risk factors for reported elder abuse and neglect: A nine-year observational cohort study. *The Gerontologist, 37*(4), 469–474.

Lai, D. W. (2011). Abuse and neglect experienced by aging Chinese in Canada. *Journal of Elder Abuse & Neglect, 23*(4), 326–347.

Lehman, H. (1989). Fraud and abuse of the elderly people. In R. S. Wolf & S. Bergman (Eds.), *Stress, conflict and abuse of the elderly people*. JDC-Brookdale Monograph.

Madrid International Plan of Action on Ageing. (2002). *Second World Assembly on Ageing adopts Madrid International Plan of Action and Political Declaration*, Spain, 8–12 April,. United Nations.

Ministry of Social Justice and Empowerment. (2007). *The Maintenance and Welfare of Parents and Senior Citizens Act, 2007*. Government of India.

Moreira-Almeida, A., Lotufo Neto, F., & Koenig, H. G. (2006). Religiousness and mental health: A review. *Brazilian Journal of Psychiatry*, 28(3), 242–250.

National Center on Elder Abuse. (1998). *National elder abuse incidence study*. American Public Health Services Association.

Paluska, S. A., & Schwenk, T. L. (2000). Physical activity and mental health. *Sports Medicine*, 29(3), 167–180.

Paris, B. E., Meier, D. E., Goldstein, T., Weiss, M., & Fein, E. D. (1995). Elder abuse and neglect: How to recognize warning signs and intervene. *Geriatrics*, 50(4), 47–51.

Paul, R. (2013). *Violence against elderly people and their mental disposition* (Unpublished doctoral dissertation). University of Calcutta.

Rowe, J. W., & Kahn, R. L. (1997). Successful aging. *The Gerontologist*, 37, 433–440.

Sharon, N., & Zoabi, S. (1997). Elder abuse in a land of tradition: The case of Israel's Arabs. *Journal of Elder Abuse and Neglect*, 8(4), 43–58.

Shimazaki, Y., Soh, I., Saito, T., Yamashita, Y., Koga, T., Miyazaki, H., & Takehara, T. (2001). Influence of dentition status on physical disability, mental impairment, and mortality in institutionalized elderly people. *Journal of Dental Research*, 80(1), 340–345.

The Hindu. (2012). *Report finds elderly enduring abuse*, 16 June, 2.

The Hindu. (April 2019). *Former MP's wife stabbed to death*, 16 April, 2.

United Nations. (2017). World population prospects: The 2017 revision. https://www.un.org/development/desa/publications/world-population-prospects-the-2017-revision.html

United Nations Population Fund. (2011). *Building a knowledge base on population aging in India (BKPAI)* (Report on the Status of Elderly in Select States of India). Author.

United Nations Population Fund. (2017). *Caring for our elders: Early responses*. Author.

United States Census Bureau. (2015) *An Aging World*. https://www.census.gov/content/dam/Census/library/publications/2016/demo/p95-16-1.pdf

Wiglesworth, A., Mosqueda, L., Mulnard, R., Liao, S., Gibbs, L., & Fitzgerald, W. (2010). Screening for abuse and neglect of people with dementia. *Journal of the American Geriatrics Society*, 58(3), 493–500.

Zhou, B., Liu, X., & Yu, P. (2018). Toward successful aging: The Chinese health criteria for the elderly. *Aging Medicine*, 1(2), 154–157.

Zoabi, S. (1994). *Violence against elderly people in the Arab sector* (Unpublished MA dissertation). Haifa University, Israel (In Hebrew).

RECOMMENDED READINGS

Biggs, S., Phillipson, C., & Kingston, P. (1995). *Elder abuse in perspective*. Open University Press.

Boulton-Lewis, G., & Tam, M. (Eds.). (2011). *Active ageing, active learning: Issues and challenges* (Vol. 15). Springer Science & Business Media.

Mackenzie, E. R., & Rakel, B. (Eds.). (2006). *Complementary and alternative medicine for older adults: A guide to holistic approaches to healthy aging*. Springer Publishing Company.

McBee, L. (2008). *Mindfulness-based elder care: A CAM model for frail elders and their caregivers*. Springer Publishing.

Nolan, M., Davies, N., & Grant, G. (2001). *Working with older people and their families*. McGraw-Hill Education.

Taylor, A. W., & Johnson, M. J. (2008). *Physiology of exercise and healthy aging*. Human Kinetics.

Wei, J. Y., & Levkoff, S. (2000). *Aging well: The complete guide to physical and emotional health*. Wiley.

Community-based Approach in Working with Vulnerable and At-risk Children

LEARNING OBJECTIVES

- Defining vulnerable children and providing information about their magnitude
- Describing the living conditions of vulnerable children
- Elaborating the problems encountered by vulnerable children
- Discussing the role of community psychologists for addressing the issues and concerns of vulnerable children
- Discussing the steps for the effective implementation of intervention programmes
- Providing detailed information about legislative and social measures for vulnerable children

ABSTRACT

Vulnerable children are those who are at risk of neglect, abuse, exploitation and maltreatment. Broadly, they include street children, child labour, slum children, children from poor families working as domestic assistant, children of CSWs, differently abled children, children without parents, children living in underdeveloped environment and school dropout children. This chapter discusses the background of vulnerable children, challenges encountered by them and consequences of various challenges they face in day-to-day life. Further, it elaborates the preventive measures and discusses at length the intervention and rehabilitative measures keeping their issues and challenges into account with special reference to the role of community psychologists and other professionals. It also highlights various legislative and social welfare measures adopted by the government for this population and suggests measures for the effective implementation of the intervention programme. At the end, it provides exercises and suggests names of some books for further reading.

Keywords: Children; vulnerable; community; neglect; abuse; prevention; intervention

6.1. INTRODUCTION

Children are the future of society. They deserve utmost care, guidance and support in terms of nutrition, education, medical care and safety for their healthy mental, social, psychological and spiritual growth. If they enjoy safety and a supportive environment with adequate support for studies, they will exhibit their potential of becoming a skilled manpower and will play a vital role in society as a responsible citizen, ensuring peace, prosperity and growth. Sadly, a large number of children do not experience their fundamental rights and undergo a lot of sufferings because of various socio-economic, familial and other reasons (Deb, 2005, 2011, 2013; Deb & Bernadette, 2014). Their number is unaccountable. The larger society is not much bothered about the welfare and safety of these disadvantaged and at-risk children.

6.2. BROAD CATEGORIES OF VULNERABLE CHILDREN

Generally speaking, vulnerable children are those who are likely to experience neglect, abuse, maltreatment and harassment (Deb, 2011). Broadly, vulnerable children include street children, child labour, slum children, children from poor families working as domestic help, children of CSWs, differently abled children, children without parents, children living in an underdeveloped environment, school dropout children and so on. This list is not exclusive. There are many more such children who may be considered vulnerable and they are children of drug addicts and alcoholics, children victim of natural calamities and children living in disorganized families where they are under constant tension on account of frequent violence.

These children are called vulnerable since they lack social support; coming from poor families, they are deprived of education, nutrition, medical care and safety. There is a general tendency among people of larger society to look at them differently and take advantage of their helpless condition. Some use them for their vested interest, while some sexually abuse them. Change in the mindset of the larger society towards these children can bring a change in their lives in terms of providing them shelter, offering them nutrition, taking them to the doctor in case of health problems and giving them basic education as an individual and/or extending them love and affection without any expectation.

6.3. DEFINITIONS OF DIFFERENT CATEGORIES OF VULNERABLE CHILDREN AND THEIR MAGNITUDE

6.3.1. STREET CHILDREN

The term 'street children' refers to 'children who live or spend a significant amount of time on the street or urban areas to fend for themselves and/or their families through "various occupations." This also denotes children who inadequately protected, supervised and cared for by responsible adults.' Like street children, other categories of children whether living with or without parents are not under proper supervision (Mitra & Deb, 2004).

The children commonly called 'street children' are best considered as children living and working in a particular urban environment. They are children out of place in the sense that they do not have what society considers having a correct relationship with major institutions of childhood—the family and education.

Generally, common people refer to street children as *children out of place*. It means these children do not have any specific place to live. Worldwide, a large number of children live on the streets and their number is increasing day by day. There is no clear estimation of this population. In fact, it is very difficult to find out the prevalence and/or magnitude of street children since they are mobile. The emergence of street children has been described as an immense tragedy worldwide. Estimation about the magnitude of street children given by different institutions varies to a great extent. India has the largest number of street children in the world. The of street children is increasing rapidly in all the metropolitan cities in India bearing a history of illegitimate extramarital sexual act, vagrant parents, maltreatment, family violence, breakdown of rural economy and urbanization.

The Anti-Slavery Society—a UK-based NGO—estimates that there are about 31 million street children across the globe. Although an exact estimate of the number of street children in India is not available, an earlier situation analysis of street children conducted in seven cities estimated that there are nearly 100,000 street children in New Delhi including children who live with their families on the streets and are engaged in rag picking, vending and so on (Pinto & Nangia, 1988). They scavenge for food in the bins on the platforms and trawl the tracks for discarded plastic for recycling. The girls are much fewer, only because most are taken away by touts and sold in brothels. Those who do survive on the platform, provide sex to the gangs of boys and men on the station in return for protection from the police and touts.

On 2 January 2018, in an interview with *BW Businessworld*, Thomas Chandy, chief executive officer of Save the Children, stated that there are about 2 million children living on the streets in India. The following case study provides a clear picture of the plight of street children.

> **Case I:** Ram, aged 13, male, having an elder sister, was staying on Sealdah railway station, Kolkata, for the last four years. He hailed from the rural areas of West Bengal. His father—a casual worker—came back home, almost every day, after having alcohol and would start abusing the people around him, especially Ram's mother. His father was irresponsible and failed to take care of the basic needs

of the family, that is, minimum food, healthcare and educational expenses. Ram thought of leaving the house for quite some time because of the unhappy family environment, which disturbed him badly. His emotional attachment with his mother and elder sister prevented him from running away from the family. One day, he came out of his house and found that a suburban train was coming. Once it reached the railway platform, he boarded it and reached Sealdah. Since then, he was staying in Sealdah railway station, which is an open area, as well as unclean and unhygienic. To take a bath, a nearby tube well was the only option for him and to attend to nature's call, he would either go to the railway tracks or the open fields. On the platform, he came in contact with other children who supported him with food. Gradually, he developed a friendship with them and got used to stealing vegetables from the farmers while they brought it to Sealdah, through suburban trains, to sell in the wholesale market. Selling stolen vegetables on the platform was his source of earning for the livelihood. While stealing vegetables, he was caught and beaten by the people on several occasions. In addition, he also experienced different forms of abuse.

With the growing number of street children, it has become a serious social issue. The local government along with NGOs should come out with a proper plan for rehabilitation of these children. Street children are deprived of their fundamental rights like other citizens of a nation. As a result, they develop a negative attitude towards the existing social system and structure. Since they are alienated from the mainstream of the society for survival, they are involved in deviant social and economic activities from the very beginning of their life. Since they do not get education, in later life, they do find it very difficult to manage a decent job for survival and lead an aimless and haphazard life. Antisocials and criminals take advantage of the miserable and helpless condition of the street children and they involve them in deviant activities. Unfortunately, by and large, our society also considers them as problem creators, street urchins and criminals. A large section of people of the high and middle class feels that street children should not be seen on the street, as it looks odd. Change of attitude of larger society towards street children is needed to bring them into the mainstream of the society.

6.3.2. Child Labour

The term 'child labour' refers to those children who are engaged in gainful work. Therefore, children working in all forms of industrial or non-industrial occupations, which are not healthy to their physical, mental, moral and social development, are covered under the definition of 'child labour'. Regarding the age limit, different laws set varying age limits for the determination of what is a child. In conjunction with 'labour', International Labour Organization (ILO) Convention No. 138 places the general limit at 15 years or, under special national circumstances, 14 years.

There are different definitions of child labour given by various agencies. Bonded child labour is any individual under 18 years of age providing services arising out of a loan/debt/advance. Bonded labour 'refers to the phenomenon of children working in conditions of servitude in order to pay off a debt'.

As per the Office of the Registrar General & Census Commissioner, Ministry of Home Affairs, Government of India (2011), the total child population in India in the age group of 5–14 years is

259.6 million. Of these, 10.1 million (3.9% of total child population) children are working, either as 'main worker' or as 'marginal worker'. UNICEF estimation says that about 33 million children in India are engaged in different forms of child labour. Among the Asian countries, India is on the top in terms of the high number of child labour. It is believed that 1 in every 11 children in India works as a child labour for survival and/or for giving support to the family. The states with the highest number of child labour in terms of chronological order are Bihar, Uttar Pradesh, Rajasthan, Madhya Pradesh and Maharashtra, as per the data given out by Save the Children. National capital Delhi is responsible for a share of 1 million child labour alone.[1] Globally, there are 150 million children who work as child labour, according to UNICEF.[2]

A case study of a child working in a tea stall in an urban area highlights how and why a child starts working for earning money. For example,

---

Case II: Md Islam, aged 13, male, came from a very poor family and has been working in a tea stall in Chennai for the last four years. Since he discontinued his education, his parents wanted him to indulge in some financial activity for earning money, that is, either working in a tea stall or any other casual work. One of his neighbours, who ran a tea stall, offered him work in his shop and he accepted the offer gladly. His day starts at 5.30 AM and he works till 10.00 PM. Sometimes, even after 10.00 PM, he works. He does not enjoy any holiday and does not get any opportunity to take rest during midday. His poor and aged parents lived in rural areas. Every month, he sends ₹600 to his parents, from his monthly salary of ₹800, keeping ₹200 in hand, towards his pocket expenses. Although he seems to be happy since he gets free meals in the shop and is able to send some money to his family, he feels the absence of his family, which he shared during interactions. A number of times, he was scolded for not being able to perform at the level of satisfaction of the owner of the tea stall. His younger brother has been studying in Class III back home and Islam wants him to continue his education.

6.3.3. CHILDREN WORKING AS DOMESTIC ASSISTANT

A domestic worker is a person who is employed in any household on a temporary or permanent basis to do the household work. They also come under child labour category. Children below the age of 16 years working in somebody's house for at least 2–4 hours in a day and/or stay in the same family and do all household chores or look after younger children may be called domestic assistant. They mostly belong to poor families and get engaged in these types of work when their parents, especially father, are unemployed or living with a single parent. Some of the children engaged in domestic work are very young.

Initially, they come to the workplace with their mother and assist them. Slowly they also start working against money. They are highly preferred since their demand is not high, and they are easily manageable. Unfortunately, their wage is very low, and they do not get adequate food and enjoy their liberty in terms of visiting their family periodically, especially the girl child who stays in somebody's house. When they fall sick, in most of the cases, self-prescribed medication is provided to them. Sadly, a good number of them experience maltreatment and abuse in all forms and bear their suffering silently.

There is no clear idea about the magnitude of child domestic workers around the world and/or in India. However, from personal experience, it has been observed that almost every urban household has at least one domestic assistant, if not two. One can imagine the total number of households in every city and the number of children working as domestic assistant. According to ILO, about 7.4 million children, especially girls, are engaged in domestic work and they mostly belong to the age group of 12–16 years. The number of child labourers between the ages of 5 years and 18 years in India as per the Census 2011 data was 33 million (Office of the Registrar General & Census Commissioner, Ministry of Home Affairs, Government of India, 2011).

The dynamics behind getting involved in work as a domestic assistant vary from place to place and in case of a child getting involved in domestic work, it is found to be more of a chain-wise relation, that is, becoming a follower of mother's profession when a child discontinues school education. For example,

---

Case III: Aruna, aged 14, female, school dropout after Class III, has been living in a slum with her parents. She has a younger sister. She discontinued her education due to lack of guidance and encouragement. Most of the children of her age group, in the same slum, do not attend school. Perhaps, that is another reason for which she lacked motivation to continue education. On the other hand, school education near the slum area, where she was going, was not effective. Teachers were not regular and failed to teach effectively to create interest among slum children and children from underdeveloped areas. Her father works as a rickshaw puller while her mother works as a domestic assistant. She visited her mother's workplace on a number of occasions while she was very young. After leaving school, she used to loiter in her locality with other children, which her mother perceived to be unsafe. For the same reason, her mother insisted her to get engaged in some work which might be safer than that of roaming in the locality with peer group members. Since her mother was known in the locality as a good woman, Aruna got a work in a household at a nominal rate of ₹1,000 per month. She went for work in the morning and came back at the end of the day. The house owner gave her food during the day. The expectation of every house is very high. A domestic assistant is supposed to do all the household chores against a meagre amount of money. Occasionally, she was scolded for minor mistakes.

6.3.4. Children of CSWs

Children of CSWs are those children whose mothers are engaged in commercial sex trade. Most of the women come in this profession because of compulsion and non-availability of social and family support. The common reasons for landing in this profession include wrong promise of marriage and having physical relation with poor rural girls prior to marriage resulting in pregnancy, poor educational and financial background, lack of skills and other situational affairs in life. The number of CSWs worldwide is huge. There is no clear estimate of their number in India. Nevertheless, it varies from a few hundreds to a few thousands in different cities. They live in a small room in some locality which is called a 'red-light area'. In every city, there is such designated place where they live alone and/or along with their child. Children of CSWs experience extreme humiliation and discrimination in the larger society. A large number of them are not admitted to school since they do not have their father's identity. They are vulnerable to HIV/AIDS in addition to the risk of sexual abuse. Since these children do not attend the school, they remain unskilled and lead a very poor quality of life. In some 'red-light areas' in India, some NGOs are working for the welfare of CSWs and their children in creating awareness about various health issues. Some NGOs introduced saving schemes for saving some money from the daily income of the CSWs, while some NGOs gave skill development training to CSWs and their children in addition to non-formal and formal education for the children.

In a study on child-rearing practices among brothel-based CSWs, Pardeshi and Bhattacharya (2006) observed that

> some commercial sex workers continued pregnancy with the hope of security and support, while others were compelled to do so, as they report late for medical termination of pregnancy. A group of sex workers (devdasis) received support during pregnancy, delivery, puerperium and child-rearing. The role and responsibilities of raising the child depended upon the kind of family support available to the mothers. Being a single parent, the stigma of the profession, odd working hours and variable family support were major challenges, while the fact that the women were earning, availability of rehabilitation centres, the homogeneous groups within the brothels, supportive peers and local non-governmental organizations were factors which helped them in the process of raising their children.

There are no data available about the total number of children of CSWs across the country. However, their number could be about 0.2–0.3 million or more. The following case study of a child of CSW is a clear example of challenges faced by these children in the society.

> **Case IV:** Neelam, aged 17, female, was living in a red-light area with her mother in Kolkata. She was studying in a nearby government school. An NGO involved in an action research project helped her in getting admitted to a school. She has been studying sincerely and passed the Class X board examination with first division marks. Prior to the NGO intervention, that is about 10 years back, she was very upset about her future since her mother found difficulty in admitting her in schools, since the father's identity was missing. One of the NGO members acted as a guardian for her, which convinced the school authority and admitted her to the school. She experienced a range of challenges in the red-light area and they included humiliation because of her mother's profession; discrimination in every stage of life, including when she a visited nearby hospital; an attempt to be sexually abused by her mother's customer and feeling of insecurity and anxiety due to lack of social support. Now, she feels confident after passing the first board examination with good marks. She wishes to study up to graduation and, after that, she will look for a job. Once she gets a job, she would like to move out of the place with her mother.

6.3.5. Differently Abled Children

According to *The Free Dictionary*:

> the term *differently abled* is sometimes used as a substitute for *disabled* or *handicapped*. *Differently abled* emphasizes the fact that many people with disabilities are quite capable of accomplishing a particular task or performing a particular function, only in a manner that is different from or takes more time than that of

people without the disability. On the other hand, *differently abled* is often criticized as an awkward euphemism and in some cases may be taken as offensively condescending by disabled people themselves. Like *challenged,* it is used most frequently in academic, government, and social service environments; its use outside those contexts may be problematic.[3]

In other words, disability is an umbrella term covering impairments, activity limitations and participation restrictions. Worldwide, the number of differently abled children is increasing. Differently abled children include children with various forms of physical disability, retarded mental growth, LD and so on. They are in helpless condition since adequate intervention facilities in terms of diagnosis of the problem- and need-based training with trained manpower are not available. Although the federal governments in India have brought up appropriate legislation, they did not translate into action across the country. Parents should update their knowledge about the disabled condition of their child and take them to an intervention centre for proper diagnosis of the condition and seek appropriate intervention which might help to improve the condition to some extent. Most importantly, it is necessary to help children with mental retardation and autism to develop skills for self-care activities. In case of children with LD, the situation could be improved, if early intervention is sought.

According to the World Report on Disability released on 9 June 2011, about 15 per cent of the global population, that is, about 1 billion people suffer from various forms of disabilities worldwide and they belong to both developed and developing countries disproportionately (United Nations, 2011). Childline reports that 1.67 per cent of Indian children aged 0–19 years suffer from disability of various kinds. About one-third (35.29%) of all differently disabled people are children in India. Unfortunately, less than 5 per cent of children with disabilities get the opportunity for school education.[4] The following case study is an example of NGO support services for differently abled people.

Case V: Vivek, 12 years, male, was born and brought up in a lower middle-class family. His parents studied up to Class X and both of them work as casual workers. He had one younger brother and one sister, and they were studying in Class II and III, respectively. Vivek could not continue his education because of LD, which was not detected at a young age. His parents as well as school-teachers punished him a number of times for not being able to perform like other children. Therefore, Vivek became a double victim of his circumstances. One day, Vivek's father visited an NGO in their locality and discussed the condition of his elder son, especially concerning his educational background. The NGO then referred the case to another NGO, which was a little far from their house, for needful support. His father visited the same NGO with Vivek, and they diagnosed him with LD. NGO professionals asked him to visit the organization for needful intervention. Finally, intervention helped in improving the situation to some extent. However, Vivek could not continue his formal education and got admitted for vocational training.

6.3.6. CHILDREN WITHOUT PARENTS

Children who lost both of their parents and/or do not have any knowledge about parents whereabouts may be considered under this category. It is very sad that a large number of children worldwide live without parents. A large number of children live without parents in rehabilitation and/or shelter homes run by the government or NGOs. They may not live on the streets and may live with grandparents and other caregivers such as uncle and aunt. Parents might have died because of natural calamities, war, parents in conflict, accident and chronic health problems, or untraceable. In some countries, there is a system to accommodate these children in shelter or rehabilitation homes run by the government and the government takes care of their expenses for proper upbringing. In addition, NGOs also work with these children, provide them with shelter and take care of them in their institute in providing nutrition, education, medical care and vocational guidance. For rehabilitation of these children, sometimes parents without children come forward for adoption legally. The Central Adoption Resource Authority (CARA) is playing a very important role in this regard ensuring proper verification of authenticity and motive of the couple prior to adoption. This approach helps a large number of children to get parents and a home environment and, in turn, it changes their life.

There are no authentic data regarding the number of children without parents in India. Undoubtedly, a large number of children without biological parents live in residential institutions or on their own. They urgently need mental health support facilities in addition to addressing their basic needs including health, nutrition, safety and education.

Case VI: Rahim, aged 10, and his younger sister Kamala, aged 8, live with their aunt since the death of their parents (in a car accident when they were also in the car). They got admitted to school along with their cousins and started attending the school. Although they were not discriminated against, these two children without parents used to feel the absence of their biological parents very much, especially when there was a parent–teacher meeting in a school and/or when there were social gatherings, where other children came with their parents. Psychologically, they used to remain upset most of the time, which was visible in their faces, though they interacted with others in social situations. Nevertheless, psychologically, they could not overcome the traumatic experience of witnessing their parents' death in the car accident.

Case VII: Kamal, aged 14, male, was living in a government-run shelter in Tamil Nadu. He lost both his parents in the Tsunami. He had been receiving formal education and his performance was reasonably satisfactory. Although he could mingle with the inmates of the shelter, sometimes, he fought with other children and for the same reason; he was punished by the home authority on a number of occasions. Sometimes, under the influence of peer group members, he got involved in group fighting and afterwards, he realized his mistakes. Normally, he was active and took part in all sports and cultural programmes of the shelter home. Due to the same reason, the authority did not take any disciplinary action against him when he was caught fighting with other children. He wants to pursue his studies to the greatest extent possible and wants to be economically independent, so that, in turn, he can help other children who are in need of care and support like him.

6.3.7. SLUM CHILDREN

A simple definition of an urban slum is a densely populated area marked by crowding, unhygienic living environment without basic municipal facilities such as sewerage system, electricity, safe drinking water, run-down housing, poverty and social disorganization.

Migration of poor people from rural to urban areas is a common phenomenon for survival. When they come to urban areas, most of them cannot afford to hire a rent a house. They look for free accommodation and finally, they land up in slum areas. Most of the slum areas do not have basic amenities in terms of safe drinking water, sanitation and sewage facility, electricity, education facility for children and living environment is most unhygienic. Very few children from the slum areas get admitted to schools. Even if they are admitted, most of them become school dropouts because of lack of guidance and supervision of their studies. However, there are instances where children from the slum areas persuaded their education successfully despite all hurdles and became doctors and joined some other profession and have been leading a good life with parents. Some of the slums are located just adjacent to railway tracks and/or highways and small children are vulnerable to accidents. Normally, during the daytime, both the parents go out for casual work for earning money and children remain alone at home. In one such slum area in Kolkata, a good number of children became physically handicapped because of a rail accident. Children were playing or sleeping in the railway track and met with an accident. In other slum areas, children are vulnerable to various health problems because of unhygienic living condition. Sometimes, some children from the slum areas get involved in criminal activities under the influence of peer group members and it becomes very difficult to bring them back to the mainstream. Therefore, NGOs should work in different slum areas for providing necessary care and services to the children for their healthy growth and development.

The projected slum population in India was about 104 million by 2017, that is, 9 per cent of the total projected population. According to the data provided in the Parliament, Maharashtra, Uttar Pradesh, Andhra Pradesh and Madhya Pradesh have maximum number of slum children in India.[5] Mascarenhas (2015) reported that every eighth urban child (0–6 years) also lives in slums. Children living in slum areas sometimes get involved in socially deviant activities under the influence of peer group members. For example,

Case VIII: Naveen, aged 14, male, who studied up to Class IV, had been living in a slum in Chennai for four years. He came to the city with his parents in search of a livelihood and discontinued his education. He has one younger sibling aged 7 and studying in Class I in a government school in Chennai. Naveen's father is a casual worker. His mother also works as a domestic help in order to provide for the family. When both the parents went out for work, both the siblings stayed alone at home. Naveen used to look after his younger brother. Naveen was also looking for a job. Naveen has a friend circle in the same slum who was involved in stealing for their pocket expenses. Sometimes, he also did the same job under peer group influence. A number of times, he also had alcohol with his friends. Once he was arrested by police on suspicion and finally, he was released when police arrested the main culprit. That was a good lesson for Naveen. Since then, he has been a little cautious in getting himself engaged in socially undesirable activities under the influence of peer group members.

6.3.8. SCHOOL DROPOUT CHILDREN

The children who got admitted to the primary level for formal education and discontinued for some reasons after sometime are called school dropout children. The number of school dropout children is more in the rural areas as compared to urban areas mostly because of distance, poor infrastructure facilities, non-availability of teachers and/or ineffective teaching methods, lack of supervision and guidance by parents, poor sanitation facilities as well as poor financial condition of the family and wrong perception about value of education. Non-availability of sanitation facilities compels girl students to discontinue education. School dropout rate is high in the families where there are small children and both the parents go to field or outside for work. In this situation, elder children look after the minors. School dropout children in rural areas, especially boys, loiter on the street most of the day with their peer group members and sometimes indulge in deviant social activities including sexual abuse of minor girls. It happens because of non-availability of constructive activities available for these children in rural areas. In some areas, there are video parlours and in most of the video parlours, adult pictures or pornography is shown. Since there is no entertainment for grown-up children in rural areas, they find video parlours attractive because of puberty phase and curious mind. Some of them try to have first-hand experience of sex and when they come across any minor girl unattended, they make an attempt to abuse them. To them, it is not abuse; rather it is saource of fun, whereas in urban areas school dropout children get involved in other deviant or risk activities such as stealing, snatching jewellery and having alcohol under the influence of peer group members. Until attempts are made to continue their education through readmission to school and motivate them for studies, these children will always remain vulnerable and unskilled. Local NGOs should initiate skill-based training programme for them which will, in turn, give them a hope for better life, and society will be benefitted in addition to their family members.

There is no clear estimation concerning the total number of school dropout children in India. It varies from source to source. However, the reality is that a large number of children discontinue education because of various reasons. For example, as per the report of the Montreal-based UNESCO Institute for Statistics and Global Education Monitoring, the total number of school dropout in India at the secondary and higher secondary level was 47 million.[6]

The number of school dropout of both boys and girls in India during 2014–2015 at the primary level was 4.36 per cent and 3.88 per cent, respectively. At secondary level, it was 17.21 for boys and 16.88 for girls. At the primary level, school dropout rate was highest in Assam (11.51 for boys and 10.09 for girls), followed by Arunachal Pradesh (10.35 for boys and 10.03 for girls). At the secondary level, school dropout rate was highest in Daman and Diu for both boys (34.45%) and girls (29.73%).[7]

Case IX: Raman, aged 15, male coming from a poor rural-based agricultural family, had discontinued his education after Class VI. His father was engaged in agricultural work and the mother was a housewife. One day, Raman was scolded and physically beaten badly by the class teacher for not completing the homework. Since then, he stopped attending school. Afterwards, most of the time, he used to loiter with other school dropout children and sometimes got involved in socially undesirable activities under the influence of peer group members. Slowly, he started smoking cigarettes and would often steal coconuts and other fruits from gardens, which invited a lot of problems for his parents. A number of times, his parents were reported about the issue and had struggled to make him understand the situation to not do the same thing in future.

6.3.9. Children from Poor Families

Children from very poor families are those children whose parents are unable to meet their basic expenses. These children remain vulnerable to exploitation, abuse and child trafficking (Deb & Ray, 2016). Most of the children from poor families do not get the opportunity to get admitted to schools. In some cases, even if they are admitted to schools, they discontinue after a short period because of lack of guidance, encouragement and support from the family. Sometimes, distance of the school, ineffective teaching, non-availability of teachers and lack of sanitation facilities compel them to discontinue education. Since they lack social network and social support, the girl child from these families is at double risk of sexual abuse and child trafficking. The people who are involved in child and women trafficking allure the elderly people of a family with utter poverty in the name of a marriage proposal for their girl child and/or with a job opportunity. When parents come across such a proposal, they think that they will be relieved from two meals a day and, in turn, there is possibility to get a share of money from the monthly income of their child, if there is a proposal for a job opportunity. In that case, parents never feel like enquiring about the authenticity of the proposal. Finally, when they hand over the girl child to somebody, these children experience sexual abuse for sometimes and then they are sold to others against huge money and become sex slaves. These children cannot return to their family anymore in most of the cases.

About one-fourth to one-fifth of the total Indian children belong to poor families, that is, BPL. Their parents fail to ensure adequate nutrition, medical care and education for their children. Sometimes children from these families got admitted to schools, but after sometime most of them discontinue because of non-payment of school fees, if admitted in private schools and lack of school uniform and books, and guidance for the study. Children from poor families, especially families with more than one girl child, become vulnerable to child trafficking (Deb et al., 2005). The following case study is the bright example of such situation.

Case X: Gita, aged 14, female, was born and brought up in a very poor family in a rural area. She had two younger sisters aged 12 and 10. Her father was working as a casual labour in agricultural fields. Sometimes, the mother would also work in the agricultural field, especially during the monsoons. Although Gita was admitted to a school, which was far away from her house, she discontinued after four years because of the distance and lack of guidance. Her younger sisters were not admitted to schools because of the same reason. One day, a stranger visited her family with a job offer for Gita and for which she was to go to the city with him. In turn, she can also send some money back to her family. After hearing all the information, her father agreed and said that after one week she can join the job. Meanwhile, her father met the *gram pradhan* (head of village) and shared information about the job offer for Gita. The *gram pradhan* asked her father not to hand over Gita to the man, until he was satisfied about her safety and security, and also asked Gita's father to bring the man to him. When the man came to know that Gita's father discussed the issue with the *gram pradhan*, he disappeared and never came back. It seems that the man was involved in child trafficking.

In sum

A large number of children in the developing countries are neglected and remain vulnerable to abuse and maltreatment. They include children living on the street, child labour, trafficked children, children working as domestic workers, differently abled children, school dropout children, children without parents, children of CSWs and children from poor families.

6.4. LIVING CONDITIONS OF STREET/ORPHAN, SLUM, CHILDREN IN CONFLICT WITH LAW AND CHILDREN OF CSWs

6.4.1. LIVING CONDITIONS OF STREET AND/OR ORPHAN CHILDREN

Thousands and thousands of children across the world live on the street which is unsafe and dirty. According to a study conducted among the street children in the city of Chennai, about 90 per cent of them live with their parents in the streets (National Labor Institution, 1992). They mostly survive working as ragpickers.

In fact, no basic facilities are available for the street children. Normally, they avail whatever facilities are available in nearby places where they reside. These children usually exercise their choice and remove themselves from the environment. They learn to survive through 'unconventional' means. A place to sleep at night and escape from the hell of abuse is always a cause of worry for these children. While some have a fixed place to sleep, others sleep wherever they find it convenient and safe. Having no permanent place also means that the children cannot store their possessions in a secured place. However, they often have to contend with the police, who would drive them off the road, platform, abandoned building and so on.

In general, people on the pavement tend to gather in a number of places and sleep in shop verandas, under bridges, trees, in bus shelters, abandoned buildings or just out in the open, railway station platforms. They are virtually excluded from urban infrastructure and facilities whatsoever and have to rely on roadside amenities for water used for drinking and cooking. Open space serves as sanitary purposes. Medical, educational and other essential services are inaccessible to them. Most of the street and/or orphan children across the country do not have access to shelter.

The local police and even the municipal cleaners create great difficulties for the street and/or children in India. For any petty thefts, they are the first ones to be accused by the police. It has been observed that the police extort about half the earnings of the rag pickers as commission. The children also had to pay some staff members of the municipality to ease the way for rag picking (National Labor Institution, 1992). Chilly winter nights, mosquito bites, regular theft and violence, susceptible to bullying, policemen, local dadas, passers-by, passengers, railway staffs, coolies harassment, accidents, sudden showers, absence of a dry place to sleep during monsoons and so on are the constant problems these children face who are out on the streets.

A large number of children are found today living on a railway station in every corner of the country. Life on a railway station has its own rhythm—mostly characterized by trains whistling in and out and the movement of large numbers of people with trains arriving and departing. Within this floating population are some people who are constant features—vendors selling various eateries/drinks, booksellers, others like the railway staff and, of course, coolies (porters). It is in this environment that children on the platforms eke out their existence: washing, bathing, earning, eating food, playing and sleeping. While some on the platform live with their family or other relations, many live on their own. Like all street children, the ones living at the railway stations are mobile groups and often do not stay in one place for long.

In some places in the cities, children on the streets sometimes share the common bathrooms and latrines, share the living areas, cook and eat in the open because of lack of kitchen space, make their living claustrophobic and deprive the residents of any sort of privacy. Although there is no water shortage in those areas where they live, many water sources are located near public toilets or garbage dumps. This increases the chances of water contamination. Defecation in the open and in public places further deteriorates their health conditions. The violence and aggressions are everyday occurrences and happen at any time of the day and night. Gang wars between two areas take place almost regularly on every street.

Inadequate food, unhygienic living conditions and the strain of work affect the health of working street children. From a number of studies, it has been reported that the majority of the children fall prey to physical weakness, fatigue, backache and muscle pain. Also, children are affected by respiratory tract infections, TB, diarrhoea, skin diseases and worm infestations.

Most problems of urban childhood have their roots in a country's rural sector. This is especially true for countries like India where thousands of children are forced to migrate from villages to cities to ultimately end up in extremely exploitative situations. Thanks to empirical research, there is now a greater understanding of the characteristics of street children in general and the nature of their daily lives. It is commonly accepted that these children constitute a fundamentally different category of children to street living children. The majority of studies on street children have focused exclusively on the children living on the streets, leaving our understanding of the psychological characteristics of street children.

Many street/orphan children end up by settling in the city street, marrying and having a family. In this manner, the street influences in propagating their generation. Abebe (2009) did a study to explore the working lives of street children in Addis Ababa, focusing in particular on an analysis of begging. Findings disclosed that 'although begging is a way of life that some children have followed since early childhood, for others it is merely a pastime activity, and a temporary survival strategy from which they will eventually "move on."'

6.4.2. Living Conditions of Slum Children and Children of CSWs

Like street children, the living environment of slum children and the children of CSWs is somewhat similar. In the slum and/or in the red-light areas where CSWs normally live, there is a designated place where children live with their parents and/or mothers. They do not frequently change the place until they are asked by the owner of the house to vacate the house, especially in the red-light areas. In the case of a slum, sometime slum dwellers are asked to vacate the place for development work, that is, road construction and/or construction of flyover.

In almost all the slums and red-light areas, the living environment is not hygienic, safe and comfortable. Because of poverty and compulsion, they live in these underdeveloped areas without any basic facilities such as no safe drinking water, no sewage facility, no electricity, and housing condition is very poor. In slum areas, people live in plastic shelters without any ventilation facilities. If there is heavy rain or storm, they take shelter in verandas of nearby buildings. Both slum children and children of CSWs are exposed to environmental hazards and violence. The children of CSWs, especially girl children, are vulnerable to sexual abuse, maltreatment, discrimination and humiliation. Male children of CSWs are used by the mother's customers for bringing alcohol and food for them and carry forward all other work as instructed by the owner of the house and other senior and powerful members of the locality. Whenever a customer comes, children have to leave the home and take shelter on the street since most of the CSWs live in single small rooms without much ventilation facility. Most of the children of CSWs are deprived of primary education and primary health facilities like slum children.

6.4.3. LIVING CONDITIONS IN THE OBSERVATION/REHABILITATION AND/OR SHELTER HOMES

Children in conflict with law or in need of care are forwarded to the observation homes for behaviour modification and/or safe shelter. In most of the government-run observation homes, all children in need of care and in conflict with law are referred by the juvenile courts and/or social welfare department. Most of the homes are overburdened, that is, the number of children is more than double, if not more, as compared to space. Keeping the increasing number of these categories of children, more number of homes should have been developed. But it did not happen in most of the states in India resulting in an overcrowded living environment with minimal facilities including lack of arrangements of vocational training and non-formal education for these children.

Training programmes available in the observation homes for these children are not beneficial for getting a job once they are released from the homes. Most of the training programmes are not skill-based. So far as hygienic condition is concerned, some homes are well maintained while others are not in good conditions. It all depends upon the head of the institution, that is, superintendent of homes. The home where the superintendent of homes is active and dynamic, overall functioning of the home is very good.

In sum

In general, the living condition of disadvantaged children is unhygienic, risky and having inadequate space, especially in the government observation homes. The places where they live are prone to health hazards that result from direct exposure to changing weather. There exist almost no facilities for sanitation and for taking bath. For drinking water, they depend upon nearby available sources, whether safe or unsafe. For nature's call, they mostly go to open space.

6.5. PROBLEMS ENCOUNTERED BY THE VULNERABLE CHILDREN

Vulnerable children encounter various problems in everyday life. Problems include neglect, abuse, maltreatment, exploitation, discrimination and deprivation from their fundamental rights being a citizen of a country. Regarding the problem of street children, Glauser stated that street children are always in anticipation that any moment they might be woken up by a policeman's boot or stick, or may be drenched by a jet of cold water from a truck, car, bus lined up for a street wash. However, a brief description of the major problems encountered by vulnerable children is discussed further.

6.5.1. LACK OF SAFE SHELTER

The basic problem vulnerable children face is lack of safe shelter. Wherever they stay and wherever they go, they are unsafe. Everywhere they are at high risk of exploitation, sexual abuse and harassment. Nowadays a good number of NGOs started working for the welfare and rehabilitation of vulnerable children in different parts of the country. A good number of fortunate children enjoy this facility, which is more needed for a girl child.

6.5.2. INADEQUATE FOOD

For earning money for bread and butter, street/destitute and child labourers work hard whole day as nobody is there to ensure two meals a day for them. Among them, some live with their parents on the street, in slums and/or in rural areas. They are relatively in better condition since either of the parents or both the parents are there with them. Children without parents and with no education work as unskilled labour and get minimum wage. A large number of them do not get the minimum nutrition and suffer from malnutrition.

6.5.3. LACK OF EDUCATIONAL FACILITIES

Most of them do not get the opportunity to study. Some might have been admitted to school and have discontinued while some had never been to school. As a result, in future when they become older, they do not get a better job. Whole life they work as unskilled labourers and are exploited.

6.5.4. NEGLECT, ABUSE AND MALTREATMENT

The most common problem vulnerable children experience is neglect in terms of nutrition, medical care, education, love and affection, and supervision of their education. A large number of them remains unattended and nobody is there to address their issues and concern.

The rehabilitation and different shelter homes are places where vulnerable children, especially those who are in conflict with law, need care and safety, and live without parents. These places are supposed to be safe and secured. However, frequent reports by print and electronic media highlight the scary situation in those places reporting sexual abuse of children across the country. For example, the Tata Institute of Social Sciences' report in Bihar disclosed an incidence of sexual abuse of both boys and girls in six shelter homes in Bihar. ActionAid's report also substantiated the same with the data from other parents of the country (Singh, 2018).

Reza (2017) did a study in Bangladesh to understand the nature of violence experienced by street children almost regularly covering a sample of 75 street children. The study yielded

insights about the types of violence endured and how age, gender, and location impacted risks faced by street children. The study also highlights the complex and varied roles that social networks and group solidarity, as well as the actions of individual peers, play in the survival of this vulnerable population.

6.5.5. Physical and Mental Health Problems

Street children experience a range of physical and mental problems and they mostly remain unattended. Beegle et al. (2009) found significant negative consequences of child labour on education and health for working for long hours in a day. O'Donnell et al. (2002) commented that 'the relationships between child labor and health are complex. They can be direct and indirect, static and dynamic, positive and negative, causal and spurious.'

Sexually transmitted infections (STIs), pregnancy, trauma, TB, uncontrolled asthma and dermatologic infestations are a few of the health problems, which are commonly present among street and orphan children and children of CSWs. Some of them also become dependent on drugs and alcohol under the influence of peer group members or by drug peddlers. They are also vulnerable to HIV/AIDS as some of them experience sexual abuse in these somatic problems, are compounded by high rates of drug and alcohol abuse as well as depression and suicide. Despite the obvious need for medical services, homeless youth are at the hands of strangers.

There is some evidence concerning health issues of vulnerable children. For example, in a qualitative study covering 48 street children from three locations, Mathiti (2006) found that

> the street children were depressed due to lack of access or substandard educational and medical facilities, or depressed because of living conditions at the shelters. Based on the findings of the study, the author suggested that the participants who were accommodated at shelters that encouraged involvement in income-generating activities were more likely to experience a compromise of their emotional well-being than their counterparts who were not involved in income-generating activities.

Franieck and Page (2017) analysed three case studies of three brothers, ages 5, 8 and 11, and observed that 'all the three children experienced family conflict. Further, their narratives were also characterized by emotional detachment, limited parental engagement, and self-centeredness.'

Street and orphan children are at high risk of psychological problems too in addition to various physical health problems as a result of both the circumstances that preceded their homelessness, and as a direct consequence of life on the streets. Like street and orphan children, slum children and the children of CSWs also encounter similar mental health challenges and remain unattended since parents, if available, are not in a position to understand the problem and to take them to mental health professionals for remedial measures. Regarding the psychological state of these children, Craig and Hodson (2000) found signs and symptoms of psychiatric disorder among 55 per cent homeless children, associated with adverse childhood experiences and rough sleeping. Sourander (1998) examined the traBharatitic events and behaviour symptoms of 46 unaccompanied refugees and found that 'refugee children are more vulnerable to emotional distress than older children.' Senanayake et al. observed that Colombian street children were mostly exposed to road traffic accidents, and physical and sexual abuse.

In case of any health problem, most of vulnerable children remain unattended, except few lucky children who are under the intervention programme of NGOs and/or live with parents. Sometimes they visit nearby/local government health centres for treatment and get free medicine. Since street/orphan and destitute children do not have anybody to follow up whether they are taking medicine on time or not, and since there is no secured and safe place to preserve medicines after one or two days, they do not take the medicine regularly. Hence, a large number of vulnerable children suffer from different health problems throughout the year.

6.5.6. Risk Behaviour

Most vulnerable children live on the streets, in slums and in red-light areas and are exposed to the risks of tobacco, alcohol and substance abuse and the subsequent addiction. Vulnerable children on the streets, in slums and in red-light areas are also used as drug peddlers and pushers (injectors). The lure of money is high. Gambling in the form of *satta* (a form of gambling) and playing cards is most common among all age groups of males and they can be seen playing cards in the park and on every street of the cities.

In this regard, South African studies have suggested that 'street children are resilient but also suicidal, engage in unprotected sex and other high risk sexual behaviour as a means of survival, have high rates of substance abuse and are physically abused and stigmatized due to their state of homelessness' (Hills et al., 2016). However, in this regard, an interpretative phenomenological analysis of the transcribed data revealed that

> incidence of violence and drug and alcohol use were common experiences of street life. Yet despite these challenges survival was made possible through personal and emotional strength, cultural values, religious beliefs, supportive peer relationships, and participation in sports activities. These protective, resilience resources should be strengthened in health promotion interventions with a focus on mental health, the prevention of violence, substance use, and daily physical activities that seems to provide meaning and hope. (Hills et al., 2016)

In another study, Johnson et al. (1996) assessed HIV risk behaviours in a sample of homeless youth in a large urban area in Chicago and examined factors associated with these behaviours. Findings revealed that

> overall, 83.7% reported at least one of these risk factors: multiple sex partners; high-risk partners; inconsistent condom use; history of sexually transmitted disease; anal sex; prostitution; and/or intravenous drug use. An index of these behaviors was associated with being male, having unmet personal needs, being interviewed in street locations, and having a history of sexual abuse.

Street children are vulnerable to a number of other problems throughout their lives. Keeping this background in mind, Bashir and Dasti (2015) attempted to examine the relationship between poly-victimization and mental health in street children of Lahore city. The results indicated that

> poly-victimization positively predicted the psychological distress and negatively predicted psychological wellbeing in street children. Further the authors concluded that the most common type of victimization was conventional crime which negatively predicts mental health of street children. The results highlight the need for designing improved services for this vulnerable group.

In sum

Disadvantaged children encounter various challenges and remain vulnerable to problems such as poor nutrition, psychological and physical health problems, and lack of access to health facilities, lack of safety, lack of educational facilities, various forms of abuse, neglect and harassment. Some of them get involved in risk behaviour unconsciously without understanding the consequences of the behaviour or under pressure.

6.6. REASONS FOR LEAVING HOME AND ACCEPTING STREET LIFE

Children feel most comfortable to live with their biological parents and siblings. Living with biological parents gives them a sense of acceptance, feeling safe, mental security and happiness. In the absence of biological parents, generally children feel unsafe and helpless, and become vulnerable to various forms of abuse, neglect and maltreatment. Therefore, hardly any child wishes to leave home when there is a congenial family environment.

Now the question arises why some children leave home? Children leave home for the most trivial of reasons, such as fear of being scolded or wounded pride at some imagined insult. Sometimes, family violence and extreme poverty force them to leave home.

A seven-year-old boy from Tirupati had run away from home after being burned with cigarette butts by his father. Should an abusive father be given guardianship? When the case came for hearing in the Juvenile Welfare Board, he was bundled into the next train to Tirupati, Andhra Pradesh, as the parents have the right to custody. The law of the land gives custody of children to parents even if they abuse their children regularly. Law does not empower children to fight abuse (Source: Report of The New Indian Express, December 2001).

Deb and Mitra (2002) carried out a study in Kolkata, India, with a view to identifying the multi-factorial causes responsible for leading children to accept a street life. A group of 40 children, 18 males and 22 females in the age group of 9–19 years, was covered in the present study. Findings disclosed that

> the factors which mostly pushed children to the street, half-dug pavements, railway platforms include influence of step-parents, death of either or both parents, and ill-treatment of grandparents, family disintegration, and gender bias of parents, effect of poverty and/or unemployment, deviant behavior of parents, parental carelessness and environmental influence. From such stressful experience these children also developed some future aspirations like other children living in normal family environment.

In Kenya, Wainaina found that

> most of the children are on the street due to family-related problems. Author further argues that most of them come from a family background of physical, emotional and/or sexual abuse. Although these findings point to family dysfunction and disintegration as the major reasons why children end up on the streets, it should be noted that most of these family problems are aggravated by poverty.

In sum

Street children leave home because of unhappy family environment, violence or under the influence of peer group members when they become school dropouts. Sometimes, they want to venture into the beauty of city life and get into a local train and are unable to return home and finally accept street for living.

6.7. CONSEQUENCES OF CHILDREN LIVING IN VULNERABLE CONDITION

Children living in vulnerable conditions finally experience the worst consequences in different forms. In most of the cases, children are forced by circumstances to land up in vulnerable conditions for which most of them are deprived of school which is the foundation for any individual for acquiring skills and knowledge for leading a quality life. In the following section, the adverse effects of their vulnerable condition have been discussed.

6.7.1. RETARDATION OF NORMAL GROWTH OF THE CHILD

Engagement of children in economic activities at an early age and deprivation from minimum nutrition retards the normal mental and physical growth of the children. As a result, the mental and physical strength of the children is burned in their early age of life, especially children who work as child labour.

6.7.2. DEPRIVATION FROM CHILD RIGHTS

An overwhelming number of vulnerable children are deprived of their fundamental rights, that is, safety, adequate nutrition, education, medical care and love as well as affection. They are also deprived of their childhood since a good number of them get engaged in economic activities because of poverty. Normally during childhood, every child gets maximum pleasure playing with peer group children and through games and sports, and engagement in recreational activities.

6.7.3. ACADEMIC BACKWARDNESS

Because of involvement in economic activities, working children remain deprived of education and thereby their inner potentials remain underutilized. A large number of other categories of vulnerable children have either never been to school or discontinue education and remain unskilled labour for life long. Hence, the nation loses a good amount of potential human resources.

6.7.4. DEVIATION FROM THE MAINSTREAM OF THE SOCIETY

The children who are involved in economic activities at an early age are deprived of basic minimal education and as a result, in later life, they do not find a good job. After some years of work, if they lose their job or the company is closed down where they used to work, no option is left to them to survive following honest and/or normal means. As a result, during unemployment period, a good number of them involve themselves in antisocial activities under slightest provocation and gradually a large number of them deviate from the mainstream of the society. There is a need to take up the programme for modification of behaviour of deviant children (Deb et al., 1997).

6.7.5. WORKING CONDITIONS AND HEALTH HAZARDS

Most vulnerable children get engaged in some economic activities for survival. Owing to the nature of different kinds of work and work environment, children become victims of different forms of health problems, both physical and mental. Children starting work at an early age have a longer period of exposure to cumulative health hazards.

6.7.6. SEXUAL ABUSE, MALTREATMENT AND EXPLOITATION

Most vulnerable children experience sexual abuse, maltreatment and exploitation (Deb & Gireesan, 2015). There are incidences of sexual abuse of both boys and girls in the shelter homes in different parts of India (Singh, 2018). Children who work as child labour are exploited by most of the employers in terms of poor salary and, sometimes, they do not get their salary which they saved with the employer on account of minor issues. Often, they experience ill treatment and discrimination despite their best services to the employer. When they suffer from minor health problems, they mostly remain unattended. Children who work in hazardous work conditions like in firecracker, chemical and stone chips industries suffer from lungs and other related health problems.

Deb et al. (1997) made an attempt to investigate the nature and workload of girl children engaged in domestic work, their wage package and the kind of problems faced by them. The majority of the girl children were found to have been receiving wages too low (ranging from US$1–10 per month) compared to the nature and volume of work performed by them (i.e., cleaning utensils, clothes, rooms, taking care of younger children, cooking and shopping), not to mention untold psychological (i.e., threatened to dismiss from the work, not allowed to enter into the house, withdrawal of food, confinement in a room) and even physical torments (i.e., being beaten up by stick, utensils, iron rod and hot iron) inflicted upon them for minor mistakes. Not infrequently, these girls become victims of sexual harassment, particularly in the upper-class families. Almost in all cases, they are treated no better than slaves and are forced to feed on leftovers of the meals served to the concerned household members. Well or unwell, they are compelled to do all types of household chores, because they are altogether deprived of medical attention. While reality stands as observed earlier, it is of utmost importance of the hour to create widespread social awareness in order to change the lots of countless neglected and abused girl children for the better which they rightly deserve.

6.7.7. CONSEQUENCES FOR BEING A CHILD OF A CSW

Evidence concerning challenges for the children of CSWs is scanty. However, available literature provides some idea about the plight of their situation in the red-light areas in particular and larger society in general. Often the children of CSWs experience social stigma and discrimination as a result of their mother's profession. Their social network and support facilities are also very poor. They hardly receive any support when needed. However, this potential vulnerability can be ameliorated by potential sources of resilience connected to support networks, parent health, parent–child bonding, education, economic situation and other environmental factors (Hogan, 1998).

Some studies based on South Asia and Kenya report that the separation of children of CSWs from parents, sexual abuse, early sexual debut, introduction to sex work as adolescents, low school enrolment, psychosocial issues arising from witnessing their mothers' sexual interactions with clients and social marginalization are the most common challenges they experience (Bletzer, 2005; Chege et al., 2002; Pandey, 2008; Pardeshi & Bhattacharya, 2006; Sloss & Harper, 2004). Grooming to enter the sex trade and trafficking is the reality for some children of CSWs since options are limited for survival as perceived by some CSWs (Hayman, 2003; Ling, 2001). In Kenya, the more educated a sex worker was, the more likely she was to prioritize education for her children (Chege et al., 2002).

A large number of children of CSWs are at high risk of HIV, congenital syphilis, fatal alcohol syndrome, physical and sexual violence and TB (Beard et al., 2014; Chersich et al., 2014; Majid et al., 2010; Shahmanesh et al., 2009). However, there are a few studies on children of female sex workers (FSWs), and none include the data on their HIV rates or causes of death.

In a qualitative study on differently abled children among rural communities in India, on the basis of the case study method, Janardhana et al. (2015) observed different forms of discrimination experienced by these children and they include denial of disability, physical restraints, social boycott, denial of property rights, decreased marital life prospects due to disabled member in family, implications on the sexuality of people with disability, women with disability, discrepancies in state welfare programmes and problems in measuring disabilities.

In sum

The children who live in vulnerable condition suffer from multiple problems such as poor cognitive and physical development, deprivation from their fundamental rights, academic backwardness, social isolation and a range of physical health challenges including HIV/AIDS because of sexual abuse. Physical punishment for stealing for survival and humiliation is very common. In addition, social discrimination is very common in their life.

6.8. PREVENTION OF FURTHER GROWTH OF STREET/ORPHAN CHILDREN, CHILD LABOUR AND CHILDREN WORKING AS DOMESTIC ASSISTANT

As stated earlier, vulnerable children are of various categories and broadly they include street children, orphan children, child labour, slum children, children from poor families working as domestic assistant, children of CSWs, differently abled children, children without parents, children living in slums just adjacent to the railway track and underdeveloped living environment, children from poor families and school dropout children. Children of all these categories are at risk of abuse, neglect, maltreatment and harassment, and their nature of risk varies as they are different from each category in terms of socio-economic and family environment. For example, the situations of street and orphan children are different. Some street children live on the street with their parents while some are alone as they do not have any information about parents' whereabouts. The second category of children may be called orphan children. Let us discuss prevention of growth of street/orphan children and child labour.

For prevention of further growth of street/orphan children and child labour, community psychologists should adopt the following strategies in association with allied organizations and/or government departments:

- *Improvement of rural infrastructure and job opportunities:* The rapid growth of street and/or orphan children in almost all cities is the result of rapid urbanization through migration.

Hence, migration should be checked arranging basic amenities and employment opportunities in the rural areas.

- *Support for income-generating programme in rural areas:* Poverty is one of the main causes behind a large number of children who come to the city for finding the means of life and finally they work as child labour. In the rural areas, awareness should be created about the sources of financial support from the banks for cultivation, income-generating activities and/ or for small business. In this regard, more NGOs should come forward and work in different rural areas. NGOs can motivate and help poor rural people to form self-help groups and initiate economically viable income-generating activities.

- *Social awareness on child rights and for prevention of child labour:* Social awareness is urgently needed to sensitize people of across society about child rights and the negative aspects of child labour and its long-term impact on child's future quality of life and overall socio-economic development of the country. Findings revealed that parents and teachers lack knowledge about child rights (Deb & Mathews, 2012). The awareness programmes need to be organized separately for different target groups. For creating social awareness, mass media, especially through television shows, non-government welfare organizations, trade union, government and various political parties, can play an important role in creating awareness about the dire consequences of child labour.

- *Prevention of family violence:* In some families, parent–child relationship is not healthy. As a result, children often witness violence in the family. Some children find it difficult to cope with a hostile family environment and therefore they prefer to run away. Hence, it is important to launch an intervention programme in the rural areas to create awareness about child-rearing practices and importance of cordial parent–child relationships. In urban areas, NGOs should identify runaway children and integrate them with the family.

- *Sensitization about family planning methods and gender-related issue:* Premarital or unwanted pregnancy and/or preference for a male child are the main causes behind an increasing number of orphan children across the society. The issue requires intensive awareness about family planning methods and gender sensitization both in the rural and urban areas for giving a clear picture about the role of both the genders, that is, both boys and girls are equally potential and productive if equal opportunity is given to them. Electronic media and NGOs can play a vital role in creating awareness about these issues.

- *Prevention of children working as domestic assistant:* Normally the children whose mother works as domestic assistant follow the same tradition. Initially, they visit the place with their mothers and assist them when they are very small. In most of the cases, mothers take their young child to their workplace since nobody is there to look after them. A good number of others admit their child to nearby schools and most of them discontinue after 2–3 years of study. They do not find much interest in the studies since teaching is not effective, school infrastructure is not good, teachers fail to teach in an interesting manner and finally nobody is there at home to supervise and guide them. Finally, they discontinue, and their mother engages them in somebody's house as full-time or part-time domestic assistant. In this regard also, the role of NGOs or community-based organizations is very important. They can think of opening a half-way home in different slums from where mothers go for domestic work and mothers can leave their child when they go for work. In addition, NGOs can think of providing guidance for studies and engaging children in some creative and vocational activities.

In sum

A number of measures might help to prevent further growth of street/orphan children, child labour and children working as domestic assistant. They include improving rural infrastructure and job opportunities, encouraging rural people for income-generating programme for prevention of migration from rural areas to urban areas, measures for prevention of family violence, creation of awareness about child rights, family planning methods and gender-related issue and sending children to school instead of engaging them in domestic work.

6.9. INTERVENTION

In order to address the issues and challenges of vulnerable children, community- and institution-based intervention programmes should be taken up by the public health professionals in which doctors, community psychologists and social workers are an integral part of the process. In this regard, community psychologists should take the lead role along with social work professionals and the Department of Social Welfare of each state. For addressing the issues of vulnerable children, it is essential to involve local NGOs and other allied organizations since they have close touch with the grassroots people. Community-based intervention programme is needed for vulnerable children who live with parents, while institution-based intervention is most suitable for street or orphan children. Since vulnerable children fall under different categories, their issues and challenges are different. The ultimate objective of intervention is to ensure that these vulnerable children do not experience further victimization and get a safe platform for healthy growth and development.

6.9.1. Ensuring Institution-based Programme for Safe Shelter and Basic Facilities for Street, Orphan and Destitute Children

So far as street, orphan and destitute children are concerned, it is very important to locate them and bring them under some intervention programme or in the shelter home ensuring safe accommodation and other basic minimum facilities. Based on the age, gender and maturity level of the children, need-based intervention programme should be arranged. Essentially intervention programmes include training on socialization process, non-formal education, arrangement of formal education for matured children with some level of literacy and getting them admitted in nearby day school or residential school. For some older children who are not interested in formal school, vocational training programme could be arranged for them based on their interest, aptitude and job market. In addition, it is very important to examine their health status and provide them immunization from time to time. It would be good if NGOs can trace the family of those children, if possible, and connect and insist them to visit their child which will be good for their mental health.

A number of studies found that institutional care is not beneficial, rather it is damaging to the development of infants and small children relative to foster care (Tizard & Hodges, 1978; Van et al., 2008). However, Whetten et al. (2009) reported that just opposite findings, that is, institutional care and support services are beneficial for children in need.

6.9.2. Arrangement of Non-formal and Formal Education for Vulnerable Children under Both Institution- and Community-based Programmes

Arrangements of non-formal education should be made for vulnerable children who had never been to school. Every effort should be made to bring all vulnerable children under intervention for education. Non-formal education will enhance their confidence and will motivate them for formal education and accordingly, they should be admitted to school for formal education with residential accommodation facilities for those who require it. Education is necessary for including values in addition to knowledge and skills among children and finally making them skilled manpower for nation-building. Regular supervision and guidance are prerequisites for ensuring the continuation of education of vulnerable children with full clarity.

6.9.3. Mental Health Intervention and Recreational Activities Including Group Activities for Children under Both Institution- and Community-based Programmes

As vulnerable children are exposed to hard reality, they experience neglect, abuse and maltreatment in addition to witnessing violence, some of them suffer from post-traumatic stress, anxiety, deprivation and fear psychosis (Deb & Mukherjee, 2009, 2011; Deb & Sen, 2006; Deb & Walsh, 2012; Deb et al., 2011). In order to address these issues, mental health intervention is essential to enhance their psychological competence and give them confidence and mental strength to cope with real-life adversities. In addition to individual counselling, group and psychotherapy, recreational and group activities should be arranged. It is believed that group activities help children to forget adverse and traumatic experience fast and resume normal activities.

6.9.4. Vocational Training for Children for Both Institution- and Community-based Programmes

Children without much formal education may be given vocational training on different trades. After vocational training, NGOs should assist them in getting work so that they can live in society with dignity and self-respect.

6.9.5. Arrangement of Night Shelter for the Street Children

Street children are subjected to all forms of abuse and maltreatment in everyday life. Besides other harassment, girl children are more prone to sexual abuse. Hence, a safe night shelter is urgently needed for these children, especially for girl children, to protect them from antisocials and from pimps. This apart, an arrangement for keeping the belongings of children is required. So night shelter should have the same arrangements. NGOs should also provide dress to these children collecting from different sources.

6.9.6. Monitoring Working Condition of Child Labour

It is very important to map all the industries where children are employed and make an effort to determine the age of the working children. The children who are below the age of 14 years should be taken back to their family and get admitted to school. Parents should be sensitized about the welfare of the child and supported with information in case of any issue and concern which compelled them to engage their minor child in economic activity.

The children who are above the age of 14 years may be allowed to work, subject to work condition, their remuneration and timings of work. If the workplace does not have proper ventilation, lighting and hygienic facilities, and children are poorly paid and work for a long period in a day, local labour inspector should warn the employer to improve the situation and increase the wages of the children as per market rate. Continuous monitoring of the workplace by concerned government employee would perhaps improve the situation. In this regard, local municipal counsellors should also be vigilant about the issue and give them a feel if they do not comply with government norm in employing children in their factory or industry, their licence will automatically be cancelled. The employer should also be asked to give minimum free time to these children for playing with friends and/or watching television entertainment programme in addition to ensuring basic literacy for them.

6.9.7. Needful Measures for Children Working as Domestic Assistant

Children working as domestic assistants also come under child labour category. But their nature of work is different. Community psychologists with the help of local NGOs should sensitize the larger society about the condition which compels some children from poor families to work as domestic assistant through community-based awareness programme and mass media. The employers should be sympathetic to them. They should treat them as human beings and provide them some care which they do with their own child instead of treating them as slaves and disregard their rights to safety, proper nutrition, healthcare and dignity. Since they are engaged for domestic work, they should perform their duties. Under no circumstances, they should be exploited, abused and maltreated. In every locality, local NGOs should spread the same messages among local community members. These children should be allowed to visit their parents periodically and little free time for relaxation. Further, the employer should teach them basic literacy so that they can read and write, which will make a big difference in their life.

6.9.8. Needful Measures for Children from Poor Families through Community-based Intervention Programme

Children from poor families are deprived of adequate nutrition, primary healthcare and education. Most of them are not admitted to schools and they remain out of school. These children are more vulnerable to sexual abuse and child trafficking. Local panchayat members need to identify the families living BPL and help them with information to improve their economic condition and/or with loan facility for taking up income-generating activities. These children should be brought up under the ICDS so that they enjoy the benefits of non-formal education and supplementary nutrition. They should be sensitized about the value of education so that they prefer to admit their children to school. Monitoring of school attendance by the local panchayat and/or community leaders of these children will ensure their safety and better future.

6.9.9. Needful Measures for Children of CSWs through Community-based Intervention Programme

Children of CSWs are deprived of their basic rights such as safety, education, healthcare and adequate nutrition and are more vulnerable to sexual abuse and join their mother's profession under adversities, especially when mothers are not able to run the profession on account of health problems and/or overage. These children are discriminated since their mothers are in the sex trade and experience humiliation as the larger society looks at them differently. Therefore, local public representatives with the help of local youth volunteers and NGOs should come forward and take up a welfare programme for these children in terms of arranging safe shelter in the locality when their mothers remain busy in entertaining their clients. In addition, efforts should be made by them to get these children admitted into school and provide them guidance in the evening hours and motivate them to pursue education sincerely in addition to ensuring free educational materials, school fees and school uniform (Deb, 2002). Some group activities for the children and their mothers should be arranged to enhance their resilience capacity and psychological competence to deal with all challenges in life. Periodic outings and educational tours would further enhance their self-confidence. The children who are not interested in general education, vocational education could be arranged for them keeping their interest and aptitude as well as market demand into account. Sports and cultural problems could also be arranged for improving group cohesiveness and for entertainment in which children from the larger community could be invited. Periodic health check-up and counselling for them and for their mothers should also be arranged.

There is a need to open daycare centres and night shelters in the red-light area where the children can be looked after during the working hours. The sex workers should be educated about weaning and nutrition. The role of peer workers and NGOs was very important in helping the women raise their children (Pardeshi & Bhattacharya, 2006).

6.9.10. Needful Measures for Differently Abled Children through Community-based Intervention Programme

Children experience different forms of disability. It could be physical, mental and LD and their issues and concerns are different. Early diagnosis of the problem is essential to decide the nature of intervention by professionals. Intervention would help to improve the condition. Parents should be sensitized to bring their children with any form of disability for early diagnosis and their role in improving the condition of the child at home. It is necessary to bring the children with disability in the organizations/centres which are engaged in dealing with differently abled children for periodic follow-up and/or regular visit depending upon the nature of the condition and as prescribed by the experts. The children who are not intellectually impaired should be encouraged to get admitted to school and continue it as education can bring quality change in their lives.

6.9.11. Needful Measures for School Dropout Children through Community-based Intervention Programme

The number of school dropout children is large. Normally children become school dropouts because of lack of supervision and discouraging and/or fearful school environment. These children should be counselled, encouraged and motivated to continue their education and get readmitted to school. In this regard, parents should be sensitized so that they get their children admitted to school. If a child became school dropout because of discouragement and/or fearful school environment, the issue should be taken up with local administration and/or with the panchayat member if the school is located in rural areas. In the case of urban school, local leaders should be contacted to do the needful in addition to talking to the principal of the school. Sometimes non-availability of sanitation facility might be the cause for school dropout of girl children. In that case, school authorities should implement the appropriate measures immediately.

In sum

Intervention programmes which are needed to improve the condition of vulnerable children include institution-based safe shelter and basic facilities for street, orphan and destitute children, non-formal and formal education for vulnerable children. Under both institution- and community-based programmes, mental health intervention and recreational activities are needed including group activities, vocational training, safe night shelter for the street children, periodic monitoring of working condition of child labour and domestic assistants, and needful measures for children from poor families, children of CSWs, differently abled children and school dropout children are required.

6.10. STEPS FOR EFFECTIVE IMPLEMENTATION OF INTERVENTION PROGRAMME

The following steps are suggested for the effective implementation of intervention programmes for the disadvantaged and vulnerable children in general and street children in particular on the basis of the author's first-hand field and research experience.

- It is necessary to identify the disadvantaged and/or street children. The NGOs which are involved in intervention and rehabilitation of vulnerable and/or street children should have a network with the councillor of local Municipal Corporation, schools, youth groups and hospitals to locate the street children. NGOs should have contact centres/places in the bus stand, railway platform and in the commercial areas.
- Community psychologists working in the NGOs should listen to their problems, basic requirements/needs and try to contact the family members, if available, for reintegration.
- Next, community psychologists should make arrangements for thorough medical examination and extend medical services, if required.
- Further, community psychologists should extend individual and group counselling for establishing a trust-building relationship so that they feel like to stay in the shelter home of

the NGO and arrange group and recreational activities for these children to make them comfortable in the shelter home. In addition, children should be engaged in daily activities of the shelter home. Their involvement in daily activities will help to develop a sense of belongingness among them.

- Family counselling should be extended if parents, or either of the parents, are available and NGOs should seek their cooperation for the future career of their child. Parents should be asked to visit their child periodically at least once a month which will make their child happy.
- Non-formal education to disadvantaged/street children should be provided to make them familiar with the socialization process. Teachers engaged in non-formal and formal education should be sensitive to children's needs and be friendly with them so that they feel comfortable to share their issues and concerns with the teachers.
- Formal education and regular educational guidance at least up to primary level and more should be arranged in case of better performance. Some children may be weak in English or Maths. In that case, special need-based guidance should be provided to them without fail.
- The aptitude and interest of the disadvantaged/street children for providing need-based and potential vocational training should be ascertained. This approach would help children to develop skills fast and, in turn, will make them employable.
- Follow-up and monitoring of performance and movement of these children are necessary as they are likely to be involved in deviant activities again under the influence of peer group members and may run away from home and/or residential school.
- Outings and cultural programmes should be organized for the children for recreation and to develop a positive feeling about life.
- Periodic feedback should be given to the children about their performance, which will motivate them to perform better. Reward system may be introduced for good behaviour and participation in institutional activities and for good educational performance.
- Precautions should be taken while selecting staff/personnel for dealing with disadvantaged/ street children. Effort should be made to select personnel with child-friendly attitude and preferably female candidates with motivation and interest in this work. Otherwise, despite all other proper arrangements, one may not get the better and/or expected results from the programme.
- Sensitization of the staff of the shelter homes about child rights and common challenges faced by them should be done so that no child experiences any abuse and feels comfortable in the shelter homes.
- Since most vulnerable children feel neglected, psychologically insecure, helpless, hopeless and depressed, shelter homes should give emphasis on mental health intervention in terms of individual and group counselling or therapy by professional psychologists. Arrangements for parents counselling is also essential so that in turn they can ensure quality parenting.
- Monitoring of performance of staff/counsellors who directly deal with the children should be done and appropriate measures should be taken. In this regard, it is important to speak to the beneficiary children to gauge their perception about the behaviour of the service providers/counsellors/trainers.
- Coordination and partnership with other similar agencies/NGOs for sharing of resources and for working together should be developed so that basic needs of vulnerable children are

addressed. One organization may not have all the facilities. So coordination and partnership with other similar agencies/NGOs will help to fill up the gaps.

- Periodic monitoring and evaluation of intervention programmes for the effective implementation of the same by an outside agency is required. Evaluation does not necessarily mean to criticize the designer of the programme and/or to find out the faults of a programme, rather it helps to understand the shortcomings in service delivery, if any, and thereby helps in taking course of corrective measures.
- One should attend and share their learning experience, whether positive or negative, in seminar/workshops/conferences so that others can learn from one's experience and replicate the positive results, if necessary.
- Information and/or outcome of an intervention programme should be disseminated through publication of papers in the journals and in periodicals for wider coverage of audiences.

In sum

Based on first-hand field experience of the authors, a number of steps have been prescribed for the effective implementation of intervention programmes. For example, identification of vulnerable children and listening to their voices to understand their issues and challenges from their perspective and taking needful measures accordingly should be done. It is very important to recruit sensitive staff who are interested to work for the welfare of these children, and training should be organized for such staff to sensitize them about the issues and rights of vulnerable children. Networking with similar NGOs is very essential for referral services and for learning from each other for delivering quality services to vulnerable children.

6.11. LEGISLATIVE MEASURES FOR ADDRESSING ISSUES AND CHALLENGES OF VULNERABLE CHILDREN

The Government of India adopted various legislative measures for addressing the issues and challenges of vulnerable children (Deb, 2013). Most of these legislative measures underwent revision from time to time for their effective implementation for safeguarding the welfare issues of vulnerable children. A brief description of constitutional and few legislative measures related to child welfare have been provided further.

6.11.1. THE INDIAN CONSTITUTION

The Indian Constitution[8] is the foundation of the Indian democratic system which ensures four fundamental rights to all citizens, namely justice, liberty, equality and fraternity. Different articles in the Indian Constitution talked about different issues. For example:

Article 14 guarantees equality before the law and article 15 prohibits discrimination based on gender, caste, race and religion while Article 21A directs all States to provide free and compulsory education to all children between the ages of six to fourteen years. At the same time, Article 24 prohibits children under 14 from being employed in factories and mines, and from working in any hazardous employment. Child trafficking and forced labor is prohibited by Article 23. Freedom of religion is conferred by article 25 (The Indian Constitution (adopted on Nov. 26, 1949, enforced on Jan. 26, 1950).

This apart, the Government of India has taken up various legislative measures for ensuring child safety and for protection of their other rights.

6.11.2. The Indian Penal Code (1860)

It is one of the major fundamental laws in India and it clearly prescribes punishment for various crimes considering their nature.

It provides for criminal liability and prosecution of offenders for simple and grievous hurt (sections 319 to 329); wrongful restraint and wrongful confinement (sections 339, 340–346) and so on. Section 372 and 373 of the IPC set punishment for selling and buying of minors for purposes of prostitution while section 376-2C spells out the punishment for rape (The Indian Penal Code 1860, Act No. 45).

6.11.3. The Immoral Traffic (Prevention) Act, 1956

For prevention of child and women trafficking, this law came into force. This act prescribed

the punishment for various acts against children and women which include (i) punishment for keeping a brothel or allowing premises to be used as a brothel (sec. 3); (ii) punishment for living on earnings of prostitution (sec. 4); (iii) procuring, inducing, or taking person for the sake of prostitution (sec. 5); (iv) detaining person in premises where prostitution is carried on (sec. 6); (iv) prostitution in or in the vicinity of public places (sec. 7); (v) seducing or soliciting for the purposes of prostitution (sec. 8); (vi) seduction of a person in custody (sec. 9) and so on. Since this law did not mandate any social agent for reporting, incidents of reporting is very law. (Deb, 2014)

This issue requires the attention of law policymakers.

6.11.4. The Child Labour (Prohibition and Regulation) Act, 1986

This act prohibits employment of children below the age of 14 years in certain occupations. This law was not effective in the prevention of child labour for various reasons, that is, lack of manpower and monitoring for the implementation of the law and determination of exact age of a child since a good number of them do not have birth certificates. At the same time, in the present socio-economic scenario of the country, it is practically very difficult to implement the law without making alternative arrangements and/or source of income for poor families especially in the rural areas.

6.11.5. The Protection of Children from Sexual Offences Act, 2012

The Protection of Children from Sexual Offences Act, 2012, was passed by the Indian Parliament for prevention of sexual abuse of children. In this law, for the first time, media, studio and photographic professionals have been mandated for reporting of sexual exploitation of children for pornography and related activities to the police as per Section 20. There is also a need to mandate other social agents, namely teachers, doctors, nurses and parents for reporting of such incidents to the appropriate authority.

6.11.6. THE COMMISSION FOR PROTECTION OF CHILD RIGHTS ACT, 2005

This is another important legislative measure for ensuring speedy trial of offences against children for violation of their rights.[9] Most of the states in India have come out with state commission for protection of child rights. As per this law, every district should have a child protection officer for overall supervision of different provisions for the protection of child rights. Although in reality, very few districts in India appointed a child protection officer, it is expected gradually every state will realize the importance of appointment of such officials.

6.11.7. THE RIGHT OF CHILDREN TO FREE AND COMPULSORY EDUCATION ACT, 2009

As per this act, every child deserves free primary education (Section 3) and every school should have 25 per cent seat reservation for socio-economically backward children. In addition, this law banned corporal punishment (CP; Section 17). The main challenge lies with the implementation of the act in ensuring the reservation of 25 per cent seats for children from poor families. There is an urgent need to give emphasis on monitoring of the situation for ensuring education for all children. Education will keep vulnerable children on the safer side and will ensure a better future.

6.11.8 THE JUVENILE JUSTICE (CARE AND PROTECTION OF CHILDREN) ACT, 2015

The Juvenile Justice (Care and Protection of Children) Act, 2000 (amended in 2015) helps ensure care and protection for vulnerable children from trafficking. This law has a special provision to

penalize the children aged between 16–18 years and involved in heinous crime and will be tried in criminal court. In addition, it recognizes certain offences against children as special offences and provides for punishment. These include cruelty against a juvenile (section 75), using a child for begging (section 76), using a child for vending, peddling, carrying, supplying or smuggling any intoxicating liquor, narcotic drug Or psychotropic substance (section 78), procuring a child for employment (section 79), and sale and procurement of children for any purpose (section 81). Section 82 clearly spelt out the punishment for applying corporal punishment against children. Further this act included few additional harmful acts of elderly people against children which were not included in the previous juvenile laws and suggested appropriate legal measures to penalize the perpetrators and they include use of child by militant groups or other adults (section 83) and kidnapping and abduction of child (section 84) (The Juvenile Justice [Care and Protection of Children] Act, 2015, No.02).

Many more legislative measures are in place for addressing children welfare issues and these include (a) the Prohibition of Child Marriage Act, 2006; (b) the National Charter for Children, 2003; (c) the Pre-Conception and Pre-natal Diagnostic Techniques (Prohibition of Sex Selection) Act, 1994; (d) the PWD Act, 1995; (e) the Guardians and Wards Act, 1890, and (f) the Young Persons (Harmful Publications) Act, 1956.

Now, the question arises whether all these legislative measures are adequate to address the welfare and safety issues of the children. It might be very difficult to answer this question in one word or sentence. However, what is needed at this hour is to create awareness among law enforcement agencies and common people about these laws and the importance of their implementation for protection of child rights. It is also very important to acknowledge the rights of children in the society. The MSJE in association with international child rights organizations and local NGOs should take appropriate measures for creating awareness about child rights and for changing the traditional and orthodox mindset of Indian population about the issue so that everybody acknowledges child rights, takes care of children welfare issues and ensures protection of their rights. At the same time, it is the obligation of the state governments to implement the legislations with proper training for the law enforcement agencies so that, as and when they come across an incident of abuse, neglect and maltreatment, they can implement the law effectively. In this regard, proper coordination between the respective Ministry of central and state governments is required for taking need-based measures.

In sum

There are a number of legislative measures adopted by the Government of India for addressing issues and challenges of vulnerable children. The Indian Constitution emphasized the child protection issue in different articles. For example, Article 21-A directs all states to provide free and compulsory education to all children between the ages of 6 years and 14 years. At the same time, Article 24 prohibits children under the age of 14 years from being employed in factories and mines, and from working in any hazardous employment. The Indian Penal Code (1860) has a number of provisions for the prevention of sexual abuse of children. Likewise, the Immoral Traffic (Prevention) Act, 1956, is a specific law for prevention of trafficking of children and women. In addition, a number of other legislations are in place for the protection of child rights.

6.12. POLICIES AND PROGRAMMES FOR WELFARE AND WELL-BEING OF VULNERABLE CHILDREN

Although several policies and programmes have been adopted for childcare in India, there is a need to take up many more initiatives for dealing with specific situations of vulnerable children across society.

Some of the prominent policies and programmes for childcare in India include

the National Policy for Children (1994), the National Policy for Education (1986), the National Policy for Empowerment of Women (2001), the National Health Policy (2002), the National Charter for Children (2004), the National Plan of Action for Children (2005), the Integrated Child Protection Scheme (2009) and the National Policy for Children (2013) (The National Policy for Children, 1994).

No doubt that a large number of Indian children under vulnerable condition have been benefitted by these policies and programmes. The big challenges for India are gender discrimination, inequality, caste system, poor rural infrastructure, lack of access to education for rural people, unemployment and so on.

Some of the important social welfare schemes for children are discussed in the following text.

6.12.1. The Integrated Child Protection Scheme

This scheme was introduced in 2009 with a view to ensuing the protection of child rights. The objectives of ICPS are

> to contribute to the improvement in the well-being of children in difficult circumstances, as well as to the reduction of vulnerabilities to situations and actions that lead to abuse, neglect, exploitation, abandonment and separation of children. These will be achieved by: (i) improved access to and quality of child protection services; (ii) raised public awareness about the reality of child rights, situation and protection in India; (iii) clearly articulated responsibilities and enforced accountability for child protection (iv) established and functioning structures at all government levels for delivery of statutory and support services to children in difficult circumstances; (v) introduced and operational evidence based monitoring and evaluation. Specific objectives of the scheme include (i) institutionalizing essential services and strengthen structures; (ii) enhancing capacities at all levels; (iii) creating database and knowledge base for child protection services; (iv) strengthening child protection at family and community level; (v) ensuring appropriate inter-sectoral response at all levels; and (vi) raising public awareness (The Integrated Child Protection Scheme (ICPS), the Ministry of Women and Child Development, Government of India).

As per this scheme, the central government should establish and strengthen a continuum of services for emergency outreach, institutional care, family and community-based care, counselling and support services in addition to placing and strengthening necessary structures and mechanisms for the effective implementation of the scheme at the national, regional, state and district levels. In reality, if this scheme is implemented, vulnerable children will be on the safer side and will enjoy their rights.

6.12.2. Integrated Child Development Services

This is another important scheme which aims to extend care and support services to 0–6 year-old children and their mothers. This scheme was launched by the Government of India on 2 October 1975 with a view to achieving five main objectives

> viz., improving the nutritional and health status of children in the age group of 0–6 years; laying the foundation for proper psychological, physical and social development of the child; and reducing the incidence of mortality, morbidity, malnutrition and school dropout; achieving effective co-ordination of policy and implementation amongst the various departments to promote child development, and enhancing the capability of the mother to look after the normal health and nutritional needs of the child through proper nutrition and health education (Integrated Child Development Services (ICDS), the Ministry of Women and Child Development, Government of India).

All categories of vulnerable children should be brought under this scheme. There are some challenges in implementing the schemes as revealed by a study (Report on Quick Evaluation of ICDS, June 2015). The findings and suggestions need the attention of health policymakers for taking appropriate corrective measures.

6.12.3. Rajiv Gandhi National Creche Scheme for Children of Working Mothers

This scheme is meant for the children of working mothers so that they can drop their young baby while they go for work. There are a number of benefits of this scheme and they include day-care facilities for children (6 months to 6 years) of working mothers in the community, improved nutrition and health status of children, physical, mental, emotional and social development of children, educating and empowering parents/caregivers for better childcare, sleeping facility for children, health check and immunization facility for child, supplementary nutrition, and preparing children below 3 years for pre-school education (Rajiv Gandhi National Creche Scheme for Children of Working Mothers; the Ministry of Women and Child Development, Government of India).

This scheme benefited a large number of working mothers to go for their work keeping their small child to a safe place.

6.12.4 CHILDLINE SCHEME

The objective of this scheme is to provide information about the vulnerable condition of a child so that immediate support could be provided to rescue the child. Keeping the need of street and destitute children in mind, this scheme was launched. Any individual can call a toll-free number (1098) and inform the situation and seek help. This is a toll-free number. There is a need to carry out an evaluation study to examine the effectiveness of this scheme.

6.12.5 THE BETI BACHAO BETI PADHAO SCHEME

This scheme launched on 22 January 2015 by honourable Prime Minister of India, Narendra Modi, intends to bring gender equality. The big gender disparity in some of the states in India, especially Punjab, Haryana and Rajasthan, insisted the Government of India to bring this scheme for bringing gender balance and rendering justice to the female child.

It is worth mentioning here that for the welfare and well-being of the girl child, the Department of Women and Social Welfare, Government of West Bengal, has brought the Kanyashree scheme with a view to ensuring education for the girl child and delaying their marriages till at least the age of 18. No doubt that such initiatives will bring a change in the outlook of the general population towards the girl child.

6.12.6. THE CENTRAL ADOPTION RESOURCE AUTHORITY

CARA is a statutory body of the Ministry of Women & Child Development, Government of India. It functions as the nodal body for the adoption of Indian children and is mandated to monitor and regulate in-country and inter-country adoptions. CARA primarily deals with the adoption of orphan, abandoned and surrendered children through its associated/recognized adoption agencies.

6.12.7. INTEGRATED SCHEME FOR STREET CHILDREN, MINISTRY OF SOCIAL JUSTICE AND EMPOWERMENT, THE GOVERNMENT OF INDIA

This scheme was launched with a view to providing street children a platform for enjoying their rights. The scheme provides shelter, nutrition, healthcare, education, recreational facilities and ensures protection from abuse and exploitation. The beneficiaries for this scheme are children without homes or family ties, children of CSWs and pavement dweller.

6.13. INTERNATIONAL POLICIES FOR WELFARE AND WELL-BEING OF GLOBAL POPULATION INCLUDING VULNERABLE CHILDREN

The SDGs of the UN is the latest policy for addressing the welfare and well-being of the global community including vulnerable children. It is a continuation of global efforts of Millennium Development Goals. Out of 17 well-defined SDGs, seven goals are directly related to child welfare and well-being, and they include ending poverty and hunger, improving health and education, gender equality, ensuring availability and sustainable management of water and sanitation for all, and making cities more sustainable and safe. Since the Government of India is a signatory to SDGs, it is the moral obligation of the government to implement all the goals in the truest sense for benefit of the human community and in turn it will ensure the protection of rights of all children in the society.

In sum

Social policies are taken up in any society to improve the condition of vulnerable population as directed by the legislative measures of the same country. For addressing the issues and challenges of vulnerable children in India, a number of social policies are taken up by the Government of India and they include

the National Policy for Children (1994), the National Policy for Education (1986), the National Policy for Empowerment of Women (2001), the National Health Policy (2002), the National Charter for Children (2004), the National Plan of Action for Children (2005), the Integrated Child Protection Scheme (2009) and the National Policy for Children (2013).

Some of the latest integrated and comprehensive social policies are '(i) The Integrated Child Protection Scheme Integrated Child Development Services; (ii) Rajiv Gandhi National Creche Scheme for Children of Working Mothers; (iii) CHILDLINE Scheme; (iv) The Beti Bachao, Beti Padhao Scheme; (v) The Central Adoption Resource Authority; and (vi) Integrated Scheme for Street Children.' The SDGs of the UN also have a number of provisions concerning the welfare and well-being of vulnerable children.

6.14. RECOMMENDATIONS

Keeping the socio-economic situation of a country, proper preventive measures and intervention programme should be taken up to improve the condition of vulnerable children. Some steps are recommended keeping the situation in India into account. Examples of which are as follows:

- First, there is a need to identify the families living BPL and/or living in slums, streets or red-light areas. These families should be provided support to improve their economic condition in the form of creating self-help groups or encouraging to start income-generating programme.
- Second, the authority of the Department of Social Welfare of every state should be active to implement the central government welfare schemes for disadvantaged children in truest sense and monitor the progress of implementation closely to ensure effective implementation.

- Third, the Department of Social Welfare of every state should strengthens network with NGOs and local community/clubs and seek their support for the effective implementation of the child welfare schemes.
- Fourth, appropriate psychological intervention programme should be in place for addressing the mental health needs of vulnerable children in addition to giving them orientation on socialization process. For the same task, trained psychologists should be appointed in different organizations and they should be provided reasonably good remuneration to attract the experienced psychologists. Otherwise, with poor remuneration, one will never get an experienced psychologist to serve the purpose.
- Fifth, while selecting the staff for NGOs and other organization, skilled manpower with a passion for working with vulnerable children should be selected.
- Sixth, there is a need to evaluate the efficacy of schemes and take appropriate measures based on the recommendations of evaluation study of the schemes.

6.15. CONCLUSION AND IMPLICATIONS

During childhood, every child needs proper care and protection including safety for their all-round healthy growth and development. In turn, they will contribute with their skills for social growth and prosperity. Sadly, a large number of children in every society remain vulnerable to various risks of neglect, abuse and exploitation in addition to retarded growth and development owing to a number of socio-economic, cultural and situational affairs either in isolation and/or in combination. Our social system should ensure basic minimal facilities for these children through amendment of appropriate legislative and social measures from time to time. All the measures meant for the welfare of vulnerable and at-risk children need to be closely monitored, evaluated and necessary changes in the programmes should be made based on inputs from the mid-term evaluation of the programmes/schemes for the realization of their effective implementation in the truest sense through.

It is the obligation of local government, especially the social welfare department and/or women and child development departments, to implement the projects with full sincerity involving the local NGOs, elected members and community leaders. In this regard, community psychologists should act as facilitators. It is very important to appoint a dynamic person in the chair of the said departments as a leader who has passion as well as experience for working with disadvantaged and at-risk children. In a number of states, sometimes it happens that the person who is heading the Department of Social Welfare neither has any experience nor passion or interest to work for disadvantaged children resulting in the poor implementation of the welfare schemes.

Under no circumstances, one should not compromise with welfare of children (Deb, 2016). Finally, it is very important for all of us as responsible citizens of the society to extend our support and cooperation for ensuring safety for each and every child. If any of us comes across any vulnerable child, we should attend the child problem immediately and inform Childline for help (tele helpline 1098). The corporate sector should also join hands with local government as part of corporate social responsibility for the effective implementation of various welfare schemes for vulnerable children in reality not in paper.

EXERCISES

One-mark Questions

1. Define vulnerable children.
2. As per law, define the age group of children.
3. Whom do we call differently abled children?
4. State the common health problems faced by street and slum children.
5. Why do some children leave home?
6. Whom do we call trafficked children?
7. How to sensitize parents of vulnerable children about quality parenting?
8. Which law banned CP?
9. How to enhance self-concept of children of CSWs?
10. What is the objective of the National Commission for Protection of Child Rights Act, 2005?
11. State the broad activities of ICPS.
12. Did any law mandate any social agent for compulsory reporting of child abuse? If yes, which law?

Five-mark Questions

1. Describe the common challenges faced by the children of CSWs.
2. How to ensure protection of rights of girl children working as domestic assistants?
3. Discuss the psychological needs of children without parents.
4. Are shelter homes safe for disadvantaged children? Justify your answer.
5. How to motivate vulnerable children for studies?
6. Discuss the role of Childline. Is Childline active?

Ten-mark Questions

1. Discuss the role of community psychologists in prevention of child trafficking.
2. What are the most common challenges in rehabilitation of street children?
3. What are the steps to be followed for the effective implementation of intervention programme for vulnerable children?
4. Elaborate the government policies for welfare of disadvantaged children.

Reflexive Questions

1. How to address the mental health challenges of vulnerable children living in slum areas?
2. How to ensure community support for the effective implementation of child welfare schemes?
3. Is there proper coordination among different organizations working with vulnerable children? Justify your answer.
4. Do children of CSWs experience discrimination? Give some examples to justify your answer.

NOTES

1. https://www.moneycontrol.com
2. https://data.unicef.org/topic/child-protection/child-labour/
3. www.thefreedictionary.com/differently+abled
4. http://www.childlineindia.org.in/children-with-disabilities.htm

5. http://timesofindia.indiatimes.com/articleshow/21927474.cms?utm_source=contentofinterest&utm_medium=text&utm_campaign=cppst
6. https://www.firstpost.com/india/unesco–47-million-youth-in-india-drop-out-of-school-by-10th-standard–2961334.html
7. https://timesofindia.indiatimes.com/india/school-dropout-rates-in-india/articleshow/62333614.cms
8. Adopted on 26 November 1949, enforced on 26 January 1950.
9. Implemented in 2006.

REFERENCES

Abebe, T. (2009, January). Begging as a livelihood pathway of street children in Addis Ababa. *Forum for Development Studies*, *36*(2), 275–300.

Bashir, Z., & Dasti, R. (2015). Poly-victimization and mental health of street children in Lahore city. *Journal of Mental Health*, *24*(5), 305–312.

Beegle, K., Dehejia, R., & Gatti, R. (2009). Why should we care about child labor? The education, labor market, and health consequences of child labor. *Journal of Human Resources*, *44*(4), 871–889.

Bletzer, K. V. (2005). Sex workers in agricultural areas: Their drugs, their children. *Culture, Health & Sexuality*, *7*(6), 543–555.

Chege, M. N., Kabiru, E. W., & Mbithi, J. N. (2002). Childcare practices of commercial sex workers. *East African Medical Journal*, *79*(7), 382–389.

Chersich, M. F., Bosire, W., King'ola, N., Temmerman, M., & Luchters, S. (2014). Effects of hazardous and harmful alcohol use on HIV incidence and sexual behaviour: A cohort study of Kenyan female sex workers. *Globalization and Health*, *10*(1), 22.

Craig, T. K. J., & Hodson, S. (2000). Homeless youth in London: II. Accommodation, employment and health outcomes at 1 year. Psychological Medicine, 30(1), 187–194.

Deb, S. (2002). Rehabilitation of the children of commercial sex workers through participatory approach. *Journal of Community Guidance and Research*, *19*(3), 299–314.

Deb, S. (2005). Child trafficking in south Asia: Dimensions, roots, facets and interventions. *Social Change*, *35*(2), 143–155.

Deb, S. (2011). Exploitation and harassment of migrant women and girl children working as domestic assistant. In S. Sarkar & M. Srivastava (Eds.), *Globalisation and gender* (pp. 200–226). Rawat Publications.

Deb, S. (2013a). Burden of child abuse and neglect in India and government response: A secondary data-based study. In U. V. Somayajulu, S. S. Raju, & C. P. Prakasam (Eds.), *Social inclusion and women health: Perspectives and issues* (Vol. 2, pp. 323–361). The Women Press.

Deb, S. (2013b). Socio-legal measures for protection of child rights in India: A review. In R. N. Srivastava, R. Seth, & J. V. Niekerk (Eds.), *Child abuse and neglect: Challenges and opportunities*. Jaypee Brothers Medical Publishers.

Deb, S. (2014). Legislation concerning reporting of child sexual abuse and child trafficking in India: A closer look. In B. Mathews & B. C. Donald (Eds.), *Mandatory reporting laws and the identification of severe child abuse and neglect* (pp. 541–546). Springer.

Deb, S. (2016). Introduction—Child safety, welfare and well-being: Need of the hour. In S. Deb (Ed.), *Child safety, welfare and well-being* (pp. 1–11). Springer.

Deb, S., & Bernadette, M. (2014). Burden of child abuse and neglect with special reference to socio-legal measures: A comparative picture of India, Philippines and Japan. In C. Jon (Ed.), *Child abuse and neglect: Worldwide* (pp. 77–106). Praeger.

Deb, S., Datta, K., & Ghosh, M. (1997). Modification of a deviant street children's behaviour: An in-depth case study. *Indian Journal of Criminology*, *25*(1), 15–22.

Deb, S., & Gireesan, A. (2015). Contexts of risks and exploitation. In Farrell Ann et al. (Eds.), *The SAGE handbook of early childhood research* (pp. 327–344). SAGE Publications.

Deb, S., & Mathews, B. (2012). Children's rights in India: Parents' and teachers' attitudes, knowledge and perception. *International Journal of Children's Rights, 20*(2), 1–24.

Deb, S., & Mitra, K. (2002). Nature and types of abuse and neglect among migrant child labour: a qualitative study. In Paper accepted for oral presentation in the 14" International Conference on child Abuse and Neglect to be held in Denver, USA between July (pp. 7–10).

Deb, S., & Mukherjee, A. (2009). Impact of sexual abuse on personality disposition of girl children. *Journal of the Indian Academy of Applied Psychology, 35*(1), 113–120.

Deb, S., & Mukherjee, A. (2011). Background and adjustment capacity of sexually abused girls and their perceptions of intervention. *Child Abuse Review, 20*(3), 213–230.

Deb, S., Mukherjee, A., & Mathews, B. (2011). Aggression in sexually abused trafficked girls and efficacy of intervention. *Journal of Interpersonal Violence, 26*(4), 745–768.

Deb, S., & Ray, M. (2016). Child abuse and neglect in India: Risk factors and protective measures. In S. Deb (Ed.), *Child safety, welfare and well-being* (pp. 39–57). Springer.

Deb, S., & Sen, P. (2006). A study on psychological trauma of young trafficked women. In D. Daro (Ed.), *World perspectives on child abuse* (7th ed., pp. 66–68). International Society for Prevention of Child Abuse and Neglect.

Deb, S., Srivastava, N., Chatterjee, P., & Chakraborty, T. (2005). Processes of child trafficking in West Bengal: A qualitative study. *Social Change, 35*(2), 112–123.

Deb, S., & Walsh, K. (2012). Impact of physical, psychological, and sexual violence on social adjustment of school children in India. *School Psychology International, 33*(4), 391–415.

Franieck, M. L. C. F., & Page, T. (2017). The family narratives of three siblings living in a 'street situation' since birth. *Early Child Development and Care*, 1–13.

Hayman, A. L. (2003, November). *When mom's a ho: Children of prostituted women* [The 131st Annual Meeting], 15–19 November. https://apha.confex.com/apha/131am/techprogram/paper_71492.htm

Hills, F., Meyer-Weitz, A., & Asante, K. O. (2016). The lived experiences of street children in Durban, South Africa: Violence, substance use, and resilience. *International Journal of Qualitative Studies on Health and Well-being, 11*(1), 30302.

Hogan, D. M. (1998). The psychological development and welfare of children of opiate and cocaine users: Review and research needs. *The Journal of Child Psychology and Psychiatry and Allied Disciplines, 39*(5), 609–620.

Janardhana, N., Muralidhar, D., Naidu, D. M., & Raghevendra, G. (2015). Discrimination against differently abled children among rural communities in India: Need for action. *Journal of Natural Science, Biology, and Medicine, 6*(1), 7.

Johnson, T. P., Aschkenasy, J. R., Herbers, M. R., & Gillenwater, S. A. (1996). Self-reported risk factors for AIDS among homeless youth. *AIDS Education and Prevention, 8*, 308–322.

Ling, B. (2001). *Growing up in the brothel*. Save the Children.

Majid, N., Bollen, L., Morineau, G., Daily, S. F., Mustikawati, D. E., Agus, N., Anartati, A. S., Natpratan, C., & Magnani, R. (2010). Syphilis among female sex workers in Indonesia: Need and opportunity for intervention. *Sexually Transmitted Infections, 86*(5), 377–383.

Mascarenhas, A. (2015). Urban children living in slums vulnerable to variety of risks: Report. *The Indian Express*.

Mathiti, V. (2006). The quality of life of 'street children' accommodated at three shelters in Pretoria: An exploratory study. *Early Child Development and Care, 176*(3–4), 253–269.

Mitra, K., & Deb, S. (2004). Stories of street children: Findings from a field study. *Social Change, 34*(4), 77–85.

O'Donnell, O., Van Doorslaer, E., & Rosati, F. (2002). *Child labour and health: Evidence and research issues*. UNICEF. http://www.ceistorvergata.it/public/CEIS/image/UCW/PaperUCW/Research%20paper/77.%20Child%20labour%20and%20health.pdf

Office of the Registrar General & Census Commissioner, Ministry of Home Affairs, Government of India. 2011. *Census of India*. Office of the Registrar General & Census Commissioner, Ministry of Home Affairs, Government of India.

Pandey, S. P. (2008). *Rehabilitation of Disadvanced [sic] Children and Women Sex Workers*. Serials Publications.

Pardeshi, G., & Bhattacharya, S. (2006). Child rearing practices amongst brothel based commercial sex workers. *Indian Journal of Medical Sciences, 60*(7), 288–295.

Pinto, R., & Nangia, P. (1988). *Children in specially difficult circumstances in Delhi. Focus on working and street children* (UNICEF Report). UNICEF.

Poonam, R. N., Seema, S. Bansode, Shinde, R., & Abhay, S. N. (2011). Street children of Mumbai: Demographic profile and substance abuse. *Biomedical Research, 22*(4), 495–498.

Report of The New Indian Express (December 2001). Malnourished 7-year-old found with cigarette butt burns, bruises, rescued from adoptive parents in Telangana. www.newindianexpress.com › states › telangana ›

Report on Quick Evaluation of ICDS (June 2015). NITI AAYOG, Program Evaluation Organisation Government of India New Delhi-110001. https://niti.gov.in/writereaddata/files/document_publication/report-awc.pdf

Reza, M. H. (2017). Street children's use of social support against everyday abuse in Bangladesh. *Child & Youth Services, 38*(4), 285–301.

Shahmanesh, M., Wayal, S., Cowan, F., Mabey, D., Copas, A., & Patel, V. (2009). Suicidal behavior among female sex workers in Goa, India: The silent epidemic. *American Journal of Public Health, 99*(7), 1239–1246.

Singh, S. (2018). Sexual abuse at six homes, physical violence at 14: Report to Bihar govt. *The Indian Express.* https://indianexpress.com/article/india/sexual-abuse-at-6-homes-physical-violence-at-14-report-to-bihar-govt

Sloss, C. M., & Harper, G. W. (2004). When street sex workers are mothers. *Archives of Sexual Behavior, 33*(4), 329–341.

Sourander, A. (1998). Behavior problems and traumatic events of unaccompanied refugee minors. Child Abuse & Neglect, 22(7), 719–727.

Tizard, B., & Hodges, J. (1978). The effect of institutional rearing on the development of 8-year-old children. *Journal of Child Psychology, Psychiatry, and Allied Disciplines, 19*(2), 99–118.

United Nations. (2011). *Panel Discussion on sports for inclusive development: Sports, disability and development: Key to empowerment of persons with disabilities and their communities.* https://www.un.org/development/desa/disabilities/panel-discussion-on-sports-for-inclusive-development-sports-disability-and-development-key-to-empowerment-of-persons-with-disabilities-and-their-communities-27-june-2011-1-15-to-2-30-p-m-confer.html

Van, I. Jzendoorn, M. H., Luijk, M. P. C. M., & Juffer, F. (2008). IQ of children growing up in children's homes: A meta-analysis on IQ delays in orphanages. *Merrill-Palmer Quarterly, 54*(3), 341–356.

Whetten, K., Ostermann, J., Whetten, R. A., Pence, B. W., O'Donnell, K., Messer, L. C., Thielman, N. M., & Positive Outcomes for Orphans (POFO) Research Team. (2009). A comparison of the wellbeing of orphans and abandoned children ages 6–12 in institutional and community-based care settings in 5 less wealthy nations. *PLOS One, 4*(12), e8169.

RECOMMENDED READINGS

Brandon, M., Schofield, G., Trinder, L., & Stone, N. (1998). *Social work with children.* Macmillan.

Deb, S. (Ed.). (2015). *Child safety, welfare and well-being: Issues and challenges.* Springer.

Deb, S. (2018). *An empirical investigation into child abuse and neglect in India: Burden, impact and protective measures.* Springer.

Deb, S., Bhadra, S., Sunny, A. M., & Sahay, S. (2019). *Childhood to adolescence: Issues and challenges.* Pearson.

Deb, S., Sunny, A. M., & Majumdar, B. (2020). *Disadvantaged children in India: Empirical evidence, policies and actions.* Springer Nature.

Erooga, M. (Ed.). (2012). *Creating safer organizations: Practical steps to prevent the abuse of children by those working with them* (Vol. 35). John Wiley & Sons.

Skinner, D. (2004). *Defining orphaned and vulnerable children* (Vol. 2). HSRC Press.

Vostanis, P. (2007). *Mental health interventions and services for vulnerable children and young people.* Jessica Kingsley Publishers.

Project-affected People and Their Rehabilitation through Participatory Approach

LEARNING OBJECTIVES

- Defining project-affected persons and families
- Understanding the reasons for taking up development projects and its consequences
- Understanding psychological attachment towards place/land
- Studying the role, methods and benefits of the participatory approach in developing rehabilitation and resettlement (RR) plan
- Understanding the process of estimating compensation for the project-affected families and basic facilities to be provided in the resettlement site
- Discussing the role of community psychologists in development and implementation of RR plan
- Understanding the salient features of the Right to Fair Compensation and Transparency in Land Acquisition, Rehabilitation and Resettlement Act, 2013

ABSTRACT

Development is a continuous process in any society. In order to meet the needs of the people of the larger society, various development projects are coming up from time to time, which requires more land, technical manpower, natural resources and communication facilities. Normally, development projects are taken up in suburban or rural areas so that it does not affect the greater population. However, wherever it is taken, the question of displacement of people is inevitable. The broad objective of the chapter is to discuss the consequences of development projects on the livelihood of displaced people, women and children, and to review the experiences of different development projects and related issues. The chapter also discusses the psychological attachment of people towards their land in addition to discussing the role of the participatory approach for developing the rehabilitation and resettlement (RR) plan and empowering the project-affected people (PAP) to share their views and participate in every step of planning and execution of the RR plan. It is believed that if PAP are involved in the process from the beginning and in deciding the compensation for them, considering the government rules and regulations, it might be easier to implement the RR plan. The chapter further highlights the role of psychologists in carrying out baseline study, planning for compensation packages and mobilizing community leaders for the finalization of the RR plan. Finally, it discusses the strengths and weaknesses of the Government of India's RR Policy.

Keywords: Development project; project-affected people; rehabilitation; resettlement; participatory approach

7.1. INTRODUCTION

With the passage of time, everything is changing very fast because of continuous development in society in different fields. Development is a continuous process and, in turn, it helps to improve the overall quality of life of the common people and makes everything comfortable, affordable and beneficial for human beings.

About 15–20 million people across the world are affected by forced displacement, annually, due to infrastructure projects such as irrigation schemes, mines, industries, power plants and roads. At the same time, a sizable number of them leave their place of residence in search of new livelihoods or to protect themselves from civil or military conflicts, highlighting the serious challenges of displacement in subsequent years. Evidence demonstrates that the majority of the displaced people belong to poor and marginalized communities and, within them, women and children experience maximum challenges.

Any development project has positives and negatives. Positive aspects include benefits of the output of the development project for people of the larger society and negatives include relocation and resettlement of people living in the area where development project is going to happen. People living in areas which the government or private industries are going to acquire may be called the project-affected people (PAP). There are different definitions of PAP.

7.2. PROJECT-AFFECTED PEOPLE

Development projects such as dams, mines, industries, roads, power plants and others need vast tracts of land for setting up and expansion of existing infrastructure. A typical thermal power plant of 2,000 megawatts would need about 1,600 hectares of land. Normally, the lands to be acquired for such projects are already in use for different purposes such as residential, agricultural, business, public utility and other activities. The persons utilizing these lands for living, cultivating and practising any other activity, with or without legal ownership, may need to give up the activity and/ or lose the land and the structure thereon, fully or partially, for the project. These persons are therefore affected adversely or negatively.

PAP refers to anyone affected by land acquisition (LA), relocation or loss of incomes associated with the project—changes in the use of land, water and other natural resources might be mentioned as factors.

Although projects often have many adverse impacts by way of displacing or affecting shelter, business or any other activity, they also have positive impacts as discussed earlier on certain populations who can be called 'beneficiaries' of the project. The concern here is for those who are affected adversely or negatively by the project since they require resettlement and rehabilitation in restoring or improving their previous living standards.

7.2.1. DEFINITION OF PROJECT-AFFECTED PEOPLE IN VARIOUS ACTS AND POLICIES

In this section, we shall look at the manner in which PAP has been defined under the various international as well as national policies and acts.

1. *Asian Development Bank's (ADB) Policy on Involuntary Resettlement, 1995:* As per ADB's policy, an affected person can be someone whose standard of living is affected entirely or partly, permanently or temporality, with or without displacements in terms of their (a) household or private business institution, (b) right on any land, water resources or any movable/ irremovable assets and (c) place of work.

2. *World Bank's Operational Policy on Involuntary Resettlement OP 4.12, December 2001 (Revised April 2004):* World Bank was one of the first international institutions to come up with a comprehensive policy on involuntary resettlement. It broadly defines the 'PAP' as people who are adversely affected by project-related relocation, acquisition and income loss. World Bank's Operational Policy on Involuntary Resettlement OP 4.12, December 2001 defines the term 'displaced persons' as people who are affectedly badly by the involuntary taking of land, which would force them to relocate their homes, lose the right of access to their properties, lose their source of living or lose access to legally designated parks and protected areas. The impact is severe in intensity and could have direct effects on the livelihood of the affected persons.

3. *The Land Acquisition Act, 1894:* In India, compensation for LA and resettlement assistance for the PAP, until very recently, was governed by the Land Acquisition Act of 1894, which has categories of 'person interested' and 'displaced person'. In Section 3(b) of the LA Act, 1894, a 'person interested' includes all people who would claim for compensation for LA under this act and are deemed to be interested if they are interested in an easement affecting the land. People who are prone to suffer displacement due to LA, including agricultural labourers and other people who are dependent on this land for the livelihood are also 'person interested' (Fernandes, 2004; Fernandes & Paranjype, 1997).

In other words, an individual should have an interest in the land, which is being acquired. Such an interest may be an absolute one, such as that of an owner or a partial one, such as that of a tenant or a licensee.

In Section 3(h) of the LA Act, 1894, a 'displaced person' is intended for them, who occupied a revenue/forest land with or without *patta* such as a fisherfolk, a grazer, an agricultural labourer, a semi-nomad, a small trader or a village artisan, who have to be displaced due to the project (Fernandes & Paranjype, 1997, p. 256).

7.3. CATEGORIES OF DEVELOPMENT-INDUCED PROJECT-AFFECTED PEOPLE

People affected by development projects can be broadly categorized into (a) directly affected by the project and (b) indirectly affected by the project.

The directly affected PAP include those whose lands and/or structures are fully or partially acquired for the project, namely (a) owners of houses, businesses, agricultural lands and other structures; (b) those using the land and/or structures of others with no ownership but are dependent on the lands and/or structures for their dwelling or livelihood purposes such as agriculture, residential tenants, labour work on the lands and commercial establishments. The directly affected PAP can be further classified into three main categories (a) title-holders, (b) non-title-holders and (c) those with customary user's rights.

The indirectly affected PAP are generally in the form of deprivation of access to common property resources and public utilities and new pressures exerted on the socio-economic infrastructure of the host population.

In sum

Development in a society is a continuous process. As any development project has some benefits, it also affects the people and their families where it is taking place in terms of displacement and losing lands. There are different definitions of project-affected families and it varies from institution to institution. Project-affected families may be broadly categorized into two groups, directly project-affected families and indirectly project-affected families. Directly project-affected families are those who live in the area where a project is established, while indirectly project-affected families are those who do not lose their lands and development project in the locality affects them indirectly. For example, they may experience more pollution, their agricultural land may be affected because of the disposal from the chemical industry and so on.

7.4. REASONS FOR TAKING UP DEVELOPMENT PROJECTS

Various types of development projects are taken up in different countries from time to time for various reasons. For example, dams are constructed for the generation of hydroelectric power so that electricity could be supplied to meet the needs of the local community. Hydroelectric power projects do not cause much environment pollution. Dams are also constructed for supplying water to agricultural fields. Fish cultivation is also done. Therefore, dams serve multiple purposes. Thermal power plants belong to another category of industries, which generate power, thus causing a lot of environment pollution in the process. A typical thermal power plant of 1,000 MW would need about 800 hectares of land.

Other categories of development projects are mining industries. Mining industries are developed for extracting natural resources and these include coal, bauxite, petroleum-related items and so on. Mining industries cause a lot of environment pollution. Therefore, there is a need to take every precautionary measure to prevent environment pollution. Setting up an automobile industry for manufacturing cars also requires a lot of land.

The earlier description clearly highlights the need for establishing various categories of industries for various developments and all of them are essential for the welfare and well-being of the society. All the industries and development projects generate a lot of employment opportunities and, automatically, a large number of small-scale industries and small business enterprises are growing up in and around the big development projects. Finally, there is a wave of social and economic development if the development projects are taken up, following the guidelines and taking into account the interests of the PAP and environmental balance.

7.5. CONSEQUENCES OF DEVELOPMENT PROJECTS ON LIVELIHOOD, WOMEN AND CHILDREN

Development projects have both positive and negative consequences as discussed earlier. As development projects are required for producing various products, by-products and materials for other industries, they also generate a lot of revenue and employment opportunities, the reflection of which is seen in the overall social and economic growth.

Similarly, development projects have been regarded as a development opportunity for the tribal people. Many tribal communities live in relatively isolated areas, which are remote, hilly and in the vicinity of the forest, characterized by poor infrastructure and lack of basic civic amenities. Hence, displacement on account of development projects could be beneficial for the tribal community if it is properly planned through the participatory approach.

At the same time, any development project, which involves the acquisition of land, brings a lot of challenges for the people residing in the same area as they need to be replaced to another area. Before we discuss the negative consequences of any development project, it is important to have some idea about the profile of the PAP. Normally, any development project is taken up in the rural areas, which is inhabited by tribal population and they are mostly illiterate and solely dependent on forest products or natural resources.

Most tribal people in India lead a hard, materially poor life but multiple natural resources along with strong community ties make life possible, even under difficult circumstances. Development destroys natural resources and community network from the life of displaced people. Adivasis/tribals largely depend on agriculture as their main source of the livelihood. Minor forest produce, such as fish and cattle, supplement their income and means of the livelihood in numerous ways. Hence, when they are displaced and settled in a new area, it becomes very difficult for them to enjoy all these natural facilities immediately. It is a time-consuming process.

Displacement is an extremely painful experience. Building one's life in a new locality is a long, difficult and arduous process. Rehabilitation cannot be treated as an appendage to the main project and carried out as an afterthought. It has to be handled with meticulous planning and execution.

The enormity and complexity of the whole process cannot be overemphasized. Consideration of displacement and rehabilitation has to be an integral part of the whole project.

Cultivation is the major occupation for most of the rural people. It takes a long time to prepare a land for cultivation. Therefore, the livelihood of the people living in the project area gets directly affected as they have to start their life afresh in a new area which may not be fertile and may not have forest and water bodies. Rural people, who largely depend upon natural resources and cultivation, always look for forest and water bodies so that, through their efforts, they can manage their life with the outputs of agriculture and forest by-products.

Limited knowledge is available about the actual impact of development projects on the poor (Neubert, 2013). According to Baker (2000):

> many are reluctant to carry out impact evaluations because they are deemed expensive, time consuming, and technically complex, and because the findings can be politically sensitive. Yet a rigorous evaluation can be powerful in assessing the appropriateness and effectiveness of programs. Evaluating impact is particularly critical in developing where resources are scarce, and every dollar spent should aim to maximize its impact on poverty reduction.

The negative consequences of losing land can be grouped into eight broad categories.

1. *Impact on the livelihood:* Since project-affected families are supposed to be replaced in new areas, their lifestyles get terribly disturbed. First, it affects their livelihood. They have to think of alternative options for the livelihood in new areas which depends on the soil of the land, climate, availability of water and other natural resources in the new areas. If the land is not fertile and water bodies are not available, they then struggle for producing agricultural items. If a forest is not present in and around the new place, they have to look for sources of fuel for cooking. Most of the tribal people in rural and remote areas depend on dry leaves and branches of trees for fuel.

2. *Impact on overall economy of the family:* Overall economic condition of the PAP undergoes a fall since they will be shifted to new areas and start everything afresh. For starting life afresh, in any new area, involves a lot of additional expenses. In a settled area, people have various sources of income, which are missing in a new area.

3. *Impact on mental health:* Human beings are conditioned to daily lifestyles wherever and with whoever they live with. Any change in lifestyle in terms of change of occupation, relocation and peer group affects the minds of human beings. Whatever be the possessions one has and wherever they sit or sleep for a long time, any change in such schedules makes one uncomfortable and it causes stress, anxiety and a feeling of uncertainty and insecurity. Therefore, during any such transition, there should be a continuous dialogue with the PAP and other community leaders and they need to be appraised about the development from time to time and their views and opinions should be given importance and, in turn, this process will give then confidence that they will not suffer much loss.

4. *Impact on health:* There is an association between physical and mental health. When an individual is mentally disturbed, they feel physically weak and less energetic and become vulnerable to physical health problems. At the same time, when people move to new areas which are not well connected to health facilities, women and children become more vulnerable to various health challenges and these include communicable diseases and non-communicable

diseases. In addition, women and children suffer from malnutrition and injury (Birley, 1995). A primary health centre is essential in every locality. It is less likely that a new area will have primary healthcare facilities. Lack of primary healthcare and immunization facilities for infants and newborn children also depends on the availability of chemist shops and qualified doctors, which will make the life of the PAP risky in new and isolated areas.

5. *Impact on education:* In case of any development project, children become the worst victims of circumstances along with women. Their education gets affected. They either discontinue education because of non-availability of educational facilities in new areas or they need to walk a long distance for attending schools. Sometime, books or other educational materials or guidance for studies may not be available. Therefore, this issue needs special attention while planning for rehabilitation.

6. *Impact on women and childcare:* A number of studies demonstrated the negative impact of the development project on women. They struggle a lot to collect drinking water and fuel for cooking, in addition to taking care of children (Parasuraman, 1993). At the same time, there might be one newborn child or infant in every family or every alternate family in a locality. When the issue of resettlement comes, childcare gets affected because of total rescheduling of lifestyles. Parents remain busy in thinking and planning for resettlement, which does not allow them to look after their small children properly. In some families, the responsibility goes to the elder children, then somehow, they manage to take care of their younger children, though it may not be similar to parental care.

7. *Impact on social network:* In due course, people develop a social network with others through regular interactions in different social situations. In turn, this helps an individual or a family during crisis. When people are relocated, they lose their social network and feel helpless if there is any crisis in the new area. Some studies have highlighted the same issue after their research (Rogers et al., 2012).

8. *Environment pollution:* The negative impact of development projects has been documented by several researchers (Dixon et al., 2013; Lattemann & Höpner, 2008; McCarthy et al., 2002; Morgan, 2012). Waste materials of some of the chemicals, pesticides and other industries cause tremendous environmental pollution, thus directly affecting the plants, animals and fishes, if they are not disposed as indicated in the proposal which was submitted to the Environment Department for getting the project approval. There are many instances where waste materials were not disposed scientifically.

In sum

The adverse consequences of development projects are many more. Displacement affects the livelihood of the project-affected families, that is, they have to look for new occupation for their survival, their lifestyles get changed and mentally they feel upset because of change of environment and losing their social network. The overall economy of the family gets affected. In addition, children education gets disturbed because of non-availability of educational institutions in and around the rehabilitation site. Mother and children also suffer from different physical health problems due to the lack of safe drinking water and proper sanitation facilities. Non-availability of health centres causes further problems for them. Environment pollution adversely affects the quality of life of the people who live in and around the development project.

7.6. PSYCHOLOGICAL ATTACHMENT TOWARDS PLACE/LAND

Psychological or emotional attachment of people to land or place is very strong, especially if the land is inherited for generations and/or if people are living in the same area for a long time and get involved in cultivation. This subject comes under environmental psychology. It is very difficult for people to give up the land or sell it to others, even if a good price is offered. Whenever any such proposal of purchase comes, instantly the people reject it.

Some research has been carried out on the subject. In this regard, Schroeder (1991) discussed the difference between 'meaning' and 'preference', defining meaning as 'the thoughts, feelings, memories and interpretations evoked by a landscape' and preference as 'the degree of liking for one landscape compared to another' (Schroeder, 1991).

However, place/land attachment is multidimensional (Scannell & Gifford, 2010) and cannot be justified simply through a cause and effect relationship. In other words, it may be stated that place/ land attachment depends on a reciprocal relationship between behaviour and experiences (Rollero & de Piccoli, 2010). Due to numerous differing opinions on the definition and components of place attachment, organizational models have been scarce until recent years (Lewicka, 2011). A noteworthy conceptual framework is the tripartite model, developed by Scannell and Gifford (2010), which defines the variables of place attachment as the three Ps: person, process and place (Lewicka, 2011).

7.7. PARTICIPATORY APPROACH FOR DEVELOPING REHABILITATION AND RESETTLEMENT PLAN

While developing the rehabilitation and resettlement (RR) plan, one should develop the same, keeping in mind the cultural background of the project-affected population, their cultural beliefs and practices, their existing natural and human resources, so that they can cope with the changing situation. In other words, the RR plan should be culture-specific, need-based and viable, so that displaced people can easily settle down in the new place. In this regard, the participatory approach would be immensely beneficial. The participatory approach means ensuring the participation of the villagers and their identified leaders from the beginning of the planning and development of the RR plan and execution of the implementation of the plan. Without the participation of the villagers or the PAP, it would be extremely difficult to ensure the smooth implementation of the RR plan.

Displacement is a continuous process, which often prompts a person to leave the original location and go elsewhere. Displacement needs to be viewed as a process rather than an event, which starts way before the actual physical displacement and continues for a long time after uprooting the people from the place. Therefore, concerned governments and/or companies should consider any displacement as a continuous process of interactions/dialogues between two parties. The process should be fully participatory and mutually beneficial for both the parties, not only on paper but also in practice. Only then, the displacement of population on account of the development project will be regarded as justifiable to the invaluable loss of human life/backward communities.

7.7.1. PARTICIPATORY APPROACH/METHOD AND ITS STRENGTHS

The broad objective of the participatory approach is to ensure the involvement of the end-users for planning and designing of any intervention programme so that community members perceive it as their own project, which is meant for their benefits. There is another similar method called participatory learning and action. They are interchangeably used in different situations. However, if community members perceive the intervention project as their own project, in which they were involved from the beginning, it would ensure maximum and effective utilization of the intervention project and its long-term sustainability. This is in contrast to traditional methods of planning of any intervention programme. This approach or method is called bottom-up approach which facilitates planning and designing on a need-based intervention basis.

It has been observed that a good participatory approach or method improves motivation, increases learning and feelings of ownership and enables the community's active participation in the development process and, finally, community members feel that they are empowered. Raising awareness about the proposed development project enables the users to make an 'informed choice' about what will become their preferred intervention project.

It has also been observed that involving and informing the end-users of any intervention programme helps in sending a vibe to the PAP that the problems and chosen solutions really reflect the needs and preferences of the users. This increases the chance that implemented solutions are really used. In contrast, the systems, which are perceived to be inconvenient, difficult to operate or, in other ways, do not correspond to the needs and preferences of the users have a high chance of not being used, or are adapted in ways that cause numerous problems or risks.

In a participatory approach, representatives from all stakeholders, namely the PAP, government representatives, representatives from local NGOs and industries, health workers and legal professionals are invited and they work together and exchange their views to find out an amicable solution to a problem. The brainstorming exercise following democratic group's learning processes help towards proper planning of an intervention project. Across the world, policymakers witnessed the benefits of the participatory approach in various water supply, sanitation and RR projects.

There are various participatory approaches or methods which involve a range of activities with a common thread. Enabling ordinary people to play an active and influential part in the decision-making process will affect their lives. This means that people are not just listened to, but also heard and that their voices shape outcomes. Social science and public health professionals often use the same approach as it is believed that knowledge, experience and suggestions of even an illiterate individual is valuable, innovative and beneficial for designing any intervention programme for them, as compared to earlier approaches, that is, designing an intervention programme based on knowledge and experience of the outside experts. Outside experts' knowledge and experience might be valuable since they worked in other situations, but the same knowledge and experience may not be applicable in another situation because of variation in two different set-ups in terms of climate, geographical location and people's attitude with respect to demographic, socio-economic and cultural backgrounds.

In the past, outside experts criticized the views of local people since they are not much educated and impose their ideas by suggesting what needed to be done, contradicting with local people and undermining the indigenous knowledge and experience of local people. Outsider's interferences demotivated local people to come forward and share their ideas and views regarding any development. In the given situation, participatory approach altered the notion and it became imperative to establish rapport, to sit down, listen and learn, to respect, to facilitate, to be nice to people, to learn not to interview, to know when not to speak and when not to be present. As a result, the outsiders now empower the local people by handing over the stick to them, which facilitates the enhancement of their confidence to contribute for planning and developing intervention projects, keeping the local need into account.

This approach could be applied to many settings—rural and urban, poor and wealthy—across the society. Location for conducting the exercise might be parks, under village trees and places where everybody will feel relaxed and comfortable. This approach or method could be followed at all stages of the project planning, development and implementation. Political parties also use the same approach for strengthening citizen engagement, claiming rights and holding the powerful to account.

7.7.2. KEY PRINCIPLES OF PARTICIPATORY APPROACHES OR METHODS

It is important to understand the key principles of participatory approaches that could be followed at appropriate stages of project planning and implementation. They are as follows:

- *The right to participate:* All the members of a group will be encouraged to participate in the discussion with open minds and place their viewpoints in taking beneficiary friendly intervention programmes. As it appears to be simple, it is very difficult to follow the same approach in reality. Maximizing the participation of the less powerful is a key feature of this approach.
- *Hearing unheard voices:* This approach encourages to come out with ideas of unheard voices and creating safe spaces that allow them to be heard. Therefore, most suppressed group of people gets the chance to share their views openly for the protection of their interest and rights.
- *Seeking local knowledge and diversity:* It is very important to get the perspective of the insiders and their diverse viewpoints, for the policymakers, so that they can adopt people-friendly policies and utilize them to the fullest extent.
- *Reversing learning:* This approach helps to come out of preconceived notions about an issue and attempts to learn from others with open minds, so that learning becomes really beneficial.
- *Using diverse methods:* A range of participatory approaches/methods helps to draw in as many people as possible to undertake learning and analysis on an equal basis.
- *Handing over the stick (or pen, or chalk):* This concept of 'handing over the stick' had emerged from the early works, using participatory approaches in some communities in South Asia and Africa. It involves those considered 'expert'—powerful or of higher status—sitting back, keeping quiet and allowing others to participate. Thinking about the relationships between more powerful and less powerful people and what those relationships imply for those who can speak and who cannot, it is an important aspect of using participatory methods.
- *Attitude and behaviour change:* Normally, the powerful people dominate in any decision-making process related to any issue in the society. Therefore, altering the existing practice of the decision-making process, the participatory approach has been encouraged and used in case of different development projects and were found to be really beneficial and people friendly.

In sum

The participatory approach is found to be beneficial in developing RR plan. It empowers the local people to decide what is good for them and what needs to be done. In the participatory approach, representatives from all stakeholders are invited and they work together and exchange their views to find out suitable solutions to a problem. In turn, the planner and policymakers get the insider perspective of development and accordingly they develop the programme which benefits most of the project-affected families.

7.8. BROAD OBJECTIVE OF THE REHABILITATION AND RESETTLEMENT PLAN

The broad objective is to develop a viable, culture-friendly and need-based RR plan for the PAP and to provide them with adequate compensation following the guidelines of the government.
Specific objectives of the RR plan are as follows:

- To ensure adequate compensation for land and other natural resources directly to the PAP
- To rehabilitate the directly affected people
- To create similar infrastructure and community services in the resettlement sites
- To improve the socio-economic conditions of the directly PAP through income-generating activities, with a view to raising their economic status at least, at par with that of the pre-rehabilitation state, so that they can fruitfully reinvest the money received as compensation on a sustainable basis
- To act as facilitator for the implementation of government welfare and development programmes in the resettlement sites
- To act as facilitator for sharing scientific knowledge with the directly PAP for cultivation, better outcome and marketing of the agricultural products
- To act as facilitator to enjoy the benefits from different government welfare programmes like Indira Awaas Yojana, scholarship for education and loan for entrepreneurship programmes
- To organize viable vocational training programmes for the people directly affected by the project
- To act as facilitator for women empowerment

7.9. PROCESS FOR DEVELOPING REHABILITATION AND RESETTLEMENT PLAN

For developing the RR plan, continuous dialogue should be initiated with the villagers or PAP in which there is a need to involve a third party who will play an impartial role. More specifically, the following steps are prerequisite to come out with an effective RR plan involving all the stakeholders. The steps include the following.

1. *Carrying out a situation analysis study:* It is very important to carry out a situation analysis study at the initial stages to understand the social situation, community dynamics and availability of resources. In particular, a situation analysis study would help to achieve the following objectives:
   - Understanding the perception/reaction of the PAP towards bringing new developments and/or commercial projects
   - Understanding the profile of the decision-makers of the proposed area to be taken up by the government or a private company
   - Understanding the nature of psychological attachment of the people towards their land
   - Understanding the expectation of the PAP
   In order to achieve the earlier objectives, qualitative data collection techniques such as informal interviews, in-depth interviews, key informant interviews, FGDs, and participant and non-participant observation methods are found to be suitable methods. In addition,

village information schedule may be used for collecting detailed information about the villagers or PAP.

As a practical example, the findings of a similar study have been presented here. Let us have a look at the findings of a study carried out in Jharkhand where an industry proposed to acquire a big land, covering four villages, for bauxite industry. The study also attempted to understand the basic problems faced by the directly project-affected villages and the people of neighbouring villages, that is, the indirectly project-affected villages. The name of the villages and name of the company are not mentioned here for confidential purpose. The objective-wise findings are discussed in the following section.

a. *Reaction of the PAP towards a new project:* Replying to a question 'whether the villagers feel that any developmental work in the area will be beneficial for them', the majority of them answered in affirmative. In fact, villagers welcomed any development project in the area, which will not be the cause of displacement.

   Further, when the issue of commercial projects and/or private investments was raised before the villagers through casual conversation, mixed responses were found. The majority of the villagers, especially elderly people, were of the opinion that it will go against the interests of the villagers and they will be displaced. On the other hand, youths, especially those who lived in the plains and studied a little bit either did not object directly or expressed positive views.

   One clear picture was observed in all the villages. The people who can help the villagers in getting work are more acceptable to the villagers.

   In addition, the perception of the younger generation and older generation in the studied villages were found to be different. Youths, who periodically interact with the people of plains, in connection with different activities, possess a more open outlook than that of their counterparts.

b. *Emotional attachment towards land:* Emotional attachment of the villagers towards the land was probed. Emotional attachment of four directly PAP towards land were found to be strong since they have been living in the place for generations. People develop cognitive–emotional bonds towards places which is known as place attachment. In this regard, humanistic geographers, for example, have described topophilia, meaning love of place and 'sense of place', which is often defined as similar to place attachment.

   However, it is expected that when the issue of compensation will be discussed with the PAP, it will be acceptable to them and, in turn, they might extend full cooperation for the smooth implementation of the rehabilitation plan.

c. *Community leaders/decision-makers:* Normally, in any tribal community, elderly people become the main decision-makers and/or has been regarded as community leaders and they are known by different names such as 'Mukhia' and 'Pahan'. However, in the four covered villages, tribal people regard only those who help them, by giving some work and/or source of earning and they are considered as the main decision-makers. The main and/or indirect decision-makers of the studied villages are both outsiders and from within the community.

d. *Main problems encountered by the villagers and prioritization of needs:* People of all the four directly project-affected villages suffer from the same problem with little variation. There is lack of basic minimal facilities in the studied villages, such as safe drinking water, water for irrigation, lack of health facilities and lack of educational facilities, poor communication and low levels of income (see Table 7.1).

TABLE 7.1
Main Problems and Prioritization of Needs

Directly Project-affected Villages	Main Problems Encountered	Prioritization of Needs
Village I	• Lack of health facilities • Lack of educational facilities • Lack of safe drinking water • Poor income • Poor communication	• Health facilities • Primary school • Work for earning money
Village II	• Lack of health facilities • Lack of educational facilities • Lack of safe drinking water • Poor income • Poor communication • Lack of irrigation facilities	• Health facilities • Secondary school • Safe drinking water facility
Village III	• Lack of health facilities • Lack of educational facilities • Lack of safe drinking water • Poor income • Poor communication • Lack of irrigation facilities	• Safe drinking water facility • Electricity • Irrigation facility • Road • Food
Village IV	• Lack of health facilities • Lack of educational facilities • Lack of safe drinking water • Poverty • Poor communication • Lack of irrigation facilities	• Safe drinking water facility • Work for earning money • Water for irrigation

Source: Deb (2005a).

The Government of Jharkhand has addressed the said problems in their new RR package, which is under finalization. The company will be adopting the same. In addition, the company will act as facilitator to implement the government welfare and development programmes from the local Block Development Office.

Efforts were made to address all these problems in the RR plan with a view towards helping the PAP to lead a minimum standard of living. In case of some developmental and welfare activities in the new settlement site, the authority of the company was asked to act as a facilitator to implement the government programmes from the local Block Development Office.

e. *Expectation of the PAP:* Normally, the expectations of poor tribal people are not much. They want some basic facilities such as safe drinking water, water for cultivation, education, health services and communication, in addition to work for survival with better wages.

The expectations of the indirectly PAP are similar to others. They also want basic minimal facilities such as safe drinking water, water for cultivation, education, health services and communication, in addition to work for survival with better wages.

2. *Initiating dialogue with the community leaders:* Based on the findings of the situation analysis study, an effort should be made to initiate dialogue with the community leaders and take them in confidence by explaining the short term and long term of any development project and ensuring the protection of their rights to them. In this regard, the government or any third party may be involved in taking up the discussion forward. It might require a series of discussions with different categories of community leaders and efforts should be made until the PAP are not convinced.

3. *Forming a supervisory committee:* It is very essential to form a supervisory committee for planning and development of RR plan and the committee members should comprise representatives from the project-affected families, from the government and/or private companies, NGO representatives, health workers and legal experts. The role of the committee is to initiate the dialogue with the project-affected families, concerning the issue and make an effort to convince them by explaining the measures to be taken to protect their interests. Further, the committee will sit together to discuss about the compensation issue and methods of providing the same in addition to the identification of suitable substitute land for them for the resettlement plan and oversee the entire implementation proofs of the RR plan. All the members of the committee will be allowed to share their views and offer suggestions for planning and development of an effective RR plan.

4. *Carrying out a detailed survey for compensation:* After convincing the leaders of the community and the other PAP, there is a need to carry out a detailed survey for collecting detailed information about all the project-affected families in terms of number of family members, their educational background and skills, area of their homestead land, cultivable and non-cultivable lands, livestock animals and natural resources such as trees and ponds.

In sum

Developing RR plan is a continuous process. The first step is to identify the community leaders in the area and initiate dialogue with them regarding the proposed development project, establish rapport with them and try to understand their reaction and views. And also give them a feeling that you are concerned about their welfare issue. It is also important to ascertain the nature and extend psychological attachment of project-affected families towards land so that need-based measures could be taken to address their emotional issues. Further, there is a need to carry out a survey in the area to understand the common people reaction towards bringing development project, their expectation and the main problems encountered by them and prioritization of their needs followed by a detailed survey of the area to identify the total project-affected families and their socio-economic condition, cultural background and resources, both human and natural.

7.10. METHOD FOR ASSESSING THE SITUATION, AVAILABILITY OF RESOURCES AND PLANNING FOR RR PLAN

Participatory rural appraisal (PRA) is the most suitable research method for understanding the rural situation in terms of the characteristics of the people, their lifestyles, beliefs and practices, local resources and other issues and concerns of the local people. In particular, PRA is a method to understand the rural social situation. It is an exercise in which rural people, irrespective of their educational and occupation backgrounds, are encouraged to participate, whereas the outsiders, that is, the researchers and third party, play the role of catalysts and facilitators to enable people to undertake and share their own investigation and analysis. This method helps local people to exchange their views and knowledge with other community leaders/members and enables them to analyse their own situation and prioritize their issues for addressing their problems. Finally, this process helps both the outsiders and the insiders to come out with a solution for any challenging situation. There are many PRA techniques. Some of the most used PRA techniques are discussed further.

7.10.1. Public/Village Meetings

The objective of this meeting with the villagers or people of proposed project sites is to appraise them about the development project and to gather information about demographic and socio-economic characteristics of the people of that area. In particular, this meeting helps to collect information about demography, occupational patterns, institutional arrangements, social security, infrastructure, resources, manpower, needs, problems, priority and opportunities.

7.10.2. Walkover Survey

The objective of this survey is to gather information about the patterns of land use, cropping, soil and tree species, and potential for area development. For this exercise, the observation method is adopted in addition to informal discussions or casual conversations with the people while walking in the area.

7.10.3. Social Mapping

This is another interesting and important exercise of the PRA technique. The objective of the exercise is to develop an insight of the physical layout of the village and spatial distribution of social groups, in addition to gaining knowledge about the access of different social groups to infrastructure and basic services. This exercise also helps to develop an understanding about social characteristics of the village in terms of their source of the livelihood, land distribution, skills of human resources and infrastructure facilities available in the area such as schools, health centre, road, housing pattern, religious places and markets. This exercise is done using a drawing sheet and pencil or preparing a map on the ground.

7.10.4. Resource Mapping

The objective of this exercise is to examine the resources available in the village and/or in the proposed project site. In particular, resource mapping helps in gaining knowledge about nature/ types of resources available and used in the villages, ownership patterns of the resources, infrastructure available to use the resources and implication for planning. This exercise is conducted by inviting knowledgeable persons from the village. Villagers map all the resources on the ground using local materials or on a drawing sheet, using a drawing pen or pencil. Finally, based on the drawing, the issues related to local resources are discussed with the villagers and analysed jointly.

7.10.5. Focus Group Discussion

The objective of FGD with a group of 10–12 villagers is to gather information about the background of the people in terms of various social groups and gender, with a view to understanding their perception and ability in resource use. In addition, FGD helps to understand the role of women in taking decisions and other related issues. FGD helps in gathering information about knowledge, perception and behaviour of people about various issues. The beauty of this exercise is cross-checking of information within the group during the discussion.

7.10.6. In-depth Interview

It is another qualitative data collection technique to collect in-depth information about various issues from different categories of people based on the need or the objective of any work. Qualitative data collected through in-depth interviews helps to understand any issue from an insider's perspective and, accordingly, appropriate measures can be taken, which will serve the purpose of the people.

In sum

For assessing the situation, beliefs and practices, availability of resources and planning for developing the RR plan, PRA is one of the best approaches. There are different participatory methods and they include public/village meetings, walkover survey, social mapping resource mapping, FGD and in-depth interview. All these methods are very helpful for understanding the insider perspectives about different issues.

7.11. ESTIMATING COMPENSATION FOR THE PROJECT-AFFECTED FAMILIES BASED ON DETAILED HOUSEHOLD SURVEY

Detailed household survey data are the basis for estimating compensation for the project-affected families following the government rules and regulations. However, efforts should be ensuring to offer adequate compensation to both directly and indirectly project-affected families.

7.11.1. Compensation and Rehabilitation Facilities

The government and/or any private company has to develop the RR package following the guidelines of the local government. Although compensation for homestead, cultivable and non-cultivable land should be decided as per the standard government rate and also keeping the market rate into account, it should be little more than the present rate, since actual displacement will take place after one or more than one year.

7.11.2. For Land and Construction of New House

After discussion with the supervisory committee members, compensation for immovable properties should be provided as per prevailing market rates and following the guidelines of the local government.

- For the construction of houses in the new resettlement site, 25–40 decimal land should be provided, free of cost, to all the project-affected families whose houses will be acquired.
- If any family does not want this land, they will be offered at least ₹100,000/- as one-time compensation.
- For the construction of houses in the new resettlement site, an amount of at least ₹100,000/- should be provided to all directly project-affected families, whose houses would be acquired and the money will be digitally transferred in the account of the head of the household. For the construction of houses, all managerial and backup support will be provided to the project-affected families by the government company free of cost.
- Valuation of all other civil structures and assets of the project-affected families will be done as per the guidance of the supervisory committee and as per law.
- A token amount of ₹10,000/- will be given to all directly project-affected families for shifting purposes at the time of resettlement. This amount might vary, depending upon the number of family members.

7.11.3. Employment

Any skilled jobs, as and when available, will be offered to the locals or PAP. However, the person should be physically and mentally fit and they should fulfil the requisite qualification.

7.11.3.1. Self-employment

Opening a big mine or industry in a new area means opening a lot of avenues of earning for the local people and it also invites developmental activities in the area. Hence, opening a mining industry in an area will create a lot of employment and self-employment opportunities. The company will support self-employment schemes such as pressure checking, tire resoling centre, cycle repairing shops, dhabas and paan shops, where some of the PAP can be supported. Apart from this, a number of indirect job opportunities will be created in the truck transport system, such as drivers and helpers, which will be offered to the PAP first.

In case of semi-manual mining, there is a scope for the deployment of large-scale workforce throughout the year. The PAP, especially the unskilled workers, will get work in the new mine throughout the year on a daily wage system.

7.11.4. Subsistence Allowance

Resettlement takes time. Hence, an amount of ₹10,000/ will be given to all the directly project-affected families every month, at least for a period of 12 months, through discussion with the supervisory committee members and local government.

In a new place, it takes some time to settle down. For getting returns from the land through agriculture, it takes some time. During this phase, if the PAP do not receive some support, it would be very hard for them to survive.

7.11.5. ORGANIZING VIABLE VOCATIONAL TRAINING PROGRAMMES FOR THE DIRECTLY PAP

It is not practically feasible for any government or company to offer employment to all unemployed people in an area. Hence, it is always advisable to organize skill-based vocational training programmes, looking into the local market needs and considering the skill/aptitude and educational background of the people, so that, after the training, one can encash the skills and earn the minimum amount of money for livelihood.

Hence, the government or company will organize or send all the eligible PAP for some vocational training programmes following the guidelines of government RR plan, so that they can start some income-generating activities. Trade for vocational training may be decided later on through discussions with the experts and supervisory committee members, so that, it becomes really useful and beneficial to the people.

After the training programme, the government and/or company will also act as facilitators to help the villagers enjoy the benefits of different government loan schemes for initiating income-generating activities or for getting employment.

7.11.6. SELECTION OF PLACE FOR RESETTLEMENT

Resettlement should be identified in nearby areas or at least within the same block or district. Prior to finalization, the area should be shown to the supervisory committee members and community leaders, that is, the representatives of the directly project-affected families.

In order to avoid any unwanted dispute and/or for the smooth implementation of the project, methods for distribution of 25–40 decimal land to each project-affected family for the construction of houses should be decided through discussions with the supervisory committee members.

However, location of an actual rehabilitation site depends upon the availability of sufficient vacant land in nearby areas.

7.11.7. ARRANGEMENTS OF OTHER BASIS FACILITIES IN THE NEW RESETTLEMENT AREA

Some basic amenities such as education facilities, health facilities, facilities for safe drinking water, water for irrigation, sanitation and communication facilities should be provided by the government or a private company in the new resettlement area. Apart from this, one community hall should be established in the new area so that community people can assemble, relax and exchange personal issues.

7.11.8. Education Facilities

One of the most important issues that require immediate attention are the educational facilities. A few steps that could be adopted by the governing bodies are provided as follows:

- The government or a company should help the local authority in the renovation of the existing local school infrastructure and/or schools, if it is not available, or building additional classrooms with drinking water and sanitation facilities.
- In case of necessity, the government or a company should help to build/construct two–three additional rooms for non-formal education for small children below the age of 6 years, so that the parents can leave their children there and can go for work.
- For the renovation of existing infrastructure and/or for the construction of additional rooms, the government or a company should provide one-time grants and the renovation and/or construction work should be done under the close supervision of the supervisory committee members or through the participatory approach. In this regard, the government or company should explore the facilities available with the local district or block office.
- The government or company should provide merit scholarship every year to deserving candidates for completing higher studies, for a period of 2–4 years. Later on, this will become part of the ongoing community development activities.

7.11.9. Healthcare Facilities

This is the major problem for the people of interior villages. For providing minimum health facilities, the following steps should be adopted by the authority of the local government.

- Primary health centres in the nearby villages of new resettlement sites should be upgraded in discussion with the respective health officials of the district or the block, so that, in case of any health problem occurs, the PAP may access minimum healthcare facilities.
- A periodic health camp (once a month or once in every two months) should be organized by the Health Department of the local government or company in the new resettlement sites.
- In the project site, the government or company should have their own medical facilities. The PAP should also have access to these medical facilities.
- The government or company must organize periodic veterinary health camps.

7.11.10. Facilities for Drinking Water

Adequate facilitates for safe drinking water is very essential in the rehabilitation site and it should be arranged by the government or company. Deep tube wells and/or hand pumps are also needed for using water for other domestic and agricultural purposes. These arrangements should also be made by the government or company. In the rural areas, for want of safe drinking water, a large number of children and elderly people suffer from waterborne diseases. Hence, this issue should be taken up seriously.

7.11.11. SHARING OF TECHNICAL KNOWLEDGE WITH REGARD TO AGRICULTURE

The PAP may not have knowledge and experience in certain types of income-generating activities. Therefore, from time to time, scientific knowledge about various income-generating activities should be shared with the PAP, by the experts, for better agriculture, through camps in the market area and/or in a convenient place. These facilities should be provided free of cost.

7.11.12. SANITATION FACILITY AND COMMUNITY POND

Lack of sanitation facilities causes different problems. First, for women and adolescents, it is embarrassing to go to open fields for excretion or urination. Second, women and adolescent girls become vulnerable to sexual abuse. Third, it brings unhygienic living environments. Therefore, it is very important to pay proper attention to this issue and make proper arrangements for sanitation facilities in the resettlement site. In addition, there is a need for community ponds for different purposes.

7.11.13. COMMUNITY HALL

The community hall is a meeting place of the community members. If there is an opportunity for building a community hall, people will be very happy and they can assemble in the same place after work or for any family, social or religious occasions. Arrangement of community halls will bring people close to each other and they can meet occasionally or/and exchange views.

7.11.14. PROPER ROADS AND/OR COMMUNICATION FACILITY

Communication facilities are essential for the development of any community or society, especially when a new area is going to be developed for the PAP. Without proper roads and transportation facilities, local people would not be able to move freely and cannot bring their agricultural products to the nearby markets. As a result, middlemen exploit the poor villagers who are involved in agricultural activities. For communication, approach roads and connection roads between the clusters should be made, in the new settlement site, by the government or private company.

7.11.15. FACILITIES FOR AGRICULTURE AND IRRIGATION

Agriculture is one of the main sources of survival for the tribal population or villagers. Hence, in the new settlement area, the following arrangements should be provided by the government or company and/or they will act as facilitators in regard to the following issues:

- Arrangements for irrigation facilities, in the form of check dams and pump machines, should be provided by the company. For maintenance of the same, responsibility should be given to the authorities of the Agriculture Department or Department of Fisheries of the local government or private company or they should hire experts from outside.

- Latest scientific methods for cultivation should be disseminated among the PAP so that they can take the advantages of the same and get maximum output from the land.
- Arrangement for soil test should be done to guide the PAP in the right direction so that agricultural products/vegetables will grow more/better in the area.
- Arrangements should be made for free distribution of seeds or at subsidized rates, in addition to fertilizers.

7.11.16. INCOME-GENERATING ACTIVITIES

Keeping the local market and potential of the area and land, the government or a company should help the displaced people run some income-generating activities to supplement their family income. Following are some of the activities, which should be explored, depending upon the situation.

1. *Horticulture:* Agroclimatic conditions of rural areas are suitable for horticultural development. Many of the tribal communities have great regard for fruit-bearing trees. Horticultural development in the tribal areas will be useful on other considerations also. In the first place, it will provide fruits both for raising the level of nutrition for the tribal people and also as a source of supplementary income. Second, trees will be steps in the prevention of soil erosion, which is an acute problem in some of the study areas.

   A programme of horticultural development in the rehabilitation site should start with the identification of fruit trees, which will be suitable for the climate conditions. Lands suitable for horticultural development may also be identified and taken up for large-scale plantation. If there were government lands, the tribes would be allowed to plant trees on them and use the yield.

   It has been observed that very sub-marginal and non-productive land is used for growing agricultural crops like paddy, while it may really be more suitable and productive for raising horticultural plants.

2. *Animal husbandry and dairy development:* Tribal agriculture continues to be based primarily on animal power. While cattle wealth is given considerable importance in the socio-economic conditions of the tribes, the status of families is being determined in many communities by the number of cattle owned, the quality of the animals used for raising the level of diet, providing adequate protein to the tribal people and also as a source of subsidiary income.

   The programmes of poultry development and animal husbandry will also aim at improving the nutritional status of the local tribals. When a programme has a focus on improving the income of the community, it should give emphasis on the marketing aspects, so that outputs are sold, and people may earn some money. For the sale of products for income-generating activities, local markets should also be explored. Thus, a balance between the economic and nutritional aspects of these programmes are taken care of.

   In the case of animal husbandry and/or livestock, care should be taken to distribute better quality animals and at least one pair of animals. Only then would villagers be able to see some profit after a phase of gestation.

3. *Plantation programmes/afforestation:* In the new settlement area, there may not be enough useful and valuable trees. Hence, a special drive should be given to plant saplings, which will

provide minor forest produce and other sources of subsistence and income. This approach will help to achieve two objectives. First, prevention of environmental pollution and, second, sources of earning money and/or saving of fuel expenses by using forest by-products.

4. *Dissemination of information about various government welfare and development programmes and act as a facilitator:* There are a number of developmental and welfare programmes of the Government of India for the marginalized population, regarding which poor people are not aware of. The government or a company should disseminate information about those programmes to the PAP and/or should act as a facilitator, so that they can enjoy the benefits from the same.

7.11.17. The Ministry of Rural Development, Government of India

A list of welfare and developmental programmes under the Ministry of Rural Development has been provided further, which the PAP can explore and make the best use of, for improving their quality of life. These programmes include the following:

- Swarnjayanti Gram Swarozgar Yojana
- Pradhan Mantri Gram Sadak Yojana (for communication and/or improvement of road condition)
- Training: National Institute of Rural Development
- Strengthening/establishment of State Institutes of Rural Development
- Strengthening/establishment of extension training centres
- Organization of training courses, seminars and workshops
- Indira Awaas Yojana
- National Food for Work Programme
- Sampoorna Grameen Rozgar Yojana
- National Social Assistance Programme
- DRDA
- Human Resource Development Programme
- National Drinking Water Mission

7.11.18. Welfare Schemes of the Ministry of Women and Child Development, and the Ministry of Human Resource Development, Government of India

A list of welfare and developmental programmes under the Ministry of Women and Child Development, and the Ministry of Human Resource Development, Government of India, has been provided further. Local governments should help the PAP to enjoy the benefits of the same welfare schemes. In this regard, local NGOs should work as facilitators for the implementation of the same schemes in the resettlement site.

- Employment and income-generating training-cum-employment-cum-production units for women
- Support to Training and Employment Programme for Women

- Balika Samridhi Yojana
- Swavalamban (Number of Voluntary Organisations Assisted and Fund Released) scheme
- Scheme of Assistance for Construction/Expansion of Hostel Building and strengthening the hostel facilities for working women with daycare centre for children
- Scheme on community-based production of nutritious foods

7.11.19. Emphasis for Protection of Women and Children's Rights in the Rehabilitation and Resettlement Plan

Women literacy is the indicator of development in any society. It has been observed that women, children and the elderly are particularly vulnerable to suffering due to displacement.

Hence, the rehabilitation packages should provide due emphasis on equal status to woman, so that they do not become subject to any harassment or maltreatment. In addition, women should be encouraged to form self-help groups for running income-generating activities. If a woman is educated and independent economically, she enjoys better status in the family and would be less vulnerable to neglect, abuse and harassment.

Research has also revealed that children are vulnerable to sufferings due to changes in life circumstances from displacement. Therefore, the issue of education facilities, educational guidance, healthcare facilities and safety for children should be given due priority in the resettlement plan.

7.11.20. Facilities for the Indirectly PAP

Basic problems encountered by the people of neighbouring villages should be addressed in order to specify their grievances. The problems of the people of neighbouring villages should be identified and prioritized in the discussions with their representatives.

- Identification of new place/land for resettlement in discussion with the committee members
- Developing culture-specific resettlement plans and implementation of the same in a phased manner

7.11.21. Implementation and Monitoring of RR Plan

For the successful implementation of the RR plan, it is urgently needed to involve the directly PAP. Otherwise, it will create a lot of problems at the later stage.

In order to ensure community participation, a supervisory committee should be formed, as discussed earlier, with representatives from all stakeholders, including the PAP, by the villagers. All issues related to planning and development of the RR plan should be discussed with an open mindset and all concerned should be given options to share their views and suggestions. Continuous evaluation among the supervisory committee members is a continuous process, and not a one-time interaction with the villagers. It should be right from the beginning of the project, that is, household survey and local resources, deciding the compensation and selection of new sites and formulation of the overall RR plan. Thereafter, development work in the resettlement site, in terms of allocation of homestead and agricultural land as compensation, houses, development of infrastructures such as houses, schools, health centres, community hall and safe drinking water, construction of water bodies and communication facilities must be carried out.

In addition, the following activities should be undertaken after the resettlement, under the close supervision of the supervisory committee:

- Awareness about technology transfer and scientific cultivation process and various government welfare and development programmes in the field of agriculture
- Distribution of good quality seeds for different agricultural products and livestock animals, as mentioned earlier
- Regular monitoring of all these activities by higher authorities and follow-up of all income-generating activities for required assistance, in case of need

7.11.22. ADDITIONAL MEASURES FOR SMOOTH IMPLEMENTATION OF REHABILITATION PLAN

Some additional measures that can be adopted to ensure smooth implementation of the rehabilitation plans are mentioned as follows:

- Identity cards should be issued to each project-affected family in order to avoid any confusion in maintaining the records.
- Periodic meeting with the supervisory committee members should be held to review the progress of the resettlement plan.
- Follow-up after the implementation of the RR plan is a prerequisite to ensure that post-resettlement issues are addressed by the government or company, that is, technical know-how support is provided to the project-affected families for running income-generating activities or forming women self-help groups and getting loans from the rural banks as committed in the RR plan. Finally, it is very important to help them in selling the output of their income-generating activities.

7.11.23. TENTATIVE TIME FRAME FOR DEVELOPMENT OF INFRASTRUCTURE AND IMPLEMENTATION OF THE PLAN

It is very important to develop a tentative time frame for the development of the infrastructure facilities and implementation of the same so that the PAP can remain mentally prepared for the same and can plan their future accordingly. As an example, a proposed time frame has been mentioned in Table 7.2 for providing an essence to the student about how it should work. The proposed time frame is overlapping as a number of development activities should be carried on at the same time for faster completion of the RR plan. However, the time frame depends upon a number of factors such as total project-affected families to be shifted, location of the new site of settlement, availability of materials in and around the area for development of infrastructure

TABLE 7.2
Activity-wise Tentative Timetable

Sl. No.	Activities	Time Frame
1.	Clearance from the respective departments of Jharkhand government	Two months
2.	Formation of a core group and discussion with the core-group members and explaining the rehabilitation facilities to be offered	One month
3.	Calculation of different forms of compensation and payment of compensation	Two months
4.	Distribution of homestead and agricultural land	Two months
5.	Construction of houses and approach roads and connecting roads between the sites	Six months
6.	Establishment of basic amenities such as drinking water, primary health centre, school, community hall, community sanitation facilities	Six months
7.	Initiating dialogue with the block officials for support from the block office, whatever permissible and available	One month
8.	Shifting from the previous area to resettlement site	Two months

Source: Deb (2005b).

facilities and availability of manpower in addition to file clearance from the respective Ministry of Infrastructure Development.

About 24 months are required to implement the RR plan, if everything goes smooth and all concerned agencies extend their cooperation. It may take more time depending upon a number of factors as mentioned before. However, the government or company should ensure the timely implementation of the RR plan, which will cause relatively less suffering to the project-affected families.

In sum

Proper compensation should be offered to all the directly and indirectly project-affected families following the guidelines of local government. Employment opportunities to be provided to the project-affected families in the development project. For any skilled jobs, as and when available, first priority should be given to the local or PAP. In addition, skill-based vocational training programmes should be organized for the people considering their skill/aptitude and educational background. Subsistence allowance to be provided to all the directly project-affected families at least for a period of 12 months. For resettlement, land should be identified within the same block or district so that people can find some cultural similarity which would, in turn, help them to remain psychologically better. While identifying the resettlement area, views of project-affected families should be sought. Some basic arrangements such as the construction of houses, sanitation facilities, safe drinking water, health centre, educational and communication facilities, community hall should be arranged in the new resettlement area prior to shifting people. Further, it is very important to provide information to people about different government welfare schemes and know-how about agriculture and income-generating programmes. The entire RR process should be closely monitored by a committee for the smooth and effective implementation of plan.

7.12. ROLE OF COMMUNITY PSYCHOLOGISTS IN RR PLAN

Community psychologists' role is extremely important in every step of the development project, that is, right from the beginning. More specifically, the role of the community psychologist is as follows:

- At the first instance, the community psychologist can carry out the survey, sensitively, to assess the nature of the land, human and natural resources available to the people of the area, followed by conducting studies to assess the nature and extent of psychological attachment towards the place/land.
- In order to sensitize the community members about the issue of development project, the community psychologist can take up the issue sensitively and take them in confidence, ensuring due compensation and explaining the participatory approach to be followed in developing the RR plan.
- During the continuous process of dialogue regarding RR, some of the PAP might be psychologically disturbed and feel emotionally insecure. Here, a community psychologist can specify the mental disturbances by conducting group therapy and/or individual counselling as a subject expert.
- Being a part of the negotiation process, a community psychologist can play an effective role in protecting the interests of the PAP.
- Finally, during the implementation process of the RR plan, they can be watchful and ensure the effective implementation of the RR plan as agreed. The presence of the community psychologist will give confidence to the villagers or the PAP to a great extent.

7.13. LATEST LEGISLATIVE MEASURES FOR PROTECTION OF THE INTERESTS OF PAP

7.13.1. THE RIGHT TO FAIR COMPENSATION AND TRANSPARENCY IN LAND ACQUISITION, REHABILITATION AND RESETTLEMENT ACT, 2013

The broad objective of this act (Ministry of Rural Development, 2013) is to adopt consultation processes with institutions of local self-government and gram sabhas for ensuring a participatory and transparent process for acquisition of land for the development of projects. The act also emphasizes upon least disturbances to the owners of the land and other affected families and fair compensation to the project-affected families, in addition to smooth RR of the same families. Further, the act provides emphasis on considering PAP as the partner in the development project, so that the LA would lead to improved socio-economic conditions of the same people.

There are 13 chapters in the law, which deal with various issues related to LA and methods adopted for the same purpose, keeping in mind the interests of the PAP. In Chapter II, it states that first, a social impact assessment should be carried out within six months of the notification issued by the appropriate government in consultation with the local government bodies with their representatives. As per Section 5 of the act, public hearing should be arranged to examine the reaction of the PAP. Further, social impact assessment report should be evaluated by an independent multidisciplinary group of experts to assess its potential benefits and make recommendations within two months from the date of its constitution. The recommendations of the expert group should be made in the local language, in addition to English, and uploaded on the government website for the information of all concerned.

Under Section 10 of Chapter III, it is categorically stated that there is a need to safeguard food security, that is, irrigated multi-cropped land should not be acquired. If it is acquired, supplementary arrangements should be made. For example, as per Subsection 2 of Section 10, 'such land may be acquired subject to the condition that it is being done under exceptional circumstances.'

Further, Subsection 3 of Section 10 states that

> Whenever multi-crop irrigated land is acquired under sub-section (2), an equivalent area of culturable wasteland shall be developed for agricultural purposes or an amount equivalent to the value of the land acquired shall be deposited with the appropriate Government for investment in agriculture for enhancing food-security.

Section 16 of the law under Chapter IV talks about the preparation of the RR Scheme by the administrators and carrying out a survey to identify the project-affected families, while Section 18 states that approved RR Scheme must be made public in the local language and uploaded on the website of the appropriate government.

Section 26 empowers collectors of districts to determine the market value of the land of project-affected families. There are certain conditions for determining the market value of the land and they include

(a) the market value, if any, specified in the Indian Stamp Act, 1899 (2 of 1899) for the registration of sale deeds or agreements to sell, as the case may be, in the area, where the land is situated; or

(b) the average sale price for similar type of land situated in the nearest village or nearest vicinity area; or

(c) consented amount of compensation as agreed upon under sub-section (2) of section 2 in case of acquisition of lands for private companies or for public–private partnership projects, whichever is higher:

Provided that the date for determination of market value shall be the date on which the notification has been issued under section 11.

Finally, the collector will calculate the total amount of compensation to be paid to the landowner by including all assets attached to the land as per Section 27.

Section 30 states the award of solatium. For example, Subsection 1 states that 'the Collector having determined the total compensation to be paid, shall, to arrive at the final award, impose a Solatium amount equivalent to one hundred per cent of the compensation amount.'

This amount shall be in addition to the compensation payable to any person whose land has been acquired.

As per Section 31, the collector shall award the RR package to project-affected families and as per Subsection 2 of Section 31, there are specific issues to be looked into while initiating the process of RR and they include the following:

1. RR amount payable to the family
2. Bank account number of the person to which the RR award amount is to be transferred
3. Particulars of house site and house to be allotted, in case of displaced families
4. Particulars of land allotted to the displaced families

5. Particulars of one-time subsistence allowance and transportation allowance in case of displaced families
6. Particulars of payment for cattle shed and petty shops
7. Particulars of one-time amount to artisans and small traders
8. Details of mandatory employment to be provided to the members of the affected families
9. Particulars of any fishing rights that may be involved
10. Particulars of annuity and other entitlements to be provided
11. Particulars of special provisions for the Scheduled Castes and the Scheduled Tribes to be provided

---

In sum

This law is very comprehensive and takes care of all the issues, keeping in mind the interests of project-affected families and social causes. The main challenge lies while implementing the law as per the provisions made in the law and satisfying the local people and informing them about the positives and negatives of the development project and getting their cooperation. Finding a suitable land, nearby, for resettlement, is always a big challenge. There is a need to closely monitor the implementation of the project, especially during resettlement.

7.14. ISSUES AND CHALLENGES WITH RESPECT TO IMPLEMENTATION OF RR PLAN FOLLOWING THE BROAD GUIDELINES OF THE RIGHT TO FAIR COMPENSATION AND TRANSPARENCY IN LAND ACQUISITION, REHABILITATION AND RESETTLEMENT ACT, 2013

First of all, the local government and/or the private company who is going to acquire land for establishing an industry need to be committed to fulfilling the agreed terms and conditions. At the initial stages, the concerned agency or government is sincere in their efforts, but slowly, as time passes, they become casual in implementing the RR plan and somehow make an effort to complete the implementation task without paying much attention to the quality issue and without addressing the day-to-day issues of the displaced people.

Second, lack of transparency is another big challenge in implementing the project. Although constituted committee members are supposed to oversee the implementation of the project, the periodic meetings are not held on time.

So far as compensation is concerned, sometimes it is not given to the PAP on time, as per the agreed terms and conditions. As a result, the PAP are unable to start their life afresh in a new area and/or to start their own businesses or agricultural activities.

While developing the rehabilitation plan, the issue of 'know-how' technology is committed by the government or private company, that is, the PAP will be provided free of cost 'know-how' technology and guidance for running their income-generating activities. In reality, it does not happen. Sometimes, for the sake of formality, once or twice, one or two experts come from outstation and brief the PAP about starting and running a specific income-generating activity. Thereafter, they are not available if the PAP have any query or face any challenge in running the income-generating activity.

7.15. CONCLUSION AND IMPLICATIONS

Displacement on account of development projects and social unrest situations is a global phenomenon for both developed and developing countries. Development projects are necessary to cope with the increasing demands of society and the latest scientific developments and finally the output of development projects benefits the larger society. Without setting up industries and/or commercial projects, it is next to impossible to improve the standard of living of the common people. New industries and/or commercial projects would generate direct and indirect sources of earning for the local people. People living in and around the new project/industry will be immensely benefited by the process.

Nevertheless, there are some disadvantages of development projects, especially when the question of acquiring large area comes into being. The people who live in the identified area are the victims of development project, though a lot of promises are made by the government or private company. However, if adequate compensation is offered and a suitable area is identified for RR, the sufferings of the PAP would be less. For developing the RR plan, the participatory approach should be followed for addressing the issues and challenges of the PAP from the right perspective. While calculating the compensation, a better price must be offered and subsidiary allowances need to be provided to each family, at least for a period of one year, until they become independent economically. Basic amenities such as safe drinking water and sanitation facilities, water bodies and minimum communication facilities, health centres and educational facilities need to be made available in the new area.

There are a number of positive implications of establishment of an industry. First, it is expected to create job opportunities for a large number of people, including the PAP. PAP may not be absorbed in higher technical positions, but they may be engaged in unskilled jobs, given their background.

Second, creation of opportunities for income-generating activities and dissemination of information about various government schemes among the villagers is necessary. It would help the project-affected villagers to avail opportunities from government loan schemes.

Third, women will be encouraged to form self-help groups for running income-generating programmes and it will also help them share technical knowledge and getting financial support from rural banks like national banks for agricultural purposes.

Fourth, there will be more small industries to supply the material to the big industry which, in turn, will create more opportunities for many more people to earn for their livelihood.

Fifth, there will be an improvement of communication facilities in the resettlement and project sites. In the remote areas where development projects are undertaken, normally, communication facilities are very poor. In some areas, it is very difficult to reach the villages since there are no proper roads. Tribal villagers are used to walking 8–10 km or even more, for visiting the local market, for selling the agricultural products and/or livestock animals and for purchasing the basic amenities from the weekly market. In the new settlement area, there would be proper and connecting roads for the villagers to travel easily. Proper roads are required for a number of reasons. First, it will help the villagers to travel from one place to another. Second, in case of any serious health issue, the patients would be able to go to the nearest health centre. Third, villagers will get the proper price of their products when they would be able to carry the vegetables and other items to the local market.

Sixth, there will be a creation of educational facilities. There are plenty of villages in remote areas where there are no educational facilities. Even if there is any such opportunity, it is located at distant places. As a result, a large number of children are deprived of basic primary education and thereby they become unskilled workers for life. Hence, the establishment of new industries will ensure educational facilities in the new area.

Seventh, a lot of other development projects will be undertaken in the new areas and they include health centres, safe drinking water facilities and water facilities for agriculture and finally, all these development activities would improve the overall quality of life of the PAP. Health facilities would ensure proper care and treatment of the health of poor people and/or further referral services.

EXERCISES

One-mark Questions

1. Define development.
2. What do you mean by an income-generating programme?
3. Define the participatory approach.
4. What is an in-depth interview?
5. What do you mean by compensation?
6. What do you mean by market value?
7. Who are indirectly affected by projects?
8. Define social discrimination.
9. What is impact assessment?
10. Why are the views of PAP important?

Five-mark Questions

1. Why is there a need for development project?
2. Who are directly affected by a project?
3. What is FGD? Discuss its strength.
4. What is social mapping? Why is it necessary?
5. Define resource mapping. How should it be carried out?

Ten-mark Questions

1. Are project-affected families provided adequate compensation? Give an example.
2. Discuss the challenges in screening directly project-affected families.
3. Discuss the impact of any development project on women.
4. How do you identify the land for resettlement of project-affected families?

Reflexive Questions

1. Discuss the advantages of PRA.
2. What are the challenges faced by project-affected families at the time of resettlement?
3. How does one deal with the issue of psychological attachment to land?
4. Discuss the role of community psychologists in preparing an RR plan.

REFERENCES

Baker, J. L. (2000). *Evaluating the impact of development projects on poverty: A handbook for practitioners.* World Bank.

Birley, M. H. (1995). *The health impact assessment of development projects.* HMSO Publications Centre.

Deb, S. (2005a). Situation analysis and proposed rehabilitation and resettlement plan. Funded by INDAL, Jharkhand, India.

Deb, S. (2005b). Rehabilitation and resettlement plan for the project affected people in Gumla District Jharkhand, funded by HINDALCO, Jharkhand, India.

Dixon, J. A., Carpenter, R. A., Fallon, L. A., Sherman, P. B., & Manipomoke, S. (2013). *Economic analysis of the environmental impacts of development projects.* Routledge.

Fernandes, W. (2004). Rehabilitation policy for the displaced. *Economic & Political Weekly, 39*(12), 1191–1192.

Fernandes, W., & Paranjpye, V. (Eds.). (1997). *Rehabilitation policy and law in India: A right to livelihood.* Indian Social Institute.

Lattemann, S., & Höpner, T. (2008). Environmental impact and impact assessment of seawater desalination. *Desalination, 220*(1–3), 1–15.

Lewicka, M. (2011). Place attachment: How far have we come in the last 40 years? *Journal of Environmental Psychology, 31*(3), 207–230. doi:10.1016/j.jenvp.2010.10.001

McCarthy, M., Biddulph, J. P., Utley, M., Ferguson, J., & Gallivan, S. (2002). A health impact assessment model for environmental changes attributable to development projects. *Journal of Epidemiology & Community Health, 56*(8), 611–616.

Ministry of Rural Development. (2013). *The Right to Fair Compensation and Transparency in Land Acquisition, Rehabilitation and Resettlement Act, 2013.* Ministry of Rural Development.

Morgan, R. K. (2012). Environmental impact assessment: The state of the art. *Impact Assessment and Project Appraisal, 30*(1), 5–14.

Neubert, S. (2013). *Social impact analysis of poverty alleviation programs and projects: A contribution to the debate on the methodology of evaluation in development co-operation.* Routledge.

Parasuraman, S. (1993). Impact of displacement by development projects on women in India. *ISS Working Paper Series/General Series, 159*, 1–12.

Rogers, J. C., Simmons, E. A., Convery, I., & Weatherall, A. (2012). Social impacts of community renewable energy projects: Findings from a woodfuel case study. *Energy Policy, 42*(C), 239–247.

Rollero, C., & de Piccoli, N. (2010). Place attachment, identification and environment perception: An empirical study. *Journal of Environmental Psychology, 30*(2), 198–205.

Scannell, L., & Gifford, R. (2010). Defining place attachment: A tripartite organizing framework. *Journal of Environmental Psychology, 30*(1), 1–10.

Schroeder, H. W. (1991, September). Preference and meaning of arboretum landscapes: Combining quantitative and qualitative data. *Journal of Environmental Psychology, 11*(3), 231–248. doi:10.1016/S0272-4944(05)80185-9

RECOMMENDED READINGS

Mathur, H. M., & Marden, D. (1998). *Development projects and improvement risks.* Oxford.

Reddy, A. A. (2016). *Rehabilitation and resettlement in Tehri hydro power project.* Partridge India.

Community Support for People Affected by Disaster

LEARNING OBJECTIVES

- Defining the natural calamities, war and violence
- Understanding the magnitude and causes of natural calamities
- Discussing the rescue and after care arrangements of disaster
- Examining the impact of disaster on mental health and addressing the same
- Discussing the disaster management strategies, policies and programme

ABSTRACT

Disaster management, many times, becomes a series of complex and overwhelming activities due to the unpredictable nature of the disaster and magnitude of destruction caused by it. It could be a sudden trigger or a slow-onset disaster due to a natural or man-made cause and could be foreseen or occur suddenly at a completely unprepared point in time. The plight it brings to a community is such that the remaining of it may continue to be traced even after generations. This chapter is an attempt to understand the lasting impact a disaster can have on the psychological build-up of a community. It introduces several prominent ideas of disaster management and rehabilitation of individuals after the disaster has occurred. Attempts have been made to closely understand the model of proactive psychosocial care that could be used at the community level depending on the intensity of the need of the individual. An overview of existing policies and programmes available in India in relation to disaster management is also provided. The chapter closes with a brief description about the role of psychologists in disaster management.

Keywords: Calamity; community; disaster; hazard; rehabilitation

8.1. INTRODUCTION

Unanticipated occurrence and massive impact, these two characteristics of a disaster make it extremely difficult for people to fight it out. This becomes particularly tiresome when the society lacks any protective mechanism in place to be used at the time of emergency. Statistics say that there would be at least one disaster per day on average, and the number seems to only increase due to increase in the population density, adverse variations in environmental components such as climate change, global warming, deforestation, pollution and whatnot. It could come in the form of earthquake, landslide, flood, drought, epidemics, war or disaster due to technical failures such as thermal power plant blast, pollution or global warming. The devastation caused in terms of physical injury and death, as well as economic downfall due to destruction of building, or road, struggle to meet the need for basic amenities, the plight of children and the elderly, differently abled, pregnant women are some of the most pressing sufferings brought by disaster. The prevalence of mental illness associated with exposure to trauma and shock is also found to be increasing; in fact, studies claim that discomfort in the psychosocial and mental illness is a major component of the burden caused due to a disaster. Scholarship on the impact of a disaster on the mental health of the affected population done worldwide gives a very clear picture of the significantly high rates of psychiatric condition among the survivors of a disaster. Most prominently diagnosed conditions associated with a disaster are PTSD, depression, anxiety, adjustment disorders and alcohol dependence. It has to be noted that a large proportion of such conditions go unattended, and also the ones which have received medical attention would belong to the undiagnosable category.

This chapter intends to understand the impact of disaster on the psychosocial well-being of a community. Through thorough literature review of available data worldwide, this chapter attempts to explore the standard of mental health post-disaster and how they are addressed. An attempt to understand techniques in disaster management and the various types of rehabilitation involved in the process is being made. A model that offers effective psychological care after the disaster is examined, considering the Indian context. Further, an overview of the available policies and programmes related to disaster management in the country is also provided. The chapter ends with an overview of the role of psychologists in disaster management.

8.2. DEFINITION OF NATURAL CALAMITIES, WAR AND VIOLENCE

This chapter discusses several distinct but closely related topics of significance. Let us familiarize ourselves with a few terms and gain clarity on their relevance in this chapter.

As defined by the United Nations Office for Disaster Risk Reduction (UNISDR), a disaster is a 'serious disruption of the functioning of a community or society involving widespread human, material, economic or environmental losses and impacts, which exceeds the ability of the affected community or society to cope with using its own resources'. On another dimension, the Centre for Research on the Epidemiology of Disasters defines a disaster as 'a situation or event which overwhelms local capacity, necessitating a request to a national or international level for external assistance; an unforeseen and often sudden event that causes great damage, destruction and human suffering'. Hence, a disaster could either be a natural calamity such as flood, earthquake, landslide and epidemic or could be man-made in nature such as war, pollution or global warming. Each disaster may include either an event that can cause a massive impact on people or could be a group of small events which occurred in a series to finally cause the impact (Brewin et al., 2008); each of them has its own unique challenges to face (McFarlane & Williams, 2012). The guidelines produced by the Central Water Commission (May, 2006) mandated the states of the country to develop their own emergency action plan for larger dams in respective states; despite this, only 192 out of 4,728 dams (96%) of the cases function without an emergency plan as understood from an evaluation report generated in 2011 (*The Hindu*, 2013).

Natural calamities could be those 'natural processes or phenomena that may cause loss of life, injury or other health impacts, property damage, loss of livelihoods and services, social and economic disruption, or environmental damage' (United Nations Office for Disaster Risk Reduction, 2014). At the same time, man-made calamity could be due to either intentional/unintentional human actions that could result in a huge emergency which involves death, injury, destruction and loss, such as war or civil strife. Keeping these two ideas in mind, one should comprehend a hazard as 'a rare or extreme event in the natural or human-made environment that adversely affects human life, property or activity to the extent of causing a disaster' (Sena, 2006).

It is important to understand that it is the degree of vulnerability of a community that makes a hazard into a disaster. Hence, whether natural or man-made, if there arises a situation of acute deprivation of basic necessities that causes significant impairment in the functioning of that community, and which requires intervention without which recovery is not possible, then such a condition could also be understood as a disaster. Be it natural/man-made disaster or sudden-onset/slow-onset disaster, the loss and destruction could be massive and of unforeseeable magnitude causing significant suffering to mankind.

8.3. MAGNITUDE AND CAUSE OF CALAMITIES

The worldwide frequency of calamities over the past two decades was such that over three million families were victims to the loss and sufferings (Roudini et al., 2017); 'In 2017, 335 natural disasters affected over 95.6 million people, killing additional 9.697 and costing a total of $335 billion' (Below & Wallemacq, 2018), out of which '183 were natural catastrophes and 118 were man-made disasters' (Swiss Re Institute, 2018). In the year 2017, Asia (136 occurrences) was found to be the most vulnerable with over 70 per cent share rate of affected people. The Red Cross Society also provided corroborating evidence and emphasized on the geographic location of Asia, particularly the east and southeast regions of Asia, as a deterministic reason for high calamity incidence (Kokai et al., 2004). An interesting trend observed in terms of the disaster loss is lower mortality but higher cost (Below & Wallemacq, 2018). *The Implementation Guide for Man-made and Technical Hazards* by UNISDR had hence also targeted on managing man-made hazards at a global panorama (UNISDR, 2018). As per the latest reports from the Red Cross Society, Asia is rated as the area with the highest proneness to disaster (International Federation of Red Cross and Red Crescent Societies, 2018) and where 'over 40% of world's natural catastrophe occurs' (International Federation of Red Cross and Red Crescent Societies, 2010). This is so for varied reasons, but mostly because of its geographic location.

The Asian continent is often struck with natural calamities such as earthquakes, tsunami, volcanic eruption, typhoons and cyclones. Turbulent wind, unbearably heavy rainfall, irrepressible flood and uncontrollable destruction, people in the Asian continent are constantly under threat of violent natural disasters (Kokai et al., 2004). Climatic changes and increasing population densities are often quoted in terms of cause and effect association with calamity incidence (McFarlane & Williams, 2012), particularly in natural calamities. Concentration of greenhouse gas in the atmosphere and its various threatening probabilities of climate variables such as temperature and precipitation are understood to be linked with the occurrence and natural calamities (Thomas, 2014). Hardest hit countries such as China. the USA and India have large geographical areas which is one powerful contributory factor that aggravates catastrophe. Fragility in utilizing the technological advancements in controlling natural calamities lead to increase in death and loss, as can particularly be seen in the Third-World countries (Weisaeth & Tonnessen, 2003). The nature of the disaster is the prime contributor to the magnitude of destruction. For instance, if there is an anticipatory period before the actual occurrence of a disaster, then evacuation systems and primary prevention strategies can reduce the impact of the aftermath.

In sum

- A disaster is a 'serious disruption of the functioning of a community or society involving widespread human, material, economic or environmental losses and impacts, which exceeds the ability of the affected community or society to cope with using its own resources', as defined by UNISDR.
- The magnitude of disaster is increasing every year, and the Asian continent is struck with maximum occurrences.

8.4. RESCUE AND AFTER-RESCUE ARRANGEMENTS

In the matter of arranging rescue and after-rescue provisions, the involvement of and coordination between the central and state governments is inevitable. The nature and extent of support which both these hierarchies of government can provide is mutually inclusive and can be rightly placed for the people in need through community participation. Hence, a rescue mission can attain its maximum success through the joint efforts of governments at various levels and its people. Along with the systematic framework of disaster management, understanding drawn from previous similar experiences, either of the same locality or any other locality, can contribute significantly in deciding better management techniques. The aftermath of the hydro-meteorological disaster at Mandakini, Uttarakhand, in 2013, left several practical understandings behind regarding issues of the disaster-prone area which are discussed below. Most importantly, the lack of effective information management and poorly fared information handling capacities by the authority had created a state of confusion that hampered the rescue operations; neither was the locality well equipped with an effective communication mechanism through which information could be passed to the emergency operations centre nor was there any means for controlling the spread of false information through media and to lessen further panic among the people. Another pressing factor was the absence of an effective warning infrastructure that could emanate forecasting and prediction from real-time data for immediate communication to the location under threat. Another notable learning from the disaster at Mandakini is the need to train a sufficient number of locals who are familiar with the locality, its terrain, routes and possible hurdles, along with the specialized rescue team of each state; this is understood to ensure the effectiveness of disaster management. It is recommended that rescue protocols adapted across regional and linguistic variations should be clearly laid down and rehearsed at the earliest to minimize further confusion (Rautela, 2013).

Prompt learning from the Indian Army's intervention in managing the 2010 flash floods in Leh (Ladakh) could show the need for readiness and immediate activation of the disaster management activities which was already set and well-rehearsed way back in time. The need for pre-hospital care intervention as well as an effective communicative network were also evidently contributing to the aforementioned intervention. Over and above, community involvement and knowledge dissemination were found to be paramount in building confidence among the public (Gupta et al., 2012). Further, drastic climatic changes resulting from unscientific human intervention are clearly ascribed as the supreme cause of disaster in an area. Changes in climatic conditions have now aggravated beyond control, that it has become extremely challenging to prevent further fragmentation of ecologically sensitive and fragile ecosystem and landscape in the country; unscientifically planned and executed developmental projects are to be blamed and further establishments of similar activities should be avoided (Kala, 2014). Working along the similar lines, a post hoc study on cyclone Aila (2009) occurred in Bangladesh stresses on the 'need to focus on Disaster Risk Reduction in parallel to the disaster preparedness planning' (Mallick et al., 2011).

For initiating an effective rescue operation, a number of issues need to be taken care of at various levels and proper coordination among all military and paramilitary forces including local community is required.

8.4.1. AT THE GOVERNMENT LEVEL

It is in the hands of the local government to initiate an immediate rescue operation with an overall objective of minimizing damages to the maximum possible extent and to rebuild the community to its original shape. The federal and local governments ensure immediate release of funds that they are expected to contribute; in majority of the times, the local government would be under huge pressure for efficiently managing the limited amount of fund and this is the immediate and most appropriate requirement of the time. In addition, voluntary donation may be invited from all sources to meet the expenses incurred. On the whole, the local government is responsible for monitoring the overall rescue operation such as arranging for helicopters, ambulances and other vehicles from the nearby places for rescue, ensuring the availability of all medical facilities in nearby health centres, providing food, safe drinking water and other essential items for people in need, and several other simple and complex coordinated chain of actions to ensure smooth rescue and recovery of the locality. The government can make effective utilization of the advancements in information and communication technology (ICT), mass media and radio for coordinating communication between the affected area and the emergency control rooms. Assigning toll-free numbers and publicizing the same for faster communication and intervention could be another mode of effective mitigation. The government, at a later stage, can address the issues related to loss and damage of house, agricultural land and crops, roads, communication networks and so on and rebuild the locality to its previous condition.

8.4.2. AT THE COMMUNITY LEVEL

The execution of the action plans and rescue operations could be successful through the active participation of community members who are familiar with the locality and the people in need. The tasks involved in the rescue operation would include searching for people from the disaster site, locating family members and children and establishing a connection with them, arranging food and safe drinking water, collecting essentials such as clothing and medicines, relocating people who are rescued to some other safe locality and the list goes on. The trained officials involved in rescue and rehabilitation mission can have the participation of the community members in providing assistance to many such activities that require familiarity and close understanding of the locality, roads and terrains, location of houses, institutions or factories in the affected area.

Disaster management involves not just the immediate rescue activities, the community can be involved in the rehabilitation and recovery phases post disaster. This involves activities such as ensuring the safety of the disaster-affected people in the camp, arranging culture-specific group activities for the elderly people in the camp, arranging games and sports for the children which would help them to come out of the traumatic state of mind, arranging mental health support services such as individual counselling, group counselling and family counselling for addressing PTSD. Once basic issues are addressed, there is a need to rebuild the community by the government in terms of houses, health centres, schools, community hall, community sanitation facilities, safe drinking water and communication and transportation facilities such as roads and bridges. The families can then be encouraged to move to their houses and resume daily-life activities including farming.

In sum

- For maximum effectiveness in rescue and after-rescue arrangements, prompt intervention of the federal and local governments is mandatory; community participation should also be ensured for maximum reach and productivity of the rescue operations.

8.5. IMPACT OF DISASTERS ON MENTAL HEALTH

Psychological aftermath and coping with a disaster varies widely in relation to the degree of exposure, damage and loss, socio-economic condition of the individual and the country, the quality of support system available and other political and cultural variables that can affect the set-up (Satapathy, 2012). Commonly seen post-disaster responses could be of various nature: emotional, psychosomatic, cognitive, behavioural and attitudinal (Satapathy, 2012). One should understand that these responses are natural and are meant to take place; it is the duration and intensity of these response conditions that make them adaptive/maladaptive in nature. The prevalence of psychopathology is estimated to increase by at least 17 per cent after a disaster (Rubonis & Bickman, 1991); stress, PTSD, depression, anxiety and adjustment problems are the commonly found conditions encountered by people. On a global frame, there has been an appreciable increase in the diagnosis as well as the documentation of disaster psychiatry, which has resulted in the creation of plenty of knowledge regarding the general behaviour of post-disaster psychopathology. Despite the complexity in terms of the uncontrollable nature, the huge physical and financial loss, the reporting of psychopathology could be even harder due to the latency effect or late-onset occurrence of illness (Green et al., 1990), some may not be fulfilling the diagnostic criteria and hence are omitted, and then there are times when symptoms would last even up to 14 years (Green et al., 1990), and there are reports which suggest that psychological distress induced by disaster can be even permanent (Bland et al., 1996). Whatever the case may be, studies across the globe have agreed upon the psychological problems emerging out of the exposure to disaster and can range from severe to chronic intensity (Bödvarsdóttir & Elklit, 2004).

Mental health disturbances associated with calamities are so devastating that they leave a lasting impression on anybody who is involved directly/indirectly. Let us base our analysis on existing data-driven understanding from the field for better understanding. Known and recorded statistics on the magnitude of natural calamities in Asia is so high that in 2015, 59.3 million people were affected and 16,046 deaths were reported (Economic and Social Commission for Asia and the Pacific, 2015). It has to be noted that in some parts of Asia-Pacific, for instance, in Indonesia, the government has declared the disaster rates to be 'as high as 2.75 disasters a day' (International Federation of Red Cross and Red Crescent Societies, 2010). Given the fact that natural calamity has become an everyday scenario in Asia, the number of research studies on the psychological correlates of such disasters are scanty; however, of late, the Asian empirical studies have shown an appreciable emergence of disaster psychiatry in the continent, paving the way to reduce stigma and provide better support for the survivors (Kokai et al., 2004). The prevalence of psychiatric illness among the calamity survivors of the Third-World countries are massive, both among the children and the adult survivors (Goenjian et al., 1995); however, there lacks validated data about the same particularly from the South Asian countries as compared to the magnitude and frequency of the occurrence of calamities in these regions of the world (Kar & Bastia, 2006).

Available scholarship on disaster psychiatry clearly predicts morbidity to illness conditions, particularly to anxiety and depression (Tol & Ommeren, 2012). In an attempt to study the psychological aftermath of the Hanshin Awaji earthquake in Japan, 'sleep disturbance, depression, hypersensitivity and irritability' were observed as a response to the stress (Kato et al., 1996); these disturbances were of clinically significant magnitude and are understood to be aligned to the 'exposure to stress, extent of loss, social disorganization and lack of community support' (Kokai et al., 2004). The destruction affecting over 1.5 million people in Pakistan due to the 2010 flood also left huge psychological burden on the country; a cross-sectional study reported high rates of PTSD (59%) and depression (54.4%), along with finding an increase in substance dependence among the individuals during their stay at the rescue camps (Mubeen et al., 2013). Anxiety disorder was the direct and immediate impact on people's mental health after the Hanshin Awaji earthquake, and was frequently reported in the first month following the disaster in 1998. Further, somatization as an externalizing response to stress was also reported among Asians (Kokai & Shinfuku, 2000).

Prevalence of PTSD among adolescents was nearly 20 per cent even after four years of 2010 Yushu earthquake in China (Dongling et al., 2017). It is worth analysing the study findings of the psychological aftermath of the 2015 earthquake in Nepal: along with depression and anxiety, distress (42%), hazardous alcohol consumption (20.4%), suicidal ideation (10.9%), aggression developed out of lack of control (33.7%) were found after four months post-earthquake (Kane et al., 2018); symptoms of PTSD and depression were prevalent among adolescents up to 40.4 per cent and 23.3 per cent, respectively (Silwal et al., 2018); 51 per cent of children from school-going age were found to have moderate to severe PTSD symptoms even after a year of the calamity (Acharya et al., 2018); and this was prevalent in both natural and technological disasters (Acierno et al., 2006).

Disaster psychiatry in all its subsidiaries are embarrassingly scant in India, however, findings of a few Indian-based studies are quoted. Anxiety symptoms and insomnia were highly reported among the public during the Nipah virus attack in Kerala that has occurred during May–June 2018 (Swathy et al., 2018). A substantial proportion of the population which suffers from non-disordered distress is often found to be left unnoticed (Brewin et al., 2008; Stanke et al., 2012; Tol & Ommeren, 2012). The result of a study conducted to understand the commodity of mental illness among the adolescents of Odisha (India) after the massive 1999 cyclone substantiates the above-mentioned predication. The prevalent illness conditions were PTSD (26.9%), major depressive disorder (17.6%) and generalized anxiety disorder (12%); the rate of comorbid psychiatric diagnosis was nearly 40 per cent; all these findings were observed even after 14 months of the calamity (Kar & Bastia, 2006). The uncontrollable monsoon rainfall and flood that pushed the state of Kerala (India) into devastation had even greater psychological payback; depression (48%) was found particularly among the geriatric population of the state in a post hoc study conducted after a month (Thomas et al., 2019); stress and anxiety ranging from moderate to severe levels were also detected among the people of flood-affected areas (Pooja & Nagalakshami, 2018). Drought is another natural calamity whose impact is, again, difficult to document due to its complex nature and accumulation over time. Along with illness conditions related to physical health like malnutrition, water-related illnesses like cholera, vector-borne illnesses (e.g., West Nile virus) and mental health issues are prevalent, in terms of distress, emotional reactions and associated behavioural alterations (Stanke et al., 2013). The indirect impact of drought on mental health has to do with economic pressure resulting from financial loss. Stress, increased alcohol or substance dependence, sleeplessness and depression are commonly reported as drought-related mental health issues. Substantiating this understanding, an Indian-based study also found that rate of stress, worry and suicide is found to increase in association with drought in an affected region (Raval & Vyas, 2013).

The differentiation between natural and man-made calamity is, in most of the cases, are arbitrary in nature. This is so because of the popular argument that natural disasters are the repercussions of unscientific human involvement on earth and ecosystem. Hence, the line between the natural and man-made calamities could be exclusive, overlapping or completely inclusive of each other. However, the nature of war makes it exclusively man-made calamity primarily with the cognitive and behavioural sequence being involved. Exposure to armed conflict is understood as a man-made calamity, where the meaning and impact of death and destruction have various dimensions on the socio-political as well as humanitarian grounds. Literature has shown a range of mental health troubles due to war, which includes PTSD, depression, anxiety, insomnia, behavioural troubles and somatic complaints, particularly seen among children and adolescents (American Psychological Association, 2010). Several studies on war-related mental health troubles have discussed the 'cumulative impact of multiple trauma-the dose effect' (American Psychological Association, 2010); the link between trauma and psychopathology is such that 'the more frequent and severe trauma exposure leads to worse psychological outcomes particularly in war' (Ellis et al., 2007). The range of war-related psychopathology as per study findings is disturbing: PTSD ranging from 7 per cent to 75 per cent (Allwood et al., 2002), depression ranging from 11 per cent to 47 per cent (Papageorgious et al., 2000). To cite the instances of terrorist attacks on the Peshawar and Kyber Pakhtunkhwa (Pakistan), the diagnosis was proximately made with both moderate (66%) and severe (11%) levels of PTSD (Abbas et al., 2017). An important drawing from various studies conducted was the additive effect of war and violence on the children's coping skills; this may make the vulnerability to adjustment and PTSD symptoms high among these children (Allwood et al., 2002). A study of a kind, conducted among the children living in the war-prone areas of Zudan, is trying to understand the comorbid interplay of trauma, depression and grief in the children in reaction to the atrocities of war. War experiences such as rape, murder (being made to kill/hurt a family member) were predictive of trauma; being raped or witnessing someone else getting raped and death of one's family were predictive of depression; while abduction, being forced to kill/fight or hiding oneself for self-protection were associated with grief in children (Morgos et al., 2008). A study conducted among the geriatric population of Vietnam ascribed war to be one of the causal factors for the high prevalence of depression among them (Leggett et al., 2012; Samy et al., 2015). A post hoc study conducted in five war-affected countries, namely Bosnia and Herzegovina, Croatia, Kosovo, the Republic of Macedonia and Serbia concluded that the rate of mental disorders, particularly anxiety and mood disorders would continue to be highly prevalent among the survivors even after several years of war (Priebe et al., 2010). Reporting and documentation of war-related data in a country like India are poorly being done and hence no authentic evidence-driven study findings could be found to be discussed. Nevertheless, the understanding about the prevalence, probability and vulnerability towards post-disaster psychopathology is clear and remains a common-level ground reality.

Be it a natural or man-made calamity, its adverse impact on people's mental health condition is devastating. Studies on disaster calamities tend to focus mainly on PTSD, depression and anxiety; however, it has also been mentioned that there are several other disordered illness conditions as well. Late-onset symptomatology, somatization, poor coping skills are the matters to be pondered upon, considering the challenge calamity could bring on mental health. Even though limited, all the study findings stress the need for psychological intervention programmes in disaster management.

In sum

- Disaster has an adverse effect on the victim's mental health status.
- Commonly reported mental illness condition in disaster psychiatry includes PTSD, depression, anxiety, hypertension, irritability and other stress-induced conditions.
- Somatization, increased dependence on substance and alcohol and adjustment disorders are found to be late responses to disaster.

8.6. DISASTER MANAGEMENT FOR COMMUNITY WELL-BEING

The Disaster Management Act, 2005, understands disaster management as 'a continuous and integrated process of planning, organizing, coordinating and implementing measures which are necessary or expedient for—prevention, mitigation, capacity-building, preparedness, prompt response, evacuation, rescue and relief and rehabilitation and reconstruction' (Ministry of Law and Justice, 2005). Management of disaster should be a continuous process, which could be successful with the active participation of all individuals at the community level and of governments at all levels. It has to be understood that disaster management should not be just the interventions after a disaster has occurred, but rather should begin way before rescue and rehabilitation. Disaster management aims to:

- Prevent or reduce the potential loss due to calamity
- Ensure timely intervention and assistance for the victims
- Achieve recovery at a fast pace

Disaster management, as depicted in Figure 8.1, in simple terms, is an interface between efforts to reduce the risk of any disaster and the efforts to recover from any destruction that has happened. Therefore, this extensive multi-level intervention programme should include 'pre-disaster planning and preparedness activities, organizational planning, training, information management, public relations and many other fields' (National Institute of Disaster Management, n.d.). It is an umbrella term for all disaster-related activities such as 'disaster preparedness, response and recovery, post disaster epidemiological surveillance, environmental management and mitigation' (Sena, 2006). As seen from the model given in Figure 8.2, the disaster management cycle has three key phases:

1. *Pre-disaster phase:* Effective prevention of disaster situations is now a growing concern in academic circle due to the understanding developed by governmental organizations: that disaster management is an aid towards sustainable regional development of a country (Hualou, 2011). The Yokohama Strategy 1994 has also identified the pre-disaster phase to

FIGURE 8.1
Phase of Disaster Management

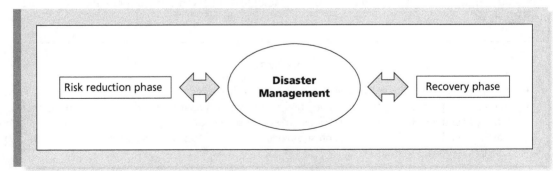

FIGURE 8.2
Phases of Disaster Management Cycle

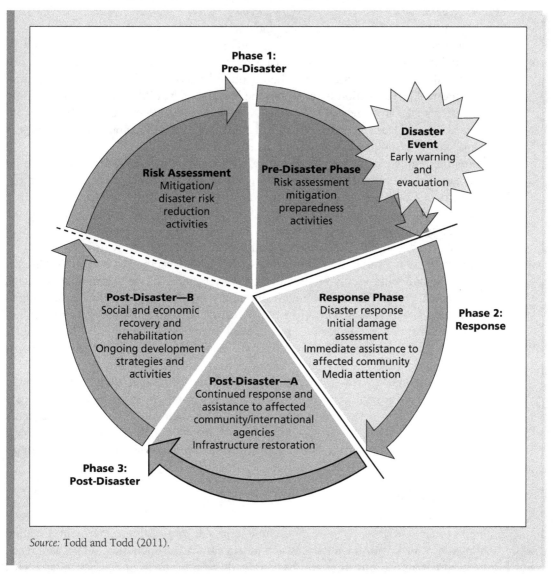

Source: Todd and Todd (2011).

be effective in achieving long-term objectives in comparison to disaster response alone. Hence, this phase targets at achieving the first aim of disaster management, which is the prevention/reduction of loss. So the term stands for the involvement of precautionary measures taken for the prevention and mitigation of disaster. Hence, all the measures taken, policies installed and programmes implemented before the occurrence of a disaster/calamity/ hazard which would ease prevention, mitigation and preparedness could be involved under this phase. It is advised that 'disaster risk reduction should become a normal practice, fully institutionalized within an agency's relief and development agenda' (Ministry of Home Affairs, 2011).

The components of the pre-disaster phase include:

a. *Prevention:* The term prevention here stands for any protective action that could be undertaken in order to cause a significant reduction in the impact of calamity/disaster; one should not misunderstand that the intention here is to state that natural calamities are preventable. Prevention here is from the harmful effect of the calamity/disaster, and the damage it can potentially cause on people and economic assets. Activities for prevention could be dependent hazard identification and vulnerability assessment and hence should be tailor-made based on the situations.

b. *Mitigation:* Mitigation should be seen in a larger canvas: 'it should address the issues of structural and non-structural interventions along with the fiscal and monetary tools' (Ministry of Home Affairs, 2011). Primary mitigation is about creating hazard resistance and reducing hazard vulnerability, while secondary mitigation is about keeping the community prepared to face the hazard. In other words, the target is to attain high resistance to disaster in communities through such pre-disaster activities.

c. *Preparedness:* It is that state of readiness needed to respond to a calamity/disaster effectively and could ideally be provided to every member of the community. Through this process, both the government and community should be equipped in responding to emergency situation appropriately, so that causalities can be reduced; and further, complications can be avoided. 'Preparedness includes designing warning systems, planning for evacuation and reallocation, planning ways for storing food and water, equipment for building temporary shelters, devising management strategies and holding disaster drills and exercises' (Sena, 2006). Some countries are practising the involvement of disaster management in their school curriculum, while in other places, emergency drills, seminars and posters on immediate response are being informally conveyed to the students; these efforts are greatly appreciated (National Graduate Institute for Policy Studies, 2007). According to Sena (2006), preparedness consists of three basic steps, which are:

   • Preparing a plan
   • Training to the plan
   • Exercising the plan

Preparedness, therefore, is more of the functional side of disaster management. Creation of public awareness through training and practice is the key component of preparedness. It is important to ensure right backup and support through legislative and civil provisions.

d. *Early Warning:* Areas which are vulnerable to disaster/calamities could be kept under supervision to identify for early signs of alert so that this information could be quickly passed around to people. 'Reliable warning, with sufficient lead-time, that is precise in space and time and its effective communication, in a decipherable manner, to the population likely to be affected by the event is the key to saving human lives and mitigating losses' (Rautela, 2013). Alert in varying ranges of restrictive measures can be set out and be guarded with the help of the authority. This could be one-way through which loss can be completely or partially avoided. Mass education by media or word of mouth could be used to spread the information.

The government of India has adopted prevention and mitigation into its developmental planning, by emphasizing their role in sustainable development on the count. Given the geographical location and landscape of India, the country is highly vulnerable to several calamities and hence calamity-specific mitigation measures are adopted as discussed below. The National Disaster Mitigation Fund (NDMF) was constituted under the Disaster Management Act, 2005, under Section 47 of IPC, where the fund was exclusively credited to be used as NDMF. India has the history of many unforeseeable earthquakes, floods, landslides and other hazards of massive intensity; because of which a few mitigation measures have been installed: National Earthquake Risk Mitigation Project (NERMP), National Building Code (NBC) for monitoring the construction activities, active involvement by the Building Materials and Technology Promotion Council (BMTPC), Ministry of Panchayati Raj are a few mentionable measures. Similarly, the National Cyclone Risk Mitigation Project (NCRMP), Integrated Coastal Zone Management Project (ICZMP), National Flood Risk Mitigation Project (NFRMP), Flood Management Program, the Drought Prone Area Program (DPAP), Desert Development Program (DDP), centrally sponsored scheme for strengthening of fire and emergency services, forest fire management, National Vector Borne Disease Control Program (NVBDCP), preventive measures against oil and chemical disaster, epidemics, rail and road safety and civil aviation are some of the popular intervention from the central and state government in the country (Ministry of Home Affairs, 2011).

The contribution by careless human interaction with the environment is undoubtedly one of the major reasons for magnification of the disaster impact (Sato et al., 2016). Hence, the need for installing sophisticated disaster mitigation intervention using information and communication technology is heightened, towards which scientists and governments strive for. Interface between different sectors of science and technological advances, along with the active involvement of various ministries of governments are required for effective disaster management.

2. *During-disaster phase:* The second phase deals with ensuring timely intervention and support during the occurrence of the disaster; addressing the second aim of disaster management. According to the National Institute of Disaster Management (NIDM), this is 'to ensure that needs and provisions of the victims are met to alleviate and minimize suffering'. This is the time for the actual execution of relief work and interventions which were planned during the pre-disaster phase. The only component of this phase is the response.

   a. *Response:* 'A set of activities implemented after the impact of a disaster in order to assess the needs, reduce the suffering, limit the spread and the consequences of the disaster, and open ways to rehabilitation' is response (Sena, 2006). Any activity done during the occurrence of disaster can be understood under this term. Organized management of the scene is very crucial, particularly in massive and paralytic calamities; the challenge continues as the duration and dynamics of disaster intensifies. Some of the common responses caused due to injury are effective handling of the causality, triage, the way of prioritizing the treatment for injury, utilization of first-aid, transportation of patients who require advance treatment, balancing between the medical resources and available medical professionals. Utilization of communication and broadcast system is a boon in several situations, but over-dependence on these systems have consequence in cases of calamities that can destroy these systems of communication. Hence, response is a set of immediate steps taken which marks the beginning of the re-establishment of functionality of systems and infrastructure (Todd & Todd, 2011).

3. *The post-disaster phase:* This phase is about the recovery, rehabilitation and development of the affected community to its initial shape. This is also the learning and realizing phase of the required risk reduction measures that has to be taken care of to prevent and mitigate the next disaster. Depending on the nature and intensity of disaster, restoration activities may demand resources of various standards, and the facilitation given to those demand from the part of the community and government would make a lot of impact. Priority should be given to the restoration of basic living amenities such as food and water and medical assistance. Reconstruction of homes, buildings, roads and rails would follow later on and could be time-consuming depending on the condition. Support from the governments through relief fund and loan, technical support through various ministries, government and private enterprises should make the restoration process faster. However, these enabling activities should be particularly made available for the vulnerable and poor sector of the affected community.

   a. *Rehabilitation:* In cases where the community has to be shifted out of their homes/ affected zones, rehabilitation facilities should be provided. This could be done through providing temporary public utilities and accommodation facilities, along with ensuring the availability of food, water, basic clothing and medical aid. Mental healthcare facilities should also be provided without much delay, in order to ensure faster recovery and coping. Further input about the rehabilitation of a community that survived a calamity is given in the following section.

   b. *Development:* This is an ongoing, step-by-step activity where the community regains its pre-disaster phase and is back to their life of routine. Encouraging participatory behaviour through improved communication and coordination, decentralizing the initiatives for recovery from the centre to its subsidiary, capacity building for risk management and quality of life, teaching disaster risk reduction as a priority are some of the guiding principles to be adopted (Ministry of Home Affairs, 2011). Along with this, the community would be equipped with better disaster reduction measures for the future.

As can be understood from Figure 8.3 disaster management includes several administrative decisions to be taken followed by operational activities. These phases are not bound by clear boundaries between these phases and the subsidiary steps under these. If the activities in the pre-disaster phase are done effectively, then the subsequent phases would be easier to face. Similarly, learning from the post-disaster phase should be wilfully incorporated into pre-prevention phase, so that it could be taken care of the next time. Nevertheless, all these interventions could successfully be done, with the help of responsible and sensitive institutions of authority and community involvement.

FIGURE 8.3
Steps Involved in Disaster Management

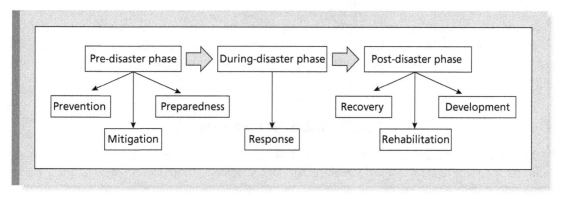

8.7. REHABILITATING THE COMMUNITY

Given the massive destruction, chaos and loss any calamity can bring to the community, rehabilitation by all means and at all levels is highly essential. This is true in the case of everybody, nevertheless, damage to the physical and psychological health of children and differently abled people are highest. 'Psychosocial vulnerabilities, impaired physical mobility, diminished sensory awareness, poor health and economic conditions' could limit the elderly even further (HelpAge India, 2007). Hence, rehabilitation should be given utmost preference among all the attempts to recover a community. Rehabilitation is the 'overall dynamic and intermediate strategy of institutional reform a reinforcement, reconstruction and improvement of infrastructure and services; aimed towards support to the initiative and actions of the affected population in the political, economic and social domain as well as reiteration of sustainable development' (National Disaster Management Authority, 2018). In simple terms, the extent of damage is such that it would affect the physical, psychological, social and economic capital of the affected zone. Hence, as seen in the following diagram, effective rehabilitation should be one that could address all these four domains (Figure 8.4).

FIGURE 8.4
Types of Rehabilitation after a Disaster

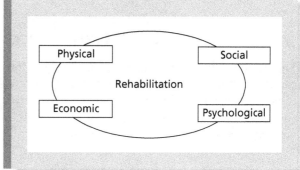

8.7.1. PHYSICAL REHABILITATION

In brief, physical rehabilitation targets at rebuilding the destroyed building, transportation, communication and other basic necessities such as water and electricity. Physical rehabilitation can also take care of strategies to reinstitute employment by working on the losses in terms of agriculture and farming. Effective strategies could be undertaken to protect the environment from another calamity, for instance, plastic waste removal from the water bodies and ensuring effective wastewater treatment to mitigate flood or epidemics. Often, governments relocate the affected community to a new area until the affected location is restored; this is a very sensitive but integral part of physical rehabilitation which must be done with sensitivity. Subsidies and loan provided by the governments to construct new houses or strengthened the affected house could also be covered under physical rehabilitation.

8.7.2. Social Rehabilitation

Social rehabilitation has to do with the revival of the affected community in terms of their social life. As mentioned earlier, a vulnerable group of the affected population, such as the elderly, children, differently abled people, children on street and women, require additional care and support to withstand the disaster. Hence, these sets of the population should be rehabilitated to areas where they can easily adjust and resocialize with ease. Along with this, attempts to revive educational institutions and workplaces back to before also require input, for ensuring recovery and productivity.

8.7.3. Economic Rehabilitation

Restoration of means of livelihood is the foremost preference of economic rehabilitation. This might be a time-consuming process in some affected cases where destruction would be severe and result in tremendous loss of essential assets for economic survival. For instance, agriculture and animal husbandry are mostly affected source of income that faces severe loss during calamities. Along with the restoration, ensuring their continuity is also important, where effective preventive measures should be taken to survive a similar situation in future.

8.7.4. Psychological Rehabilitation

The trauma of death, injury and scars and destruction of one's own home, workplace or native land can leave a lasting impression of pain and shock in the psychological well-being of the survivors. Hence, rehabilitation should be done by keeping into account the disturbed state of mind of the survivors. Aids to stress management and coping should be provided in order to ensure fast recovery. Let us elaborate our understanding about this issue in the following session.

8.8. ADDRESSING PSYCHOLOGICAL TRAUMA AND ARRANGEMENT OF SAFE SHELTER

The disabling impact of calamities/disaster on the psychological well-being of the affected community has called attention to several social scientists across the world. Evidence has proved, time and again, about the need to provide the right intervention, at various stages of requirement,

FIGURE 8.5
Model on Post-disaster Psychological Care Delivery

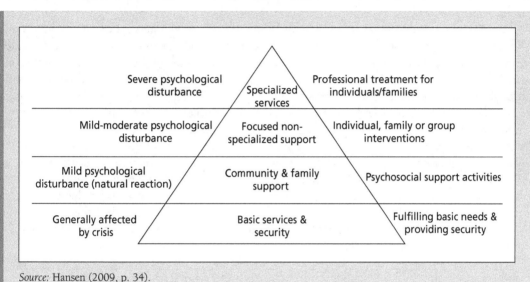

Source: Hansen (2009, p. 34).

to the survivors: it may range from provision of basic needs such as food and water to even a stage where treatment and medical care be given to people with severe psychological challenge. An approach to rehabilitation which addresses both the physical and psychological need of a community is found to successfully enhance the strength of the affected population to recover from the unanticipated downfall. Community involvement has also established its unique role in recovery mechanism and has found to ease the adaptive capacity of the community, as they themselves would feel the need to recover. Psychological rehabilitation should adopt a strength-based approach; where along with immediate recovery from stress and trauma, the community should be trained in capacity building, social support, coordination and team spirit.

The model shown in Figure 8.5 is in the shape of an upright pyramid with four layers or stages representing the four levels at which psychological support needs to be given. Psychological support should be given at the levels of the individual, family and community at various degrees of intensity based on the status of one's psychological well-being. Before addressing any psychological disturbance as an illness, it is important to understand that some reactions to disaster/calamity/destruction is natural and would settle down in due course of time; therefore, the tendency to label such responses as an illness must be avoided. The period of grief is natural and needed for the healthy functioning of the individual; if needed, support and resources should be provided at the right time. In the immediate aftermath of the disaster, the intervention must address their basic psychosocial needs, after which specialized services should be provided. However, the generally observed trend in India is either the complete absence of any psychosocial support provided, or such provision is made available only during the immediate days. No follow-up or provision of higher levels of supportive intervention is generally seen. As discussed earlier, the prominently observed illness conditions such as PTSD, depression, anxiety and behavioural disorders need highly professional mental healthcare support and hence there definitely is a need for mental health service providers who are trained in post-disaster psychological needs of a community.

Covering the whole of the affected population, psychosocial intervention, at its very basic, should be able to meet the basic needs such as food, water, clothing and shelter to every individual who is affected by the calamity. The people who face mild psychological distress in the community, which is quite natural and appropriate, need to be provided with basic psychosocial activities through outreach activities such as sensitizing them about stress, coping styles and such similar topics. This could be done with the help of *Anganwadi* workers, elected representatives, Primary Health Centres (PHCs) of the locality, general hospitals and so on. If the intensity of the calamity is so massive, then, it is not practical to coordinate professionals into this level of intervention. Instead, a team of non-professional community facilitators can be formed to act as a psychological first aid to reach the community for support (Mooney et al., 2011). The psychological first aid can also identify the individuals from the community who require additional psychological care and intervention and be referred to higher levels of the pyramid, that is, either the focused non-specialized support for those suffering from mild to moderate disturbance or specialized services for those with severe psychological disturbance.

In sum

- Disaster management is an interface between efforts to reduce the risk of any disaster and the efforts to recovery from any destruction that has happened and is multi-staged.
- The pre-disaster phase includes prevention, mitigation, preparedness and early warning. The during-disaster phase primarily deals with the prompt and appropriate immediate response given to the occurrence of the disaster. The post-disaster phase has to do with rehabilitation and development of the affected community.
- The four types of rehabilitation are physical, social, economic and psychological rehabilitation.

8.9. DISASTER MANAGEMENT POLICIES AND PROGRAMMES

The Government of India has a clear consensus on the provision of relief fund associated with calamities. The authority figure for the division and distribution of relief funds is the Finance Commission of the country who decides on the policies regarding disaster relief assistance. The Calamity Relief Fund (CRF) instituted by the 11th Finance Commission is present in each state of the country, of which 75 per cent is contributed by the central government and the remaining 25 per cent by the state government. Based on the guidelines laid by the national committees, the fund is released to the state in need of the CRF. Chief secretary of the state does the recommendation for the relief fund, the CRF, depending on the state-specific norms. However, in situation where the fund in need is more than the fund available in the CRF, the state can seek help from the National Calamity Contingency Fund (NCCF). The decision regarding the allocation of funds from NCCF is done by a high-level committee under the deputy prime minister and is done based on the assessments done.

The government has instituted several ways of monitoring at the centre and state level in the form of policies and programmes. The multi-ministerial approach involves active involvement of various departments, each of which is concerned with specialized primary or secondary functions.

Due to the complexity and unpredictable nature of a calamity, various ministries are linked to disaster management at the national level: the prominent nodal ministries of the mitigation for different disasters include Ministries of Home Affairs, Defense (Indian Coast Guard and Border Road Organization), Road Transport and Highways, Civil Aviation, Railways, Health and Family Welfare, Agriculture and Farmers Welfare, Earth Sciences, Water Resources, River Development and Ganga Rejuvenation, Housing and Urban Affairs, Environment, Forests and Climate Changes, Mine, Atomic Energy, and Earth Science (National Disaster Management Authority, 2018).

At the national level, there is the Central Relief Commissioner (CRC) at the Ministry of Home Affairs, who comes under this ministry and is the nodal officer to coordinate all involvements related to disaster management. The crisis management group includes nominated nodal officers from each of the above-mentioned ministries/departments; this group is chaired by the CRC who is the prime authority of the country's decisions regarding the management of any disasters. The National Crisis Management Committee (NCMC) controls the Crisis Management Group (CMG) and is headed by the cabinet secretary by given directions to all the ministries and departments for the needed action taken by each of these units. Annually, each of this ministries/organizations develops disaster management projects from their concerned field, which will be reviewed and sanctioned by the CMG as contingency plans. In most of the cases, these would be coordinated activities between the central and the state. During the time of any disaster, the CMG provides active involvement and assistance needed for the affected state through the respective resident commissioner. The emergency operations centre/control room at the nodal Ministry of Home Affairs works under the CRC and deals with the exchange of information across the concerned ministries/departments along with file maintenance. As mentioned earlier, there exists a provision for a contingency action plan (CAP) which is dealt by the national CAP. The main function of CAP is to identify effective initiatives that need to be undertaken and determine the plan, procedure and focal point of administration. Parallel to the central government involvement, there are state-wise initiatives which may or may not be under the direct control of the central government. State relief manual is one such programme which is a set of codes installed at the state level where specific roles of each of the departments and officers concerning disaster management are written down. These undergo periodic review and update based on the state-specific needs as well as its history and previous history. A few of the key national-level bodies working towards disaster management in India are:

- Cabinet Committee on Security (CCS)—evaluate national security
- NCMC—superintend command and control of the response to the disaster
- National Disaster Management Authority (NDMA)—draft disaster management related policies and rules
- National Executive Committee (NEC)—assists NDMA in its smooth functioning as well as prepares national-level plans.
- National Disaster Response Force (NDRF)—works closely with the state governments in dealing with disasters.
- NIDM—education (dissemination of information) and capacity building. (National Disaster Management Authority, 2018)

A similar set-up is present at the level of state government as well, where there is a State Crisis Management Committee where the chief secretary is the chairman. All the concerned ministries/departments at the state level come under this body, concerning disaster management. Like at the central government, the control role of the relief commissioner is in close contact with the climate monitoring and weather forecasting units to be vigilant about early warning signs. The Disaster Management Act, 2005, mandates the institution of the following:

- State Disaster Management Authority (SDMA)
- State Disaster Response Force (SDRF)
- State Emergency Operation Centre (SEOC; National Disaster Management Authority, 2018).

The district-level disaster management wing under the control of the collector/deputy commissioner; there is District Level Coordination and Relief Committee in close alliance with the elected representatives, governmental and non-governmental agencies to work towards disaster management. The committee is in close association with the armed forces and other organizations such as the ministries of communication and transportation, to assess effective response and rescue. The district magistrate acts as the coordinator of all the prevention-mitigation-preparedness-related activities of the district together with the District Disaster Management Authority. A similar system of coordinated activity at block/*taluka* level is planned to be developed in due course of time (National Disaster Management Authority, 2018). Thus, through effective coordination and teamwork, the committee keeps the community prepared before the strike of the calamity, and also, effectively intervene at the strike of the calamity.

8.10. ROLE OF COMMUNITY PSYCHOLOGIST IN DISASTER MANAGEMENT

The contributions that could be made by a community psychologist in disaster management can be huge and multidimensional. Involvement of psychology and its impact on people can be seen in every level of disaster management including 'mitigation, advance preparedness acute response to events and long term psychosocial effects' (Percy et al., 2011). Preventive medicine, the actual principle behind disaster mental health, is the trend shifter by placing 'relief of the individual' at the centre of disaster management; it is this approach that has integrated community to health promotion, prevention and rehabilitation of illness affecting a larger population (Math et al., 2015). A systematic review conducted on the tsunami-hit region of Myanmar proves that psychosocial support given to the survivors and community can significantly facilitate improvement in both physical and psychosocial well-being of the individuals (Htay, 2006); all of these highlights the major role a community psychologist can and should play in disaster management. A model on the role of community physiologist in disaster management is shown in Figure 8.6.

A community psychologist on the field affected by any disaster would have to deal with people having different state of mind, survivors and kin of people who are dead or injured, people who have lost their families, properties, children, pregnant women, mothers with newborn babies, differently abled people, wounded, the elderly and so on. The magnitude of their pain and the extent of their recovery can vary based on factors such as their age, status of education, degree of exposure, personality, coping styles, the intensity of trauma and devastation, range of social support and so on. Apart from individual cases, a community psychologist would have to deal with families who are together in sharing the load of destruction, which the disaster has brought them, and also the community as a whole. The dynamics of the community can vary depending on their

FIGURE 8.6

Model on the Role of Community Psychologist in Disaster Management

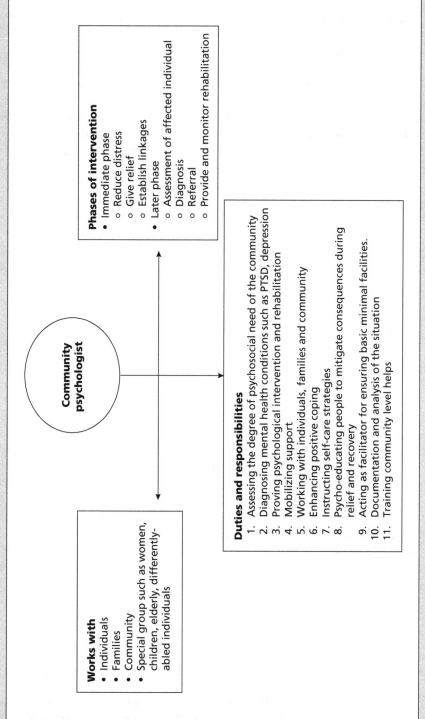

Works with
- Individuals
- Families
- Community
- Special group such as women, children, elderly, differently-abled individuals

Community psychologist

Phases of intervention
- Immediate phase
  ○ Reduce distress
  ○ Give relief
  ○ Establish linkages
- Later phase
  ○ Assessment of affected individual
  ○ Diagnosis
  ○ Referral
  ○ Provide and monitor rehabilitation

Duties and responsibilities
1. Assessing the degree of psychosocial need of the community
2. Diagnosing mental health conditions such as PTSD, depression
3. Proving psychological intervention and rehabilitation
4. Mobilizing support
5. Working with individuals, families and community
6. Enhancing positive coping
7. Instructing self-care strategies
8. Psycho-educating people to mitigate consequences during relief and recovery
9. Acting as facilitator for ensuring basic minimal facilities.
10. Documentation and analysis of the situation
11. Training community level helps

Source: Sekar et al. (2005).

level of preparedness, leadership, their past experiences and support they receive in all terms towards recovery.

Involvement of community psychologist is crucial at all levels of disaster management. Immediately after the disaster, a psychologist works towards reducing the distress among the survivors, apart from arranging the basic facilities needed for the individuals. This could be done by encouraging ventilation, empathetic behaviour, social support and active listening, by motivating them in externalizing their interest in productive involvements, recreation and spirituality in the case where it is applicable. They have to address issues related to extreme stress and trauma caused by disaster, sudden displacement, loss/damage of lives and properties, difficulties in adjusting to the environment at the camps, uncertainties about their future life and disturbances due to psychiatric conditions. In later phases of intervention, once the situation is under better control, the psychologist can do psychological assessments in diagnosing commonly found conditions, such as PTSD, depression, anxiety and so on, provide appropriate treatment options, do referral, counselling and other intervention strategies for people who are in need. Rehabilitation and follow-up for people whose condition requires advanced care should also be provided.

The duties and responsibility of a community psychologist in a disaster-hit locality are many and they include: assessing the degree of psychosocial need of the community, diagnosing mental health conditions such as PTSD, depression and so on, providing psychological intervention and rehabilitation, mobilizing support, working with individuals, families and community, enhancing positive coping, instructing self-care strategies, psycho-educating people to mitigate consequences during relief and recovery, acting as a facilitator for ensuring basic minimal facilities, training community-level helpers, developing a psychological model for addressing the mental health issue of disaster-affected people, training of manpower for delivering the services to disaster-affected people, extending psychological support services to disaster-affected people in terms of individual, family and group counselling as per need, organizing sports, cultural and spiritual activities to engage people in group activities so that they can come out of their traumatic experiences, trying to connect people of relief camp with their family members and relatives, coordinating with concerned government and NGOs for adopting effective strategies for dealing with the situation, sensitizing people of the relief camp about their safety issue, acting as facilitator for ensuring basic minimal facilities, encouraging people in the relief camp to start life afresh and documenting and analysing of the situation. They are also bound to address the delayed responses such as loss of productivity after disaster recovery, increased dependence on substance and alcohol, suicidal ideation and attempts, and numerous other difficulties associated with restarting a new life from scratch after the disaster. Thus, in several such ways, a community psychologist can instigate the process of rebuilding personal, family and community lives of the survivors of the disaster.

In sum

- Community psychologist plays a crucial role in disaster management; they work with individuals, families, communities and also among people who require special attention such as women, children, the elderly and the differently abled.
- They intervene in (a) immediate phase primarily to reduce stress and ensuring the availability of immediate and basic facilities and (b) later phase to do assessment, diagnosis and provide intervention for people who need support.

- Their duties and responsibilities are many and may include assessing the degree of psychosocial needs of the community, diagnosing mental health conditions, providing psychological intervention and rehabilitation, mobilizing support, psycho-educating people to mitigate consequences during relief and recovery, acting as facilitator for ensuring basic minimal facilities, training community-level helpers, training of manpower for delivering the services to disaster-affected people, trying to connect people of relief camp with their family members and relatives, coordinating with concerned government and NGOs for adopting effective strategies for dealing with the situation and encouraging people in the relief camp to start life afresh and documenting and analysing the situation.

8.11. CONCLUSION AND IMPLICATIONS

Given the magnitude of destruction and distress brought to a community by disaster, recovery would require input, hard work and coordinated effort by a large group of people. The proactive involvement of the community members would ease out the recovery process and fasten up the reconstruction. Disaster management is not just about the phase after the occurrence of disaster; rather, the pre-disaster phase that plays a crucial role in prevention and mitigation as well as in creating preparedness among the community should be done with precision and be backed up with scientific understanding gathered from the past experiences as well as by utilizing the nexus of information and communication technology. Community participation would make sure the execution of an approach—which is relief-centric, individual-oriented and is working towards the restructuring of the community. The role of community psychologist in every stage of disaster management is crucial, as it would ensure that disaster management services related to mental healthcare would be tailor-made based on the unique need of the individual and community. Hence, management of disaster is an everyday process that requires the involvement of every member in the community.

Natural calamities have a number of negative implications. It does not only cause loss of lives and property but also destroys the entire community and people suffer from PTSD. It takes a long time to rebuild the community. A good number of people become homeless and orphan, losing their close family members. Like the elderly, children are the worst victims of the situation. It affects their education in addition to physical and mental health.

EXERCISES

One-mark Questions

1. What is a hazard?
2. Define a disaster.
3. Explain the term 'economic rehabilitation'.
4. What is meant by mitigation?
5. What is the difference between a hazard and a disaster?
6. What do you understand by 'psychological first aid'?

7. What is preparedness?
8. What is PTSD?
9. What are the most commonly observed causes of disasters?
10. State any two legislative measures taken for disaster management in India.

Five-mark Questions

1. Community involvement is the key to speedy recovery after disaster. Justify the statement.
2. What are the types of rehabilitation after a disaster?
3. Critically analyse the components of the pre-disaster phase.
4. Explain the objectives of disaster management.
5. Critically evaluate the role of a community in rebuilding the affected area.
6. What are the causes of a disaster?

Ten-mark Questions

1. Analyse the model on post-disaster psychological care.
2. With the backup of evidence, explain the impact of a disaster on the mental health of survivors.
3. Explain the cycle of disaster management from the Indian context.
4. How does psychological rehabilitation improve the well-being of the community?

Reflexive Questions

1. The involvement of the community contributes extensively to the success of disaster management. Reflect.
2. What are the various roles played by community psychologists in disaster management?
3. Reporting and documenting the information regarding a disaster is important for mitigation and preparedness. Discuss.
4. The magnitude of mental illness and need for psychological intervention are topics which are unexplored in disaster management. Elucidate.

REFERENCES

Abbas, S. A., Hassan, A., & Ali, S. (2017). Impact of terrorism on the development of posttraumatic stress disorder (PTSD) among the residents of Khyber Bazaar and its immediate surrounding areas in Peshawar, Khyber Pakhtunkhwa, Pakistan. *Pakistan Journal of Pharmaceutical Sciences, 30*(1), 205–212.

Acharya, S., Bhatta, D., & Assannangkornchai, S. (2018). Post-traumatic stress disorder symptoms among children of Kathmandu 1 year after the 2015 earthquake in Nepal. *Disaster Medicine and Public Health Preparedness, 12*(4), 486–492. https://doi.org/10.1017/dmp.2017.100

Acierno, R., Ruggiero, K., Kilpatrick, D. G., Resnick, H., & Galea, S. (2006). Risk and protective factors for psychopathology among older versus younger adults after the 2004 Florida hurricanes. *American Journal of Geriatric Psychiatry, 14*(12), 1051–1059. https://doi.org/10.1097/01.JGP.0000221327.97904.b0

Allwood, M. A., Bell, D. J., & Husain, S. (2002). Children's trauma and adjustment reactions to violent and nonviolent war experiences. *Journal of American Academy of Child & Adolescent Psychiatry, 41*(4), 450–459. https://doi.org/10.1097/00004583-200204000-00018

American Psychological Association. (2010). *Resilence & recovery after war: Refugee children and families in the United States.* https://www.apa.org/pubs/info/reports/refugees-full-report.pdf

Below, R., & Wallemacq, P. (2018). *Annual disaster statistical review 2017.* Centre for Research on the Epidemiology of Disasters. https://www.cred.be/annual-disaster-statistical-review-2017

Bland, S., O'Leary, E., Farinaro, E., Jossa, F., & Trevisan, M. (1996). Long-term psychological effects of natural disasters. *Psychosomatic Medicine, 58*(1), 18–24.

Bödvarsdóttir, I., & Elklit, A. S. K. (2004). Psychological reactions in Icelandic earthquake survivors. *Scandinavian Journal of Psychology, 45*(3), 3–13.

Brewin, C. R., Scragg, P., Robertson, M., Thompson, M., & Ehlers, A. (2008). Promoting mental health following the London bombings: A screen and treat approach. *Journal of Traumatic Stress, 21*(1), 3–8. https://doi.org/10.1002/jts.20310

Dongling, L., Hui, C., Ling, M., Wenqian, B., Zailiang, L., & Changying, C. (2017). Post-traumatic stress disorder and its predictors among bereaved Tibetan adolescents four years after the Yushu earthquake: A cross-sectional survey in China. *Journal of Clinical Nursing, 26*(7–8), 1095–1105. https://doi.org/10.1111/jocn.13481

ESCAP. (2015). *Disasters in Asia and the Pacific: 2015 year in review.* Economic and Social Commission for Asia and the Pacific. https://www.unescap.org/sites/default/files/2015_Year%20in%20Review_final_PDF_1.pdf

Ellis, B., Kia-Keating, M., Yusuf, S., Lincoln, A., & Nur, A. (2007). Ethical research in refugee communities and the use of community participatory methods. *Transcultural Psychiatry, 44*(3), 459–481. https://doi.org/10.1177/1363461507081642

Goenjian, A. K., Pynoos, R. S., Steinberg, A. M., Najarian, L. M., Asarnow, J., Karayan, I., Ghurabi, M., & Fairbanks, L. A. (1995). Psychiatric comorbidity in children after the 1988 earthquake in Armenia. *Journal of the American Academy of Child & Adolescent Psychiatry, 34*(9), 1174–1184.

Green, Bonnie, L., Lindy, J. D., Grace, M. C., Gleser, G. C., Leonard, Anthony, C., Korol, M., & Winget, C. (1990). Buffalo creek survivors in the second decade: Stability of stress symptoms. *American Journal of Orthopsychoatry, 60*(1), 43–54. https://doi.org/10.1037/h0079168

Gupta, P., Khanna, A., & Majumdar, S. (2012). Disaster management in flash floods in Leh (Ladakh): A case study. *Indian Journal of Community Medicine, 37*(3), 185–190. https://doi.org/10.4103/0970-0218.99928

Hansen, P. (2009). *Psychosocial interventions: A handbook.* International Federation Reference Centre for Psychosocial Support. https://www.cstsonline.org/assets/media/documents/Psychosocial%20interventions%20A%20handbook%20LowRes.pdf

HelpAge India. (2007). Disaster management. https://www.helpageindia.org/our-work/welfare-development/disaster-management/

Htay, H. L. A. (2006). Mental health and psychosocial aspects of disaster preparedness in Myanmar. *International Review of Psychiatry, 18*(6), 579–585. https://doi.org/10.1080/09540260601108952

Hualou, L. (2011). Disaster prevention and management: A geographical perspective. *Disaster Advances, 4*(1), 1–5.

International Federation of Red Cross and Red Crescent Societies. (2010). *Disasters in Asia: The case for legal preparedness.* https://www.ifrc.org/Global/Publications/IDRL/reports/IFRC_IDRL_Report_EN.pdf

International Federation of Red Cross and Red Crescent Societies. (2018). *Leaving millions behind: World disaster report 2018.* https://reliefweb.int/sites/reliefweb.int/files/resources/B-WDR-2018-EXECSUM-EN.pdf

Kala, C. P. (2014). Deluge, disaster and development in Uttarakhand Himalayan region of India: Challenges and lessons for disaster management. *International Journal of Disaster Risk Reduction, 8*, 143–152. https://doi.org/10.1016/j.ijdrr.2014.03.002

Kane, J., Luitel, N., Jordans, M., Kohrt, B., Weissbecker, I., & Tol, W. (2018). Mental health and psychosocial problems in the aftermath of the Nepal earthquakes: Findings from a representative cluster sample. *Epidemiology and Psychiatric Sciences, 27*(3), 301–310. https://doi.org/10.1017/S2045796016001104

Kar, N., & Bastia, B. K. (2006). Post-traumatic stress disorder, depression and generalised anxiety disorder in adolescents after a natural disaster: A study of comorbidity. *Clinical Practice & Epidemiology in Mental Health, 2*(17), 1–10. https://doi.org/10.1186/1745-0179-2-17

Kato, H., Asukai, N., Miyake, Y., Minakawa, K., & Nishiyama, A. (1996). Post-traumatic symptoms among younger and elderly evacuees in the early stages following the 1995 Hanshin-Awaji earthquake in Japan. *Acta Psychiatria Scandanavica, 93*(6), 477–481.

Kokai, M., & Shinfuku, N. (2000). PTSD in Asian society. *Encyclopedia of Clinical Psychiatry, S6*, 309–318.

Kokai, Masahiro, Fuji, S., Shinjuku, N., & Edwards, G. (2004). Natural disaster and mental health in Asia. *Psychiatry and Clinical Neurosciences, 58*, 110–116. https://doi.org/10.1111/j.1440-1819.2003.01203.x

Leggett, A., Zarit, S. H., Nguyen, N. H., Hoang, C. N., & Nguyen, H. (2012). The influence of social factors and health on depressive symptoms and worry: A study of older Vietnamese adults. *Aging and Mental Health*, *16*(6), 780–786. https://doi.org/10.1080/13607863.2012.667780

Mallick, B., Rahaman, K. R., & Vogt, J. (2011). Coastal livelihood and physical infrastructure in Bangladesh after cyclone Aila. *Mitigation and Adaptation Strategies for Global Change*, *16*, 629–648. https://doi.org/10.1007/s11027-011-9285-y

Math, S. B., Nirmala, M. C., Moirangthem, S., & Kumar, N. C. (2015). Disaster management: Mental health perspective. *Indian Journal of Psychological Medicine*, *37*(3), 261–271. https://doi.org/10.4103/0253-7176.162915

McFarlane, A. C., & Williams, R. (2012). Mental health services required after disaster: Learning from the lasting effects of disaster. *Depression Research and Treatment*, *2012*(970194), 1–13.

Ministry of Home Affairs. (2011). Disaster management in India: A report by Ministry of Home Affairs. India Water Portal. https://www.indiawaterportal.org/articles/disaster-management-india-report-ministry-home-affairs

Ministry of Law and Justice. (2005). *The Disaster Management Act, 2005*. https://cdn.s3waas.gov.in/s365658fde58ab3c2b6e5132a39fae7cb9/uploads/2018/04/2018041720.pdf

Mooney, M. F., Centre, J., Paton, D., Karanci, A. N., East, M., Gardner, D., & Johnston, L. (2011). Psychosocial recovery from disasters: A framework informed by evidence. *New Zealand Journal of Psychology*, *40*(4), 26–38.

Morgos, D., Worden, J., & Gupta, L. (2008). Psychosocial effects of war experiences among displaced children in southern Darfur. *Omega*, *56*(3), 229–253.

Mubeen, S. M., Nigah-e-mumtaz, S., & Gul, S. (2013). Prevalence of post-traumatic stress disorder and depression among flood affected individuals of Sindh, Pakistan: A cross-sectional survey in camps five months after the flood. *Pakistan Journal of Medical Research*, *5*(4), 111–115.

National Disaster Management Authority. (2018). *National disaster management plan (NDMP) revised/draft–1/2018*. https://ndma.gov.in/images/pdf/NDMP-2018-Revised-Draft-1-2018OCT16-A.pdf

National Graduate Institute for Policy Studies. (2007). *Disaster education*. https://www.preventionweb.net/files/3442_DisasterEducation.pdf

National Institute of Disaster Management. (n.d.). *Understanding disasters*. https://nidm.gov.in/PDF/Disaster_about.pdf

Papageorgious, V., Frangou-Garunovic, A., Iordanidou, R., Yule, W., Smith, P., & Vostainis, P. (2000). War trauma and psychopathology in Bosnian refugee children. *European Child and Adolescent Psychiatry*, *9*(2), 84–90.

Percy, C., Chen, Y. F., Bibi, A., Dodson, E., Evans, T., Klingberg, D., & Bruggen, M. van der. (2011). The contribution of human psychology to disaster management: Mitigation, advance preparedness, response and recovery. *WIT Transactions on the Built Environment*, *119*(14), 195–208. https://doi.org/10.2495/DMAN110181

Pooja, V. K., & Nagalakshami, K. (2018). Stress, anxiety & depression among flood affected people in Kerala. *International Journal of Education and Psychological Research*, *7*(4), 179–181.

Priebe, S., Bogic, M., Ajdukovic, D., Franciskovic, T., Galeazzi, G. M., Kucukalic, A., Lecic-Tosevski, D., Morina, N., Popovski, M., Wang, D., & Schutzwohl, M. (2010). Mental disorders following war in the Balkans. *Arch Gen Psychiarty*, *67*(5), 518–528.

Rautela, P. (2013). Lessons learnt from the deluge of Kedarnath, Uttarakhand, India. *Asian Journal of Environment and Disaster Management*, *5*(2), 43–51. https://doi.org/10.3850/S1793924013002824

Raval, V., & Vyas, K. (2013). *Drought readiness and anxiety of new and experienced Indian Farmers* (Paper No. 46295). Munich Personal RePEc Archive. https://mpra.ub.uni-muenchen.de/46295/1/MPRA_paper_46295.pdf

Roudini, J., Khankeh, H. R., & Witruk, E. (2017). Disaster mental health preparedness in the community: A systematic review study. *Health Psychology Open*, *4*(1), 1–12. https://doi.org/10.1177/2055102917711307

Rubonis, A., & Bickman, L. (1991). Psychological impairment in the wake of disaster: The disaster–psychopathology relationship. *Psychological Bulletin*, *109*(3), 384–399.

Samy, A. L., Khalaf, F., Z., & Low, W. Y. (2015). Mental health in the Asia-Pacific region: An overview. *International Journal of Behavioural Sciences*, *10*(2), 9–18. https://doi.org/10.14456/ijbs.2015.39

Satapathy, S. (2012). Mental health impacts of disasters in India: Ex-ante and ex-post analysis. In Y. Sawada & S. Oum (Eds.), *Economic and welfare impacts of disasters in East Asia and policy responses* (pp. 425–461). Economic Research Institute for Asean and East Asia.

Sato, H., Takeda, K., Matsumoto, K., Anai, H., & Yamakage, Y. (2016). Efforts for disaster prevention/mitigation to protect society from major natural disasters. *FUJITSU Science and Technology*, *52*(1), 107–113.

Sekar, K., Bhadra, S., Jayakumar, C., Aravindraj, E., Henry, G., & Kishorekumar, V. (2005). Facilitation manual for trainers of trainees in natrual disasters. NIMHANS and Care India.

Sena, L. (2006). Disaster prevention and preparedness (Lecture notes, Jimma University). https://www.cartercenter.org/resources/pdfs/health/ephti/library/lecture_notes/health_science_students/lln_disaster_prev_final.pdf

Silwal, S., Dybdahl, R., Chudal, R., Sourander, A., & Lien, L. (2018). Psychiatric symptoms experienced by adolescents in Nepal following the 2015 earthquakes. *Journal of Affective Disorders*, 234, 239–246. https://doi.org/10.1016/j.jad.2018.03.002

Stanke, C., Kerac, M., Prudhomme, C., Medlock, J., & Murray, V. (2013). Health effects of drought: A systematic review of the evidence. *PLOS Currents Disasters*, 5, 1–39. https://doi.org/10.1371/currents.dis.7a2cee9e980f91ad7697b570bcc4b004

Stanke, C., Murray, V., & Amlôt, R. (2012). The effects of flooding on mental health: Outcomes and recommendations from a review of the literature. *PLOS Currents Disasters*, 1, 1–17. https://doi.org/10.1371/4f9f1fa9c3cae

Swathy, S. S., Sidharthan, M., Issudeen, M., Shibukumar, T. M., Kumar, A., & Tharayil, H. M. (2018). Psychological interventions during Nipah viral outbreak in Kozhikode district, 2018. *Indian Journal of Psychological Medicine*, 40(4), 387–389. https://doi.org/10.4103/IJPSYM.IJPSYM_249_18

Swiss Re Institute. (2018). Natural catastrophes and man-made disasters in 2017: A year of record-breaking losses. *Sigma* (1). https://www.swissre.com/dam/jcr:1b3e94c3-ac4e-4585-aa6f-4d482d8f46cc/sigma1_2018_en.pdf

The Hindu. (2013). Over 4,500 large dams lack emergency action plan, 4 July. https://www.thehindu.com/news/national/over-4500-large-dams-lack-emergency-action-plan/article4880921.ece

Thomas, J. J., Prakash, B., Kulkarni, P., Murthy, M. R. N., & Thomas, J. J. (2019). Prevalence and severity of depression among people residing in flood affected areas of Kerala. *International Journal of Community Medicine and Public Health*, 6(3), 1143–1146.

Thomas, V. (2014). Confronting climate-related disasters in Asia and the Pacific. *Review of Economics*, 65(2), 121–136.

Todd, D., & Todd, H. (2011). *Natural disaster response lessons from evaluations of the World Bank and others*. http://documents.worldbank.org/curated/en/621591468350106378/pdf/657860NWP0Box30at0disaster0response.pdf

Tol, W. A., & Ommeren, M. Van. (2012). Evidence-based mental health and psychosocial support in humanitarian settings: Gaps and opportunities. *British Medical Journal*, 15(2), 1–5.

UNISDR. (2018). *UN highlights urgent need to tackle man-made and technological hazards*. https://www.undrr.org/news/un-highlights-urgent-need-tackle-man-made-and-technological-hazards

United Nations Office for Disaster Risk Reduction. (2014). Risks & disasters. https://www.undrr.org/publication/unisdr-annual-report-2014

Weisaeth, L., & Tonnessen, A. (2003). Responses of individuals and groups to consequences of technological disasters and radiation exposure. In R. Ursano (Ed.), *Terrorism and disaster: Individual and community mental health interventions* (pp. 209–235). Cambridge University Press.

Community-based Intervention for HIV/AIDS

ABSTRACT

HIV/AIDS is a global public health challenge, which affects people of all age groups and all communities with little variation. Nevertheless, the situation is under control worldwide due to multiple strategies adopted by all the nations. What is required now is to ensure sustained care and support facilities to people who get infected by the disease, so that they can lead a life of quality and their manpower is also utilized. This chapter provides a definition of the disease and basic information for creating awareness among students in addition to discussing the psychosocial impact of the disease and social stigma attached to it. It also delineates the need and importance of counselling services in terms of mental health support facilities and ensuring protection of individual identities and their rights in social life. At the same time, it describes who could be the right people for delivering the counselling services, as all the students who study psychology and/or social work are not suitable for performing the same role. Further, it discusses micro-skills in counselling, aims of pre- and post-blood test counselling, prevention, community-based intervention and rehabilitative measures to be adopted to address the issues effectively and efficiently. Skill development training, career counselling and placement opportunities are some of the issues discussed in the chapter for the benefit of the students. Finally, the chapter gives an overview about the National AIDS Control Programme with special reference to care and support services for the people living with HIV/AIDS and draws conclusion and recommends some measures for a close monitoring of the situation.

Keywords: HIV/AIDS; counselling; role of psychologist; community; intervention; India

9.1. INTRODUCTION

This universe has witnessed a number of challenges which adversely affected human civilization. Human immunodeficiency virus/acquired immunodeficiency syndrome (HIV/AIDS) pandemic is one such public health challenge which has taken the lives of millions of people worldwide. At the beginning of the pandemic, health workers, policymakers and administrators were helpless for want of proper knowledge about the issue, which caused a lot of confusion in addressing the issue scientifically. During the window period, the HIV infection was spread among a large number of people since the HIV test did not reveal the infection and was negative. The window period is the time between HIV infection and the point when the test will give an accurate result. However, gradually, scientific studies disclosed information about the dynamics of the virus, cause and consequences of the disease, including medical and psychological interventions, resulting in effective policies and programmes for combating the disease. Joint efforts by national and international agencies succeeded in arresting the faster spread of the disease across the world with some variations. What is needed now is to ensure effective care and support services for the HIV/AIDS-affected people across the society, so that they can lead a life of quality. Before we proceed to discuss about various aspects of the disease, let us have a look at the current global and national scenarios of HIV/AIDS in terms of the magnitude of the problem.

9.1.1. HIV/AIDS: GLOBAL SCENARIO

HIV/AIDS is a pandemic that affected 37.9 million people worldwide in 2018. Out of the total HIV-infected people in 2018, 36.2 million were adults, while the number of children below 15 years of age was 1.7 million. It is estimated that about 1.7 million people worldwide got this infection in 2018.[1]

Most of the children infected by HIV during pregnancy, childbirth or breastfeeding belong to Sub-Saharan Africa. About three-fourths of the HIV-infected people (75%) had knowledge about their HIV status while one-fourth (25%) were waiting to confirm their status. It is very important to ascertain the HIV status for ensuring proper treatment, care and support services for better prognosis. Unfortunately, the majority of the HIV-infected people belonged to low- and middle-income countries such as Africa, Asia and the Pacific, Europe and North America. This health problem does not affect the individual alone. It also affects all the family members, the community and the economy of the nation as a whole. Nevertheless, sincere efforts by the international community and country-specific policies and programmes are able to arrest the problem to some extent, resulting in a declining trend of the HIV infection in all the countries.

9.1.2. HIV/AIDS: Scenario in India

According to the National AIDS Control Organization (NACO, 2017), there were about 2.14 million people living in India with HIV. Of them, 22 per cent belonged to the 15–49 years age group. The country witnessed 87,580 new infections in 2017. India holds the third position in terms of the highest number of people with HIV/AIDS after South Africa and Nigeria. However, there is a clear trend of decline of new infections in India, and it was possible because of multiple strategies jointly adopted by NACO and other allied organizations.

The NACO report further provides a clear picture of the prevalence of HIV infection, geographically and location wise. Mizoram had the highest adult HIV prevalence in the country (2.04%), followed by Manipur (1.43%), Nagaland (1.15%), Telangana (0.70%), Andhra Pradesh (0.63%), Karnataka (0.47%), Goa (0.42%), Maharashtra (0.33%) and Delhi (0.30%).[2]

In sum

HIV/AIDS is a global public health challenge affecting a large number of people worldwide. Latest data of 2018 indicates that about 37.9 million people were affected by this pandemic across the world. The African continent is the worst affected region followed by India. According to NACO, there are about 2.14 million people living with HIV in India. The youth of Mizoram and Manipur are badly affected by this health problem.

9.2. UNDERSTANDING THE HIV/AIDS SCENARIO

HIV weakens the body's immune system (or the defence system) and makes a person susceptible to a range of minor health problems. In normal circumstances, human beings are able to resist all such viruses which cause minor health ailments. After entering the body, HIV attacks the CD4 cells and it multiplies inside the CD4 cells. As a result, infected CD4 cells are destroyed and reduced. Ultimately, this situation leads to greatly reduced/compromised immunity of the body. In other words, HIV reduces the ability of the body's immune system to defend the body against the introduction of foreign substances (antigens).

AIDS is the much-advanced stage of the HIV infection, when a person's immune system completely breaks down. As a result, a person becomes vulnerable to numerous health problems such as TB, pneumonia, several forms of cancer and ultimately death. Let us explain the abbreviated form of AIDS. The term 'acquired' means transmitted from one infected person to another; it is neither innate nor inherited. The 'immune system' means the body's system of defence while 'deficiency' indicates not functioning to the appropriate degree. When a person reaches the AIDS stage, it demonstrates that the body's immune system is depleted, and it is unable to defend itself against infections. Finally, the word 'syndrome' refers to a group of signs and symptoms of illness, which result from the destruction of the body's defence, caused by HIV.

A person with HIV infection will not manifest any physical symptoms at the initial stage and will lead a life like a normal person. This stage is called HIV non-symptomatic. Once the disease progresses, the person will manifest different minor health problems and will also show certain physical symptoms. This stage is called HIV symptomatic. Evidence demonstrates that HIV antibodies are detectable only three weeks to six months after the first infection. This phase is called the 'window period'.

9.2.1. COMMON SYMPTOMS OF HIV

The first symptom of HIV is fever. Subsequently, people start experiencing other mild symptoms such as fatigue, swollen lymph glands and a sore throat. At the initial stage, the virus starts moving into the bloodstream and starts replicating it in large numbers. Slowly, the immune system of the infected person starts inducing an inflammatory reaction.

Other common symptoms of HIV and AIDS include rapid weight loss, continual fevers, extreme fatigue, tiredness, prolonged swelling of lymph glands, pain in the groin, neck or armpits, aching muscles and joint pain, skin rash, nausea, vomiting and diarrhoea continuously for more than a week, dry cough and sweating at night as well as sores near the mouth, genitals or anus.

9.2.2. STAGES OF HIV

Broadly, there are three stages and they include the following:

Stage 1. Acute HIV infection: In this stage, the majority will have a flu-like illness which is referred to as the natural response of the body to HIV infection. It happens 2–4 weeks after getting the infection. Flu-like symptoms include fever, chills, rash, muscle aches, sore throat, fatigue, swollen lymph nodes, mouth ulcers and so on. These symptoms may last for a few days to several weeks and it varies from person to person. If one experiences most of these symptoms, one should go for a blood test for ascertaining the HIV status. If the blood test result is found to be HIV positive, one should modify their behaviour and undergo appropriate medication as suggested by a specialized doctor.

Stage 2. Clinical latency: During this stage, the virus multiplies at very low levels. It is important to remember that people in this stage may not feel sick or have any symptoms. This stage is known as chronic HIV infection. Evidence suggests that without any HIV treatment, one may be in this stage for 10 or 15 years. However, one may also pass through this stage faster.

If one undergoes HIV treatment religiously, as suggested by a doctor, and keep an undetectable viral load, one can protect their health in addition to preventing transmission of the disease. But if the viral load is detectable, one can transmit HIV during this stage, even when there is no symptom. However, it is essential to get checked by a doctor from time to time.

Stage 3. AIDS: If one has got HIV and is not under medication, the virus will gradually weaken the immune system and lead to AIDS, the last stage of HIV infection. The common symptoms of AIDS, as mentioned before, are rapid weight loss; recurring fever or profuse night sweats; extreme and unexplained tiredness; prolonged swelling of the lymph glands in the armpits, groin or neck; diarrhoea that lasts for more than a week; mouth, anal or genital sores; pneumonia; red, brown, pink or purplish blotches on or under the skin or inside the mouth, nose or eyelids; memory loss, depression and neurological disorders and so on. These symptoms are similar to some other diseases. Therefore, one should certainly perform a blood test for confirmation.

9.2.3. MODES OF HIV INFECTION

Evidence clearly highlights that HIV is transmitted through direct contact of some bodily fluid containing HIV, such as blood, semen, vaginal fluid, seminal fluid and breast milk. Primarily, transmission can come in the form of anal, vaginal or oral sex, blood transfusion, use of contaminated needles, sharing needles, exchange of blood between mother and child during pregnancy, childbirth, through breastfeeding or through some other exposure to one of the above infected bodily fluids.

People involved in risk behaviour are mostly vulnerable to HIV. Risk behaviour, as mentioned before, includes unprotected sex, having sex with multiple partners, men having sex with men, getting infected blood and blood products. Research data indicates that the major mode of transmission of the virus (86%) is unprotected sexual contact.

There are some misconceptions about the methods of transmission of the virus. One might get the virus if one uses the same utensils, stays in the same room, gives kiss to an infected person or use the same toilet are a few. Over a period of time, massive awareness campaigns about HIV and AIDS have been successful to clear the misconceptions about the HIV infection. As a result, social stigma and misconceptions related to the virus have gone down to a great extent.

9.2.4. Methods of Prevention

For prevention of HIV transmission, every individual should be careful about certain issues. For example, one should abstain from unprotected sexual relationships in addition to having one faithful sexual partner only. One should never use unsealed needles or share the same needle used by another intravenous drug user. While taking blood, one should check the label of the blood, whether it is from the licensed government or private blood banks and see that the product has been tested for HIV, malaria, venereal disease research laboratory, hepatitis C virus and hepatitis B virus. Every pregnant mother should test her blood for ascertaining the HIV status for prevention of transmission of the virus from mother to child. If HIV is found to be positive, timely medication may prevent HIV transmission to the newborn child. For prevention through breastfeeding, suitable feeding options have to be adopted. In this regard, a mother should seek guidance from the doctor or counsellor of integrated counselling and testing centres (ICTCs).

In sum

The full form of HIV is human immunodeficiency virus, while that of AIDS is acquired immunodeficiency syndrome—the advanced stage of the HIV infection. The common symptoms of HIV are prolonged high fever, rapid weight loss, extreme fatigue, tiredness, swelling of lymph glands, pain in the groin, neck or armpits, aching muscles and joint pain, skin rash, nausea, vomiting and diarrhoea continuously for more than a week and so on. There are three stages of HIV and they include acute HIV infection, clinical latency and AIDS. The modes of transmission of the virus are through sexual contact, sharing of needles with an infected person, infected mother to a newborn child and taking blood from unreliable sources. So far as preventive measures are concerned, one should have only one faithful sexual partner, even if one wishes to have sex with others, one should use a condom in every sexual contact. One should never share a needle with another person and should always ensure not to use any used needle. A pregnant mother should go for a blood test for ascertaining HIV status and take the doctor's advice if it is found to be positive and finally one should always take blood from a reliable source.

9.3. PSYCHOSOCIAL IMPACT OF HIV/AIDS

HIV/AIDS has a range of psychosocial impacts, not only on the mental and physical health but also on the social life of an individual. It also affects the family dynamics, family relationships as well as mental health of all the family members, including children's education and their social network. Let us look at the initial response of HIV-infected individuals once they come to know about their HIV status.

9.3.1. THE INITIAL RESPONSE

The initial response after knowing the seropositive result is a feeling of shock and surprise, followed by a feeling of guilt, shame, distress, embarrassment and so on. Some of them also suffer from psychological stress by thinking about the method of disclosing the seropositive result to family members, especially to the life partner, if married.

9.3.2. PSYCHOLOGICAL IMPACT OF HIV/AIDS

Depression is one of the common psychological symptoms in case of any patient suffering from any chronic health problem, including people with HIV/AIDS and suicidal ideation is one of the signs of severe depression. Regarding depression, one study revealed that more than half of the subjects (53.3%) were suffering from severe depression, which affected HIV/AIDS-infected women to a greater extent (Deb, 2004). Two latest studies have reported lower incidents of depression compared to the Kolkata study. For example, Peng et al. (2010) revealed psychiatric morbidity, including depression, in 46 per cent HIV/AIDS-infected male prisoners, which is a little lower compared to the Kolkata study findings. Grov et al. (2010) also found that 39.1 per cent of HIV/AIDS-infected persons exhibited symptoms of major depression. Both male and female HIV/AIDS patients suffer from depression with equal intensity. 'Multivariate modelling of one of the latest studies successfully explained 42 per cent of the variance in depression which was significantly related to increased HIV-associated stigma, increased loneliness, decreased cognitive functioning, reduced levels of energy, and being younger' (Grov et al., 2010). Another cross-sectional study by Marwick and Kaaya (2010) covering 220 HIV-positive outpatients at a dedicated Tanzanian HIV/AIDS care centre revealed that 'depression or mixed anxiety was found in 15.5 per cent of subjects, with 4.5 per cent suffering from other anxiety disorders'. Some of the underlying causes of the low prevalence of depression in the earlier studies might be better socio-economic conditions of the patients and their better access to care and support services. In contrast, HIV/AIDS-infected patients in West Bengal come from a lower socio-economic background, with a lack of social support and poor access to healthcare facilities because of distance and poverty. Also considering the fact that most of the subjects have very low levels of education, there is the possibility that they are unable to understand and accept the hopeful aspects of this condition (HIV/AIDS) and ignore the negative outlook of the society at large. Thus, they succumb psychologically much before the actual disease manifests any adverse effects on them.

Similarly, the people diagnosed with AIDS react with extreme depression and thoughts of suicide (Kelly et al., 1993). However, a large number of them wish to change their lifestyle, that is, reducing high-risk behaviour to healthy lifestyles in terms of diet, exercise and compliance with the doctor (Taylor, 2006). Some even think of helping others so that they do not indulge in any risk behaviour and become a victim of similar situations like them.

9.3.3. Stigma and Discrimination

At the initial stage of the pandemic, people with HIV/AIDS experienced social stigma as well as social discrimination, not only in social life, workplace and family but also in the health centres. For example, people with HIV were asked to leave the house, terminated from their jobs, job opportunities to youth and adults with HIV/AIDS were denied, children were denied admission in schools and/or asked not to come to the school and social boycott. Unfortunately, in the health centres too, they experienced a range of discrimination, which includes not issuing health card, providing food to the patient from a distant place, denied health check-up by the doctors and not talking to them with patience and care and giving them a feeling that they are not good people and so on. As a result, people with HIV/AIDS were discouraged to come forward for individual and family counselling as well as medical care and guidance. Some even got involved in more high-risk behaviours to spread the disease fast so that they get more people with HIV to strengthen their group capacity or raise their voice for better care and support facilities. Stigma also acts as a barrier to preventive behaviour. For example, men or women with HIV wish their partner to use condoms for safety but might be hesitant to ask because of the stigma associated with HIV.

It has been observed that all the family members of a person with HIV experience social discrimination. Social support was lacking for most of the families in the community, if any family member was suffering from HIV/AIDS. There are instances of neglect in the hospitals where appropriate care was denied.

About 10–12 years back, social stigma was very strong in the Indian society. Unfortunately, pregnant women in India usually get the blame for being HIV infected even though they got the infection from their husband (Thomas et al., 2009). In some communities, social stigma was so strong that even after the death of a person with HIV/AIDS; their dead bodies were not allowed to be cremated/buried, out of a notion that through the smoke, the virus might spread.

In a study in Kolkata, 'a number of participants reported multiple types of discrimination. Among these, 16 (38.1%) reported 2 types and 8 (19%) reported 3 types of discrimination, while 18 (42.9%) reported only 1 type of discrimination' (Deb, 2004).

9.3.4. Discrimination in the Family

Family was the most common setting where discrimination occurred against the people living with HIV/AIDS (PLWHA). Qualitative data towards this end highlights the reality. For example,

> 'Disclosed the result to everybody. They behaved very badly. The family members along with neighbours motivated the landlord and drove them away from the house.'—Participant (male)

> 'Annoyed parents suggested a divorce.'—Participant (male)

> 'Mother-in-law is not a good person. Used abusive words after hearing the news. Asked to test the child and refused to help. Others were also not supportive.'—Participant (female)

'She is a dirty woman. She got the virus (*poka*). In-laws used to blame her for this virus.'
—Participant (female)

'Some hatred was shown by neighbour's family members.'—Participant (female)

'Discrimination by father compelled me to leave home.'—Participant (male)

9.3.5. DISCRIMINATION AT HEALTH CENTRES

Unfortunately, health centres were the place where people with HIV and AIDS experienced more discrimination. It was more about 10–15 years back. In this regard, Deb (2004) disclosed,

discrimination occurred most often at the time of admission to the hospital and while staying in the ward—both were reported by 36.8% (7/19) of the participants. Other situations where discriminatory treatment was reported included dealing with the confidentiality of the report, as reported by 3 out of the 19 (15.8%), and testing the blood for HIV (5.3%, 1/19). Two (10.5%) did not provide any information about the occasions when they encountered discrimination in a health center. Many (36.8%, 7/19) reported more than one occasion.

Further, the same study by Deb (2004) found,

nearly eighty percent (78.9%, 15/19) of those who experienced health center discrimination considered that the medical services they received were different from the services received by other patients. A same proportion (78.9%, 15/19) of victims of discrimination believed that the discriminatory attitude of the health personnel affected the medical care they provided. Approximately half (47.4%, 9/19) and 60% (63.2%, 12/19) of the discriminated stated that the medical staff who were aware of their seropositive status did not attend to them properly or did not behave properly with them during their visit.

However, over a period of time, a lot of changes have been observed in the social perception of HIV/AIDS and perhaps it is because of the multi-level awareness programmes covering all categories of the population across society. Now, a person with HIV/AIDS enjoys better care and support facilities in the family, in their social life and also in the hospital set-ups and workplace.

9.3.6. REACTION OF COMMON PEOPLE TOWARDS THE INFECTED PERSON

Recent evidence indicates that family is the first place where the infected person experiences maximum discrimination in the form of expression of hatred, using abusive language, being non-caring and non-supportive, breaking relationships with their life partners, instigating the infected person to leave the house or to commit suicide and many in-laws blaming the daughter-in-law for bringing the infection into the family. The verbatim responses of some of the subjects, mentioned in a recent study given below, provide glaring examples of different forms of discrimination experienced within the family.

'Relatives suggested that I should die. So suicide was an option. I was afraid. Did not disclose to neighbours the correct test results to avoid social discrimination.'—Subject (male)

'It was a disease, family advised not to say to anyone.'—Participant (male)

9.3.7. GRIEF AND BEREAVEMENT

Grief and bereavement are very common among people with HIV/AIDS although death is a normal phenomenon. People with HIV/AIDS develop a strong notion of early death despite the availability of a range of care, treatment and support facilities. Evidence indicates that bereavement of a partner can have adverse effects on the immune systems of HIV-positive men and women. In a study, Kemeny et al. (1995) observed, 'a person with HIV who had been bereaved by the death of their partner showed a significant increase in immune activation and a significant decrease in proliferative response to mutagenic stimulation'.

9.3.8. DISINTEGRATION OF SUPPORT SYSTEMS

In any crisis situation in life, social support helps an individual or a family to cope with the stressful situation and come out of the crisis phase. People with HIV/AIDS badly need social support and support from the family so that they fight the mental stress caused by the disease. It is believed that a person with social support will have more mental strength and is less vulnerable to depression or hopelessness. Ironically, in a civilized society, people with HIV/AIDS do not get social support, even from the educated group of people. Therefore, social disintegration makes a person with HIV/AIDS more vulnerable to highly stressful situations, leading to severe depression and development of suicidal ideation.

In sum

HIV/AIDS has an adverse effect on mental health and social life. In addition to experiencing social stigma, fear of boycott by family members is very high among the infected people. Some of the people with HIV/AIDS suffer from high anxiety, hopelessness, depression and fear of death. They not only experience discrimination in the family but also in the health centres and in the community, despite several awareness programmes in different social and community set-ups.

9.4. NEED AND IMPORTANCE OF HIV/AIDS COUNSELLING

In simple words, counselling is a confidential dialogue between an individual/couple/family and a counsellor which empowers them to take a decision about personal issues. In other words, counselling is a process in which an experienced person sensitizes a person who is confused or in trouble to take a suitable decision from among the available solutions, considering the pros and cons of a situation. Counselling is an important element of HIV care as it deals with the psychological needs of the individuals when the individual encounters a range of psychosocial, economic and health-related challenges in life. Perceived social stigma and discrimination make challenges in life manifold. Therefore, offering counselling services to a person with HIV is a mandate for all nations.

According to WHO,

HIV/AIDS counselling as a confidential dialogue between a client and a counselor aimed at enabling the client to cope with stress and take personal decisions related to problems arising from HIV/AIDS. The counseling process includes the evaluation of personal risk of HIV transmission, facilitation of preventive behavior and evaluation of coping mechanisms when the client is confronted with a positive result.

Counselling is very important in HIV/AIDS as a preventive measure and for behaviour modification as there is no complete cure from the disease. Counselling in HIV/AIDS through ICTC is the entry point to extend care and support services to an individual with risk behaviour in sensitizing them about their risk behaviour and its consequences. In particular, counselling helps in sensitizing a person about their risk behaviour so that a person does not indulge in any more risk behaviour and/or take precautionary measures for safety. At the same time, counselling helps in ensuring support from the family members of a person with HIV/AIDS which is very much needed when one is diagnosed as HIV positive. At the time of availing counselling and testing services, a person's queries are clarified by providing scientific information about various aspects of the disease and the person undergoes HIV test in a supportive and confidential environment. People who are found HIV negative are sensitized to reduce their risk behaviour, while the people who are diagnosed HIV positive are offered psychosocial support including treatment and care.

Counselling also helps to provide hope to a person with HIV/AIDS that their life is very important for their family members, children and even for the larger society. There are a number of examples where a person with HIV/AIDS, after blood test counselling, dedicated themselves to the welfare of other people like them, in terms of ensuring diagnosis, treatment and resolving family crises. When a person develops AIDS, continuation of medication as prescribed by a physician is essential and in turn, retroviral therapy helps a person to lead a reasonably better life. In order to ensure compliance with the physician's medication, counselling for antiretroviral therapy (ART) is found to be highly beneficial. Specific counselling practised in the field of HIV/ AIDS includes pre-test counselling, post-test counselling, adherence counselling, couples counselling, crisis counselling and grief or bereavement counselling.

Evidence concerning benefits of counselling is plenty. For example, a study carried out in Zimbabwe among HIV-infected women demonstrated the important role of counselling in providing psychological support. Further, the study indicated that counselling services should be provided for a longer period in case of people who are suffering from severe psychological distress (Krabbendam et al., 1998). In another study in Uganda, counselling services offered by NGOs through district hospitals were found to be highly beneficial to the family members along with the person having HIV/AIDS to cope with the stressful situation. As a result of supportive counselling, over half of the clients (56.9%) made plans for the future and 51.3 per cent wished to make wills. Further, the study disclosed that there was a high level of acceptance towards PLWHA by families (79%) and the community (76%; Kaleeba et al., 1997). Similarly, another study in Uganda among PLWHA men and women helped them to accept the present status of their life and move ahead with available medication and support facilities. Further, the study observed the positive impact of ART adherence (Nyanzi-Wakholi et al., 2009).

Studies carried out in India among STD clinic attendees and clients of FSWs witnessed positive behavioural change in terms of increased usages of condoms, on account of multiple counselling sessions (Bentley et al., 1998; Lipovsek et al., 2010).

Evidence from across the world also highlights poor treatment adherence because of psychosocial and behavioural factors such as stigma, disclosure issues, lack of social support, interpersonal relationship, especially among partners of married couples, depression and experience of traumatic events in life (Joglekar et al., 2011; Murray et al., 2009). These issues require effective and culture-specific counselling sessions for boosting the morale of the person, increasing their levels of self-esteem and confidence and creating a desire for living a healthy life.

Finally, the counsellors should address the issues and challenges of people with HIV/AIDs holistically and strengthening their coping capacity and creating a supportive environment for them.

In sum

Individual and family counselling are found to be very beneficial for people with HIV/AIDS as there is no complete cure from the virus. Counselling helps to give mental strength to the patient and self-disclosure. In turn, it ensures family acceptance and family support to the patient. It also helps to find a new meaning in life for doing something for others and family members.

9.5. MICRO-SKILLS IN COUNSELLING

As mentioned above, counselling is a process that empowers the client with correct information so that they are able to take an appropriate decision to resolve their personal problem. In order to play the role of an effective counsellor, one needs certain interpersonal and communication skills. Communication happens between a counsellor and counselee in case of individual counselling or the counsellor and family members in case of family counselling or a counsellor and a group of people in case of group counselling. Broadly, communication could be of two types, verbal and non-verbal. It is very important that a counsellor understands the experience or problem of a counselee and of the situation, from the perspective of a client. One of the most important steps in counselling is establishing rapport with the client and making them feel that a counsellor maintains confidentiality about the information shared by a client. In turn, this approach will make a client comfortable.

The micro-skills which are prerequisite for effective communication between a counsellor and a client for creating a supportive client–counsellor relationship include the following.

9.5.1. ACTIVE LISTENING

Active listening is very important and a client can very well understand from the facial expression or body gesture of the counsellor whether they are listening carefully or not. Active listening involves understanding the client socially, emotionally and intellectually. It also demonstrates that a counsellor is listening, hearing and paying attention to each and every issue shared by the client. Active listening requires patience. It also needs a relaxed posture, occasional nodding of the head, not interrupting while a client is narrating their feelings and encouraging the client to speak about their feelings and whatever they want to share. It is also very important to minimize internal and external distractions such as noises, worries, ideas and sudden thoughts during counselling sessions. During counselling, proper eye contact or body posture are essential indicators of active listening. Further, acknowledging the clients' feeling help to facilitate free expressions and a deeper understanding.

9.5.2. Questioning

Asking questions to the client during counselling is necessary to understand the client's issues and challenges from the right perspectives and helping the client to introspect for having proper insight about the issues and challenges they are facing. Questioning should be done for clarification of any issue and not for fulfilling the unnecessary curiosity of the counsellor. A number of counsellors feel tempted to ask unnecessary questions for their personal curiosity. While asking questions, a counsellor should remember that they ask one question at a time and there should not be any ambiguity in the question. The counsellor should ask a question while maintaining eye contact with the client. Questions should be very brief and clear. When a counsellor asks a question, it should be open-ended which will allow the client to narrate their feelings. Under no circumstances should closed-ended question like 'Yes' or 'No' be asked. Examples of closed-ended, open-ended and lead questions are given as follows for better understanding.

Examples of closed-ended questions:

- Do you have multiple sex partners?
- Did you use a condom during every sexual contact with CSWs?

Examples of open-ended questions:

- What are the challenges you face when you visit a health centre?
- According to you, how do you overcome social discrimination?

Examples of leading questions:

- Don't you think that you should use a condom during every sexual contact?
- Do you think that healthcare providers discriminate against people with HIV/AIDS?

9.5.3. Using Silence

During counselling sessions, silence plays a very important role. When a client first visits a counsellor with some objective, they might take time to reveal the information which they could not to any other person before. So a counsellor should give time to the client to think about what they want to say or share. In fact, there is no need to have a continuous dialogue between a client and a counsellor during counselling sessions. There should be some slots for silence in between discussion and/or sharing feelings of a client. Silence allows a client to proceed at their own pace. Silence allows a client to think about what to express and how to express it in addition to providing space to experience and internalize the feelings. Also, silence gives the freedom to a client whether to continue the discussion with the counsellor or to withdraw as some of the clients make a judgement about a counsellor regarding their personality and trustworthiness.

9.5.4. Non-verbal Behaviour (Body Language)

Non-verbal behaviour, which is body language, plays an equally important role in communication during a counselling session between a client and a counsellor. In reality, most of the communication during counselling is non-verbal. From non-verbal communication, both client and counsellor communicate a lot of information and they develop a good understanding. A sensitive counsellor welcomes non-verbal communication. Examples of broad non-verbal behaviour during counselling include body language and paralinguistics. Body language includes gestures, facial expressions, posture, proper eye contact, mirroring, body orientation, body distance, shifting legs, tapping fingers and so on. There are a range of paralinguistic behaviours and they are sighs, grunts, voice volume, voice frequency, voice pitch change, nervous giggles, cough and so on.

9.5.5. Accurate Empathy

Generally speaking, some psychologists confuse the term 'empathy' with 'sympathy'. Sometimes a counsellor promises something to a client, that is, 'don't worry; I am going to solve your problem soon'. It is a clear example of sympathy. In simple terms, sympathy has a shade of compassion towards the person with the problem. In other words, the term sympathy indicates direct support to a client while empathy attempts to bring equality between a counsellor and a client, which is, the client has the capacity to address their problem. Empathy denotes proper understanding of the client's feelings and thoughts. In simple terms, empathy can be explained as 'putting one's feet into client's shoes'. Accurate empathy means entering the client's world and look at things from the client's perspective. Empathy facilitates the client in self-expression without inhibition.

In sum

Micro-skills in counselling help to deliver effective mental health support services to the client. The basic micro-skills for a counsellor are active listening, questioning, using silence, non-verbal behaviour, that is, body language and accurate empathy.

9.6. STAGES OF COUNSELLING

Counselling is a process. In one session, the problem of the client may be resolved, that is, bringing insight into a client, while in the case of some clients, it requires multiple sessions. However, broadly, the stages of counselling are as follows:

- *Rapport building:* Building rapport with the client is the first and most important step towards success in counselling. When a client is entering the room of a counsellor, if the counsellor stands up and welcomes the client and asks them to sit and then the counsellor takes a seat, it makes a big difference in establishing a good rapport with the client. Further, ensuring confidentiality of information through proper eye contact, creating a congenial environment with adequate privacy, ensuring free expression of feelings and ventilation help a lot for rapport establishment.
- *Assessment and analysis of the problem:* It could be done by defining and focusing especially on the problem. At the same time, it is also important to examine the nature and seriousness of the problem. Thereafter, it is also necessary for a counsellor to clarify the boundaries of the counselling relationship in addition to understanding the client's beliefs, knowledge and concerns and assessing the impact of the problem on the client's life. There is also a need to explore the support facilities and insight of the client and finally, facilitating a summary of the problem by the client.

- *Provision of ongoing supportive counselling:* In this stage, a client is encouraged to express their thoughts and feelings. Identifying different options, exploring existing coping skills and developing further coping skills, enabling behaviour change, monitoring progress towards identified goals, providing referral if necessary are other issues concerning ongoing supportive counselling.
- *Planning and initiation of steps:* In this stage, a client is motivated towards behaviour change, setting achievable goals and planning to achieve the goals by identifying the options based on existing coping skills and developing further coping skills.
- *Implementation of the plan:* In this stage, a plan of action is developed for the client in discussion, with the client, and putting the plan into action following appropriate intervention strategies by the client, with the counsellor reinforcing and monitoring behaviour change.
- *Termination and follow-up:* Finally, it is necessary to assess the progress of behaviour change and coping resources. Further, the counsellor reinforces follow-up by ensuring that the client is acting as per plans. Managing of issues by the client is monitored by the counsellor. The counsellor also follows up the coping strategies of the client through daily functioning by availing the support facilities. Finally, the counsellor successfully ends the counselling process and encourages the client to meet the counsellor in future, if needed.

9.7. QUALITIES OF A COUNSELLOR

Like every profession, the profession of psychological counselling also needs some special skills. Every student studying psychology is not suitable for this profession. One should have some specific qualities. First of all, a person with a psychology background should have a passion for this profession and then only they can do justice to the profession. Second, a counsellor should be sensitive and emotionally mature. Third, a counsellor should have patience to listen to the views of the counselees and should encourage free expression of feelings of the client. Fourth, a counsellor should encourage the client to think differently to solve their problems. Fifth, a counsellor should refer the cases to other professionals, if required, without any inhibition. Sixth, a counsellor should ensure the confidentiality of information shared by a client. Seventh, a counsellor should avoid discussions with the client about irrelevant issues.

Key counselling skills include genuineness, listening, unconditional positive regard, believing the client, cultural sensitivity, making the client aware of the various alternatives, recognizing their own limitations, patience, not blocking the free expression of feelings, being non-judgemental, staying focused, being empathetic and finally, should have knowledge and staying updated about the latest development of the subject.

In sum

Stages of counselling include rapport building, assessment and analysis of the problem, provision of ongoing supportive counselling, planning and initiation of steps, implementation of the plan and termination and follow-up. Regarding the qualities of a counsellor, it is very difficult to come out with a yardstick to measure the same. Nevertheless, one should have a psychology background and passion for this profession, one should be emotionally mature and sensitive, one should have the patience to listen to the views of the counselees and encourage free expression of feelings, one should ensure confidentiality of information and refer the case to other professionals, if necessary.

9.8. OBJECTIVES OF PRE- AND POST-TEST COUNSELLING

Pre- and post-test counselling of people involved in high-risk behaviour are essential for their welfare and well-being. It ensures safety for people involved in high-risk behaviour; it also helps people to lead a quality life. Nevertheless, patient compliance is required for helping them. Let us have a clear idea about the objectives of pre- and post-test counselling.

1. *Pre-test counselling:* Pre-test counselling is offered in ICTC of the hospital. The broad objective of pre-test counselling is to sensitize the person involved in high-risk behaviour to undergo HIV test voluntarily. In order to prepare the person for the HIV test, a counsellor makes an effort to understand the nature of risk behaviour one was involved in and providing them detailed information about the efficacy of the HIV test. The issues which are discussed during pre-test counselling include mode of transmission of HIV, preventive measures, difference between HIV and AIDS, benefits of a blood test for ascertaining HIV status, available intervention facilities and so on. Further assessment is also done to understand whether a client is able to sense their vulnerability towards HIV infection, which is called 'risk appraisal'. Efforts are also made by the counsellor during pre-test counselling to understand the coping strategies of the client so that they can guide the client once the blood test report is available. Risk reduction plan is developed and risk reduction goals are set up during pre-test counselling. The client is also mentally prepared by the counsellor to accept the HIV report and deal with their anxiety and stress until they receive the report. For the blood test meant to ascertain the HIV status, written consent is taken from all the clients. Pre-test counselling is non-threatening, supportive and client friendly.

2. *Post-test counselling:* Like pre-test, post-test counselling is also equally important. The broad objective of post-test counselling is to review the HIV-related information provided to the client during pre-test counselling, disclose the HIV test result to the client, inform them about the window phase, if the result is negative, encourage them for a retest, sensitize the client for behaviour modification and disclosure of information to the family members. In addition, a counsellor should assess the anxiety and stress level of the client. In most of the hospitals, HIV test results are provided to the client on the same day and the implications of HIV test results are informed and explained to the client and their understanding of it is judged. As stated earlier, if the report is negative, a counsellor should discuss the window period and the client should be asked for retesting. Risk reduction plan is reviewed and adherence to it is assessed. Adherence concerning safer sex practices is emphasized and if married, partner blood testing for ascertaining HIV status is also recommended. The big challenge for the counsellor is if the report comes positive. If the report is positive, the counsellor should assess the psychological reaction of the client to the test and the client is given time to release their emotional outburst. Further, the counsellor sensitizes the client to adopt coping strategies which they adopted during any crisis phase earlier in life and brief the client about healthy lifestyles. The counsellor also plays the role of a third party to disclose the information to family members with consent from the client and ensures support facilities for the client. Subsequently, counselling sessions are planned with mutual convenience in addition to sensitizing the client about the testing of blood of the partner and safer sexual practices, assessment of pre-ART and opportunistic infection. Social support facilities from the family and others are discussed during post-test counselling.

9.9. SPECIFIC ROLES OF PSYCHOLOGISTS IN HIV/AIDS

The role of psychologists in HIV/AIDS prevention, intervention and rehabilitation is very important. They play multiple roles in addition to pre- and post-test counselling in the voluntary counselling and testing centre of a hospital, as discussed in the previous section. In particular, the role played by the psychologists include the following.

9.9.1. CRISIS COUNSELLING

People experience different crises in life and overcome the same adopting different strategies. Strategies for dealing with crisis vary from individual to individual, depending upon their coping mechanism. In the case of HIV/AIDS, it is more of an individual's reaction or response to the situation. Therefore, the individual's perceived crisis is an issue to be addressed by a professionally trained counsellor sensitively. This type of counselling is to be extended to a person with HIV/AIDS until the issue is psychologically accepted by the person and they start thinking positively and accept the reality to address the issue logically by taking appropriate measures. In turn, the process of crisis counselling minimizes the severity of the traumatic situation since they are educated and receive social support from the dear ones and dialogue is established with near ones affected by the crisis. It also facilitates and strengthens the coping strategies of the client. Ultimately, crisis counselling helps in identifying the trigger and also develops strategies to remove it.

9.9.2. GRIEF COUNSELLING

Grief or bereavement counselling offered by psychologists is found to be beneficial when one loses dear ones in life. In most of the cases, it happens because of premature death due to an accident or sudden health problem. In case of the death of a person on account of HIV/AIDS, a counsellor needs to counsel the family members, especially the life partner and/or children, as they are the most psychologically affected. The main objective of grief counselling is extending empathy and sensitizing the client to accept the reality, that is, the death of the close ones and remain psychologically strong as life should move on. As evidence says, the family member of a person with HIV/AIDS experience discrimination in social life. This issue should also be addressed during grief counselling and bringing back the life partner and/or children to normal life. The impact of grief on closer ones include withdrawal from daily routine, not having food on time, loss of interest in studies for children, loneliness, blaming oneself for not taking proper care of the person who died, loss of hope, depression and so on. The manifestation of grief varies from person to person, age, gender, nature of relationship with the person and nature of economic dependence on the person who died. Few sessions of grief counselling may help an individual to come out of thought fixation and resume daily-life activities.

9.9.3. ADHERENCE COUNSELLING

Adherence counselling is another important role played by the psychologists in case of HIV/AIDS. As we know, HIV/AIDS is a clinically manageable health condition with the help of adherence counselling. Due to the advent of ART, now HIV/AIDS is a manageable health condition. Earlier

ART was very expensive. Now, the Government of India has made ART free of cost, and it is offered in most of the hospitals in India. Evidence indicates that ART suppresses replication, if it is taken on time as prescribed by a doctor. Adherence to ART is therefore vital in this treatment. Any irregularity in following the prescribed regimen can lead to resistance to the HIV drugs, and therefore, can weaken or reverse its effect. Adherence is defined as 'the act or quality of sticking to something—to adhere to something'. In the context of ART, adherence means a more collaborative process between the patient and the provider. The patient's cooperation with the doctor for effective intervention, that is, prescribed regimen is essential. Adherence to the recommended regimen should be more than 95 per cent to avoid the development of ART drug resistance. This means that missing more than three doses per month is associated with increased risk of drug resistance and failure to treatment (NACO, 2007). Even though in case of HIV, adherence counselling is mainly associated with antiretroviral treatment, it should also be included in the context of any other long-term treatment like AKT (treatment for TB; NACO, 2006). Assessing the commitment of the client to take the treatment life long, making a client aware of the treatment and its side effects, explaining the possible barriers of the treatment, identifying the ways to overcome them, communicating with the healthcare provider and possible resistance are some of the aspects of the adherence counselling process. Now, adherence counselling has become an integral part of the treatment of people suffering from HIV/AIDS. In the process of adherence counselling, a counsellor should be able to identify the barriers to adherence counselling. Common barriers include forgetfulness, fear of side effects, general negligence, distance of the ART centre, lack of transportation facilities, lack of support in the family, negligence caused by family violence on account of the disease and several other religious and socio-economic factors. Adherence counselling is teamwork that is to be performed by doctors, nurses, pharmacists and patients. The counsellor should also involve other family members so that a person with HIV does not forget to take the medicine on time. Some of the reminder strategies found to be effective may be prescribed. They include alarms and marking dates in the calendars.

9.9.4. Couple Counselling

Couple counselling by psychologists for married people with HIV/AIDS is very crucial for disclosure of the HIV status and ensuring good and supportive couple relationship. The main threat for a person when identified with HIV is how to disclose the information to the life partner. The immediate conclusion is rejection, separation, humiliation and family violence. The perceived reaction from the life partner causes a lot of stress and anxiety in addition to frustration, feeling of shame and guilt and some even develop suicidal ideation. Sometimes, a blame game starts in the relationship. In some cases, a person with HIV/AIDS indulges into addictions when they perceive non-cooperation from the life partner, which makes the person vulnerable to other risks. The broad objective of couple counselling is to help the individual with HIV/AIDS to maintain the harmony in relationship and strengthen mutual understanding instead of focusing on the source of the infection within the couple. Rather, couple counselling helps to build careful, supportive and healthy couple relationships. During counselling, a counsellor should listen to both the individuals carefully, by paying equal respect. In addition to couple relationship, other worries such as children's education and future, financial crisis, safer sex and the health status of the infected partner are to be addressed and solutions need to be found in the given situation through discussion. If both the partners are infected and suffer from ill health, there can be issues pertaining to caregiving and support from other family members, which might be different than HIV-discordant couples. This issue should also be discussed and further strategies need to be identified. Therefore, couple counselling is found to be very important to help couples to have open discussions and exchange views with each other. In fact, in such a situation, a counsellor creates a favourable environment to establish a dialogue between couples to think positively, face life challenges, remain mentally strong and move ahead in life despite other several challenges. The counsellor also acts as a facilitator to empower couples to deal with their emotional crisis.

9.9.5. FAMILY COUNSELLING

Family counselling is different from couple counselling. In family counselling, all the family members are involved to address any crisis or challenging issue while in couple counselling, mostly the couples are involved in the discussion for resolving an issue through discussion. In family counselling, a psychologist's role is very important. The family counsellor attempts to involve all the family members to ensure support from others in addressing any issue jointly. In the case of HIV/AIDS, when people from a joint family or from a family with more than two members are there, everybody's participation is important, except small children. When the issue of HIV status is to be disclosed, it should be disclosed with the consent of the person. Disclosure of health status to all the family members ensures acceptance and cooperation in fighting social stigma and giving mental support to the person with HIV/AIDS.

9.9.6. TELECOUNSELLING

There is another equally important way to extend counselling to people with HIV/AIDS who are hesitant to come and meet the counsellor physically out of a feeling of shame and disclosure of personal identity. In case of telecounselling, the psychologist plays a very important role as a counsellor. In India, the toll-free number of telecounselling is 1098. A counsellor should be very sensitive in rendering telecounselling and encourage a client to call again if they feel like contacting for clarification of any other issues. A good number of the younger population prefer telecounselling across the world.

9.9.7. PREVENTION OF PARENT-TO-CHILD TRANSMISSION (PPTCT) COUNSELLING

Psychologists also act as PPTCT counsellor in extending counselling services to pregnant mother when she comes to the health centre for regular physical health check-ups. The objective of PPTCT counselling is to sensitize a mother about the necessity of checking the HIV status for safety of the newborn, since preventive measures are available. In most of the cases, the pregnant mother agrees for a voluntary blood test for ascertaining HIV. If it is found to be HIV positive, they are asked for a confirmatory test after one month. Even if that is positive, a prevention method is followed for the prevention of HIV transmission from mother to a child as advised by a doctor.

9.9.8. Targeted Intervention Counselling

Psychologists also play an important role in the targeted intervention programme in sensitizing the vulnerable people, that is, people working as daily wage earners in market areas, working in constructions sites, in transport and dock areas and/or other commercial places. They need to work in those areas by running a counselling unit, performing street plays, distribution of leaflets, small group meetings after work hour and/or as per their convenience. When a counsellor works with them, they need to refer the cases to nearby hospitals for testing of blood for ascertaining the HIV status.

9.9.10. Training of Trainers

Psychologists along with other professionals such as doctors, administrators and social workers act as very good trainers because of their basic knowledge about human psychology and teaching pedagogy. In the Global Fund to Fight AIDS, Tuberculosis and Malaria (GFATM) project, psychologists played a crucial role as a trainer since most of the training modules are based on psychological principles.

9.9.11. Programme Manager

Psychologists also work as a programme manager in different HIV/AIDS intervention programmes. A psychologist knows how to motivate others and engage them in work adopting different strategies. Educational background also helps to get along with others in running any community-based intervention programme.

In sum

A person with psychology background and with some basic training on HIV/AIDS counselling can play multiple roles in dealing with people suffering from HIV/AIDS such as pre- and post-blood test counselling, crisis counselling, family counselling, grief counselling, adherence counselling, tele-counselling, PPTCT counselling and targeted intervention counselling. In addition, they can act as a trainer for trainees and programme manager. A large number of psychologists are working in the field of HIV/AIDS in India in various capacities successfully and efficiently.

9.10. PREVENTION

Multiple preventive measures were adopted by NACO for the country, and they implemented the programmes with the help of State AIDS Prevention and Control Societies of every state. In this regard, local NGOs and educational institutions play very important roles as they have a close connection with the local community, people with high-risk behaviour, and youth as well as the students.

Red Ribbon Club is one concept to sensitize the students of educational institutions about HIV/AIDS across the country. Red Ribbon Club arranges lectures by experts to disseminate information about the issue among students in addition to arranging debates and discussions among students, poster competition, essay writing competition and street plays to communicate the message about social stigma, the mental health status of people with HIV/AIDS, family conflict, available support facilities and so on.

Distribution of leaflets, posters, pamphlets, organizing workshops, seminars, conferences, training for health professionals, using FM radio and other electronic and print media are found to be beneficial in creating awareness among people of all sections of the society about HIV/AIDS, resulting in reduction of incidence of any new HIV infection. The impact of various approaches concerning prevention of HIV/AIDS may not have a similar impact across the country. It depends upon the organizer and their creativity and nature of engagement in organizing various programmes.

9.10.1. ROLE OF MEDIA AND NGOs IN PREVENTING HIV

The role of both electronic and print media is very important to address any social and health issue in creating awareness among common people through sharing of scientific information. Although for the prevention of HIV media has played a significant role in India, it could be more proactive by introducing many more innovative programmes during prime time, especially when family members normally watch TV at home at the end of the day. Along with media, NGOs also play an important role in India in the dissemination of information by joining hands with the local governments and directly working with people involved in high-risk behaviour and change their behaviour in the process. For example, NGOs distributed condoms in red-light areas after sharing information about the mode of transmission of the diseases so that a CSW uses condoms during every sexual contact with the client. Initially, it was difficult in some red-light areas to convince a client to use condoms. But intervention of NGOs in this regard helped a lot to sensitize them about their safety and safety of CSWs.

9.11. INTERVENTION

The broad objective of any intervention programme is to address the issues and challenges of the victim of any problem. In case of HIV/AIDS, intervention aims to address physical, mental, social, legal and economic aspects of HIV/AIDS-affected people, their family dynamics and to examine their social support facilities. Addressing social stigma, which affects the mental health of the family members and disclosure of information to the life partner and other family members with the consent of the HIV/AIDS victim is also a part of the intervention programme. Until family support is ensured, it is very difficult to ensure mental support to the person.

9.11.1. NACO CARE, SUPPORT AND TREATMENT FACILITIES

In this regard, NACO has come out with a policy for providing care, support and treatment to the HIV-positive people including people with AIDS. A person with HIV always remains vulnerable to asymptomatic ailments for the initial six to eight years. Since immunity of a person with HIV goes down, the person becomes more likely to get different opportunistic infections (OIs). Therefore, a person with HIV requires both medical and psychosocial support facilities. Immediate diagnosis and treatment for OIs help a person to live longer with a better quality of life.

In the National AIDS Control Programme II (NACP II), emphasis was given on low-cost care and support and treatment for common OIs. In addition to ensuring availability, accessibility and affordability of ART treatment to the poor, NACP III also focused on improving family and community care through psychosocial support to the individuals, especially to the poor women and children affected by the pandemic. Improving compliance of the prescribed ART regimen and addressing the stigma and discrimination associated with HIV also got priority in NACP III.

9.11.2. CARE AND SUPPORT FOR CHILDREN WITH HIV

About 50,000 children below 15 years become the victim of HIV every year. Hence, NACP III had a provision for early diagnosis and treatment of children with HIV. In order to provide quality care to children with HIV, special training programmes for counsellors were organized across the country. In addition, efforts were made to make support facilities available to these children through referral and outreach activities in terms of nutrition, education, recreational facilities, foster care facilities and skill development programme.

Efforts made by NACO for combating HIV/AIDS in India during the last three decades yielded some positive results, that is, achievements of 66 per cent reduction in new infections since 2000 and 54 per cent reduction in AIDS-related deaths since 2007. It was possible because of the support and cooperation from people with HIV and AIDS, staff of all health centres, effective role of counsellors, community-based organizations, academics and researchers, development partners, private sectors and international organizations.

In NACP IV (NACP IV, 2017–2024), the emphasis for the next seven years is on 'ending of AIDS'. Currently, the vision of NACO is that of 'paving the way for an AIDS-free India' through attaining universal coverage of HIV prevention, treatment to care and continuum of services that are effective, inclusive, equitable and adapted to needs'.

By 2020, 'the focus of NACP is to achieve the following targets:

- 75 per cent reduction in new HIV infections
- 90–90–90: 90 per cent of those who are HIV positive in the country know their status, 90 per cent of those who know their status are on treatment and 90 per cent of those who are on treatment experience effective viral load suppression
- Elimination of mother-to-child transmission of HIV and syphilis
- Elimination of stigma and discrimination'

By 2024, 'NACP further wishes to achieve the following targets:

- 80 per cent reduction in new HIV infections
- Ensuring that 95 per cent of those who are HIV positive in the country know their status, 95 per cent of those who know their status are on treatment and 95 per cent of those who are on treatment experience effective viral load suppression'

In order to achieve the targets as stated above, the following five broad strategies are adopted by NACO under NACP IV (2017–2024).

- *'Intensifying and consolidating prevention services with a focus on high-risk group (HRG) and vulnerable populations:* With respect to this strategy, efforts have been made to reach the unreached population who are socially alienated with quality care and support services, through different approaches.
- *Expanding information, education and communication services for (a) general population and (b) HRG with a focus on behaviour change and demand generation:* In this regard, communication strategies for HRGs, vulnerable groups and unreached populations have been developed in such a way that they help to change the risk behaviour following culturally sensitive approaches. In addition, efforts are being made to create awareness among the general population, particularly women and the youth, about HIV/AIDS.
- *Comprehensive care, support and treatment:* It includes (a) ART including second-line ART, and management of opportunistic infections; (b) facilitating social protection through linkages with concerned departments/ministries. The programme emphasizes on public–private partnerships towards comprehensive care and treatment for people with HIV/AIDS. Further, efforts have been made to minimize social stigma and discrimination at all levels, including healthcare settings, so that people with high-risk behaviour do not hesitate to visit the health centres.
- *Strengthening institutional capacities:* It refers to the phased integration of HIV services with the routine public sector health delivery systems, streamlining the supply chain mechanisms and quality control mechanisms and building capacities of governmental and non-governmental institutions and networks.
- *Strategic information management systems (SIMS):* This strategy would help to take up evidence-based measures, monitoring and evaluation of the intervention programme in addition to tracking the epidemic, situation analysis and identifying the clusters with a high incidence of HIV/AIDS. In turn, SIMS would help in the effective management of overall HIV/AIDS intervention programmes.'

In sum

Last three decades of efforts by NACO, State AIDS Prevention and Control Societies and international organizations such as UNAIDS and GFATM and others towards prevention yielded some positive results in creating awareness among a cross-section of society about the virus and in improving quality of life of the people who were suffering from HIV/AIDS through effective counselling. However, there is a need to reach out to the unreached in sharing information about the virus and bringing them under the intervention programme in addition to improving the quality of care and support services to the infected people.

9.12. SUSTAINABLE DEVELOPMENT GOALS

SDGs adopted by the UN in September 2015 are the latest social yardstick to transform the world into a better living environment, following the inclusive approach. The basic principle of SDGs is 'leaving on one behind'. Every nation is keen to achieve the targets related to all the 17 well-defined goals adopting appropriate situation-specific strategies. Goal 3 of SDGs is ensuring healthy lives and promoting well-being for all at all ages. Regarding some of the major health issues such as AIDS, TB, malaria and neglected tropical diseases and combat hepatitis, water-borne diseases and other communicable diseases, it has been envisaged to end all these health problems by 2030.

9.13. INTERNATIONAL EXPERIENCE OF POSITIVE IMPACT OF INTERVENTION PROGRAMME

Worldwide, several intervention programmes are taken up by various agencies to prevent HIV transmission and for behavioural change. All these programmes had varied impact on different communities. For example, in an intervention programme with Latina immigrants living in farm worker communities, Rojas et al. (2019) found positive results in increasing condom use during vaginal and anal sex with male partners, self-efficacy for condom use, intentions to negotiate safe sex and HIV-related knowledge from baseline to six months, post intervention. The findings of the study confirmed the efficacy of intervention programmes, as demonstrated by previous researches.

Global data indicates that women engaged in sex work (WESW) are most vulnerable to HIV. In most of the developing countries, women come into sex trade due to poverty and compulsion and they remain marginalized as long as they survive. One recent study in Uganda by Ssewamala et al. (2019) found that when WESW have access to more capital and/or alternative forms of employment and start earning formal income outside sex work, they lead better lives and thereby reducing their STI/HIV risk. Therefore, there is a need to impart skills among WESW and in this regard, the local social welfare department and NGOs should take the initiative to organize skill-based training programmes for helping them to switch over to other professions.

As stated before, health professionals are coming out with innovative strategies for prevention of HIV transmission and behavioural change of most vulnerable groups across the world. A few strategies such as text messaging, online peer support group and coaching strategies were found to be very beneficial among the youth (Swendeman et al., 2019).

Jiang et al. (2019) undertook a study in Zhejiang, China, to assess the quality of life status and related factors among young HIV-infected men who have sex with men (MSM) aged 16–24 years. The findings indicated that 'for improving the QOL of this population, greater emphasis should be placed on improving social support, self-efficacy and ART adherence, in addition to reducing discrimination, disease progression and high risk behaviours'.

Evidence also highlights the positive impact of training in enhancing the knowledge of the participants. In one such training conference, as part of the health promotion programme of a high school in Milan (Italy), it was aimed to evaluate the impact of training conferences on the awareness of STIs among adolescents aged 16–17 (Orlando et al., 2019). Pre- and post-design clearly indicated a higher awareness about the spread and the mode of transmission of STIs, of high risk sexual and behavioural practices and prevention methods. The findings of the study justified the need to carry out similar awareness programmes among adolescents across the society, especially where adolescents are involved in risk behaviour.

In another intervention study, Mi et al. (2019) examined the mediating role of social support and self-efficacy which was underlying the relationship between HIV disclosure to family members and ART adherence. People living with HIV in China provided data on HIV disclosure, ART adherence, perceived social support on medication adherence, adherence of self-efficacy and social–demographic information. The path analyses revealed that disclosure to family members had significant indirect effects on adherence via social support and self-efficacy.

PLWHA are vulnerable to psychological distress primarily because of social stigma and low availability of mental health resources. The situation is similar in China. Therefore, Yang et al. (2018) made an attempt to examine the efficacy of interventions in reducing psychological distress and enhancing resilience among the people with HIV/AIDS. Cognitive restructuring to address depressive thought patterns, behavioural activation to decrease isolation and paced breathing to reduce anxiety were some of the strategies to reduce psychological distress and strengthen their resilience. Evidence demonstrated a significant reduction in HIV-related distress, depression, problems with adjustment, as well as improvements in resilience and perceived social support due to the intervention. Therefore, the same model of intervention may be replicated elsewhere for helping people with HIV/AIDS.

Bareki and Tenego (2018) assessed the knowledge, attitudes and practices of healthcare workers towards HIV post-exposure prophylaxis (PEP). Findings disclosed that the majority of respondents (70.7%) had adequate knowledge about PEP, and they possessed a positive attitude towards PEP. The study further observed that a significant number of healthcare workers had been exposed (53.7%) to risk. Although the participants were knowledgeable, they showed inadequate practices with regard to HIV PEP.

9.14. THE ROLE OF GFATM PHASE 7 IN HIV/AIDS INTERVENTION IN INDIA

In order to empower HIV/AIDS counsellors, GFATM played an important role in India. It is an international effort to save the lives of millions of people worldwide who are suffering from HIV/AIDS, tuberculosis and malaria. In India, currently, GFATM is in the seventh phase. HIV counselling is one of the subcomponents of GFATM 7 in India. This is the first time that the importance of involvement of academic institutions like universities in combating the challenge posed by HIV/AIDS is being appreciated. GFATM 7 is active in 38 universities across India, covering almost all the states and union territories. GFATM 7 proposes to implement its programme in collaboration with allied agencies working in the fields like State AIDS Prevention and Control Societies in each state. The goal of the programme is to strengthen human resource and institutional capacities of the national health system in HIV/AIDS, to enable accelerated growth of NACP III and the Government of India. The GFATM team in all the institutes is committed to achieve the following threefold objectives: (a) enhancement of the quality of trainers; (b) improvement of the quality of training infrastructure and training systems and (c) support and supervision of the training institutions and counsellors.

The role of higher learning institutes was found to be very effective in several ways. First, organizing the training programme by trained academics from different public health streams was a very good initiative to engage academics in achieving the national mission. The training program for counsellors should be carried out systematically

The GFATM orientation and refresher training programmes focused on three broad areas, namely knowledge, attitude and skills, that is, enhancement of knowledge of the HIV/AIDS counsellors about various aspects of the disease, changing their negative attitude towards the disease and patients and imparting skills to them to deliver effective counselling services to the client and their family members. The training manual, which was developed by NACO, was followed across the country. The first author of the book was one of the resource persons in developing the NACO manual for training of counsellors as mentioned before.

The NACO *HIV Counselling Training Modules* was developed through six regional consultations and field-testing in which the first author of the book played a crucial role as one of the resource persons (NACO, 2006).

The NACO modules broadly cover ICTC-related issues with special emphasis on risk reduction and facilitating HIV test decision in addition to addressing issues related to HIV testing and care for pregnant women and infant feeding. Other areas covered in the NACO training manual include treatment preparedness, adherence and follow-up counselling of patients when one comes for ART, crisis intervention and problem-solving counselling, family counselling, mental health issues and suicide prevention in HIV, the role of TB and STIs and their correlation with HIV/AIDS, group counselling, managing psychological distress, grief and bereavement counselling, counselling for occupational stress and burnout, legal and ethical issues, nutrition counselling and home-based care.

9.14.2. IMPACT OF TRAINING ON **HIV/AIDS** COUNSELLORS

Under the GFATM project, the Calcutta University centre, like other 38 universities, organized a series of orientation programmes for HIV/AIDS counsellors using the NACO models to enhance their knowledge and skills for better management of the cases in the field situation. All the training programmes were subjected to evaluation following pre and post design. It would be interesting to share the findings of the evaluation of one such training programme for the students.

The resource persons for the training programme were the master trainers as well as professionals from the State AIDS Prevention and Control Societies, Calcutta School of Tropical Medicine, medical colleges and several NGOs. In order to give better training to the ICTC counsellors, a group of professionals from different disciplines working in the field of HIV/AIDS were trained as master trainers under the GFATM project across the country and had also been exposed to the ICTC work set-up so that they can train the ICTC counsellors professionally.

9.14.2.1. Evaluation of the Orientation Training

The basic design of the evaluation of the orientation training was a pre-training and post-training design, as mentioned before, to evaluate the effects of the 12-day induction training on ICTC counsellors' knowledge, attitude and skill development related to different aspects of HIV/AIDS, following the self-administration method. Since learning is comprised of an affective domain (attitude), a cognitive domain (knowledge) and a psychomotor domain (skill/practice), these three areas were used to evaluate changes in the ICTC counsellors' behaviour as an outcome of the training intervention.

9.14.2.2. Tool Used for Evaluation of the Orientation Programme

The pre- and post-training knowledge and skill questionnaire for ICTC counsellors (NACO, 2006) was used here. It comprised of 30 items, 11 each on knowledge and attitudes and 8 on skills. It was developed by NACO (Ministry of Health and Family Welfare, Government of India) with technical support from WHO, UNICEF and Centers for Disease Control and Prevention (2006). The content of the questionnaire was based on the standard NACO module for training of HIV counsellors. The face validity of the questionnaire was assessed by a group of 38 experts. Out of the 30 items in the questionnaire, 20 were open-ended, 8 had a dichotomized response choice pattern (yes/no or true/false) and 2 provided multiple choices for responses. The items related to three major domains, which included the following.

1. *Knowledge:* It intends to measure the amount and accuracy of the information possessed by the counsellor, which is relevant to the area of HIV/AIDS counselling. It consists of 11 items (7 open-ended, 3 with dichotomized response choice pattern and 1 with a multiple-choice response pattern). It is designed to assess factual knowledge in the areas of HIV transmission (processes and principles), the window period, risk behaviours, diagnostic procedures for detection of HIV in the human body, questioning skills in counselling and self-care strategies for counsellors. The items carry different weights, from one to three marks. The possible score for this domain ranges from 0 to 20. Examples of questions in this section are as follows:
   a. What do we call the interim period between a person getting infected with HIV and the detection of HIV antibodies?
   b. List three self-care strategies for counsellors.
2. *Attitude:* This domain covers items that assess the respondents' attitude, views and opinions about various aspects of HIV/AIDS counselling and targeted intervention. This section differs from the previous one as it assesses attitude and views about topics that are more likely to be coloured by preconceived notions, biases and prejudices. It consists of eight items, including one case study (five open-ended and three with dichotomized response patterns). Two of the items deal with the importance of HIV counselling and group supervision for counsellors, three items cover issues such as dos and don'ts in specific counselling situations—occupational exposure to HIV, sexual assault, partner intimation and disclosure. The rest of the items deal with perceptions about targeted intervention and HRGs, namely FSWs, injecting drug users, MSM, prisoners and the youth. Scores for this domain range from 0 to 16. Examples of questions in this section are as follows:
   a. When a client discloses an incident of sexual assault, what are the first three things that should be done before conducting a forensic interview?
   b. List three ways HIV can be transmitted in prison.
3. *Skills:* Items in this domain pertain to the awareness of specific techniques and steps to be followed in HIV counselling. It consists of 11 items, including 2 case studies (8 open-ended, 2 with dichotomized response patterns and 1 with multiple-choice response patterns). The items relate to areas such as follow-up testing, pre-test counselling, active listening skills, post-test counselling (for both reactive and non-reactive clients), determining the seropositive status of the client, PEP, services for MSM, suicide risk assessment, counselling for breastfeeding and referrals. Possible scores for this domain range from 0 to 33. Examples of questions in this section are:
   a. What are the three indications that a client is at high risk for suicide?
   b. What are the five things that should be covered when giving someone a positive HIV test result?

The total score on the questionnaire was obtained by adding the scores obtained in each domain. Total scores range from 0 to 69. Scoring is done in accordance with the scoring standard developed by NACO, which provides the correct answers for the close-ended items and for the open-ended items, the lists of all the possible responses that may be scored. The items carry different marks—based on the scoring rationale of awarding 1 mark for every correct response. The closed-ended items carry one mark each, while in case of the open-ended items, which ask for several pieces of information, the marks allotted range from 1 to 5. For instance, in Item 2—'list 3 ways in which HIV is not transmitted'—the subject is awarded a score of 1 for every correct answer, with a maximum score of 3 points. Thus, a respondent obtains full score if they can name at least three ways by which HIV is not transmitted; 2, if they can name at least two; 1, if they name only one; and 0, if they provide no correct answer or fail to respond to the item. However, for the first question, only a complete set of three answers, mentioning the three routes of HIV transmission gives the respondent a score of 1. Any less than that would amount to a score of 0. A respondent's status in terms of their performance may be found out using the following classification:

Score Range, 47–69 = Superior/Grade A; 24–46 = Average/Grade B; and 0–23 = Poor/Grade C

9.14.3. FINDINGS OF THE EVALUATION STUDY

Findings indicate statistically significant improvement in overall scores, especially in three broad domains such as knowledge, attitude and skill development ($p < 0.001$) after the training. In other words, it might be stated that after the training, mean scores for knowledge, attitude and skills, and the three components combined increased significantly with very large effects (Table 9.1; Deb et al., 2016). All participants experienced an increase in knowledge, attitude and skill score, with little variation.

TABLE 9.1

Overall Knowledge, Attitude and Skills of the 24 ICTC Counsellors: A Comparison between Pre- and Post-training Scores

	Pre-Training M (SD)	Post-training M (SD)	T-value[a]	Cohen's d[b]
Knowledge (Max. score = 20)	10.63 (1.91)	14.75 (2.44)	7.79[c]	1.93
Attitudes (Max. score = 16)	6.08 (2.15)	10.25 (2.27)	9.28[c]	1.93
Skills (Max. score = 33)	9.04 (3.37)	15.92 (4.17)	9.86[c]	1.85
Total (Max. score = 69)	25.75 (6.49)	40.92 (7.62)	12.27[c]	3.38

Source: Deb et al. (2016).
Notes: ICTC = Integrated counselling and testing centre; M = mean; SD = Standard deviation
[a] Paired *t*-test
[b] Cohen's *d* of 0.2, 0.5 and 0.8 indicate small, medium and large effect size, respectively (Cohen, 1988).
[*]$p < 0.05$; [**]$p < 0.01$.
[c]$p < 0.001$.

However, there was a scope for further improvement and to elevate all the participating counsellors to Grade A. The success of this training programme also depended on the contributions of time and cooperation from our master trainers, resource persons and all our partner agencies. The study indicates that intensive training can significantly improve knowledge, attitude and skills of the ICTC counsellors. As a result, the ICTC counsellors feel more confident and comfortable to deal with people having high-risk behaviour, motivate them for blood testing, alter their risk behaviour, prepare a reactive person to cope with the stressful situation and facilitate care and support services. It was also observed that after the training, the biggest areas of change were in two domains, that is, knowledge and attitude. Empowering the ICTC counsellors with enhanced knowledge, positive outlook and skills, through professional training, will facilitate HIV prevention. In a country like India, where population explosion and poor health infrastructure are major problems in delivering effective health services, the success of this type of training is a hope to curb incidences of HIV infection and extending better care and support services for the beneficiary.

Further, in-depth analysis of pre- and post-training data indicates that special emphasis should be given on the following areas in future training programmes since comparison of pre- and post-training data did not reveal any significant changes:

- *Knowledge domain:* Knowledge regarding window period, incubation period, testing exposed babies, risk behaviour and testing kits for HIV.
- *Attitude domain:* Discussion of sexuality with the client.
- *Skill domain:* Testing to rule out window period, HIV test algorithm, counselling for feeding options and referral services.

Refresher trainings are needed for the ICTC counsellors to ensure skill development of all the counsellors and to keep them updated with the latest development in the subject in every aspect of HIV/AIDS. Finally, there should be some flexibility to cover some of the relevant issues in the training, like sessions on relaxation techniques and conflict management. Care should be taken to recruit counsellors with social science backgrounds, preferably masters in psychology, social work or sociology and sustainable interest should be ascertained. At the same time, it is important to ensure job security with a good salary.

In sum

Support from the GFATM project for organizing orientation and refresher training for the counsellors was found to be very effective as revealed by a number of systematic studies and feedback from the participants. In turn, the trained counsellors could deliver better and quality counselling services to the people with HIV/AIDS in the community.

9.15. REHABILITATION

The broad objective of rehabilitation is to ensure the acceptance of the person with HIV/AIDS by the family members and non-discrimination in the health centre and workplace so that they can live in the society with dignity. In the truest sense, rehabilitation should be both in terms of occupation and practice, so that a person can live an independent life in society and is able to support the family. If a person does not have any employable skills, an effort should be made to provide them with some skill-building training for immediate employment or for self-employment. In case of a young person, vocational and career counselling should be offered at the institutional or the community level through NGOs, so that they can opt for interest-oriented career options in life. When vocational and/or carrier counselling is offered, the market demand for the same vocation should be taken into account. NGOs, along with all the State AIDS Prevention and Control Societies should act as facilitators for the placement of people with HIV/AIDS.

9.16. RECOMMENDATIONS

Although there is a perceived change in the society about HIV/AIDS in terms of social acceptance and quality healthcare in the health centres because of continuous awareness, a lot more work needs to be done to address some of the issues related to HIV/AIDS. These include the following:

- Creating awareness about reproductive health among adolescents and youths through educational institutions. In this regard, NGOs should reach out to school dropout youths and adolescents through a community-based approach.
- Sensitizing schoolteachers to teach reproductive health issues, following proper pedagogy, instead of sidelining the topic and asking the students to study the subject on their own.
- Closely monitoring the awareness programme in states like Manipur with the incidence of a new infection.
- Bringing all the people with HIV/AIDS under intervention programmes, especially in the rural areas and people working in the transport and construction industries.
- Sensitizing rural mothers and women from the lower social strata about family planning methods and their benefits.
- Addressing issues and concerns of the third gender community, especially about sexuality, and offering them health services and counselling.
- Addressing social perception about the third gender community and ensuring social acceptance.
- Periodic review and revision of NACO policies and programmes and taking up need- and culture-specific programmes.
- Monitoring all intervention programmes across the country periodically and taking appropriate measures.
- Improving the documentation of data/information and using them for the improvement of the situation.
- Periodic evaluation of training programmes and all overall programmes related to HIV/AIDS and taking respective corrective measures.

9.17. CONCLUSION AND IMPLICATIONS

HIV/AIDS has taken the lives of thousands and thousands of people all over the world. India is also one of the worst-affected countries like the African countries. Nevertheless, well-planned prevention activities, based on evidence and intervention programmes across the society, along with the joint efforts of the government, international organizations and local NGOs can arrest the pandemic. Now, the incidence rate of new infection has gone down significantly, along with social discrimination, to a great extent. What is required now is to extend quality care and support services to PLWHA. Every nation has taken several measures, including the Government of India, to improve the quality of life of people with HIV/AIDS.

There are many implications of HIV/AIDS. First, it affects the physical, mental and social health of an individual. Second, a large number of people experience discrimination in health centres, workplaces and even at home. Third, the productivity of the people with HIV/AIDS goes down, causing huge financial loss. Fourth, expenditures increase for the prevention of the disease and the treatment. Fifth, family dynamics gets affected in addition to childcare. Sixth, this disease causes fear psychosis among the common people.

EXERCISES

One-mark Questions

1. What is HIV/AIDS?
2. What are the common symptoms of HIV?
3. Define HIV/AIDS counselling.
4. What are the immediate reactions of a person after knowing the results of the blood test?
5. Define stigma. How is it related to HIV?
6. What is the role of voluntary counselling and testing centre?
7. What do you mean by targeted intervention?
8. Is HIV common among the gay population?
9. What do you understand by intervention?
10. What is rehabilitation?

Five-mark Questions

1. What are the common methods of transmission of HIV?
2. How do you prevent HIV transmission?
3. Do people with HIV experience discrimination in health centres? If so, why?
4. Is social support beneficial for people with HIV/AIDS?
5. What are the objectives of pre- and post-test counselling?
6. What is the role of media in preventing HIV?

Ten-mark Questions

1. Discuss the importance of HIV/AIDS counselling.
2. Are the professionals, belonging to the psychological stream of study, suitable for HIV/AIDS counselling? Justify your answer.
3. Discuss the importance of micro-skills in counselling with some practical examples.
4. Why is ART important? Explain.

Reflexive Questions

1. What are the implications of the high incidence of HIV/AIDS in the Indian society?
2. Could GFATM project train HIV/AIDS counsellors effectively across the country? Discuss.
3. Is the support of family members beneficial for people with HIV/AIDS? Discuss.
4. Discuss the various challenges faced by the people with HIV/AIDS.

NOTES

1. https://www.hiv.gov/hiv-basics/overview/data-and-trends/global-statistics
2. http://naco.gov.in/sites/default/files/HIV%20Facts%20&%20Figures.pdf

REFERENCES

Bareki, P., & Tenego, T. (2018). Assessment of knowledge, attitudes and practices of HIV post exposure prophylaxis among the doctors and nurses in Princess Marina Hospital, Gaborone: A cross-sectional study. *Pan African Medical Journal*, *30*(1), 233.

Bentley, M. E., Spratt, K., Shepherd, M. E., Gangakhedkar, R. R., Thilikavathi, S., Bollinger, R. C., & Mehendale, S. M. (1998). HIV testing and counseling among men attending sexually transmitted disease clinics in Pune, India: Changes in condom use and sexual behavior over time. *AIDS*, *12*(14), 1869–1877.

Deb, S. (2004). *A study of psychosocial and economic problems encountered by the commercial sex workers with HIV/AIDS in Kolkata*. Department of Women and Child Development, Ministry of Human Resource Development, Government of India.

Deb, S., Mitra, C., Sun, J., & Majumdar, B. (2016). Capacity enhancement of ICTC counsellors through residential training on HIV/AIDS. In S. Deb & A. Shukla (Eds.), *HIV/AIDS in India: A public health approach on contemporary trends* (pp. 297–310). Global Vision Publishing House.

Grov, C., Golub, S. A., Parsons, J. T., Brennan, M., & Karpiak, S. E. (2010). Loneliness and HIV-related stigma explain depression among older HIV-positive adults. *AIDS Care*, *22*(5), 630–639.

Jiang, T., Zhou, X., Wang, H., Luo, M., Pan, X., Ma, Q., & Chen, L. (2019). Psychosocial factors associated with quality of life in young men who have sex with men living with HIV/AIDS in Zhejiang, China. *International Journal of Environmental Research and Public Health*, *16*(15), E2667.

Joglekar N., Paranjape R., Jain R., Rahane G., Potdar R., Reddy K. S., & Sahay S. (2011). Barriers to ART adherence and follow ups among patients attending ART centres in Maharashtra, India. *Indian Journal of Medical Research*, *134*(6), 954–959.

Kaleeba N., Kalibala S., Kaseje M., Ssebbanja P., Anderson S., van Praag E., Tembo G., & Katabira E. (1997). Participatory evaluation of counseling, medical and social services of the AIDS support organization (TASO) in Uganda. *AIDS Care*, *9*(1), 13–26.

Kelly, J. A., Murphy, D. A., Bahr, G. R., Koob, J. J., Morgan, M. G., Kalichman, S. C., Stevenson, L. Y., Brasfield, T. L., Bernstein, B. M., & St Lawrence, J. S. (1993). Factors associated with severity of depression and high-risk sexual behavior among persons diagnosed with human immunodeficiency virus (HIV) infection. *Health Psychology*, *12*(3), 215–219.

Kemeny, M. E., Weiner, H., Duran, R., Taylor, S. E., Visscher, B., & Fahey, J. L. (1995). Immune system changes after the death of a partner in HIV-positive gay men. *Psychosomatic Medicine*, *57*(6), 547–554.

Krabbendam, A. A., Kuijper, B., Wolffers, I. N., & Drew, R. (1998). The impact of counseling on HIV-infected women in Zimbabwe. *AIDS Care*, *10*(2), 25–37.

Lipovsek, V., Mukherjee, A., Navin, D., Marjara, P., Sharma, A., & Roy, K. P. (2010). Increases in self-reported consistent condom use among male clients of female sex workers following exposure to an integrated behaviour change program in four states in Southern India. *Sexually Transmitted Infections*, *86*(Suppl 11), i25–i32.

Marwick, K. F., & Kaaya, S. F. (2010). Prevalence of depression and anxiety disorders in HIV-positive outpatients in rural Tanzania. *AIDS Care*, *22*(4), 415–419.

Mi, T., Li, X., Zhou, G., Qiao, S., Shen, Z., & Zhou, Y. (2019). HIV disclosure to family members and medication adherence: Role of social support and self-efficacy. *AIDS and Behavior*, *24*, 1–10.

Murray, L. K., Semrau, K., McCurley, E., Thea, D. M., Scott, N., Mwiya, M., Kankasa, C., Bass, J., & Bolton, P. (2009). Barriers to acceptance and adherence of antiretroviral therapy in urban Zambian women: A qualitative study. *AIDS Care*, *21*(1), 78–86.

NACO. (2006). *HIV counselling training modules for VCT, PPTCT and ART counsellors*. Ministry of Health and Family Welfare, Government of India with technical support from WHO, UNICEF and CDC.

NACO. (2007). *ART guidelines*. Ministry of Health and Family Welfare, Government of India.

NACO. (2017). *National strategic plan for HIV/AIDS and STI 2017–2024*. http://naco.gov.in/national-strategic-plan-hivaids-and-sti-2017-24

Nyanzi-Wakholi, B., Lara, A. M., Watera, C., Munderi, P., Gilks, C., & Grosskurth, H. (2009). The role of HIV testing, counseling, and treatment in coping with HIV/AIDS in Uganda: A qualitative analysis. *AIDS Care*, *21*(7), 903–908.

Orlando, G., Campaniello, M., Iatosti, S., & Grisdale, P. J. (2019). Impact of training conferences on high-school students' knowledge of sexually transmitted infections (STIs). *Journal of Preventive Medicine and Hygiene*, *60*(2), E76.

Peng, E. Y. C., Lee, M. B., Morisky, D. E., Yeh, C. Y., Farabee, D., Lan, Y. C., Chen Y. M., & Lyu, S. Y. (2010). Psychiatric morbidity in HIV-infected male prisoners. *Journal of the Formosan Medical Association*, *109*(3), 177–184.

Rojas, P., Ramírez-Ortiz, D., Wang, W., Daniel, E. V., Sánchez, M., Cano, M. Á., Ravelo, G. J., Braithwaite, R., Montano, N. P., & De La Rosa, M. (2019). Testing the efficacy of an HIV prevention intervention among Latina immigrants living in farm worker communities in South Florida. *Journal of Immigrant and Minority Health*, 1–7. https://doi.org/10.1007/s10903-019-00923-4

Ssewamala, F. M., Bahar, O. S., Tozan, Y., Nabunya, P., Mayo-Wilson, L. J., Kiyingi, J., Kagaayi, J., Bellamy, S., McKay, M. M., & Witte, S. S. (2019). A combination intervention addressing sexual risk-taking behaviors among vulnerable women in Uganda: Study protocol for a cluster randomized clinical trial. *BMC Women's Health*, *19*(1), 111.

Swendeman, D., Arnold, E. M., Harris, D., Fournier, J., Comulada, W. S., Reback, C., Koussa, M., Ocasio, M., Lee, S. J., Kozina, L., Fernández, M. I., & Rotheram, M. J. (2019). Text-messaging, online peer support group, and coaching strategies to optimize the HIV prevention continuum for youth: Protocol for a randomized controlled trial. *JMIR Research Protocols*, *8*(8), e11165.

Taylor, S. E. (2006). *Health psychology*. Tata McGraw-Hill Education.

Thomas, B., Nyamathi, A., & Swaminathan, S. (2009). Impact of HIV/AIDS on mothers in southern India: A qualitative study. *AIDS and Behavior*, *13*(5), 989.

Yang, J. P., Simoni, J. M., Dorsey, S., Lin, Z., Sun, M., Bao, M., & Lu, H. (2018). Reducing distress and promoting resilience: A preliminary trial of a CBT skills intervention among recently HIV-diagnosed MSM in China. *AIDS Care*, *30*(Suppl 5), S39–S48.

RECOMMENDED READINGS

Clark, H. R. 2011. *The Cure for HIV & AIDS*. B. Jain Publishers.

Deb, S., & Shukla, A. (2017). *HIV/AIDS in India: A contemporary public health trends*. Global Vision Publishing House.

DeJong, J. (2003). *Making an impact in HIV and AIDS: NGO experiences of scaling up*. ITDG.

Liamputtong, P. (Ed.). (2013). *Stigma, discrimination and living with HIV/AIDS: A cross-cultural perspective*. Springer Science & Business Media.

Pequegnat, W., & Szapocznik, J. (Eds.). (2000). *Working with families in the era of HIV/AIDS*. SAGE Publications.

Rajamanickam, M. 2006. *Psychology of perspective of HIV and AIDS*. Concept Publishing Company.

Webb, D. (1997). *HIV and AIDS in Africa*. Pluto Press.

Weinreich, S., & Benn, C. (2004). *AIDS, meeting the challenge: Data, facts, background*. WCC Publications.

WHO, Regional Office for South-East Asia. 2006. *Antiretrovirals for HIV: A compilation of facts and product information*. Author.

Interventions at School: Role of Community Psychology

ABSTRACT

Education is essential for everybody for leading a quality and meaningful life. It not only ensures skills and knowledge but also grooms a child with some values, and finally one becomes a responsible citizen. However, during school days, a good number of students experience a range of challenges such as academic pressure, poor teaching, CP, psychological abuse and poor support facilities, which lead to development of anxiety, depression, adjustment problems, suicidal ideation, suicide and so on. All these challenges need immediate attention of the school administrators in terms of mental health support facilities and sensitization of teachers and parents, so that students enjoy their studies and move ahead in life. This chapter provides an overview of the challenges faced by the students. Parents are the first social agents to the children who impart basic orientation on the socialization process in which learning is an integral part. If parents teach children in a friendly manner, explaining various issues by citing simple examples and bringing down their level to the level of children, learning for children will become very enjoyable, and children will also become more curious to learn new subjects with interests. If parents do not take much interest to teach their wards at home with interest and patience, children struggle to learn new things. The chapter elaborates the role of teachers in schools in developing an interest among students towards studies with special reference to their personality, method of teaching, communication skills and updated knowledge on the subjects and their passion for teaching. Available evidence concerning effective teaching and its association with students' motivation, interest and performance in studies are discussed in the chapter in addition to discussing characteristics of a good teacher and implications of parents and teachers' role in child education.

Keywords: School; intervention; community psychology; parents; teachers; students; academic pressure; mental health challenges; guidance and support

10.1. INTRODUCTION

Children go to school for gaining knowledge and skills which make them productive and responsible citizens. Therefore, education is essential for every child, and it is also the fundamental right of a child to get quality education. Although it is very difficult to define quality education, one can have an idea about quality education of a school based on the overall academic performance of the students.

The broad objective of education is to ensure physical, mental and spiritual development of the children so that they can lead a quality life and can also contribute towards social growth and development. Education also helps children in assimilation of knowledge, developing ability in understanding and interpreting the situation from the right perspective, character building and personality development, bringing out the fullest potential of children, gaining self-confidence and becoming independent in life.

For the overall mental, social, career, personality and spiritual development of children, a child-friendly environment, both at home and in school, is essential in addition to basic care and support facilities, such as adequate nutrition, medical facilities, education, recreational facilities, safety and security, love and affection, as outlined by the UN Convention on the Rights of the Child (UNCRC; United Nations, 1989). Therefore, education should be imparted in such a manner that children find it interesting and enjoyable, and thereby become motivated. However, in some developing countries such as India and China, children/students experience tremendous pressure and/or stress right from their primary education and throughout their career due to a number of factors such as overpopulation, less number of perceived good academic institutions compared to total population, resulting in over-competition, unemployment and over expectation of parents (Deb et al., 2011; Sun, 2011). Even in some of the developed countries, in case of higher technical education, students experience academic stress.

Unfortunately, a large number of children in the developing countries are out of school and some discontinue education at an early stage because of numerous factors such as distance, lack of teaching staff, lack of guidance and encouragement, non-availability of restroom in the school that is especially applicable for girl children, harsh disciplining method and poverty. Now the question arises, how to ensure education to all children? It requires multiple strategies and involvement of community leaders. As poverty is one of the main barriers of education for children of poor families, there is a need to make every effort to improve the economic condition of the poor. In addition, effort should be taken by the government to open schools in interior rural areas in reasonably convenient locations so that children from interior areas can attend the school. Community mobilization by the community leaders for bringing all the children to the school could be another good strategy as community leaders have close ties with the community members.

In sum

Education is an integral part of our life and every individual should get the opportunity for education. Children require education for their holistic development so that they are able to lead a quality and meaningful life and are also able to contribute towards social development. Sincere efforts should be made by the local administration and community leaders to admit all the disadvantaged children in schools and see that they continue education to the maximum levels.

10.2. THE INDIAN EDUCATION SYSTEM

In a resource-challenged nation, partly due to the large-scale non-availability of audiovisual aids and other technologies that encourage practical learning and application of knowledge and partly due to an inability to switch from the colonial methods of education, the Indian school education system is textbook oriented, where the stress is on rote memorization of lessons, which requires systematic study for long hours every day. The elaborate study routines occupy a student from morning till late evening hours, leaving hardly any time for socialization and recreation. In India, the school education system has two broad categories of educational boards. The first category includes three central boards which cover all India, namely the Central Board of Secondary Education (CBSE), the Council for the Indian School Certificate Examinations and the National Open School. The second category includes the state-level boards. Every state has its own school board, and it offers courses within the state. Interestingly, the curriculum of all the boards, irrespective of the category, varies to a great extent. Students studying under some state boards get good scores since the curriculum is less and methods of examination and evaluation are easier, while the curriculum of the central boards and methods of examination and evaluation are comparatively much more difficult. This variation in curriculum calls for uniformity so that every student across the country faces a similar situation. Less number of educational institutions as compared to population causes higher competition among students. A student starts experiencing competition at the time of entry to the primary level, and it continues up to the higher secondary level and beyond. Grade 10 final examination is very important as it determines the selection of the education stream in a good school. Students with high scores only get admission in their preferred educational stream. In India, the common preference is science stream so that one can study either medical or engineering as it might help them to get a job and establish in life first.

Another feature of teaching in schools is that teachers wish to complete the curriculum within the time frame and hardly pay attention to whether the students could follow the class and understood the subject or not. As a result, a large number of students lose interest in studies and perform poorly as compared to their potential. In some schools, teachers are not sincere in teaching the subject, and it happens mostly in the government schools since the job of government schoolteachers is secured, while in private schools, teachers teach effectively, otherwise they might lose the job. Sometimes, ineffective teaching in schools and sometimes parents' anxiety insist them to engage private tutors for their children after Grade 8. Further, once one chooses an education stream at Grade 11, they cannot switch to another stream, that is, from humanities and commerce to science stream or vice versa, therefore causing tremendous stress among such children.

The New Education Policy (NEP) 2020 proposes a transformational change in our education system through a comprehensive framework to address most of the aforementioned concerns. Expanding the mandatory schooling age range, instituting a single regulatory body for higher education, a four-year undergraduate programme with multiple entry and exit points and blurring the contour among science, arts and commerce streams are some of the promising changes recommended by the policy. However, it demands time to fully implement the NEP effectively and in the truest sense, and it is also expected that effective implementation of NEP will address all the challenges faced by the students in the following section.

10.3. ROLE OF SOCIAL SUPPORT AND ITS BENEFITS

Social support in any form, whether mental, physical, financial, is found to be beneficial for needy people. In different crisis situations in life, when people experience crisis and/or feel helpless, social support succours people to regain self-confidence, and they become mentally strong.

Like other social agents, children also suffer stress and crisis during their developmental phase in terms of socialization, the dos and don'ts about their behaviour and over or unrealistic expectations of parents and teachers. During the development phase, children also need social and mental support from the parents, teachers, friends and significant others for their social, personality and career development. A number of studies highlighted the benefits of social support. For example, individuals with high levels of perceived social support are more hopeful, better adjusted and have lower levels of depression and stress, and higher self-esteem and sense of well-being (Dumont & Provost, 1999). More precisely, social support has been associated with better adjustment during the transition from elementary to middle school (Hirsch & Dubois, 1992).

In sum

The Indian education system is very competitive since the number of educational institutions is limited as compared to the need, which causes tremendous stress for students at all levels. Therefore, students need support from parents, siblings, teachers and significant others to pursue their education.

10.4. CHALLENGES FACED BY THE STUDENTS

The scenario of the school's academic, physical and social ambience varies across the country and types of school. For example, in some private schools, administrators are very much concerned about quality education and students' mental health while in some private schools, students are under tremendous stress and a strict disciplining method is followed. Variations in terms of quality education and student's safety and care have also been observed in government schools. Nevertheless, in the following section, an overview is given about the common challenges faced by the students.

10.4.1. ACADEMIC LOAD

Vast school curricula, especially at Grades 11 and 12, are big challenges for students in India. Do students really need to study such a vast curriculum? This issue requires the special attention of the school education policymakers. Brainstorming among academics, school teachers and school administrators would help to examine the relevance of the vast academic curriculum and revise the curricula accordingly. Perhaps, there is a need to revise the school curricula, considering the social relevance into account and the academic load should be reduced substantially. Vast academic curricula cause academic pressure for students.

10.4.2. ACADEMIC PRESSURE

Since the number of good schools is limited in every state in India as compared to the population of students, there is always a high competition at the time of entry at the primary level. As a result, parents put a lot of pressure on their ward to perform better in the interview. Students who are successful in securing admission in those schools are appreciated by the parents, whereas the students who fail to get admission in the good school do experience psychological abuse and even, sometimes, physical abuse. Thereafter, when a student moves to a higher level, academic pressure increases to perform better without considering the capacity of a child. In order to ensure better performance, parents appoint a number of private tutors and after the school hours, some students go to private coaching centres while in case of some students, private tutors come home for teaching the same subject which was taught in the school. Here, the question of quality of education comes. Had there been quality teaching in the schools, perhaps students would not require visiting a private coaching centre. However, this logic may not be true in the case of every school. Sometimes, despite quality school education, parents also engage private tutors. It has been observed that on an average, 4–5 private tutors are engaged for special support to the students, especially the parents who can afford. There are instances where it has been observed that even parents with poor income wish to spend more money for the education of their children. For attending double education, nowadays most of the children do not enjoy their childhood and hardly find time for games and sports, resulting in compromising with the holistic growth and development of children. Evidence indicates that about 30–40 per cent students experience academic stress.

Among the variety of sources of stress experienced by children as mentioned before, academic and study-related issues are significant contributors to stress in childhood (Bjorkman, 2007). Verma and Gupta (1990) have defined *academic stress* as 'mental distress with respect to some anticipated frustration associated with academic failure, anticipation of such failure, or even an awareness of the possibility of failure' (p. 7). Now the question arises 'why some students experience stress in response to academic situations?' Students undergo stress since grades and/or test scores indirectly set the yardstick to judge them as good or bad. Parents, siblings, relatives, teachers and people of the larger society interpret the status of the child/student on the basis of grades and marks, which are referred to in most of the social situations while introducing the child. A child can sense it very well. Results of an Australian study support the aforementioned statement as the study revealed that school-related situations are the main sources of stress (Kouzma & Kennedy, 2004).

A study in China reveals that a heavy burden from academic activities is the cause of academic stress among Chinese students (Sun, 2011). Previous researchers found that students with low academic grades are more likely to be stressed (Bjorkman, 2007; Li et al., 2007).

Students in Indian schools across the country experience academic pressure from the parents and teachers for better performance. In this regard, one Kolkata-based study covering the students of Grades 11 and 12 revealed that 'nearly two-third (63.5%) of the students, irrespective of grade, reported stress because of academic pressure. Further, the study reported that about two-third (66%) of the students reported of having parental pressure for better academic performance' (Deb et al., 2011).

10.4.3. Ineffective Teaching

There is a common complaint about government schools across the country that a good number of teachers do not teach effectively. They do not teach effectively since they are not knowledgeable and they do not have teaching skills or they are knowledgeable, but they are demotivated for some reasons. It is very important to find out the answer to the aforementioned question and take appropriate measures. From personal experience as part of a governing body of a number of Kendriya Vidyalayas (KVs), I have observed that the authority of a KV runs the system appointing a large number of contractual teachers every year. Since a contractual teacher's contract is for one year and they are less paid, they are not motivated to teach effectively. Hence, it is important to fill up all the vacant posts of government schools with full-time permanent teachers by knowledgeable candidates, with teaching skills only. Under no circumstances should an academic administrator compromise with quality while selecting a teacher. In a large number of private schools, the scenario is almost the same. They run a school with contractual teachers, paying less salary and therefore they fail to attract good teachers which affects the quality of education adversely and also demotivate students.

10.4.4. Disciplining Method

Disciplining of students is necessary to develop good habits and also to improve performance in all aspects, including academic performance. Every academic institution has some rules and regulations for all the staff and students so that a system is run smoothly, and everybody follows the same. Disciplining children is a little challenging since they are immature. Therefore, there is a need to reinforce the rules and regulations to the students, instead of resorting to CP for minor mistakes. In some schools, teachers resort to harsh CPs, which not only cause physical pain but also affect their dignity and some even get demotivated. A student might commit a mistake and it requires proper handling sensitively. With positive words, a teacher can change a student forever.

If a teacher uses derogatory comments for committing a mistake by a student, it might adversely affect a student psychologically. Therefore, a teacher should always be sensitive to students' issues and extend their support and encourage them for better academic performance. Only encouraging words can bring a miraculous change in the life of a student. In a study in Tanzania's O-level secondary schools, it was found that

> corporal punishment was the most common form of punishment in secondary schools. The majority of teachers supported its continued use, but believed in moderation. The majority of students and teachers were unaware of national laws to restrict corporal punishment. Students reported disliking the practice and believed it was ineffective and resulted in emotional, as well as physical, distress. (Feinstein & Mwahombela, 2010)

In a recent study in Puducherry, India, it has been observed that

> 62% of the students reported experiencing school corporal punishment (CP) in the past 12 months, with males and those attending public schools being significantly more likely to report school CP than females and those in private schools. Youth who reported school CP reported more anxiety and depression. That relation was more pronounced in youth who reported family tension. (Deb et al., 2017)

10.4.5. LACK OF EXTRACURRICULAR ACTIVITIES INCLUDING GAMES AND SPORTS

The curriculum of the CBSE is designed in such a way that students get at least one period in a day for games and sports and/or extracurricular activities. On the other hand, the curriculum of some of the state boards does not have much scope for extracurricular activities. From the morning, students attend one class after another and become exhausted by the end of the day. Even some school engage students after school hours for special coaching. Hence, students from a good number of private schools hardly get any chance for physical activities. They are trained to work hard for extraordinary academic performance.

10.4.6. LACK OF BASIC FACILITIES SUCH AS SAFE DRINKING WATER, RESTROOM AND SAFETY

These basic facilities are missing mostly in rural schools and even in some urban government schools. Even if a restroom is present, it remains unclean. Safety is also an issue for some schools. Some children experience CP and psychological abuse. Some also experience sexual abuse in the hands of school staff and school bus drivers, and some are bullied by senior students.

10.4.7. MENTAL HEALTH CHALLENGES FACED BY THE STUDENTS

School students suffer from a range of mental health problems such as adjustment problems, examination phobia, anxiety, depression and suicidal ideation. The incidence of suicide among students is increasing day by day. The students who come from poor families and are poor in terms of communication skills suffer from more adjustment problems, while some students, who are intellectually backwards, suffer from examination phobia. Results of a Kolkata-based study on adolescent students show that

> anxiety was prevalent in the adolescents with 20.1% of boys and 17.9% of girls found to be suffering from high anxiety. More boys were anxious than girls. Further, it was observed that adolescents from Bengali medium schools were more anxious than adolescents from English medium schools. Adolescents belonging to the middle class (middle socio-economic group) suffered more anxiety than those from both high and low socio-economic groups. (Deb et al., 2010)

Likewise, the students whose parents have high expectation from their child undergo psychological stress and some even suffer from anxiety and depression.

One study carried out among Mexican schoolchildren with LD indicates

> that a higher percentage of children with LD were at risk for anxiety (22.3% vs. 11.5%) and depression (32% vs. 18%). Findings demonstrate that that there is an increased awareness of co-morbid depression and anxiety among students with LD and there is a need to promote early identification and intervention in schools. (Gallegos et al., 2012)

Evidence from the developed countries highlights that 'educational stress among students attending secondary schools has significant associations with mental health problems, such as depression, anxiety, and suicidal ideation' (Ang & Huan, 2006; Bjorkman, 2007). In this regard, one recent study in Kolkata reported that parental pressure for better academic performance caused high anxiety among adolescents in comparison with adolescents who did not experience the same. Likewise, in case of emotional adjustment, self-concept, self-confidence and parental pressure had negative effects (Deb & Bhattacharya, 2012).

A number of studies carried out among Indian school students reported mental health problems faced by the children and adolescents for school-related distress, exhibiting symptoms of depression, high anxiety, frequent school refusal, phobia, physical complaints, irritability, weeping spells and decreased interest in schoolwork (Rangaswamy, 1982; Verma & Singh, 1998). Some children also lose interest in studies due to lack of encouragement and academic pressure (Shah, 1991; Verma & Gupta, 1990). The situation is similar in other Asian countries like China (Lee & Larson, 2000). One of the studies in Kolkata, India, reported examination-related anxiety among 81.6 per cent students, especially among female students who studied in the local language (Deb et al., 2011). The study further revealed that about one-third (32.6%) of the students revealed symptoms of psychiatric illness.

A cross-sectional study conducted among school students in Chandigarh, India, found that

> out of 2402 students, 1078 (45.8%) had psychological problems, half (1201 students) perceived problems in their role as students, about 930 (45%) reported academic decline while about 180 (8.82%) students reported that life was a burden. The study further observed that about 122 (6%) reported suicidal ideation, and around 8 (0.39%) students reported suicidal attempt. (Arun & Chavan, 2009)

10.4.8. Non-availability of Mental Health Support Services in Schools

Most of the schools in India do not have a psychologist to deal with the challenges of the students. As a result, students remain unattended if they suffer from stress and/or abuse. In some states and/or in the locality, though there are psychologists, social stigma and lack of knowledge on mental disorder among community members are the main barriers to seeking mental health support services. A good number of children suffer from common childhood disorders such as LD, autism and ADHD, which require proper diagnosis and intervention. Timely diagnosis and intervention can improve the situation substantially and, in turn, children can lead a much better life. However, due to lack of knowledge about these problems among the primary school teacher, these problems never get the attention of the teachers and children grow with the same problem and fail to cope with school academic demand.

10.4.9. LACK OF SUPPORT FACILITIES FOR BACKWARD STUDENTS

The students who are coming from poor families under the Right to Education Act, 2012, hardly get any special attention from the schoolteachers. Very few schools have special support facilities for disadvantaged children to bring them to the levels of other students. Most of their parents are also not in a position to guide their children in studies. As a result, these students suffer from inferiority complex and are unable to perform well like other students and, after a few years, they become school dropouts.

10.4.10. CHALLENGES IN ENSURING EDUCATION FOR ALL AND SCHOOL DROPOUTS

In order to ensure education to disadvantaged children, the Right of Children to Free and Compulsory Education Act, 2009 (MHRD, 2009), has been passed by the Indian Parliament and as per the same law, 25 per cent seats should be provided to economically disadvantaged children in all schools across the country. Data are lacking about the effective implementation of the law in terms of providing seats to the disadvantaged children. However, in some states, the law is followed while in some states it is not implemented owing to a number of reasons, such as lack of knowledge among the poor people about the law, denial of admission by the school authorities, especially in the private schools.

A large number of schoolchildren in the rural areas become dropouts because of lack of guidance and family compulsive situation, that is, looking after younger children and poverty. Sometimes, distance and non-availability of teachers and restroom in the schools discourage children to continue education.

In sum

School academic and social ambience as well as quality of teaching vary from school to school, irrespective of category, that is, private or public schools. However, as students gain knowledge and skills while attending the school, a large number of them also experience a range of challenges during school days and they include high academic load, academic stress, ineffective teaching, harsh disciplining methods, lack of basic facilities such as safe drinking water, restroom and safety, lack of relaxation facility in terms of games and sports, and lack of mental health support facilities for students. Some of them also suffer from mental health challenges such as adjustment problem, examination anxiety and depression.

10.5. RISK FACTORS FOR MENTAL HEALTH CHALLENGES AMONG SCHOOL STUDENTS

Sufficient evidence is available pertaining to multi-factorial causes for mental disorders in children and adolescents. Poverty, social disadvantage (Duarte et al. 2003; Patel & Kleinman, 2003), parental mental disorder (Leinonen et al., 2003) or substance abuse (Obot & James, 2004) and discordant intra-parental relationships are causes of mental disorders among children and adolescents. Mental disorder among children adversely affects the concentration in studies and finally the academic performance (Patel et al., 2007). Children who experience any forms of violence and abuse are more likely to suffer from mental health challenges.

So far as the risk factors pertaining to academic stress are concerned, available evidence indicates that socio-economic background of the family, that is, the educational background of parents, parental pressure for better academic performance, income, gender, educational grade and the number of private tutors are responsible for the same (Deb et al., 2011). Rural school location, low school connectedness, perceived poor academic grades, gender, older age and frequent emotional conflicts with teachers and peers are other risk factors of mental health challenges for students.

10.6. IMPACT OF ACADEMIC STRESS

High academic demand and/or pressure have an adverse impact on mental health of students. Association between academic failure and depression has been well established by a number of previous studies (Kellam et al., 1983; Sun, 2011). At the same time, studies have also reported that 'depressive mood is associated with academic problems or low academic achievement' (Hilsman & Garber, 1995; Kaslow et al., 1984).

Suicide among students in India is increasing on account of academic failure or for not being able to perform as per expectations of parents and significant others. In India, every day, 24 students commit suicide because of academic failure (Ministry of Home Affairs, Government of India, 2015). As per the Crime in India data, the rate of suicide among students has jumped from 6.23 in 2000 to 24 per day in 2015. These data are alarming and this issue needs immediate attention of education policymakers. In an Indian study, suicidal ideation was found in 6 per cent of the school students in Chandigarh while 0.39 per cent attempted to commit suicide (Arun & Chavan, 2009).

In sum

There are a number of risk factors for mental health challenges among students and they include poverty, social disadvantage, parental mental disorder or substance abuse, discordant relationships between parents, child abuse and neglect, poor communication skills among students, high academic demand and parental pressure for better academic performance and so on. Academic stress causes mostly anxiety and depression among students and even suicidal ideation.

10.7. THE ROLE OF SCHOOL ADMINISTRATION

The role of school administration as well as teachers is very important for improving the situation, which is creating a student-friendly atmosphere in the school, in terms of effective teaching and creating a fear-free academic environment for optimal utilization of students' potentials through their active engagement in the studies. In order to improve the overall performance of the students and for inculcating good habits, parents' support and cooperation are essential.

In the following section, the role of teachers and parents is discussed at length with some practical examples.

10.8. ROLE OF SCHOOLTEACHERS

The role of a teacher in a school is to impart knowledge by explaining the subject/concept in a simple language so that all the students in a class can follow the same. Along with teaching a subject, a teacher should clarify the confusion of the students, if any, with patience, instead of ignoring and/or discouraging the student. Once the concept is clear to the students, they will be encouraged to study the remaining part of a subject with interest. Therefore, the teacher's role is very important in developing students' special interest in a subject and for motivating the students in studies. Through effective teaching, a teacher in a school becomes very popular among students and every student wishes to attend all the classes of the same teacher and, finally, the same teacher becomes a role model for the students. In other words, a good teacher plays the role of a friend, philosopher and guide.

Teacher's role is not confined to the classroom only. A teacher is supposed to engage in multiple tasks, related to the profession. The teacher needs to prepare the lesson plans, plan for systematic teaching throughout the year and intimate the students about lesson plans at the beginning of an academic session, teach on a regular basis, set questions papers, evaluate periodically the performance of students, prepare grade papers, manage the classroom, meet with parents and work closely with other school staff. In today's advanced society, a teacher's role is a multifaceted one and every role they play should be done with utmost care. In this working situation, the role of the school principal is very crucial in motivating all the teaching and non-teaching staff through active leadership. If the principal is sensitive to teachers' challenges and issues and motivates the teachers through reward a system for effective teaching, the students will be ultimately benefitted.

10.8.1. Characteristics of a Good Teacher

An important matter of concern when discussing school intervention is the characteristics that is expected from a good teacher. A few relevant ones are listed below:

1. *Good academic background:* A teacher should have a good academic record. It is expected that a teacher with a good academic record studied sincerely while they were a student and is knowledgeable. A knowledgeable person can impart knowledge and will be more engaged in classroom teaching since they have knowledge. Therefore, while selecting a candidate for

the teaching profession, the selection committee members should never compromise with quality. Selecting a single unqualified candidate under compulsion and/or for recommendation of a teaching position will be highly damaging and disastrous for the students' welfare. Students will suffer for years and they will lose their interest in the particular subject.

2. *Passion for teaching and learning:* A person who has no interest in teaching and learning may not contribute effectively in teaching. Sometimes, a person opts for teaching profession since they failed to engage in other jobs. These types of candidates, after acceptance of the teaching job, neither teach effectively nor are they satisfied. Their mere presence in the school does not benefit the system. Therefore, the passion of a person for a teaching is very important and while selecting a candidate for a teaching position, these issues should be given importance. Normally, most of the schoolteachers in Indian schools accept teaching position because of compulsion. Therefore, it is important to make the teaching position attractive by providing better salary packages to attract the best candidate for teaching positions.

    The teacher who teaches the subject in an interesting manner by giving practical examples makes it easier for students to follow. The teacher as an educator must take into account the student's learning styles, abilities and personalities.

3. *Good communication skills:* In the teaching profession, communication skill in English is very important along with advanced knowledge in a subject. A teacher with good communication skills can impart knowledge among students more effectively and in an efficient manner. Hence, while selecting a candidate, the communication skills of a candidate should be ascertained through demonstration of a lecture before the selection committee.

4. *Teaching methods:* Teaching methods vary according to the level and/or grade of the students. While teaching, the teacher must bring down their level to the level of the students so that effective communication takes place and students also understand the subject easily. A teacher should prepare the lesson plan for an academic year giving equal weightage to completing the entire syllabus prior to each periodic examination and should share the same lesson plan with the students on the first day of the academic year so that the students also can prepare for them accordingly. Unfortunately, a good number of teachers do not understand the value of developing lesson plans and share the same with the students. A few days prior to the examination, students are not sure of syllabus or the question paper to be set for an examination. Some teachers do not take the classes regularly and fail to meet the expectation of the students. Some are very poor in evaluating the answer scripts. These special characteristics demoralize young students and give a bad name to the profession of teaching.

    Teachers should be punctual in taking classes and should teach in such a manner that a student does not need to attend another private tutor for studying the same subject. It is not only a waste of time but also an additional economic burden for parents. It deprives a child of enjoying normal childhood activities, that is, playing with other children and enjoying the leisure time as outlined in the UNCRC (United Nations, 1989). According to Article 31 of the UNCRC, every child has the right to leisure, play and participate in cultural events, which is good for their mental refreshment, comfort and happiness. Unfortunately, almost all the students in Indian schools are forced to attend multiple private tutors for clarification of their queries, since school teaching is not effective. A large number of contractual teachers teach in such a manner that students' queries are not clarified during school hours and they are compelled to attend the same teacher after school hours. This unofficial double education system needs immediate attention of the education policymakers for the interest of the larger student community.

A teacher should adopt the most interesting methods for teaching by giving practical examples. Sometimes, it could be participatory using audiovisual aids, while sometimes the teacher should take the students outside the classroom in a natural environment for teaching, if possible. While teaching, individual differences should be taken care of and, accordingly, a teacher should teach. Good teachers have a responsibility to respond and alter their teaching methods as per the students' needs and taking the advancement of society into account. In other words, a teacher should be flexible with an open mindset.

5. *Pleasing, balanced personality and leadership quality:* Personality of an individual matters a lot in social relations whether in the classroom or in the community, along with leadership qualities. A person with a pleasing and balanced personality, with a smiling face, becomes easily acceptable to others. When the acceptance of a person is good to others and/or rapport is established, it becomes easier for them to communicate information or reach students effectively following different pedagogy. Hence, it is very important for a teacher to greet students while they enter the classroom with a smiling face. A smiling face of a teacher creates an anxiety-free learning environment in the classroom which is very much required to understand the so-called difficult subjects such as maths, physics and chemistry, and encourages students to attend the class, understand the subject and/or clarify their confusions, if any. Therefore, the overall leadership quality of a teacher enables them to manage the class well and make the classroom effective in disseminating information.

6. *Availability to students within and outside the class:* A teacher should be punctual in going to class every day. Punctuality of teachers will make students punctual, sincere and attentive. A good teacher will always come to class with proper preparation so that they can teach the subject systematically and proceed according to the lesson plan prepared at the beginning of a session. A teacher should also be available for the students for clarification of any queries after the class hours with smiling faces and will also encourage students to come forward with any queries.

7. *Believing in disciplining students in non-abusive forms and encouraging the students:* Disciplining students in school is important for the formation of good habits such as attending classes regularly and on time, being attentive in the classroom, taking class notes, taking part in school cultural and social activities and completing the homework. If any student performs well, it should be encouraged and appreciated in front of other students and, in turn, this process will motivate other students to perform well for getting the appreciation. If any student fails to perform up to the expectation of a teacher, they should not be criticized in front of others. That particular student should be given feedback in private, in a constructive manner with encouragement so that a student does not feel much disappointed and rather feel encouraged improving the performance. Encouragement is the best approach to improve the performance of students. A teacher should never resort to CP for disciplining students. CP is banned legally in India. If any teacher punishes a student physically, as per the Section 17 of the Right of Children to Free and Compulsory Education Act, 2009, and Section 82 of the Juvenile Justice (Care and Protection of Children) Act, 2015 (Ministry of Law and Justice, 2015), it is considered a punishable offence.

8. *Giving right feedback to the students and parents:* It is very important to give the right feedback to the students and their parents. Not giving proper feedback about a student's performance is unethical. Appreciating a student for poor performance will not be beneficial for a student. Sometimes, some teachers unnecessarily become very critical about a student if they do not have a liking for them for some reason. As a result, a teacher may not give the right feedback. Parents need proper feedback so that they can take appropriate corrective measures at home while teaching to improve the child's performance.

9. *Accepting parent's feedback and/or open to new ideas or criticism:* Normally, people find it difficult to accept feedback, if it is not positive or is critical, even if it is right. A person with an open mind always welcomes any criticism, and introspects and makes an effort to change themselves. A teacher should also be open to criticism instead of being adamant. If we accept the right feedback and/or are open to criticism, there is a scope to overcome our limitations. For a teacher, it is very important to get the students' feedback which will help the teachers to decide the future styles of teaching for the benefits of the students instead of remaining with a preconceived notion.

10. *Having updated knowledge and interest to learn further:* There is no end to learning. It is a lifelong process. A teacher should also make an effort to become updated about the latest development in their subject so that, in turn, when they go to class, they can impart the latest knowledge to the students. In turn, the students feel more interested and develop a good impression about that particular teacher and are also benefitted.

11. *A teacher needs to be a good human being and the role of spirituality:* It is very important to become a good human being. A good human being with a good heart can impart knowledge with full interest effectively. A good person's presence in any social set-up is beneficial for the neighbouring community. In the educational institution also, a good teacher with advanced knowledge makes a difference in the teaching–learning process. Spirituality makes an individual think positively about others and students. A spiritual person is more committed to their profession. Therefore, arranging some special lectures in the school on values of spirituality will be beneficial for the teachers as well as for the students.

12. *The teaching mission of a teacher:* A good teacher will have a proper plan to teach students effectively. They will always be systematic in teaching with updated information so that students can follow them and, in turn, students will also become interested in the subject since they create a supportive environment. The supportive learning environment facilitates students' attitudes towards overall learning which has a very powerful influence on their attitudes towards the learning process.

10.8.2. Challenges for a Teacher

There are a number of challenges for teachers to teach in an educational institution. Poor infrastructure in terms of educational support materials, that is, non-availability of blackboard, LCD facilities, lack of essential items and reference books, poor seating arrangements, resulting in the diversion of attention of students in classroom teaching are some of the common challenges. School administration should pay attention to these challenges and make needful arrangements. There are some schools in India with more than 50 students in a classroom. Teaching a large number of students, especially young children, sometimes becomes challenging. Another challenge is addressing the diverse intellectual needs and behaviour problems of some of the students in the same class.

Lack of encouragements from the school authority and poor support system sometimes becomes demotivating factors for some teachers. Hence, the principal of a school should be sensitive and introduce a reward system for motivating the well-performing teachers.

Lack of promotion, poor salary or insecurity for being a contractual teacher are discouraging for some teachers. Sometimes, increased workload due to inadequate number of teachers and additional responsibilities demotivates them. Therefore, filling up of all the vacant posts by permanent teachers in a school is important, in addition to revising the service benefits of attracting the best talent in the school teaching profession.

In sum

The role of teachers is very important in motivating students in studies. A knowledgeable teacher with a pleasing personality, who is passionate about teaching and having teaching skills, can generate interest among students about a particular subject, for even subjects like mathematics. In some institutions, teachers also teach in difficult situations such as large class size, non-availability of audiovisual facilities, job uncertainty, that is, working as a contractual teacher, work pressure and lack of encouragement from the authority.

10.9. ROLE OF PARENTS

The role of parents in child education is very important since they are the first social agents in a child's life (Maccoby, 1992). Among both parents, the mother's role is more crucial as the child is closely monitored and brought up by her. A child's cognitive development starts in the family through interaction with mother, father, siblings and other family members. During the growing up stage, a child learns what they observe in the behaviour of family members and tries to imitate the same behaviour. Therefore, responsible behaviour among children could be inculcated from the early stage through responsible and disciplined behaviour of elderly members of a family. During early childhood development, parents should try to train the child for the formation of good habits such as having food on time, toilet training, free mingling with other children, sharing with others and social manners like how to talk and behave with others. In other words, this process of development is called socialization process. Thereafter, parents keep on guiding and supporting their children for better education, better career and to become a responsible and productive citizen. Therefore, it might be stated that parents are the first and lifelong teachers and guide for a child.

Parenting styles make a big difference in the life of children and adolescents for all-round quality care and guidance. Evidence further clearly demonstrates that along with parenting styles, parenting behaviours also play an important role in the upbringing of children and adolescents. Out of four broad categories of parenting styles, namely authoritative, authoritarian, permissive and uninvolved, authoritative parenting styles are found to be more beneficial for positive outcomes in children and adolescents (Morris et al., 2017). On the contrary, uninvolved parenting styles are found to bring out the worst in adolescent outcome (Weiss & Schwarz, 1996). So far as parenting behaviour is concerned, parental warmth and support, inductive reasoning and open parent–child communication are found to be facilitating in the positive outcome of adolescents. Different roles played by the parents during the developmental stage are described in brief in the following section.

10.9.1. SPECIFIC ROLE OF PARENTS FOR CHILDREN EDUCATION AND QUALITY UPBRINGING

Parents play an irreplaceable job in education and quality upbringing of a child. There are a few relevant concerns that the parents should ensure in order to ensure effective parenting:

1. *Parents should ensure congenial and disturbance-free family environment:* Congenial and/or disturbance-free happy family environment is prerequisite for the healthy psychological upbringing of children. Therefore, parents should be very careful to ensure tension-free family environment through exchange of smiles among themselves and in maintaining good interpersonal relationships with extended family members and neighbours. In turn, good interpersonal relationship ensures peace of mind and happiness in the family and in the neighbouring environment, which gives a sense of security and comfort to a child. In addition to this, parents should take care of other basic needs of the child, that is, adequate nutrition, medical care and safety. Nowadays, television channels engage family members to a great extent in different entertainment programmes and there is a general tendency to enjoy the programme with high volumes or, unconsciously, the TV volumes remain high which distract the attention of the students in studies. Parents should be very careful about this issue and ensure distraction-free environment during study hours. At the same time, parents should not allow their children to watch TV for a long time. Watching TV for longer duration does not give children the chance to develop their own interests in different subjects and explore on their own, because it controls the emotion of the children (Carlo et al., 2017; Den Hamer et al., 2017).
2. *Understanding child psychology by parents:* Every parent should pay attention to their child's liking and their voices, that is, what they want, like and wish to communicate. Accordingly, if parents deal with their child's needs and psychological desires, a child will develop a feeling of acceptance and, in turn, it will facilitate better parent–child understanding and strong emotional bondage. Therefore, every parent should study some literature on child psychology, that is, how to deal with children and guide them.
3. *Parents should act as role models for the child's learning:* At home, a child learns various things through activities from their parents, that is, playing together, reading together, counting together, through observation of parents' activities, which are crucial for a child when a child starts attending preschool education. In other words, it might be stated that, in a natural setting, at home, a child learns various things without any stress, and these become guiding principles for a child to follow in other social settings.
4. *Parents concern, attention and engagement in children education:* The parents who are concerned about their child's welfare and quality upbringing pay proper attention to their child's education. Paying proper attention to the child means spending quality time with them, taking interest in their studies and study-related activities, guiding them for systematic

studies and encouraging them for good habits, which include waking up on time and studying during morning and evening, during a particular time. Evidence suggests that parental engagement in different forms for child education has a positive impact on student achievement in terms of higher grades and test scores, enrolment in higher-level programmes and advanced classes, better social skills, improved behaviour, lower dropout rates, higher graduation rates and a greater likelihood of commencing tertiary education (Hill et al., 2004; Hong & Ho, 2005).

In addition, parents should spend some leisure time with children, playing games with them and discussing general issues. This style of upbringing makes the children feel responsible about their studies and other responsibilities. As parents should make their children conscious about their rights, they should also remind them about their certain responsibilities. Parents should also impart knowledge about dos and don'ts with utmost care. After putting their children in pre-primary school and even later stages, parents follow up with their children's classwork and homework in addition to teaching basic lessons at home.

5. *Parents' disciplined lifestyles:* Parents' lifestyles and good habits have a tremendous impact on the education and outlook of a child. The parents who lead a disciplined life can give quality time to their children and look after every welfare aspect of their child. Disciplined parents get up early in the morning and, throughout the day, they follow a routine systematically and children also automatically follow the same lifestyle which helps them to accomplish their day-to-day task on time, including studies. Children of disciplined parents study during particular times religiously.

6. *Parents' education, occupation and interest in studies:* The parents who are educated are able to guide their children for education better than that of the parents who are less educated or illiterate (Davis-Kean, 2005; Sebastian et al., 2017). However, it does not necessarily mean that every educated parent is interested to teach their child. There are examples where parents are not much educated, but they encourage their children for studies ensuring all required educational facilities and engaging private tutor. Hence, parents' interest is also necessary in educating children.

7. *Providing all educational support and clarifying queries of children:* Admitting a child in the best schools and providing them with all necessities are important. In the course of study, parents should sit with their child and teach them and clarify their confusion, if any. Timely teaching at home and clarification of confusion will facilitate faster progress and, in turn, this process of learning will develop special interest among children towards studies.

8. *Teaching the subject interestingly with practical examples:* When parents teach their wards at home, they should teach the subject in an interesting manner so that the child develops a special interest. Sometimes, practical examples could be cited, making some fun and/or simple games would be very interesting for children. Once the child finds interest, they will get involved in the study and that learning process will be spontaneous and joyful. While teaching a child, parents should encourage their child to come out with ideas and listen to them carefully. This approach will help a child to think about an issue and, gradually, a child's imagination power and thinking process will be stronger. There is also a need to bring down the level of parents to the level of a child for effective communication.

9. *Encouraging children for good performance and studying storybooks:* Encouraging children for good performance is extremely rewarding in motivating students in studies (Delin & Baumeister, 1994). Even if a child's performance is not good in any particular subject,

constructive criticism with encouragement is beneficial in motivating the child in the subject. Thereafter, a child will study hard to get appreciation. On the contrary, it has been observed that praising children for good performance may negatively affect children's responses to achievement situations (Mueller & Dweck, 1998). The second school of thought is of the view that if good performance by children is appreciated, thereafter, these children may become overconfident and may not study seriously resulting in underperformance.

Every parent loves their child and every parent wishes to communicate the same feelings to their child through different means. Giving small gifts on different occasions and for small achievements is very much encouraging for children. Presenting study books and books on moral values and/or books on great personalities would be more rewarding for gaining knowledge and development of moral values among children.

10. *Telling stories to children about great personalities:* Parents should tell stories about positive case studies and/or provide information about great personalities to their children. This approach would help to develop a mission in life and would also encourage them to study sincerely.

11. *Allowing children for games and extracurricular activities with other children for natural growth:* During childhood, the activity which gives maximum pleasure to a child is playing with other children. Therefore, small children should be allowed to play with other children, irrespective of their socio-economic background. This process of free mingling allows children to develop social skills which are prerequisite in later life when they go to a new environment. The children, who were allowed to mix up with other children, can cope with any new situation faster than the children who were not allowed to play with other children.

12. *Taking children on educational tours by parents:* Periodic educational tour to historical places, botanical gardens and libraries, and interaction with students from other schools enhance the practical broad-based knowledge and provide a wider outlook. Encouraging children to visit libraries will facilitate curiosity about various subjects and will make a child more confident and curious about new knowledge, which is necessary for a good mental health.

Rabindranath Tagore, a Nobel laureate from West Bengal, India, was primarily an educationist. Tagore believed in 'naturalism' for framing educational model. According to Tagore, in education, freedom is the basic guiding force for inculcating interest within a student about a subject. Through the observation of nature, a student will develop an interest in a subject. Based on this understanding, Tagore had established Shantiniketan to fulfil his desired goal of a nature-based education system.

13. *Empowering children to take their educational responsibilities:* Other than teaching their child regularly, parents should empower their child to develop a routine for study and encourage self-monitoring. In order to mark the progress of a child's study, parents should give examples and ask their child to follow the same so that, gradually, children become independent, though parents' monitoring should be a regular process. Parents should encourage their child to study the syllabus throughout the year systematically, preparing the notes on each topic, checking the notes, writing periodic tests at home and, finally, emphasizing the need for revision of the syllabus. Reading loudly is the best option for faster learning, retention and recognition.

14. *Parents should visit the school and enquire about child progress and any challenges:* In addition to teaching and guiding children at home, parents should visit the school to enquire about the child's performance and/or any challenges. Based on the teacher's feedback, parents can

think of adopting appropriate strategies for guiding children in the right direction for better performance and improved interpersonal relationships.

15. *Parents need to pay attention to the child's safety and balanced nutrition:* During the development phase, parents need to take care of the basic needs of their children. They should also be very careful about the safety of their child at home and in the educational institution. Therefore, parents should discuss with their child the nature of violence they might experience and what the child should do if they encounter the same challenge. CP, sexual abuse and poor teaching are the common challenges a child might experience. If parents appoint a private tutor, the performance of the private tutor should be monitored instead of depending upon them blindly. From time to time, parents should also enquire if they see that their child is withdrawn and/or inattentive.

16. *Parents need to provide balanced love and affection:* As for healthy physical development, a child needs a balanced diet. Parents should provide balanced love and affection for keeping them on track. Overindulgence may cause problems for a child; strict and/or indifferent attitude towards a child is also not good. A child should feel that they are very much wanted and parents should teach them to behave properly and nicely to others and be particular about their day-to-day activities, including studies.

17. *Encouraging child interest-oriented learning methods:* Learning methods vary from child to child. In a house, two siblings follow two different styles of learning and both of them might be successful. Therefore, it would be better not to force a child to follow the learning method of another child. They might be encouraged to follow the method of learning of another child. If they adopt it, it is fine. Otherwise, a child should be encouraged to follow their own style of learning.

18. *Parents' learning habit:* Parents should observe when children are studying. Their learning habit will teach a child to study every day at a particular time and will also develop interest among them to study a new subject. Parents should appreciate the progress of their child's study and reward them for good performance. Reward should be in terms of presenting a new storybook or any other educational item, which will be encouraging for a child.

19. *Monitoring children activities:* Parents should monitor their children's activities to ensure that they do not waste much time playing online games and/or video games. If parents find that their child is spending more time playing online or video games, they should intervene sensitively and fix the time limit for this type of games.

10.9.2. Challenges/Obstructions in the Family for Child's Learning

Challenges and obstructions in the family can have a detrimental impact on the learning process of the child:

1. *Mental illness of parents:* Parents with mental health challenges fail to provide minimum care to their children. As a result, children remain unattended and also feel insecure. These children require support from the extended family members for their education (Leijdesdorff et al., 2017; Stallard et al., 2004). Some of the common challenges faced by the children of those parents include (a) blaming self for their parents' difficulties, and experiencing anger,

anxiety or guilt; (b) feeling embarrassed or ashamed as a result of the stigma associated with their parents' mental illness; (c) social isolation and/or discrimination on account of parents' mental illness; (d) increased risk of facing challenges at school; (e) vulnerability to become dependent on drugs under peer group influence when parents support is missing and (f) vulnerability to depression and demotivation in studies.

2. *Parental indifferent attitude to child education:* Unfortunately, a large number of parents with low levels of education do not give value to education because of their compulsive situation, that is, poverty. To them, the immediate need is very important, which is arranging money for daily needs. As a result, rural parents, especially parents living BPL, prefer to engage their children in family agricultural activities or childcare, for looking after younger ones when they go to the field or outside for work. First-hand experience of the author says that rural people often refer to unemployment issues and raise a question about the value of education.

3. *Parental indulgence:* Some parents, especially parents with easy source of money, give more pocket expenses to their children to show their deep love for their children without realizing that more money might urge their ward in a negative direction. Additional money will lead them to unnecessary purchases of different items and will deviate them from education to other directions. As a result, some children get spoiled easily because of overindulgence by the parents.

4. *Parents dependence on substance:* Evidence indicates that the parents who are dependent on substances fail to play their responsible role for quality upbringing of their children in terms of care and guidance for child education, providing timely nutrition and ensuring other support as and when they require. In turn, this environment demotivates children to study effectively. The findings of the previous studies highlight that children of substance-abusing parents are vulnerable to developing physical, emotional and behavioural problems (Kilpatrick et al., 2000; Peleg-Oren & Teichman, 2006). Therefore, substance-dependent parents need immediate attention for de-addiction and rehabilitation with the help of extended family members and friends.

5. *Disciplining children following harsh method:* Some parents are impulsive and/or short-tempered. Without providing quality time to their child and supervising and guiding their studies, they develop over expectation from their child. Even some parents set a target to their child, that is, a child has to get 95 per cent and above, otherwise they will be punished. Sometimes, parents apply harsh punishment which is highly demoralizing for a child. Evidence clearly indicates that parental CP is positively associated with children's behavioural and mental health problems (Deb et al., 2017; Lansford, 2017).

In sum

Like teachers, the role of parents in the child's education is equally important. Parents should provide the basic facilities, should be child friendly and should spend quality time with them and listen to them patiently. Parents should also ensure a happy family environment and clarify their confusion related to all academic issues and supervise their studies closely. There are some constraints in some families which adversely affect the children, such as mental health challenges of parents causing neglect, parent's dependence on substances, family violence and harsh disciplining methods for which parents should consult psychologists to resolve the issues for the interest of the children.

10.10. INTERVENTION IN SCHOOL

There is an urgent need to recruit professional psychologists in every school, proportionate to students so that they can deliver a range of quality services. Broadly, the nature of services of a psychologist includes conducting sensitization programmes, addressing issues related to the stress of the students and other challenges faced by the students. A range of social, emotional and behaviour programmes is needed for addressing various problems of students to enhance their psychological competence and skills for dealing with daily life challenges and academic demands (Sklad et al., 2012). A brief account of the services of psychologists is provided further.

10.10.1. SENSITIZATION PROGRAMME FOR PARENTS, TEACHERS AND STUDENTS

The role of parents for quality upbringing of children is very important. Some parents do provide quality care and supervise the education of their children, while some are indifferent or lack parenting skills. Therefore, sensitization of parents about various issues for ensuring quality parenting and support to children is essential through school-based intervention programmes.

A good number of teachers also need inputs to become student-friendly and teaching effectively based on students' feedback. The authorities of very few schools in India make an effort to gather students' feedback about teaching methods and the challenges faced by them in the school. Therefore, sensitization programmes for school authorities and teachers about student issues such as quality of teaching, abuse and neglect experienced, common childhood disorders such as LD, autism, intellectual disability and ADHD would be immensely beneficial for taking needful measures and in providing quality education and creating positive schooling ambience.

Like parents and teachers, sensitization programmes in terms of group counselling are needed for students to make them aware about some of the important issues such as health and hygiene, reproductive health and child rights so that they become more resilient and/or more psychologically competent to deal with different situations in life.

A section of students does manifest externalizing behaviour, that is, aggression and hurting or disturbing other students. Some even disturb the teachers in the classroom, while some get pleasure violating the school norms, that is, not coming to school on time or without school uniform. The children with conduct disorder normally come from disturbed family environments. They require special intervention in order to change their behaviour and engage them in studies. Cognitive behaviour therapy and social skills training are found to be beneficial for changing the behaviour of adolescents with conduct disorder, including emotional disorder (Kaufman et al., 2005; Maag, 2006).

10.10.2. MENTAL HEALTH SUPPORT SERVICES

As discussed before, students experience a range of challenges such as academic load, stress, harsh disciplining methods, adjustment problems, anxiety and depression, which require support services by a trained psychologist in a sensitive manner. In order to deliver professional psychological support services, individual and group counselling play an important role in enhancing their resilience capacity, in addition to behaviour therapy, cognitive behaviour therapy and family therapy. The objective of individual counselling is to address the sensitive issues of the students by maintaining confidentiality, while group counselling is aimed to address common issues of the students. Therefore, every school should recruit trained psychologists to deal with student's issues and challenges, and other related issues.

A meta-analysis study found that, for addressing depression and anxiety of school students, mostly cognitive behaviour therapy, interpersonal therapy or psycho-education were followed. Most were associated with short-term improvements or symptom reduction at follow-up (Neil & Christensen, 2007). However, there is a need to examine the long-term impact of all these psychological intervention programmes to reduce anxiety and depression among school students.

10.10.3. EXTRACURRICULAR ACTIVITIES, GAMES AND SPORTS

Children get maximum pleasure out of extracurricular activities, and games and sports. Sufficient evidence is available about the benefits of extracurricular activities including games and sports for holistic growth and development of children. These activities help children to become rejuvenated to study hard. In some schools, children enjoy extracurricular activities though for limited periods, while in some schools, authorities engage children in studies ignoring extracurricular activities and sports. It requires strict instruction from the school policymakers and they should monitor the situation periodically.

10.10.4. STUDENTS' PROTECTION COMMITTEE

Every school should have a Students' Protection Committee comprising teachers, school administrators, students' representative and an NGO representative and they should meet periodically to discuss issues related to students and come out with solutions.

10.10.5. SPECIAL LECTURE FOR ACADEMIC MOTIVATION AND SPECIAL CLASS FOR BACKWARD STUDENTS

Motivation of students in studies varies. Some are self-motivated, while some need inputs and/or continuous encouragements for better academic performance. Therefore, special lectures by psychologists or educationists as to how to prepare for examinations would be beneficial to motivate the students in studies. Encouraging words and clarifying the queries of the students, especially about mathematics, physics and chemistry, are needed.

Some students are a little intellectually backward, they need special coaching in the school after the school hours for clarification of their queries. If school authorities are able to arrange special classes for those students who have some queries or confusion about any content, it would benefit them.

10.10.6. HEALTH CAMP IN THE SCHOOLS

A periodic health camp is a must in all the schools for health check-ups during the formative years of children. Some children suffer from vision problems while some from anaemia and others suffer from some other problems. Periodic health check-ups would help to diagnose the health problem and take appropriate measures. In addition, preventive measures about some health problems should be adopted through sensitization programmes in the schools.

10.10.7. Educational Tour

Periodic educational tours such as visiting a science museum, botanical garden, library and a place of historical importance and other higher learning institutes need to be arranged in every school to give exposure to the students. Educational tours are highly motivating for students and they develop some vision about life.

10.10.8. Redressal System

Every school should have students' redressal system as per the Right to Education Act, 2012, and the Juvenile Justice (Care and Protection of Children) Act, 2015. These two laws particularly protect the interest of the children in addition to other legislative measures and social policies. If any student experiences CP and/or sexual abuse, they should be encouraged to report the incident to the school authority. In turn, the school authority should take immediate measures for the protection of rights of the children. Otherwise, parents can take up the issue with the higher school authority.

10.10.9. Research and Documentation

In order to understand the efficacy of various school-based intervention programmes, there is a need to carry out research from time to time and, accordingly, inputs should be given to the school authorities for translating the findings into action.

In sum

School-based intervention programmes are prerequisite for ensuring positive schooling environment. Sensitization programme for parents, teachers and students on various important issues such as quality parenting, effective teaching methods, child psychology, life skills development and child rights would help them to realize their roles and responsibilities. Other school-based intervention programmes include mental health support facilities for students and other staff by trained psychologists, periodic health check-ups, establishing a Students' Protection Committee, arranging educational tours, games and sports for students, special lecture for motivating students and arrangement of special classes for disadvantaged children and redressal mechanism.

10.11. RECOMMENDATIONS FOR TEACHERS, PARENTS, STUDENT COUNSELLORS/PSYCHOLOGISTS AND POLICYMAKERS

In order to address academic stress and other related issues, teachers, parents and students should be brought under the purview of intervention programmes. The following steps are proposed for different stakeholders, including education policymakers, based on evidence and personal experience.

10.11.1. For Parents

Recommendations for parents are as follows:

- Developing friendly relationship with children so that they feel comfortable and are able to open up and speak their mind while addressing their issues. Parents need to strike a balance between love and discipline, that is, not giving indulgence or not becoming too strict.
- Giving quality time to children, ensuring conducive family environment, providing adequate facilities for study, clarifying their confusion about any academic issue, supervising their studies closely and encouraging them even for small achievements.
- Visiting the educational institution and/or attending the parent–teacher meeting in the educational institution to enquire about academic progress of the children and deciding the future stream of study in discussion with the child, considering their aptitude, interest and future prospect into account.
- Restrain from any form of child abuse, since it is a violation of child rights as per the UNCRC (United Nations, 1989).
- Giving frequent and timely feedback to the child, both positive and negative, in a constructive manner so that they can take appropriate measures for future studies and this process will enhance the self-confidence of the child.
- Nurturing children's self-worth, competence, autonomy and self-efficacy. Providing freedom to children to engage in academically challenging pursuits. One must not hesitate to consult a psychologist or psychiatrist if they witness any unusual behaviour in the child.

10.11.2. For Teachers

Recommendations for teachers are as follows:

- Remember that every child is unique and potent. Therefore, while teaching, efforts should be made to address the queries of all the students in a class.
- Do not apply CP for correcting and/or modifying the behaviour of a student. Child maltreatment in any form, namely psychological, physical and sexual, has far-reaching negative effects on mental health, personality, social adjustment and career development of the students. Rather, think of some other strategy to motivate students for better academic performance.
- After teaching a subject in the class, ask students in a friendly manner whether they have understood the same and then explain the same subject in simple language, if required. Do not give too much pressure for better academic performance.
- Teaching subjects throughout the year in a systematic manner is important so that students can complete the course in time and revise the same properly.
- Introducing reward system for motivating students for better performance in such a way so that others do not feel demotivated and at the same time they become more sincere and perform well.
- Encouraging students to actively participate in classroom activities. Participation enhances their self-confidence and self-esteem and develops teamwork.

- Incorporating a variety of teaching activities such as role-play, brainstorming, discussions, demonstrations and audiovisual presentation. Reassuring students that they can do better if they try. Continuous encouragement from the teachers could be rewarding for improving the performance of the students.
- Be enthusiastic in the classroom. A teacher's enthusiasm is a crucial factor in student motivation.
- Students must be given feedback about their performance at the right time. It is necessary to be specific when giving negative feedback. The student's weakness needs to be addressed not in front of other students.
- Avoiding demeaning comments about a student in the classroom. Students are influenced more by positive comments than by negative comments. A smile, a pat, addressing by name, saying 'very good' and so on motivate students.
- Help the students develop systematic habits. Preparation of timetable, fixing a place to study, time management, taking notes and completing everyday assignments are skills that need to be inculcated in students.

10.11.3. School Authorities

WHO's health-promoting school model talks about an integrated approach to health and has been implemented widely in the developed countries. However, school-based interventions must address a number of domains after carrying out a need assessment such as (a) strategies for dealing with violence in the educational institutions (perpetrator and experience), including addressing gender issues; (b) strategies for preventing, acknowledging and seeking help for mental disorders such as depression, anxiety and suicidal behaviours; (c) strategies for prevention of tobacco and alcohol use and (d) strategies for addressing learning difficulties and disabilities. The authorities of educational institutions should address the following issues:

- Be careful while recruiting permanent and contractual teaching staff. Under no circumstances should a single incompetent candidate be recruited for teaching.
- Monitoring teaching methods closely and giving feedback to the respective teachers, if required, in such a manner that teachers take up teaching job more seriously.
- Adopting a 'student protection policy' for creating a student-friendly environment in the educational institutions. Student protection policy in the school should comprise teachers, parents, student's representative, legal professionals and social activists.
- Organizing meaningful parent–teacher meeting periodically, that is, once every month, to give feedback about the students to their parents/guardians.
- Organizing short-term workshops for the teachers to reorient them about effective teaching methods and to update them about the latest advancement in the respective subjects, so that they can teach more effectively.
- Recruiting student counsellors or psychologists in every school to deal with behavioural and emotional problems of the students and develop motivation in them for better academic performance.
- Organizing workshop on life skill development in every school for the students to prepare them to cope with stressful situations in life including academic stress.
- Sensitizing parents and teachers about the need and importance of students' mental health and carry out necessary actions to address the issues at the school level.

10.11.4. Role of Psychologists at Schools

The role of psychologists in a school is very important in order to identify the students with some problems. It could be LD or any other childhood disorders. Early identification of childhood disorders normally helps in improving the situation and thereby helps the children to lead a better life. School psychologists can sensitize the teachers to act as a mentor to the students (Sedlak, 1993). Further, psychologist's role is also very important to design and extend mental health support services to the abused and maltreated students and students with academic stress in a school (Phasha, 2008). School psychologists focus on the psychosocial, developmental and cultural factors that facilitate or interfere with student's positive functioning, choice of attitudinal and motivational patterns, use of best-fit strategies and least use of interventions-needed approach. To address the targeted behavioural and emotional problems of today's youth, for example, school avoidance, dropout behaviour, academic stress, substance abuse, gang activity, teenage pregnancies and suicidal ideation, a wide range of professional expertise is needed, with mechanisms for case coordination, ongoing consultation and programme development for action planning, along with quality assurance advocacy. There may be also a focus on health education, with mental health services and guidance, to reiterate and focus the need for primary prevention.

10.11.5. Policymakers

There is an urgent need to relook at the present curriculum and modify the same, keeping the issue of relevance into account. Second, there is a need to bring uniformity in curriculum across the country, whether state board or CBSE. Third, there is a need to critically examine the present evaluation system of students' performance, considering the latest global assessment trend into account. Fourth, promoting research and encouraging the academics and researchers to take up more research to understand the effectiveness of different programmes taken up by the federal government and central school boards for the welfare of the students should be done.

10.11.6. Guidelines for Students for Systematic Study and for Exam Preparation

Students need guidance from the parents and teachers for systematic study. Some students do get guidance while some do not. Following are the guidelines for systematic preparation throughout the year for better performance: (a) students should develop their own timetable for study at home, keeping their other commitments in mind; (b) from the very first day of an academic session, students should engage themselves in studies, attending all the scheduled classes in the school on time, study all the subjects, irrespective of whether a particular class was conducted in the school or not. While attending the class, students should take the notes of important points being taught in the class. Consulting the textbooks, class notes and other related study materials, the students should prepare their own notes; (c) students should read the chapter of the textbook first, thoroughly, a number of times, prior to attending the classes. This approach will help them to understand the subject easily when the teacher teaches it. During the class, if any point is not clear, students should get the issue clarified with the teacher instead of suppressing the query, thinking about what others will interpret about their gesture. If necessary, they should consult a knowledgeable person or get information from the internet. After returning from the school, students should take rest for some time and then study the subjects which were discussed in the school, thoroughly, with full attention; (d) if students face any challenge related to study or any other issue, they should share the same with the parents instead of suppressing the issue. Otherwise, this challenge might be a barrier for focusing attention in future classes; (e) every day, students should study on time as per their timetable and study with full concentration in a room which is totally distraction-free, namely no sound, no music, no television, no mobile phone and so on; (f) one should develop a habit of studying on their own in the same way as one loves to play with their friends spontaneously; (g) do not try to memorize the subject in one attempt. First, one should read a chapter a number of times, understand the meaning and then one should attempt to memorize the subject question wise. This process might require more than two–three attempts and even more for some students. After the full understanding of a chapter, students should develop their own notes, considering notes taken during the class and consulting more than one book, as discussed before and get it checked by an experienced person. Thereafter, students should attempt to memorize some of the important questions. Student, should also practise writing answers on their own. If a student understands the concept, they can answer any question even if they do not memorize the same. After completion of one chapter, students should read the next chapter following the same process. In between, one should revise the previous chapter and important questions and write them along while reading the subsequent chapters; (h) one should not study one subject for a long period. After studying one subject for about 1–2 hours, one should read another subject, taking a small break in between for relaxation. This process would cause less stress; (i) every day, one should go for some physical exercise or extracurricular activities for relaxation and take balanced diet and should not involve oneself in internet gaming or mobile for a long time. Students should also read individual interest-oriented storybooks/novels for mental refreshment; (j) prior to every exam, students should practise the previous year's question papers and write mock tests at least twice, arranged by the schoolteachers or by parents at home. This process will help students to understand their weakness, time management and prepare them accordingly. In turn, this approach will help them remain stress-free, in addition to giving them more confidence for writing the final exam and (k) the guidelines, as suggested earlier, for effective study would be interesting, enjoyable and stress-free for school students if they engage themselves in the study spontaneously from the beginning of an academic session and study meaningfully throughout the year with full concentration and keep themselves away from all distractions to the best extent possible. Following this approach, academic stress could be converted to joyful learning.

10.12. A CONCEPTUAL MODEL FOR WELFARE AND WELL-BEING OF STUDENTS

In order to impart quality education, a school should have a safe and supportive environment in addition to good administration and qualified teachers with passion for teaching and skills. In addition, a school should have a Students' Protection Committee for addressing students issues and reward system for motivating students for good performance. A school should also have a mental health professional for taking care of mental health issues of the students and motivate them in

FIGURE 10.1
Depicting the Positive Outcome of Encouraging and Supportive School Environment

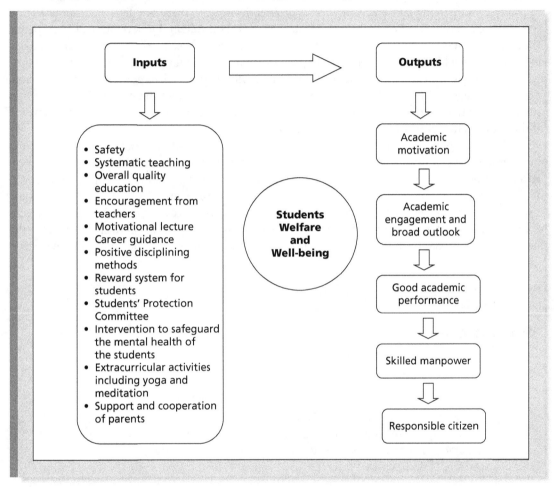

studies through various extracurricular activities. In turn, it is expected that positive schooling environment will have good positive outcome in terms of producing skilled and responsible manpower for nation building. Positive outcome of encouraging and supportive school environment is depicted in Figure 10.1.

10.13. CONCLUSION AND IMPLICATIONS

Education helps an individual to lead a quality and meaningful life, adjusting with all social agents and contributing to the society. Therefore, every child should attend school, be motivated to study sincerely and their issues and challenges should be addressed sensitively through school-based intervention programmes. The role of parents and teachers is very important in the child's education, moral and social development, good habit formation and career growth. Parents and teachers should be sensitive to children's needs and they need to listen to their voices. In addition to guiding children for study, both parents and teachers should be friendly so that there is effective communication between them. Primary school teachers can play an important role in the development of students. They are often the sole source of a student's learning experience. What students learn at the primary- and middle-school levels can shape how they are in the future. Finally, the teachers should play the role of a caregiver in the classroom in terms of providing physical, emotional and intellectual support for students in various capacities. Systematic study throughout the year under the care and guidance of parents and teachers will definitely reduce the academic stress and examination anxiety of the students to a great extent, prior to the examination.

Quality education, addressing students' issues and challenges and promoting positive schooling environment have multiple implications. First, students will enjoy the education and will perform better if school environment is safe and supportive. Second, good performance of the students will help them secure admission in reputed higher learning institutes and, in turn, they will become responsible and skilled manpower resources and contribute towards national growth and development. Third, the number of crimes as well as health expenditure will decrease. Finally, the family will be very happy looking at the positive role of their child within the family and in society.

EXERCISES

One-mark Questions

1. What is the objective of education?
2. Define academic stress.
3. What do you mean by CP?
4. Define examination anxiety.
5. Are extracurricular activities beneficial for students? Why?
6. What is the role of a Students' Protection Committee in schools?
7. Which method of learning is beneficial, part learning or whole learning?
8. How can school dropouts be prevented?
9. How can you ensure safety in school?
10. What is the objective of the Right to Education Act, 2012?

Five-mark Questions

1. What is the impact of academic stress?
2. Elaborate upon the risk factors for mental health challenges of school students.
3. Discuss the role of teachers in imparting values among students.
4. Is teaching method important for imparting knowledge among students? Justify your answer.
5. What are the challenges faced by the teachers while teaching? Discuss.

Ten-mark Questions

1. Discuss with examples the challenges faced by students in schools.
2. How do you motivate students in studies? Discuss the methods of preparation before the examination.

3. Discuss the role of parents in quality child upbringing.
4. Is the role of a psychologist important in a school? Justify your answer.

Reflexive Questions

1. Is it necessary to revise school curriculum every five years? Justify your answer.
2. How do you ensure quality education in schools? Discuss.

REFERENCES

Ang, R. P., & Huan, V. S. (2006). Relationship between academic stress and suicidal ideation: Testing for depression as a mediator using multiple regression. *Child Psychiatry & Human Development*, 37(2), 133–143.

Arun, P., & Chavan, B. S. (2009). Stress and suicidal ideas in adolescent students in Chandigarh. *Indian Journal of Medical Sciences*, 63(7), 281–287.

Bjorkman, S. M. (2007). *Relationships among academic stress, social support, and internalizing and externalizing behavior in adolescence* (PhD dissertation, Northern Illinois University), United States. Publication No. AAT 3279173.

Carlo, G., White, R., Streit, C., Knight, G. P., & Zeiders, K. H. (2017). Longitudinal relations among parenting styles, prosocial behaviors, and academic outcomes in US Mexican adolescents. *Child Development*. doi:10.1111/cdev.12761

Davis-Kean, P. E. (2005). The influence of parent education and family income on child achievement: The indirect role of parental expectations and the home environment. *Journal of Family Psychology*, 19(2), 294.

Deb, S., & Bhattacharya, B. (2012). Relationships between parental pressure for better academic performance and mental health variables of adolescents of 11th and 12th standard. *International Journal of Education and Management Studies*, 2(1), 1–6.

Deb, S., Chatterjee, P., & Walsh, K. M. (2010). Anxiety among high school students in India: Comparisons across gender, school type, social strata, and perceptions of quality time with parents. *Australian Journal of Educational and Developmental Psychology*, 10(1), 18–31.

Deb, S., Kumar, A., Holden, W. G., & Rowe, L. S. (2017). School corporal punishment, family tension, and student's internalizing problems: Evidence from India. *School Psychology International*, 38(1), 60–77.

Deb, S., Majumdar, B., & Sun, J. (2011). *Academic stress, parental pressure, anxiety and mental health among Indian school students.* Paper presented at the International Conference on Students' Mental Health: Issues and Challenges, 25–26 July 2011, Puducherry, India.

Delin, C. R., & Baumeister, R. E. (1994). Praise: More than just social reinforcement. *Journal for the Theory of Social Behaviour*, 24(3), 219–241.

Den Hamer, A. H., Konijn, E. A., & Bushman, B. J. (2017). Measuring exposure to media with antisocial and prosocial content: An extended version of the content-based media exposure scale (C-ME2). *Communication Methods and Measures*, 11(4), 289–299.

Duarte, C. C. H., Berganza, C., Bordin, I., Bird, H., & Miranda, C.T. (2003). Child mental health in Latin America: Present and future epidemiologic research. *International Journal of Psychiatry in Medicine*, 33(3), 203–222.

Dumont, M., & Provost, M. A. (1999). Resilience in adolescents: Protective role of social support, coping strategies, self-esteem, and social activities of experience of stress and depression. *Journal of Youth and Adolescence*, 28(3), 343–363.

Feinstein, S., & Mwahombela, L. (2010). Corporal punishment in Tanzania's schools. *International Review of Education*, 56(4), 399–410.

Gallegos, J., Langley, A., & Villegas, D. (2012). Anxiety, depression, and coping skills among Mexican school children: A comparison of students with and without learning disabilities. *Learning Disability Quarterly*, 35(1), 54–61.

Hill, N. E., Castellino, D. R., Lansford, J. E., Nowlin, P., Dodge, K. A., Bates, J. E., & Pettit, G. S. (2004). Parent academic involvement as related to school behavior, achievement, and aspirations: Demographic variations across adolescence. *Child Development*, *75*(5), 1491–1509.

Hilsman, R., & Garber, J. (1995). A test of the cognitive diathesis-stress model of depression in children: Academic stressors, attributional style, perceived competence, and control. *Journal of Personality and Social Psychology*, *69*(2), 370–380.

Hirsch, B. J., & DuBois, D. L. (1992). The relation of peer social support and psychological symptomology during the transition of junior high school: A two-year longitudinal analysis. *American Journal of Community Psychology*, *20*(3), 333–347.

Hong, S., & Ho, H. Z. (2005). Direct and indirect longitudinal effects of parental involvement on student achievement: Second-order latent growth modeling across ethnic groups. *Journal of Educational Psychology*, *97*(1), 32.

Kaslow, N. J., Rehm, L. P., & Siegel, A. W. (1984). Social-cognitive and cognitive correlates of depression in children. *Journal of Abnormal Child Psychology*, *12*(4), 605–620.

Kaufman, N. K., Rohde, P., Seeley, J. R., Clarke, G. N., & Stice, E. (2005). Potential mediators of cognitive-behavioral therapy for adolescents with comorbid major depression and conduct disorder. *Journal of Consulting and Clinical Psychology*, *73*(1), 38.

Kellam, S. G., Brown, C. H., Rubin, B. R., & Ensminger, M. E. (1983). Paths leading to teenage psychiatric symptoms and substance use: Developmental epidemiological studies in Woodlawn. In S. B. Guze, F. J. Earls, & J. E. Barrett (Eds.), *Childhood psychopathology and development* (pp. 17–55). Raven Press.

Kilpatrick, D. G., Acierno, R., Saunders, B., Resnick, H. S., Best, C. L., & Schnurr, P. P. (2000). Risk factors for adolescent substance abuse and dependence: Data from a national sample. *Journal of Consulting Clinical Psychology*, *68*(1), 19–30.

Kouzma, N. M., & Kennedy, G. A. (2004). Self-reported sources of stress in senior high school students. *Psychological Reports*, *94*(1), 314–316.

Lansford, J. E. (2017). Family and cultural contexts of parental discipline and children's adjustment: Introduction to the special section. *International Journal of Behavioral Development*. https://doi.org/10.1177/0165025417708343

Lee, M., & Larson, R. (2000). The Korean 'examination hell': Long hours of studying, distress, and depression. *Journal of Youth and Adolescence*, *29*(2), 249–272.

Leijdesdorff, S., van Doesum, K., Popma, A., Klaassen, R., & van Amelsvoort, T. (2017). Prevalence of psychopathology in children of parents with mental illness and/or addiction: An up to date narrative review. *Current Opinion in Psychiatry*, *30*(4), 312–317.

Leinonen, J. A., Solantaus, T. S., & Punamaki, R. L. (2003). Parental mental health and children's adjustment: The quality of marital interaction and parenting as mediating factors. *Journal of Child Psychology Psychiatry*, *44*(2), 227–241.

Li, J.-H., Feng, X.-L., Mei, S.-L., & Yao, D.-L. (2007). Investigation of study pressure effects on mental health of junior high school students in Changchun. *Medicine and Society*, *20*(2), 56–57.

Maag, J. W. (2006). Social skills training for students with emotional and behavioral disorders: A review of reviews. *Behavioral Disorders*, *32*(1), 4–17.

Maccoby, E. E. (1992). The role of parents in the socialization of children: An historical overview. *Developmental Psychology*, *28*(6), 1006.

MHRD. (2009). *The Right of Children to Free and Compulsory Education Act*. Author.

Ministry of Home Affairs, Government of India. (2015). *Crime in India report 2000*. Author.

Ministry of Law and Justice. (2015). *The Juvenile Justice (Care and Protection of Children) Act, 2000*. Author.

Morris, A. S., Criss, M. M., Silk, J. S., & Houltberg, B. J. (2017). The impact of parenting on emotion regulation during childhood and adolescence. *Child Development Perspectives*. doi:10.1111/cdep.12238

Mueller, C. M., & Dweck, C. S. (1998). Praise for intelligence can undermine children's motivation and performance. *Journal of Personality and Social Psychology*, *75*(1), 33.

Neil, A. L., & Christensen, H. (2007). Australian school-based prevention and early intervention programs for anxiety and depression: A systematic review. *Medical Journal of Australia*, *186*(6), 305–308.

Obot, I. S. A., & James, C. (2004). Mental health problems in adolescent children of alcohol dependent parents; Epidemiologic research with a nationally representative sample. *Journal of Child & Adolescent Substance Abuse*, *13*(4), 83–96.

Patel, V., Alan J. F., Sarah, H., & Patrick, M. (2007). Mental health of young people: A global public health challenge. *The Lancet*, 29–40.

Patel, V., & Kleinman, A. (2003). Poverty and common mental disorders in developing countries. *Bulletin of the World Health Organization*, 81(8), 609–615.

Peleg-Oren, N., & Teichman, M. (2006). Young children of parents with substance use disorders (SUD): A review of the literature and implications for social work practice. *Journal of Social Work Practice in the Addictions*, 6(1–2), 49–61.

Phasha, T. N. (2008). The role of the teacher in helping learners overcome the negative impact of child sexual abuse: A South African perspective. *School Psychology International*, 29(3), 303–327.

Rangaswamy, K. (1982). Tension headache in adolescents. *Journal of Psychological Researchers*, 26(2), 70–72.

Sebastian, J., Moon, J. M., & Cunningham, M. (2017). The relationship of school-based parental involvement with student achievement: A comparison of principal and parent survey reports from PISA 2012. *Educational Studies*, 43(2), 123–146.

Sedlak, A. J. (1993). *Estimating the national prevalence of child abuse from sentinel data*. American Statistical Association.

Shah, B. (1991). Adolescents' school adjustment: The effect of family climate. *Indian Educational Review*, 26(1), 88–95.

Sklad, M., Diekstra, R., Ritter, M. D., Ben, J., & Gravesteijn, C. (2012). Effectiveness of school-based universal social, emotional, and behavioral programs: Do they enhance students' development in the area of skill, behavior, and adjustment? *Psychology in the Schools*, 49(9), 892–909.

Stallard, P., Norman, P., Huline-Dickens, S., Salter, E., & Cribb, J. (2004). The effects of parental mental illness upon children: A descriptive study of the views of parents and children. *Clinical Child Psychology and Psychiatry*, 9(1), 39–52.

Sun, J. (2011). *Educational stress among Chinese adolescents: Measurement, risk factors and associations with mental health* (Unpublished doctoral dissertation, submitted to the School of Public Health, Queensland University of Technology), Brisbane, Australia.

United Nations. (1989). *Convention on the rights of the child*. https://www.ohchr.org/en/professionalinterest/pages/crc.aspx

Verma, S., & Gupta, J. (1990). Some aspects of high academic stress and symptoms. *Journal of Personality and Clinical Studies*, 6(1), 7–12.

Verma, S., & Singh, M. B. (1998). Perceived causes of behavior problems among Indian adolescents. *Psycholingua*, 28(2), 151–158.

Weiss, L. H., & Schwarz, J. C. (1996). The relationship between parenting types and older adolescents' personality, academic achievement, adjustment, and substance use. *Child Development*, 67(5), 2101–2114.

RECOMMENDED READINGS

Bowen, J., Jenson, W. R., & Clark, E. (2003). *School-based interventions for students with behavior problems*. Springer Science & Business Media.

Deb, S. (2018). Positive schooling: Concept, characteristics, situation analysis and implications. In S. Deb (Ed.), *Positive schooling and child development* (pp. 1–26). Springer.

Doll, B., & Cummings, J. A. (Eds.). (2007). *Transforming school mental health services: Population-based approaches to promoting the competency and wellness of children*. Corwin Press.

Sandoval, J. H. (Ed.). (2001). *Handbook of crisis counseling, intervention, and prevention in the schools*. Routledge.

PART C
Research and Practice

Understanding and Supporting Community

- Use of research methodologies in community psychology
- Importance of qualitative and quantitative data collection methods
- Role of culture and its implications
- Implementation of community-based programmes
- Implications of the global community

ABSTRACT

This chapter deals with the nuances of community research and practices. The developmental trajectory in the field of community psychology, in different parts of the world, has been traced here to have a better understanding of the same in the Indian scenario. The relatively nascent discipline of community psychology boasts of unique methodological stances in addressing different community issues. The use of both qualitative and quantitative research paradigms has been detailed. They may be used either singularly or in a mixed research modality to address varied societal issues. The significance of culture has also been stressed in the chapter to provide a contextual bearing on community psychology. The need for community programme designs along with community programme evaluation has been clarified by the authors. The current status of the discipline, which is heading towards a global community, has also been stressed and its implications discussed.

Keywords: Research methods; qualitative methods; quantitative methods; programme development; programme evaluation; global community

11.1. INTRODUCTION

Community-based research is needed for a better understanding of issues and challenges affecting the people of all age groups in a community. There is a strong influence of cultural beliefs and practices on the well-being and quality of life of common people, with respect to various issues that also require investigation, in order to bring a change in the outlook of the common people. The ultimate objective of community-based research is to improve the quality of life of people so that every individual enjoys their life as long as they survive, by maintaining good interpersonal relationships with family members and significant others and remaining productive, and their presence in the community becomes meaningful.

Community psychologists rely on empirical answers, systematic observation and measurement. Actions of all individuals are based on research findings, and research is used to understand the impact of those actions. Community-based research provides evidence collected from the field through observation and via the interaction of the community members with the policymakers, for taking appropriate measures at the local, regional and national levels. Community psychologists find it important that they must share control with the community members to enhance the knowledge gained from research. A good community research design along with a collaborative equation with the community can produce greater insight into community behaviour at large, which may not be available otherwise. Both community members and community professionals, in the form of community psychologists, plan and implement research in the community at large.

New methodologies of research have been found to be appropriate, for community psychology in particular, since its inception from the Swampscott Conference. This is due to traditional laboratory methods favoured by psychologists, which have been found to be less suitable to study people's behaviour in social and cultural contexts. Most research in community psychology bank on certain principles which have been narrated in the following section.

11.1.1. PRINCIPLES IN RESEARCH ON COMMUNITY PSYCHOLOGY

Research on community psychology should be guided by established principles and hence this session is dedicated to discuss in brief, some of the important principles in research on community psychology

1. *Research embodies social values:* Community psychology is intricately related to the value of the research, along with action, for bringing about advancement in society. For this, several values need to be internalized, namely citizen participation and collaboration, social justice, respect for human diversity and search for community strengths. This is expected to help address different social issues to help arrive at a global community.

   The fundamental values and assumptions in community research essentially bank on three different philosophies of science. It is to be noted that one's beliefs about what scientific knowledge is, through what methods it is obtained and how it is related to action constitute the *philosophy of science*. Each philosophy involves a family of related perspectives, and not just any single school of thought (Campbell & Wasco, 2000; Nelson & Prilleltensky, 2005). Table 11.1 discusses the different philosophies of science for community psychology research.

Table 11.1
Different Philosophies of Science for Community Psychology Research

Philosophy of Scientific Discipline	Epistemology and Psychological Stance	Methodological
Post-positivist (A critique of positivism)	Knowledge is derived from field observation and in interaction with the community.	Cause-and-effect relationships, hypothesis-testing, modelling and experimental methods are emphasized. Adopts experimental methods, hypothesis-testing and psychological measurement to community settings.
Constructivist (or Postmodernism)	Close interaction and/or collaboration between researchers and participants are the basis for gaining knowledge. Dismisses ideals of value-free objectivity. Seeks to understand a particular social context and what it means to the people who experience it.	Understands real-life situations, interprets the situation from the lived experiences of participants; qualitative methods are of focal interest; testing hypotheses about causes and effects are less important. It emphasizes on qualitative research and on some feminine researchers
Critical	Knowledge is shaped by power relationships and the location with social systems. Asks questions about who is able to define the nature of research relationships and who has the power to state what is true.	Research and action are integrated; the researcher pays attention to 'unheard voices,' and challenges injustice using a variety of methods. Critical community research may use specific research methods drawn from either post-positivist or constructivist approaches.

In psychology, positivism has been dominant. A few of its common elements, which are important in psychology are pursuit of value-free neutrality and objectivity in research, and an ultimate goal of understanding cause-and-effect relationships through hypothesis testing while controlling extraneous factors. Positivist science attempts to construct generalized laws on the basis of research findings. This vision is critiqued as no observer is value-free, that is, one is always a member of a culture and is influenced by it. Moreover, the 'generalizability' of research findings is limited to particular qualities of cultures, historical circumstances and settings (Gergen, 2001). These and other critiques have led to post-positivist thinking.

Constructivist approaches have mainly been the focus of community psychology in the last two decades. They tend to address the collaborative researcher–community relationship. They are also referred to as contextualist or postmodernist philosophies of science. Knowing thus occurs in a relationship and is a product of a social connection between the researcher and the research participant. Critical approaches, on the other hand, highlight the integration of research and action as well as the significance of the social system. An activist stance may be adopted by a critical approach to research. All three scientific philosophies are useful in community psychology research and a study may incorporate elements of more than one of these three philosophies (Nicotera, 2007).

Values play important roles during the initial framing of any research question. The strength points of the participants, instead of their weaknesses, are of greater focus by community psychologists. They usually approach any social issue by targeting towards competence development of participants. In addition, they tend to address dysfunction in social environments rather than in individuals.

2. *Research needs to be linked to action:* Community research needs to be designed in ways that promote human welfare at the ultimate level. In fact, interventions may be developed and evaluated so as to prevent behavioural problems or to promote the well-

FIGURE 11.1
Action Research Cycle

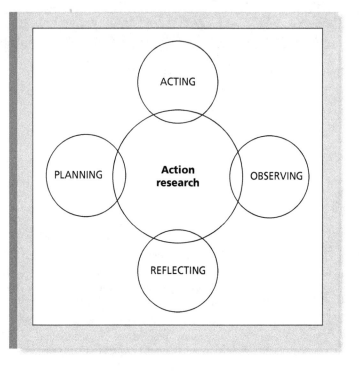

being of the community. In addition, research needs to be relevant to social policy (Kazdin, 2000). Besides, community psychology essentially follows an *action research tradition* to infer how the ecological context impacts individuals and vice versa. Action research is an outlook to enquire, rather than a specific research method. Action research employs a participative process to remain grounded in experience. This may be diagrammatically sketched as shown in Figure 11.1.

Here, research-based evidence insists directly towards action which further results in additional research. Existing theories also get enriched due to the same. This model has much applicative value in small community-based organizations, that is, NGOs, which engage in different activities at the local level and also evaluate the programmes. As such, a community psychologist works like a laboratory psychologist (experimental psychologist), with the former being engaged in social intervention, while the latter primarily being engaged in the manipulation of variables. In many instances, generative research in the community makes the use of correlations to understand the association and their extent between different variables.

3. *Research needs collaboration between researchers and participants:* The community psychologist serves as a *participant conceptualizer* as well as an *active participant in the social setting.* They enable in bringing the conceptual and methodological tools of psychology to solve community problems and thereby serve as a participant conceptualizer. At the same time, they collaborate with other members of the community and play the role of an active participant in the social context (Bennett et al., 1966).

Collaboration between the two has its benefits. The research is expected to be better with higher applicative value. This is because the community worker takes advantage of the knowledge and perspectives of the participants and the research is expected to 'mirror' their stance to a greater extent. Moreover, interventions based on findings of community research have a lasting impact on participants. Knowledge is mostly socially constructed. Creating an intervention based on community research demands hard work on the part of the community professionals. They may need to conduct an elaborate literature review to design interventions suitable to the community (Blakely et al., 1987).

4. *Research involves complexity in the real world:* This is true because researchers who study naturally occurring processes or interventions in the natural context are not able to isolate a few variables to examine their sole effects, unlike the psychologist who manipulates variables in the laboratory. Many creative research paradigms are followed by community psychologists who are challenged by such crises. Some of the disciplines of social science such as anthropology, sociology and social work use qualitative data collection techniques for a better understanding of the real-life situation. The community worker may also take the help of quantitative methods like survey research, when the research has little or no control over the phenomenon under study. True experiments may also be conducted, but less frequently. In addition, clever quasi-experimental designs may be chalked out to exploit naturally occurring variations to understand social phenomenon. The community researcher need to take account of different possible explanations for a phenomenon, sometimes called rival hypotheses, before making inferences. They must also consider whether the phenomenon has greater probability of occurrence in the same manner in other social contexts.

5. *The researcher should pay attention to the situational context and need to be associated with the multi-tiered analysis of variables:* Comprehension of the relationship between individuals and settings is of much focus in community psychology. The psychologist is interested to understand the nature of the interaction that the context has on one's behaviour. As such, characteristics of social settings, like the neighbourhood, and their impact on behaviour are of great focus. This is because failure to consider contextual effects may result in erroneous attributions of causality to the behaviour of individuals in the community at large. Thus, it is necessary for community research to be context dependent so that the community psychologist is able to unfurl meaning in terms of its different layers of analysis.

6. *Research needs to be culturally anchored:* Community psychologists also need to consider the cultural milieu encompassing any behaviour. Culture refers to values, norms, behaviours, and 'blueprint for living' that vary among individuals based on different national origins, and/or socio-economic background. Cultural anchoring makes research meaningful by increasing the cultural appropriateness of research efforts (Kazdin, 2000).

Hence, community research needs to take into account the clever designs by paying attention to social and cultural contexts in which participants dwell and follow certain essential values. In order to understand the nuances of community research, the global contexts of community psychology need to be brought to the foreground. Community psychology has developed in different countries and has taken a global form at present. This has been narrated in the upcoming section.

In sum

The broad objective of community-based research is to address the issues and challenges that adversely affect the community, keeping the situational and cultural context as well as social values into account. Emphasis is also given on understanding the insider's perspectives of the issues and the role of culture in behaviour determination. In most of the community-based research, researchers prefer to have collaboration with the community members for the benefit of the research. Action and intervention research are highly preferred in such research.

11.2. COMMUNITY PSYCHOLOGY: A BURGEONING INTERNATIONAL FIELD

It was as early as the 1970s and 1980s when community psychology began to emerge in different parts of the world having different contexts. Working with indigenous people and learning from them are of great focus in different countries.

11.2.1. STATUS OF COMMUNITY PSYCHOLOGY IN NORTH AND LATIN AMERICA

The formative pillar of community psychology in North America hails from Canada where six different areas were highlighted in research practices, namely 'values and ethics, community mental health, health promotion and prevention, social network intervention, promotion of inclusion, and community economic development' (Nelson et al., 2007). Further, community psychology is also taught at the university level in several universities of Mexico. Indigenous psychology aimed at the community well-being, taking into account several cultural traditions and responding to poverty and other social issues, has often interested community psychologists to probe into such areas.

Community psychology had its genesis in Latin America as an independent offshoot during the 1970s (Comas-Diaz et al., 1998). Such movements grew out of social psychology and social change movements.

11.2.2. OVERALL STANDING OF COMMUNITY PSYCHOLOGY IN EUROPE, AUSTRALIA AND NEW ZEALAND

Community psychology emerged as a field of study in Portugal and Spain, as fascist regimes were pushed out of power in the 1970s. It extended in the northern parts of Europe and Australia, and gradually spread to different areas as the discipline was getting consolidated in the USA and in Canada (Reich et al., 2007). Further research in the allied field took place in New Zealand (Robertson & Masters-Awatere, 2007). Shared cultural history appears to contribute to community psychology movements in Australia and New Zealand. Different parts of Europe, like Italy, had its origin of community psychology movements in the area of CMH.

11.2.3. STATUS OF COMMUNITY PSYCHOLOGY IN ASIA

Community psychology in Asia has its major focus in Japan where a professional society was organized in 1998. Development of cross-cultural models to enhance community psychology perspectives has been much encouraged in Japan (Sasao & Yasuda, 2007). Besides, the discipline had also been applied to address issues in school, so as to promote the adaptation of students in the long run. Community psychology is regarded as an emerging field in other Asian countries such as Hong Kong and India (Reich et al., 2007). However, traditions of addressing social conflicts date back to many years. The need is felt to understand the emerging discipline, especially in the Indian context, to be able to enrich community psychology as an indigenous discipline in the nation and to move towards a global psychological perspective of the community in the long run.

11.2.4. COMMUNITY PSYCHOLOGY IN INDIA

The concept of community psychology in India emerged as a reaction to the hospitalization model of training mental health programmes. Professor Durganand Sinha is regarded as the father of community psychology movement in India who made a pioneering contribution in the analysis of the community development programme (CDP) in his book *Indian Villages in Transition* in 1969. He opined that the CDP had to be designed in a way such that human factors were considered as part of social change in the village community.

In 1987, at Lucknow, the Community Psychology Association of India (CPAI) was established in Lucknow University with the goal of helping the communities. Another noteworthy event was the foundation of the *Indian Journal of Community Psychology* in 2004, which documents research in the area of community psychology. The need is felt for action-oriented research and participation of the whole community in defining development and describing relations between organizations and people to plan strategies for national development.

For addressing the mental health challenges at the community level, community psychology in India played an important role. The National Mental Health Programme (NMHP) was launched in India in 1982 with a broad objective to focus upon severe mental disorders. Thereafter, the Government of India initiated the National Rural Health Program on 12 April 2005 to provide accessible, affordable and quality healthcare to the rural areas, especially the vulnerable groups.

In April 2011, the MoHFW formed a committee with mental health professionals to come out with a new framework of NMHP and plan, with the objective to train mental health professionals, considering the prevalence of various types of mental health challenges and stressing the need for delivering effective mental health services through out-patient and in-patient departments and so on.

However, mental health issues in India have a number of challenges as well.

1. There remains a huge gap between necessity and treatment in reality. There is a huge 'treatment gap' in the population. It is greater in the countryside.
2. Stigma and inequity associated with mental illness are rampant, which hinder socio-cultural development within the society.
3. Lack of skilled individual possessions for mental health concern and behaviour often serves as a major hindrance in rendering appropriate community health services to the participants.

4. The passive role of the government, both at the central and the state level, further serves as a hindrance at the administrative level.

5. Unavailability of appropriate mental health services, predominantly in situations where individual resources are scanty, along with economic constriction and infrastructure, tends to chiefly obstruct mental health services in the countryside rural regions.

6. Low mental health literacy of the community at large also serves as a hindrance towards societal development. This relates to lesser comprehension and perception on the part of the participants about mental disorders, which could otherwise assist their acknowledgement, management or preclusion.

Nevertheless, in spite of these challenges, there have been quite a few noteworthy community programmes in India. For example, NGOs across the country created awareness among the CSWs about preventive measures of HIV/AIDS through condom promotion. In addition, they united the CSWs for creating better and supportive work environment so that clients cannot dominate them so far as sexual behaviour is concerned. Participation of CSWs and their cooperation in this initiative of NGOs helped to change the situation and improved their quality of life to some extent.

It is thus expected that community psychologists will work jointly with other public health professionals for the promotion of mental health and community development. The need is palpably felt by the author to comprehend the different methodologies currently in use in community psychology. This has been discussed in the forthcoming section of the present chapter.

In sum

Community psychology emerged as an independent branch of psychology during the 1980s, in industrial countries such as Canada, the USA and Australia, with special focus on certain issues in research practices, namely values and ethics, CMH, health promotion and prevention, social network intervention, promotion of inclusion and community economic development. The need for community-based research was felt to understand the insiders' perspectives of their issues and challenges, especially indigenous people and/or people living in interior areas. In India, the first community psychology association, CPAI, was established in 1987 in Lucknow University, with an objective to help within the community. However, this subject did not get much attention from academics and researchers in India. This branch is relatively new in India as compared to other branches of psychology.

11.3. RESEARCH METHODS IN COMMUNITY PSYCHOLOGY

Community psychology has different approaches towards planning and conducting research. They may be termed *participatory community research*, *participatory action research*, *action research*, *collaborative research* and *community science* (Jason et al., 2004; Trickett & Espino, 2004; Wandersman et al., 2005). These are meant for facilitating community partnership and citizen participation in community research. Here, participation may be referred to as a process which involves capacity building over time (Bess et al., 2009).

However, participatory approaches are not devoid of limitations. Some of the major limitations include the following:

- Participatory methods often demand more time and risk from citizens, who, in turn, are required to master new roles to get themselves empowered in the process.
- Open acceptance of each community member must be practised in an unconditional manner. However, this is often compromised, and the community research loses its viability (Hazel, 2007).
- Participatory methods do not erase existing power differentials, which must be acknowledged and dealt with. Even participatory research may have negative consequences for the community. Researchers must be vigilant regarding the process and actual outcomes of their studies (Isenberg et al., 2004).

It must be taken into account that the use of different research methods in community research depends on the questions that are to be probed by the researcher. Often, qualitative and quantitative research methodologies are used singularly or in a mixed paradigm to strengthen a specific investigation. They usually yield complementary forms of knowledge which help to enrich the understanding of the interrelationships of the individual with their community. The multiple methodologies may also be used in participatory community research. Community research needs to take into consideration the contextual and cultural factors in order to have a better understanding of the dynamics coming into play. Thus, community psychology addresses different issues using varied methodologies to arrive at different forms of knowledge.

11.3.1. CHARACTERISTICS OF QUALITATIVE RESEARCH METHODS IN COMMUNITY PSYCHOLOGY

Qualitative research methods rely on an in-depth understanding of community issues, considering the issues related to different social and cultural contexts. Exploration of change and flux in social relationships, in the societal and cultural context and over time, are often the interest points of researchers. These include in-depth interviewing, ethnography, participant observation, case studies, life histories, discourse analysis and conversation analysis (Jupp, 2006). In other words, 'qualitative research helps in providing detailed analysis of complex, dynamic, and meaningful lived experiences across a variety of social and cultural contexts' (Camic et al., 2003). This is much important in advancing scientific knowledge in community psychology (Tebes, 2005). Most qualitative research methodologies share a number of common features.

1. *Contextual meaning:* Qualitative research wishes to understand the situation of an individual or a phenomenon, considering the contexts of an individual's real-life situation. This approach encourages the community members to speak about the issues which are bothering them from their perspectives (Brodsky, 2001).
2. *Participant–research collaboration:* Research participants and community researchers create personal and mutual relationships on the basis of the context over time. This approach is highly beneficial for understanding diverse social and cultural contexts (Camic et al., 2003).

3. *Purposeful sampling:* The researcher in qualitative research usually tries to unfurl multi-layered meanings of reality by engaging in a detailed analysis. Researchers may also use their experiential knowledge for the said purpose (Cosgrove & McHugh, 2000).

4. *Listening:* The community researcher attempts to be an 'active listener' by setting aside preconceptions and understanding the participants as they are observed against their context. They improve their skills of being an active listener in the process by initiating free-flowing discussions on issues through open-ended questions.

5. *Reflexivity:* Community researchers embrace reflexivity into their systems by stating their interests, values, preconceptions and personal statuses or roles, as explicitly as possible, not only to the participants but also in the research report. The basic assumptions of the researchers are also examined in the light of what they learn from the participants. This brings about a practical transparency in the research process (Miller & Banyard, 1998; Rappaport, 2000).

6. *Thick description:* The data obtained through qualitative research methods are essentially 'thick' in terms of personal experiences and filed observations. Talking to more than one participant in the field, one could cross-check the information and thereby ensure the reliability of information (Stein & Mankowski, 2004).

7. *Data analysis and interpretation:* Data analysis in qualitative research requires identifying repeating themes and comparing distinct categories or stages in the form of codes. This framework enables in bringing forth a comparison of responses. Researchers can test the validity of themes or categories that emerge in the process by collecting and analysing more and more data until a stage of saturation is attained (Stewart, 2000).

8. *Checking:* The community researcher may cross-check the information based on observation and key informants' interviews.

9. *Multiple interpretations:* Multiple interpretations or accounts of a single topic may emerge, which reflect the presence of 'multiple realities' as perceived from different angles by participants. This enriches the notions of thick description and realism (Tolman & Brydon-Miller, 2001).

10. *Generalization:* Generalization of findings is less pertinent than understanding the meaning among the participants sampled. Converging themes are then obtained from multiple cases or studies by community professionals.

There are four essential steps in conducting any qualitative research and they include asking, witnessing, interpreting and knowing (Stein & Mankowski, 2004). They help in attending to the 'unheard voices' of the participants, especially the weaker sections of the society. In addition, they provide a deeper and contextual understanding of a culture, a community or population. The different steps of qualitative research as mentioned before may be schematically depicted by Figure 11.2.

The first step of *asking* involves identifying the potential participants for a study and clarifying the researcher's assumptions and values. This is followed by the next act of *witnessing*, which concerns how the researcher and participants would create knowledge by means of developing a collaborative relationship. The researcher poses open-ended questions to which the participants describe experiences and ideas. This is often followed by the researcher providing an attentive, empathic and affirming audience. Participants' words are recorded in some way. The ensuing act of *interpreting* involves analysis of the information gathered through asking and witnessing, making wider sense of patterns in the experiences of participants. This act raises the question regarding whose story is it? Whether it is the primary purpose to communicate the experiences and voices of

FIGURE 11.2
Different Steps in Qualitative Research

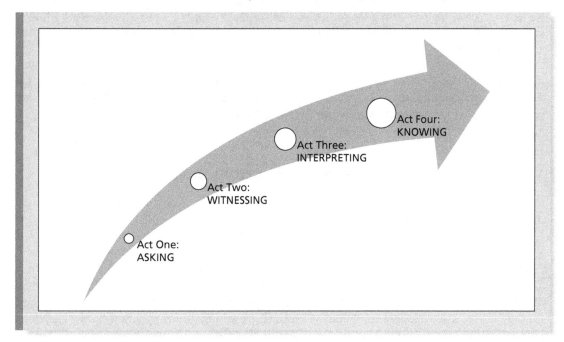

participants or to classify, analyse or critique those experiences? This is finally followed by the final act of *knowing*, which involves knowing the products of qualitative research and whether they are useful to further the interests or capacities of the research participants. This includes academic reports as well as other results.

In sum

The approaches which are followed in community research are participatory community research, participatory action research, action research, collaborative research and community science. Addressing emerging issues of community life by following appropriate approaches is the main focus of community research, aimed towards improving the situation through collaborative approach. In a community set-up, especially in the rural areas, qualitative research methods for investigation of culture-specific issues are found to be most suitable as they help in understanding and interpreting different social phenomena in great detail.

11.3.2. QUALITATIVE DATA COLLECTION TECHNIQUES

It involves a direct interaction process between a researcher and a participant of a study or a small group of people. Gubrium and Holstein (2001) argue that modern research interview is founded on three basic premises, namely *democratization of opinions, researcher–researched duality* and *respondents as being 'vessels' of knowledge.* In-depth interviewing essentially banks on delving into the participants' 'deeper self' to produce genuine data (Johnson et al., 2002). It facilitates self-disclosure of participants about their issues and challenges freely and frankly without any inhibition (Douglas, 1985). However, the sensitivity of a researcher in asking questions about sensitive issues also matters a lot.

Here, the researcher attends to the participants and also takes account of their experiential processes. Interviews are usually recorded, and transcripts are then prepared, for which, the analysis can be based on the participants' actual words. The findings from qualitative interviewing may have limited generalizability. Nevertheless, the findings of a qualitative study are applicable for the community where the study is carried out.

11.3.2.1. Informal/Unstructured Interview

It is one of the methods of qualitative data collection without using any structured questionnaire. This type of interview is conducted in a casual setting, such as over tea/coffee or lunch or when the respondent is free and is willing to spare 10–15 minutes with the researcher to answer a few questions. The duration of the informal interview should not be more than 20 minutes. A researcher is aware of the objective of their study and, accordingly, they mentally decide what questions need to be asked to the study subjects to gather the required information, following an informal interaction method. Since the researcher does not open any notebook or question paper, the respondent does not feel inhibited to respond to any question spontaneously. Therefore, informal/unstructured interview method is found to be very beneficial in collecting data from the study subjects in a community setting, or for other purposes, to understand an issue from an insider's perspective. An informal interview is most suitable for selecting a candidate for a particular job to assess whether the candidate would be suitable for a particular working environment.

There are some advantages and disadvantages of informal/unstructured interview. This interview process is flexible and comfortable for the study subjects, it is interactive and there is a scope to clarify the issue of discussion. It also helps to understand the subject better from the subject's body language and it is practical to examine an issue and verify the answer on the spot, if necessary. On the other hand, it is time-consuming and interruptions might occur. Due to the casual setting, some study subjects may not be comfortable with this approach of interview and feelings of insecurity among the study subjects regarding the confidentiality of information are also viable.

11.3.2.2. In-depth Interview

An in-depth interview is another open-ended and discovery-oriented qualitative data collection technique that is suitable for community research. It is a one-to-one data collection method using an in-depth interview guide. This method of data collection allows the subjects to reveal their mindset the way they think about an issue without any inhibition. This method helps to gather detailed information about an issue of a study from the study subjects. It is flexible like an informal interview. The main objective of an in-depth interview is to explore a study subject's point of view, experiences, feelings and perspectives about an issue in detail. Although this could be conducted over phone to collect data, it is advisable to conduct it face to face. This type of interview should not last for more than 30–40 minutes for a single study subject.

There are many advantages of an in-depth interview. For example, this type of interview helps to establish a good rapport with the study subjects so that they feel comfortable and, in turn, the good rapport with the study subjects helps in generating more insightful responses regarding sensitive and personal issues. Second, for a researcher, this method is advantageous while asking follow-up questions and probing the questions further in order to have a better understanding of the knowledge, attitudes and perceptions of a study subject about any issue. Third, the body language of the study subjects could be assessed by the researcher and accordingly a researcher can take the interview process forward to make it more engaging and exciting. Fourth, research based on in-depth interviews could be done with a small number of study subjects. Fifth, this method of qualitative data collection is highly insightful, and it helps to identify highly valuable findings quickly.

The main disadvantage of an in-depth interview is that it is time-consuming. Second, to conduct an in-depth interview, a researcher should be sensitive and trained for proper transcription and analysis of the data. Third, on many occasions, the interview setting may not be suitable for having a detailed discussion about an issue with the study subjects. Fourth, in case of a large study, where a researcher requires more help for data collection, there is a possibility of difference in approach towards data collection.

11.3.2.3. Focus Group Discussion

An FGD involves a discussion with a group of 8–10 individuals in an interviewing mode. The group members may be homogenous or heterogeneous, depending upon the issue of investigation. In FGD, a researcher plays the role of a facilitator and initiates the discussion on various issues one by one, ensuring that every member participates in the discussion and shares their views openly, without any inhibitions. A researcher is assisted by another investigator for recording of discussions and other purposes. Prior to recording of the discussion, the participants should be ensured that information shared by them will be used for research only and the recording will be deleted once the study is completed. It should start with self-introduction and all the participants should sit in a circle, so that everybody can see each other. It should be ensured that there is no disturbance while the discussion is on. Ideally, an FGD should not last for more than one hour.

H. J. Rubin and I. S. Rubin (1995) are of the opinion that each participant is regarded with equal status and respect in a focus group and their opinions are valued by the facilitator. The main advantage of FGD is that this method of data collection from a small group of subjects helps in collecting rich information and the information is then cross-checked by the group members during the discussion. After conducting 4–5 FGDs, a researcher can have a better understanding of any issue to be able to draw a conclusion. FGDs are also very stimulating to the respondents at times (Fontana & Frey, 2005). However, FGDs also have their own challenges. For example,

1. One or two of the participant/s could dominate the group and hinder its effectiveness;
2. Inhibition to share personal views about sensitive issues;
3. It is difficult to deal with shy participants in FGDs and
4. The facilitator needs to be skilled to be able to ask questions simultaneously while recording the responses whenever needed (Merton et al., 1956).

11.3.2.4. Observation

Observation is a very powerful and one of the most reliable methods of qualitative data collection in a natural environment, without informing anyone from the community about their behaviour and, at the same time, the nature of different social interactions is being observed by a researcher. This method of data collection facilitates first-hand experience about an issue in the community set-up. There are two broad categories of observation. They are participant and non-participant observation. Participant observation means that a researcher will become a part of the community and live there while carrying out a study so that they can directly observe what is going on and can learn about various cultural beliefs and practices, and also interact with the community members. In other words, participant observation is an observational mode of research in which the observer participates in a group in order to record the behaviours of interest. On the other hand, non-participant observation means that a researcher will visit an area with some objective in mind and will observe what is going on and, if necessary, they will interact with some community members and will come back with their observation of the community and will conclude about the issue of the investigation. Non-participant observation involves the observer to remain passive for they do not participate in the group for the observation of the behaviour of interest.

Observation is somehow similar to ethnographic methods of data collection in natural settings, about language, behaviour, community/family rituals and so on. Anthropologists mostly use ethnographic methods of data collection. However, gradually researchers from other branches are also using ethnographic approaches.

There are some limitations of the observation method. They include the following:

1. Not all phenomena can be observed in situations. Biographical processes are difficult to observe. This is also applicable for comprehensive knowledge processes.
2. Participant observation can hardly be standardized and formalized beyond a general research strategy, and it does not make sense to consider this as a goal for further methodological developments (Luders, 2004).
3. The researcher's notes, analysis and interpretation can be affected by selective observation, selective memory and selective interpretations.

However, if a researcher is trained, sensitive and committed, they can overcome the aforesaid limitations. One should remember that qualitative research can investigate an issue where the quantitative method fails.

11.3.2.5. Case Studies

Community psychologists may use the case study approach while using archival data (e.g., minutes of group meetings, newspaper reports, police statistics and so on). They provide an in-depth analysis of a single case or multiple cases which possess the characteristics under consideration. Case studies are reported to be a very good method for understanding the cultural, social or community contexts of any issue. They can also provide relevant and contextual description. Case studies also serve as sources of ideas about behaviour in the community set-up; they provide opportunities for much innovation; they can effectively study rare phenomena; serve as challenges to theoretical assumptions and serve as tentative support for psychological theories. This method also serves as a complement to the nomothetic investigation of human behaviour. However, the case study method is still criticized because of its difficulty to draw cause-and-effect relationships as it is a source of bias during data collection and interpretation, and also because of the underlying problem of generalization from a single individual.

Hence, qualitative methods often use different narratives in community research. *Data triangulation, respondent validation* as well as *verisimilitude* are often addressed to combat chances of an anecdotalism in community research (Silverman, 2000). Data triangulation involves the use of different methods to have a better understanding of the same phenomenon. Respondent validation relates to using respondents as mediators who engage in the process of validating the data by providing their feedback. Finally, verisimilitude refers to the process of eliciting a personal experience in the reader, which is similar to the original experiences of the research participant. This further validates the research process and its findings (Brodsky, 2003; Stein & Wemmerus, 2001).

The following section will attempt to sketch the different quantitative research methods commonly used in the field of community psychology.

11.3.2.6. Participatory Rural Appraisal

This method of qualitative data collection is suitable for designing rural development programmes based on rural people's understanding of their issues and challenges. Therefore, active participation of the local people is essential in this exercise. This method helps in getting an insider's perspective of an issue. This method of data collection helps to consider the knowledge, experiences and opinions of *rural* people in the planning and management of development projects and programmes. According to Vashishtha and Kunwar (2004):

> Participatory Rural Appraisal (PRA) is a methodology for interacting with villagers, understanding them and learning from them. It involves a set of principles, a process of communication and a menu of methods for seeking villagers participation in putting forward their points of view about any issue and enabling them to do their own analysis with a view to make use of such learning. It initiates a participatory process and sustains it.

There are different exercises under PRA and some of them are social mapping, resource mapping, developing seasonal calendars, mobility mapping and so on. These types of exercises are conducted for different purposes. For example, social mapping is an exercise to identify households and human resources in terms of income, land owned by a family, other family resources, educational qualification of the people of each household, family income and so on. This type of information is helpful to understand the well-being of the people of a community/village and to assess how any development project might affect people of different social groups of a village. Resource mapping is another exercise which is done to identify the natural and man-made resources and their locations in a community. Information about local resources helps to plan future development projects for the welfare of the common people.

Exercises pertaining to seasonal calendars are useful for better understanding of the weather in a community and the crops that grow there during different seasons. In turn, this information helps in planning income-generating activities for the poor through self-help groups. In order to understand movement patterns of an individual or a group of the community during different seasons, mobility mapping is conducted. The beauty of PRA is that it could be done with people without any basic educational background.

In qualitative researcher sensitivity, skills of the researchers in collecting the data and familiarity with the local culture, in addition to communication skills and their commitments, are the answers to reliability and validity of the qualitative data.

11.3.3. Quantitative Data Collection Techniques

Quantitative methods tend to follow a positivist paradigm but can be effectively used within community settings to delve into the multilevel influence of environmental factors on participant health and well-being (Luke, 2005). The commonalities of quantitative research methods may be stated as follows.

1. *Measurement and comparison:* Measurement and comparison of the quantitative data can be feasible through such methods.
2. *Numbers are data:* On the one hand, while researchers using qualitative methods look for patterns in words and narratives, researchers using quantitative methods seek patterns in numbers on the other.
3. *Cause and effect relationship:* These methods are able to offer knowledge regarding cause-and-effect relationship among the variables in an investigation. Hence, prediction of consequences is possible using such research methods.
4. *Generalization:* Conclusions can be generalized at least to some extent across settings, contexts and communities.
5. *Standardized measures:* Standardized measurement instruments are preferred to ensure reliable and valid findings of research studies unlike qualitative research methods.

More particularly, the tools used for quantitative research are discussed further.

11.3.3.1. Structured Questionnaire

A structured questionnaire is used to collect detailed background information about the study subjects in addition to their opinion about various issues. Predetermined modes of responses are provided against all the questions. Therefore, a respondent has to give their answer against a question within the given options only. In most of the community-based research, structured questionnaires are used.

11.3.3.2. Semi-structured Questionnaire

This type of questionnaire elicits both qualitative and quantitative data. It helps to understand the subject's perspective of an issue as it allows the expression of the respondent's personal views about various issues, in addition to collecting the quantitative data.

11.3.3.3. Standardized Psychological Tools

In almost all the social science studies, especially in psychological studies, researchers use multiple standardized psychological study tools for measuring different psychological aspects of the study subjects that are developed by others or researchers. If it is developed by others, one needs to culturally adapt the tools. For any standardized psychological tool, one should find out its psychometric properties.

11.3.3.4. A Comparative Picture of Qualitative versus Quantitative Research Methods

Both qualitative and quantitative research methods have their own strengths and weaknesses. However, combining both the methods, especially in a community-based study, if applicable, one can complement each other and thereby can learn the topic of investigation better and present the results of a study in a more interesting manner.

    Thus, qualitative and quantitative research methods may be compared as follows (Table 11.2).

TABLE 11.2
Comparison of Qualitative versus Quantitative Research Methods

Qualitative Research	Quantitative Research
Data collection methods are informal interviews, in-depth interviews, focus group discussions, observation and so on.	Data collection methods include structured interview schedule, semi-structured questionnaire and standardized psychological tools.
Primarily follows inductive process for formulation of theories and hypotheses.	Primarily follows the deductive process to test previous concepts, constructs and hypotheses.
More subjective as this approach tries to understand an issue from the insiders' perspectives.	More objective as this approach draws conclusions about an issue based on observed effects of a programme on community members.
Attempts to understand the social and cultural contexts of an issue.	It is mostly objective and number based.
Based on small sample and collects in-depth and more detailed information.	Based on large sample and collects information about issues which do not require in-depth probing.
Mode of response is not fixed, and it is more of exploratory and descriptive.	Mode of response is predetermined.
Mostly content and thematic analysis is carried out to capture the subject's point of view in the context of a culture and a situation.	Statistical tests are used for meaningful interpretation of data.
Skills and sensitivity of the researcher are the answer to their liability and validity of data.	Psychometric properties of study tools ensure reliability and validity of data along with proper methods of administration of the study tool at the time of data collection, ensuring ethical considerations.
It is time-consuming and requires special training of a researcher to conduct it and analyse the descriptive data.	Less time-consuming and does not require rigorous training.
Follows natural life situation model.	Follows human behaviour model.

In sum

There is a range of qualitative data collection techniques in community research and they include an informal/unstructured interview, in-depth interview, FGD, PRA and so on. All these methods are suitable in situations where people are mostly illiterate, and some issues require in-depth understanding from cultural perspectives. In addition, quantitative data collection techniques are also in use in community research where one wishes to collect basic information about a community and its population. Broadly, quantitative data collection techniques are structured questionnaires, semi-structured questionnaires and standardized psychological study tools. Both qualitative and quantitative data collection techniques have their own strengths and weaknesses. However, if one combines both the approaches, if applicable, for a particular research, one can gather good information.

11.4. RESEARCH DESIGN

There are multiple research designs for carrying out studies in the community on various issues. Each research design has its own strength and each one of them is applicable and suitable for different topics of investigation. A brief description of some of the commonly used research designs is provided further with some practical examples.

11.4.1. SURVEY RESEARCH DESIGN

For community-based research covering a large population, survey research is one of the best options for measuring various parameters/issues in applied social research. The data collected through this type of research design help in providing a clear picture about population characteristics and thereby taking need-based decisions for the policy formulation of a particular community with respect to some specific issues. For example, one can think of doing a survey to gather information about the health status of children in a community, that is, how many children up to 18 years of age have all the immunizations. Another good example of a survey research is to find out the total population of elderly people in a community, who are above 60 years of age, and their health status. In that case, all the households of a community are to be covered in the study.

11.4.2. BASELINE STUDY DESIGN

A baseline study design is another type of study which is carried out to gather baseline information about a particular issue, design an intervention programme based on the same information and, finally, comparing the same information after the implementation of the intervention programme with end-line data/information to ascertain the effectiveness of the intervention programme. Ideally, in this type of study, the same study tool should be used for collecting data for both baseline and end-line studies.

In other words, it might be stated that baseline study gives information which may be termed as performance indicators to understand the present situation with respect to some issues of a community prior to the implementation of any intervention project. Baseline data are the basis for designing need-based intervention programmes. For example, one proposes to enhance the knowledge, change the perception and alter the behaviour of adolescents, if they are found to be involved in risk behaviour, through an intervention project. In that case, one has to ascertain the current level of knowledge, perception and behaviour of adolescents about various aspects of reproductive health and, on the basis of baseline data, one will design the intervention programme and will provide inputs to the adolescents following various methods. After the intervention, one can think of collecting the end-line data using the same questionnaire and comparison of end-line data would help to assess whether the intervention was beneficial for improving the knowledge, perception and also altering the risk behaviour of the adolescents.

11.4.3. Cross-Sectional Study Design

A cross-sectional study design proposes to gather information about certain issues from all categories of the population at one point in time. This type of study design helps to get a clear picture of the trend of any issue in the community. In other words, this type of study design is often referred to as snapshots of the population about certain characteristics. A practical example of a cross-sectional study design would be a psychological study to ascertain the prevalence of depression among people of a particular community. A researcher can attempt to understand the same issue among people across different age groups and social backgrounds of a community.

11.4.4. Correlational Study Design

A correlational study design attempts to understand the nature of relationships between different variables occurring naturally. In other words, a correlational study design attempts to find whether two or more variables of a study are related or not. If they are related, whether there is a positive or negative relation. For example, whether long study hours have any correlation with the performance of the students. One more practical example could be whether obesity in adolescents has any association with lifestyle and/or food habits.

11.4.5. Epidemiological Study Design

Normally, an epidemiological study design is followed when there is the occurrence of a health problem, all of a sudden, and it affected people of different age groups. The objective of epidemiological study is to find out when and how a disease affects people of a particular community at a point of time, irrespective of their age, gender and socio-economic background. In other words, epidemiological study proposes to ascertain the common symptoms of a disease and risk factors involved in the same. The findings of the epidemiological studies help the policymakers to take appropriate preventive measures of the same. In this type of study, a researcher tries to find out the cause and effect relationship of a disease.

11.4.6. Cross-cultural Study

A cross-cultural study design is a type of study where a researcher compares the behaviour of people of different cultural groups to find out the impact of culture on behaviour, family life and outlook of people. Cross-cultural study could be between two or multicultural groups of the same society or between the population of different countries.

Cross-cultural psychologists also focus on both universal behaviours and unique behaviours of the population. For example, what rituals are followed immediately after the birth of a child and over a period of one year, among different cultural groups of a society?

11.4.7. ACTION RESEARCH

Action research is another population study design used in case of community research. It is somewhat similar to an intervention study. In action research, the documentation system should be very strong and objective. Periodic monitoring of the implementation of project activities is essential to ensure effective delivery of services to the target groups. In addition, one should carry out the midterm and end-term evaluations of the intervention.

11.4.8. LONGITUDINAL STUDY DESIGN

A longitudinal study design is mostly based on observation in which a researcher collects information about the same subject for a period of one or two years. The duration of longitudinal study could be more depending upon the issue of investigation. In market research, longitudinal study design is very popular as it gives an estimate to the researcher to ascertain the purchase behaviour of consumers, that is, whether common customers of a retail shop buy the same product over a period of time. Ascertaining brand awareness of a particular product over a period of time is another issue suitable for longitudinal study.

11.4.9. INTERVENTION STUDY DESIGN

Intervention study design intends to provide inputs to the community or a group of population to improve their behaviour or knowledge about an issue, following different methods suitable to a certain culture. In an intervention study, cooperation from the target group is necessary. In case of an intervention study, one should attempt to examine the impact of the intervention. For example, whether the target groups found the intervention programme to be beneficial and, if so, how? Assessment of impact would help to improve future intervention programmes.

11.4.10. RANDOMIZED FIELD EXPERIMENTS

Here, participants are randomly assigned to experimental or control groups to obtain homogenous pretest conditions as far as experimental and control groups are concerned. Random assignment of participants to the different groups helps to control different confounding variables when the sample size is large (Sullivan, 2003). Randomized field experiments are unsurpassed for their clarity of cause–effect interpretations (Weissberg et al., 2003). However, 'experiments require substantial prior knowledge of the context to propose social innovations worth testing and to choose measurements' (Lipsey & Cordray, 2002).

11.4.11. Non-equivalent Comparison Group Design

Such research designs come to help whenever assignment of participants to experimental or comparison conditions is not random (Linney & Repucci, 1982). This approach is practical and less intrusive than randomized experiments. However, the control of confounding variables is much weaker, and clarity of interpretation and confidence in conclusions are compromised.

11.5. ETHICAL ISSUES IN RESEARCH

The simple definition of ethics is a moral code of conduct for an individual to behave in a society. In research, ethics play an important role for conducting quality research. Ethical issues in research, especially where a researcher deals with a community and human beings, are very important for a number of reasons. First, it ensures the protection of the rights of the study subjects. Second, it helps in generating quality data. Third, it sensitizes a researcher to be truthful and avoid any error in presenting the data. Fourth, it sensitizes a researcher against fabricating, falsifying or misrepresenting field evidence.

The main ethics that need to be followed while doing any research in the community are (a) explaining the objective of any research to the community or study subjects in simple local language which will be understandable, and obtaining their consent (verbal or written) for participation in the research; (b) explaining the implication of giving consent, that is, how much time one has to give to the researcher for acting as a study subject and whether there are any direct or indirect benefits; (c) confidentiality of the information/data needs to be ensured; (d) whether any risk is involved in being a study subject needs clear explanation; (e) date and time of the interview for data collection should be decided as per the convenience of the study subjects; (f) study subjects should be informed that they can withdraw from the study at any point of time if they are not comfortable in answering some questions; (g) feedback about the outcome of the study, that is, what emerged from the study, and proposed recommendations should be shared with the study subjects/community members at the end of the study and (h) a copy of the study report should be shared with the concerned government and non-government organizations, in addition to writing articles for journals towards dissemination of information.

In sum

In any research, design plays a very important role to carry out the study systematically, thus integrating all the components of the study in a coherent and logical way. In simple words, design indicates how a researcher proposes to carry out a study. For every research, one should adopt the most suitable design. It helps to follow appropriate methods for selection of study subjects, measurements to be used and data analysis. Like design, ethics in community research is very important. Ethics mean a certain code of conduct that must be followed while carrying out a study, which includes obtaining informed consent of the study subjects prior to joining a study, ensuring confidentiality of information, deciding the date and time of the interview as per the convenience of the study subjects and so on. In turn, ethical issues followed in a research help to protect the rights of the study subjects and ensure quality data.

11.6. CULTURE AND ITS RELEVANCE IN COMMUNITY PSYCHOLOGY

Understanding diverse cultures and settings is mandatory for community psychology as all research, including laboratory studies, occur within a cultural backdrop. It becomes pertinent to understand how cultural dynamics have their role to play in the manifestation of behaviour in the community at large. Four methodological issues involving culture as an important variable come to the forefront (Bond & Harrell, 2006; Tebes, 2000). First are queries concerning the assessment of cultural or ethnic identity. Another important and associated issue which concerns understanding accurately is the diversity within each culture that accounts for population heterogeneity (Sasao & Sue, 1993). Issues regarding assumptions of methodological equivalence across cultures also crop up (Burlew, 2003). Moreover, research studies have found that inter-group studies were more likely to emphasize the deficits of a culture or population, while intra-group studies more often emphasized strengths (Martin et al., 2004). Thus, the nature of research designs is often the culprit of the underlying differences or similarities that may be later reflected in the results, due to inherent unique features of the research design(s) instead of the genuine existence of any such trend(s).

Thus, there is a dire necessity of cultivating an understanding of one's own culture to realize how experiences have shaped one's world view. An awareness of one's own limited knowledge and a genuine willingness to learn are crucial in understanding community psychology (Mock, 1999). The community psychologist needs to recognize that this is an ongoing learning process, which essentiates them to become culturally anchored. It is desirable if they can intricately intermingle their own experiential knowledge in the process and immerse themselves genuinely in the community as a citizen to 'soak' in the flavours of the community. The community professional may also skilfully create safe settings for discussions where researchers and citizens can personally explore difficult issues of culture and power; how one's own culture influences and limits one's world view; strengths of different cultural world views and values; personal effects of social injustice and oppression, and so on. A valuable way to learn about cultures is to study its narratives in the form of shared stories that express important values, historical events, folkways and emotions (Tandon et al., 1998).

The need is felt to evaluate different community programmes by researchers to have an understanding of the relative position by stakeholders. This is attempted to be addressed in the following section.

11.7. COMMUNITY DEVELOPMENT PROGRAMMES AND NEED FOR COMMUNITY RESEARCH

Common people in both urban and rural communities experience a range of issues and challenges related to physical and mental health in addition to economic and social issues such as social stigma and discrimination. These problems vary from community to community and depend on the location of the community as well. In order to address all these problems, there is a need to conceptualize a viable intervention project. In this regard, community psychologists can play an important role in extending need-based services to the community, based on evidence. For delivering any services to the community, money is required. For generating money, one needs to develop a need-based project proposal for funding. There are several national and international organizations that fund potential project proposals for funding the upliftment of a community and/or addressing any special problem of a community which affects a large number of any population. If an NGO or any organization, including academic institutions, is knowledgeable and skilled in writing project proposals, funding would not be an issue. The first author of the book has long experience in writing research/intervention project proposals for various national and international funding agencies. A student studying at the undergraduate or postgraduate level should have a basic idea about writing a project proposal for funding, whether it be an intervention or research proposal.

11.8. SKILL DEVELOPMENT PROGRAMMES FOR THE YOUTH AND WOMEN

With increasing population in India and other developing countries where government jobs are limited, there is a need to impart skills among youth and women through skill-based development programmes. Compared to job opportunities in urban areas, it is much less in rural zones. Therefore, there is a need to identify skill-based trades for which there are job markets or one can think of initiating their own business, based on acquired knowledge and accordingly design the short-term skill-based training programmes for youth and women. Recently, the Government of India has also specially emphasized upon skill-based training programmes so that after gaining skills, a youth or a woman can think of starting their own business or may get a job. The Government of India has also come up with a number of schemes towards this end. Skill-based training programmes are more required for the rural youth as job opportunities are very limited in the rural areas as well as their expectation of a salary is reasonably less as compared to urban youth and women. In this regard, a psychologist can play an important role in the community by providing guidance to the local NGOs in designing market demand-oriented skill-based training programmes, in addition to dissemination of information about various government schemes among the urban and rural unemployed youth and women, so that they come forward and take advantage of the same facilities.

Some of the most popular skill-based training programmes of the Ministry of Skill Development and Entrepreneurship, Government of India, are as follows.

- *Pradhan Mantri Kaushal Vikas Yojana:* The objective of this scheme is to impart skills among youths so that they may get a job based on their skills in the industries and lead a meaningful life. The scheme proposes to cover about 10 million Indian youths, based on training schemes and proposes to train about 10 million Indian youths on different skill-based schemes which are in high demand in many industries in India. The National Skill Development Corporation has been assigned to organize the training programmes across the country. In order to encourage the youth, some financial assistance has been provided to the youth by the government.
- *National Apprenticeship Training Scheme:* This is another demand-driven scheme which arranges five different categories of apprenticeship, based on issues such as trade apprentice, graduate, technician, technician (vocational) and optional trade apprentices. Six Regional Directorates of Apprenticeship Training located at Kolkata, Mumbai, Chennai, Hyderabad,

Kanpur and Faridabad are responsible for the implementation of the scheme. Eligible youths receive monthly stipends for attending the apprenticeship from the employer.

- *Skill Development Initiative*: The objective of this scheme is to train youths in different employable skills. In other words, this training is called vocational training. These training programmes are organized by the registered vocational training providers under the government, private and industrial establishments. This is a 100 per cent centrally sponsored scheme.

A number of NGOs are also engaged in organizing different short-term skill-based training programmes for women across the country, which help them to initiate their own business and/or to run a self-help group.

11.9. SKILLS OF COMMUNITY PSYCHOLOGISTS

Accurate self-awareness of one's emotions; self-disclosure in the process of building trust; clear communication of aims, viewpoints and values; humility; having good linguistic skills along with curiosity for gaining 'insider' knowledge are some important qualities that are desirable among community psychologists. In addition, Stark (2009) classified skills required by efficient community workers into *action skills* (e.g., consulting, community organizing, community development, coalition building, conducting evaluation and research) and *social skills* (e.g., active listening, rapport building, conscientiousness, group facilitation, conflict resolution and so on). A community psychologist requires assessing the specific needs of the community to solve issues of the community, using behavioural techniques and by developing programmes on human service, bringing about the prevention of problems and building competencies. It thus becomes mandatory for the community professional to take into consideration cultural factors that may be associated with any research. This is detailed in the upcoming section of the chapter.

11.10. SUSTAINABILITY OF COMMUNITY-BASED DEVELOPMENT PROGRAMMES

From time to time, various community development projects are taken up and implemented across the society with a good intention and with the support from the government and non-government organizations. For long-term benefits of any development project, the involvement of community members and their support are very important. In all the development projects, support is provided for a specific period for achieving some specific objectives. Some of them can sustain and function well even after the support is withdrawn by the government and other organizations while some development projects discontinue and/or are unable to function well because of a number of factors such as lack of financial support, poor leadership, lack of engagement of the local community members, external interference and differences of opinion among the local community members. Therefore, it is crucial to ensure sustainability of any development project so that the local people can continue to enjoy the benefits of the project. It requires the involvement of the local community members in the project from the inception and some of the community leaders are identified by the community members, who are given a specific role and responsibilities, so that they have a clear idea about various aspects of the development projects. Their first-hand experience will help them to run the project systematically once the funding agency withdraws from the project. For ensuring sustainability of any development project, psychologists can play the role of facilitators and/or community mobilizers in engaging community members in the project through sensitization about the potential benefits of any development project.

11.11. WRITING PROJECT PROPOSAL FOR COMMUNITY-BASED INTERVENTION PROGRAMME

For the implementation of any intervention programme, one needs financial support for which one needs to find a potential funding agency and learn to write a good project proposal for funding. The format for writing a project proposal varies across different funding agencies.

Broadly, the guidelines for writing a project proposal for intervention are as follows.

- *Title of the project proposal:* It should be very clear, precise and without any ambiguity.
- *Introduction:* One should give an overview of the issue with evidence so that an evaluator can have an idea about the issue of investigation or the services clearly. The length of the introduction should not be very long. It could be within 2–3 pages and again it depends upon the issue.
- *Justification of the project:* One should clearly justify the necessity for taking up the same project based on the secondary data.
- *Objective of the project:* One can think of writing both broad and specific objectives. Objectives should be very clear without any ambiguity and it should be achievable.
- *Potential significance of the project:* In this section, one should write the benefits of the project, that is, how the community will be benefitted from the project.
- *Baseline study:* For any intervention project, there is a need to carry out a baseline study to gather detailed information about an issue. In turn, the baseline data help in designing a need-based intervention project.
- *Activity plan:* The specific activities to be undertaken need to be explained in this section and strategies to be adopted for taking up the activities must also be explained.
- *Monitoring and documentation of implementation of the project:* Monitoring and documentation are very important to ensure the timely implementation of the project. It helps to identify the challenges in the implementation of a project and suggests corrective measures so that future activities of the project could be implemented on time, thus rectifying the mistakes or any challenges. In any project proposal, monitoring and documentation mechanisms should be properly explained, and it would be considered as a positive point of a project proposal.
- *Midterm and end-term evaluations of the project:* Any intervention project should be subjected to midterm and end-term evaluations. Midterm evaluation helps in understanding whether a project could achieve what it intended to achieve in the middle of the project and, if not, why? Accordingly, corrective measures are suggested for the future effective implementation of project activities. The broad objective of end-term evaluation is to assess the overall effectiveness of the project after the implementation of the study. Sometimes, cost-effective analysis is also done to examine whether benefits of the project were worthy, when compared to money invested in the project.

- *Manpower for the proposed project:* In this section, a clear idea should be given about manpower requirement for a project, that is, other than the project manager, how many project staff are required at different junctures, with justification, and their background in terms of education, professional and field experience. If there is a scope, some of the community members with some level of educational background may be engaged in implementing the project with some honorarium.
- *Time frame:* How much time is required for a particular project to complete needs to be clearly mentioned in a proposal. Activity-wise time frame in the form of graphical presentation would be very interesting.
- *Estimated budget and its justification:* There is a need to provide a budget based on recurring and non-recurring expenditure with proper justification. If it is a long-term project, year-wise budget under different broad heads is desirable. One can add 10–15 per cent overhead charges in the proposal for the use of office space, furniture, electricity and other facilities of an organization.
- *References:* At the end of a project proposal, one should provide detailed references, which are referred to in the introduction as well as the weblink, if available, so that one could cross-check the information.

The broad outline for writing a research proposal is somehow similar to a project proposal. In a research proposal, one needs to give more emphasis on literature review and based on existing knowledge, one should develop a conceptual model for verification. There is a need to develop a hypothesis or research questions and, finally, verify the same or find out the answers to these questions. At the same time, in case of a research proposal, the principal investigator should have a good academic and research background. For any study, research proposal should be approved by the Institutional Ethics Committee and one should clearly specify the ethical issues to be considered for protecting the interest of the study subjects. There is no standard guideline about the length of a research proposal. It depends upon the issue of investigation and guidelines of a funding agency. Past research experience in the related field and any publication in a standard international journal adds to the strength of a proposal and helps to get the funding.

11.12. MONITORING AND PROGRAMME EVALUATION

Monitoring and evaluation of any intervention project is prerequisite for the funding of any project that is funded by any international funding agency. As discussed before, monitoring is a process to check the process of the implementation of an intervention project. It helps to identify the gaps in implementation and encourages the programme manager to take corrective measures. The broad objective of evaluation of any project is to assess the effectiveness of the programme. In other words, evaluation of a programme helps to know whether a particular programme is beneficial for the community as well as the individual members of the community.

There are a number of issues to be looked into during the evaluation of a programme. These include the cost-effectiveness of the programme, any shortcomings in delivering the services to the community and reasons behind it and/or whether there are alternative options for implementing a particular project in a much better way. The different steps in programme evaluation may be schematically depicted in Figure 11.3.

11.13. GLOBAL COMMUNITY: A ROAD MAP OF COMMUNITY PSYCHOLOGY IN THE FUTURE

The need is felt by a global community to emerge into the feeling of 'connectedness' of all citizens for the overall well-being of the community at large. It may be considered as a superordinate society which does not take into consideration factors of ethnocentricity, cultural bias, indigenous psychologies and the like in its development. Community psychology is thus heading towards an international field consequently.

FIGURE 11.3
Steps in Programme Evaluation

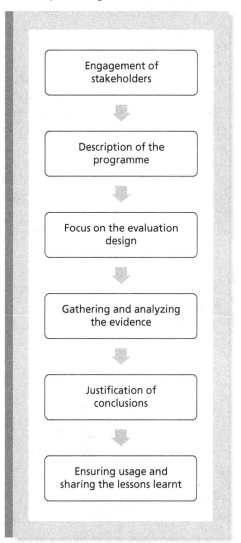

In sum

Understanding cultural perspectives of an issue is one of the main focuses of community research. For a better understanding of the community and its cultural beliefs and practices, participatory research is beneficial. A student of the postgraduate level should have some idea as to how to write a project proposal which is provided in this section in brief. Any programme should be monitored periodically to ensure proper and effective implementation. Further, programmes need to be evaluated to examine their effectiveness in taking corrective measures for future programmes. As mentioned before, supporting the community in various ways, based on evidence, is the ultimate objective of community psychology research. The youth are the future of a nation and since it is very difficult to ensure a government job for every youth, skill-development programmes and the concept of self-help groups for rural and poor women are going to play a crucial role in a country like India.

11.14. CONCLUSION AND IMPLICATIONS

Human resources are the most important components of worldly life. Solving the physical, mental and financial strength struggles of all community members should be the target of all sciences to attempt the betterment of life on the earth. Social-strength-wise, people vary a lot and, in a country like India, countless people live BPL. The conscience and consciousness of able individuals need to have prominent focus on these layers of the society, not only to help these poor people but also to enrich and ensure the quality of life of everybody as far as it is practicable. Community research, community methods, community approaches to so many different mental and social issues seem to be the means of arriving at solutions. Since community psychology is the device to adopt such attempts within the scientific parlance, we must salute this branch of psychology with its methods and contents to come to our aid in many ways. Not only the planning and design of a community project but also its implementation demands the joint efforts of too many people. Hence, awareness of these is the new avenue towards psychology as a science and it needs to be opened by all the interested and able beings. Saving human resources can be the glory point of 'humanity'.

Community-based research has many implications. It helps to understand the issues from the insider's perspectives as it adopts mostly qualitative data collection techniques such as in-depth interviews, FGD, observation and, mostly, all the research is done in a natural setting. Quantitative study findings are also beneficial, especially when it is carried out among educated people who can read a questionnaire and are able to provide a well-thought response. In turn, findings of the studies help to design need-based CDPs. Monitoring of the implementation of the programme helps to ensure the smooth implementation of the programme as per plan. Finally, midterm and end-term evaluations give an idea about the efficacy of the programme and its cost-effectiveness, that is, how far the community-based programme has benefitted the target groups.

EXERCISES

One-mark Questions

1. What is a global community?
2. What does project evaluation mean?
3. What is a community programme design?
4. Mention the epistemological bases of community psychology.
5. What does a supportive community mean?
6. What is community service?
7. Mention any two primary features of quantitative research methods.
8. What is an action research?
9. What is meant by ethnography?
10. What is a case study?

Five-mark Questions

1. What are the aims of community research?
2. Why is cultural context important in community research?
3. Mention the skills that a community psychologist must possess.
4. How can stakeholders evaluate community programmes?
5. Differentiate between post-positivist and constructionist paradigms of research.
6. Distinguish between focus group interview and qualitative interview.

Ten-mark Questions

1. How can community research be conducted?
2. Discuss the significance of qualitative research methods in community psychology.
3. Discuss the status of community psychology in India.

Reflexive Questions

1. Critically examine the status of community psychology in the global context.
2. Critically examine the role of mixed research methods in community studies.
3. Is the observation method of data collection a scientific one? Justify your answer.

REFERENCES

Bennett, C., Anderson, L., Cooper, S., Hassol, L., Klein, D., & Rosenblum, G. (1966). *Community psychology: A report of the Boston Conference on the Education of Psychologists for Community Mental Health.* Boston University.

Bess, K., Prilleltensky, I., Perkins, D., & Collins, L. (2009). Participatory organizational change in community-based health and human services: From tokenism to political engagement. *American Journal of Community Psychology, 43*(1–2), 134–148.

Blakely, C. H., Mayer, J. P., Gottschalk, R. G., Schmitt, N., Davidson, W. S., Roitman, D. B., & Emshoff, J. G. (1987). The fidelity-adaptation debate: Implications for the implementation of public sector social programs. *American Journal of Community Psychology, 15*(3), 253–268.

Bond, M. A., & Harrell, S. P. (2006). Diversity challenges in community research and action: The story of a special issue of AJCP. *American Journal of Community Psychology, 37*(3–4), 157–166.

Brodsky, A. (2001). More than epistemology: Relationships in applied research with underserved communities. *Journal of Social Issues, 57*(2), 323–336.

Brodsky, A. (2003). *With all our strength: The Revolutionary Association of the Women of Afghanistan.* Routledge.

Burlew, A. K. (2003). Research with ethnic minorities: Conceptual, methodological, and analytical issues. In G. Bernal, J. Trimble, A. K. Burlew, & F. Leong (Eds.), *Handbook of racial and ethnic minority psychology* (pp. 179–197). SAGE Publications.

Camic, P., Rhodes, J., & Yardley, L. (2003). *Qualitative research in psychology: Expanding perspectives in methodology and design.* American Psychological Association.

Campbell, R., & Wasco, S. M. (2000). Feminist approaches to social science: Epistemological and methodological tenets. *American Journal of Community Psychology, 28*(6), 773–791.

Comas-Diaz, L., Lykes, M. B., & Alarcon, R. (1998). Ethnic conflict and the psychology of liberation in Guatemala, Peru, and Puerto Rico. *American Psychologist, 53*(7), 778–792.

Cosgrove, L., & McHugh, M. (2000). Speaking for ourselves: Feminist methods and community psychology. *American Journal of Community Psychology, 28,* 815–838.

Douglas, J. D. (1985). *Creative interviewing.* SAGE Publications.

Fontana, A., & Frey, J. H. (2005). The interview: From neutral stance to political involvement. In N. K. Denzin & Y. S. Lincoln (Eds.), *The SAGE handbook of qualitative research* (2nd ed., pp. 695–727). SAGE Publications.

Gergen, K. J. (2001). Psychological science in a postmodern context. *American Psychologist, 56*(10), 803.

Gubrium, J. F., & Holstein, J. A. (2001). From the individual interview to the interview society. In J. F. Gubrium & J. A. Holstein (Eds.), *Handbook of interview research* (pp. 3–32). SAGE Publications.

Hazel, K. (2007). Infusing practice into community psychology graduate education. *The Community Psychologist, 40*(2), 81–86.

Isenberg, D. H., Loomis, C., Humphreys, K., & Maton, K. (2004). Self-help research: Issues of powersharing. In L. A. Jason, C. Keys, Y. Suarez-Balcazar, R. Taylor, & M. Davis (Eds.), *Participatory community research: Theories and methods in action* (pp. 123–138). American Psychological Association.

Jason, L. A., Keys, C., Suarez-Balcazar, Y., Taylor, R., & Davis, M. (Eds.). (2004). *Participatory community research: Theories and methods in action.* American Psychological Association.

Johnson, R. B., Onwuegbuzie, A. J., & Turner, L. A. (2007). Toward a definition of mixed methods research. *Journal of Mixed Methods Research, 1*(2), 112–133.

Jupp, V. (Ed.). (2006). *SAGE dictionary of social research methods.* SAGE Publications.

Kazdin, A. E. (Ed.). (2000). *Encyclopedia of psychology* (Vol. 2). Oxford University Press and American Psychological Association.

Kingry-Westergaard, C., & Kelly, J. G. (1990). A contextualist epistemology for ecological research. In P. Tolan, C. Keys, F. Chertok, & L. A. Jason (Eds.), *Researching community psychology: Issues of theory and methods* (pp. 23–31). American Psychological Association.

Linney, J. A., & Reppucci, N. D. (1982). Research design and methods in community psychology. In P. Kendall & J. Butcher (Eds.), *Handbook of research methods in clinical psychology* (pp. 535–566). Wiley.

Lipsey, M., & Cordray, D. (2002). Evaluation methods for social intervention. *Annual Review of Psychology, 51,* 345–375.

Luders, C. (2004). Field observation and ethnography. In U. Filck, E. Von Kardoff, & I. Steinke (Eds.), *A companion to qualitative research* (pp. 222–230). SAGE Publications.

Luke, D. (2005). Getting the big picture in community science: Methods that capture context. *American Journal of Community Psychology, 35*(3–4), 185–200.

Martin, P., Lounsbury, D., & Davidson, W. (2004). AJCP as a vehicle for improving community life: An historic-analytic review of the journal's contents. *American Journal of Community Psychology, 34,* 163–174.

Merton, R. K., Fiske, M., & Kendall, P. L. (1956). *The focused interview.* The Free Press.

Miller, K., & Banyard, V. (Eds.). (1998). Qualitative research in community psychology [Special issue]. *American Journal of Community Psychology, 26*(4), 485–696.

Mock, M. (1999). Cultural competency: Acts of justice in community mental health. *The Community Psychologist, 32,* 38–41.

Nelson, G., Lavoie, F., & Mitchell, T. (2007). The history and theories of community psychology in Canada. In S. M. Reich, M. Reimer, I. Prilleltensky, & M. Montero (Eds.), *The history and theories of community psychology: An international perspective* (pp. 13–36). Springer.

Nelson, G., & Prilleltensky, I. (Eds.). (2005). *Community psychology: In pursuit of liberation and well-being.* Palgrave Macmillan.

Nicotera, N. (2007). Measuring neighborhood: A conundrum for human service researchers and practitioners. *American Journal of Community Psychology, 40*(1–2), 26–51.

Rappaport, J. (2000). Community narratives: Tales of terror and joy. *American Journal of Community Psychology, 28*(1), 1–24.

Reich, S. M., Riemer, M., Prilleltensky, I., & Montero, M. (Eds.). (2007). *International community psychology: History and theories.* Springer Science + Business Media.

Robertson, N., & Masters-Awatere, B. (2007). Community psychology in Aotearoa/New Zealand: Me tirowhakamuri a kiahangaiwhakamua. In S. M. Reich, M. Riemer, I. Prilleltensky, & M. Montero (Eds.), *International community psychology: History and theories* (pp. 140–163). Springer.

Rubin, H. J., & Rubin, I. S. (1995). *Qualitative interviewing: The art of hearing data.* SAGE Publications.

Sasao, T., & Sue, S. (1993). Toward a culturally anchored ecological framework of research in ethnic-cultural communities. *American Journal of Community Psychology, 21,* 705–728.

Sasao, T., & Yasuda, T. (2007). Historical and theoretical orientations of community psychology practice and research in Japan. In S. M. Reich, M. Riemer, I. Prilleltensky, & M. Montero (Eds.), *International community psychology: History and theories* (pp. 164–179). Springer.

Silverman, D. (2000). *Doing qualitative research: A practical handbook.* SAGE Publications.

Stark, W. (2009). *Community psychology in Europe: Potentials and challenges.* Plenary Presentation at the 7th European Congress of Community Psychology, Paris.

Stein, C. H., & Mankowski, E. S. (2004). Asking, witnessing, interpreting, knowing: Conducting qualitative research in community psychology. *American Journal of Community Psychology, 33*(1–2), 21–36.

Stein, C. H., & Wemmerus, V. (2001). Searching for a normal life: Personal accounts of adults with schizophrenia, their parents and well-siblings. *American Journal of Community Psychology, 29*(5), 725–746.

Stewart, E. (2000). Thinking through others: Qualitative research and community psychology. In J. Rappaport & E. Seidman (Eds.), *Handbook of community psychology* (pp. 725–736). Kluwer/Plenum.

Sullivan, C. (2003). Using the ESID model to reduce intimate male violence against women. *American Journal of Community Psychology, 32*(3–4), 295–304.

Tandon, S. D., Azelton, L. S., Kelly, J. G., & Strickland, D. A. (1998). Constructing a tree for community leaders: Contexts and processes in collaborative inquiry. *American Journal of Community Psychology, 26*(4), 669–696.

Tebes, J. (2000). External validity and scientific psychology. *American Psychologist, 55*(12), 1508–1509.

Tebes, J. (2005). Community science, philosophy of science, and the practice of research. *American Journal of Community Psychology, 35*(3), 213–230.

Tolman, D., & Brydon-Miller, M. (Eds.). (2001). *From subjects to subjectivities: A handbook of interpretative and participatory methods.* NYU Press.

Trickett, E. (2009). Community psychology: Individuals and interventions in community context. *Annual Review of Psychology, 60*(1), 395–419.

Trickett, E. J., & Espino, S. L. R. (2004). Collaboration and social inquiry: Multiple meanings of a construct and its role in creating useful and valid knowledge. *American Journal of Community Psychology, 34*(1–2), 1–70.

Vashishtha, P., & Kunwar, N. (2004). Women self help groups in Uttar Pradesh. *Indian Journal of Extension Education, 4*(1&2), 177–179.

Wandersman, A., Kloos, B., Linney, J. A., & Shinn, M. (Eds.). (2005). Science and community psychology: Enhancing the vitality of community research and action [Special issue]. *American Journal of Community Psychology, 35*(3/4), 253–258.

Weissberg, R. P., Kumpfer, K., & Seligman, M. (2003). Prevention that works for children and youth: An introduction. *American Psychologist, 58*(6–7), 425–432.

RECOMMENDED READINGS

Bond, M., Hill, J., Mulvey, A., & Terenzio, M. (Eds.). (2000a). Feminism and community psychology [Special issue: Part I]. *American Journal of Community Psychology, 28*(5), 585–755.

Bond, M., Hill, J., Mulvey, A., & Terenzio, M. (Eds.). (2000b). Feminism and community psychology [Special issue: Part II]. *American Journal of Community Psychology, 28*(6), 759–911.

Hazel, K., & Onanga, E. (Eds.). (2003). Experimental social innovation and dissemination [Special issue]. *American Journal of Community Psychology, 32*(4), 359–370.

Pimavera, J., & Brodsky, A. (Eds.). (2004). Special issue: Process of community research and action. *American Journal of Community Psychology, 33*(3/4), 177–279.

Revenson, T., D'Augelli, A., French, S., Hughes, D., Livert, D., Seidman, E., Shinn, M., & Yoshikawa, H. (Eds.). (2002). *Ecological research to promote social change: Methodological advances from community psychology.* Kluwer Academic/Plenum.

Glossary

Acquired immunodeficiency syndrome: It is an advanced stage of the HIV infection. When a person's immune system completely breaks down, he becomes vulnerable to numerous health problems such as tuberculosis, pneumonia, several forms of cancer and ultimately death.

Activity limitation: It is a difficulty encountered by an individual in executing a task or action.

Activity theory: This theory which is offered by Robert Havighurst states that the elderly people remain engaged in some activities, considering them as productive and enjoy ageing.

Attention-deficit hyperactive disorder: It is a condition where areas of attention and activity are compromised. The individual may express inattention and hyperactivity either in isolation or simultaneously.

Autism spectrum disorder: It is a pervasive neurodevelopmental disorder characterized by impairments in social communication and restricted, repetitive patterns of behaviour, interests or activities. They are a group of conditions where social communication is predominately affected. They also exhibit behavioural difficulties.

Baseline study design: It is a type of study which is carried out to gather baseline information about a particular issue and design an intervention programme based on the same information and finally, comparing the same information after implementation of the intervention programme with end-line data/information to ascertain the effectiveness of the intervention programme.

Biopsychosocial model: It is developed by George L. Engel and explains the interaction between the biological, psychological and social factors, which explains all the health and illness outcomes of an individual.

Child labour: They are children working in all forms of industrial or non-industrial occupations, which are not healthy to their physical, mental, moral and social development.

Community: It is understood to be a social group of people belonging to a specified area who share common geography, culture, government or personal characteristics.

Community-based rehabilitation: It is a means of empowerment for differently-abled individuals through the provision of equal opportunities in the community, thereby invoking among them a feeling of inclusion and acceptance.

Community mental health: It is a comprehensive paradigm where the mental health needs of a community are addressed, met and facilitated within the community through the right usage of community resources.

Community psychology: It is a derivative in the discipline of psychology that studies individuals from the context of community interactions; the transactions between individuals and their environment is the prime lesson in this discipline.

Continuity theory: This theory, offered by Robert Atchley, states the ability of an individual to continue the same habits, preferences, lifestyles and maintaining social networks and relationships whey they grow old, that is, they do not much differentiate their habits and lifestyles as they age.

Correlational study design: It attempts to understand the nature of relationships between different variables occurring naturally. In other words, a correlational study design attempts to find whether two or more variables of a study are related or not.

Cross-cultural study design: It is a type of study where a researcher compares the behaviour of people of different cultural groups to find out the impact of culture on behaviour, family life and outlook of people.

Cross-sectional study design: It proposes to gather information about certain issues from all categories of the population at one point in time. This type of study design helps to get a clear picture of the trend of any issue in the community.

Disability: It is an umbrella term covering impairments, activity limitations and participation restrictions.

Disaster: It is a serious disruption of the functioning of a community or society involving widespread human, material, economic or environmental losses and impacts, which exceeds the ability of the affected community or society to cope with using its own resources.

Disaster management: It is a continuous and integrated process of planning, organizing, coordinating and implementing measures which are necessary or expedient for prevention, mitigation, capacity-building, preparedness, prompt response, evacuation, rescue and relief and rehabilitation and reconstruction.

Disengagement theory: This theory is contributed by Elaine Cumming and William E. Henry; according to which, people withdraw themselves from social interactions when they become old with a notion that they are going to die soon.

Domestic workers: They are the ones who are employed in any household on a temporary or permanent basis to do the household work.

Ecological model of human development: A theory propounded by Bronfenbrenner (1979) has been defined as the mutual accommodation between an active, growing human being and the changing properties of the immediate context where the individual person develops.

Empowerment: It means providing self-confidence to people, imparting knowledge and skills among them so that they can take their own decision in a given situation.

Epidemiological study design: It is followed when there is the occurrence of a health problem, all of a sudden, and it affected people of different age groups. The objective of epidemiological study is to find out when and how a disease affects people of a particular community at a point of time, irrespective of their age, gender and socio-economic background.

Focus group discussion: A focus group discussion involves a discussion with a group of 8–10 individuals in an interviewing mode. The group members may be homogenous or heterogeneous, depending upon the issue of investigation. In FGD, a researcher plays the role of a facilitator and initiates the discussion on various issues one by one, ensuring that every member participates in the discussion and shares their views openly, without any inhibitions.

Health-seeking behaviour: It is any activity undertaken by individuals who perceive themselves to have a health problem or to be ill for the purpose of finding an appropriate remedy. It is the decision or an action taken by an individual to maintain, attain or regain good health and to prevent illness.

Human immunodeficiency virus: It is a virus which weakens the body's immune system (or the defence system) and makes a person susceptible to a range of minor health problems.

Impairment: It is a problem in the body function/structure.

In-depth interview: An in-depth interview is another open-ended and discovery-oriented qualitative data collection technique that is suitable for community research. It is a one-to-one data collection method using an in-depth interview guide. This method of data collection allows the subjects to reveal their mindset in the way they think about an issue without any inhibition.

Informal/unstructured interview: It is one of the methods of qualitative data collection without using any structured questionnaire. This type of interview is conducted in a casual setting, such as over tea/coffee or lunch or when the respondent is free and willing to spare 10–15 minutes with the researcher to answer a few questions.

Intellectual disability: It is that condition arising out of an individual's compromised cognitive development in comparison to their age group. It is understood as a significantly reduced ability (a) to understand new or complex information and to learn and apply new skills and (b) to cope independently, that begins before adulthood with a lasting effect on development.

Learning disability: It is a group of conditions that is characterized by significant limitations in both intellectual functioning and in adaptive behaviour, which covers many everyday social and practical skills.

Life course: It is a sequence of socially defined events and roles that the individual enacts over time.

Life course perspective: It is a multidisciplinary theory proposed by Glen H. Elder Jr which tries to understand the mental, physical and social health of individuals by incorporating both lifespan and life-stage concepts, resulting in determining the health trajectory.

Linked lives: Lives are lived interdependently; and socio-historical influences are expressed through this network of shared relationships.

Longitudinal study design: It is based on observation in which a researcher collects information about the same subject for a period of one or two years. The duration of longitudinal study could be more depending upon the issue of investigation.

Mental health: It is a state of well-being in which the individuals realize their own abilities, can cope with the normal stresses of life, can work productively and fruitfully and are able to contribute to their community.

Mental Healthcare Act: It is an act that provides for mental healthcare and services for persons with mental illness and to protect, promote and fulfil the rights of such persons during delivery of mental healthcare and services and for matters connected therewith or incidental thereto.

Natural calamity: It is a natural process or phenomenon that may cause loss of life, injury or other health impacts, property damage, loss of livelihoods and services, social and economic disruption or environmental damage.

Non-equivalent comparison group design: It is a research design to help whenever assignment of participants to experimental or comparison conditions is not random.

Observation: It is a very powerful and one of the most reliable methods of qualitative data collection in natural environment, without informing anyone from the community about their behaviour; and at the same time, the nature of different social interactions is being observed by a researcher.

Palliative care: It is an approach that improves the quality of life of those patients and their families which are facing life-threatening illnesses, through prevention and relief from suffering.

Paraprofessional force in psychology: It is a unique feature of the community-based intervention programme, who can function in communities by instigating its potential for group work towards a common cause.

Participation restriction: It is a problem experienced by an individual in getting involved in life situations (for example, impairments leading to unemployment).

Participatory rural appraisal: This method of qualitative data collection is suitable for designing rural development programmes based on rural people's understanding of their issues and challenges. Therefore, active participation of the local people is essential in this exercise. This method helps in getting an insider's perspective of an issue. The method of data collection helps to consider the knowledge, experiences and opinions of rural people in the planning and management of development projects and programmes.

Persons with disabilities: They are people who have long-term physical, mental, intellectual or sensory impairments which in interaction with various barriers may hinder their full and effective participation in society on an equal basis with others.

Positive ageing: It is a process of developing and maintaining the functional ability that enables well-being in older age. It is multidimensional, encompassing the avoidance of disease and disability, the maintenance of high physical and cognitive function and sustained engagement in social and productive activities

Primary prevention: It is a type of prevention strategy that targets to prevent the actual occurrence of any illness among the people at risk.

Project-affected persons: They refer to anyone affected by land acquisition, relocation or loss of incomes associated with project–changes; use of land, water and other natural resources might be mentioned as factors.

Quality of life: It is a subjective and a multidimensional concept which speaks about some standard levels for emotional, physical, environmental and social well-being.

Randomized field experiments: In this design, participants are randomly assigned to experimental or control groups to obtain homogenous pre-test conditions as far as experimental and control groups are concerned.

School dropout children: They are children who got admitted to primary level for formal education and discontinued for some reasons after some time.

Secondary prevention: It is a type of prevention strategy that focuses on early identification and intervention.

Semi-structured questionnaire: This type of questionnaire elicits both qualitative and quantitative data. It helps to understand the subject's perspective of an issue as it allows the expression of the respondent's personal views about various issues, in addition to collecting quantitative data.

Specific learning disabilities: It means a disorder in one or more of the basic psychological processes involved in understanding or in using language, spoken or written, which may manifest itself in an imperfect ability to listen, speak, read, spell or to do mathematical calculations.

Standardized psychological tools: These tools are used for measuring different psychological aspects of the study subjects that are developed by others or researchers.

Street children: They are children who live or spend a significant amount of time on the street or urban areas to fend for themselves and/or their families through 'various occupations'. This also denotes children who inadequately protected, supervised and cared for by responsible adults.

Structured questionnaire: It is used to collect detailed background information about the study subjects in addition to their opinion about various issues. Predetermined modes of responses are provided against all the questions.

Tertiary prevention: It is a prevention strategy that involves providing services to individuals who have already developed problems.

Index

CPSIA information can be obtained
at www.ICGtesting.com
Printed in the USA
LVHW100956221220
674776LV00015B/146